# CIVIL WAR PRISONS & ESCAPES

## A Day-by-Day Chronicle

ROBERT E. DENNEY

*Foreword by Edwin C. Bearss*

Sterling Publishing Co., Inc. New York

ACKNOWLEDGEMENTS

First, I would like to thank my wife, Frances, for her patience in dealing with my long hours and weeks while completing this book.

My gratitude and appreciation to the many employees of the Library of Congress and the National Archives who assisted me in my research at their wonderful facilities. Thanks also to the Virginia Historical Society, Richmond, Va., for its assistance.

I must thank two employees of the Van Noy Library, Ft. Belvoir, Va., Jane Townsend and Phyllis Cassler, for their assistance and interest in my ongoing projects.

Special thanks to my friend and magician at the Library of Congress, Gayle Harris, for her assistance and encouragement.

I am fortunate to know the nation's expert on Civil War history, Edwin C. Bearss, Chief Historian for the National Park Service, and I am even more fortunate that he consented to write the Foreword for this book. For the Foreword I am truly grateful.

Last, but certainly not least, my gratitude to my editor, Keith L. Schiffman, for his patience and guidance.

**Library of Congress Cataloging-in-Publication Data**

Denney, Robert E.
    Civil War prisons & escapes : a day-by-day chronicle /
by Robert E. Denney ; foreword by Edwin C. Bearss.
       p.  cm.
    Includes index.
    ISBN 0-8069-0414-3
    1. United States—History—Civil War, 1861-1865—Prisoners and prisons.
2. Prisoners of war—United States History—19th century. 3. Prisoners of war—
Confederate States of America—History.
I. Title.    II. Title: Civil War prisons and escapes.
E615.D46 1993
973.7'7—dc20                                 93–23889
                                                      CIP

10  9  8  7  6  5  4  3  2  1

First paperback edition published in 1995 by
Sterling Publishing Company, Inc.
387 Park Avenue South, New York, N.Y. 10016
©1993 by Robert F. Denney
Distributed in Canada by Sterling Publishing
℅ Canadian Manda Group, One Atlantic Avenue, Suite 105
Toronto, Ontario, Canada M6K 3E7
Distributed in Great Britain and Europe by Cassell PLC
Villiers House, 41/47 Strand, London WC2N 5JE, England
Distributed in Australia by Capricorn Link (Australia) Pty Ltd.
P.O. Box 6651, Baulkham Hills, Business Centre, NSW 2153, Australia
*Manufactured in the United States of America*
*All rights reserved*

Sterling ISBN 0-8069-0414-3 Trade
                 0-8069-0415-1 Paper

This book is dedicated
to both my maternal
great-grandfathers:
Corporal Eliab Hickman
Company E, 92nd Regiment
Ohio Volunteer Infantry,
who survived the war and
the horror of Andersonville,

and

Private Mathias Fox
Company D, 197th Regiment
Ohio Volunteer Infantry,
who served but a short time,
but served well.

# CONTENTS

*Better send no more prisoners to Tuscaloosa. Accommodations exhausted. Lunatic Asylum will not be leased. To seize it would disorganize the institution and arouse the indignation of a loyal and Christian people.*
    —John G. Shorter, Gov. of Alabama, in a letter to Confederate Secretary of War, Judah P. Benjamin, December 19, 1861

*It is currently reported here that the [Union] enemy have organized a regiment of negroes at Port Royal officered by white men, and that this regiment is now probably in the vicinity of the city. As these negroes are slaves in open insurrection they are liable by the laws of the state to be hung whenever taken.*
    —Wm. P. Miles, of Charleston, S.C., in a letter to President Jefferson Davis, June 11, 1862

*A large portion of the prisoners who have been in confinement any length of time are reduced to almost skeletons from continued hunger, exposure and filth.... No wood tonight and it is very cold. The nights are long and are made hideous by the moans of suffering wretches.*
    —John Ransom, Union Sgt., incarcerated at Belle Isle Prison, November 24, 1863

# FOREWORD

## BY EDWIN C. BEARSS

Since September 1955, when I reported for duty at Vicksburg National Military Park to begin my career as a historian with the National Park Service, I have led several thousand interpretative tours of our nation's battlefields and military-related sites. Participants in these tours represent a wide and diverse constituency as to education, age, culture, and economic status.

There are, however, more grim reminders than today's landscaped battle sites of the Civil War that illustrate man's inhumanity to man: these are the prisoner-of-war camps and stockades. Statistics, grave sites, official reports, letters, diaries, reminiscences—and the trial of Maj. Henry Wirz, the commandant of the Confederate prison for Union prisoners of war at Andersonville, Georgia—combine to underscore that these facilities, whether administered by the Union or the Confederacy, whether located near a small village in southwest Georgia or on a rocky island in Lake Erie, were places where thousands of Americans suffered and died.

In 1903, Adjutant General of the Army Frederick Ainsworth reported that his study of Union and Confederate records documented that 211,411 Union soldiers were captured during the war, of whom 31,218 died while prisoners. The same sources listed 462,634 Confederate soldiers captured, of whom 25,956 died while in captivity. There was a 12.9 percent mortality rate for Northern prison pens and a 15.5 rate for Southern.

If, in the years following 1865, in an effort to heal the wounds of that terrible fratricidal conflict, a memorial had been erected in the national capital on which were incised only the names of the Americans who had died as prisoners of war, it would have been as awe-inspiring as today's Vietnam Memorial. The number of names included on such a memorial would be less by 1,001 than the 58,175 Americans who died from all causes in Vietnam, but this number would far exceed the 27,704 American battle deaths in the Korean War, or the 50,510 American battle deaths in World War I.

Of the 33 principal places used by the Confederates for the confinement of Union prisoners, Andersonville is the only one recognized and administered by the United States Government as a National Historic Site. Eight others are identified by historical markers. Only Camp Lawton is listed in the National Register of Historic Places, and its listing is as an archaeological site.

Confederate prisoners were held at 32 different facilities by United States forces. Nine of these are listed in the National Register of Historic Places, and three of these, Forts Warren and Mifflin and Johnson's Island, have been designated National Historic Landmarks.

In October 1970, the Congress, "To provide an understanding of the overall prisoner-of-war story of the Civil War on-site and to interpret the role of prisoner-of-war camps in history," established Andersonville National Historic Site to be administered by the National Park Service.

Among the most vexing problems to confront the Civil War belligerents was how to handle prisoners of war. Standard practices prevailing among European powers in the 1850s provided that a war prisoner was entitled "to all of the privileges and subject to all the inconveniences which the usages of civilized nations impose upon prisoners of war." They could either be required to give a parole not to bear arms against their captors, not to visit certain localities, and not to give aid and comfort to the foe, or they could be confined in prison pens.

Even before the opening battles at Manassas in July 1861 and Wilson's Creek in August of the same year, United States regulars and Confederate volunteers had already surrendered and been paroled. After the battle of 1st Manassas, where the South captured almost 1,000 Federals, and the action at Hatteras Inlet, where the Union made prisoners of a number of Confederates, the two governments sought to establish a mutually accepted policy of providing for the parole and exchange of prisoners of war. In carrying out these negotiations, President Lincoln and his agents had to exercise care to avoid any tacit recognition of the Confederate government.

In July 1862, following Confederate successes in the Seven Days' Battles before Richmond, and the passage by the United States Congress of a joint resolution calling on Secretary of War Edwin M. Stanton for information on progress in solving the impasse in negotiations, which had broken down in February, Maj. Gen. John A. Dix was notified that President Abraham Lincoln wanted Dix to take charge. Dix was cautioned to avoid any recognition of the Confederacy. On July 18, 1862, Dix met with the Confederate representative, Maj. Gen. Daniel H. Hill, and a cartel was drafted providing for the parole and exchange of prisoners. This draft was submitted to and approved by their superiors. Four days later, on the 22nd, the cartel was formally signed and ratified by Generals Dix and Hill.

With the announcement of the Dix-Hill Cartel, hopes for exchange of the thousands held in prison camps, North and South, so long promised, were realized. During the next several months, thousands of prisoners were exchanged at Aiken's Landing on the James River in Virginia, and at Vicksburg, Mississippi. Differences in interpreting the cartel soon posed problems for the agents of exchange and for their respective governments.

In answer to the Emancipation Proclamation and receipt of news that the United States was encouraging recruitment of black regiments (composed of former slaves and led by white officers), the Confederate Congress on May 1, 1863, passed a joint resolution declaring that captured white officers of black troops were to be put to death, as they were to be considered guilty of inciting servile insurrection. Captured black soldiers were to be turned over to the states, to be punished or returned to their masters. This resolution led on May 25 to a stoppage in the exchange of officers, although the exchange of enlisted personnel continued.

Secretary of War Stanton's decision of October 27, 1863, to postpone the parole and exchange of any prisoners in accordance with the Dix-Hill Cartel had drastic consequences for tens of thousands of Union and Confederate soldiers and their families. In the weeks and months following, Stanton's decision, which was reaffirmed by Lt. Gen. Ulysses S. Grant soon after his promotion to command of all Union armies in March 1864, had far-reaching and tragic repercussions. The great battles that marked Grant's war of attrition, beginning in May 1864, resulted in the capture of tens of thousands of prisoners for whom there was little or no hope of exchange. These soldiers were concentrated in prison pens under conditions that even a public conditioned to World War II death camps, the Bataan Death March, the prison pens of North Korea and Koje-do, and the "Hanoi Hiltons" would have difficulty understanding.

The story of Civil War prisons, the suffering and high death rate among those held, and the question of who was responsible for the breakdown of the Dix-Hill Cartel are, after 130 years, still emotional and highly charged issues. Robert Denney has chosen this subject for his second book, *Civil War Prisons & Escapes: A Day-by-Day Chronicle.*

Denney has recently joined the legion of Civil War authors. His first endeavor, *The Civil War Years: A Day-by-Day Chronicle of the Life of a Nation,* published in November 1992, was listed by the Military History Book Club as an alternate selection. Bob Denney's service in two wars, his familiarity with the pluses and minuses of computers in the organization of data, his longtime study of President Lincoln and the Civil War, and personal experiences with the military and political bureaucracies have given him the tools to tell the story of *Civil War Prisons & Escapes* "like it was."

Denney, before he became a historian, had two successful careers, the first in the military and the second in computers. Denney joined the U.S. Marine Corps in 1947 immediately after his graduation from high school. He served with the 1st Marine Division in north China and Guam, and was discharged as a platoon sergeant in May 1950. This was seven weeks before the Korean War erupted, when Kim Il Sung's combat-ready divisions stormed across the 38th Parallel. Denney saw the handwriting on the wall. He re-enlisted, this time casting his lot with the U.S. Army. As a staff sergeant and a member of an intelligence unit, Denney operated in North Korea with partisan units from Christmas 1951 until he was wounded, decorated, and evacuated to Japan in mid-July 1952. In the years between the Korean and Vietnam conflicts, Denney, as he rose in rank from first sergeant to captain, became a pioneer in the employment of helicopters, as the Army developed air-mobile capability. Denney, after two brief trips to Vietnam in 1965, spent 1966 there as a Project Officer for the Army Material Command, and returned to the United States with a second Purple Heart and other decorations. Denney retired from the Army in September 1967, after 20 years' service.

Bob Denney, like more than one hundred million other citizens of the United States, had two forebears who served as soldiers in the Civil War. One of these—Cpl. Eliab Hickman of Company E, 92nd Ohio Volunteer Infantry—a soldier in the Army of the Cumberland, was captured by the Confederates near Cassville, Georgia, and survived the horror of Andersonville.

With such a background, it is easy to understand why Denney chose to write of Civil War prisons, the prisoners, the guards, and the men charged with their administration. To do so, Denney employs words of the actors in this tragic drama culled from the *Official Record,* journals, and reminiscences. The story is told chronologically, as the book's subtitle indicates; the author, to provide continuity, provides paragraphs setting the stage and giving the context. As a former marine, I found Denney's pithy remarks regarding the bureaucracy and life in the military on target. These give a special flavor that is much appreciated to the story of *Civil War Prisons & Escapes,* which historians and would-be historians who have not been in the military and denied the pleasure of seeing the elephant cannot achieve.

# PROLOGUE

uch has been written about the prison camps of the Civil War, most of which has been dedicated to the stories of Andersonville, Elmira, Salisbury, and other prisons whose treatment of their prisoners became infamous.

This book will view the prisoner problem from a different outlook, the situations in the various prison camps and why they were operated as they are reported to have been. I make no excuses for any individual, group, army, or government in the handling of prisoners during the war. There was certainly enough blame to go around considering the inhumanity displayed. While researching and collecting the information for this book, I've been very careful to record *only* what the protagonists said or wrote, providing only clarifying remarks or comments. I've also tried to present a brief background of the other events of the war, such as the various campaigns, etc., but only to place events in their proper perspective.

It's unfortunate that many of the records kept by the Confederate government at various locations during the war were destroyed or lost when the fighting was concluded. The records kept by the Union and the *Official Records*, which contain much of the extant Confederate material, are sometimes the only sources readily available.

Diaries, which are used freely, are a great source of information about the period and they provide color to the text. Most diaries are very enlightening.

I have tried to show that there was much more involved in the prisoner-of-war issue than modern literature depicts. To write a horror story of a particular prison, such as Andersonville or Elmira, which would be dramatic, hardly tells the story of the people involved and their response to their situation. The organizational and logistical problems alone were staggering and have been but little discussed. Not all the protagonists were hard-hearted brutes who delighted in tormenting helpless prisoners. Most of those involved were hard-working, diligent, and honorable people who were doing their best in a bad situation.

Being a prisoner of war presents many physical and psychological problems to the individual. The axiom that "no man loves his jailor" isn't always true, but it is most often the case. The prisoner focuses his resentment upon the nearest target, his jailor.

Prisoners also present problems to the individuals and governments responsible for their security, care, and feeding. In the American Civil War, neither the North nor the South was prepared for the problems of the prisoners.

We must also remember that there were other "prisoners" involved in the war. There were civilians who became prisoners of state who, while faring somewhat better than the soldiers, were still incarcerated for extended periods, often without being charged with a specific crime.

In February 1861, the United States Army had less than 16,000 officers and men of all ranks, most of these serving on the western frontier in scattered companies. One year later, after the surrender of the garrison at Ft. Donelson, Tenn., U.S. Grant immediately took custody of *over 15,000 prisoners of war!* This was the first large surrender of the war and the administration of these prisoners would largely set the tone for the control and care of prisoners thereafter.

While the concept of receiving prisoners of war may sound easy to understand, imagine for a minute what your reaction would be to suddenly be responsible for food,housing, clothing, medical care, and control of this many people, be they military or civilian. How would they be fed? How many were sick or wounded, how many badly sick or wounded? Where to put them? These, and a myriad of other questions, demanded immediate answers; immediate resources were limited or not adequately known. There was no precedent for this situation in American military history because no American armies of this size had existed before.

Since no government wants to keep prisoners forever, how could they be sent back to their own government? The answer, in the Civil War, was a *Cartel of Exchange.*

## CARTEL OF EXCHANGE

Historically, prisoners of war were treated more as hostages than as prisoners. Some cartels existed between warring factions but their operations were seldom placed in writing. In most cases the prisoners were left to the mercies of their captors.

During the War of 1812, a cartel was written between the United States and England concerning the prisoners' treatment and their exchange. That cartel was largely negotiated, on the part of the United States, by the father of John Henry Winder, who later, by a twist of fate, became the Confederate Commissary-General of Prisoners. The cartel of 1812 was the basis for the one eventually adopted by the Union and Confederacy.

Briefly, the cartel defined the basis for exchange. A general was exchanged for a general *or* for a specified number of colonels *or* for majors *or* enlisted

men, etc. A detailed description of the cartel is attached as Appendix I. The cartel between the factions did not legally get resolved until mid-1862, but this did not necessarily mean that exchanges were not taking place under its general provisions. Wide latitude was given local commanders, who usually opted for prisoner exchange as early as possible. The cartel remained in effect for the period of the war, but was suspended for a period in 1863 and 1864. This suspension, about which there were many recriminations, caused untold suffering in the prison camps, both North and South.

## MR. LINCOLN'S PROBLEMS

President Abraham Lincoln had a major problem. Cartels of Exchange were made between existing governments. *The Southern Confederacy was considered by the Federal government to be in insurrection, not a separate government.* To agree to a cartel with the Confederate government was, in effect, to recognize that such a government existed. Lincoln was not ready to do this for many reasons; recognizing the Confederacy as a legal government would lend credence to it and permit foreign governments to recognize the Confederacy as a separate nation. Lincoln, first and foremost, meant to restore the Union, which meant that he couldn't recognize the war as anything other than a rebellion.

The South issued Letters of Marque to armed vessels to prey on Northern shipping. A Letter of Marque (shown in Appendix II) was a recognized instrument of warfare that *was issued by a legal government.* Ergo, if Lincoln did not recognize the Confederacy as a separate government, the Letter of Marque was not legal, and the ship's crews operating under such letters became pirates and were subject to hanging. Several instances arose early in the war that created major problems for both North and South regarding agreement to the cartel.

## THE PRISON CAMPS

During the war there were basically four types of prison compound. The most sheltered type contained actual barracks, or buildings, which protected the prisoners from the elements. These were more prevalent in the North: Elmira, Douglas, Morton, Butler,

Johnson's Island, Chase, Ft. McHenry, Ft. Warren, Governor's Island, Alton, Nashville, Louisville, Ohio State Penitentiary, etc. In the South, Libby and Castle Thunder in Virginia and Castle Pinckney in Charleston were about the only ones of this type.

The second type had partial shelter for the prisoners, the larger number of prisoners being without permanent shelter. Mostly in the South, these included Cahaba, Macon, the Insane Asylum in Columbia, and Salisbury.

Third, were those prisons which relied solely on tents for shelter. Point Lookout and Ship Island were about the only long-term prisons of this type used by the North. The Columbia Prison, Belle Isle, Millen, and Florence were located in the South.

Fourth, were those who left it to the prisoner to find his own shelter, nothing being provided at all. The most infamous of all was Andersonville. Belle Isle almost became that way for a period of time, as did Florence. The large prison pen at Belle Plain near Fredericksburg, Va., at one time held over 5000 prisoners in an open field for nearly 45 days.

As the war progressed, the camps in the North improved, while those in the South worsened.

## TREATMENT OF PRISONERS

The United States Army had specific regulations (shown in Appendix III), prior to the war, covering the treatment of prisoners after capture.

These same regulations (with name changes) were adopted (Appendix IV), by the Confederate Army when that Army came into existence. Basically, the regulations required that prisoners' personal property was to be respected (the prisoners were not to be robbed of personal effects or clothing) and the prisoners were to be provided with the same rations and medical treatment as that provided to the soldiers who captured them.

The respect for personal property was handled differently in different areas of the conflict and at different times during the war. As the war progressed, the practice of taking blankets, money, and even clothing from prisoners became commonplace on both sides, but especially in the Confederacy. This practice was abhorred on both sides, but it continued. The robbing of the prisoners and then not replacing the items, especially clothing and blankets, caused much suffering, especially among Confederate prisoners incarcerated in northern climates.

The second item, concerning rations and medical treatment, would be controversial during the war and for as long as one veteran was still alive. Considering the rations that were issued to both armies, the prisoners might have been better off if rations had not been considered, and they had been provided with normal foodstuffs. The diet of the common soldier, North and South, left much to be desired.

The regulations also prohibited the abuse of prisoners while in captivity. This was largely adhered to by the troops in the field; the opponents understand each other better at the fighting level. When prisoners, North or South, came into custody of noncombatants such as militia, home guards, etc., the treatment often became abusive. The rear-echelon guards became intolerable in many cases.

The caretakers of the camps, i.e., the commandants, were mostly officers who were trying to do a very difficult job, and this difficulty was reflected in their correspondence over a long period of the war. Not one of them, including Capt. Henry Wirz, deliberately set out to be demonic. All had their problems with their respective governments, especially when competing for resources.

## PAROLES AND
## THE EXCHANGE SYSTEM

Paroles of prisoners of war were last used during the American Civil War. The romantic nature of warfare existed in the minds of all men. With this romantic concept came the idea of personal honor. A person's word of honor given was a sacred trust that could not be broken, except at the peril of being ostracized by one's fellow man. An example is shown in Appendix V.

During the early stages of the war, officers were paroled as a matter of course and sent North (or South) to arrange for an "equivalent" to be returned in their stead. When the "match" was made, each was declared "exchanged" and was free to engage in military activities again. Ultimately, there were thousands of paroled officers and men who became game pieces in a giant chess game. Much acrimony would result in the question of who had been exchanged and who had not during the late months of 1863.

The Confederacy had unilaterally announced an exchange of prisoners without the North's acquiescence, which made that same exchange illegal according to the cartel's terms.

Basically, the exchange-and-parole system worked so long as both sides adhered to the rules of the game. When one side or the other violated the rules, problems developed rapidly.

## PRISONER NUMBERS AND DEATHS

The first major battle of the war, at Manassas, Va., in July 1861, yielded few prisoners for either side. Those captured by the South were sent to Richmond, some to remain for just a few days, others for several months. As a rule, the occasional capture of cavalry vedettes, infantry pickets, etc., of either side accounted for but few men and these men were usually exchanged within a short period of time. It wasn't until large masses of troops began to be captured that major problems arose.

In 1866 the United States War Department went through a lengthy process to determine how many prisoners were held by each side during the Civil War. Also computed was how many of these prisoners died during captivity. The initial figures showed that the North held 220,000 Confederates, of whom 26,436 died while in prison. The South held 126,000 Federal prisoners, of whom 22,576 died while being held. These figures are debatable.

In 1906, James Ford Rhodes, a Northern historian, recomputed the numbers and determined that the South held 194,000 Federals (vice 126,000 in the original report), and the North held only 215,000 Confederates. While Rhodes's figures in total prisoners varied, he concluded that the number of deaths in the prisons was probably correct. With the latter figures, the death rate was about 12 percent in the Northern camps and 15.5 percent in the South.

Yet a third set of figures for Northern prisons, compiled by Col. Robert C. Wood, former Confederate officer, in the late 1800s is shown in Appendix VI.

The number of deaths among the prisoners varied greatly from prison to prison. Often, the number of deaths was influenced by disease rather than by harsh treatment or deliberate starvation, although this was the main theme played in the press and among the returned prisoners. For example, smallpox, the deadly disease of the era, took 387 prisoners' lives at one prison camp for Confederates in 30 days, representing about 10 percent of the prisoner population, and many of the prisoners told tales of their Union jailors deliberately using "bad" vaccine. Many of the prisoners, especially those from the South, arrived at the camp afflicted with smallpox and it spread like wildfire. The problem was not so prevalent with Federal prisoners, who were vaccinated as a normal course during their training.

Other diseases took their toll on the prisoners, especially diarrhea. The South issued unbolted cornmeal to the prisoners which contained the bran from the kernel. This bran, unlike bran from wheat, was hard, flinty, and indigestible. It immediately caused stomach disorders, and many of these disorders hung on for the rest of the prisoner's life. Nearly every camp commandant in the South, including Wirz, complained loudly about this bran, but nothing was done to correct it. Following the war, many disability pensions involved diarrhea or dysentery.

Another major factor in prison deaths was the state, both physical and mental, of the individual prisoner when he arrived at the camp. John Ransom tells of healthy prisoners arriving at Andersonville who would, within a very short time, disintegrate and die, their mental capability not being enough to stand the shock. Many reports from the prisons of the North indicate that the Confederate prisoners arriving at those locations had been exposed to the elements prior to and during the battles in which they were captured, to be followed by days of transportation to the prison itself. Often these men were wounded or already sick. Usually, if they survived for the first two weeks, their life expectancy improved.

# 1861

New Year's Day in Washington, and President Buchanan held the usual New Year's Levee at the White House, but the holiday cheer was missing. In South Carolina, the Governor had sent a very arrogant letter to President Buchanan about Maj. Anderson's move to Sumter. The Governor believed that an agreement had been reached with the President to leave Anderson at Ft. Moultrie and that Anderson's move was a breach of confidence. In Charleston Harbor, the state also seized Ft. Johnson, which had been previously abandoned.

At a Cabinet meeting, Gen. Winfield Scott, the aged Commander of the U.S. Army, favored sending a fast steamer to resupply Anderson as soon as possible. Scott believed that a commercial steamer would be less conspicuous and generate less of a threat. In this belief, he would be wrong.

It became quite the vogue in the South to take over Federal forts located within the various states. South Carolina seized old Ft. Johnson, in Charleston Harbor, on the 2nd; Georgia seized Ft. Pulaski, at Savannah, on the 3rd; Alabama took the U.S. Arsenal at Mt. Vernon, Ala., on the 4th, followed by Ft. Gaines and Ft. Morgan, near Mobile, on the 5th; the arsenal at Apalachicola, Fla., was seized by Florida State troops on the 6th, who then took over the old Spanish fort at St. Augustine on the 7th. All of the seizures, except Ft. Johnson, were done by states that were still in the Union.

In most of the fort seizures, the number of captives was few, and of these captives several joined the Southern cause in one capacity or another.

On the 9th, Mississippi voted to secede from the Union, causing wild rejoicing in the South. In Charleston, S.C., the commercial steamer *Star of the West* arrived at Charleston Harbor to resupply the Federal garrison at Ft. Sumter. The Confederate gunners fired on the ship, the wheel was put about and the steamer left.

Also on the 9th, North Carolina seized Ft. Johnson, at Wilmington, to be followed on the 10th by Ft. Caswell. Louisiana troops seized Fts. Jackson and St. Phillip, guarding the city of New Orleans, on the 10th.

Florida became the third state to secede on the 10th by a vote of 62 to 7. Alabama was the fourth state to secede the following day (11th) with wild parties held in the streets of Montgomery.

Ft. Pike, La., was taken over by state troops on the 14th. On the 15th, the State of Florida demanded that Ft. Pickens be turned over to the state. The Federal officer in command refused. The actual commander was on leave of absence in Maryland at the time; Maj. John Henry Winder would play an important role in the treatment of Federal prisoners in the South.

It was not until the 19th that Georgia voted to secede (by a vote of 208 to 89). One of those opposing secession was Alexander H. Stephens, later

Vice-President of the Confederacy. Georgia seized the Federal arsenal at Augusta on the 24th, while the Louisiana Legislature voted to secede, the sixth state to leave the Union.

Ft. Macomb, near New Orleans, was taken by Louisiana troops on the 28th, and the U.S. revenue cutter *Robert McClelland* was surrendered to Louisiana State authorities in New Orleans. Another revenue cutter, the *Lewis Cass*, was surrendered to Southern authorities in Mobile.

The last day of the month, the Federal Mint in New Orleans and the U.S. revenue schooner *Washington* were seized by the Louisiana authorities.

A busy month indeed. Five more states had left the Union, many forts had been seized, and the slide into war quickened.

## FEBRUARY 1861

In Texas, Lt. Col. Robert E. Lee departed for Virginia on an extended leave of absence to handle some personal matters at the family home, "Arlington." Also in Texas, a vote to secede passed by 166 to 7.

On the 9th, Jefferson Davis was elected President of the Confederacy for six years with no renewal of options. Alexander Stephens, of Georgia, who had voted against secession, was elected Vice-President, with the same options.

On the same day that Jefferson Davis was notified that he had been elected President of the Confederacy (the 11th), the President-elect of the United States left Springfield, Ill., for Washington. Lincoln would never see his Illinois home again. The 16th, Davis arrived in Montgomery, Ala., to assume his new duties.

In Louisiana, William T. Sherman, formerly head of the school at Alexandria that would later become Louisiana State University, turned over his accounts and prepared for his departure North. Sherman would return to Louisiana, but in a far different role.

Lincoln made his way slowly across the states to Washington, speaking at many places on the way: Pittsburgh on the 15th; Cleveland on the 16th; Buffalo on the 17th; Albany on the 18th; New York on the 19th; Philadelphia on the 21st; and into Baltimore on the 23rd.

When Brevet Maj. Gen. David E. Twiggs, USA, in Texas, surrendered all the military establishments in that state to the Confederacy, the cry of "Treason!" was heard from many quarters.

After being inaugurated on the 18th, Davis rushed into his Cabinet appointments, selecting many who had held public office in the United States.

The politicians in Washington were trying to reach some accommodation with the states' rights issue and the expansion of slavery. Nothing would work—the war was coming.

## MARCH 1861

Lt. Col. Robert E. Lee arrived at "Arlington," the family home on the Potomac, on the 1st. Across the river in Washington, Lincoln worked on his Cabinet nominations.

On the 4th, in a ceremony on the Capitol steps, Lincoln became the 16th President of the United States. Security was very tight. Troops lined the streets and cavalry was available for quick reaction.

Also on this day, the "Stars and Bars," was raised for the first time over the Confederate Capitol in Montgomery, Ala.

On the 16th, Robert E. Lee was promoted to full Colonel in the United States Army after 32 years of service. Two days later, the venerable Sam Houston, then Governor of Texas, refused to take an oath of allegiance to the Confederacy. He felt that Texas should go it alone since it had already seceded from one government. He resigned as Governor on the 29th and went into retirement.

## APRIL 1861

In Richmond, on the 4th, the Virginia State Convention *rejected* by a vote of 89 to 45 a motion to pass an ordinance of secession and to have it voted on by the State residents.

Lincoln, on April 6, sent an emissary to Gov. Pickens in Columbia, S.C., to inform the Governor that Ft. Sumter would be supplied *with provisions only*, no reinforcements of men or guns.

On April 7, Gen. Beauregard notified Maj. Robert Anderson that no further interaction would be allowed between Ft. Sumter and Charleston. The fort was now essentially cut off.

The following day, Lincoln's emissary, R.S. Chew of the State Department, arrived at Columbia and delivered his message to Gov. Pickens. Pickens read the message to Gen. Beauregard. Beauregard placed all Confederate forces in the area on alert. No one was taking a backward step at this challenge. The next day, in Charleston, S.C., the *Mercury* newspaper declared that the resupply of the fort meant war.

In Montgomery, Ala., the Confederate government was between a rock and a hard place. If it permitted the resupply of the forts at Charleston and Pensacola, it was tacitly agreeing that these forts belonged to the Union government and that the secession movement was meaningless. If the Confederates repelled the resupply and reinforcement, it meant that they would be branded the aggressor. Confederate Secretary of State Robert Toombs told Davis on the 9th that to fire on the national flag would be:

suicide, murder and will lose us every friend at the North. You will wantonly strike a hornet's nest which extends from mountain to ocean, and legions now quiet will swarm out and sting us to death. It is unnecessary; it puts us in the wrong; it is fatal.

On the 10th, the Confederate Secretary of War informed Beauregard that if he were sure that the attempt would be made to resupply the fort, he should demand its immediate surrender and evacuation. If refused, Beauregard was to take whatever action he deemed necessary to reduce the fort.

On April 11, Col. James Chesnut, a former U.S. Senator and the husband of the famed Civil War diarist Mary Chesnut; Capt. Stephen D. Lee, late of the U.S. Army; and Lt. Col. A.R. Chisolm, a representative of Gov. Pickens, left the dock at Charleston and went to Ft. Sumter to demand its immediate surrender. There they met with Maj. Robert Anderson and discussed the demand. After a consultation, Anderson declined to surrender but stated that he would probably be starved out in a few days anyway, if not battered to pieces by artillery.

Shortly past midnight on April 12, Roger Pryor and three men went out in a boat flying a white flag to Ft. Sumter to again confer with Maj. Robert Anderson about the surrender of the fort. To these men Anderson replied that he would evacuate the fort on the 15th unless he received additional instructions or supplies, not realizing that a relief fleet was lying just outside the harbor, awaiting day-light to enter. To the men in the boat, anything less than immediate surrender was not acceptable, and they then informed Anderson that firing would commence within one hour if he did not surrender. Anderson, realizing what was coming, shook the hands of the four men and told them, "If we do not meet again in this world, I hope we may meet in the better one." The boat left for Cummings Point about 3:20 A.M., arriving there at 4 A.M.

At Cummings Point, Roger Pryor, a Virginian, was offered the honor of firing the first shot, but he declined. Another Virginian, a 67 year-old fire-eater and avid secessionist named Edmund Ruffin, gladly accepted the honor, and at 4:30 A.M. pulled the lanyard on the gun. Sumter was fired upon. The war had begun.

In Charleston, people gathered on the rooftops to watch the display of artillery as Beauregard's 47 guns began the bombardment. The crowd, in a holiday mood, cheered as the shells struck home and the fort was battered. Beauregard's gunners threw over 4000 rounds at the fort, tearing up the earthen works, dismantling guns, and making life miserable for the defenders. The flag was shot from its staff only to be nailed up again by a courageous sergeant. There could be no doubt of the outcome. Anderson was outgunned and beyond hope of help from the outside. The firing continued all day Friday and through the night.

On April 13, the defenders, now down to few rations and little water, stoically stood the bombardment. At last, honor satisfied, Anderson capitulated to his former artillery student and agreed to the surrender terms offered on Thursday, the 11th. Roger Pryor returned to Sumter to participate in the ceremonies which took place in the fort hospital. No casualties as the result of enemy fire had occurred on either side during the bombardment. The surrender was signed and Anderson was permitted to fire a fifty gun salute to his flag. Sumter was gone, and Anderson and his defenders were the first prisoners of war.

The next day, large crowds on boats gathered in the harbor to see the Federals leave the island fort and board boats to take them North.

On April 15, Lincoln took action that would do more to solidify the South than any that had been taken so far. Lincoln issued a call for 75,000 volunteers to serve for three months and called for a special session of Congress for July 4th. While some Northern states quickly affirmed their commitment to supply troops, North Carolina and Kentucky just as quickly refused.

The calls to the then-border states of Virginia, North Carolina, Tennessee and Arkansas for troops led to action to join the South in most cases. In Tennessee, Gov. Isham Harris declared that "Tennessee will furnish not a single man for the purpose of coercion, but fifty thousand if necessary for the defense of our rights and those of our Southern brothers." This furnished a prime excuse for Harris to "ask the Confederacy for protection" and to take the state into the Southern camp even though the voters had already refused such a move by a majority of 10,000 votes.

Preparations among the various states, North and South, filled the rest of the month with frantic activity. Troops had to be obtained to defend Washington. The blockade had to be put in place on the Southern ports. The Southern states were organizing troops and getting them armed.

On April 18, Robert E. Lee refused command of all Union forces, resigned his commission and went back to "Arlington." In Washington, five companies of troops arrived from Pennsylvania via Baltimore for the defense of the capital. When coming through Baltimore they had been met with cold stares and ugly looks, but no overt action had been taken against them.

The following day, April 19th, the 6th Massachusetts Volunteer Infantry Regiment arrived in Baltimore and was marching from one station to another en route to Washington when a large crowd of Southern sympathizers began to throw rocks and bricks and fired into the ranks of the troops. These troops, unlike those of the day before, were armed, and returned the fire, killing twelve civilians and wounding several more. The troops picked up their four dead, packed them in ice and sent them home and then went on to Washington with their 17 wounded.

George W. Brown, the Mayor of Baltimore, by now a very nervous man, wrote a letter to President Lincoln which was hand-carried by emissaries explaining the stance of the people of that city:

Sir: This will be presented to you by the Hon. H.

Lennox Bond, George W. Dobbin and John C. Brune, esqs., who will proceed to Washington by an express train at my request in order to explain fully the fearful condition of affairs in this city. The people are exasperated to the highest degree by the passage of troops and the citizens are universally decided in the opinion that no more should be ordered to come.

The authorities of the city did their best today to protect both strangers and citizens and to prevent any collision but in vain; and but for their great efforts a fearful slaughter would have occurred.

Under these circumstances it is my solemn duty to inform you that it is not possible for more soldiers to pass through Baltimore unless they fight their way at every step.

I therefore hope and trust and most earnestly request that no more troops be permitted or ordered by the Government to pass through the city. If they should attempt it the responsibility for the blood shed will not rest on me.

Again on the 21st, a delegation from Baltimore called upon Lincoln to protest the killings of citizens in Baltimore the previous Friday (the 19th), calling it "a pollution" of Maryland soil. Lincoln replied that he must have troops to defend the capital. Dissatisfied, the Marylanders returned to Baltimore and cut the telegraph wires, burned bridges, and tore up miles of track. The city of Washington was now cut off from any rail support, Harpers Ferry being held by Confederate Thomas J. Jackson and his 8000 men, who were searching the houses in Maryland near Harpers Ferry for arms.

On April 21, three days after refusing to take command of the Union forces, Robert E. Lee accepted the command of the forces of the State of Virginia. He would not be appointed commander of the Army of Northern Virginia for yet another year.

At last, on the 25th, a sufficient number of Federal troops arrived in Washington so that everyone could breathe a little easier.

On April 27, the Confederate Congress, meeting at Montgomery, Ala., voted to move the new capital to Richmond, Va. Montgomery was too small a town and did not have sufficient resources to handle such a large group of people as would be present with the new government.

On the 27th, Lt. Gen. Winfield Scott directed Brig. Gen. Benjamin F. Butler, at Annapolis, Md., that:

The undersigned, General-in-Chief of the Army, has received from the President of the United States the following instructions respecting the Legislature of Maryland now about to assemble at Annapolis, viz:

It is left to the commanding general to watch and await their action, which if it shall be to arm their people against the United States he is to adopt the most prompt and efficient means to counteract even if necessary to the bombardment of their cities and in the extremest necessity suspension of the writ of *habeas corpus.*

In the absence of the undersigned the foregoing instructions are turned over to Brig. Gen. B.F. Butler, of the Massachusetts Volunteers, or other officer commanding at Annapolis, who will carry them out in a right spirit—that is with moderation and firmness. In the case of arrested individuals notorious for their hostility to the United States the prisoners will be safely kept and duly cared for but not surrendered except on the order of the commander aforesaid.

In Richmond, Va., on April 29, an astute (and bigoted) observer had met with several of the current and future leaders of the Confederate States of America and had witnessed the secession of Virginia from the Union. John Beauchamp Jones, aged 51, was a self-imposed refugee from New Jersey who had long supported the Southern cause in his newspaper in Burlington, N.J., and in his books and articles. When South Carolina seceded, Jones realized that he would not be able to remain in the North in the event of a national conflict. His outspoken mannerisms led to almost immediate difficulty with his neighbors in New Jersey and Philadelphia. On April 9th he departed from Philadelphia and travelled to Richmond, via Baltimore and Washington, D.C., leaving his family and most of his books and papers in New Jersey. He arrived in Richmond on the 12th and lodged in a boardinghouse, the Exchange Hotel being too expensive for his purse. He was destined to play an important role in the coming conflict as an "inside" observer of events in the Confederate government and as a constant critic of the military establishment, although he was employed by the Confederate War Department. He maintained a diary throughout the war that was originally published in 1866 in two volumes as *A Rebel War Clerk's Diary.*

Jones, John B., Rebel War Clerk, Richmond, Va.:

At fifty-one, I can hardly follow the pursuit of arms; but I will write and preserve a DIARY of the revolution. I never held or sought office in my life; but now President Tyler and Gov. Wise say I will find employment at Montgomery. The latter will prepare a letter to President Davis, and the former says he will draw up a paper in my behalf.... To make my DIARY full and complete as possible, is now my business.

### May 1 (Wednesday)

On this day, one of the major protagonists in the administration of prison camps in the South departed from Baltimore, Md., on his way to Raleigh, N.C., to offer his services to his adopted state, North Carolina. John Henry Winder was born in 1800 on his family estate in Maryland. Winder was the descendant of a prominent Maryland family and the son of the commander of the American troops who had been defeated at Bladensburg, Md., on August 23, 1814, a defeat that led to the burning of Washington, D.C., by the British. Winder, at age 14, was just beginning his life as a cadet at West Point at the time of the defeat. Winder, though the family name was disgraced at West Point, continued his education there with a grim determination to make the Winder name once again one to be proud of. After his graduation as a Lieutenant, and until his resignation in April 1861, Winder served his country faithfully and well. Despite his being stubborn, hot-tempered, and profane, his contemporaries considered him an efficient, honest, and courageous officer. He had served at several posts during his long military career, including a twenty-year tour at Ft. Johnson near Wilmington, N.C., where he met and married his second wife (his first wife had died). His experience at Ft. Johnson, as commissary officer, would hold him in good stead later during his service in the Confederacy. His family, still located in Baltimore, were widely respected lawyers and farmers and often served in the state legislature. There were mixed feelings within the family about the secession of South Carolina from the Union, brothers and cousins often taking opposing sides. Winder considered himself a Southerner by adoption due to his long tenure in North Carolina and decided to resign his commission and go to North Carolina to offer his services. On April 20, 1861 he forwarded his resignation as Major of the 3rd Regt. of Artillery and Commander of Ft. Pickens, Fla., to the Adjutant-General of the United States Army in Washington, D.C. On April 30th, he received notification that his resignation had been accepted. He booked immediate passage on the railroad leaving Baltimore. He was never to see Baltimore again.

### May 2 (Thursday)

John Henry Winder passed through Washington, D.C., where he boarded a steamer for Norfolk, crossed over to Portsmouth, and took a train to Raleigh, N.C., arriving there late in the afternoon.

In Washington, more troops were arriving daily; most were as unprepared for their role as the first that came. Among these were the New York Fire Zouaves in their flashy uniforms.

### May 3 (Friday)

Today, Lincoln expanded his call for volunteers to an additional 42,000, these to serve for three years. He also increased the size of the regular army and navy. He did all of this while Congress was out of session.

### May 5 (Sunday)

Maj. Gen. Benjamin F. Butler today seized the railroad relay house on the tracks leading to Annapolis and Baltimore, thus securing a route to Washington. Butler, a noted criminal lawyer and state legislator in Massachusetts, would later use his training well during negotiations with the South on the exchange of prisoners. In Butler, Robert Ould, the Confederate Agent of Exchange, would face a formidable opponent.

Benjamin Franklin Butler was born in Deerfield, N.H., on November 5, 1818. He studied law and became a power in state politics. In 1860, he was a delegate to the Democratic Convention held in Charleston, S.C., and voted for Jefferson Davis as the Presidential candidate 57 times. After Ft. Sumter was fired upon, he formed a regiment in Massachusetts and took it to Washington, D.C., where he was appointed the first Major General of Volun-

teers by Lincoln. He would prove to be one of the worst choices for this role that could be found. Almost everything military Butler touched went sour until finally, in January 1865, Grant had him relieved of command. Butler resigned his commission in November 1865. He returned to politics and while serving as a United States Representative, he was very active in the impeachment of Andrew Johnson. He also ran, unsuccessfully, for president. He died on January 11, 1893 in Washington, D.C.

### May 6 (Monday)

John Henry Winder met with Gov. John W. Ellis of North Carolina. Ellis asked Winder to serve on a state advisory board where Winder's military experience would be useful. Winder agreed and left for Montgomery, Ala., to secure his commission and appointment.

On this date, the states of Tennessee and Arkansas passed Secession Ordinances and left the Union officially. This made the 9th and 10th states to join the Confederacy. In Montgomery, Ala., President Davis approved a bill of May 3rd declaring that a state of war existed between the United States and the Confederacy.

### May 7 (Tuesday)

In Maryland, arrests were being made of those who had destroyed the railroad bridges in late April to prevent additional troops from coming through Baltimore headed towards Washington. The Governor of the State and the Mayor of Baltimore, in collusion with the antigovernment element, talked out of both sides of their mouth when dealing with the Federal authorities. Judge M. Nelson, in Frederick County, west of Baltimore, requested assistance in arresting and disarming hostile citizens in the city of Frederick.

The Governor of Tennessee, Isham Harris, took action within the Legislature to join the state to the Confederacy, *without* a vote by the citizens of the state. In Knoxville, Tenn., a riot occurred between pro-Union and secessionist factions. This ill will would continue throughout the war.

### May 9 (Thursday)

In Montgomery, Ala., the Confederate Congress authorized the President to accept into volunteer service for the duration of the war those forces deemed necessary. The South, like the North, initially accepted volunteers for one year. This changed rapidly in the South and soon all troops were "in for the duration."

### May 10 (Friday)

John H. Winder arrived at Montgomery, Ala., to find the city in chaos. Thousands were trying to get appointments to the government, get government contracts, or settle grievances. Winder also found that the appointment he had sought had been given to someone else. He returned to Raleigh, N.C., disillusioned. He reached Raleigh on May 21st, where he wrote a long letter of protest to Gov. Ellis.

### May 13 (Monday)

John B. Jones departed Richmond, Va., on Sunday bound for Montgomery, Ala., for an interview with Jefferson Davis. After travelling all night, he arrived in Wilmington, N.C.

Jones, John B., Rebel War Clerk, Wilmington, N.C.:

We traveled all night, and reached Wilmington, N.C. early in the morning. There I saw a Northern steamer which had been seized in retaliation for some of the seizures of the New Yorkers. And there was a considerable amount of ordnance and shot and shell on the bank of the river. The people everywhere on the road are for irremediable, eternal separation. Never were men more unanimous. And North Carolina has passed the ordinance, I understand, without a dissenting vote. *Better still, it is not to be left to a useless vote of the people.* [italics added]

Jones' comment on the "vote of the people" is true. The first public vote on the secession showed that the "people" did not desire to leave the Union. The North Carolina Legislature ignored that vote and opted to secede. A similar event occurred in Tennessee where the public vote held a 10,000 majority *to remain in the Union.* That vote too was ignored, and Tennessee was led into the Confederacy primarily by its pro-Southern Governor, Isham Harris.

### May 19 (Sunday)

Having arrived in Montgomery, Ala., four days previously, John B. Jones had been busy indeed. On the 16th he visited the Capitol and presented his papers to the Virginia delegation, from whom he received immediate support for his endeavors. On the 17th, Jones met President Jefferson Davis and told him he was looking for temporary employment, preferably in the War Department. Davis suggested that he see the Secretary of the Treasury, intimating that the War Department would not be a very busy place. On the 18th, Jones again saw President Davis, who again suggested the Treasury Department. Jones believed that the War Department would better suit his diary.

Jones, John B., Rebel War Clerk, Confederate War Department, Montgomery, Ala.:

The Secretary of War sent for me this morning, and said he required more assistance in his correspondence, then increasing daily; but the act of Congress limiting salaries would prevent him from offering me an adequate compensation. He could only name some ten or twelve hundred dollars. I told him my great desire was employment, and facilities to preserve interesting facts for future publication. I was installed at once, with Maj. Tyler, in the Secretary's own office. It was my duty to open and read the letters, noting briefly their contents on the back. The Secretary would then indicate in pencil marks the answers to be written, which the major and I prepared. These were signed by the Secretary, copied in another room, and mailed. I was happy in the discharge of these duties, and worked assiduously day and night.

### May 24 (Friday)

Maj. Gen. Benj. F. Butler, now commanding at Ft. Monroe, Va., took the first action of the war concerning Negro slaves who escaped into Union lines. Today, Butler refused to release three Negro slaves who had entered his lines, stating that they were "contraband of war," thus giving a new twist to the slave issue.

Butler was visited by Maj. J.B. Cary, CSA, who demanded to know with regard to the Negroes what course Butler intended to pursue. Butler's response was they were to be treated as "contraband of war" and not returned to their master. Cary then asked if Butler

did not feel myself [Butler] bound by my constitutional

obligations to deliver up fugitives under the fugitive-slave act. To this I replied that the fugitive-slave act did not affect a foreign country which Virginia claimed to be and that she must reckon it one of infelicities of her position that in so far at least she was taken at her word; that in Maryland, a loyal State, fugitives from service had been returned, and that even now although so much pressed by my necessities for the use of these men of Col. Mallory's yet if their master would come to the fort and take the oath of allegiance to the Constitution of the United States I would deliver the men up to him and endeavor to hire their services of him if he desired to part with them. To this Maj. Cary responded that Col. Mallory was absent.

### May 27 (Monday)

At Ft. Monroe, Va., Maj. Gen. Benj. F. Butler was gaining more runaway slaves than he could easily handle. These fell into a different category from the male laborers he had previously taken in from Virginia. Today, Butler further informed Lt. Gen. Scott in Washington:

> The inhabitants of Virginia are using their negroes in the batteries and are preparing to send the women and children south. The escapes from them are very numerous and a squad has come in this morning to my pickets bringing their women and children. Of course these cannot be dealt with upon the theory on which I designed to treat the services of able-bodied men and women who might come within my lines.... Up to this time I have had come within my lines men and women with their children, entire families, each family belonging to the same owner.

Butler proposed to put those capable of it to work, issue rations for all, and charge the rations against the pay the workers would receive. Three days later, Simon Cameron, Secretary of War, approved Butler's plan of action.

### May 28 (Tuesday)

On this date at Manassas Junction, Va., George H. Terrett, Colonel, CSA, former commander of the City of Alexandria, Va., reported to Gen. P.G.T. Beauregard the circumstances surrounding his evacuation of that city and the capture of a troop of Confederate cavalry commanded by Capt. Ball:

> Sir:... In regard to the capture of Capt. Ball and his troop I have to report that on the morning of the 24th instant about 1.30 A.M. Capt. Ball came to my quarters and reported that one of vedettes stationed at the Chain Bridge, about three miles west of Georgetown, D.C., had informed him that a squadron of cavalry had crossed over to the Virginia shore. I immediately ordered my command under arms to await further orders. About 5.30 A.M. an officer was sent from the steamer *Pawnee*, Northern Navy, to inform me that an overwhelming force was about entering the city of Alexandria and it would be madness to resist and that I could have until 9 A.M. to evacuate or surrender. I then ordered the troops under my command to assemble at the place designated by me on assuming command in Alexandria that I might either resist or fall back as circumstances might require. As soon as the troops were formed which was promptly done I repaired to the command, and then ascertaining that the enemy were entering the city by Washington street and that several steamers had been placed so that their guns could command many of the principal streets I ordered the command to march and proceeded out of the city by Duke street. Capt. Ball accompanied me as far as his quarters, a little west of the railroad depot where he halted, and I proceeded to the cars which were about half a mile from the depot, where I had ordered them to be stopped, and from orders given before marching out of the city the cavalry was to follow in my rear for the purpose of giving me information in regard to the movements of the enemy. Capt. Powell followed my instructions and why Capt. Ball did not I am unable to report.

At Columbus, Ohio, the *Ohio State Journal* ran an article describing the activity at Camp Jackson, on the edge of the city, which resulted in a new camp, Camp Chase, being constructed four miles west of the city.

> Workmen were engaged yesterday in taking down the barracks at Camp Jackson, for the purpose of removing to a new camp to be organized four miles west of the city. It is to be regular camp, and will contain one hundred acres. The land has been plowed, harrowed, and rolled smooth, and will make a good place for drilling purposes.

This was the beginning of Camp Chase, which would be a training center and then be partially converted into a prison camp for Confederate prisoners of war, and later, a Camp of Parole for returning Federal prisoners. The first Confederates held at Camp Chase were members of the 23d Virginia Regt., who were captured in the Kanawha Valley of western Virginia. These men arrived at Chase on July 5, 1861, and stayed but a short while before being exchanged. The largest number of prisoners at Camp Chase was in 1863, when over 8000 were incarcerated at that post.

### May 30 (Thursday)

Secretary of War Simon Cameron today notified Maj. Gen. Benj. Butler, at Ft. Monroe, Va., that Butler should retain any slaves entering his lines, employ them and keep records of their service.

### June 2 (Sunday)

In Northern Virginia, Gen. P.G.T. Beauregard took command of the Confederate forces around Manassas. There was light reconnoitering on both sides, but few prisoners taken. Those who were captured were exchanged by flag of truce between the local commanders.

In western Virginia, the Union and Confederate forces were milling around in the rain, the commanders trying to locate the enemy, the soldiers trying to keep dry.

### June 3 (Monday)

The Confederate privateer *Savannah*, under Capt. Baker, captured the American brig *Joseph* on the high seas. The *Savannah* was operating under a letter of *marque* from the Confederate government dated May 18, 1861. The *Savannah* was almost immediately taken by the U.S.S. *Perry*, Lt. Parrott. Capt. Baker and his crew were categorized as pirates, the United States not recognizing the letter of *marque* as a legal instrument.

In a minor action in western Virginia the Federal forces routed the Confederates at Philippi. The Confederates' flight became known as the "Philippi Races," a name the South did not enjoy. No prisoners were taken during this engagement.

### June 8 (Saturday)

In Tennessee, the voters in the western part of the state voted 2 to 1 *for secession*. In the eastern part of the

state, the vote was 2 to 1 *against secession*. Either way, Tennessee was already committed to the Confederacy.

### June 10 (Monday)

At Big Bethel, Va., the first serious battle of the war was fought between 2500 Federals from Ft. Monroe and 1200 Confederates. The Federals lost this one, losing 79 men, five of whom were probably captured. The Confederates lost 1 man.

Following the death of North Carolina Gov. Ellis, Henry T. Clark became Governor *ex officio*. In that capacity, he notified Confederate Secretary of War L.P. Walker, in Richmond:

Sir: Your communication of the 8th was laid before me today addressed to the late Gov. Ellis. Mr. Winslow informs me that after his conversation with the President he made on his return home particular inquiries as to the proper place for the proposed depot of prisoners. Neither at Hillsborough nor at Greensborough are there any buildings of capacity suitable. Upon application at Allemance, which in every way is a proper place, he found that the proprietor objected to it and declined to permit the buildings to be used. He ascertained that at Salisbury, to which place there are railroad communications north, south, and west and where supplies are cheap, a very large and commodious building could be purchased for $15,000. It was constructed for a cotton factory, can be made secure and comfortable for about 1500 to 2000 [prisoners] and would probably sell for $30,000 to $50,000 when the war is over. We will furnish the proper troops to guard. Should this be decided upon it had better be withheld from the public until the purchase is made.

With this beginning, one of the South's worst prisons got its start.

### June 14 (Friday)

Union troops, under the command of Col. Lew Wallace, entered Romney, western Virginia, after a long march from Cumberland, Md. After a brief skirmish with Confederate forces, Wallace returned to his base in Maryland.

### June 16 (Sunday)

On this day Henry (Heinrich Hartmann) Wirz of Milliken's Bend, La., a physician of that area, enlisted in Co. A, 4th Battalion, Louisiana Volunteers. This organization was sent east to serve in what later became the Army of Northern Virginia.

Wirz was born in Zurich, Switzerland, in November 1823. Wirz, in the 1840s, served a short prison term for "something to do with money." Wirz was well read, and he spoke German, English and French. His first wife died young, leaving him with two children who resided with his parents in Zurich. They did not migrate to the United States with their father in 1849.

Arriving in the United States, Wirz initially settled in Kentucky and five years later married a widow with two young daughters. Shortly after their marriage, the Wirz family moved to Milliken's Bend, La. On February 25, 1855, Wirz fathered a daughter (called Cora), the only child of his second marriage.

### June 21 (Friday)

John Henry Winder had returned to North Carolina from his visit to Montgomery, Ala., completely disgusted with the way the new Confederate government was doing things. He waited around Raleigh for a period, during which time the Confederate capital was moved to Richmond, Va. Earlier this month Winder went to Richmond to seek a commission in the Confederate Army. At Richmond, Winder found lodgings at the Spotswood Hotel and went to visit Jefferson Davis and his old friend Samuel Cooper. Cooper, a former U.S. Army Colonel, was now the Adjutant-General of the Confederate Army and the ranking general. On this date, Cooper forwarded a commission as a Brigadier General in the provisional army and designated Winder inspector general of all the military camps in the Richmond area. Winder wasted no time in accepting the appointment.

Brig. Gen. John H. Winder began his duties by becoming familiar with Richmond and its environs. His duties included the fitting out of the soldiers with uniforms and weapons before they were sent to the field, processing discharges of those unfit for service, capturing and returning Confederate soldiers deserting their units, and the care of the wounded and sick soldiers in the area. Quite a task, considering that the population of Richmond had doubled in less than four months, the city now full of office seekers, drunken soldiers, gamblers, prostitutes, and saloons. Richmond was like the Wild West towns later in the century. To accomplish his task, Winder discovered a truth that would haunt him for the entire period of the war: he would never have adequate staff to accomplish his mission.

### June 22 (Saturday)

The pro-Union sentiment brought a rally in Greeneville, Tenn., where the citizens declared their preference for the Union. Even though this part of the state would remain under Confederate control until late in the war, it furnished more troops for the Federal forces than for the South, and it was also a haven for escaped Union prisoners from the Carolinas and Georgia.

### June 28 (Friday)

The Confederate privateer *Jefferson Davis*, the former slave-trading ship *Echo*, was now involved in raiding American shipping on the high seas under a letter of *marque*. Today Capt. Louis M. Coxetter sailed the privateer from Charleston, S.C., to begin raids which resulted in the capture of several Union ships off the coast.

### July 1 (Monday)

In Baltimore, the arrest of the Board of Police Commissioners was in full swing. These noteworthy gentlemen, Southern sympathizers all, were incarcerated at Ft. McHenry. Some would later be sent to Ft. Warren in Boston Harbor.

After completing the arrests, Maj. Gen. N.P. Banks notified Lt. Gen. Scott that "the board of police was arrested this morning at 4 o'clock. Troops have been stationed at the principal squares of the city. All is perfectly quiet. We greatly need cavalry for patrol duty."

### July 2 (Tuesday)

To date, the Union and Confederacy had met only in minor battles, and the number of prisoners being held by either side was fairly small. In Richmond, no proper "prison" had yet been established for prisoners of war. In fact, the Richmond *Dispatch* of this date complained that the 75 to 100 Union prisoners being held at a depot on Main Street were wandering around the city almost free of constraint. Brig. Gen. Winder, who had the responsibility for these prisoners, largely ignored the newspaper's complaints. At the same time that Winder was being criticized by the Richmond papers for being lenient, the Northern papers were charging him with cruelty to those same prisoners in his charge.

### July 5 (Friday)

Gen. Robert E. Lee, commanding the area of Richmond, Va., today wrote Brig. Gen. John H. Winder, Confederate Commissary-General of Prisoners in Richmond:

> General: The President has learned that the crew of the privateer *Savannah* has been indicted by the grand jury of New York for treason and piracy, which he views as indicating an intention of not considering them as prisoners of war. I have consequently been directed to recall the paroles granted to Lt. Col. Alexander H. Bowman and Capts. Lyman M. Kellogg and Daniel Chase, belonging to the Army of the United States Government, and to place them with the rest of the prisoners of war in close confinement. You are therefore instructed to demand the written paroles given to the officers named, and to express to them the regret felt at depriving them of privileges which it would have been the pleasure of the President to have continued until they were exchanged but for the necessity he is under of awarding to them the same treatment extended the prisoners of the Confederate States.
>
> You will therefore take measures strictly to guard all the prisoners of war under your charge, granting to them every kindness and attention in your power compatible with their safe-keeping. You are also at liberty to explain to the prisoners the reason for the change in their treatment.

### July 6 (Saturday)

On this date Capt. William Smith, a privateer with a letter of *marque* from the Confederate government, captured by force the United States merchant ship *Enchantress* on the high seas. Smith's ship, the *Savannah*, was an armed merchant vessel with a specific mission to prey on United States shipping on the high seas.

Another Confederate privateer, the *Jefferson Davis*, operating east of Cape Hatteras, captured the brig *John Welsh*.

### July 7 (Sunday)

The Confederate privateer *Jefferson Davis*, Capt.

Louis M. Coxetter, captured the American schooner *S.J. Waring* about 150 miles east of Sandy Hook, N.J., the entrance to New York Harbor. A prize crew was put aboard and the ship sent to Charleston. On the 16th, one William Tilghman, a Negro crewman of the *Waring*, overwhelmed the prize crew from the *Jefferson Davis*, took possession of the schooner and sailed to New York, where it arrived on July 22.

### July 8 (Monday)

In Richmond, the war clerk's diary recorded his prejudice this day against John Henry Winder. This prejudice would last throughout the war and, in some cases, be wholly without foundation. Jones will take exception to every effort of Winder's and vilify him wherever possible.

Jones, John B., *Rebel War Clerk*, Confederate War Department, Richmond, Va.:

> There is a stout gray-haired old man here from Maryland applying to be made a general. It is Maj. J.H. Winder, a graduate of West Point, I believe; and I think he will be successful. He is the son, I believe, of Gen. Winder whose command in the last war with England unfortunately permitted the City of Washington to fall into the hands of the enemy. I have almost a superstitious faith in *lucky* generals, and a corresponding prejudice against unlucky ones, and their progeny. But I cannot suppose the President will order this general into the field. He may take the prisoners into his custody—and do other jobs as a sort of head of military police; and this is what I learn he proposes. And the French Prince, Polignac, has been made a colonel; and a great nephew of Kosciuszko has been commissioned a lieutenant in the regular army. Well, Washington had his Lafayette—and I like the nativity of these officers better than that of Northern men, still applying for commission.

One of the major problems in Richmond, and Washington, was the number of drunken soldiers roaming the streets. In Richmond, the Mayor, with fewer than 100 policemen, tried to solve the problem by closing the bars on Sundays and no later than ten P.M. during the week. This only seemed to put the drunks on the street earlier, and they became rowdier. The city's jails were full of soldiers who had been arrested for public drunkenness and disorderly conduct.

### July 11 (Thursday)

At the mouth of the Delaware River where it empties into Delaware Bay, some 48 miles south of Philadelphia, lies Pea Island. Just east of the island is New Jersey and to the west is Delaware City. During settlement of the area in Colonial days a Dutch ship loaded with peas was abandoned in the river after running aground. The peas grew, the island grew, and eventually the resulting land became large enough for a fort to be built on it during the Revolutionary War. A subsequent fort, named Ft. Delaware, was still standing during the Civil War. It was converted into a prison for Confederate soldiers, and it was used throughout the war.

In Missouri, the pro-Southern faction was getting more and more violent. Even the presence of pro-Union state militia was enough to set off the volatile atmosphere. In Neosho, Mo., the commander of a militia rifle company had a rather bad experience.

Conrad, Joseph, Capt., Rifle Co. B, Third Regt.. Missouri Vol., Springfield, Mo.:

Sir: In accordance with your order I most respectfully make hereby a statement of facts concerning the surrender of myself and men at Neosho July 5, 1861.

After you [Col. Franz Sigel] had left Neosho on the 4th of July I observed that the city was very unquiet. I took all necessary precautions by placing extra sentinels and sending out patrols every half hour day and night. The Fourth passed off quietly.

On the 5th day of July the same precaution was taken. About 11 o'clock I heard the cannonading, whereon I immediately dispatched a patrol of twenty men under the command of Lt. Damde to inquire if possible the cause of it. At 1 o'clock I received orders signed by Brigade Quartermaster Richardson to retreat with my command if necessary. Lt. Damde with his patrol returned about the same time. They had scarcely returned—in fact had not been in camp more than ten minutes—before the enemy came pouring in in all directions to the number of about 1200 to 1500 men under the command of Col. [Thomas] Churchill and Maj. [James] McIntosh (Arkansas Rangers). Finding it impossible for me to

hold my post with success, after due deliberation—after due consultation with my officers and men—I concluded that it would be best to make the surrender as it was required—namely unconditionally. We were after the surrender of our arms placed in the court house where we remained until Monday, the 8th.

I must mention here that the officers of the Arkansas Rangers as well as of the Missouri troops behaved themselves quietly, accommodatingly and friendly both towards myself and men; but their privates on the contrary in a most insulting and brutal manner.

On the 8th we were released, we officers having before given our parole of honor not to serve any more against the Confederate States of America during the war, my men having been sworn to the same effect. We left Neosho on the evening of the 8th, at 5:30 o'clock, with an escort of about thirty men under the command of Capt. Boone for our security and protection, the people of Neosho and farmers of that vicinity having threatened to kill us in the streets. Capt. Boone escorted us about four miles from the camp. After innumerable hardships and dangers, without food and water, our canteens having all been stolen from us by the Southern troops, we at last reached Springfield, my men all broken down having traveled the distance of eighty-five miles in fifty hours with hardly any food at all.

Having made this statement I respectfully place the same in your hands to judge my actions.

### July 12 (Friday)

Confederate Brig. Gen. Robert Selden Garnett was retreating into the Cheat River valley of western Virginia. The Federal forces were well into the Great Kanawha Valley and their meeting with Brig. Gen. Henry Wise's Confederate force was nearing.

### July 13 (Saturday)

In western Virginia on the 10th, Union Maj. Gen. George B. McClellan placed three Union brigades at Buckhannon and one at Philippi ready to move against Confederate Gen. Robert S. Garnett's smaller forces at Rich Mountain and Laurel Hill. On the 11th, at Rich Mountain, Brig. Gen. Rosecrans successfully moved 2000 troops over very rough terrain and attacked the rear of Confederate Lt. Col. [John] Pegram's force of 1300, cutting off the Southern retreat. Federal losses were only 12 killed and 49 wounded. No reliable record of Confederate losses is available. Pegram's men managed to scatter and escape. Also on the 11th, north of Rich Mountain at Laurel Hill, Federal Gen. T.A. Morris's troops demonstrated against Gen. Robert S. Garnett's Rebel force, causing Garnett to evacuate his positions. On the 12th, Garnett was retreating into the Cheat River valley while part of the Confederate troops from the Rich Mountain fight escaped to Staunton, Va. McClellan came into Beverly, western Virginia about noon. Garnett's troops crossed Cheat Mountain in the rain and entered the Cheat River valley. About noon the Federals caught up and a fight was made at Corrick's Ford in which Garnett was killed, giving him the dubious honor of being the first General Officer to be killed, North or South. His body was recovered by Federal troops who returned it to his family. Pegram was forced to surrender 555 of his troops. This was one of the largest groups of soldiers captured to date.

From Beverly, western Virginia, Maj. Gen. George B. McClellan wired Col. E.D. Townsend, in Washington, concerning the number of prisoners of war he was about to have custody of:

> Have received from Pegram proposition for surrender with his officers and remnant of his command, say 600 men. Have accepted surrender agreeing to treat them with kindness due prisoners of war, but stating that it was not in my power to relieve them from any liability incurred by taking arms against the United States. They are said to be extremely penitent and determined never again to take arms against the General Government. I shall have nearly 900 or 1000 prisoners to take care of when Pegram comes in. The question is an embarrassing one. Please give me immediate instruction by telegraph as to the disposition to be made of officers and men taken prisoners of war. I recommend that course as in many instances calculated to produce an excellent effect upon the deluded masses of the rebels.
>
> The latest accounts make the loss of the rebels killed some 150.

### July 14 (Sunday)

In response to McClellan's telegram yesterday, Union Gen. Winfield Scott, in Washington, replied on this date:

> You have the applause of all who are high in authority here.
>
> Discharge all your prisoners of war under the grade of commissioned officers who shall willingly take and subscribe a general oath....
>
> As to the officers among your prisoners permit all to return to their homes who willingly sign a written general parole....
>
> But you will except from this privilege all officers among your prisoners who have recently been officers of the U.S. Army or Navy and who you may have reason to believe left either with the intent of bearing arms against the United States. The captured officers of this description you will send to Ft. McHenry.

### July 15 (Monday)

Federal Secretary of the Navy Gideon Welles today wrote Lt. E.G. Parrott, U.S.S. *Perry*, congratulating him on the capture of the Confederate privateer *Savannah* on the high seas. The *Savannah*, Capt. William Smith, was taken to Philadelphia, where the Confederate crew was incarcerated as pirates.

Gen. Winfield Scott, General-in-Chief of the U.S. Army, directed Maj. Gen. George B. McClellan, in western Virginia, to release the enlisted prisoners and those officers who will take a parole *except those who are known or supposed to have recently resigned from the Army or Navy of the United States with the intention of entering the ranks of the rebels.* The latter category of prisoner was to be sent to Ft. McHenry in Baltimore, to Maj. Gen. Nathaniel Banks, and then they were to be transferred, under guard in an armed steamer, to Ft. Lafayette, New York, for incarceration. This would affect several officers who had resigned their commissions and "gone South" to serve the Confederacy.

### July 16 (Tuesday)

Out from the camps around Alexandria and Washington moved McDowell's over 1400 officers and 30,000 men. All five of the division commanders and eight of the 11 brigade commanders were Regular Army officers, some with much field experience. The march to Manassas (Centreville) was a nightmare.

The troops had little training in marching. The long lines of troops and artillery would snake down a road, stop for a while, move for a short distance, stop for a longer while, and move again. The troops drank all their water in the first three hours (in a hot sun) and had no place to get more.

There was much breaking of ranks to sit in the shade or to pick blackberries. Equipment that seemed light enough in Alexandria now weighed tons and was discarded along the road.

In Richmond, Robert E. Lee appointed Winder to command of the camp of instruction located outside the city at the fair grounds but cancelled the order two days later. Winder remained in his duties as Inspector General. About this same time Winder was given the responsibility of dealing with the prisoners of war in the city of Richmond.

### July 17 (Wednesday)

About this date, Richard Bayley Winder, second cousin to John Henry Winder, would join the 39th Virginia as a commissioned officer. A year later, then a Captain, Richard joined Gen. John H. Winder's command at Richmond and remained with him throughout the war.

### July 18 (Thursday)

At noon McDowell's army approached Centreville, 22 miles and two and one-half days after leaving his camps around Alexandria. The temperature was nearing 90°F, the men were out of water and did not have the cooked rations they were to have had before they left Alexandria. Confederate Gen. Joseph E. Johnston was hurrying from the Shenandoah Valley.

McDowell decided to reconnoitre the area and sent a brigade-size force from Brig. Gen. Daniel Tyler's division to Blackburn Ford, where Col. I.B. Richardson took the brigade further than it was supposed to go and met Beauregard's troops in a bloody clash which accomplished little except to cause the Federals to retreat.

### July 20 (Saturday)

At Centreville, Va., the opposing armies were assembling troops, getting them fed and ready for battle.

McDowell completed his preparations and assignments. About 2:30 A.M. the 21st, McDowell had all his troops in motion towards the Confederates.

### July 21 (Sunday)

Knowing that the battle would begin, several U.S. congressmen and their ladies with picnic baskets and wine travelled to Centreville by carriage to see the battle. Traffic and constant jockeying for position on the field interfered with troop movements and control. One congressman would later be captured and sent to Libby Prison in Richmond.

Union Gen. McDowell attacked the force at Manassas around a little creek called Bull Run. The battle was confused and chaotic, and resulted in a Federal retreat. The Union losses were about 460 killed, 1124 wounded, and 1312 taken prisoner or missing. This was the largest group of prisoners the South had to contend with to this date. The Union captured but few of the missing 13 Confederates. Gen. Beauregard ordered the prisoners removed to Richmond.

### July 22 (Monday)

The Federal troops defeated at Manassas began to straggle into Washington, most of them having walked the distance in a matter of a few hours, after taking more than two days to get there. Many of the wounded were in terrible shape when they arrived, and they only found inadequate hospital facilities there.

### July 23 (Tuesday)

In Richmond, the relatively few Union prisoners were housed in Harwood's Tobacco Factory at Main and 26th Streets. When the prisoners taken at Manassas arrived, this caused a sudden overload, and additional buildings were needed. The next facility was Ligon's Warehouse and Tobacco Factory at the intersection of Main and 25th Streets. Water and gas pipes were put into the buildings and troughs were used as latrines. Into these buildings went the prisoners from the July Battle of Manassas and the later (October) Battle of Ball's Bluff. One of the more distinguished prisoners was Alfred Ely, a congressman from New York, who was taken on the Manassas battlefield. Neither of the buildings now in use was furnished with cots, eating facilities, or other essential items.

### July 25 (Thursday)

In Richmond, the prisoners from Manassas were in the city and the wounded arrived hourly. Many of the physicians of the city headed for the battle-field to assist.

Jones, John B., Rebel War Clerk, Confederate War Department, Richmond, Va.:

Our prisons are filled with Yankees, and Brig. Gen. Winder has employment. There is great pressure for passports to visit the battle-field. At my suggestion, all physicians taking amputating instruments, and relatives of the wounded and slain, have been permitted by the Secretary to go thither.

### July 27 (Saturday)

On the western frontier, the Seventh U.S. Infantry commander, Maj. I. Lynde, surrendered his command without firing a shot to an inferior Confederate force commanded by Capt. John R. Baylor. The Seventh Infantry officers, after giving their parole, were free to leave for United-States-held territory. A number of the captured Federal troops deserted to the Confederates, including a hospital steward, one sergeant, and twenty-four privates. Maj. Lynde would be recommended for court-martial when he reached Union territory.

Two days previously Col. William Johnston, CSA, reported to Acting Gov. Henry T. Clark of North Carolina concerning the status of the proposed prison buildings at Salisbury, N.C.:

I proceeded to Salisbury to obtain the necessary information in relation to the Chambers factory and appurtenances proposed to be purchased for the use of the Confederate States as a prisoners' depot. The lot comprises sixteen acres with and contiguous to the corporate limits of the town of Salisbury, and contains the principal factory building, about ninety by fifty feet, three stories high, with an engine house at one end about sixteen by eighty feet, constructed of good brick; also six brick tenements with four rooms each, and a larger superintendent's house of framed materials, with smith shop and two or three inferior buildings. The property was originally used as a cotton manufacturing establishment.... Without making any accurate calculations as to the cost of repairs for the purposes intended I should think $2000 would be amply sufficient.... The location of the property is very eligible, shaded by a beautiful

grove of oaks and well supplied with good water.... The government is authorized to occupy the building immediately.

The problem of prisoners in North Carolina was rapidly becoming more acute. Acting Gov. Clark notified Confederate Secretary of War Walker that the governor had neither lodging nor money to purchase food for the prisoners sent him after the battle at Manassas, Va. A further problem was furnishing guards for the proposed prison at Salisbury. The state did not want to use "combat available" troops, as these troops were needed in the Army of Northern Virginia. The use of locals conscripted specifically for this purpose was under discussion.

### July 29 (Monday)

In Richmond, Brig. Gen. John H. Winder was having problems keeping a staff. It seems that those assigned him were then reassigned at about the time they learned their duties. Winder wrote the Secretary of War:

Sir: The duties of my position are very heavy both indoors and out, and they are rendered still more so by the frequent changes made in the officers detailed to assist me. There have already been six officers detailed for duty with me (not including those at the prison). Of the six only one remains. These officers do not remain long enough to acquire sufficient knowledge of the details to assist me much.... I would respectfully ask that ... I may be permitted to select two or three young, active men at such compensation as the Secretary of War may designate. The writing connected with the prisoners of war is enough to occupy one person.

To add to the confusion, the captives from Bull Run, as well as the wounded (from both sides), began to arrive in Richmond in numbers. Winder had no place prepared for them, having only recently been given that responsibility, so he placed them in the city's alm house. This was only a stopgap, and more permanent quarters would soon have to be found.

About this same time the tinder was lit between Winder and Lucius Bellinger Northrop. Northrop, a former student of Winder's at West Point in 1830, had been wounded during the Seminole War and was physically incapable of performing the role of a soldier. He retained his commission, however, and went on to study medicine, building a good practice in Charleston, S.C. When the war started, Northrop, 50, resigned his commission in the Union Army and went to Richmond. President Davis appointed him a Colonel and placed him in charge of the commissary for the Confederate Army. This was a poor choice on Davis's part, for Northrop had no training in this type of operation.

Unfortunately, both Winder and Northrop had much the same temperament. Both were strong-minded, and it didn't take long for the sparks to fly. They would spend countless wasted hours writing letters to, and about, each other, until Winder died in February 1865.

In North Carolina, Acting Gov. Henry T. Clark had a problem. It seems that a group of Union prisoners had been sent to Raleigh unannounced, and Clark had no idea

in what manner I shall treat the prisoners of war sent on here by Lt. Todd a week since. They were sent on here without any previous notice. I had no quarters for them and no instructions from you how I should treat them. Rather than embarrass you I received them from Lt. Todd, and have had them shut up in a house ever since with a full company of volunteers guarding. The officers on their parole are walking about the streets. They are without money and have applied to me for what may be necessary to meet their demands (daily), and I am provided with no funds for them but have ordered each of them served with soldier's rations.... They have been furnished with food and with clothes....

They are odious to our people and the guarding of them is regarded as degrading among our volunteers.... Under these circumstances I would most respectfully ask not to be encumbered with more, and suggest that perhaps some State further south might better do it, but make some provision for those already sent.

Jones, John B., Rebel War Clerk, Confederate War Dept., Richmond, Va.:

Today quite a number of our wounded men on crutches, and with arms in splints, made their appearance in the streets, and created a sensation. A year hence, and we shall be accustomed to such spectacles.

## July 30 (Tuesday)

The Confederate Secretary of War, L.P. Walker, notified Gov. Henry T. Clark of North Carolina that the arrangement to buy the factory at Salisbury, N.C., for use as a prison for Union prisoners of war was satisfactory. The owners even agreed to take Confederate bonds in payment! This was not a good long-term investment on their part.

At Ft. Monroe, Maj. Gen. Benj. F. Butler was having a time with the Negroes who had entered his lines seeking freedom. He referred to them as "contraband of war" and put them to work preparing fortifications. He asked for a opinion from the Secretary of War in Washington as to the legal status of these former slaves.

## July 31 (Wednesday)

Rumor is the worst enemy of the soldier. Near Manassas, Va., Gen. Joseph E. Johnston, CSA, wrote Maj. Gen. Irwin McDowell, USA, concerning a very vicious rumor.

Sir: Information has been given me that two soldiers of the Army of the Confederate States whilst upon picket duty were hung near Centreville on the night of the 17th instant. The object of this communication is to ascertain the nature of the offense which required this ignominious punishment and upon what evidence the decision was based. If not done by your authority I must demand that the perpetrators of this violation of the usages of civilized warfare be delivered to me for such punishment as the nature of their offense demands, or be punished by yourself.

## August 1 (Thursday)

In Richmond, Surgeon-General S.P. Moore visited the buildings being occupied by the Union prisoners. His report to the Confederate Secretary of War stated:

I visited the buildings occupied by the prisoners yesterday afternoon. The upper building has on the first floor fifty-two officers, including five surgeons; the latter are assisting the medical officer in his attendance on sick prisoners. The second and third floors contain 261 men. In the lower building are 551 prisoners. The police of these buildings is very bad, especially the lower one. The yard of the upper building requires much policing. From the crowded state of these buildings it is feared that a pestilence may make its appearance, and if it should the city would be the sufferer. It is therefore recommended that an additional building be had so as to make a more proper distribution for these men.

Today, Maj. Gen. Irwin McDowell, USA, responded to Gen. Joseph E. Johnston, CSA, concerning two Confederate soldiers allegedly hanged by Federal forces in July:

General: I have to acknowledge the receipt of your letter of the 31st ultimo by flag of truce. You state information has been given you that two of your soldiers whilst upon picket duty were hung near Centreville on the night of the 17th of July. This is certainly utterly without foundation, and should be classed with those rumors and accusations made against you as well as against me by people with overheated imaginations. It has as little truth as the charge generally believed here that you fired on our hospital knowing it to be such, and that your troops bayoneted all our wounded who fell into their hands, a charge I have not hesitated even against most positive direct evidence to put down as false.

I have never heard of the hanging of any man by the troops under my command and am confident not one has been hung. At the time you state, the evening of the 17th, we were not in possession of Centreville. All of your men who have fallen into my hands have been treated with every consideration of which their position admitted.

### August 3 (Saturday)

In Richmond, Judah P. Benjamin, former U.S. Senator from Louisiana and now head of the Department of Justice in the Confederate government, struck to the heart of the problem with the capture and trial of the crew of the privateer *Savannah*. The United States government intended to try the crew as pirates, although the crew had been operating under a letter of *marque* from the Confederate government. William M. Browne, Assistant Secretary of State, requested an opinion from Benjamin as to how counsel could be provided the privateer crew during their trial. Benjamin replied:

I beg to say that I would cheerfully give any aid in my power to the counsel charged with the defense of

the captain and crew of the *Savannah* but I am totally at a loss to see what can be done here.

The counsel desires parol proof of the action of this Government. We can send no witnesses to New York. We can furnish no such proof in time of war. *The question appears to me to be much more of a political than of a legal character. If the United States refuse to consider this Government as even belligerent I do not see what effect the offer of parol proof could have. If we be recognized as belligerents the action of the public authorities of a belligerent nation can in no manner be authenticated so conclusively as by its seal.* [italics added]

Regarding the location of a prison at Salisbury, N.C., Lt. Col. R.H. Riddick, Assistant Adjutant-General for that state, wrote Gen. Samuel Cooper, Adjutant-General, CSA:

Salisbury is located in the most productive region of the State. I have no doubt that if Col. Johnson, our Commissary-General of Subsistence, were authorized to do so he could make a contract for subsisting the prisoners at a much less cost than to issue to them the usual army ration. Fruits, vegetables (garden) and fresh meats are produced in great abundance with a very limited market for them. That county has furnished nearly 1000 men for the war, which of course increases the usual surplus productions in that proportion. I am creditably informed that more wheat has been raised in that part of the State than can be stored away in the usual granaries.

This "surplus" of production will plague the South all during the war. Most areas of the South grew huge quantities of food but had no means of shipping it to the needed points (such as Richmond). It seemed incongruous that the prisoners who were to occupy Salisbury during the war were so ill-fed.

### August 7 (Wednesday)

The passage of information between the warring factions was a constant, and worrisome, thing for the duration of the war. That, coupled with the fact that newspapers would print *anything* created problems on both sides.

Jones, John B., Rebel War Clerk, Confederate War Department, Richmond, Va.:

The New York *Herald* has been received, containing a pretty accurate list of our military forces in the different camps of the Confederate States, with the names and grades of the general officers. The Secretary told me that if he had required such a list, a more correct one could not have been furnished him. Who is the traitor? Is he in the Adjutant-General's office?... For my part, I have no doubt there are many Federal spies in the departments. Too many clerks are imported from Washington.

### August 8 (Thursday)

In Richmond, as in Washington, spies, both real and imagined, were on everyone's mind. Brig. Gen. J.H. Winder in Richmond was taking an active role in investigating those suspected of spying, much to the chagrin of many of the citizens. To control movement of the population in the South, a system of "passports" was enacted on this date for those wishing to travel outside of their immediate area. These passports were controlled by Gen. Winder's department and the investigation of those requesting passports was handled by Winder's men.

Winder recruited thirty civilians to act as agents for his department; fourteen of these were from Maryland and a few were from New York or Philadelphia. To the citizens of Richmond, these men were aliens and were treated as such—thoroughly despised by the populace. To further add to the ill feelings, several of Winder's men were Jews and Richmond was generally an anti-Semitic city. While some of these agents were honest and capable, most were arrogant and abused their powers.

Also in Richmond, the Confederate Congress enacted a law directing that all aliens leave the country within 40 days. This was primarily to clear out the large numbers of foreign speculators in cotton and tobacco who were in Richmond and largely underfoot of the government officials. The law also was meant to reduce the number of "spies" and "foreign agents" believed to be in the capital.

The crew of the rebel privateer *Petrel*, captured by the U.S.S. *St. Lawrence*e, was brought to the port of Philadelphia on this date and held as pirates.

The Confederate Secretary of War, L.P. Walker, directed that Brig. Gen. John H. Winder take immediate action to relieve the crowding of the prisoners within Richmond. This directive was in response to the Surgeon-General's letter of August 1. Winder reminded the Secretary that the overcrowding had been caused by the Surgeon-General taking over one of the buildings then used as a prison for use as a hospital. Another building was, in fact, procured for use as a prison and would be occupied on this date.

Maj. Gen. Benj. F. Butler, in Hampton, Va., had asked the Secretary of War, Simon Cameron, for clarification on what to do with Negroes entering Union lines to escape slavery. He, Butler, being an avid (almost rabid) abolitionist, had construed a way around the old Federal Fugitive Slave Laws, which required the return of all "runaway" slaves, by treating them as "property" and, as such, classed as "contraband of war." Cameron, ever the sly fox, said the Fugitive Slave Laws *must be respected in the states of the Union*; however, *for the states in insurrection the situation was different*. In essence, if a slave in Kentucky, Maryland, Missouri, the District of Columbia, or elsewhere in the North ran away, that slave must be returned to the master, but in the Southern states different rules applied. The slaves, of course, had no say in this discussion. Cameron did concede, however, that those slaves now classed as "contraband" could not be returned. This concept of "contraband" would have far-reaching effects when the freed Negroes entered the Union army and were captured by the South.

### August 9 (Friday)

In Missouri, the clash between the Federal and Rebel forces was fast approaching. The two Confederate forces were being led by Maj. Gen. Ben McCulloch and the Missouri State Guard was headed by former governor Sterling Price.

On this date the *Ohio State Journal* reported that:

Capt. J.W. Free arrived here at a late hour last night from Lexington, Perry County, Ohio, with a company of one hundred and fifty men. This company brought with them from Zanesville one hundred and ten Rebel prisoners, which the Seventeenth Ohio Regiment had sent to that place. Among the number were one preacher, one lawyer, and one doctor.

### August 10 (Saturday)

At Wilson's Creek, Mo., the second "major" battle of the Civil War—and the first in the western theater—was fought on this day. The battlefield was amid rolling hills and brush-choked gullies with poor visibility. The battle ended with about 186 Federals captured and no Confederates taken prisoner. The Federals lost nearly 25 percent of their force in the battle.

### August 16 (Friday)

Lincoln, at long last, declared the Southern states in a state of rebellion and forbade all commerce with them. This ended, at least legally, the trade in cotton, etc. in the sub-rosa market place. It also made clearer the status of the prisoners of war held by the South at this point. Both Congress and the military had urged Lincoln to agree to a cartel so that prisoners could be exchanged. Lincoln, rightly, had refused because of the legal repercussions of such a recognition of the South.

### August 17 (Saturday)

In Richmond, War Clerk Jones recorded actions relating to the expulsion of aliens from the Confederacy:

The President has issued a proclamation, in pursuance of the act of Congress passed on the 8th instant, commanding all alien enemies to leave in forty days; and the Secretary of War has indicated Nashville as the place of exit. This produces little excitement, except among the Jews, some of whom are converting their effects into gold and departing.

### August 18 (Sunday)

After several successful captures of American shipping, the Confederate privateer *Jefferson Davis*, Capt. Coxetter, wrecked on the bar at the entrance to St. Augustine, Fla., thus ending her short career.

### August 19 (Monday)

At Columbus, Ohio, the *Ohio State Journal* reported:

Twenty-eight prisoners arrived Saturday from West Virginia via Cincinnati; and of these, twenty-three are on parole. They will be immediately transferred to Richmond, Va. The reporter heard one of them remark that if they took Washington City they would not burn it, for there were too many good buildings there; and as they wished to make it the capital of the Confederacy sometime, these buildings would be needed.

### August 20 (Tuesday)

Today, the *Ohio State Journal* in Columbus ran another article concerning the prisoners held at that city:

GONE. The secessionists who attracted eager crowds at the American Hotel yesterday left for their homes in Virginia today. They were released on parole not to take up arms against the government again.

These same prisoners were probably recaptured later in the war, parole or no parole.

### August 24 (Saturday)

On this day, President Jefferson Davis named Pierre A. Rost commissioner to Spain. He also named James M. Mason to Great Britain and John Slidell to France. Their mission was to gain recognition for the Confederacy and to act as purchasing agents for arms, materials, etc. Rost's trip would be uneventful. Mason and Slidell were destined to take a slight detour.

In Washington, two alleged spies, Mrs. Rose Greenhow and Mrs. Philip Phillips, were arrested on charges of corresponding with the Confederates.

### August 27 (Tuesday)

With a force of eight ships and nine hundred men, Maj. Gen. Ben Butler arrived off Cape Hatteras, N.C., and the U.S. Navy began bombardment of Fts. Clark and Hatteras. Clark was abandoned early with little or no opposition. Hatteras resisted. Butler put some troops ashore, but with great difficulty, due to heavy wind and seas.

### August 28 (Wednesday)

Federal War Department General Orders No. 69, of this date, directed that: "II. All enlisted men in the volunteer service who have been taken prisoners by the enemy and released on parole will be discharged from the service." This action cleared many of the problems encountered in trying to exchange prisoners between the warring factions—no parolees, no exchanges.

The Confederate forces at Cape Hatteras, N.C., surrendered to the Union forces commanded by Flag Officer Silas Stringham and Maj. Gen. Benjamin Butler. The prisoners were removed to the Federal fleet and sent to New York Harbor for incarceration.

Some civilians in the South had their own ideas of how to handle the prisoner-of-war situation. One James Phelan of Aberdeen, Miss., today wrote President Davis:

Let the Yankee prisoners be confined and then give notice to the United States government that after a certain day no more food, clothing, or medicine will be furnished said prisoners by the Confederate States, and that the United States must take care of them. Should they refuse, let them starve. We have delivered our souls.

### September 1 (Sunday)

Brig. Gen. U.S. Grant assumed command in the area of Cape Girardeau in southeast Missouri.

### September 2 (Monday)

Today, 678 prisoners of war, officers and men, captured at Fts. Clark and Hatteras in North Carolina arrived aboard the U.S. Flagship *Minnesota*, Flag Officer Stringham, in New York Harbor.

In Richmond, President Davis received a helpful suggestion from Mr. W.A. Wilson of Ft. Sullivan, Tex., about the Federal prisoners of war:

Honored Sir: You will please pardon the liberty I take in addressing you and offering a suggestion with regard to the prisoners which we have taken. Learning from the papers that the Federal Government will not exchange, and they consuming our sustenance in the meantime, and knowing that your mind is ever filled with pressing and important business is the cause of my writing and calling your attention to the importance of having a railroad connecting this State with Louisiana for military, mail and other purposes, and suggesting the propriety of having those prisoners accomplish the work. They might as well work, as they have to be fed.

### September 5 (Thursday)

The Mayor of Richmond, Va., appealed to the local Army Inspector General, Brig. Gen. John Henry Winder, for assistance in keeping order in Richmond. Winder, with his usual efficiency, immediately responded. He obtained a large tenement building, took the soldiers from the city's jail, and marched them to the tenement where they were placed under guard. The wayward soldiers would remain there until released to their units after trial for their offenses.

Today, Tazewell W. Trice, of Cotton Plant, Ark., wrote President Davis on his idea on treatment of the prisoners of war:

The people of these parts are complaining at the disparity of treatment of prisoners on the part of the Yankees and that of the Confederacy; and while we regret the necessity of retaliation, yet we see no alternative left but to do so, and Lincoln and his partisans think we are afraid. We would suggest that all that you have of the Lincoln party in the East be handcuffed and sent to Ft. Sumter, there to be placed on bread and water, and, further, that Gens. Pillow, Hardee, and McCulloch be instructed to break the left legs of all that they now or hereafter may have in their possession and then turn them loose.

### September 9 (Monday)

In Washington, Charles Henry Winder, a respected attorney and brother to Brig. Gen. John H. Winder, CSA, was arrested as a disloyal citizen for his forthright stand on the rights of the southern states to secede. He was held in the Old Capitol Prison until his release on parole about October 15th. He would remain free for the remainder of the war.

### September 10 (Tuesday)

In Philadelphia, one of the prominent citizens of the city who believed that it was wrong to start a war over secession was William Henry Winder, another brother of Brig. Gen. John Henry Winder, CSA. He wrote Secretary of War Simon Cameron letters denouncing the Union stance on secession. William Henry also publicly, and loudly, denounced Lincoln's policy towards the South. He also refused to take an oath of allegiance to the Union. Secretary of War Cameron ordered his arrest on this date and directed that he be taken to Ft. Lafayette in New York for imprisonment. Winder would remain there until mid-October when he would be removed to Ft. Warren prison in Boston Harbor. At Ft. Warren, William Henry would be held for the next 15 months without charges being brought against him. William Henry was finally released on November 27, 1862.

### September 12 (Thursday)

The Federal government ordered the arrest for disloyalty of Maryland legislators who were scheduled to convene in Frederick on Sept. 17th. The arrests were ordered because the legislators were rumored to be about to vote to secede from the Union. Arrests began on this day and continued through the 17th, the prisoners being sent to Ft. Warren in Boston Harbor. Maryland remained loyal to the Union.

### September 20 (Friday)

At Lexington, Mo., the siege that began on the 12th by Maj. Gen. Sterling Price ended today with the surrender of Col. James A. Mulligan's Irish Guard command of 2800 Federals. Price (former Governor of Missouri) delayed assaulting for five days while Mulligan waited for relief that never came from Union forces under Maj. Gen. John Frémont. On the 18th, Price assaulted Mulligan's works to no avail. The following day, the 19th, another attempt was made that met with more success; this time the Confederates used dampened bales of hemp which they rolled forward as they advanced to protect the assaulting troops. Finally, on this date, Mulligan capitulated. Price, with an additional 2800 muskets available, called for the people of Missouri to join him.

### September 29 (Sunday)

Col. Gustavus Loomis, commanding Ft. Columbus, N.Y., reported to the Adjutant-General in Washington that two prisoners had died within Castle William at the fort. Loomis strongly recommended that the prisoners be removed to other locations before the onset of cold weather because the quarters were unheated.

### September 30 (Monday)

On Governor's Island, N.Y., Andrew Norman, an Orderly Sergeant captured at Ft. Hatteras, N.C., on August 29, wrote Simon Cameron, Union Secretary of War:

The undersigned are orderly sergeants of the companies taken prisoner at the surrender of Ft. Hatteras, on the coast of North Carolina, on the 29th ultimo. Our men are now suffering very greatly from disease. Today 115 of the 630 are confined by disease which threatens to prostrate us all.

In this conflict now being waged between the two sections of our country prisoners have been discharged by both parties, as at Rich Mountain, Springfield and Lexington, upon their parole not to bear arms until released from their obligation. We ask for our men that they may be permitted to return to their homes upon the same pledge. We are assured that a knowledge of our condition would incline you favorably to consider this application. The officer having the care of us, Lt. Case, of this post, has been active in kindness to us but the want of room and the presence of contagious diseases among us, unused as we are to this climate, defy all his efforts to protect us against it by force. Four of our men have died within the past five days and as many others are dangerously ill.

Surgeon William J. Sloan, USA, inspected the quarters of the prisoners from Cape Hatteras and wrote the following report to Col. G. Loomis, commanding Ft. Columbus, N.Y.:

Sir: I have the honor to report that the condition of the Ft. Hatteras prisoners in the castle at this post is such as to require the immediate attention of the Government. They are crowded into an ill-ventilated building which has always been an unhealthy one when occupied by large bodies of men. There are no conveniences for cooking except in the open air, no means of heating the lower tier of gun rooms and no privies within the area. As the winter approaches I cannot see how these 630 men can be taken care of under the above circumstances. These men are without clothing and are not disposed to use the means prescribed by me for the prevention of disease unless compelled to do so. Everything necessary in a sanitary point of view has been urged upon them but is only carried out by the persistent efforts of the officer in charge of the castle. Under all these circumstances with the effect of change of climate and the depression resulting from their situation disease must be the result.

There are now upwards of eighty cases of measles amongst them, a number of cases of typhoid fever, pneumonia, intermittent fever, &c. I have taken the worst cases into my hospital and am preparing it with beds to its full capacity for other cases. Every building upon the island being crowded with troops, with a large number of tents, I know not how the condition of these prisoners can be improved except by a change of location to some other place for all or a portion of them, the present condition of things resulting principally from deficiency of quarters and not from causes within our control.

## October 1 (Tuesday)

A major problem arose when the privateers were captured on the high seas after attacking United States shipping. It was really a question of legality and the recognition of the "letter of marque" being used by the privateer. Today, the question of issuing "letters of marque" by the South which allowed privateering on the high seas was settled for the Union when Secretary of the Navy Gideon Welles rejected their issue on the grounds that such issuance would be "a recognition of the assumption of the insurgents that they were a distinct and independent nationality."

## October 3 (Thursday)

Quartermaster-General of the Union Army M.C. Meigs wrote Simon Cameron, Secretary of War, about the establishment of a "depot for prisoners" upon one of the islands in the west end of Lake Erie. He recommended the appointment of Lt. Col. William Hoffman, USA, to the post of Commissary of Prisoners for the Union forces. Lt. Col. Hoffman, at the time, was a paroled prisoner and could not take active field command against the Confederacy.

## October 5 (Saturday)

Brig. Gen. Benjamin Huger, CSA, at Norfolk, Va., reported to Gen. Samuel Cooper in Richmond that:

Col. Wright, from Roanoke Island, reports that on the 1st October he and Capt. Lynch with three steamers and 150 men, Third Georgia Regiment, fell in with and captured the Lincoln steamer *Fanny*, 2 officers and 48 men, loaded with quartermaster's and commissary stores and ammunition. What disposition shall I make of the prisoners?

## October 7 (Monday)

Quartermaster-General M.C. Meigs, in Washington, directed that Lt. Col. William Hoffman, Eighth Infantry, in New York, was to be appointed as Commissary-General of Prisoners, to inspect the group of islands known as Put-In-Bay, and Kelley's Island in Lake Erie, off Sandusky, Ohio, with reference to leasing them to build a depot for prisoners of war.

## October 8 (Tuesday)

In New York, Surgeon William J. Sloan, USA, wrote Col. G. Loomis, commanding Ft. Columbus in New York Harbor, about the condition of the Confederate prisoners taken at Cape Hatteras:

Colonel: I have the honor to report that the condition of the sick prisoners has not improved. Deaths occur almost daily and there continues to be a large number of cases of measles, pneumonia, typhoid fever, &c. I have taken as many cases into the hospital as can be accommodated. The sickness will continue and increase so long as a large body of men is crowded together in Castle William. If 100 are removed to Bedloe's Island as contemplated and including a large proportion of the sick there will be better facilities for improving the condition of those remaining.

## October 16 (Wednesday)

John Yates Beall (pronounced Bell) was born in Jefferson Co., Va., on Jan. 1, 1835. He attended the University of Virginia and returned home in 1856. When Virginia seceded from the Union in April 1861, Beall joined the Second Virginia Regiment which became a part of the famed "Stonewall" Brigade. Following the Battle of First Manassas he returned home to the Shenandoah Valley for a short period of time and on this day took part in a battle which involved Col. Turner Ashby's Brigade near his home. Severely wounded in this battle, he was medically discharged from the Confederate Army. Restless, he went west to Iowa and then to Canada, where he conceived the idea of freeing the Confederate prisoners at Camp Douglas in Chicago and on Johnson's Island near Sandusky, Ohio. Further plans called for the formation of a group of Confederate privateers on the Great Lakes which would plague U.S. commercial shipping. Evidently little, or no, thought was given to the reaction of the Canadian government to an enterprise of this kind. Beall left Canada for Richmond in January 1863.

## October 21 (Monday)

Up the Potomac River from Washington, Federal Col. Edward D. Baker led troops across the river to assault the Confederate force reported to be in the area of Leesburg, Va. The expedition turned into a disaster. Baker's men were routed and fell back to the bluff about dusk. They attempted to get across the river but not enough boats were available, and many of the Union troops drowned. The Confederates shot many of the Federals while the latter were trying to get down the bluff in the dark, creating mass confusion. The loss to the Union force was 49 killed, 158 wounded, and 714 missing (some of whom were drowned and whose bodies were never recovered). The remainder became prisoners of war and were transferred to Richmond and later to Salisbury, N.C.

### October 23 (Wednesday)

Special Orders No. 284, War Department, Washington, directed that Lt. Col. William Hoffman, Eighth Infantry, be detailed as Commissary-General of Prisoners from October 7th. He was to report to Quartermaster-General Meigs for instructions. Hoffman would hold this post for the duration of the war.

Working on instructions given prior to his official appointment, Hoffman had surveyed the islands off Sandusky, Ohio, for a possible site for a "depot for prisoners of war." The site chosen was on Johnson's Island in Sandusky Bay, which afforded the best possible security. Hoffman wrote QM-Gen. Meigs of his plans for the depot:

In order to form an estimate of the cost and time necessary to establish a depot I have assumed that one-story wooden buildings framed, covered with shingles, ceiled overhead, and for officers all round, with upright weather boarding battened would be most suitable and economical. A building 105 feet long, 24 feet broad, with 9-foot walls, divided into three rooms, heated by two stoves in each room, would accommodate 180 men and would cost $800. A building 112 feet long, 29 feet wide, containing twelve rooms, 14 by 16, divided into groups of four rooms by halls, would quarter 48 officers and would cost $1100. It would lessen the cost somewhat to put two or three building of these dimensions together and if they could be built two stories high it would still more diminish the cost.... A hospital, store-houses and kitchens will be required and probably mess-rooms as there will be scant room for eating in the

quarters. The vicinity of Sandusky to Johnson's Island would render it unnecessary to have large store-houses on the island. On the outer island stores for three months would have to be kept on hand for the winter.

... I would suggest a substantial plank fence to inclose the ground on three sides, a high open picketing closing the fourth side towards the water for security in winter time. A gate at one end of the angles with a blockhouse sufficiently large for the guard. A small blockhouse also at the angle near the water to guard that front. Sentinels should be posted at suitable points around the inclosure on elevated platforms so they could overlook the inside grounds....

Sandusky is a cheap and abundant market for lumber, and I have consulted with an experienced builder there who would give any required security to put up seventeen buildings of the kind I have described by the 10th of December and at the cost I have named, adding the cost of delivering the lumber to the island.

The guard for the depot should consist of 100 to 150 men. One officer and about thirty men would be required daily for guard service.... Both blockhouses should be armed with a small howitzer on a suitable carriage and canister ammunition. A guardboat would be required at all times when the bay is free of ice.

Obviously, the protection of the prisoners from the elements and the security of the prisoners were uppermost in the planning for the depot.

General Orders No. 90, United States War Department, issued on this date, provided for the pay of officers and men taken by the enemy as prisoners of war to be paid to their lawful dependents— to persons presenting a written authority from the prisoner to draw his pay; or without such authority, to his wife, the guardian of his minor children, or his widowed mother in the order named. This solved a major problem for the families of those in uniform. While present for duty in their respective units, the individuals had the responsibility of sending money home, there being no allotment system as currently used in the modern services.

In Washington, Gen. Winfield Scott directed that the Commanding Officer, Western Department, in St. Louis, Mo., take steps to have Maj. Isaac Lynde, Seventh Infantry, placed under arrest on his arrival at Jefferson Barracks from Ft. Leavenworth, status to be reported immediately to Gen. Scott. Maj. Lynde surrendered his command in New Mexico to a much smaller Confederate force without firing a shot. Gen. Scott was perturbed and was looking for adequate reasons for the surrender.

### October 26 (Saturday)

Today, Quartermaster-General Meigs, in Washington, directed that Lt. Col. Hoffman establish "a depot for prisoners of war on Johnson's Island, in Sandusky Bay, according to the plans which you have submitted...." Thus, one of the major Union prisoner stockades for officers was established.

### October 29 (Tuesday)

William Sydney Winder, son of Brig. Gen. John H. Winder, was this day commissioned a 1st Lieutenant in the Confederate forces. He was assigned to work with his father and remained in that assignment for the rest of the war. His most important assignment was as Adjutant-General of the post at Andersonville, Ga.

### November 1 (Friday)

Capt. W.E. Prince, commanding U.S. First Infantry at Ft. Leavenworth, telegraphed the Federal Adjutant-General in Washington that, pursuant to instructions, Maj. Isaac Lynde had been placed under arrest upon his arrival at Leavenworth. Disposition instructions on Maj. Lynde were requested by Capt. Prince.

### November 4 (Monday)

Maj. Gen. John E. Wool, at Ft. Monroe, Va., today wrote Confederate Maj. Gen. Huger, Commanding Department of Norfolk, that a party of refugees was being sent to Norfolk along with letters and other items:

I send herewith by flag of truce and commend to your courtesy and care Mrs. Mary P. Dimitry, her daughters Mary E. and Matilda, her sons Alexander, Robert, Thomas and Ernest, and a white nurse; Mrs. Mary White and five children, the oldest boy being eleven years of age; Miss Mary K. Ellis, Mr. Frederick Pinckney and his wife Sophia Pinckney. I also send under cover to you two packages, one containing three letters with $12 in gold inclosed therein and

addressed respectively to J.C. Barnes, A.F. Smith, and John R. Heywood; the other package contains letters for prisoners and others in the South.

The arrangements to purchase the factory at Salisbury, N.C., for use as a prison depot had finally been consummated and prisoners would be there shortly.

### November 5 (Tuesday)

Federal Acting Secretary of War T.A. Scott, in Washington, telegraphed Maj. Gen. J.E. Wool, Ft. Monroe, Va.:

General: You will on receipt of this letter adopt such measures as may be necessary to send a staff officer with a flag of truce across the lines to ascertain from the enemy whether they will permit supplies of clothing, blankets and other articles to be sent to our men now prisoners of war.

### November 9 (Saturday)

Gen. Wool contacted his counterpart in Richmond concerning the shipment of clothing, etc. to the Federal prisoners. Maj. Gen. Benjamin Huger, CSA, Dept. of Norfolk, responded to Gen. Wool:

My Government will allow blankets and articles of clothing necessary for the comfort of prisoners of war to be sent to them. Any such articles you may send to me will be promptly forwarded by the Southern Express Company, and money may be sent to pay the freight here or it may be paid on delivery.

Confederate Secy. of War Judah P. Benjamin today directed Brig. Gen. John H. Winder to perform a rather onerous chore:

Sir: You are hereby instructed to choose by lot from among the prisoners of war of highest rank one who is to be confined in a cell appropriated to convicted felons and who is to be treated in all respects as if such convict, and to be held for execution in the same manner as may be adopted by the enemy for the execution of the prisoner of war, Smith, recently condemned to death in Philadelphia.

You will also select thirteen other prisoners of war, the highest in rank of those captured by our forces, to be confined in the cells reserved for prisoners accused of infamous crimes, and will treat them as such as long as the enemy shall continue so to treat the like number of prisoners of war captured by them at sea, and now held for trial in New York as pirates.

As these measures are intended to repress the infamous attempt now made by the enemy to commit judicial murder on prisoners of war, you will execute them strictly as the mode best calculated to prevent the commission of so heinous a crime.

### November 10 (Sunday)

Today in Richmond, Brig. Gen. John H. Winder visited Libby Prison and held an assembly of all Union officers then incarcerated in that facility. Winder read a letter from Confederate Acting Secretary of War Judah Benjamin directing that a colonel would be selected by lot and held as a hostage for William Smith, recently convicted, and condemned, of piracy in Philadelphia. An additional ten Union field officers and three captains would also be selected by lot and held hostage for the thirteen Confederates being tried for piracy in New York. The fate of all these officers would be the same as those on trial in the North.

Col. Michael Corcoran, 69th New York Militia, was the individual selected to be held hostage for Smith and would be considered a condemned felon.

The thirteen officers selected for hostages for the New York piracy trial were: Col. Wood, 14th N.Y.; Col. Willcox, 1st Michigan; Col. Lee, 20th Mass.; Col. Cogswell, 42d N.Y.; Col. Woodruff, 2d Ky.; Lt. Col. Neff, 2d Ky.; Lt. Col. Bowman, 8th Pa.; Maj. Revere, 20th Mass.; Maj. Potter, 38th N.Y.; Maj. Vogdes, 1st U.S. Artillery.; Capt. Bowman, 15th Mass.; Capt. Rockwood, 15th Mass.; and Capt. Keffer, Baker's California Regt.. The thirteen officers were to be removed from Libby Prison and sent to the county jail in Richmond.

### November 11 (Monday)

Having received Gen. Huger's positive response on the 9th, Gen. John Wool at Ft. Monroe, Va., wired T.A. Scott, Acting Secretary of War, in Washington:

Sir: Herewith you will perceive that an arrangement has been made by which clothing, blankets and other articles necessary for the comfort of prisoners of war may be sent to them. This has been accomplished without compromising the Government in any respect…

The Salisbury, N.C., *Carolina Watchman* of this date informed the local populace:

The Government has bought the old Salisbury Factory, and is now preparing to fit it up for a prison to accommodate some thousands or more of Yankees who are encumbering the tobacco factories of Richmond. Our citizens don't much like the idea of such accession to their population; nevertheless, they have assented to their part of the hardships and disagreeables of war, so bring them along. We will do the best we can with them.

Brig. Gen. John H. Winder today notified the Confederate Secy. of War, Judah P. Benjamin, of the selections made yesterday at Libby Prison, providing the names and organizations of the selected officers. These prisoners, to be held as hostage for the privateers captured on the high seas, were sent to the local jail for incarceration.

### November 14 (Thursday)

Capt. H. McCoy, CSA, in Richmond was selected to be the Quartermaster for the newly acquired prison at Salisbury, N.C. He was directed to proceed immediately to that post for duty.

### November 16 (Saturday)

At Columbus, Ohio, Col. William Hoffman, Federal Commissary-General of Prisoners, notified Adj. Gen. Lorenzo Thomas that an "establishment for prisoners of war" was being prepared at Camp Chase outside of the city. This would be the old training camp built previously.

### November 25 (Monday)

In Baltimore, Md., the Superintendent of the Adams Express Company, S.M. Shoemaker, notified Col. T.A. Scott, Assistant Secretary of War in Washington, that the Adams Express Company would transport, free of charge, any blankets or other articles destined for the prisoners of war in the South from any city in the North to a named destination.

The regiments in the North were organized by the various states and then transferred to the Federal government as complete units. With the casualties of wounded and prisoners reducing the regiments, the Union Adjutant-General's Office issued General Orders No. 102, this date:

II. The Secretary of War directs that all officers and enlisted men of the volunteer service now prisoners in the hands of the enemy or reported as missing in action, or that may be hereafter taken prisoners or reported missing in action, be transferred to skeleton regiments to be formed by the Governors of the respective States and to consist entirely of such prisoners and missing officers and men. The vacancies thus occasioned in the organized regiments will be filled by the Governors of the various States to which the regiments belong.

Capt. James B. Ricketts, 1st U.S. Artillery, had been shot four times and captured during the Battle of Manassas (Bull Run) in July. Held at Libby Prison in Richmond, he requested that an exchange with a Confederate artillery officer who also was wounded and captured be effected at the earliest possible time. He would not be exchanged until January 1862.

Quartermaster-General Meigs in Washington telegraphed Maj. Gen. John E. Wool at Ft. Monroe, Va., that 2000 suits of infantry clothing, including underclothing, shoes, overcoats, blankets and forage caps had been forwarded for Union prisoners who were in Confederate hands. Gen. Wool was to immediately forward these items to Richmond under a flag of truce.

## November 27 (Wednesday)

Confederate Secy. of War Judah P. Benjamin today received a letter from Burton Craige of Salisbury, N.C., who was visiting Richmond:

Dear Sir: When in your office this morning I omitted to mention to you that before I left home (Salisbury, N.C.) I saw Capt. McCoy, who was sent out to examine and prepare the old factory for a prison. It is much out of repair and will not be fit for the safekeeping of prisoners for a long time. I see from the morning papers that some prisoners are to leave here today for that place. If such an order was issued it ought to be countermanded for the place is wholly unfit for their safe-keeping.

## December 2 (Monday)

On this date, Dr. Braxton Craven, president of Trinity College (later to become Duke University), High Point, N.C., arrived at Salisbury, N.C., with his "Trinity Guards" to administer the Confederate prison recently opened at that location. Dr. Craven's student body had been seriously depleted with the outbreak of war and he was acting as both military commander and professor for the "Guards."

## December 4 (Wednesday)

The House of Representatives in Washington adopted a resolution calling for the Secretary of War to investigate the activity of Maj. Isaac Lynde, Seventh Infantry, at Ft. Fillmore, New Mexico, in which he surrendered his command to an inferior Confederate force without firing a shot. The House believed it was treason, or cowardice, or both.

## December 5 (Thursday)

At Ft. Monroe, the wheels of the bureaucracy finally moved enough to start the clothing for the Union prisoners held by Richmond on their way. Maj. Gen. Wool, USA, wrote to Maj. Gen. Huger, CSA:

Six boxes addressed to Lt. I.W. Hart, Twentieth Regiment Indiana Volunteers, at Norfolk, containing the following articles of clothing for prisoners of war: 53 woolen blouses, 53 caps, 53 shirts, 53 blankets, 53 pairs of trousers, 53 pairs of drawers, 53 pairs of shoes, 53 pairs of socks, and 37 greatcoats. Also nineteen cases addressed to First Lt. Charles L. Peirson, Twentieth Regiment Massachusetts Volunteers, a prisoner of war in Richmond, containing the following articles for distribution to Massachusetts troops, prisoners of war: 350 blankets, 350 overcoats, 700 flannel shirts, 700 pairs of socks, 700 pairs of drawers, 350 pairs of trousers, 350 pairs of shoes, 301 towels, 170 handkerchiefs.

## December 9 (Monday)

At Salisbury, N.C., the first 119 Union prisoners arrived to occupy the newly outfitted prison. These prisoners included 46 from the Battle of Manassas and 73 crewmen from the Federal ship *Union* which had run aground on Bogue Island off the North Carolina coast. The local populace came out to see just what a "live Yankee soldier" looked like. Both groups, prisoners and residents, were shocked. Before long, the initial prisoners were paroled and were given the freedom of the town. By the end of the month the prisoners were again restricted to the prison grounds.

### December 10 (Tuesday)

A deputation of citizens from New York called on President Lincoln today to convince him of the importance of prisoner exchange. The deputation consisted of Judge Henry E. Davies, New York Court of Appeals, and Messrs. Richard O'Gorman, New York lawyer, and James W. Savage. Lincoln was still wrestling with the problem of Southern recognition if he agreed to a cartel to exchange prisoners.

In Richmond, Quartermaster-General A.C. Myers wrote Maj. J.L. Calhoun, in Montgomery, Ala., concerning the buildings selected as a prison at Tuscaloosa, Ala.:

Sir: Capt. Griswold, assistant quartermaster, who has been placed in charge of the prison depot at Tuscaloosa has made a report to Brig. Gen. Winder which has been submitted to this office. From it it appears that the paper-mill which was rented by the agent appointed by you as a suitable place for the custody and accommodation of the prisoners of war sent to Tuscaloosa is in every respect unsuitable for that purpose. It is represented that this building is utterly untenable; that there is no flooring in the first story and in a large room in the rear no sills upon which flooring can be laid; that the grounds are low and damp, the walls moldy; that there are no windows and that there are large apertures in the brick-work. It is also represented that there is no water conveniently near; that there are no chimneys and no appointments for heating the building or cooking the food for the prisoners. In short, it appears that with reference to the number of prisoners to be accommodated, the necessary arrangements for their custody and reasonable comfort, and the degree of expenditure necessary and essential to render this building even approximately suitable for the purpose for which it was designed, the conduct of the agent has been such as to merit the severest animadversion. The contract which he has made therefore is not approved, and the Department disclaims any responsibility on the part of the Government arising out of it. Your agent therefore will take measures to have the contract which he has made abrogated, or if that cannot be done he must meet the responsibility it entails personally. The Government will not recognize or be bound by it.

One would hope that a new agent was appointed and that the next contractor was more careful in the selection of a site.

This same day QM-Gen. Myers wrote Capt. Elias Griswold to rent the local Lunatic Asylum, if it could be had at a reasonable rent, and to erect other buildings as needed.

### December 17 (Tuesday)

Today, 9 officers and 240 enlisted personnel departed Ft. Warren, located in Boston Harbor, for Ft. Monroe and eventual exchange.

### December 19 (Thursday)

The Governor of Alabama, John G. Shorter, telegraphed the Confederate Secy. of War, Judah P. Benjamin, today:

Better send no more prisoners to Tuscaloosa. Accommodations exhausted. Lunatic Asylum will not be leased. To seize it would disorganize the institution and arouse the indignation of a loyal and Christian people.

### December 20 (Friday)

To Gov. Shorter's wire of yesterday, Secy. of War Judah P. Benjamin in Richmond responded, "I shall send no more prisoners to Tuscaloosa. Never thought of seizing asylum."

Dr. Braxton Craven, prison administrator at Salisbury Confederate Prison, wrote Judah Benjamin, the Confederate Secretary of War, concerning Craven's duties and his authority. Benjamin's reply indicated that both Craven and his "Trinity Guards" might be integrated into the Confederate Army. Craven refused to consider this because he had been led to believe that he would *not* be required to enter military service. With this stalemate, Craven and his "Guards" returned to High Point, N.C., in January 1862.

### December 24 (Tuesday)

The Federal Secretary of War notified Maj. Gen. John E. Wool, commanding at Ft. Monroe, that the Sanitary Committee [Sanitary Commission] desired to send medical supplies to Richmond to be used to treat the sick and wounded of the Union prisoners of war at that location. Gen. Wool was to make arrangements for their transfer upon arrival.

### December 25 (Wednesday)

To the prisoners, North and South, this would be a bleak, lonely Christmas. Those in the North, not being used to the winter weather, would suffer the most. All would suffer from the pangs of homesickness and from a desire to see family and friends.

In St. Louis, Mo., Maj. Gen. Halleck notified the Adjutant-General in Washington that he had almost 3000 prisoners of war at that location and no place to put them. It seems that the Governor of Illinois had a nearly empty state prison at Alton, Ill., that could be used. Would Washington authorize the use of the prison?

### December 30 (Monday)

Union Secretary of State Wm. H. Seward today wrote Maj. Gen. Wool at Ft. Monroe requesting "The Rev. Dr. Wilmer, of Philadelphia, is proceeding to Virginia. I will thank you to allow him to pass freely."

However, when the Reverend Doctor's baggage was routinely searched it was found to contain 107 spools of silk, 31 rolls of tape, 26 new shirts, 48 pairs of boots, 650 envelopes, 6 reams of paper, 31 pairs of socks, 2 gross of pens, 15 penholders, 11 silk vests, 2 silk dresses, 2 dozen handkerchiefs, 2 pieces of silk, 25 gross of buttons, 50 papers of pins, 100 papers of needles, 50 spools of thread, 5 pieces of grey cloth, 10 pounds of coffee, and 50 pairs of pants. Feeling that such a large volume of trading goods would be too much for the Reverend Doctor to carry, all of these items were confiscated.

### December 31 (Tuesday)

In Washington, Lincoln was discouraged by the activity, or lack thereof, during this, the first year of the war. No major Union victories had been gained: conversely, the loss at Manassas in July still rankled. He had a general commanding the major force who would not move and was arrogant and self-seeking. Late in the day he visited the Quartermaster-General of the Army, Montgomery C. Meigs. During his visit Lincoln remarked,

> General, what shall I do? The people are impatient; Chase has no money, and tells me he can raise no more; the General of the Army has typhoid fever. The bottom is out of the tub. What shall I do?

The first year of the conflict ended. Many skirmishes had been fought but only two major battles, Manassas in the east and Wilson's Creek in the west, had been fought. Few prisoners were taken in either battle and the problem, while there, was not fully addressed. Lincoln had the same problem he started with, that of recognition of the South. If he acquiesced to a formal exchange agreement, he would then be tacitly acknowledging that the Confederacy was a separate nation. The Southerners would have won their point, and foreign recognition of the Confederacy could result.

# 1862

As yet neither side had come to grips with the prisoner problem, although they were working on solutions. Exchanges had been consummated between field commanders, keeping the prisoner population to workable levels. In the North, a few prisons had been provided for and more were in the planning. In the South, little had been done except adding more buildings at Richmond and providing for the prison at Salisbury. It was to prove a cold, bitter winter not only to the soldiers in camp, but also to the prisoners already incarcerated. None of the prisoners was psychologically prepared for confinement, and many adjustments would have to be made.

In Washington, Lincoln still wrestled with the problem of a prisoner exchange cartel.

### January 1 (Wednesday)

At Ft. Warren, Mass., the Confederate emissaries to Britain and France who had been imprisoned were released today. They were sent to Provincetown, Mass., to board the British warship H.M.S. *Rinaldo* and to continue their trip to Europe. Confederates Mason and Slidell and their secretaries were released due to British demands, and the affair was finished.

In the Shenandoah Valley, Gen. Thomas J. Jackson moved towards Romney in western Virginia, the ultimate goal being the Baltimore and Ohio Railroad and the locks of the Chesapeake and Ohio Canal—an attempt to cut the Union's communications with the west.

### January 5 (Sunday)

In the lower Valley early yesterday morning Jackson captured Bath, chasing the Federals to the Potomac. Jackson ordered the shelling of Hancock, Md., and sent men to burn the bridges north and west of that town.

### January 6 (Monday)

As the Union forces near Hancock, Md., were reinforced, Jackson withdrew, abandoning any hope of crossing the Potomac and raiding north.

### January 7 (Tuesday)

Jackson's column was struggling with a severe ice storm. Jackson's column, nearly frozen, reached Unger's Store, while on the northwestern turnpike east of Romney, Union forces defeated the Confederates at Hanging Rock Pass.

### January 8 (Wednesday)

The United States House of Representatives today adopted a resolution that "the President of the United States be requested to communicate to this House what if any steps the Executive Department has taken for the systematic exchange of prisoners."

The number of Federal prisoners confined at Salisbury, N.C., had increased to 295, from the 119 initially held there on December 9, 1861.

### January 9 (Thursday)

The Governor of North Carolina, Henry T. Clark, wrote Confederate Secretary of War Judah P. Benjamin in Richmond concerning the prison depot at Salisbury:

Sir: When it was first proposed to establish a prison depot in North Carolina there was such a local prejudice against such an establishment that I hesitated to give any aid or sanction to it; but since it has been established I am informed that the prejudice has been entirely removed. I do not know how many prisoners we may be blessed with, but if it is desirable to remove all of them from Richmond I am informed that the prison depot at Salisbury will only accommodate a part, about 800 or 900, with building extensive outhouses for them. The grounds in Salisbury are sufficiently large (sixteen acres) for any buildings temporary or otherwise that would be needed; but should it become necessary for more extensive accommodations, and as building and improving are always expensive, particularly now for the want of materials, I would suggest the purchase of Olin College, in the adjoining county of Iredell.

At Annapolis, Md., the ships carrying the Union troops who would later assault the coast of North Carolina sailed for Ft. Monroe.

### January 10 (Friday)

In the west, Brig. Gen. U.S. Grant moved his troops towards Columbus, Ky., through miserable weather. The march to Columbus would be long, tiring, and fruitless.

In Washington, the rising tide of resentment over the conduct of Secretary of War Simon Cameron would soon cause his resignation.

### January 11 (Saturday)

At Hampton Roads, Va., the fleet departed, carrying Brig. Gen. Ambrose E. Burnside and his expedition to Cape Hatteras, N.C. In Washington, Lincoln finally rid himself of Simon Cameron by accepting Cameron's resignation as Secretary of War and appointing him Minister to Russia. Cameron would soon resign that post and return to the States and run again for Congress.

Maj. George C. Gibbs, CSA, was assigned as commander of the prison at Salisbury, N.C., on this date.

### January 13 (Monday)

It was not an uncommon thing for civilians to be arrested and sent to prison for some minor infraction of rules or through some misunderstanding. Once there, it was difficult to get out because those who knew the circumstances of the arrest were not available to provide information. It appears that this happened to several prisoners at Camp Chase, Ohio, and Lt. Col. Hoffman tried to get some of them released. Today, Hoffman wrote the Adjutant-General in Washington:

There are several prisoners of war at Camp Chase, some of them quite advanced in years, whose friends in Virginia have presented petitions for their release on their taking the oath of allegiance, and if it is thought advisable to release any on those terms some of these men are good subjects for it. Generally they are civilians who have been taken upon some suspicious conduct of little consequence, but two of them are charged with having been a short time in some rebel organization, though not so when captured. The petitions or other papers are authenticated by affidavits or signatures of officials. If it is approved I will select a few, not over twelve, of the most favorable cases and direct them to be released.

In Washington, Lincoln said he would nominate Edwin M. Stanton, of Ohio, as the new Secretary of War, replacing Cameron.

In the Shenandoah Valley, "Stonewall" Jackson resumed his march after remaining at Unger's Store since January 7th. When Jackson's troops began the march, the day was sunny, but a storm developed in the late afternoon.

The Federal fleet from Ft. Monroe arrived off Hatteras Inlet and began crossing the bar into Pamlico Sound, N.C.

### January 14 (Tuesday)

Gen. Thomas J. Jackson's men spent a very rough day in rain and sleet on the road to Romney.

Off the coast of North Carolina, the flotilla from Ft. Monroe was riding out a vicious storm that was scattering the fleet and causing much distress among the troops aboard the ships.

### January 15 (Wednesday)

Edwin M. Stanton was today confirmed by the Senate to be the new Secretary of War, an office he would hold for the remainder of the war.

Jackson's column finally reached Romney in western Virginia after two rough weeks on the road.

### January 17 (Friday)

Lt. Col. William Hoffman, Federal Commissary-General of Prisoners, today notified Surgeon-General Dr. C.A. Finley, in Washington, that Finley was authorized to hire a civilian physician to care for the needs of his guards and the prisoners located on Johnson's Island, Sandusky Bay, Ohio. Hoffman requested sufficient supplies for 1000 officers and men for a six-month period to be provided by the local Army medical purveyor, Surgeon R.S. Satterlee.

Yesterday, Jackson ordered an attack on Cumberland, Md., but had to cancel it for lack of troops. Today, for the second time, he did the same thing. One of his units had but 15 men able to walk.

In the Hatteras area of North Carolina, the Union fleet was still scattered and several ships were aground because of the storm.

### January 18 (Saturday)

At Romney, Jackson finally ordered his troops back into winter quarters at Bath (Berkeley Springs) and Moorefield. Loring's Division, a recent newcomer to Jackson's command, remained at Romney, referring to the town as a "pigpen."

### January 19 (Sunday)

Today a battle was fought in Kentucky that had more names than any other fought during the war. At Mill Springs, or Logan's Cross Roads, or Fishing Creek, or Somerset, or Beech Grove, the Confederates and Federals squared off with about an equal force of 4000 each. At the end of the scrap, the Federals had lost about 261, 15 of whom were captured. The Confederates lost about 533, 99 of whom were prisoners.

### January 20 (Monday)

Secretary of War Edwin Stanton today in Washington ordered "that two commissioners be appointed to visit the city of Richmond, in Virginia, and wherever else prisoners belonging to the Army of the United States may be held, and there take such measures as may be needful to provide for the wants and contribute to the comfort of such prisoners at the expense of the United States."

At Hatteras Inlet, N.C., the amphibious operations fleet had finally crossed the bar and entered the Sound and was preparing for the assault on Roanoke Island.

### January 21 (Tuesday)

Today was Gen. Jackson's 38th birthday, and after remaining in Romney since January 16, Jackson accompanied Garnett and the Stonewall Brigade back to Winchester.

In the west, a reconnaissance of the area around Ft. Donelson, Tenn., was being completed by the Union gunboats preparatory to an assault. On the Tennessee River, another reconnaissance was being conducted of the area around Ft. Henry.

### January 26 (Sunday)

In Illinois, the governor offered the use of the prison at Alton to house prisoners of war. The facility had fallen into disuse and would require some work to get it ready. On this day, Maj. Gen. Henry Halleck, in St. Louis, notified Maj. R. Allen to prepare the prison:

> Major: A quartermaster or agent should be sent to Alton prison tomorrow morning to provide fuel, &c., for the occupation of the place by the prisoners of war and a garrison of say four companies. Fire should be built in all the stoves for a day or two to dry the place of all dampness. The well should be cleaned and pumped out, or provisions made for a supply of water from the river; also tables and benches in eating rooms, &c.

### January 27 (Monday)

The Reverend Bishop E.R. Ames, of Indianapolis, and the Honorable Hamilton Fish, of New York, today accepted appointments as Commissioners to visit prisoners held by the Confederacy.

At Norfolk, Va., the Confederacy rejected a proposal by Maj. Gen. Wool to exchange Col. Corcoran, 69th New York, currently held in Richmond, for William Smith, captain of the Confederate privateer *Savannah*. Smith had been convicted of piracy and now was incarcerated in Philadelphia. The Southern reply stated:

> [Our] Government will not take into consideration any proposition for exchange of our privateers taken in our service on the high seas until there is an absolute, unconditional abandonment of the pretext that they are pirates, and until they are released from the position of felons and placed in the same condition as other prisoners of war, and we decline receiving any proposal in relation to the hostages whom we are forced unwillingly to treat as felons as long as our fellow-citizens are so treated by the enemy.

### January 29 (Wednesday)

Maj. Gen. Benj. Huger, CSA, at Norfolk, wrote Gen. Wool that on January 24 a light-boat was wrecked on the Southern coast and seven crewmen were saved. Huger is willing to return the seamen as noncombatants. However, the North is holding similar personnel in prison. Huger asked if this policy was to continue, and, if so, he would keep those seven seamen in jail until he heard from Gen. Wool. The anxiety of the seven seamen must have been very high, facing an unknown future.

### January 30 (Thursday)

Secretary of War Edwin Stanton, in Washington, wrote his newly appointed Commissioners regarding their duties:

> The Rev. Bishop Ames and Hon. Hamilton Fish.

> Gentlemen: Persons who have been in the military service of the United States as officers and soldiers are now held as prisoners in the city of Richmond, Va., and in other places in the South; some of them are sick, some wounded, many in a state of destitution and all are objects of public sympathy and deep solicitude to this Government. You have been appointed the humane and Christian duty of visiting these prisoners in the places where they are confined and to relieve their necessities, supply their wants and provide for their comfort according to your discretion. You are also to make or procure a list of all the prisoners so held in captivity, designating their names, the time and place where captured, the service to which they belonged, their present state and condition,... for the purpose of effecting their exchange or

release. Your message being purely an errand of mercy this Government expects and desires that you should not seek, obtain or report information or have communication on any subject not immediately relating to its humane and Christian object.... You will proceed directly to Fortress Monroe and communicate with Gen. John E. Wool, commanding there, who is instructed to take such measures as may be right and proper to procure you a safeguard and passage to Richmond or other places to enable you to perform the duties of your appointment.... You may give assurance that on like condition prisoners held by the United States may receive visitation and relief.

Secretary Stanton also directed Surgeon-General C.A. Finley to provide whatever medicines were necessary and desired by Messrs. Ames and Fish for use by the Union prisoners held by the Confederacy.

Quite often people who were trying to improve the lot of the prisoners failed to carry through on their good intentions and, often as not, created additional problems for others. This seemed to be the case at Wheeling, western Va., where an individual who signed himself as "Follower of the Cross" wrote Brig. Gen. Rosecrans about the conditions of the local prisoner compound. Maj. Joseph Darr, Jr., had the opportunity to reply to the General's inquiry into the matter:

> Sir: In reply to the communication addressed to you by a "Follower of the Cross" respecting the condition of the prison and its inmates under my charge I have to request that you appoint some one to examine its and their condition and report to you. Changes have been daily made to improve the appearance of the prisoners, and the only obstacle I have found in the way was their own disposition to be filthy and neglect cleanliness. The prison has been completely whitewashed and every article furnished to keep it clean. The commissary department is well attended to. It is true the prisoners need clothing which Lt. Col. Hubbard was directed some time ago to furnish them, as the "Followers of the Cross" did not carry out their benevolent designs to attend to it, though repeatedly furnished with lists of what was necessary.

### January 31 (Friday)

Today Edwin Stanton, Union Secretary of War, issued Orders No. 15 directing that prisoners of war would receive the same pay during imprisonment as during normal active duty.

In Richmond, Secretary of War Judah P. Benjamin, having learned that Messrs. Hamilton Fish and Bishop Ames were being sent South to visit the Union prisoners, instructed Maj. Gen. Benjamin Huger, CSA, at Norfolk on how the emissaries were to be handled:

Sir: The newspapers announce the early arrival of two gentlemen from the United States, Messrs. Hamilton Fish and Bishop Ames, charged by the enemy with some mission the exact nature of which we do not fully comprehend in relation to the prisoners of war held by us. As these gentlemen will probably present themselves under a flag of truce within your command I deem it prudent to inform you in advance of the views of the Government.

You are therefore instructed if these gentlemen present themselves to direct the officer of your boat to inform them that he will cheerfully take charge of any communication they may have addressed to you or any other public officer and that an answer will be sent them at Ft. Monroe. If they ask to have an interview with you the officer will inform them that he will communicate to you their desire for an interview and will send them an answer at Ft. Monroe whether you can receive their visit and will ask them to give him a written request addressed to you soliciting an interview and explaining the object for which they seek it.

You are requested to communicate to the Department whatever may occur between your officer and these visitors before sending them an answer, and not to permit them to come to Norfolk until you receive special instructions to that effect.

## February 1 (Saturday)

In the west, the assaults on Fts. Henry and Donelson were getting started. At Hatteras, the Union ships were still getting organized for the assault on Roanoke Island.

## February 3 (Monday)

In the west the troops were set in motion for the assault on Ft. Henry on the Tennessee River. Grant's troop-laden steamers left Cairo and Paducah at 6 P.M.

## February 4 (Tuesday)

Just north of Ft. Henry, Tenn., the Union troops disembarked from the transports onto very soggy terrain before marching on Ft. Henry. Everything quickly became bogged down in the rain.

## February 5 (Wednesday)

The Union kept up their approach to Ft. Henry, and the 3000 troops left inside the fort were becoming nervous. The fort was partly inundated from the heavy rains and the flooding Tennessee River.

## February 6 (Thursday)

Today, Flag Officer Foote and his Federal gunboat armada captured Ft. Henry without using ground troops. Using four armored and three wooden gunboats, the fire from the fleet was sufficient to cause Confederate Brig. Gen. Tilghman to surrender, having sent most of his men cross-country to Ft. Donelson. Foote's gunboats opened fire on the open fort about 11 A.M. and Tilghman, after striking the flotilla with 59 shots from his artillery, lowered the flag about 2 P.M. and surrendered 12 officers, 66 men and 16 patients after losing a total of 21 casualties. Heavy rains had prevented Grant's 15,000 troops from reaching the fort in time for the assault. Tilghman and his men were held for Grant.

## February 7 (Friday)

On this date, an additional 493 Federal prisoners arrived from New Orleans at Salisbury, N.C., for incarceration. This brought the total to about 800.

The assault on Roanoke Island finally began with the Union fleet moving towards its objective, bombarding Ft. Bartow at Pork Point.

Brig. Gen. Grant directed that Gen. McClernand "cause to be furnished from the rebel property captured cooking utensils for 100 men including the usual outfit of tin cups, plates, &c., necessary for a soldier for the use of prisoners taken at this point [Ft. Henry]."

Grant further communicated with the Commander of U.S. Forces at Paducah, Ky.:

Inclosed find a roll of Confederate prisoners taken at Ft. Henry and sent forward for safe-keeping until properly discharged. Security demands that the officers should not be paroled in Paducah but confined to a house (you can select the property of any notoriously disloyal person for the purpose) and not allowed to hold communication by letter or otherwise with citizens except with such restrictions as you may deem prudent.... Officers and soldiers held as prisoners are allowed U.S. soldiers' allowance of rations and no more and must cook or provide cooks for themselves. Any article of luxury wanted by the prisoners may be allowed them where they have the means of purchasing themselves.

## February 8 (Saturday)

Earlier, Maj. Gen. Burnside had moved his Federal force into Albemarle Sound at Hatteras and begun the advance on Roanoke Island aboard the ships of Commodore Louis M. Goldsborough. The battle for Roanoke Island resumed about 9 A.M. this day, and by 4 P.M. the obstructions sunk by the Confederates had been cleared sufficiently for the Federal gunboats to enter Albemarle Sound, the Confederate gunboats being overwhelmed by the Federal fleet. The 7500 Federals quickly took control of the island from the 2000, or more, Confederates commanded by Gen. Wisc. Most of the Confederates were taken prisoner and processed for parole.

## February 9 (Sunday)

Confederate Brig. Gen. Gideon J. Pillow assumed command of Ft. Donelson. Pillow had been sent to Donelson as the second-in-command to Brig. Gen. Floyd. This was a poor choice in a pair of commanders.

## February 10 (Monday)

With Roanoke Island in Union hands, the Federal fleet sailed for Elizabeth City, N.C. That city was captured with little trouble.

In the west, Flag Officer Foote sent his gunboats downriver to be refitted and readied for the assault on Ft. Donelson.

## February 11 (Tuesday)

At Ft. Donelson, Federal Gen. McClernand was approaching from Ft. Henry, and Grant was approaching from downriver. Federal gunboats were racing up the Cumberland to support the assault on the fort as Brig. Gen. Simon Bolivar Buckner, CSA, arrived.

## February 12 (Wednesday)

At Ft. Donelson, Grant now had his troops in a ring around the Confederate fort, which had an open side on the river. Foote and his Federal gunboats were on the way.

At Columbus, Ohio, Col. R.P. Buckland, the Commander at Camp Chase, asked Secretary of War Stanton if it was permissible to let the Confederate prisoners in his care visit Columbus.

At Ft. Lafayette, N.Y., a group of prisoners taken from aboard the privateers *Petrel*, *Jefferson Davis*, and *Savannah* who were nonnatives of the South, but who were caught there when hostilities began, asked to take the oath of allegiance to the United States and be released from prison. No record of any action taken.

## February 13 (Thursday)

At Ft. Donelson, Confederate Brig. Gen. Floyd arrived and took command from Brig. Gen. Pillow. Some skirmishing had taken place between the ground forces, and the Federal gunboat U.S.S. *Carondelet* had bombarded the fort in the morning. The fair weather of the morning turned into an afternoon of freezing rain and sleet with the temperature falling to only 10°F at night.

## February 15 (Saturday)

Yesterday, the assault on Ft. Donelson was begun by Gen. Grant and Flag Officer Foote with the Federal fleet bombarding the fort. The fort replied with artillery using plunging fire. Foote's flagship was hit 59 times and disabled. Today, Brig. Gen. Pillow organized an assault on McClernand's Federal line, being aided by the troops of Gen. Buckner. After a hot fight, McClernand's line was broken and the road to Nashville was open, but nobody used it immediately. An argument within the Confederate camp resulted in Pillow ordering the troops back into the fort. McClernand, taking advantage of this and with the help of Gen. Lew Wallace, advanced, and the troops occupied their old positions by nightfall. The Federals could have easily lost this one. Floyd, after a council, decided to surrender and to flee the fort, turning his command over to Pillow. Pillow, seeing the handwriting on the wall, decided to follow Floyd, turning the command over to Gen. Buckner. Floyd took an available steamer, loaded his staff and Virginia brigades aboard and left for Nashville. Pillow and his staff escaped across the river in a flatboat, and made their way to Nashville.

One of the commanders within Ft. Donelson was thinking of everything but surrender. Nathan Bedford Forrest led his Confederate cavalry out of Donelson, through a freezing creek, and to safety. Forrest's was the only organized body of troops to escape.

On Roanoke Island, N.C., the processing of the prisoners taken was completed, all being placed on parole and held for exchange. Shortly they would be sent to Elizabeth City, N.C., and turned over to the Confederate authorities. This saved the expense of transporting them north, feeding and housing, and then exchanging them. The list included 2 colonels; 4 lieutenant-colonels; 6 majors; 34 captains; 37 first lieutenants; 64 second lieutenants; 3 third lieutenants; 2 quartermasters; 5 quartermaster-sergeants; 3 adjutants; 3 sergeants-major; 2 commissary-sergeants; 2 orderly-sergeants; 4 aides-de-camp; 1 captain of artillery; 1 Navy lieutenant; 1 engineer; 144 sergeants, 126 corporals; 9 musicians; 1989 privates, 3 surgeons, 7 assistant surgeons; 2 company physicians; 5 hospital attendants; and 29 servants, for a total of 2488.

### February 16 (Sunday)

Confederate Brig. Gen. Simon B. Buckner, left in command by default at Ft. Donelson, asked Grant for terms for surrender. Grant gave his now famous reply, "No terms except unconditional and immediate surrender can be accepted. I propose to move immediately upon your works." Buckner believed and accepted. The bag of Confederate prisoners was between 12,000 and 15,000. This was the largest group of prisoners up to that time taken in any American war. The surrender was electrifying, both North and South, for it opened the door to Nashville, and to much of Tennessee.

Brig. Gen. Ambrose E. Burnside, USA, today wrote Maj. Gen. Benjamin Huger, CSA, about the exchange of prisoners taken at Roanoke Island, N.C. Burnside's proposition on the exchange of "equivalent" ranks reads like a latter-day baseball-card trade:

The following is the basis I propose:

For one colonel—one lieutenant-colonel and major or three majors or seven captains.

For lieutenant-colonel—two majors or four captains or six first lieutenants.

For major—two captains or four first lieutenants.

For captain—two first lieutenants or three second lieutenants.

For first lieutenant—two second lieutenants.

For second lieutenant—four sergeants or six corporals or ten privates or in same proportion for other grades in the commutation.

At Ft. Donelson, Tenn., the Confederates surrendered by Confederate Brig. Gen. Simon B. Buckner were being assembled. Grant issued Special Field Orders No. 10 directing:

All prisoners taken at the surrender of Ft. Donelson will be collected as rapidly as practicable near the village of Dover, under their respective company and regimental commanders, or in such manner as may be deemed best by Brig. Gen. S.B. Buckner, and will receive two days' rations preparatory to embarking for Cairo. Prisoners are to be allowed their clothing, blankets and such private property as may be carried about their person and commissioned officers will be allowed their sidearms.

This same day, Gen. Buckner wrote Grant about problems between the two forces. The guarding of this large a number of prisoners was entirely new to both captured and captor alike. Buckner explained his problem:

General: It is with much regret that I am forced to call your attention again to the cruel situation in which my men are placed by the ignorance of some of your executive officers on guard. Thousands of these men have been standing nearly all day in the mud without food and without fire. Whenever my officers attempt to collect their men they are arrested at almost every corner of the street by some of your guards.

The arrangements suggested by me this evening to employ four or five of your officers to assist in this collection is ineffectual. Fifty messengers could not accomplish it. If you wish to give effectual relief to my men your police orders will necessarily have to undergo material modifications.

On my way from your headquarters this evening I met opposite my quarters Capt. Dodge, of one of your cavalry regiments, having in charge two of my colonels who by the orders of some officer for some unknown purpose were to be marched through the mud to your headquarters, although one of the officers was paroled specially by Gen. Smith. There seems to be no concert of action between the different departments of your army in reference to these prisoners.

As a means of remedying this and the other existing evils I suggest either that your interior guards be permitted to respect my pass, or that you appoint a provost-marshal or other officer who shall hold his office in my headquarters, vested with authority to issue passes for all necessary purposes connected with the administrative duties of the prisoners.

Gen. Grant responded immediately by directing that passes issued by Confederate Brig. Gen. Buckner should be respected by all inside guards. This permitted the orderly collection of the Confederate units. Gen. Buckner requested that the Union medical officer contact the Confederate medical officer to discuss the disposition of sick and wounded prisoners.

Montgomery, J.J., Lowry's Scouts, Confederate prisoner, Ft. Donelson, Tenn.:

The idea of being a prisoner had never entered my mind until I heard, Sunday morning, February 16, 1862, that Ft. Donelson had surrendered. I could not believe it, as we had been successful in every engagement for three days, both on land and water. The weather was bitter cold, but I lost no time in starting to Dover, a mile distant. The first information I had was that our officers had held a council of war. Gen. Floyd said that he would not surrender; but Gen. Buckner said that he would surrender rather than sacrifice two-thirds of the men to save one-third. I then asked for Floyd, and was told that he had landed his men across the river, and that Col. Forrest had gone also. Having no time to lose, I hastened to the river, where I found the steamer *Gen. Anderson* waiting to carry off Pillow [Floyd]—horses, negroes, and baggage. I went to headquarters and made every effort to get aboard, but appealed in vain, as they were afraid the boat would sink. However, I saw three horses and two negroes with baggage taken on afterwards. It was then early daylight, and I returned to camp with no hope, only to submit to whatever might happen.

## February 17 (Monday)

Indiana Gov. Oliver P. Morton put the wheels of government in motion. Morton telegraphed Gen. Halleck in St. Louis that Indiana could care for 300 wounded at each of three locations: Evansville, New Albany, and Indianapolis. Morton could also accommodate 3000 prisoners if necessary. The Governor was going to Donelson with an extra train, ten doctors and lots of nurses.

Iowa's Adjutant-General H. Price also wired that 3000 prisoners could be accommodated at Davenport at 16 cents per day, providing the government furnished the building, fuel and guards. A government building for 1200 was available immediately.

Illinois offered space for 3000 to 4000 Confederate prisoners at Springfield and additional space in Chicago for 8000 or 9000.

General-in-Chief Maj. Gen. George B. McClellan notified Gen. Halleck in St. Louis to send Gens. A.S. Johnson, Pillow, and Buckner to Ft. Warren, Boston Harbor, under strong guard at once. There was a major mixup here. Gen. A.S. (Albert Sydney) Johnston had been the overall commander of the Confederate western forces and hadn't been captured at Ft. Donelson. Gen. B.R. Johnson, CSA, was at Donelson, but had escaped. The only one captured was Buckner! All of the general officers named had served in the United States Army as officers at one time and were to be considered traitors. This position was later changed and they were treated as opponents only.

Halleck, in St. Louis, notified both Grant (at Donelson) and Sherman (at Paducah) to send 500 of the sick and wounded, both Union and Confederate, to Cincinnati by boat. Halleck specifically stated that all sick and wounded were to be treated alike.

Union Brig. Gen. Don Carlos Buell, based in Louisville, was in communication with Gen. Albert S. Johnston, CSA, in the vicinity of Bowling Green, Ky. Both generals appointed officers to confer on the problem of prisoner exchange. The treatment of medical officers was a special case, as indicated by Buell's letter to Johnston:

I accept your proposition in substance in regard to medical officers, and in order that the rule on that subject may be as definite as possible I propose the following for your consideration: Medical officers taken as prisoners of war while in the discharge of their professional duties either on the field of battle or else-where may be retained to take charge of their own sick and wounded as long as their services are required. When not required for that purpose they will be sent back to their own lines under a flag of truce without parole or exchange. While employed with their sick and wounded they will be allowed all proper facilities and indulgences necessary for that object but will be liable to the usual terms of parole for prisoners of war.

This arrangement is not to be construed as interdicting either party from the adoption of rigor-ous measures towards medical officers who abuse the privileges meant to be extended to them in their pro-fessional character.

Montgomery, J.J., Lowry's Scouts, Confederate prisoner, Ft. Donelson, Tenn.:

On Monday I took deck passage on a steamboat, not knowing my destination. The weather was still very cold. We arrived at Alton, Ill., the following Satur-day, and were marched to boxcars, into which were crowded fifty to a car. Eighteen hours afterwards we emerged at Chicago.

### February 18 (Tuesday)

Maj. Gen. McClellan, in Washington, tele-graphed Gens. Halleck, Buell, and Rosecrans that "the Secretary of War directed that no arrangements either by equivalents or otherwise will be made for the exchange of the rebel generals Johnson, Buckner, Pillow and Tilghman, nor for that of prisoners who had served in our Regular Army, without special orders from these headquarters."

In St. Louis, Maj. Gen. Halleck telegraphed Brig. Gen. Cullum in Cairo, Ill., to send 3000 of the Confederate prisoners each to Springfield, Ill., and Indianapolis, Ind., the remainder to be sent to Chicago, and captured officers, after giving their parole in writing, to be sent to Camp Chase in Columbus, Ohio. The prisoners taken at Ft. Donel-son were being scattered around the countryside.

Halleck finally sent word to McClellan in Wash-ington that the only Confederate general captured at Ft. Donelson was Buckner. Halleck also counter-manded his previous order about giving Confeder-ate officers parole. Notification was sent to Grant, Sherman, and Cullum that the officer prisoners were to be sent to St. Louis under strong guard.

Halleck received a telegram from three concerned citizens in Cairo to the effect that "We think it unsafe to send prisoners to Springfield, Ill.; there are so many secessionists at that place." The prisoners were to be sent anyway.

To add to the confusion, Union Brig. Gen. E.A. Paine, at Cairo, Ill., telegraphed Halleck:

There are 11,000 prisoners here now. Shall I send some to Indianapolis, say 3000? Gov. Morton is here and says that they can be guarded. Gov. Yates, of Illi-nois, says that they cannot be guarded at Springfield, Ill. It certainly is not safe to send them to Spring-field.... Answer immediately.

### February 19 (Wednesday)

Brig. Gen. Don Carlos Buell, USA, at Louisville, notified Maj. Gen. Halleck at St. Louis, Mo.:

...a warrant has been issued and an officer sent by the State authorities to arrest and claim the custody of Gen. Buckner on the charge of treason against the State of Kentucky. The feeling against him is so intense among a large portion of the people of the State that his presence would seriously endanger the good order of the community, and I request that he shall be under no circumstances be sent here or turned over to civil authority.

In Cairo, Ill., Union Brig. Gen. G.W. Cullum had been busily supervising the transportation of the sick, wounded and Confederate prisoners of war to sites in the North. Most of this activity had been going on for nearly two weeks and Cullum was get-ting weary, as indicated in his telegram to Maj. Gen. Halleck in St. Louis:

My Dear General: It is mighty hard to play every-thing from corporal to general and to perform the functions of several staff departments almost unaided as I have done the past two weeks.... By some strange accident several of your telegrams did not come into my hands till after I had telegraphed urgently to you today to know the disposition of the prisoners. All but 1500 had then gone up the Mississippi, being nearly 10,000. Of the remaining, 1000 went well guarded tonight and 500 will follow in the morning to Camp Douglas [Chicago, Ill.].

For want of steamer and guards I was compelled to send officers as well as men, but had them separated and have instructed the commanding officer at Camp Douglas to continue to keep them apart. The officers came down with pistols and sidearms saying it was so agreed by Gen. Grant. I have disarmed them, sending their swords and pistols to the commanding officer at Camp Douglas to be governed by your instructions in the matter.... I am completely fagged out, and being among the little hours of the morning I must say good night.

### February 20 (Thursday)

Maj. Gen. John E. Wool was informed today that Brig. Gen. Howell Cobb, CSA, had been authorized to act as Agent for Exchange for the Confederate government. Cobb was currently in Norfolk, Va.

In the vicinity of Hatteras, N.C., Maj. Gen. Ambrose E. Burnside, commanding the Union offensive in that area, was in contact with Maj. Gen. Benjamin Huger, CSA, commanding at Norfolk, regarding the exchange of prisoners taken during the assault on Roanoke Island, N.C. Between Burnside and Huger the petty problems that would later snag the exchanges were not present, both accepting the commonsense approach to the problem.

In the west, the movement of the prisoners taken at Ft. Donelson had become a nightmare for both captor and captive. Some of the prisoners had been aboard steamers for several days and had been ill fed, in some cases not fed at all. Efforts were being made to provide cooked rations to the prisoners as rapidly as possible, but the effort was falling behind.

In Shelbyville, Tenn., M.J. Waldron wrote Col. W.W. Mackall that "considerable many of the Ft. Donelson soldiers who have escaped are passing through here all going to their native places. Most of them have arms. They act as though they were deserting."

Capt. John Adams, CSA, in Memphis, Tenn., also had 225 Federal prisoners and a need for some place to send them. They were currently housed and fed for 40 cents per day by contract.

### February 21 (Friday)

The prisoners arriving at Chicago presented several unexpected problems for the authorities in that city. First, the guards with the prisoners were from Grant's army and would be returned to the field as rapidly as possible—which meant immediately.

There were insufficient local guards to take over the security at once. Some overlap of duties must be accommodated. Second, due to the large number of officers captured, there were no facilities to house them all. The mayor reported complaints of the local citizenry about Confederate officers being feasted in the city's hotels.

On the James River in Virginia, steamers were running from Norfolk and Richmond to exchange prisoners. On one such trip, a heavy fog disrupted the proceedings and prevented the boats from meeting at the appointed time. Charles C. Fulton, in charge of the exchange for the Navy, reported to Capt. G.V. Fox, Asst. Secretary of the Navy, in Washington, on the event:

Notice having been received by Gen. Wool that some 400 exchanged prisoners would be sent down James River yesterday the *George Washington* and *Express* left at about noon for the appointed meeting place. The rebel boat was appointed to meet them at 3 o'clock but at that hour she was not in sight, and shortly after a heavy fog set down making it impossible to move in any direction. The two boats were fastened together and having dropped anchor waited for the rebel boat to appear. The fog did not lift till late in the evening when the wind blew so fresh that the boats dragged their anchors and had to be separated. This morning at sunrise the expected prisoners made their appearance on the *William Allison*, which it seemed had also anchored for the night a few miles above us. She immediately came alongside, and the roll of prisoners being called, they were transferred to our boats. The return passage was made without any incidents and we arrived here about 10 o'clock this forenoon. The prisoners will be immediately sent North.

### February 22 (Saturday)

At Ft. Donelson, Grant tried to get treatment for the Confederate wounded and sick at Donelson and Clarksville. Several Confederate surgeons are available and could be set to work in this area.

I send a petition of surgeons now held as prisoners at this place. There are still some 200 sick and wounded prisoners and probably 120 wounded at Clarksville. These latter were not taken as prisoners at the fort but fell into our hands by taking possession of Clarksville. I would suggest the propriety of liberating such of the prisoners as are not likely to be fit for duty soon and a sufficient number of surgeons to take care of them.

At Indianapolis, five trains of prisoners arrived and the prisoners were taken to the fairgrounds and placed in the stables. These would be their quarters for some time to come.

### February 23 (Sunday)

Discussions resumed on prisoner exchange when the new Confederate agent, Gen. Howell Cobb, replacement for Gen. Benjamin Huger, met with Union Maj. Gen. John E. Wool. At this time it was agreed that the cartel written by Brig. Gen. Winder's father during the War of 1812 would be used as a basis for any new agreement for exchange. The real problem was the surplus of prisoners. This surplus occurred when one side exchanged more prisoners than did the other. The side with the surplus awaiting exchange would be required to keep them in a noncombatant role until such time as the exchange was consummated in writing. This meant feeding and housing essentially nonproductive military elements. The North would later discharge the men rather than provide housing and rations. Basically, prisoners were to be exchanged within ten days of their capture, if possible. In some instances, where wounds were too serious for the prisoner to be moved, the delay was only in the transportation of the prisoner to his own government—the exchange took place on paper with the patient being paroled.

Montgomery, J.J., Lowry's Scouts, Confederate prisoner, Camp Douglas, Chicago:

It was Sunday, and we had no fire and nothing to eat or drink, only a tin cup full of hot coffee for each man at Bloomington, Ill. We were marched to Camp Douglas prison, in Chicago. With what I could steal from the commissary, I did not suffer much from hunger. I did not believe there was any wrong in such stealing. All the time I was planning to make my escape, but was foiled by being stricken down by erysipelas. After getting up I renewed my energies for escape, knowing it an issue of life or death.

Bateman, Francis M., Pvt., 78th Ohio Vol., Ft. Donelson, Tenn.:

My dear parents. I have written before but I did not mail all finished to you. Did not know where to tell you to address your letters. I have had the Diareah the last three days and I feel weak and trembly. This will account for such poor penmanship. This [?] our position [?] shelling. We therefore changed our camp just before we got to it the enemy were whipped. We then changed our camp again [?] within the entrenchment close to the Cumberland River. [?] very high. This fort & entrenchment enclose a portion of land at least 15 miles square and is as strong as the famous pass of Thermopaly. I don't see how in the world we ever took it. If the secesh had not been such cowards, we would have lost 50,000 men before we could have taken it. We lost about 100 men the enemy about the same. We captured some 20,000 men (prisoners) 27,000 small arms 130 cannon mules & horses 800 wagons besides immense quantities of munitions and provisions. The Gunboats & 15,000 men have gone up to Nashville with the intention of taking it. We expect a hard battle soon. Col Leggett is provost marshall of Dover a little place about the size of West Zanesville. It has a court house and is a county seat & is situated within the enclosure & the 78th have to stay here and guard it. Some of our men while strolling about the entrenchment yesterday found a secessionist in a brush heap with both leggs shattered by a cannon ball his hands both froze off. His face frozen until it was black. He was in his shirt sleeves and had been lying there ever since last Friday a week on the cold ground & was still able to faintly ask for a drink of water. Be sure to write me & tell me how the army is at other places and what prospects the times present for there is no such thing as a newspaper here. I would like to know how Price is getting along in Missouri and whether our troops have attacted any other place lately. "Where is Marshall" The captain is coming around & asking in every tent are there any men who are unable to march tomorrow. We will likely soon start somewhere likely to Nashville. Give my love to grandfather and mother to my brothers & sisters, &c. That quarter that mother put in that box of troches proved very good. I never opened the troches until the other day when we went 8 miles on a march to flank the enemy. I was hungry and faint. I opened my box of troches to take one for my cough when I found a quarter with this I bought me some bread which revived me.

**February 24 (Monday)**

At Camp Douglas, Ill., there was only one surgeon for a prisoner population of over 7000. Some thought was being given to employing some civilian surgeons to help with the treatment of the sick.

The Mayor of Chicago, Julian S. Rumsey, was trying to cope with the problem of the prisoners of war at Camp Douglas but things were getting too far out of control. He wired Maj. Gen. Halleck in St. Louis on this date:

There are now about 7000 prisoners here at Camp Douglas. There is not even a fence about the barracks. The troops there are all skeleton regiments and artillery companies, with most of their men absent. The guard that accompanied the prisoners here has not expected to do duty here. There is not sufficient force under the present discipline to properly guard the prisoners. I suppose there are 1000 stand of arms at the camp, but the city is entirely destitute. I have seen two men guarding 300 feet with no other arms than a stick. A few of the city police have taken, with a small guard accompanying, 1000 to 1500 prisoners one to two miles through the city and located them at the camp.

The secession officers are not kept separate from the men, and our best citizens are in great alarm for fear that the prisoners will break through and burn the city. I am assured by men familiarly acquainted with these people that there is the utmost danger, and I am sure there is nothing to prevent such destruction but their temporary ignorance. I ask that you will immediately give the necessary orders to have the camp put in better order, the expense of which can be but small, and there be the other necessary orders issued to secure our city's safety. Its destruction would surely do away with the glorious victory at Donelson. I have tried for two days to avoid calling upon you, but now feel it my imperative duty.

Halleck, in St. Louis, could find little sympathy for the Mayor of Chicago, even if the Mayor did have a real problem. Halleck replied:

Detain the guard in my name till the prisoners are safely guarded. Send all officer prisoners of war to Columbus, Ohio. My orders in this respect have been shamefully neglected. Raise a special police force if necessary. I have taken these Confederates in arms behind their intrenchments; it is a great pity if Chicago cannot guard them unarmed for a few days. No troops can be spared from here for that purpose at present.

In Washington, Quartermaster-General Montgomery C. Meigs wired Col. Wm. Hoffman, Federal Commissary-General of Prisoners, in Sandusky, Ohio:

Colonel: The following is a copy of a telegram this day directed to you at Sandusky, Ohio, and which is now confirmed:

Visit Chicago, Indianapolis and other places to which the prisoners taken in Tennessee have been sent. Report what is absolutely necessary to prevent their suffering. Quartermasters are in charge. Besides the rations allowed by regulations without regard to rank, the United States will supply such blankets, cooking utensils and clothing as are necessary to prevent real suffering. Much clothing not good enough for troops has by fraud of inspectors and dealers been forced into our depots. This will be used. Make requisition on this office by telegraph and the supplies will be ordered forward.

The *Ohio State Journal* in Columbus, Ohio, reported on the arrival of prisoners to be incarcerated at Camp Chase:

Nine prisoners captured near Fayetteville, Ky., by Col. Scammon of the Twenty-Third Ohio, arrived Saturday last and "took lodgings" at Camp Chase. The visitors are to be increased soon by a fresh arrival of the Southern chivalry. The secession sympathizers who hung their jaws on the reception of the Ft. Donelson news, ought to turn out *en masse* and give their Southern brethren a cordial welcome.

At Elizabeth City, N.C., a total of 2458 paroled Confederate prisoners were landed on this date. These soldiers had been captured at Roanoke Island, paroled and sent to the nearest Confederate port for exchange.

**February 25 (Tuesday)**

The arrival of yet more Confederate prisoners at Camp Chase was reported by the *Ohio State Journal* in Columbus, Ohio:

Another detachment of one hundred and four

Southern prisoners arrived about half past nine last night. They were all officers, including Buckner's staff, captured at Ft. Donelson. They were generally fine-looking men; and, being all officers, are undoubtedly of the upper crust of chivalry of the South. There appeared to be no uniformity of dress; each seemed to consult his own taste or convenience—perhaps the latter.

The sympathies of the crowd were awakened by the appearance among the prisoners of a woman, the wife of one of the officers, who had clung to her husband in his reverses and was determined to share his captivity. She was sent in advance of the others in charge of a special guard. There were also several contrabands in the company, brought along as servants. We doubt very much, however, whether the contrabands will be held as prisoners, but rather contrabands of war.

It is rumored that twelve hundred more prisoners will arrive at 12 o'clock today.

## February 26 (Wednesday)

On November 2, 1861 the steamer *Osceola*, a Union troop transport, foundered during a gale off the coast of South Carolina and the crew abandoned ship, landing near Georgetown, S.C., where they were taken prisoner. J.T. Morrill, the former Master of the *Osceola*, was recently returned to the North and on this day sent a letter to Secretary of War Stanton relating his experiences.

I left New York on the 24th of October in command of the steamer *Osceola*, a transport belonging to the [T.W.]Sherman expedition. The steamer foundered in the gale of November 2. With the crew I landed in two boats at Georgetown, S.C. We were taken prisoners on landing by Capt. Godbold, of the South Carolina troops. After remaining two days on North Island I was transferred to Charleston and my men to the Marion Court-House jail. While in the Charleston guardhouse I had good quarters and could get anything that I ordered. The commanding officer was brutal in his treatment; the others were kind and gentlemanly. I was transferred to the jail about the 27th of November and put in a room with three Federal officers. The others who belonged to our mess—Cols. [Orlando] Willcox, Woodruff, [G.W.] Neff, and Maj. Potter— were kept in their cells (the condemned) in the tower. Our fare consisted of one-half pound of meat (bone

included) and three biscuits daily; two ounces of coffee for five days and other small stores in proportion; the fuel was altogether insufficient to cook our provisions, being one small stick of yellow pine for two days for the whole mess. Those of us who were not in the condemned cells had the run of the yard from 9 A.M. to 4 P.M.; those of our number who were in the condemned cells had not the use of the halls, nor were the rest of us allowed to go to visit the tower. When the fire occurred in Charleston we were locked in our cells and remained unvisited and without food until 5 o'clock of the next day. We all suffered from the smoke and confinement. It was so light during the night that notwithstanding the smoke I could read fine print. In cells next to ours were confined five murderers (condemned) who had the same privileges as ourselves, liberty of the yard, &c. They were offered their liberty if they would join the Southern army but they refused. Our treatment was severe, and when we were ordered to be transferred to Columbia we were told to expect still worse fare and greater privations. But in this we were happily disappointed.

We reached Columbia on the 1st of January and at once marched to the jail of that town. It is an ordinary brick building, three stories in height and twenty by forty feet. The outer windows are well barred and secured. The yard in the rear, surrounded by a fence twenty feet high, is twenty by fifty feet. Confined in this building were, including myself, 310 Northern citizens. Thirty-two of our number, ranking as officers, had the lower floor and occupied its six rooms; the remaining 278 of our number occupied the other two stories, less two small rooms devoted to other purposes. Extreme ventilation was necessary for comfort. Our rations of meat and bread were double what they had been at Charleston, but we had no coffee or vegetables. Our treatment was good and the officers kind and gentlemanly. While there $300 were sent me from New Orleans by a friend and $300 from New York. Of these sums I was allowed to receive $100.

Among our prisoners was Capt. Nichols, of the brig *E.K. Eaton*, who was taken prisoner by the privateer *Sallie* which is well known to have had no commission. Capt. Nichols has been very badly treated, being kept on low rations, being furnished with bread alone, which he was expected to trade off for bull beef. He entrusted his sextant with an officer named McDowell, who was at times in charge of the jail, which he was to sell. He did so and never returned the proceeds to Capt. Nichols. The same dishonest practice was exercised upon Col. [Michael] Corcoran in regard to a watch which he wished to dispose of for the benefit of himself and his fellow prisoners. Lt. Dempsey, of the Sixty-ninth New York Volunteers, was also the victim of their special ire on account of a letter which he managed to send out of the prison "through the underground." An order was issued for his release and that of Capt. Farrish, of the Seventy-ninth New York Volunteers, two months and more ago by Gen. Huger. They are still in confinement and they are supposed to be kept there by order of Gen. [Roswell] Ripley, whom we considered our worst enemy. He is exceedingly bitter, though a Northern man. It is generally understood that Gen. Ripley kept back for two months and upward the clothing that our Government had sent out for its destitute soldiers in the enemy's hands.

My candid opinion is that they will not release Col. Corcoran and the other field officers as long as they can invent an excuse or get up a pretext for keeping them. They now hold them as hostages for the bridge burners [privateersmen]. I don't believe they will release Col. C. and the others any time without their being named. They are especially afraid of Corcoran on account of his influence among the Irish. It was the impression of the South Carolinians whom we saw and Irish soldiers who stood guard over us said "that Corcoran could rally the Irish of Charleston to fight with him under the old flag."

I was exchanged for Capt. Berry, who was named by Gen. Huger to me as the person whose release I was to procure. I reached this city on the 12th instant. I left 307 in the jail at Columbia, and none of the names of my fellow-prisoners have appeared in the last two lists of returned Federal soldiers. Should you desire it I will send you a list of them.

The feeding of the prisoners on the boats on the rivers in the west had still not been solved completely. Fully cooked rations had been provided for several days and an attempt to cook the rations on board each boat for the guard and prisoners was made. The results were somewhat spotty. The kitchens and cooking facilities on the boats were, in most cases, filthy and the amount of food wasted in preparation was appalling. Another solution would have to be found to feeding the prisoners while en route.

## February 27 (Thursday)

In Richmond, President Davis suspended the writ of *habeas corpus* in Norfolk and Portsmouth, Va., on this date. Brig. Gen. John H. Winder was appointed Provost-Marshal of Richmond and charged with implementing martial law in Henrico Co., Va. The loss of personal liberties would chafe the people sorely. Winder's broom would sweep Richmond from end to end and bring much resentment from the populace.

## March 1 (Saturday)

There were, as yet, no provisions for handling exchanged prisoners of war arriving from the South. This would be solved later by establishing a "camp of parole" near Annapolis, Md., and one in Chicago. Meanwhile, the prisoners were being brought to Washington, D.C., for processing. As usual, the paperwork took longer than anyone expected. Quartermaster-General Montgomery C. Meigs directed some action on the part of the Quartermaster at Washington:

Colonel: The Secretary of War is informed that the prisoners arriving here from Richmond and Ft. Monroe are not well provided for at this place; that they have sent on their baggage from Baltimore in many cases under the impression that they would be detained here only a day, and that some hundreds have been detained seven or eight days getting their accounts settled and waiting to be paid off. During this time they have slept on the floor of the buildings near the depot. Some forty have gone into hospitals unable, enervated as they are by long confinement, to resist the effects of exposure. One has died. They represent that they have neither beds nor straw; that they get but one meal a day, and that the building is very filthy.

The Secretary desires that the best provision possible be made for them. It is probable that there will be for some time to come a succession of prisoners arriving and always some to be taken care of. He considers the prisoners as in charge of the Quartermaster's Department and wishes them well cared for, and holds the Quartermaster-General responsible for its being done by the officers of the department. You will please at once take the necessary measures to have the building examined, put in thorough police and the wants of the prisoners supplied.

### March 2 (Sunday)

The Confederates evacuated Columbus, Ky., today, leaving the town to the Federals, who quickly occupied the place. Most of the guns were sent to Island No. 10 on the Mississippi, the next point of defense.

### March 3 (Monday)

The *Ohio State Journal* in Columbus, Ohio, reported that two days previously, on Saturday, an additional 720 Confederate prisoners arrived for Camp Chase. These prisoners were not too friendly when the local citizenry attempted to quiz them. The prisoner population at Camp Chase now numbered about 1200.

### March 5 (Wednesday)

The Federal prisoners of war at Memphis were to be transferred to Mobile and then further forwarded to Tuscaloosa, Ala., for confinement.

The first of the Union forces reached Savannah, Tenn., just northeast of Corinth, Miss. Another 80 troop transports, escorted by gunboats, soon followed.

Col. William Hoffman, Federal Commissary-General of Prisoners, visited the prison for Confederate soldiers outside of Indianapolis, Ind., today. A problem existed with the care of the sick and wounded prisoners—these being mostly captured after the fall of Ft. Donelson in February. In his report to Maj. Gen. Montgomery C. Meigs, Quartermaster-General of the Army, Hoffman expounds:

I visited the prisoners at Camp Morton today and found them as well cared for as could be expected under the circumstances.

I have approved of the construction of some further accommodations for them suggested by Capt. Ekin, assistant quartermaster, and some few improvements to promote the health and comfort, all of which can [be] done at trifling expense. By this means the prisoners at Terre Haute will be provided for.

There are a great many sick among the prisoners and many are being sent to the hospital every day. They were much exposed to inclement weather before their capture which, with much unavoidable exposure since, is now resulting in very general sickness. Three to six die daily.

This state of things has rendered it necessary to provide hospitals for them in the city. The city hospi-
tal is occupied exclusively by sick volunteers and prisoners of war, and I have consented, if you approve it, that while so occupied the necessary expenses, which amount to _____ per week, be borne by the Government. It is under the charge of the physicians employed by the State to attend the sick at Camp Morton. One other building which will accommodate 300 sick, has been rented for $104 per month, and another, which will provide for 125, has been rented for $60 per month. The latter building I propose to give up as soon as the number of sick is sufficiently reduced to admit of it.

The expenses of the two hospitals will amount to $225 each per month, independent of the rent, viz: Attending physician, $100; steward, $40; two matrons, $30; apothecary, $25. Ward masters and attendants will be detailed from the prisoners.

To make more convenient and permanent provision for the sick than can be had here now it is suggested that an addition be made to the city hospital capable of holding 300 patients. The hospital contains all the necessary convenience of dispensary, kitchen, &c., and 300 more patients would only require a few more attendants and nurses, with some enlargement of the cooking apparatus. The addition could probably be put up for $2500, and as many expect there will be a great many sick and wounded of our own troops to be provided for even long after the close of the war, this expenditure would perhaps be good economy in the end. The city authorities give their consent to the arrangement and place the building entirely at the control of the Government, and I refer the matter to you.

The expenses incurred in providing for the sick prisoners will, I presume, be paid by the Quartermaster-General.

A bake house at Camp Morton would provide a fund with which many necessaries for the troops and prisoners there might be purchased that must now be furnished by the Government, and I recommend that one be built immediately. At present the flour is given to the baker, who returns only 20 ounces of bread for 22 ounces of flour.

### March 6 (Thursday)

The U.S.S. *Monitor*, after several problems, sailed from Long Island, N.Y., for Hampton Roads, Va., where destiny awaited.

### March 7 (Friday)

Today, John V. Farewell, President of the Y.M.C.A., wrote Secretary of War Stanton that the chapel built at Camp Douglas was being used as a place of confinement for prisoners and asked that the practice be discontinued.

In northwest Arkansas, Confederate Gen. Earl Van Dorn's columns had flanked Brig. Gen. Curtis's Federal force and attacked them from the rear. The Federals quickly reacted and put up a good fight. Brig. Gen. Benjamin McCulloch was killed by a sharpshooter during the fight, causing much confusion in the Confederate ranks. Confederate Brig. Gen. James McIntosh was also killed. Curtis concentrated his forces at nightfall and awaited the attack by Van Dorn on Saturday.

### March 8 (Saturday)

Yesterday in Arkansas, the battle of Pea Ridge (or Elkhorn Tavern) was joined between Federal forces under Gen. Curtis and the Confederates under Gen. Van Dorn. With about 11,000 troops engaged, Curtis lost about 1384 with about 201 of those being captured. Van Dorn started with about 14,000 and lost about 800, 200 of whom were captured. Only one major battle would be fought again in this area until 1864.

### March 9 (Sunday)

The landmark battle between U.S.S. *Monitor* and C.S.S. *Virginia* (formerly *Merrimack*) was fought today at Hampton Roads. This fight would redefine the course of naval warfare for all time.

### March 14 (Friday)

At New Bern, N.C., the Federals under Gen. Burnside captured the town, taking over 500 prisoners, with a Federal loss of about 471, 90 of whom were killed. The Confederate prisoners were loaded on transports and sent to prisons in the North.

On the Mississippi River, the Confederates evacuated New Madrid, Mo., moving most of their forces to Island No. 10.

### March 16 (Sunday)

The Federal prisoners in Richmond had been allowed to visit the local markets, under guard, and buy what produce, etc., they needed for their consumption, that is, until now. The local civilian population of Richmond began to complain loudly that the prisoners were buying up "their" food and creating shortages. The visits by the prisoners were stopped. Instead, the prison commanders turned guards into buying agents who went to market for the prisoners.

### March 17 (Monday)

In Alexandria, Va., Federal troops embarked for the trip to the Yorktown Peninsula to begin to move on Richmond.

Grant arrived at Pittsburg Landing, Tenn., and assumed command, placing his headquarters at Savannah, north of the Landing.

### March 18 (Tuesday)

At Corinth, Miss., the Confederate troops of Gen. Albert Sidney Johnston began arriving from Murfreesboro, Tenn. Due to shortage of transportation and bad roads, it would take more than a week for all the troops to close up.

### March 25 (Tuesday)

For several days, Gen. Thomas Jackson had been playing "tag" with the Federal forces in the Shenandoah Valley, keeping his "foot cavalry" very busy.

### April 1 (Tuesday)

In Virginia, McClellan was still moving men and matériel to the Yorktown area on the Peninsula. It took much time to move over 100,000 men. In the Shenandoah Valley, Jackson was still giving Gen. N.P. Banks a run for his money.

### April 3 (Thursday)

At Corinth, Miss., Gen. Albert Sydney Johnston ordered his Confederate force to move towards the Shiloh and Pittsburg Landing area, where Grant had his Federal army.

### April 4 (Friday)

Yesterday and today, movement of the Confederates from Corinth, Miss., towards Shiloh Church, Tenn., continued.

In the west, a canal was cut through the swamps so that small boats could move around Island No. 10. During the night, and during a storm, the

Federal gunboat *Carondelet*, Commander Henry Walke, ran past the Confederate batteries on the island and gained the open river below. The Confederates spotted the gunboat from the island and the night turned into a hellish scene with the storm, lightning, roar of the thunder and naval guns. Walke had strengthened his gunboat by piling cordwood around the boilers, adding extra deck planking and anchor chains for armor protection.

On the Virginia Peninsula, McClellan moved 100,000 troops against a Confederate force of less than 20,000, and failed to make a crossing of the Warwick River, giving Confederate Gen. Joseph E. Johnston time to shift his forces from the Culpeper and Richmond areas to the Peninsula. All available Confederate forces were sent to the Peninsula to defend Richmond.

### April 5 (Saturday)

In the west, the news of the gunboat running past Island No. 10 had electrified the local troops. The Northern papers, including Greeley's *Tribune*, made light of the announcement at first.

In Virginia, on the Peninsula, the siege of Yorktown began, finally.

In the vicinity of Shiloh Church, Tenn., Gen. Albert S. Johnston again failed to attack Grant. Johnston couldn't seem to get get his troops aligned until late in the day and then decided to wait until the next day. The Federals still did not realize that the Rebels were nearly on them, although some pickets reported large troop movements, but no one, including Sherman, believed them.

### April 6 (Sunday)

On the Mississippi, Gen. John Pope finalized his plans for the assault on Island No. 10. He would also attack the Rebel troops at Tiptonville, Tennessee.

The Battle of Shiloh began early this morning. By nightfall, many of Grant's troops would be at the banks of the Tennessee River and thoroughly demoralized. The battle would be hard-fought and the carnage would be terrible, including the death of the Confederate commander, Gen. Albert S. Johnston. Gen. P.T.G. Beauregard assumed command of the Confederate force. Federal reinforcements arrived in the night.

### April 7 (Monday)

Through a wild, stormy night, the Federals at Pittsburg Landing huddled near the river with most units staying in their defensive positions opposing the Rebels. Early on this day Grant counterattacked and forced the Confederates beyond his original lines, regaining all of his lost ground. Of the nearly 62,000 Federals engaged, 1754 were killed, 8408 wounded, and 2885 missing for a total of 13,047. Johnston's forces numbered about 40,000, with losses of 1723 killed, 8012 wounded, and 959 missing, for a total of 10,694.

The total casualties of 23,741 for both sides were more than at the Battle of Waterloo. The battlefield was cleared of wounded and prisoners and these were loaded on a seemingly endless stream of steamers leaving Pittsburg Landing for the North.

Opposite Island No. 10 on the Mississippi River, Gen. John Pope got his floating artillery, in the form of U.S.S. *Carondelet*, Commander Walke, and U.S.S. *Pittsburg*, Lt. Egbert Thompson. The gunboats were in position to assault Tiptonville on the Tennessee side of the river. Pope used the gunboats to bombard the Rebel gun positions, driving the crews from their guns. The Union troops landed under the cover of the gunboats and quickly cut off the escape of the Rebels. The Rebels, after a short defense, surrendered at both Tiptonville and Island No. 10. The Mississippi was now open to Ft. Pillow. Some 5000 men, 20 pieces of artillery, 7000 stands of arms, and large quantities of ammunition and provisions were captured on Island No. 10. The Southern prisoners were sent north as rapidly as possible.

### April 9 (Wednesday)

Yesterday and today at Shiloh Church, Tenn., the cleanup went on. Beauregard put the Confederate forces in defensive positions and awaited developments.

The *Ohio State Journal* in Columbus, Ohio, reported that yesterday some thirty Confederate officers from Camp Chase were transferred to Ft. Warren in Boston, Mass. Most of these officers had been on parole in the city. In a parting shot, the newspaper said, "The Knights of the Golden Circle shed buckets of tears at parting with their Southern brethren." The Knights were later called "Copperheads" in Ohio,

Indiana, and Illinois and became a large organization that sympathized with the South.

### April 16 (Wednesday)

In Richmond, President Davis signed an act of the Confederate Congress which provided for the conscription of every white male between eighteen and thirty-five years of age for three years' service.

At Pittsburg Landing, Tenn., Maj. Gen. Halleck had taken command of the Union forces; Grant was getting too much publicity.

### April 18 (Friday)

Below New Orleans, the bombardment of Fts. Jackson and St. Philip began the assault on the Crescent City. Farragut was moving north.

### April 25 (Friday)

After forcing the passage of the forts below New Orleans yesterday, Farragut's fleet arrived on the river fronting New Orleans and the city surrendered. Maj. Gen. Benjamin F. Butler would soon take command of the city for the Federal government.

### April 26 (Saturday)

The garrison of Ft. Macon, N.C., formally surrendered to Federal forces and the 400 prisoners were embarked for travel north.

### May 3 (Saturday)

The number of Federal prisoners at Salisbury, N.C., had increased to about 1400 by this date. Since the prison was built to accommodate 2500, there was still no serious crowding.

In the Corinth, Miss., area, some skirmishing was going on between Beauregard's and Halleck's forces. In the Valley, Jackson's troops crossed Brown's Gap and headed for the railhead at Mechum's Station, still annoying the Union forces.

### May 5 (Monday)

On the York Peninsula, the Army of the Potomac entered Yorktown and continued towards Williamsburg yesterday. Clashes occurred between Union and Confederate units of Gens. Longstreet and D.H. Hill's troops. Today, more heavy fighting took place as Gen. Joseph E. Johnston withdrew towards Richmond, fighting a rearguard action.

### May 8 (Thursday)

Two days previously, Federal troops occupied Williamsburg as the Confederates were leaving town. McClellan used ships and boats to land troops at West Point, Va., closer to the fighting.

At Corinth, Miss., Halleck was being passed by snails in his "race" to contact the Confederates under Beauregard.

In the Allegheny Mts., Jackson soundly defeated a 3000-man Federal force commanded by Gens. Robert Milroy and Robert Schenck. The Federals retreated with Jackson in pursuit.

### May 12 (Monday)

Two days previously, the Confederates abandoned the Norfolk Navy Yard, burning nearly everything that was flammable and sinking C.S.S. *Virginia*.

On the Mississippi, Farragut, already the master of New Orleans, accepted the surrender of Natchez, Miss.

### May 15 (Thursday)

On the York Peninsula, Confederate Gen. Joseph Johnston withdrew his forces across the Chickahominy River and into defensive positions.

At Corinth, Miss., Halleck was still losing the race with the snail on the way to battle.

### May 20 (Tuesday)

While the armies idled at Corinth, Miss., Mr. D.W. Vowles wrote Gen. Thomas A. Harris in Missouri concerning his brother, Dr. Newton Vowles:

Dear General: I wrote you some days since and sent it to Mobile to be mailed. I did not in it communicate to you fully the progress of affairs here and cannot do so now as I write you in a hurry....

Old Capt. Robards, from Hannibal, reached our camp yesterday direct from his home.... He says my brother, the old doctor, was sent to Alton in irons. He was chained very heavily, as they thought him very vicious, says the captain, Robards.

Dr. Foster is there (in Alton) in advance of my brother and condemned to be shot. The sentence has been approved by Gen. Halleck. The charge was bridge burning and railroad tearing up. I wish you would take some action or have some action taken to mitigate this penalty of our old friend Foster.

The boys are bushwhacking in Northeast Missouri. There are no troops there except the Gamble militia or home guards. He reports the boys are taking small parties of Feds every day in that region; they take no prisoners. No quarter is shown by either side.

### May 21 (Wednesday)

Beginning on this date, about 200 Federal prisoners per day left Salisbury, N.C., sent for exchange. This continued until about May 29th, when the last 70 of 1400 departed. The prison was left with only 49 officers incarcerated. These prisoners, who had relied on the enlisted personnel for cooks, now had to fend for themselves. Among these officers was Col. Michael Corcoran of New York, who had been designated as a hostage for the captain of the Confederate raider *Perry*. Whatever punishment was meted out to the Confederate privateer, Corcoran would receive the same. Corcoran was finally released in August 1862, and he returned to New York a hero. Corcoran was later promoted to Brig. Gen. and served in Virginia. He was killed when his horse threw him, and he fell on his head, fracturing his skull. He died on December 22, 1863, and his body was returned to New York.

### May 23 (Friday)

In the Shenandoah Valley, Jackson's command was now 16,000 strong and had been nimbly skipping around the Valley ahead of the Union forces. Today, Jackson hit Banks's troops at Front Royal and sent them running back towards Winchester with the Confederates in hot pursuit, trying to cut off the Federals before they could escape.

### May 24 (Saturday)

Jackson failed to cut Banks's retreat to Winchester. Lincoln ordered McDowell's 20,000 troops to the Valley to try to capture Jackson's force. Jackson was scooping up prisoners by the hundreds.

### May 28 (Wednesday)

The question of the crews of the privateersmen who were captured operating under letters of *marque* for the South had finally been resolved. The North had agreed to treat them as prisoners of war like any other captive. The South then decided to release the prisoners being held hostage for those privateersmen. Both sides thought they had a finished deal until today, when some prisoners were sent to be exchanged for the hostages and the South refused them.

At Ft. Monroe, Va., Maj. Gen. John E. Wool, Federal Agent for Exchange, notified Secretary of War Edwin M. Stanton:

My flag of truce has just returned from Petersburg with Col. Hanson, Capt. Robertson and Lt. Whitaker, all of whom I sent up for exchange, the first to be exchanged for Col. Corcoran.

Maj. Gen. Huger refuses to make any exchanges until the exchange of the privateersmen. He says he regrets he cannot agree to the exchange of any of the hostages until the privateersmen are delivered, when all will be exchanged or released on parole to be exchanged. Can you inform me whether the privateersmen have left New York for this place? If so, when is it probable they will be here? The hostages and privateersmen will be exchanged simultaneously at City Point.

This appears to be the only condition on which Maj. Gen. Huger will make any exchanges. Answer at once if convenient.

In Columbus, Ohio, a problem of prisoner security came up which was handled neatly by Col. Henry B. Carrington, 18th Infantry. The prisoners at Camp Chase, four miles from the city, were threatening insurrection and the only guard available was a few citizens. Carrington reported to Washington:

Upon the pressing requisition of Gov. Tod and Gov. Dennison to send a force to Camp Chase immediately to prevent threatened insurrection of prisoners in the absence of all guard but a few citizens I spent last night there with a strong detachment of Eighteenth Infantry. Shall I delay marching the Eighteenth until a guard is organized or shall I move them South at once? The emergency was so pressing last night that I responded to the requisition without suspending other preparations for march.

### May 30 (Friday)

In the Shenandoah Valley, Jackson had chased Banks across the Potomac and threatened Harpers Ferry. However, Frémont and McDowell were coming up fast with nearly 30,000 troops in an attempt to box Jackson in and close the net.

On the Peninsula at Seven Pines, the forces of McClellan and Johnston engaged in some heavy skirmishing, warming up for the major battle to come.

At Corinth, Miss., Halleck found that Beauregard had quit the game and pulled out without Halleck having even a clue as to what was happening.

**May 31 (Saturday)**

Henry Wirz, now a Sergeant in Co. A, Fourth Battalion, Louisiana Volunteers, was wounded in the right arm, the bone being badly shattered. The arm was useless and he eventually had to learn to write with his left hand. He would be hospitalized for a few weeks.

Yesterday in the Shenandoah Valley, Jackson began a retreat to avoid the trap being laid for him. On the Peninsula, heavy rains had flooded the area around the Chickahominy, making movement impossible.

Today, on the Peninsula, Johnston attacked two of McClellan's Corps which were south of the Chickahominy, beginning the Battle of Fair Oaks (Seven Pines). Confederate progress was slowed and then stopped by a Federal attack. Gen. Johnston was wounded and evacuated from the field, leaving the army leaderless for the remainder of the day.

Maj. Gen. Benjamin F. Butler, now in New Orleans, arrested the local sheriff for treason and put him on a boat for Ft. Warren, Mass. Butler wrote Secretary of War Stanton of his actions:

Sir: Having been convinced by strong proof collected since this city has been occupied by my command that Mr. Adolphe Mazureau has been and still is engaged in plotting treason against the United States Government, I ordered him to be arrested and to be held in safe confinement until such time as he could be safely transferred to Ft. Warren, Mass., as a political prisoner. The arrest was made as directed and Mr. Mazureau was brought before me and is sent forward on board the transport *McClellan*. The charges against him and the evidence of his guilt elicited are as follows:

CHARGE 1.—That Adolphe Mazureau is the president and leading man of a secret society known as the Southern Independence Association, of which every member is solemnly sworn to "allegiance to the

Southern Confederacy and to oppose forever the reconstruction of the old Union at the peril of his life if necessary, whatever be the fate of the war and to whatever extremities and disasters treachery or incapacity may reduce the country," and "each and every member further pledges himself to assist to the utmost of his power in carrying out all laws of the Confederate Congress and all laws of the respective States composing the Southern Confederacy which have for their object resistance to the United States by armed force or otherwise, the retaliation of injuries, the confiscation of property, and the detection and dispersion or punishment of spies and enemies in our midst."

That being sheriff of the city of New Orleans he has been untiring in his efforts to drive Union men from the city unless he could force them into the Confederate service.

He has aided the Confederate cause in every way within his power.

The Civil War was the last war in which prisoners were paroled on their honor not to engage in any military activity until properly exchanged. Both North and South adhered to this pledge and held it to be a sacred word of honor. In New Orleans, Gen. Butler found that a few of the prisoners taken during the capture of the city had violated their parole after being captured and released. These men were tried, convicted and sentenced. General Orders, No. 36, Department of the Gulf, dated this day, described their situation.

Abraham McLane, Daniel Doyle, Edward C. Smith, Patrick Kane, George L. Williams and William Stanley, all enlisted men in the forces of the supposed Confederate States, captured at the surrender of Fts. St. Philip and Jackson, have violated their parole of honor under which they, prisoners of war, were permitted to return to their homes instead of being confined in prison, as have the unfortunates of the U.S. soldiers who falling into the hands of rebel chiefs have languished for months in the closest durance.

Warned by their officers that they must not do this thing they deliberately organized themselves in military array, chose themselves and comrades officers, relying as they averred upon promises of prominent citizens of New Orleans for a supply of arms and equipments. They named themselves the

Monroe Life Guard, in honor of the late Mayor of New Orleans.

They conspired together and arranged the manner in which they might force the pickets of the United States and thus join the enemy at Corinth.

Tried before an impartial military commission, fully heard in their defense, these facts appeared beyond doubt or contradiction and they were convicted.

There is no known pledge more sacred; there is no military offense whose punishment is better defined or more deserved. To their crime but one punishment has ever been assigned by any nation—death.

This sentence has been approved by the commanding general. To the end that all others may take warning, that solemn obligations may be preserved, that war may not lose all honorable ties, that clemency may not be abused and that justice be done—

It is ordered: That Abraham McLane, Daniel Doyle, Edward C. Smith, Patrick Kane, George L. Williams and William Stanley be shot to death under the direction of the provost-marshal immediately after reveille on Wednesday, the 4th day of June next, and for so doing this shall be the provost-marshal's sufficient warrant.

The sentence was carried out.

Maj. Gen. Don Carlos Buell, USA, currently in Tennessee, was having problems with his supply lines in keeping rations flowing to the various commands. Added to this, one of his division commanders notified Buell that "the enemy, unable to feed their prisoners of war, have sent to him on parole without previous notification 1400 of those taken at Shiloh. They are on their way to Columbia [Tenn.]. What shall be done with them?"

## June 1 (Sunday)

East of Richmond on the Chickahominy, the last day of the Battle of Seven Pines was being fought, with a new general in charge for the Confederacy. Gen. Robert E. Lee had been assigned the command of the Army of Northern Virginia, effective this date. After trying to make sense of the chaos, Lee finally decided to have his troops return to defensive positions and wait to see what happened. Seven Pines accomplished nothing except to swell the number of dead, wounded, and captured on both sides.

## June 3 (Tuesday)

Montgomery, J.J., Lowry's Scouts, Confederate prisoner, Camp Douglas, Chicago:

Very early on the morning of June 3, 1862, I waked my partner, W.G. Kerr, and told him to get on his clothes, that there were no pickets outside. We went through the kitchen window and over a twelve-foot fence without trouble. Kerr got near the top, when he fell back, but he tried it again, and on reaching the top said: "Didn't I come a climbing?" When over, we were in the commons next to the city. We walked leisurely along until we reached the streetcar track, and took the first car for the city. Knowing that they published the daily arrivals, we had told some of the boys our assumed names, so they could tell as to our safety. We stopped at the Briggs House, took dinner and supper, and then rode in an omnibus to the Air Line depot, where we bought tickets for Louisville, Ky., taking a sleeping car. We missed connection there, and stopped over until the next morning when we went on to Nashville, arriving there that evening, and stopped for the night at Dr. Hodge's, corner of Broad and Cherry Streets. Taking a walk, we eluded the pickets, and, avoiding all public roads, went unmolested to Giles County.

## June 9 (Monday)

In the west, the city of Memphis was now in Union hands and would remain so for the rest of the war. In the Shenandoah Valley, Jackson defeated two Union brigades at Port Republic. Yesterday, Maj. Gen. Richard Ewell defeated Frémont's army at Cross Keys.

On this date, Secretary of War Stanton wrote Maj. Gen. George B. McClellan concerning the cartel for prisoner exchange:

You are authorized to arrange a cartel for the exchange of prisoners taken on either side before Richmond on such terms as you deem expedient. But it should not extend to any other prisoners than those taken by the operating armies before Richmond, as the enemy have violated the agreement made by Gen. Huger with Gen. Wool and have repudiated Gen. Huger's authority. This instance will no doubt put you on your guard in your negotiation.

The finalization of a cartel was a very time-consuming and tedious business. Gen. Huger had done excellent work in formulating the cartel with Gen. Wool only to have the rug pulled out from under him by the Confederate government on the matter of exchange of the privateersmen, the Confederate government insisting that only those prisoners would be exchanged for the hostages they had been holding in retaliation. All would suffer along for a while.

In Louisville, Ky., Andrew Johnson, Lincoln's appointed Governor of Tennessee, wrote Maj. Gen. Halleck:

> There are a large number of East Tennesseeans now confined in prison in Alabama and are being treated worse than beasts. I have been making efforts for some time to have them released. In Mobile they have seventy, many of them our very best citizens, who committed no offense save being for the Union. Can you not make some arrangement through Beauregard to have them all released? I have arrested a number of traitors here who will be released or handed over or exchanged for them if the arrangement can be made. Many in this region would now rather be sent to the infernal regions than to be sent South. I hope you can make some arrangements by which these oppressed men can be immediately released.

This, the above, presents an interesting picture. The Confederate government arrested citizens of Tennessee for being pro-Union—traitors to the Southern cause. These political prisoners were placed in prison in Alabama without warrant. Andrew Johnson decries the imprisonment of Union sympathizers and at the same time imprisons "traitors" who are pro-South—a not uncommon line of thought on both sides of the fence. Everything depended upon one's perspective.

In Booneville, Miss., Maj. Gen. John Pope wrote Maj. Gen. Halleck concerning the status of the prisoners of war and the plight of the civil population in his area of operations:

> Many of the prisoners of war desire to take the oath of allegiance and return home. Shall they be permitted to do so? The deserters who are and have been coming in in considerable numbers I have permitted to go on to Hamburg and find their way home as best they could. The prisoners of war who at first desired to be exchanged wish also now to take the oath. I don't know how you desire to treat such cases. I have just heard from Col. Sheridan. He is in

Baldwyn with his regiment and has pushed his advance towards Guntown. The enemy drive away and carry off everything for miles around; many families, even the wealthiest, destitute and starving—nothing whatever has been left them. The cavalry I sent out passed many fine houses of persons in good circumstances where the women and children were crying for food; everything had been taken, all the male members of the family carried away and forced into the army. Many represent the enemy as suffering greatly for food.

Mississippi would continue to be a difficult place for friend and foe alike, but not as bad as Missouri. Bands of deserters and marauders savaged the countryside, robbing everyone without discrimination. It was often difficult to tell the good guys from the bad guys.

### June 11 (Wednesday)

Mr. Wm. Porcher Miles of Charleston, S.C., wrote President Davis in Richmond today concerning the arming of Negroes at Port Royal, S.C.:

> Sir: It is currently reported here (upon the authority of a circumstantial statement in the New York *Herald*) that the enemy have organized a regiment of negroes at Port Royal officered by white men, and that this regiment is now probably in the vicinity of the city. As these negroes are slaves in open insurrection they are liable by the laws of the State to be hung whenever taken. Some of our citizens seem to apprehend the possibility of their being treated as prisoners of war and are much excited at the mere thought of such a course. I have assured them that I do not contemplate for a moment any such proceedings on the part of the Government. But to satisfy these gentlemen I have promised to write to you on the subject. It has been suggested whether it might not be expedient to warn the enemy that slaves taken in arms would be summarily dealt with, as well as all whites aiding and abetting them in open insurrection. It does not seem to me necessary to make any such proclamation in advance, but military commanders might be instructed how to proceed in the cases of such captured negroes. As our people have naturally much feeling on this subject I trust it may be my excuse for troubling you with this letter.

The letter was referred to the Secretary of War,

George W. Randolph, for attention. Randolph, in response, directed that "Negroes will not be treated as prisoners of war subject to exchange, but will be confined until Congress passes an act with regard to them." The disposition of the Negro prisoners would be defined by President Davis on the 23rd of December, this year.

In New Orleans, the former sheriff of New Orleans, Adolphe Mazureau, previously arrested for openly supporting the Southern cause and using his office to harass pro-Union citizens, was sent aboard the steam transport *Ocean Queen*, along with one Pierre Soulé, to be taken to New York for incarceration.

Gen. Robert E. Lee, acting as advisor to President Davis in Richmond, wrote Maj. Gen. George B. McClellan that he had designated Brig. Gen. Howell Cobb as the Agent for Exchange for the Confederacy to act in matters concerning the exchange of prisoners between the armies in front of Richmond. He expressed disappointment that the matter could not be extended to a general exchange.

In Batesville, Ark., Maj. Gen. S.R. Curtis, USA, had received a communication from Maj. Gen. T.C. Hindman, CSA, which threatened immediate retaliation for the hanging of prisoners by the Union forces. This was not an uncommon situation since rumor seemed to be the medium most commonly believed on both sides. Gen. Curtis responded to Gen. Hindman:

General: Your letter of the 8th instant stating that you had been informed I was going to hang men who had fired on U.S. soldiers in Izard County and that I had published an order declaring this a war of extermination, and as a probability of such reports being true expressing a remarkable zeal on your part to avenge such conduct by "hanging every Federal officer and soldier" you hold, and declaring that you will "put to death without mercy every soldier and citizen of the United States who falls into my (your) hands," is duly received.

As there is no truth in the reports you have received of my threat to hang or exterminate, the terrible vengeance so lavishly avowed by you will not require notice. There was a company of about seventy rebel soldiers attacked by my body guard in Izard County and twenty-two taken prisoner; 50 guns, 20 revolvers and some 20 bowie knives were taken. They were supposed to be regularly organized troops

and sent to the rear as prisoners of war.

To prevent this war descending into one of rapine and assassinations I have published the following order which I intend to apply to such unauthorized bands as Gen. Price in a former negotiation with me refused to exchange as prisoners of war because they were private marauders. I will call your attention to the conduct of some of your soldiers who recently robbed and burned the house of Mr. Peoples, who fled to the Union flag for shelter. I have heard of many threats and have proof of innumerable acts of barbarity practiced by your troops which I trust will receive proper attention on your part, so that your soldiers may not extend that species of warfare which you so graphically enunciate. The U.S. soldiers are here to restore peace, not to invade the homes of the citizens of Arkansas, and the people who fire on us only prolong an unfortunate and unnatural civil war that destroys the peace of society.

## June 12 (Thursday)

Near Tuscumbia, Ala.., Maj. Gen. Don C. Buell, USA, was trying to conserve his resources. He wired Maj. Gen. Halleck in St. Louis:

I have just seen the War Department order placing all paroled prisoners on leave of absence. The effect of course is virtually to disband them but still allow them pay. We have some 1500 at Nashville that have not been allowed to disperse. If they could be exchanged they might be put into service immediately.

On the Peninsula in Virginia, Sgt. Henry Wirz had returned to Co. A, Fourth Battalion, Louisiana Volunteers, for duty even though his right arm was useless and he was in almost constant pain from the wound. On this day, Wirz was cited for "bravery on the field of battle," and given a field promotion to Captain.

A delegation from Kentucky called upon President Lincoln today to protest the exchange of Maj. Gen. Simon B. Buckner, CSA, for Federal Gen. Benjamin Prentiss. Buckner, a native Kentuckian, was wanted for treason in that state by the pro-Union government.

## June 13 (Friday)

Following the capture of Fts. Henry and Donelson in February of this year, Nashville was occupied shortly thereafter and remained in Union hands for the duration of the war. The Military Governor of Tennessee, Andrew Johnson, caused the arrest of several civilians who, if allowed to remain free, would have caused problems. Johnson felt that these persons would best be held outside the state boundaries and therefore requested the Lincoln administration to provide a secure facility in which to hold them. On this date, Adjutant-General L. Thomas, in Washington, notified Andrew Johnson, Union governor of Tennessee, that arrangements had been made at Ft. Mackinac, Mich., for fifteen political prisoners from Tennessee. Come winter those prisoners would be in for a bad time.

At many of the prison camps in the North the problem of visitors and gawkers was increasing. The guards did not know which, if any, of these people were present for nefarious purposes. To provide an additional measure of control, the War Department authorized the Commissary-General of Prisoners to:

...declare martial law over a space of 100 feet outside and around the limits of the camp where prisoners of war are confined whenever you deem it necessary, and bring to punishment by short confinement or trial by court-martial ... persons trespassing upon such spaces....

Maj. Gen. John Pope, operating in northeastern Mississippi, notified Union Maj. Gen. Halleck, then at Corinth, of a problem that Pope was having with Confederate deserters:

Gen. Asboth reports to me from Rienzi that the woods and swamps east of him are swarming with deserters from the enemy. They are making their way homeward. What is to be done with them? Had they not better be suffered to go? It would take reams of blanks to administer oaths to them. I have not hitherto meddled with them as I could not feed them. Thousands have passed on their way home and as many more are coming every day. They endeavor to pass without coming into camp.

Meanwhile, at Louisville, Ky., Brig. Gen. J.T. Boyle, USA, commanding the area, requested that Secretary of War Stanton not send the prisoners from Kentucky currently located at Camp Chase, Ohio, back to that state. Boyle stated that the prisoners "return emboldened to assassinate the men who arrested them."

## June 14 (Saturday)

As yet there was no cartel with the South for the exchange of prisoners between the warring factions. The Governor of Ohio advocated the parole of the Confederate prisoners located in his state and their return to the South. Without a binding cartel, the South was free to do as it wished with the returned prisoners. This point is made to Gov. Tod by Secretary Stanton:

The question in relation to prisoners is now under consideration. If they are paroled great complaint is made by the friends of our prisoners in the South. No trust can be placed in their parole. I think it is cheaper to keep them where they are than to send them back as recruits, for the rebel Government will release them by law from their parole and force all into the ranks who do not go voluntarily, so that we shall only have to fight and take them again.

In response to Maj. Gen. Pope's request for the disposition of Confederate deserters, Maj. Gen. Halleck telegraphed from Corinth, Miss.:

I think it will be well to make as many of the enemy give their parole as possible; still it would not be worth while to pursue those who have deserted and are on their way home. I would come and see you but have for several days been confined to my tent with the "evacuation of Corinth."

In Indianapolis, the only officer who commanded a prison camp during the war who had a monument raised to him *by the inmates of the prison after the war*, Col. Richard Owen, was to be reassigned to a field command. Owen's record in handling the prisoners at Camp Morton was outstanding. No stories of cruelty, short rations, etc., occurred during his command of that facility.

In Richmond, Gen. Robert E. Lee appointed Brig. Gen. Howell Cobb as the Agent of Exchange for the South in the dealings with the Federal authorities.

## June 15 (Sunday)

Gen. Braxton Bragg, CSA, communicated with Maj. Gen. Henry W. Halleck at Corinth concerning the exchange of prisoners captured in Missouri during previous engagements. He also made a sharp complaint about another matter.:

I must avail myself of the occasion to bring to your notice an act recently committed by an officer of your command without precedent to my knowledge in regular warfare. On the morning of 30th ultimo [30 May] a cavalry detachment from your army under command, as I learn, of Col. Elliott, of the Second Iowa Cavalry, made a descent on Boonesville, on the Mobile and Ohio Railroad and a depot for our sick, and burned a train of cars and the railroad depot, in so doing burning to death not less than one sick soldier in a car and three in the railroad depot, as well as consuming the bodies of some of our dead.

Lt. Col. W. Hoffman, USA, Union Commissary-General of Prisoners to Hon. E.M. Stanton:

I have visited Ft. Delaware and find accommodations there for 2000 prisoners; 600 are there, of which 300 are to be released on parole by order from Gen. Wool. The island is a very suitable place for the confinement of prisoners of war, and I recommend that Col. Crosman be directed to have immediately erected sheds for 3000 more prisoners, making 5000 in all, and it is possible that even a greater number may be conveniently guarded there.

## June 16 (Monday)

On this date, Gen. Braxton Bragg, commanding the Western Department of the Confederate Army, wrote Maj. Gen. H.W. Halleck, commanding U.S. Forces at Corinth, Miss., concerning the exchange of prisoners. In his correspondence he touched upon the release of noncombatant personnel:

As early as 13th of April Gen. Beauregard I find informed Gen. Grant that at an early day he would release on parole all medical officers of the U.S. service in his hands. I can but think it in the clear interest of humanity and of both services that medical officers should not be regarded as other or combatant prisoners of war. I hope you will agree with me and permit Surgeon Benjamin to be absolved from his engagement to return within your lines on the day prescribed; that is, I hope he will be placed on the same footing with other medical officers released by Gen. Beauregard and yourself in May.

I have also to suggest that chaplains should be treated in the same way and released if captured with the least delay practicable.

Lt. Col. William Hoffman, Federal Commissary-General of Prisoners, today notified Capt. A.A. Gibson at Ft. Delaware, Del., to send all officer prisoners of war to the prisoner depot at Johnson's Island, Sandusky, Ohio. He further directed, "If possible arrange it so that they may arrive at Sandusky during the day, as it will be very difficult to cross them to the island at night."

## June 17 (Tuesday)

In the Shenandoah Valley, Jackson was shuttling his troops by rail to the Piedmont as fast as the trains could move them.

It appears that not all prisoners of war were being treated equally. On this date, the Army Assistant Adjutant-General E.D. Townsend notified Brig. Gen. James S. Wadsworth, the Military Governor of Washington, D.C.:

General: It appears that there is an officer of the rebel forces at Willard's Hotel named William Monaghan, a captain of the Sixth Louisiana Volunteers. It is not known whether he is on parole or not. The Secretary of War desires that he as well as any others who may be at large here under any circumstances be immediately put in confinement as in the case of prisoners of war.

The prisoners were not necessarily limited to military personnel. Some civilians were held as hostages for the safekeeping, or return, of other civilians. In one case, at least, the holding of a rebel civilian served a dual purpose. Brig. Gen. Wadsworth, Military Governor of Washington, D.C., notified Secretary of War Stanton:

Sir: In reply to your request for a report in the case of J.C. Gunnell, confined in the Old Capitol Prison,... he was arrested on the application in writing of thirty-one well-known Union citizens of Fairfax County [Va.].

Mr. Gunnell at the outbreak of the rebellion was the acting sheriff of that county, and was perhaps the most active influential secessionist in the county. He was particularly obnoxious to the Union men, and is charged that he was instrumental in procuring several to be arrested and others to be driven from the county. Having fled on the approach of the Union troops on the evacuation of Manassas he returned a few weeks later and it is charged that since his return he has threatened Union men or at least warned them as to the consequences which might follow their attendance of Union meetings, &c.

I hold Mr. Gunnell under arrest for another reason. The rebel authorities hold in prison at Richmond from thirty to forty citizens of Fairfax County for no offense but their attachment to the Union. Some of these cases are known to me as the most cruel and merciless persecutions on record. I have said to the friends of Mr. Gunnell that if they would procure the release of one of these men I would release him.

### June 18 (Wednesday)

The problem of exchange of prisoners has not been resolved to date. Today, Edwin Stanton, Secretary of War, responded to a request from Maj. Gen. McClellan on the Peninsula:

The Adjutant-General has just submitted to me your telegram ... respecting the exchange of prisoners. This subject has for several months been under the direction of Gen. Wool who has had several negotiations with Howell Cobb and Gen. Huger. The last arrangement made was broken off by the rebel authorities denying Huger's authority to make arrangement for Corcoran's exchange. It is believed that their real reason for breaking off was to obtain an arrangement that would secure the release of Gen. Buckner. The President has for some days been considering the question of agreeing to a general exchange but has not yet decided because strong opposition is manifested to the exchange of Buckner.

The Union authorities issued General Orders, No. 60, under which medical officers held as prisoners of war were to be released.

The Confederacy established a prisoner of war camp at the Fair Grounds in Lynchburg, Va., where prisoners were held prior to being exchanged or sent to other facilities. Col. George C. Gibbs, commanding the 42d North Carolina, telegraphed Brig. Gen. John H. Winder in Richmond of the situation at Lynchburg as regards accommodation and rations for the prisoners:

General: I wrote to you on the 15th instant.... I proceed now to make to you a detailed report of the condition of the prisons and prisoners. On yesterday I received from Lt. Col. Cunningham, then commanding, 30 commissioned officers, 2230 noncommissioned officers and privates, making 2260 prisoners, exclusive of three negroes, one of whom is said to be a slave. I inclose list of officers. The premises occupied as a prison are entirely unsuited to the purpose, but the assistant quartermaster at this post reports that he can obtain no other. The sleeping quarters of the prisoners are vacant (open) stalls, or such tents as they can construct with their blankets or oilcloths. The officers are in a different part of the grounds from their men. With a large and vigilant guard, two companies of which have been performing this duty for four and one-half months, I hope to prevent escape, but if the premises had been constructed for the express purpose they could not have been better contrived to permit the escape of prisoners. Lumber cannot be had to repair the fences, gates or sheds. There is no hospital, and for the reason stated one cannot be erected. There are several sick among them, but no death since their transfer to me. I have no prison surgeon or assistant. In consequences of some misunderstanding between captain and assistant quartermaster and captain and assistant commissary of subsistence the prisoners were without food for the twenty-four hours ending at noon today, and up to this time neither fuel nor well or water buckets have been supplied. The latter officer, Capt. Galt, signs himself as commanding the post. I have directed that no person be permitted to enter the inclosure except by my order. To prevent the possibility of unpleasant feeling (as I cannot obey orders from Capt. Galt) please cause an order to be issued on the subject. Meantime I consider myself in command of the post.

### June 25 (Wednesday)

The Seven Days' Battle began today when McClellan ordered his forward units to advance on his left flank which, he said, was to be a general movement forward.

On June 12, Col. Wm. Hoffman, Federal Commissary-General of Prisoners, directed Capt. H.M. Lazelle to visit the permanent camps at Albany, Utica, Rochester and Elmira, N.Y., as well as the U.S. Barracks at Buffalo, N.Y., to determine their suitability for use as prison camps. Capt. Lazelle completed his tour at Elmira and on this date submitted a report.

At Elmira there were four distinct camps which had been used as camps of instruction for the troops recruited in New York. Most of the camps had similar arrangements, buildings, mess facilities, etc., varying only in the number in each camp. A description of Camp Rathbun will suffice for all camps.

This camp is located about one mile to the west of the town on a fine road and is easily accessible at all seasons. Its situation is quite as high as the surrounding country on firm, hard, gravelly soil covered with greensward which does not during the most violent storms become soft, as it gently slopes towards a stream on the south side and is partially drained. There is not in its vicinity either marsh or standing water nor dense forest or shrubbery which could generate malaria or disease, and the whole country about Elmira is exceedingly healthful and no forms of low fever prevail. The camp is abundantly supplied with fine, pure limestone water from two large wells on the ground. Fuel is plentiful.... The ground is shut in on three sides by a low fence of about 4½ feet in height.... The fourth side is bounded by a running stream of soft water about 25 feet wide used for bathing purposes.... The buildings were all built by the Government and both they and the grounds are exclusively under its control, and at present are in the charge of Col. E.F. Shephard, of the New York Volunteers, whose headquarters are at Elmira. He has at present about fifty men, volunteer troops, in their occupancy.... The buildings are new, wooden, one story in height, with pitched roofs, and have firm floors of plank free from dampness. They are covered with boards placed with the edges together both on the sides and roofs of the buildings, and the joints or seams so formed are again covered by an outer board, making a nearly waterproof covering. They are well ventilated by square windows placed sufficiently near each other.

The quarters of the men consist of 20 buildings 88 by 18 feet each, containing two small rooms, one 24 by 7 and the other 8 by 5, and a remaining room extending throughout the interior is not thus inclosed. Each building is designed for the accommodation of 100 men.... The barracks are all furnished with wooden bunks placed end to end on each side of the long sides of the buildings. They are arranged in 2 tiers, 12 sets of 2 double bunks, one above the other, thus giving each side 48 men and leaving a passage of about 8 feet wide through the building.... The ridge pole of each is about 15 feet high and the roof or eaves on the inside about 8 feet....

In front of the men's barracks are two long buildings of 120 by 16 feet each. One contains 5 equal rooms and is used for the quarters of the field and staff, the other, containing 3 rooms, is used by the sutler. In front of these buildings and under one roof are two mess halls of 144 by 41, separated by a kitchen 64 by 41. Against the kitchen is built a shed 13 feet wide. Each hall is complete with tables and benches and will seat 1000 men each. The kitchen is complete with cooking facilities and apparatus, contains a steam-engine, large ranges, furnaces, boilers, &c., sufficient to cook for 2000 men at once.... There is no bake-house. The rations are furnished, cooked and placed on the tables for the men by contractors, who find all the table furniture and cooking utensils used both by the men and themselves, at 30 cents each ration.

The sinks are insufficient, incomplete and filthy. The whole camp, with this exception and the absence of straw ticks for the bunks, is fitted for the accommodation of 2000 men, and with some changes of their interior the quarters of the men will admit very readily of 3000.

The remaining camps at Elmira—Arnot Barracks, Post Barracks, and Camp Robinson—each contained much the same facilities, the same seating capacity for the mess halls, and the same conditions at the sink(s).

Although these sites were available, Hoffman would not opt for their use until May 1864, at which time he would select those next to the Chemung River. A portion of the site selected was *below* the level of the Chemung River and contained a large pond which was not drained at the time the camp was built. This mistake would prove fatal to many Confederate prisoners.

### June 26 (Thursday)

The second of the Seven Days' Battle began with fighting around Mechanicsville when Confederate Gen. A.P. Hill attacked at 3 P.M. after waiting for Jackson to come up. Hill's troops pushed through Mechanicsville and the Federals fell back into strong prepared positions. Hill threw his men at the position and the attack failed. Jackson was still not on the field. During the night the Federals withdrew to other prepared positions around Gaines Mill.

Gen. Samuel Cooper, Adjutant and Inspector

General of all Confederate forces, today issued General Orders, No. 45, which stated:

II. Medical officers taken prisoners of war by the armies of the Confederate States will be immediately and unconditionally discharged.

III. The Government of the United States having recognized the principle that medical officers should not be held as prisoners of war, and having ordered the immediate and unconditional release of all medical officers now on parole so held, all medical officers of the Confederate States now on parole are hereby discharged from their parole.

### July 1 (Tuesday)

On June 27th, the Confederates attacked the line held by Union Maj. Gen. Fitz John Porter and sustained heavy casualties. An evening attack by Hood and D.H. Hill at Gaines Mill succeeded and Porter withdrew back into the Union lines.

On the 28th, things were fairly quiet, with McClellan starting his long wagon trains towards the James River where he could be easily supplied. Lee, meanwhile, realigned his forces for another attack.

On the 29th, at Savage's Station, Lee was attacking McClellan's force, which was fighting a rear-guard action all day. Thousands of dead and wounded littered the battlefield.

On the 30th, yesterday, Lee tried to attack McClellan across White Oak swamp and at Glendale, and was checked. McClellan drew his forces onto Malvern Hill, where he was protected by artillery and Federal gunboats on the James River.

Today, Lee made one of his few mistakes as a commander—he ordered an assault on Malvern Hill. The Confederates bravely gave it a go, but the odds were against them. McClellan was well protected by artillery and the Confederates became cannon fodder. The Federal gunboats could, and did, get into position to rake the flanks of the Confederate lines, creating terrible casualties.

When the fighting stopped, the Seven Days had cost the South nearly 20,000 casualties, about 4000 more than those of the North.

General Orders No. 46, dated this date, as issued by the Confederate Adjutant-General's Office, directed: *All chaplains taken prisoners of war by the armies of the Confederate States while engaged in the discharge of their proper duties will be immediately and unconditionally released.*

### July 3 (Thursday)

The Seven Days' Battle was over, and the wounded, both Union and Confederate, were being taken care of within the means of the caretakers. McClellan had withdrawn to Harrison's Landing, leaving Gen. Lee's army with custody of a large number of Federal wounded who were currently tended by Union surgeons left with them when the Federal troops withdrew to Malvern Hill. Since there were no *legal* arrangements to exchange these men, the local military authorities took steps to alleviate the suffering.

Surgeon L. Guild, CSA, wrote to Maj. R.G. Cole, USA, Asst. Commissary Officer, at Crew's Farm, Va., concerning supplies needed for the Federal wounded:

Major: I am instructed by Gen. Lee to give you such information as will enable you to issue the special supplies requisite for the Federal sick and wounded within our lines. There are 400 at Mrs. Watts' house, near Gaines' Mill. They are entirely unprovided for and will need a full supply. This place is most accessible from some point on the York River railroad, at or near Savage Depot, being distant therefrom about three miles. About 3000 are at Savage Depot, on the York River railroad. They were provided to some extent with hard bread, prepared vegetables, coffee, &c., but are without meat of any kind. There are 500 in the vicinity of the battlefield of Monday, June 30, 1862, immediately on the Charles City road. They are entirely without subsistence. One thousand more will be found just beyond the battlefield of Tuesday, July 1, at Pitt's house, and at another house nearby. I would respectfully suggest that an intelligent agent be sent with each supply that there may be no mistake in the distribution.

Acting Surgeon John Swinburne, USA, remained with the Federal sick and wounded at Crew's Farm, Va. He wrote Confederate Gen. R.E. Lee concerning his charges:

Sir: I am left here by order of Gen. McClellan to look after the welfare of the sick and wounded, and since there are numbers of them placed in temporary hospitals extending from Gaines' house to this place, an area of twelve to fifteen miles, and inasmuch as it is impossible for me to oversee and insure proper attention as to medication, nursing, and food, I would therefore propose that some suitable arrangement be made either for condensing them at Savage Station, that these ends might be attained, or, what would be still more agreeable to the demands on humanity, viz, the unconditional parole of these sufferers. From what I have seen and know of you and your ideas of humanity I feel assured that this application will meet with favor, even if the Federal Government does not recognize the principle of mutual exchange of prisoners. I trust that this rule ought not be extended to the unfortunate sick and wounded. The real prisoners of war should be treated as belligerents, while humanity shudders at the idea of placing the wounded on the same footing. Your surgeons have performed miracles in the way of kind attention both to us surgeons as well as the wounded. If this proposition does not meet with favor I will, with your approbation, communicate with the Federal Government that some basis of transfer may be arrived at. The majority, in fact all medical directors in your army with whom I have conferred, fully agree with me as to the humanity of carrying out this proposition.

### July 4 (Friday)

Gen. R.E. Lee, CSA, responded to Acting Surgeon Swinburne, USA, at Crew's Farm, Va., concerning the sick and wounded:

Sir: I regret to hear of the extreme suffering of the sick and wounded Federal prisoners who have fallen into our hands. I will do all that lies within my power to alleviate their sufferings. I will have steps taken to give you every facility in transporting them to Savage Station. I am willing to release the sick and wounded on their parole not to bear arms against us until regularly exchanged, but at present I have no means of carrying such an arrangement into effect. Certainly such a release would be a great relief to them. Those who are well and in attendance upon the hospitals could not be included in such an arrangement, except such as are left for that purpose, but will be sent into the interior until regularly exchanged.

Confederate Secretary of War George W. Randolph wrote Gen. R.E. Lee on the York peninsula:

General: I have already ordered an examination into the condition of the sick and wounded of the enemy at Gaines' farm and Savage's, and on a report made this morning I directed them to be all collected at Savage's, where they can be properly attended. Lt. Col. Shields, under Gen. Winder's orders, has been charged with this duty and I think that you need give yourself no further trouble about it. The sick and wounded of the enemy at the points mentioned are reported to be about 1700.

### July 11 (Friday)

Jones, John B., Rebel War Clerk, Confederate War Dept., Richmond, Va.:

Gen. Howell Cobb has been sent down the river under flag of truce to negotiate a cartel with Gen. Dix for the exchange of prisoners.... We have some 8000 prisoners in this city, and altogether, I dare say, a larger number than the enemy have of our men.

### July 12 (Saturday)

Today, President Lincoln signed legislation that created the Medal of Honor as an award for valor in conflict with the enemy.

Lincoln also directed Secretary of War Stanton to write authorization for Gen. Dix to negotiate a general exchange of prisoners with the South. This was the beginning of the cartel.

### July 13 (Sunday)

In Page County, Va., Union Brig. Gen. A. Steinwehr issued an order directing that Maj. William Stedman, an officer of Steinwehr's brigade, arrest five of the most prominent citizens of the county to be held as hostages. These hostages were to be shot if any of Steinwehr's men were shot by bushwhackers.

Moore, R.T., Color-Sgt., 32d Tenn. Infantry, prisoner, Camp Morton, Indianapolis, Ind.:

The flag of the Thirty-Second Tennessee was ... carried by me with the regiment to Russellville, and then via Clarksville to Ft. Donelson, and into the fight on the hill outside of the works on Saturday morning, February 15, 1862, when we were ordered to capture a battery that was severe upon us with shot and shell; but we failed to take it.... When it was known that we were prisoners, or soon would be, I pulled the flag off its nice cedar staff, rolled it up, and put it in my bosom, where I kept it concealed for several days. While on the Ohio River, just before reaching Cairo, Col. Cook, having learned that I had it, asked for it, whereupon I surrendered it to him....

After landing at Cairo the commissioned officers were separated from the noncommissioned officers and privates, and we (the latter) were taken first to Lafayette, Ind., kept there about four weeks, and then taken to Camp Morton, Indianapolis.

On the night of July 13, 1862, J.H. Harrelson, of the Forty-First, and R.M. Franklin and I, of the Thirty-Second Tennessee Regiments, scaled the tall plank fence during a downpour of rain. However, the guards saw and shot at us. The rain drowned the noise we made in climbing the wall and in jumping to the ground, and that allowed us to get well under way before the guards discovered us. The "Halt!" rang out and bullets whistled, one of them passing close to my head. After running across an opening and away from the light, we ran through a cabbage patch, which was ankle deep in mud and water from the rain. Harrelson fell over a large cabbage head, and I tumbled over him. Franklin thought that we were both shot. You may imagine how we suffered with cold after running ourselves down. We were all perfectly wet; even the matches were too wet to burn. We went out about five miles on the Cincinnati railroad and after concealing ourselves in a brier thicket, we huddled together like little chickens to keep warm.

About eight or nine o'clock, to our great joy, the sun came out, and soon warmed us. We got some sheaves of wheat from a field nearby, which served for beds and food. At night we went back to the city, arriving there in time to get a lunch before train time.

### July 14 (Monday)

Moore, R.T., Color-Sgt., 32d Tenn. Infantry, escaped, en route to Canada:

Having purchased tickets, we boarded a northbound train at 10:20 P.M., July 14, and started for Canada, passing out in plain view of the lights in Camp Morton. To avoid suspicion, we bought tickets to local stations *en route.*

### July 16 (Wednesday)

Moore, R.T., Color-Sgt., 32d Tenn. Infantry, escaped, arrival in Canada:

On July 16, at about 2 P.M., we reached the "promised land," having safely crossed the Detroit River and landed in the flourishing town of Windsor, Canada. We crossed in a skiff rowed by one Mr. Cunningham. There we were under the British flag. True, we were far from home, but were free from guards with guns and bayonets, and free to work or starve, for we were without a dollar in the world and our clothes were nearly worn out. Mr. Franklin had a sister in Pennsylvania, who, with her husband, Mr. McEntyre, visited him soon after our arrival. I hired out to do farm work a couple of months, during which time I engaged to teach a country school. The next three years I taught in the village, or town, of Leamington, and courted the girls and had a good time generally.

Correspondence from Col. Joseph H. Tucker, 69th Illinois Volunteers, commanding Camp Douglas, Chicago, to Col. Hoffman, Commissary General of Prisoners:

Colonel:... I forward herewith statement respecting five women who have been found among the prisoners. I shall be happy to receive any instructions regarding them which you may see occasion to give.

Particulars respecting the five female prisoners in Camp Douglas:

*Rebecca Parish*, born in Lee County, Ga.; about twenty-eight years of age; has always lived in Sumter County, Ga., till this year; has been three years and a half married; her parents live in Barbour County, Ala.; removed with her husband, a soldier in the Confederate service, and two children to Island No. 10 about the 1st of March last. Her husband and two children had died by the middle of April, since which time she has lived under the protection of her brother, and on the 15th of April she was taken prisoner with her brother, a soldier in the Confederate service, at Island No. 10. Having no friends there and no money to take her home, she preferred remaining with her brother, although the medical men in charge at Madison, Wis., would have given her liberty and sent her back as far as Cairo.

*Harriet Redd*, born in Wayne County, Miss.; is about twenty-four years of age; has lived the greater part of her life in Pike County, Ala. Her parents live in Wayne County, Miss.; two years and a half since she removed with her husband to Pike County, Ala., where she remained till her husband joined the Confederate Army, last January, and was taken prisoner with him at Island No. 10, while an invalid and has so continued and lives with her husband in this camp.

*Araminta Palmer*, born in Pike County, Ky., is about twenty-two years of age; has mostly lived in Great Bend, [Meigs] County, Ohio; was married about two years since; went to Columbus, Ky., with her husband about a year and a half since, where her husband, an invalid, was sworn to support the Confederacy. Her husband has been dead ten months; was a cook in the Confederate hospital at Island No. 10 when taken prisoner on the 8th of last April. Has no relations within 800 miles of her and has been sickly in camp. Her parents are good Union people.

*Amelia Davis*, born in East Brandon, Vt., is about thirty-three years of age; left Vermont at the age of 18; has lived in many parts of the Union; has been married twice. Her present husband is a seafaring man, whom she married in Baltimore two years since. Both husband and wife were respectively employed as cook and stewardess on board the steamer Red Rover when taken by Gen. Buell at Island No. 10 and both sent prisoners to Camp Douglas together with a little boy eight years of age. Does not know that she has any relatives alive.

*Bridget Higgins*, born in Galway, Ireland; came to America in 1857; was married in Baltimore. Her husband was obliged to join the Confederate Army about the 1st of October last and became a member of the Nelson Artillery. She has followed the fortunes of her husband since and they were taken prisoners at Island No. 10. Does not know that she has any relatives in this country. Is in delicate health.

In Richmond, Brig. Gen. John H. Winder reported to the Secretary of War that of this date the Confederacy held Federal prisoners as follows: Richmond, 236 officers, 40 medical personnel, 7571 enlisted men; Lynchburg, 2248 all ranks; Alabama prisons, 592 all ranks; and Salisbury, N.C., 780 all ranks. Total of 11,467 with incomplete returns.

French Forrest, Chief of the Confederate Naval Bureau, notified the Confederate Secretary of War that a total of 49 naval personnel were being held by the Federals and should be considered in any exchange of prisoners.

### July 17 (Thursday)

Capt. John M. Galt, CSA, today transferred commissary stores to Capt. J.V.L. Rodgers, the assistant quartermaster for Federal prisoners at Lynchburg, Va., imprisoned at the Fair Grounds. The supplies consisted of: 6000 pounds of bacon; 138 barrels of flour; 35 bushels of beans; 1400 pounds of rice; 1680 pounds of sugar; 16 bushels of salt; 42½ gallons of vinegar; and 10 gallons of whiskey. This was to feed 2248 prisoners.

### July 19 (Saturday)

Maj. Gen. John Dix, USA, called on President Lincoln today, at Lincoln's request, to discuss the exchange of prisoners. Immediately after the discussion, Dix left for Ft. Monroe, Va.

### July 22 (Tuesday)

On this date, the Union Secretary of War issued a General Order directing that Federal commanders could seize the property, without compensation, of the citizens of Virginia, South Carolina, Georgia, Florida, Alabama, Mississippi, Louisiana, Texas and Arkansas if that property were convenient to the service of their various commands.

The long discussed cartel was finally agreed to, but not as yet signed. Maj. Gen. John A. Dix, USA, and Maj. Gen. D.H. Hill, CSA, finally agreed upon the last article of the pact, and it was forwarded to the respective governments for approval.

### July 23 (Wednesday)

In an action that would create severe problems with the cartel, although it was not directly related to the cartel, Maj. Gen. John Pope, commanding the Union army in Northern Virginia, issued General Orders No. 11 which stated:

Commanders of army corps, divisions, brigades and detached commands will proceed immediately to arrest all disloyal male citizens within their lines or within their reach in rear of their respective commands. Such as are willing to take the oath of allegiance to the United States and will furnish sufficient security for its observance shall be permitted to remain at their homes and pursue in good faith their respective avocations. Those who refuse shall be conducted south beyond the extreme pickets of this army and be notified if found again anywhere within our lines or at any point in rear they will be considered spies and subject to extreme rigor of military law. If any person having taken the oath of allegiance as above specified be found to have violated it he shall be shot and his property seized and applied to the public use.

The *Ohio State Journal* at Columbus, Ohio, reported on this date:

Yesterday two squads of prisoners were taken to Camp Chase. The train from the East brought twenty bushwhacking Confederates captured in Virginia. Several of them were wounded and on crutches.

The afternoon train from the South brought twenty-eight more, captured recently in Kentucky, among them a Col. Jones. They marched from the depot to Messrs. Hawkes & Company's stage office, where omnibuses were provided to carry them to the prison. Among the number attracted by them through curiosity were several paroled Union prisoners, who were not very choice in their language in denouncing the authorities for their accommodating spirit exercised towards these men.

The prisoners at Camp Chase are quiet and submissive since their attempt some days ago to dig out. The three prisons contain some 1676 men.

### July 31 (Thursday)

During the month of July, Capt. John M. Galt, Quartermaster, delivered to Capt. J.V.L. Rodgers rations for the Federal prisoners at Lynchburg Fair Grounds. The 2248 prisoners were issued 33,484 rations of fresh beef, 40,651 rations of bacon, 74,135 rations of flour, 33,714 rations of beans, 40,421 rations of rice, 400 rations of coffee, 59,805 rations of sugar, 74,135 rations of salt, 10,000 rations of vinegar, 3000 rations of candles, 5500 rations of soap, and 30 gallons of whiskey.

In Richmond, President Jefferson Davis wrote Gen. R.E. Lee, commanding the Army of Northern Virginia, concerning items he considered violations of the recently signed cartel:

Sir: On the 22d of this month a cartel for a general exchange of prisoners of war was signed between

Maj. Gen. D.H. Hill, in behalf of the Confederate States, and Maj. Gen. John A. Dix, in behalf of the United States.

By the terms of that cartel it is stipulated that all prisoners of war hereafter taken shall be discharged on parole until exchanged.

Scarcely had that cartel been signed when the military authorities of the United States commenced a practice changing the character of the war from such as becomes civilized nations into a campaign of indiscriminate robbery and murder.

The general orders issued by the Secretary of War of the United States ... on the very day that the cartel was signed in Virginia directs the military commanders of the United States to take the private property of our people for the convenience and use of their armies without compensation.

The general orders issued by Maj. Gen. Pope on the 23d of July, the day after the signing of the cartel, directs the murder of our peaceful inhabitants as spies if found quietly tilling their farms in his rear, even outside his lines, and one of his brigadier-generals, Steinwehr, has seized upon innocent and peaceful inhabitants to be held as hostages to the end that they may be murdered in cold blood if any of his soldiers are killed by some unknown persons whom he designates as "bushwhackers."

Under this state of facts this Government has issued the inclosed general orders recognizing Gen. Pope and his commissioned officers to be in the position which they have chosen for themselves—that of robbers and murderers and not that of public enemies entitled if captured to be considered prisoners of war....

You are therefore instructed to communicate to the Commander-in-Chief of the Armies of the United States the contents of this letter and a copy of the inclosed general orders, to the end that he may be notified of our intention not to consider officers hereafter captured from Gen. Pope's army as prisoners of war.

### August 1 (Friday)

The Confederate War Department in Richmond, reacting to the orders issued by Brig. Gen. Steinwehr on July 13th, the Federal government on July 22d, and Maj. Gen. John Pope on July 23d, issued General Orders No. 54. In highly emotional language, the General Order denounced the directives issued by the Federals as cruel and barbarous. To counter the various threats contained in the Federal directives, the Confederate government ordered:

Therefore, it is ordered that Maj. Gen. Pope, Brig. Gen. Steinwehr, and all commissioned officers serving under their respective commands, be, and they are hereby, specially declared to be not entitled to be considered as soldiers, and therefore not entitled to the benefit of the cartel for the parole of future prisoners of war. Ordered further, that in the event of the capture of Maj. Gen. Pope or Brig. Gen. Steinwehr, or of any commissioned officer serving under them, the captive so taken shall be held in close confinement so long as the orders aforesaid shall continue in force and unrepealed by the competent military authorities of the United States, and that in the event of the murder of any unarmed citizen or inhabitant of this Confederacy by virtue or under pretext of any of the orders hereinbefore recited, whether with or without trial, whether under the pretense of such citizens being a spy or hostage, or any other pretense, it shall be the duty of the commanding general of the forces of this Confederacy to cause to be immediately hung, out of the commissioned officers prisoner as aforesaid, a number equal to the number of our own citizens thus murdered by the enemy.

In essence, the Confederate government stipulated Gens. Pope and Steinwehr, and their commissioned officers, were not to be considered prisoners of war if captured, and that if any citizen were harmed because of the previously issued Federal orders, for any reason, an officer of the Federal army would be hanged.

### August 2 (Saturday)

With the possibility of a general exchange of prisoners imminent, Gen. Lee wrote Gen. D.H. Hill in Petersburg, Va.: "A letter from Gen. McClellan informs me that our prisoners at Ft. Warren were to leave that place on July 31 on the steamer *Ocean Queen* for James River.... In firing on the enemy's fleet in the river caution will be necessary so as not to inflict loss on the returning prisoners."

### August 3 (Sunday)

The first prisoner exchange under the recently agreed-upon cartel took place on this date at Aiken's Landing on the James River. A total of 3021 Feder-

als were traded for 3000 Confederate prisoners. The exchanges moved rapidly and the prisons at Macon, Atlanta, Mobile, Salisbury, Charleston, and other places emptied rapidly. They would soon refill.

### August 5 (Tuesday)

In eastern Tennessee the natives were reluctant to take Confederate money for goods or services, requesting that payment be made in specie. Maj. Gen. Kirby Smith, CSA, commanding in that area, ordered Brig. Gen. T.J. Churchill at Loudon, Tenn., "Let the commissary and quartermaster take the necessary supplies, and if Confederate money is refused in payment arrest those refusing."

### August 12 (Tuesday)

After the fighting around Cedar Mountain, Va., both Jackson and Pope slowed down, waiting for Lee and McClellan, who were, supposedly, coming from the Peninsula. McClellan, nursing a sore ego, was slowly withdrawing his troops from the Peninsula.

Today Maj. Gen. John Pope ordered that two Confederate soldiers, Sgt. James A. Neil of the ambulance train of the enemy, and Pvt. Jesse Hurdleston, of the 19th Georgia, who were taken prisoners while in the act of relieving the sufferings of some of the Federal wounded upon the field, be unconditionally released in consideration of the humanity displayed by the two men.

### August 17 (Sunday)

Yesterday, McClellan finally got most of his troops up from the Peninsula into Alexandria and Aquia Creek, Va. Little "Mac" was supposed to provide support to Pope, who had major problems heading his way. Lee was coming into Gordonsville and joining up with Jackson.

Today, 1100 Confederate prisoners left Camp Chase, Ohio, for Vicksburg, Miss., and exchange. They were to be taken to Cincinnati by train where they would board steamers for the trip down the Ohio River to the Mississippi River and thence to Vicksburg.

### August 18 (Monday)

The Federal prisoners held hostage for the privateers confined in Union jails for piracy had been freed under the general exchange of prisoners and had returned north. Today, Lincoln invited Secretary of War Stanton and Maj. Gen. Halleck to a dinner the President was giving for newly returned prisoners Gens. George A. McCall and Michael Corcoran, and Cols. Orlando B. Willcox and Alfred M. Wood.

### August 20 (Wednesday)

Today, Lee began his advance on Pope, pressing rapidly. Pope withdrew back across the Rappahannock and waited for some support from McClellan, which would never arrive.

### August 21 (Thursday)

Along the Rappahannock, skirmishing became heavier as Lee pressed Pope, looking for an advantage.

In Richmond, the situation of the Union enlisting and arming former slaves had become a real problem. The South, under its State Laws, considered the escaped slaves found under arms to be in insurrection and subject to immediate hanging. The North considered them free and capable of making their own decisions. General Orders, No. 60, issued by the Confederate government and signed by Gen. Samuel Cooper, stated:

I. Whereas, Maj. Gen. Hunter, recently in command of the enemy's forces on the coast of South Carolina, and Brig. Gen. Phelps, a military commander of the enemy in the State of Louisiana, have organized and armed negro slaves for military service against their masters, citizens of this Confederacy; and whereas, the Government of the United States has refused to answer an inquiry whether said conduct of its officers meets its sanction and has thus left to this Government no other means of repressing said crimes and outrages than the adoption of such measures of retaliation as shall serve to prevent their repetition:

Ordered, That Maj. Gen. Hunter and Brig. Gen. Phelps be no longer held and treated as public enemies of the Confederate States, but as outlaws, and that in the event of the capture of either of them, or that of any other commissioned officer employed in drilling, organizing or instructing slaves with a view of their armed service in this war, he shall not be regarded as a prisoner of war but held in close confinement for execution as a felon at such time and place as the President may order.

### August 26 (Tuesday)

At Bristoe Junction, Va., chaos was starting and wouldn't stop until Maj. Gen. John Pope was severely beaten. Confederates led by Maj. Gen. Thomas J. Jackson got behind Pope's forces and captured the station and cut the Orange and Alexandria R.R., Gen. Pope's lifeline, cutting off all communication with Washington. Jackson had circled to the west of Pope and was ready to descend on Manassas Junction. Pope, meantime, had not the faintest clue where anybody was in relation to himself. He did know, however, where McClellan was—sitting at Alexandria pouting and throwing excuses around for not sending troops to Pope.

Because of his disability caused by wounds, Capt. Henry Wirz had been assigned to the command of Brig. Gen. John H. Winder, in Richmond, as acting adjutant-general. On this day, Wirz was placed in charge of the military prison in Richmond. This assignment would last until Sept. 26 of this year.

The paroling of civilians of the Confederacy by the Union when they took an oath of allegiance to the United States had become a real problem to the Confederacy. This type of individual claimed to have taken the oath as a condition of the parole and was therefore not subject to conscription in the Confederate army.

Not so, said the Confederate government. General Orders, No. 62, issued this date, stated that this loophole had been closed:

II. It is hereby announced that no oath of allegiance to the United States and no parole by a person not in military service pledging himself not to bear arms against the United States will be regarded as an exemption from service of the armies of the Confederate States, but persons liable to conscription taking such oath or giving such parole will be enrolled for service. If captured by the enemy they will be demanded and paroled as prisoners of war.

### August 27 (Wednesday)

At Manassas, Pope, already outflanked by Jackson, left his lines and moved north towards the old Manassas battlefield. Jackson, having moved from Bristoe Station was now at Manassas Junction rail depot and destroying everything that he couldn't get on wagons and send south. Longstreet was coming up in support of Jackson. Pope was about to be in a world of trouble but didn't realize it just yet.

In Richmond, Capt. Henry Wirz began his new duties as commander of all C.S. prisons in Richmond. His immediate orders called for a roster of prisoners currently being held.

### August 28 (Thursday)

Pope arrived about noon in Manassas to find that Jackson had taken everything he could and burned the rest and then withdrawn, but Pope knew not where. Jackson, meanwhile, was sitting behind an unfinished railroad grade north of and parallel to the Warrenton Turnpike just west of the old Bull Run battlefield awaiting Pope's next move. Pope, thinking that Jackson had gone towards Centreville, headed in that direction and slammed into Jackson's force at Brawner's Farm before he knew what was happening. Longstreet and Lee approached Thoroughfare Gap. The stage was set for defeat.

### August 29 (Friday)

At Manassas, Pope believed he had Jackson trapped and ordered attacks against his positions. Jackson, in a strong position along the unfinished railroad grade, was hard pressed, but perservered. Meanwhile, more trouble arrived in the form of Longstreet and Lee as they arrived and took position at a right angle to Jackson.

In Washington, Halleck urged McClellan to send troops to support Pope. McClellan developed a strong case of the "slows" and couldn't seem to get the troops on the road.

### August 30 (Saturday)

At Manassas, Pope, believing the Confederates had retreated, attacked Jackson's line, which was the Confederate left flank. Longstreet attacked from the Confederate right flank and rolled up Pope's army, sending them into retreat towards Centreville. Pope was beaten, but the army didn't panic and go into a rout. There were plenty of Federal prisoners to fill the vacancies in Richmond.

### August 31 (Sunday)

At Manassas the wounded were gathered for evacuation, the dead were buried, the discarded equipment recovered for later use, and the battered

units rested. McClellan finally sent two corps from the Army of the Potomac to reinforce Pope. Lee got ready to attack Pope again by turning the Union right flank. He moved Jackson to a position just west of Chantilly with Longstreet following along.

In Richmond, H. Wirz notified Capt. N. Montgomery on Belle Isle that an additional 2000 prisoners would arrive at Belle Isle the next day. He directed that Montgomery inform him of any additional guards and tents that would be required.

### September 1 (Monday)

After Manassas, Lee was not yet finished. He sent Jackson around the Federal right, where Jackson ran into Federal Gens. Isaac Stevens and Philip Kearny. In the midst of a heavy rainstorm the fighting swirled around Chantilly until evening. During this scrap both Stevens and Kearny were killed, a real blow to the North. Pope held on and withdrew towards Centreville, pressured by Lee. As night fell, Washington was safe, but Lee was very close.

### September 2 (Tuesday)

From Centreville, Pope was pulling back into the entrenchments around Washington, closely followed by Lee, with skirmishing at Fairfax C.H., Vienna, Falls Church, and Flint Hill. Lincoln, reluctantly, returned McClellan to command of all the armies in northern Virginia, a move hotly opposed by Secretaries Stanton and Chase. Pope was now without a command. Lee waited near Chantilly and thought of what to do next.

The Federals evacuated Winchester, much to the delight of Jones in Richmond, who recorded in his diary, "Winchester is evacuated! The enemy fled, and left enough ordnance stores for a campaign."

### September 3 (Wednesday)

Lee withdrew to Leesburg, but there was still skirmishing around points in northern Virginia. Lee, now close to the fords of the Potomac, began to plan the invasion of Maryland. War Clerk Jones crowed in Richmond:

The enemy themselves report the loss, in killed and wounded, of *eight generals*! And Lee says, up to the time of writing, he had paroled 7000 prisoners, taken 10,000 stand of small arms, 50 odd cannon, and immense stores!

## September 5 (Friday)

Gen. John Pope, without an army, left Washington for Minnesota, where he would fight Indians. Meanwhile, Lee was crossing the Potomac fords and was approaching Frederick, Md. The citizens of Baltimore and other cities went into panic.

Capt. Henry Wirz, the new commander of prisons in Richmond, reported to Brig. Gen. John H. Winder about a shooting:

General: James Owens, Company E., City Battalion, whilst on post No. 3 discharged his gun at a Federal prisoner, name unknown, who amused himself since last evening putting his head out of the window, and when told by the sentinels on post to take it in would abuse them. Said Owens being on post, the prisoner at his game again, fired at him, not with the intention to hit him, but merely to frighten him; unfortunately the ball went in through the open window and through the ceiling, killing instantly one John Hickey, citizen prisoner from Philadelphia. I had Owens immediately put under arrest until further orders.

Wirz also informed Capt. N. Montgomery, Belle Isle Prison commander, that the sale of pies, fruit, and other things at the prison would no longer be condoned.

## September 10 (Wednesday)

On the 6th, Jackson entered Frederick, Md., and camped. On the 7th, McClellan, in his latest grandstand play "to save the country," was moving at a very slow pace northwest, not knowing where Lee (or anybody else) was at any given time.

On the 8th and 9th Lee regrouped his army in and around Frederick. On the 9th he issued his famous Special Order 191, which outlined the movements of his army and the fact that he had divided his forces. Meanwhile he was covering the gaps along South Mountain in an effective screening operation.

Today, McClellan finally found out that Lee had evacuated Frederick, so he decided to move in that direction.

On this date at Camp Marietta, Ohio, an Ohio farmer named Eliab Hickman was mustered into the Union army and became a member of Co. E, 92nd Ohio Volunteer Infantry. Hickman, described as aged 26, 5 feet 8 inches tall, sandy complexion and sandy hair, was from Centre Township, Noble County, Ohio. He was married to Rosanna and they had three children. His enlistment actually took place on July 30, 1862, and was for three years. Hickman would survive the horrors of Andersonville Prison and the war. He would eventually return to Ohio, and he and Rosanna would have ten more children.

## September 12 (Friday)

McClellan still didn't have a clue about the whereabouts of Lee. Today, McClellan moved into Frederick, Md., and Jackson was at Martinsburg, twenty miles from Harpers Ferry, where he was to contain the garrison at that site.

Maj. Gen. John Dix, Federal Agent for Exchange, wrote his counterpart in Richmond:

I send you back Miss Walters of Norfolk. She was detected in conveying a letter surreptitiously from Aikens to Norfolk, and we have advised her not come again within our lines.

The Confederate Secretary of War today received a communication from Rep. E.L. Gardenhire, Confederate Congress, concerning a captured Federal officer:

Sir: Six weeks ago, more or less, Col. John H. Morgan, the famous partisan chief, attacked and captured a Pennsylvania battalion near Tompkinsville, Ky. Amongst the prisoners taken was a Maj. Jordan, commanding said battalion. This prisoner was sent to Madison, Ga., for safekeeping. He is there now if not exchanged. In regard to this fellow Jordan I wish to bring to your notice the following facts:

1. Two months before his capture he came with his battalion to Sparta, Tenn. He made an order on the ladies of the town to cook for 600 men in one hour and upon failure he said he would turn his men loose upon them and he would not be responsible for anything they might do. The ladies understood this as a threat of rape. They were forced into compliance with his demands.

2. A few days before he was captured he with a part of his command was at Selina, a little village in Buchanan County, Tenn. He told the ladies there that unless they cooked for his command they had better sew up the bottoms of their petticoats.

These facts can be proven by the most indubitable

testimony. I will state that they occurred in the District which I have the honor to represent here and I have deemed it due to the ladies of these places to bring the facts to the notice of the Government that the proper steps may be taken to punish the barbarous wretch for the grievous insult.

The Secretary of War, G.W. Randolph, referred the above matter to President Davis for instructions. President Davis instructed Randolph that the prisoner be held pending inquiry into the matter. Randolph then referred the matter to Brig. Gen. Winder on October 1st for action. Not until November 26, 1862, was the matter resolved. Jordan wrote a denial of the charges, which was duly forwarded to Richmond. The Secretary of War found that while Jordan had behaved in an ungentlemanly and brutal manner, there was no overt act that would deprive him of his exchange under the rules of war. Jordan was ordered paroled or exchanged.

### September 13 (Saturday)

The Union Army camped in and around the town of Frederick, Md., soon after the Confederates had left. A stroke of luck led a member of the 27th Indiana Volunteer Regiment, one Barton W. Mitchell, to find a copy of Lee's Special Order 191 and to send it on to McClellan's headquarters.

### September 16 (Tuesday)

On the 14th, now that McClellan knew Lee's plan, he sent another Union general, Franklin, towards Harpers Ferry to oppose Jackson. Franklin went through Crampton's Gap easily, but then stopped for some unknown reason, giving the Confederates time to react.

By the 15th, Jackson had taken Harpers Ferry and the garrison. Lee was now trying, desperately, to gather his forces.

Today, Lee began to gather his forces at a little town in Maryland named Sharpsburg, near which flowed Antietam Creek. Here would be fought the single bloodiest day of the war.

### September 17 (Wednesday)

On this Wednesday, 23,110 Americans would be reported as killed, wounded, or missing in action—12,410 Union and 10,700 Confederates. Casualties would occur at the rate of about 2000 per hour, or about 35 per minute, during the period from 6 A.M. to 6 P.M., the bloodiest single day in American history.

Prisoners in the battle at Antietam would be few, considering the numbers of troops engaged.

### September 22 (Monday)

In Maryland, McClellan let Lee escape back across the Potomac with most of the Rebel army intact.

In Richmond, the Chairman of the Committee supervising the Army Medical Department, Augustus R. Wright, wrote a letter to the Secretary of War, G.W. Randolph, describing their visit to a prisoner of war hospital in Richmond:

Mr. Secretary: You will find inclosed a resolution passed this morning at a session of the committee on the medical department. In the discharge of our duties we visited the hospital of the sick and wounded of our enemies now in our custody. All of the wards are in a wretched condition. The upper ward was such as to drive the committee out of it almost instantly. The honor of our country will not permit us to bring the matter to the attention of Congress, thereby making the matter public.

We attach no blame to the Secretary of War. We know that in his almost overwhelming labors this matter has escaped his attention. We address you in the full confidence that you will have this condition of things altered at once. We think that the hospital for prisoners ought to be on average at least with those of our own soldiers.

### September 26 (Friday)

Capt. Henry Wirz, acting adjutant-general of the Confederate Provisional Army, had been serving as the commander of the prisons in Richmond, Va. He departed for Montgomery, Ala., this date to search for missing records on Federal prisoners of war, the results to be given to the Confederate Agent for Exchange, Robert Ould. Upon his return to Richmond, Gen. Winder assigned Wirz to command the prison at Tuscaloosa, Ala. His health failing from his wound, Wirz requested a leave of absence to visit Europe. Before departing, President Davis appointed him a special plenipotentiary on a mission to

Paris and Berlin. He would leave for Europe within a few weeks, not to return until February 1864.

The prisoners, both North and South, who had been paroled were not to participate in combat, or combat support, operations until exchanged. In Richmond, rumors were reported by John B. Jones.

Jones, John B., Rebel War Clerk, Confederate War Dept., Richmond, Va.:

It is stated that several hundred prisoners, taken at Sharpsburg, are paroled prisoners captured at Harpers Ferry. If this be so (and it is said they will be here tonight), I think it probable an example will be made of them. This unpleasant duty may not be avoided by our government.

## October 1 (Wednesday)

In Richmond, the starving time of the winter of 1862–63 was coming nearer. The coming season would be very severe for the inhabitants, the local troops, the patients in the hospitals, and the Union prisoners in Libby and on Belle Isle. This would result in the removal of the prisoners from Libby and Belle Isle in the coming year. There was food available throughout the countryside, but no means of transporting it in large quantities was available. John B. Jones recorded: "How shall we subsist this winter? There is not a supply of wood or coal in the city— and it is said that there are not adequate means of transporting it hither. Flour at $16 per barrel, and bacon at 75 cts. per pound, threaten a famine."

## October 7 (Tuesday)

Jones, John B., Rebel War Clerk, Confederate War Dept., Richmond, Va.:

Some 2500 Confederate prisoners arrived from the North last evening. They are on parole, and will doubtless be exchanged soon, as we have taken at least 40,000 more of the enemy's men than they have captured of ours.

## October 13 (Monday)

The Confederate Agent for Exchange, Robert Ould, reported in Richmond that ten thousand Confederate prisoners had been exchanged in Vicksburg, Miss.

At Castle Thunder in Richmond, Mrs. T. Webster, a native of Maryland, has been confined for some period of time as a political prisoner. Today, she addressed a plea for her freedom and exchange to President Davis:

My Honorable President: I say my, for I own no other; will no other own. I come to you, a poor weak woman whose future looks, oh, so cheerless. I come to you, the relict of him who has paid the penalty of his wrongdoing, if wrong he did, of which I know nothing. I come to begging. I wish to go home. It was hinted an exchange. Oh, sir, exchange me, a Southern-born, a South-adoring woman. No, no; rather let me remain here in my people's prison and die than exchange me for one of my own countrywomen. They say I might harm some one. Does a mother harm her child, a child her mother? The South is my mother. I will not harm her. Her glory is my pride. I look to her like a bleeding bird for succor. I have suffered. Oh, you can feel for the suffering; let me go home where I may seek some spot, and unnoticed pass the remainder of my dreary, dreary days. I will pray for you; do you no harm. There is nothing so ingenuous as fear but I fear nothing. I am protected here and my Holy Mother knows my heart, but I have ties in Maryland—interests there. Please let me go home.

President Davis forwarded this plea to the Secretary of War who, in turn, sent it to Brig. Gen. John H. Winder for inquiry. Winder replied that it was decided by the Secretary some time since to release the woman and send her home; however, the Secretary thought she would compromise many friends of the South upon her return. She was retained in prison.

## October 14 (Tuesday)

The Confederate Secretary of War directed that Gen. R.E. Lee, Army of Northern Virginia, inform the Federal authorities that prisoners taken by the Confederate partisan forces would not be exchanged until, and unless, the Federals consented to return Confederate partisans who were taken prisoner. This was a very critical point as regards the area of Missouri where large bodies of Confederate guerrillas were in operation. The normal practice there was to consider such guerrillas "outlaws" with no military standing; they were treated as criminals.

### October 16 (Thursday)

Rations for the prisoners in Libby Prison and on Belle Isle were poor to awful. This did not reflect a shortage of food in Richmond, based on the entry of John Jones in his diary:

Jones, John B., Rebel War Clerk, Confederate War Dept., Richmond, Va.:

I traversed the markets this morning, and was gratified to find the greatest profusion of all kinds of meats, vegetables, fruits, poultry, butter, eggs, etc. But the prices are enormously high. If the army be kept away, it seems the supply must soon be greater than the demand. Potatoes are $5 per bushel, and a large crop! Half-grown chickens at $1 each! Butter at $1.25 per pound! and other things in the same proportion.

### October 28 (Tuesday)

The Battle of Perryville, Ky., fought on October 8th, yielded only about 250 prisoners each for the opposing sides. Bragg, retreating into Tennessee with his long wagon trains of loot, provided little rest for the Federal prisoners. The Confederate prisoners were sent north to Ohio. Rumors, as usual, were rife in the Confederate capital. John B. Jones recorded some in his diary for this date.

Jones, John B., Rebel War Clerk, Confederate War Dept., Richmond, Va.:

Gen. Bragg is here, but will not probably be deprived of his command. He was opposed by vastly superior numbers, and succeeded in getting away with the largest amount of provisions, clothing, etc., ever obtained by an army. He brought out 15,000 horses and mules, 8000 beeves, 50,000 barrels of pork, a great number of hogs, 1,000,000 yards of Kentucky cloth, etc. But before leaving Kentucky, Morgan made still another capture of Lexington, taking a whole cavalry regiment prisoners, destroying several wagon trains, etc. It is said Bragg's train of wagons was forty miles long! A western *tale*, I fear.

### November 3 (Monday)

In northern Alabama, western North and South Carolina, and eastern Tennessee, some of the citizens of the Confederacy who were eligible for conscription were withdrawing into the hills to avoid the draft.

### November 5 (Wednesday)

In what would be a shock to McClellan, President Lincoln ordered his replacement, assigning Maj. Gen. Ambrose E. Burnside as the commander of the Army of the Potomac.

### November 7 (Friday)

Rations were getting short in Richmond for both the military and civilians. The Confederate government had taken control of the railroads, and the shipment of food and supplies for other than military purposes was almost stopped. Those items which were in very short supply in Richmond affected both the civil population and the Federal prisoners in Libby and on Belle Isle. A major result, not unexpectedly, was price gouging by the few dealers who had commodities to sell.

Jones, John B., Rebel War Clerk, Confederate War Dept., Richmond, Va.:

Yesterday I received from the agent of the City Councils fourteen pounds of salt, having seven persons in my family, including the servant. One pound to each member, per month, is allowed at 5 cts. per pound. The extortionists sell it at 70 cts. per pound. One of *them* was drawing for his family. He confessed it; but said he paid 50 cts. for the salt he sold at 70 cts. Profit $10 per bushel! I sent an article today to the *Enquirer*, suggesting fuel, bread, meat, etc. be furnished in the same manner. We shall soon be in a state of siege.

Last night there was a heavy fall of snow.

### November 8 (Saturday)

Braxton Bragg, commander of Confederate forces in Tennessee, reported the number of prisoners taken during the recent Kentucky campaign as: 9 Colonels, 5 Lieutenant-Colonels, 55 Captains, 13 Staff Officers, 5 Majors, 95 Lieutenants, and 4666 enlisted personnel—a total of 4848. This total did not include those captured by Gen. E.K. Smith's and Maj. Gen. Withers' division—over 1000 more.

The walk to Tennessee must have been tiring for the prisoners, not knowing when they would be exchanged.

### November 9 (Sunday)

The almost unheated prison at Libby and the camps on Belle Isle would have been very uncomfortable this day. John B. Jones reported the temperature at 38°F with snow still on the ground.

### November 10 (Monday)

Col. William Hoffman, Federal Commissary-General of Prisoners, today directed Brig. Gen. Daniel Tyler, commanding Camp Douglas, Ill., to form a "fund" for the benefit of the troops in the paroled camp.

General:... At the camp of paroled troops where the regular company organizations are so much broken up the surplus rations may be commuted into a general fund to be disbursed under the direction of the commanding officer for the benefit of the troops, and the fund may be used for the purchase of any articles that will really conduce to the comfort of the men, whether for furniture, for fixtures about their quarters, for the extension of the accommodations of the camp.... The ration is much larger than can be consumed by the men and the amount of the reduction is left to your discretion. What ever is saved will be paid for by the commissary, who will be the treasurer of the fund and who will disburse it on your order, which will be his voucher.... When organized companies leave the camp its proportion of the fund should be turned over to the commander and his receipt taken for it.

On August 1, 1862, the Confederate government issued General Orders, No. 54, which placed Maj. Gen. John Pope, USA, and his officers in a status of outlaws proscribing them from being treated as prisoners of war, if captured. The Confederate government, learning that Pope was no longer in the Virginia area of operations and that his order of July 23, 1862, had been rescinded, issued General Orders, No. 84, dated this date, rescinding General Orders, No. 54.

### November 12 (Wednesday)

In Richmond, the Confederate government changed the point for exchange of prisoners from Aiken's Landing, Va., to City Point, Va., at the conflux of the James and Appomattox Rivers. The Office of the Adjutant-General wrote Maj. Gen. S.G. French in Petersburg concerning the site at City Point:

General:... The major-general commanding directs me to say that he desires you to take measures without delay to provide for the reception of the prisoners at the Point as soon as possible. It will be necessary to construct a wharf at the landing. Meantime some other expedient must be used for that purpose, as the first boat will probably arrive on Saturday. Inasmuch as these boats arrive without notice it will be necessary to establish a camp at the Point for their accommodation until cars can be sent to convey them to Petersburg with an officer, to be empowered by Mr. Ould to receipt for the prisoners, and with authority to control the camp, with a surgeon and medical stores and a depot of commissary and quartermaster stores. A large proportion of the prisoners will arrive sick or wounded, so that houses at or near the Point should be procured for their shelter. The guard furnished should number at least seventy-five men, that number being necessary to prevent the prisoners from straggling into the country.... A camp be also established in the vicinity of Petersburg ... to which the paroled prisoners will be removed.... The camp of paroled prisoners at this point has given more annoyance and trouble than any other of the many charges upon the command in Richmond, and you will be fortunate and deserve unusually if you succeed where we have well-nigh failed in managing it satisfactorily. The men arrive full of the idea of deserving unusual privileges because of their capture and will at once besiege your officer for furlough, pleading the unusual merit of their position, and upon being refused, as they must be,... they become exceedingly unruly, mutinous and difficult of management. You will find it necessary to employ a large guard, therefore, and forbid their entering the town except in limited numbers daily.

The prisoners who are sick or wounded should be provided for in a hospital, which should be set apart for that purpose, properly guarded. It may now and then occur that a prisoner will bring an infectious or contagious disease into our lines, and provisions must be made to guard against and dispose of such cases promptly.

## November 14 (Friday)

In Richmond, John B. Jones despaired of any control being maintained over the Confederate government in its present state. The Federal prisoners in the South were directly affected by the lack of definitive policy regarding their welfare.

Jones, John B., Rebel War Clerk, Confederate War Dept., Richmond, Va.:

Never before did such little men rule such a great people. Our rulers are like children or drunken men riding docile horses, that absolutely keep the riders from falling off by swaying to the right and left, and preserving the equilibrium. There is no rule for anything, and no stability in any policy.

In Savannah, Ga., Confederate Brig. Gen. H.W. Mercer wrote his headquarters in Charleston, S.C., concerning the capture of Union colored troops:

General:... A few days since Capt. Brailsford, of the Lamar Rangers, landed on St. Catherine's Island and while there encountered six negroes in Federal uniforms with arms (muskets) in their hands. Capt. B. killed two of them and captured the other four. One of these negroes, a boy named Manuel, is now in the possession of Messrs. Blount & Dawson, negro brokers in this city, for sale, to prevent which I have just ordered one of my officers to take him out of their hands and to lodge him in jail, there to await the decision of Mr. Randolph.

If I may be permitted to express an opinion upon this subject I most earnestly request that these negroes be made an example of. They are slaves taken with arms in hand against their masters and wearing the abolition uniform. Some swift and terrible punishment should be inflicted that their fellows may be deterred from following their example.

This is by no means the first case that has arisen and I much fear unless something be done to prevent similar outrages it will not be the last.

Gen. P.G.T. Beauregard, commanding the Charleston area, forwarded the above letter to Richmond for a decision. In Richmond, the Secretary of War, James A. Seddon, sent the matter to President Davis with a message that "with his concurrence my decision is that the Negro be executed as an example."

## November 18 (Tuesday)

Returning Federal prisoners of war were sent to Camp Parole near Annapolis, Md., while awaiting release on furlough or return to their units. The discipline at the camp was almost nonexistent and even the inmates of the camp asked for help in getting it corrected. M. Shaw, Co. D, 44 NY Volunteers wrote Secretary of War Stanton:

Cannot something be done to lessen the perpetration of crime by the paroled soldiers kept at Annapolis? Drunkenness, fighting, burglary, robbery, gambling, &c., are witnessed by us daily, and even murder is not of unfrequent occurrence. A person is not safe to step out to meeting or anywhere else after dark. There are probably fifty gambling stands in full blast every day. A great deal of liquor is smuggled into camp and its disgraceful effects are daily seen. If we are not soon to be exchanged—and it still thought to be an injury to the Union cause to allow paroled soldiers to return to their homes—there ought to be something done to put down the reign of rowdyism here, and I believe that you only need to become acquainted with the condition of things here to do something in this matter.

## November 20 (Thursday)

For some time the status of partisan forces, properly commissioned by the Confederate government, was in question. Originally treated as outlaws and marauders, as of this date they were to be treated as normal prisoners of war and were to be exchanged when captured.

## November 22 (Saturday)

Political prisoners were also held at Camp Chase, Ohio. Today, the *Ohio State Journal* reported:

There have been examined up to this time three hundred and twenty-seven political prisoners by special commission, and two hundred and seventy of them discharged by order of the Secretary of War, together with fifty-seven others reported upon by the War Department. There are yet about four hundred prisoners confined at Camp Chase, anxiously waiting a hearing.

## November 29 (Saturday)

Several complaints had been sent to the Secretary of War concerning the discipline and status of the parolees at Camp Parole near Annapolis, Md. Col. William Hoffman, Federal Commissary-General of Prisoners, today wrote Lt. Col. George Sangster, commanding Camp Parole:

Colonel: Complaints are made to the War Department by soldiers of great disorders at your camp—drunkenness, gambling, fighting, and even murders are among the crimes enumerated.

Inform me immediately of the state of discipline of your command, what guard you have, including officers, and what orders they have in relation to the preservation of good order; what your system of police is and what is the cause of want of good discipline if such is the fact. All the troops at Camp Parole, except those taken at Harpers Ferry or since the 1st of November, have been exchanged and are liable to perform all the duties of a soldier. Require them to be drilled twice a day and see that all officers attend the drills. As soon as you can assemble fifty men of any one company make an estimate of arms and send it to me. Detail the best officer you have for the purpose to perform the duties of commissary and place him in charge of the department; he will receive and receipt for the stores and will make all issues. Have this department under your immediate eye and report promptly all irregularities.

Till you receive orders on the subject you will permit no exchanged officer or soldier to leave the camp unless by orders through me or from higher authority. This is not intended to take from you the privilege of giving passes for the day.

### December 7 (Sunday)

Jones, John B., Rebel War Clerk, Confederate War Dept., Richmond, Va.:

Last night was bitter cold, and this morning there was ice on my wash-stand, within five feet of the fire. Is this the "sunny South" the North is fighting to possess? How much suffering must be in the armies now encamped in Virginia! I suppose there are not less than 250,000 men in arms on the plains of Virginia, and many of them who survive the war will have cause to remember last night. Some must have perished, and thousands, no doubt, have frozen limbs. It is terrible, and few are aware that the greatest destruction of life, in such a war as this, is not produced by wounds received in battle, but

by disease, contracted from exposure, etc. in inclement seasons.

In such weather as Jones described, the prisoners at Belle Isle in the middle of the James River must have had a horrible time trying to keep warm.

### December 8 (Monday)

The shortages of food were being felt in Richmond this winter. The problem, as always, was transportation to get the food to the proper place. Prices were rising beyond normal, and it would get much worse.

Jones, John B., Rebel War Clerk, Confederate War Dept., Richmond, Va.:

The President of the Central Railroad says that Messrs. Haxhall, Crenshaw & Co., who have the gigantic contract with the government to furnish flour, and who have a preference of transportation by the contract, are blocking up their depots, and fail to remove the grain. They keep whole trains waiting for days to be unladen; and thus hundreds of thousands of bushels, intended for other mills and the people, are delayed, and the price kept up to the detriment of the community. Thus it is that the government contractors are aiding and abetting the extortioners. And for this reason large amounts of grain may fall into the hands of the enemy.

### December 9 (Tuesday)

At Falmouth, just across the river from Fredericksburg, Burnside issued orders for his Grand Division commanders to issue 60 rounds per man, prepare 3 days' cooked rations, and be prepared for an assault on the Rebels across the river on pontoon bridges which were coming up to span the Rappahannock for the crossing.

### December 11 (Thursday)

About 4:45 A.M. the alert was given to the Confederates that the Yankees were building pontoon bridges for the assault on Fredericksburg, Va. Barksdale's Mississippians and Perry's Floridians were placed in brick buildings whose blank rear walls faced the river to the north. Loop-holes were knocked in the brick and firing posts were assigned that looked directly out on the pontoons. When the fog lifted, the firing began and it became down-right dangerous to be on the bridges. The engineers left their positions to scamper back out of the fire only to be driven back to work by their officers until about 10 A.M., when Burnside had had enough. He told his artillery to demolish those houses, and they used over 140 guns to pour nearly 5000 rounds of heavy artillery into the city. Barksdale's and Perry's men came back, however, and shot a few more of the engineers before, eventually, a bridgehead was established and the Yanks poured over the bridges and into the city. The Confederates withdrew and it was nearly 7:30 P.M. by the time things were quiet again.

## December 12 (Friday)

A very dense fog covered most of Fredericksburg, Va., limiting visibility to just a few yards. Burnside's men came to the pontoon bridges installed yesterday and crossed the river, heading for the heights above the town where Lee's entrenchments had been waiting for weeks. The fog didn't lift until noon and then it was too late to organize the assault, so it would be done tomorrow.

## December 13 (Saturday)

More fog this morning. Sunrise at 7:17 A.M., but you couldn't tell it. The Confederates waited in their entrenchments. About ten o'clock the fog thinned and the artillery opened up. On Marye's Heights the Confederates watched the Federals align their ranks and prepare to charge up the hill. At 11:30 A.M. the assault began and it was slaughter of the worst kind. Wave after wave of blue-clad troops lined up, went up the hill, and was shot down. This went on until about 3:30 P.M. when a lull occurred. When the assault was resumed, a total of five charges were made by sunset, about 4:15 P.M., and all had been repulsed. A sixth charge was ordered and met the same fate. At 6 P.M. the fighting was called for darkness. The Federals would recross the river in the early hours of Tuesday, ending a futile exercise that killed nearly 1300 Union troops, wounded about 9600, and left almost 1800 as prisoners. The South lost about 600 killed, 4100 wounded, and 650 missing.

One unit of the 4th Brigade (Brig. Gen. James H. Lane), A.P. Hill's Light Division, Jackson's Second Army Corps, was the 37th North Carolina Volunteer Infantry which had been recruited around Statesville, N.C. Pvt. Marcus C. Dellinger, a member of Co. D, 37th N.C., had been conscripted into the Confederate Army on August 15th, barely four months previously, just in time to visit Sharpsburg, Md., on September 17th. Today, Dellinger was wounded in the knee and evacuated to Chimborazo Hospital No. 3 in Richmond, arriving there on Tuesday, December 16th. He would be furloughed on January 10, 1863, for 60 days, during which time he went home to recuperate. He would return to the 37th in March 1863, and be promoted to Corporal. He stayed with the regiment during the trying days of Chancellorsville, Gettysburg, Grant's march to Petersburg, and the siege of Petersburg. When the defenses at Petersburg collapsed, he was captured at that place on April 2, 1865, and sent to Point Lookout, Md., as a prisoner, arriving there on April 4th. With the close of the war, Dellinger took the oath of allegiance and was released on June 11, 1865, and went home to Statesville. He later migrated to Texas and then to New Mexico, where he died on November 16, 1926, at Portales.

## December 15 (Monday)

Yesterday, Lee did not follow up his victory by attacking the Union line. It would have been too expensive to do so.

Today, on the Union side, the recriminations began. Maj. Gen. Joe Hooker would be one of the first, and most vocal, of Burnside's critics, a fact that would be remembered by Lincoln in days to come.

## December 23 (Tuesday)

President Jefferson Davis, by proclamation on this date, provided the basis for a major problem in the exchange of prisoners between the United States and the Confederacy. Davis, basing his proclamation on old State law, then prevalent throughout most of the South, proclaimed that *all negro slaves captured in arms be at once delivered over to the executive authorities of the respective States to which they belong to be dealt with according to the laws of said States ... that the like orders be executed in all cases with respect to all commissioned officers of the United States when found serving in company with armed slaves in insurrection against the authorities of the different States of this Confederacy.*

In essence, former slaves who entered the Union military service, if captured, were subject to punishment for armed insurrection and they were returned to their former masters or placed in labor gangs for public work, the former master, when identified, being paid for their labor. At the time all officers in the colored regiments were white and the proclamation provided for them to be turned over to the various State governments for punishment as if involved in insurrection against the State government.

### December 25 (Thursday)

In the field and prison camps, North and South, the soldiers spent a cold, cheerless Christmas. Many, especially in the west, spent the day skirmishing along the Mississippi River and in central Tennessee.

### December 26 (Friday)

In Tennessee, Maj. Gen. Rosecrans's Union force moved southeast from Nashville towards Murfreesboro, where Gen. Braxton Bragg's Confederates held the line on the Stones River. The Union advance would culminate in the Battle of Murfreesboro, to come in five days.

In the Mississippi region, Sherman landed his troops along the Yazoo River near Steele's Bayou in an attempt to outflank the Confederate line at Vicksburg. On the 27th and 28th, Sherman's troops would advance through the swamps and cold flooded bayous to reach the bluffs around Vicksburg.

### December 29 (Monday)

Arriving at what he thought was the best place for an assault, Sherman advanced his troops near Chickasaw Bayou to assault the defenses of Vicksburg. Of the 31,000 Union troops involved, 208 would be killed, 1005 wounded, and about 563 missing. This would compare to only 63 killed, 134 wounded, and 207 missing among the Confederate

defenders. The defenses at this point were too good to crack. Sherman ceased the attack. The Federal prisoners would be held for a few days in Vicksburg and then sent east.

### December 30 (Tuesday)

Pvt. Eliab Hickman, Co. E, 92nd Ohio Volunteer Infantry, had participated in all the regimental campaigns and was still present for the muster of November/December of his regiment. The muster roll indicated, however, that Hickman owed the regimental sutler $4.33.

### December 31 (Wednesday)

Completing his slow approach to Murfreesboro, Rosecrans went through some heavy skirmishing yesterday without making contact with the main Confederate force under Braxton Bragg. The Union force arrived late yesterday, but did not attack.

This morning Bragg attacked the Federal right just before dawn, with strong columns of gray-clad infantry. Rosecrans prepared to attack the Confederate right shortly after, where the line was weakest.. The Union was driven back to the Nashville Pike with their backs to Stones River, where they held. The armies would remain in position for the long, cold night in which no fires were permitted on either side. The troops spent a very miserable night, many without adequate covering.

Several things regarding prisoners of war had been sorted out during the year. The cartel was at last in being and was being used, at least for the time. Exchanges had taken place and the mechanics and procedures were being worked out. Several serious problems remained—notably the South's stand on the status of the Union Negro soldiers and their officers. This was to cause much dissention in the coming year.

# 1863

Many lessons had been learned from 1862 about the handling of prisoners of war; not all of them were retained by the recipients. On both sides, the movement of the prisoners improved. On both sides, the treatment of the prisoners did not improve, but grew worse. The cartel of July was operating, although it would take a serious beating during the coming year.

### January 1 (Thursday)

In Tennessee, the fighting at the Battle of Murfreesboro (Stone's River) paused while the two armies got their second wind. Bragg, so far, had the best of it, even if the casualties were running high. The weather was certainly not cooperating, the troops being repositioned in the cold.

Today, Lincoln's Emancipation Proclamation went into effect. It did little to free the slaves in the Northern states, but it provided a major moral force in the South and in Europe, where to support the South would be to support slavery—not a popular idea with the common man.

### January 2 (Friday)

Lt. W.L. Nugent, CSA, at Deer Creek, Miss., wrote the Commanding General at Grenada, Miss., concerning a group of Confederate prisoners put ashore on December 31, 1862:

…list of prisoners, C.S. Army, left at Greenville, Miss., this county, by the steamer *Minnehaha*.… These prisoners were sick and were put off without any provision being made for their well being and comfort. Without bedding, rations or medicines, these disabled soldiers were roughly thrown into a deserted hotel in a small village on the river, whose inhabitants may be numbered by the half dozen.… The citizens in the neighborhood have already given away all their surplus bedding, have no medicines and can barely supply the poor soldiers with enough to eat.…

These soldiers are a portion of the prisoners brought down for exchange and ordered back by the Federal commander at Vicksburg. Eight hundred and fifty remained on the boat and were to be carried to Memphis or Helena. I understand the *Minnehaha* put off a case of smallpox below Greenville. The obvious effect if not intent of this policy will be to scatter a violent plague throughout the whole country.

### January 3 (Saturday)

Yesterday, Bragg and Rosecrans went at it again. Maj. Gen. John C. Breckinridge's troops attacked the Union line and got their noses bloodied. Bragg couldn't seem to make up his mind what he wanted to do—fight or retreat.

Bragg withdrew during the night towards Tullahoma, Tenn. The toll was terrible. Bragg, with about 35,000 troops, lost 1294 killed, 7945 wounded, and 2500 missing, mostly prisoners. Rosecrans, left in possession of the field, was the dubious winner. He started the battle with about 41,400. Of those, he lost 1677 killed, 7543 wounded, and 3686 missing, again, mostly prisoners. The Federal prisoners would be sent to Richmond and from there further south. The Confederate prisoners would be sent north, mostly to Indiana and Illinois. But first, there was the long, cold march back to Nashville.

Bragg had announced a great victory in a telegram to Richmond. Now he would have to tell them that he had withdrawn—hardly a victory.

After the bloody fighting at Fredericksburg, Va., in the last month, Maj. Gen. Ambrose Burnside still wanted to try crossing the Rappahannock River again. Fortunately, he delayed.

### January 6 (Tuesday)

Washington Turner, a citizen of Jasper, Tenn., was arrested on May 1, 1862, by Federal forces for some nebulous reason and held without trial for several months before being released. Turner wrote President Davis of his ordeal on this date:

On the 1st of last May eighty-three men belonging to Gen. O.M. Mitchel's division came from Bridgeport, Ala., and pillaged my store of every article of any worth, and on the 5th of June last Gen. Negley sent ten soldiers (Federal) piloted by one of our tories and demanded $500 in cash and my person. The captain said he was directed by Gen. Negley if I did not pay the $500 to take property to that amount. Not getting the cash they took $900 or $1000 of property, some of them relics of my deceased wife to her little son. They took me from a sick bed and made me march with troops trained without anything to eat except crackers and bacon; no tents to lie in or blankets to cover with, but was compelled to line on the cold ground without any covering whatever. From our homes we were marched near Chattanooga, Tenn., and put in a filthy stable; from thence to Shelbyville, Tenn., and put in a slaughter house, 140 feet deep without ventilation and a hospital above had with large cracks in the floor, and nothing to eat but crackers and hot water which they termed coffee. Gen. Negley issued an order prohibiting the ladies or citizens of Shelbyville from furnishing us with any article of diet whatever saying we

were furnished with the same rations that the Federal soldiers were, which was false. From thence we were taken to the State Penitentiary and incarcerated with thieves, murderers and assassins ... where I remained near four months, while my little children were robbed of everything they had to eat and scared and insulted by a brutal soldiery.... I never lived in their lines. Gen. Negley sent his cavalry six miles from his road of travel to rob and arrest me.... I understand that Gen. Negley was taken prisoner at Murfreesborough. If so, please give orders concerning his case.

### January 11 (Sunday)

Since the 4th, Union Gen. McClernand had been leading a force up the Mississippi and Arkansas rivers to take Ft. Hindman. They finally reached the fort on the 10th and the preparatory bombardment began while the troops were put into position. The gunboats, moving to within 60 yards of the fort, were raked by the fort's eleven guns, but little damage was done to the boats.

Today, the bombardment intensified and with about 2½ hours of well-directed fire, the fort was a shambles and the commander surrendered. Part of the Confederate force went on upriver, to be followed by part of the Union gunboats. The expedition continued.

Overall, there would be about 5000 Confederate prisoners collected during this expedition. Among them would be a Pvt. Thomas Didimus Richards, Co. H, 24th Texas Infantry. Richards enlisted in Live Oak Co., Tex., age 23, on March 11, 1862, for the duration of the war and was mustered in on April 10, 1862, as a part of Capt. John H. Conner's Co., 2d Regt., Carter's Brigade of Texas Lancers, which later became Co. H, 24th Texas Cavalry (Dismounted). He fought in several engagements in Texas, Arkansas and Louisiana before being captured at Ft. Hindman (Arkansas Post), Ark., on this date as a part of the 24th Texas Cavalry (Dismounted) (Lt. Col. T.S. Anderson), First Brigade (Col. Robert R. Garland), of the Confederate forces commanded by Brig. Gen. Thomas J. Churchill. The prisoners would be transferred to Camp Butler, Springfield, Ill., arriving there on January 31st. He was transferred east to be paroled at Richmond in accordance with the wishes of the Confederate government, and was a patient in the Petersburg, Va., hospital on April 18, 1863. Upon return to the west, the 24th and 25th Texas Cavalry (Dismounted) were consolidated into the 25th, and the 24th designation was no longer used. Mustered out in April 1865, Richards returned to Texas. He died in 1916 as a result of injury to his lung caused by the kick of a mule.

### January 12 (Monday)

President Davis issued a message on this date that would have far-reaching effects on the status of the prisoners of war on both sides. The cartel for exchange of prisoners had been signed on July 22, 1862, and concerned only the exchange of prisoners—it had no political overtones or criteria. Davis, reacting to the Emancipation Proclamation issued by Lincoln which had gone into effect on January 1st, placed the cartel squarely into the political arena with the following message.

The public journals of the North have been received containing a proclamation dated the first day of the present month signed by the President of the United States in which he orders and declares all slaves within ten States of the Confederacy to be free, except such as are found in certain districts now occupied in part by the armed forces of the enemy.

We may well leave it to the instincts of that common humanity which a beneficent Creator has implanted in the breasts of our fellowmen of all countries to pass judgment on a measure by which several millions of human beings of an inferior race, peaceful and contented laborers in their sphere, are doomed to extermination, while at the same time they are encouraged to a general assassination of their masters by the insidious recommendation "to abstain from violence unless in necessary self-defense." Our own detestation of those who have attempted the most execrable measure recorded in the history of guilty man is tempered by profound contempt for the impotent rage which it discloses. As far as regards the action of this Government on such criminals as may attempt its execution I confine myself to informing you that I shall unless in your wisdom you deem some other course more expedient deliver to the several State authorities all commissioned officers of the United States that may hereafter be captured by our forces in any part of the States embraced in the proclamation that they may be dealt with in accordance with the laws of those States providing

for the punishment of criminals engaged in exciting servile insurrection. The enlisted soldiers I shall continue to treat as unwilling instruments in the commission of these crimes and shall direct their discharge and return to their homes on the proper and usual parole.

### January 15 (Thursday)

On December 23, 1862, President Davis issued an Executive Order defining the status of captured former slaves and the officers who serve in Negro regiments. The order followed on the heels of Lincoln's Emancipation Proclamation, which caused a real furor in the South. Jones comments on Davis's speech:

Jones, John B., Rebel War Clerk, Confederate War Dept., Richmond, Va.:

The President's message is highly applauded. It is well written; but I do not perceive much substance in it....

The President says he will, unless Congress directs differently, have all Federal officers that we may capture, handed over to the States to be dealt with as John Brown was dealt with. The Emancipation Proclamation, if not revoked, may convert the war into a most barbarous conflict.

### January 17 (Saturday)

Federal prisoners from the battle at Stone's River (Murfreesboro) have started arriving in Richmond and the already short rations are going to get much shorter. Those 3500-plus prisoners would require a lot of food.

Jones, John B., Rebel War Clerk, Confederate War Dept., Richmond, Va.:

Shall we starve? Yesterday beef was sold for 40 cts. per pound; today it is 60 cts. Lard is $1.00. Butter $2.00. They say the sudden rise is caused by the prisoners of Gen. Bragg, several thousand of whom have arrived here, and they are subsisted from the market. Thus they injure us every way.

Prior to this time, a prisoner could be paroled and sent back to his country without an exchange having taken place. At a later time when enemy personnel of equal rank were paroled, the two names would be linked and both declared "exchanged." Today, the ground rules changed. Robert Ould, Confederate Agent for Exchange, wrote Lt. Col. Ludlow, his Union counterpart:

> In your communication of the 14th instant you desire to know whether the Federal commissioned officers now prisoners will be released. I have already furnished you with an official copy of the proclamation of President Davis dated December 23, 1862. In conformity therewith officers will not be released on parole but will be exchanged for those of corresponding rank. If you have any Confederate officer in your possession and will deliver him an officer of like grade will be delivered to you and they will be mutually declared to be exchanged.... The Federal officers, however, now in our possession will not be surrendered to you on parole.

### January 18 (Sunday)

Jones continued his complaints against the fates of war that caused shortages of food and other necessities. No thought for the thousands of prisoners of war on Belle Isle at Richmond who had little clothing, little shelter, and less food from which to extract calories to keep warm.

Jones, John B., Rebel War Clerk, Confederate War Dept., Richmond, Va.:

> It was bitter cold last night, and everything is frozen this morning; there will be abundance of ice next summer, if we keep our icehouses.
>
> In these times of privation and destitution, I see many men, who were never prominent secessionists, enjoying comfortable positions, and seeking investments for their surplus funds. Surely there must be some compensation in this world or the next for the true patriots who have sacrificed everything, and still labor in subordinate positions, with faith and patient suffering. These men and their families go in rags, and upon half-rations, while the others fare most sumptuously.
>
> We are now, in effect, in a state of siege, and none but the opulent, often those who have defrauded the government, can obtain a sufficiency of food and raiment. Calico, which could once be bought for 12½ cts. per yard, is now selling at $2.25, and a lady's dress of calico costs her about $30.00. Bonnets are not to be

had. Common bleached cotton shirting brings $1.50 per yard. All other dry goods are held in the same proportion. Common tallow candles at $1.25 per pound; soap, $1.00; hams, $10; opossum, $3.00; turkeys, $4 to 11.00; sugar, brown, $1.00; molasses $8.00 per gallon; potatoes $6.00 per bushel.

> These evils might be remedied by the government, for there is no great scarcity of any of the substantials and necessities of life in the country, if they were only equally distributed. The difficulty is in procuring transportation and the government monopolizes the railroads and canals.

In Tennessee, Gen. Braxton Bragg's Confederate army and Gen. Wm. S. Rosecrans's Union army were still facing each other, although generally quiet. Rosecrans had a real problem which he had been trying to solve for some time without adequate result. The Confederates were using a flag-of-truce as a ruse to enter Union lines and capture Federal troops and/or gain intelligence. Then the Union prisoners would be robbed of their equipment and clothing, declared "paroled," and returned to the Union lines. This use of the "flag" was a favorite trick of Gen. John H. Morgan, who used it often. Rosecrans notifies Bragg that hereafter all persons entering Union lines under the "flag" will be taken prisoner while being examined as to their true mission.

### January 21 (Wednesday)

Lt. Col. Wm. H. Ludlow, Union Agent for Exchange, notified Secy. of War Stanton that:

> a dispatch from Mr. Ould, Confederate agent for exchange of prisoners, informs me that all officers now in the hands of the Confederates and captured before the 12th of January, the date of Jeff. Davis's message, will not be released on parole but will be exchanged for those of corresponding rank. All officers captured after the 12th instant will be handed over to the Governors of the States where captured, as indicated in Jeff. Davis's message.

### January 22 (Thursday)

In the west, McClernand's Arkansas River expedition was coming to an end. This was largely a sideshow developed by McClernand for his own aggrandizement and Grant had finally had enough. He included McClernand's command as a part of his [Grant's] larger army organization which effectively reduced McClernand's stature to that of a Corps commander. McClernand went to Lincoln, an old Illinois acquaintance, about it, but McClernand was told to go back to work.

Yesterday, Col. John S. Clark, USA, wrote to "any Officer of Confederate Army" that "under a flag of truce and in the absence of any officer to confer with I have taken the liberty to land some 250 citizens, mostly women and children. They have been left at their own request and without restraint. I commend them to your kindness." A singular thing to do.

### January 26 (Monday)

Lincoln relieved Maj. Gen. Ambrose Burnside today and placed Maj. Gen. Joseph Hooker in command of the Army of the Potomac.

### January 27 (Tuesday)

In Richmond, a group of 794 Federal prisoners was being moved to City Point for exchange. The train that was to carry them to that location had backed up closer to the canal bridge than usual, which caused the line of prisoners to form on the bridge for boarding. While they were waiting, the bridge collapsed, throwing between sixty and seventy of the prisoners into the canal. All were saved except two members of the 30th Indiana Volunteers, who drowned. The commander of Camp Parole, Md., Lt. Col. George Sangster, reported to Col. Hoffman on February 2nd that 350 of them were sent to the hospital at Camp Parole with diseases, broken legs and arms, many bruised badly internally and externally.

### January 30 (Friday)

Col. Wm. Hoffman, Federal Commissary-General of Prisoners, sent Capt. H.W. Freedley to Camp Morton, Ind., to inspect the facilities. On this date, Freedley reported that the buildings were "much dilapidated and sadly in need of repairs." He recommended that buildings at nearby Camp Carrington be moved into Camp Morton and the entire facility be repaired before it was used as a hospital for prisoners of war.

### February 4 (Wednesday)

Special Orders No. 32 issued at Charleston, S.C., this date directed that "all prisoners of war in this city (except officers and negroes) of the land and naval service of the United States will be sent forthwith and turned over to Brig. Gen. Winder at Richmond." It further stated that "all officers ... will be sent for further confinement to Columbia, S.C."

### February 5 (Thursday)

Yesterday, Union Quartermaster-General Meigs informed Col. Robert Allen in St. Louis that the 5000 prisoners taken at Ft. Hindman (Arkansas Post) would be transferred to Richmond, rather than Vicksburg, for exchange. It appeared that some of the prisoners desired to take the oath of allegiance and remain in the North. Some were of Irish, German and Polish nationality and had been conscripted into the Confederate forces and did not want to return.

Col. Hoffman authorized the repair of the facility at Camp Morton, Ind., for use as a hospital for prisoners.

The *Ohio State Journal*, Columbus, Ohio, today reported the arrival of three women from Tennessee:

The ten o'clock train from the South last night brought three women from Nashville who have elected themselves to a term of repose at Camp Chase. It seems that they were decidedly brisk in forwarding contraband information to Southern leaders and giving money and aid to their soldiers. They are of one family, being mother and daughters.

### February 8 (Sunday)

After much trouble with the facilities and personnel at Camp Parole, Md., things were now in good working order. Lt. Col. Sangster reported to Col. Hoffman:

[I] inclose ... complete rolls of 740 men who arrived here on the 5th instant from Richmond.... On their arrival here I had them in barracks in half an hour after reaching the dock, and in eight hours after their arrival every man had clean clothes on, with a good overcoat and blanket and plenty of good food with comfortable quarters. Every man's name was taken down and his clothing charged to him. Had I not had these new barracks to put them in I feel satisfied that we should have lost several lives from the severeness of the weather and the naked condition of the men.

## February 11 (Wednesday)

In Richmond, Va., the shortage of food caused some weird events. Jones may have stretched the truth just a little.

Jones, John B., Rebel War Clerk, Confederate War Dept., Richmond, Va.:

> Some idea may be formed of the scarcity of food in this city from the fact that, while my youngest daughter was in the kitchen today, a young rat came out of its hole and seemed to beg for something to eat; she held out some bread, which it ate from her hand, and seemed grateful. Several others soon appeared, and were as tame as kittens. Perhaps we shall have to eat them!

## February 15 (Sunday)

John Yates Beall returned to Richmond from Canada to find out what service he could perform for the Confederacy. In Richmond, he was eventually appointed as an Acting Master in the Confederate Navy, which entitled him to be called Captain. He recruited crews for two sloops and planned his raiding on Chesapeake Bay.

## February 19 (Thursday)

At Ft. Monroe, Va., a problem had developed concerning the desertions from the First Regiment Mounted Rifles stationed at Suffolk, Va. It seemed that men from this regiment were deserting to the Confederates, turning over their equipment, and getting, in exchange, paroled. This effectively took them out of danger for several months. The Union command decided that henceforth these men would be treated as deserters, not as returned prisoners of war. That effectively stopped the practice.

The Salisbury, N.C., newspaper, the *Carolina Watchman*, reported that:

> …about 450 Yankee deserters had come in from time to time, took an oath of allegiance to the Confederate Government and had been discharged from prison on their parole of honor.

Many of the Union prisoners who took the oath in Salisbury, N.C., were released and took employment throughout the area on farms, in shops, etc.

## February 21 (Saturday)

Pvt. Eliab Hickman, Co. E, 92nd Ohio Volunteer Infantry, was reported to be in the hospital at Nashville, Tenn. He was reported as such by the unit muster rolls of February through August of 1863.

## February 23 (Monday)

The Adjutant-General of Illinois wrote Col. Hoffman on this date that the Governor had received letters from members of the 21st Regiment of Illinois Volunteers concerning their treatment upon being returned as prisoners of war. The letters alleged:

> …that some thirty members of this regiment were reported at the paroled camp at Annapolis on or before the 12th instant who on passage from Richmond and since arrival at Annapolis have received harsh treatment from officers in charge; allowed to go without rations for thirty-six to forty hours, and for two days after landing at Annapolis not provided with quarters, subsistence or blankets.

The Governor requested that corrective action be taken.

## February 24 (Tuesday)

Admiral David D. Porter, USN, commanding the Mississippi Squadron, had grown tired of his boats being fired upon by hidden snipers along the river banks. It wasn't so bad when the gunboats were fired upon; they had a means to fire back. It was the unarmed steamers that he was riled about. So, the Admiral issued the following:

> Persons taken in the act of firing on unarmed vessels from the bank will be treated as highwaymen and assassins and no quarter will be shown them.
>
> Persons strongly suspected of firing on unarmed vessels will not receive the usual treatment of prisoners of war but will be kept in close confinement.
>
> If this savage and barbarous Confederate custom cannot be put a stop to we will try what virtue there is in hanging.
>
> All persons no matter who they are who are caught in the act of pillaging the houses of the inhabitants along the river, levying contributions or burning cotton will receive no quarter if caught in the act, or if it is proved upon them.

Maj. Gen. C.L. Stevenson, CSA, commanding at

Vicksburg, Miss., complained loudly about the warning issued by Admiral Porter and threatened retaliation.

## February 28 (Saturday)

The returns for the various prisons in the North for this month showed that at Camp Douglas, Ill., the death rate was 387 for a prisoner population of 3884—*10 percent for the month!* This was the result of a smallpox epidemic.

At Camp Chase, Ohio, the Confederate officer prisoners were receiving large amounts of money from their friends and were on a spending spree. The big-ticket items were new uniforms (Confederate, of course) and boots to replace the ones they were wearing when captured. The commander of the prison was dubious about allowing this practice and requested advice. The answer was not long in coming from Col. Hoffman. No uniforms were to be purchased by the prisoners.

## March 3 (Tuesday)

Col. William Hoffman sent Capt. H.M. Lazelle, his assistant, to Camp Parole to inspect the facility and report. Lazelle, a very intelligent and observant officer, reported at some length on this date.

Federal prisoners sent to Camp Parole ... arrive there by water conveyance and in detachments ranging in number from a few hundred in some to several thousand in others.... No intimation is received ... of the sending of these prisoners to Camp Parole until the boat touches the wharf at Annapolis with them on board. They generally arrive in a state of extreme destitution, with little or no clothing and that covered with filth and vermin. They are often physically emaciated and suffering from hunger and disease.... Upon landing at the wharf they are conducted to what are termed the College Green Barracks. These consist of eight wooden frame buildings each 90 by 20 feet, one story in height, with sides and roof boarded and battened.... At present three of these buildings have been set aside for the reception of prisoners. In rear of them is a cook house well provided with cooking utensils necessary for cooking for 600 men at a time.... Upon arriving here the prisoners are formed and their number compared with the accompanying rolls. When this is done a list is immediately made of all who are in need of clothing ... and

in almost all cases a complete suit, including overcoat and blanket, is issued to each soldier upon the day of his arrival. Before he is allowed, however, to put on any article of clothing the men are marched to the river, made to throw away their old clothing and cleanse themselves. They remain two or three days in these barracks until they are provided with clothing and until accommodations are set aside for them at Camp Parole, about two miles from these barracks.... While here the prisoners are provided with full rations regularly issued, the cooking of which is done by details from among them, with the exception of bread, which is sent from the Navy-Yard Hospital. They are also well provided with fuel....

I now desire to call your attention to the guards at Camp Parole.... There are thirty infantry posts about the camp at which are nominally thirty sentinels, but great carelessness prevails among them while on post and their duty is very indifferently performed and very often totally neglected.... To establish this I will refer to some of the daily practices at the camp by the prisoners—the constant habit of defecating all about the immediate vicinity; the constant passing of sentinel's posts whenever convenient; the stopping of the fuel wagons by the soldiers of one part of the camp when the fuel is designed for another part; the interference by soldiers with the delivery of the particular quantity of fuel designed for any company, regardless of the teamster of the cavalry patrol accompanying the team, they not unfrequently tossing the black teamster in a blanket if he remonstrates; the destruction of wooden buildings by the soldiers for the purpose of using the boards whenever convenient; the seizing of the tents in camp which may be vacated by exchanged men leaving and doubling the canvas of their own by placing these tents over those occupied, and many other irregularities....

*Discipline* ... the general discipline of the camp ... is extremely slack as the above facts will illustrate. There are no parades, except for morning and evening roll calls.... Of the eleven paroled officers at Camp Parole but four are convalescents, so as to be reported for duty, and consequently two of the battalions are without any commissioned officers at all, and Col. Sangster has but two permanent assistant officers, his major and his adjutant, besides these four, in the whole camp of nearly 6000 men.... The disposition generally manifested by the paroled offices is to avoid duty if possible rather than attend to the wants of their men, and the spirit exhibited seems to be a prominent desire to complain and encourage discontent among the men rather than to remedy their discomforts.... At present one paroled officer having the Fourth Battalion in charge is alone in command of the 2900 men of whom it is composed....

... There is much complaint among the men about a want of cooking utensils and such common furniture as a tin plate, cup, knife and fork... One reason of the unequal distribution of the articles referred to is that on the departure of troops the articles of camp furniture left behind in their tents are immediately seized upon by the companies remaining instead of being turned in to the quartermaster's department and reissued.... Col. Sangster does everything in his power but he lacks experience, and as he is not properly assisted there is but little method in the labor....

Generally speaking the soldiers seem comfortably provided with quarters for the present with the exception of the Fourth Battalion of 3000 men, which is composed of Western troops.... Upon arriving at Camp Parole some of them for a week or more occupied the log frames constructed for huts without roofs, others lived in crowded tents or others occupied huts.... This induced some few of them to go to the forest with their blankets and construct for themselves shelters, a few others constructed pits covered with boughs in which they lived.... These facts were unknown to the commanding officer.... I saw but one privy for the men in the whole camp and that badly constructed, with the vault filled to the top. I was told that the others had been pulled down by the soldiers, they desiring to use the lumber for their quarters....

The police of the camp is far from being good, nor is the rubbish sufficiently far removed from the camp vicinity....

The sutler's store is more a refreshment saloon than sutler's store, though a tolerable assortment of necessary articles is kept. Oysters in every style and a species of lager beer are sold without restriction.... The hospital of the camp is in excellent condition, being well supplied with every necessary for the sick....

The ground immediately outside the present camp is so covered with accumulations of rubbish and filth and the sites of old tents and huts as to have rendered it unfit for any considerable expansion in any direction.

## March 5 (Thursday)

Lt. Col. F.A. Dick, Provost-Marshal-General of St. Louis, Mo., had been investigating actions by several wealthy and influential women in the St. Louis area. These ladies were collecting letters to be sent to the Confederacy as well as carrying on a correspondence with persons in the South. Col. Dick had sufficient evidence to arrest them, but didn't know where to incarcerate them if he did.

## March 6 (Friday)

General Orders, No. 25, published by the Adjutant and Inspector General's Office, Richmond, on this date republished "An act to protect the rights of owners of slaves taken by or employed in the Army," as passed by the Confederate Congress. In addition to defining the actions to be taken by the various functionaries, the Act also provided for the establishment of depots for recaptured slaves. The former slaves were to be held at these depots while their presence was advertised in the local press. The owner(s) could then claim the slaves and take them into custody. A total of 19 camps were designated to be established.

## March 9 (Monday)

Yesterday, the Adjutant-General in Washington notified Col. Hoffman that Capt. Lazelle's report concerning the status of Camp Parole at Annapolis had been reviewed. Col. Hoffman was authorized to take immediate action to designate the necessary officers to correct the situation at that facility.

George Williams of Wellington, Mo., wrote Charles Buford in Scott, Mo., concerning his son, Lloyd B. Williams, Co. G, 10th Texas Infantry, who was a prisoner at Camp Douglas, Ill.:

Dear Buford: I rec'd a letter on Friday night last from which I learned that Lloyd is a prisoner at Camp Douglas he wrote me that he had the misfortune to lose all his clothes & for me to send him money to buy more on Saturday I sent him money by Adam's Express Company but is very common for our mail to be robbed about every two weeks consequently it is uncertain whether or not he gets it So this morning it occurred to me to write you & ask this favor of you to send the fellow say $10 & inform me of the fact & I would remit to you till you did get it if you have any acquaintance in Chicago please ask him to look after Lloyd he was sick & had been for twenty five days and it would be two weeks before he would be able to walk Say to Bussel or Charlie if they would take cars & run up to Camp Douglas & see Lloyd I would be under lasting obligation to them moreover I would gladly pay any & all expenses incurred all they would have to do would be to draw on me for the amount.

I wrote to Lloyd not to ask to be exchanged but ask to be parolled & then make his way to Rock Island & you would assist him in getting work by which he could at least pay his board for I would rather he would work at two bits a day than be in the army his constitution unfits him for a soldier I had hoped that he was in Texas tending his sheep had he been here I think I could have kept him strait I have had a good deal of trouble to keep Euk in the traces but have managed thus far to keep him down I thought at one time that I would send Euk but I know it would be doubtful whether or not he would be allowed to pass and I knew he would not be permitted to see Lloyd.

Well Buford we are still having a rough time here. Some fifty negros left on thursday night & about as many horses So you see we will soon be without negroes and horses I have lost none this far but I recon my time will come soon this blessed war is working wonders for Mo. Buford I beg'd you to write soon but up to this time I have got no letter Sam was in bed when I wrote you he still there it soon be six months since he was taken down with Typhoid fever & he is now unable to sit up as long as a half hour at a time Susan has bad health.

write me at once & tell me all about your family where is Pattie & her little one; and above all tell me when the war will end for I do want to visit Rock Island mighty love to all

### March 11 (Wednesday)

Capt. H.W. Freedley, sent by Col. Hoffman to inspect the facility at Camp Douglas, Chicago, Ill., reported today on his inspection.

I find the condition of the prisoners at Camp Douglas much improved. The barracks have all been repaired. The fence which was partly torn down by the paroled men has been reconstructed....

The medical department is under the charge of Dr. George H. Park, surgeon Sixty-fifth Illinois Infantry. I found the hospitals generally neat and clean and are well supplied with cots and bedding. The sick prisoners are well cared for.... There has been and still is a large amount of sickness here. This is to be attributed mainly to the fact that when these prisoners came up the river they were crowded upon transports without proper protection from the weather and without proper facilities for cooking their rations. They were delayed en route, many of them sick, with only the clothing they had on their backs. They had been subjected to much exposure for some days previous to their capture and were literally broken down in health and spirits. On their arrival 800 were under medical treatment.... Besides the diseases usually found in camps smallpox is prevailing to some extent. There are now 125 cases under treatment.... The mortality of the prisoners is quite large, but this is to be attributed to their wretchedly broken-down condition. Their general health has greatly improved since their arrival at the camp. Three hundred and eighty-seven prisoners have died in the month of February; 262 now sick in hospitals, while a number are being prescribed for and receiving treatment in their quarters. This is exclusive of the 125 cases of smallpox....

... There has been but little clothing furnished by Government, only in extreme cases, but here have been large contributions by their friends.... The total number of prisoners at present confined in this camp is 3520. They are principally from the States of Texas and Arkansas.

Some concern was expressed by the local community about the smallpox hospital and the care given the patients at Camp Douglas. To allay the fears, a joint committee of Army and civilian doctors was appointed to investigate the possible danger. The report showed that all precautions were being taken.

### March 12 (Thursday)

At Richmond, Capt. Turner, commanding the prison, wrote Capt. W.S. Winder, the Asst. Adj.-Gen. of the command, of a problem. It seems that when the latest batch of prisoners arrived there were four missing—including one Brig. Gen., one Capt., and two Privates. When inquiry was made as to their whereabouts, it was found that the four were staying at the Ballard Hotel for the night. This seemed a little unusual, so Capt. Turner took action to reunite them with their fellows at the local prison. He sent someone to collect them and that person was told by a Lt. McClellan that they were not to be disturbed. Turner then went down and explained the facts of life to Lt. McClellan, who decided that they could, after all, be disturbed. The prisoners went to the lockup.

### March 19 (Thursday)

In Alexandria, Va., the paroled and exchanged prisoners' camp was almost deserted. Most of the men occupying the camp were guards and administrative personnel; only 32 of 342 were prisoners awaiting shipment. The tentage and other equipment in the camp was not being taken care of and was rotting, or becoming unserviceable. The inspector recommended that the personnel be transferred to other duties and the camp closed.

### March 21 (Saturday)

Robert Ould, Confederate Agent for Exchange, notified Col. A.C. Myers in the War Dept. that:

…if the exigencies of our army require the use of trains for the transportation of corn pay no regard to the Yankee prisoners. I would rather they should starve than our own people suffer. I suppose I can safely put it in writing, "Let them suffer." The words are memorable and it is fortunate in this case they can be applied properly and without the intervention of a lying quartermaster.

### March 23 (Monday)

There were reported to be about 100 prisoners in the Old Capitol Prison in Washington and the number was increasing. Maj. Gen. Halleck wrote to Quartermaster-General Meigs suggesting that some of them be sent to the Tortugas prison if transportation became available.

### March 24 (Tuesday)

Capt. Freedley, assistant to Col. Hoffman, had been on another inspection, this one to Camp Butler, Ill.:

This camp is situated on the Great Western Railroad about six miles east of Springfield.... There are at present confined in this camp 1620 prisoners of war who were captured at Arkansas Post, and are principally from the States of Texas, Arkansas and

Louisiana.... The rations issued to the prisoners I find to be quite as large as they can consume. They are cheerful and contented, and all agree in saying that their provisions are much better in quality and larger in amount than those issued to them when in the service of the Confederate States....

The discipline of the camp is not good. A loose manner of performing all the duties of a soldier seems to prevail. There is a decided want of force and of energy among the officers.... The police of the camp was very poor. No attention whatever had been paid to it. Large amounts of filth and offal had been permitted to accumulate in the vicinity of the prisoners' quarters until they were almost too filthy to visit. This was partly excused as it had rained almost daily for some weeks. The camp had never been dry since the prisoners arrived.... The camp was indeed exceedingly muddy and it was almost impossible to enforce any police regulations, but had proper attention been paid to drainage there would have been no necessity for its being in such a wretched condition....

The prisoners' barracks, internally and without, were exceedingly filthy, the prisoners taking no means or trouble to insure their own cleanliness or comfort although every necessary means was within their reach.... The prisoners on their part were content to remain ... amidst filth and vermin.

... The barracks occupied by the prisoners are sadly in need of repairs. New bunks should be constructed, additional modes of ventilation provided while repairs in floor and roof are required. There have been no repairs to this camp for some time and it presents a general appearance of neglect....

... I have inspected the hospitals and find [in] them but little improvement over the barracks as regards cleanliness.... The buildings used as prisoners' hospitals are illy adapted to the purposes.... Besides the hospitals above referred to there was a small building separated from the camp and without the inclosure that is used as a smallpox hospital. It contained seven prisoners, all varioloid cases. The sanitary condition of the prisoners has improved but little since their arrival. The principal causes of their unhealthy condition are exposure in transportation to this camp; long confinement on transports without sufficient clothing to protect them from the weather; prostration and reduction before capture, together with a total neglect of all sanitary regulations and of personal cleanliness. The mortality rate of the camp is quite large; 103 persons died during the month of February.

In one of the most vituperative letters seen in any Civil War archive, Daniel Harvey Hill, West Point Class of 1842, and then Maj. Gen. in the Confederate Army, wrote John Gray Foster, West Point Class of 1846, and currently Maj. Gen. in the United States Army, from Goldsboro, N.C., concerning Foster's censure of Hill for the burning of Plymouth, N.C.

Sir: Two communications have been referred to me as the successor of Gen. French. The prisoners from Swindell's company and the Seventh North Carolina are true prisoners of war and if not paroled I will retaliate five-fold.

In regard to your first communication touching the burning of Plymouth you seem to have forgotten two things. You forget, sir, that you are a Yankee and that Plymouth is a Southern town. It is no business of yours if we choose to burn one of our own towns. A meddling Yankee troubles himself about everybody's matters except his own and repents of everybody's sins except his own. We are a different people. Should the Yankees burn a Union village in Connecticut or a codfish town in Massachusetts we would not meddle with them but rather bid them God speed in their work of purifying the atmosphere.

Your second act of forgetfulness consists in your not remembering that you are the most atrocious house-burner as yet unhung in the wide universe. Let me remind you of the fact that you have made two raids when you were weary of debauching in your negro harem and when you knew that your forces outnumbered the Confederates five to one, your whole line of march has been marked by burning churches, schoolhouses, private residences, barns, stables, gin-houses, negro cabins, fences in the row, &c. Your men have plundered the country of all that it contained and wantonly destroyed what they could not carry off. Before you started on your freebooting expedition towards Tarborough you addressed your soldiers in the town of Washington and told them that you were going to take them to a rich country full of plunder. With such a hint to your thieves it is not wonderful that your raid was characterized by rapine, pillage, arson and murder. Learning last December that there was but a single weak brigade on this line you tore yourself from the arms of sable beauty and moved out with 15,000 men on a grand

marauding foray. You partially burned Kinston and entirely destroyed the village of White Hall. The elegant mansion of the planter and the hut of the poor farmer and fisherman were alike consumed by your brigands. How matchless is the impudence which in view of this wholesale arson can complain of the burning of Plymouth in the heat of action?

But there is another species of effrontery which New England itself cannot excel. When you return to your harem from one of these Union restoring excursions you write to your Government the deliberate lie that you have discovered a large and increasing Union sentiment in this State. No one knows better than yourself that there is not a respectable man in North Carolina in any condition of life who is not utterly and irrevocably opposed to union with your hated and hateful people. A few wealthy men have meanly and falsely professed Union sentiments to save their property and a few ignorant fishermen have joined your ranks but to betray you when the opportunity offers. No one knows better than yourself our people are true as steel and that our poorer classes have excelled the wealthy in their devotion to our cause.

You knowingly and willfully lie when you speak of a Union sentiment in this brave, noble and patriotic State. Wherever the trained and disciplined soldiers of North Carolina have met the Federal forces you have been scattered as leaves before the hurricane.

In conclusion let me inform you that I will receive no more white flags from you except the one which covers your surrender at the scene of your lust, your debauchery and your crimes. No one dislikes New England more cordially than I do, but there are thousands of honorable men even there who abhor your career fully as I do.

Daniel H. Hill, was born in South Carolina on July 12, 1821, the youngest of 11 children. After West Point, he served in Mexico, then left the army and taught at Washington College, Lexington, Va., and at Davidson College in N.C. When the war began he was superintendent of the North Carolina Military Institute. Hill was an excellent officer and a good leader of troops, but he couldn't keep his mouth shut, constantly complaining about his superiors. During the war he had the brass to complain about two full generals—Lee and Bragg—which did not sit well with President Davis. Recommended for promotion to Lt. Gen., the promotion was never confirmed because of his personality and attitude towards his superiors.

In his letter to Foster, Hill neglected to look at reality. First, North Carolina initially refused to secede in a vote of the people but was taken out of the Union by the State Legislature. Secondly, there was a strong, and growing, resistance to the Confederacy in western North Carolina, where it had been threatened to raise the Stars and Stripes over one of the courthouses. While North Carolina furnished more troops and suffered the most casualties of any Southern state, the feeling for the Southern cause was nowhere universal within the state.

### March 25 (Wednesday)

Col. William Hoffman wrote Col. D.H. Rucker at the Depot Quartermaster in Washington:

The Secretary of War directs that transportation to their homes be furnished to the destitute citizens recently released from the prisons in Richmond and now in this city and I have therefore to request that you will cause transportation to be provided.

### March 26 (Thursday)

The paroled prisoners at Camp Parole, Md., had been ordered to help build new barracks for their use to replace buildings that were partially wrecked by them. The prisoners refused, stating that being parolees they were not allowed to engage in any *military* activity. This situation was bucked all the way up to Maj. Gen. Halleck in Washington. Halleck directed that the work in no way violated the prisoner cartel, and that the troops should be put to work.

### March 31 (Tuesday)

Special Orders, No. 90 from HQ, Dept. of the Tennessee, U.S. Grant commanding, directed that a new prison camp to hold 1000 prisoners be built on one of the islands in the Mississippi River between Columbus, Ky., and Memphis, Tenn.

### April 4 (Saturday)

Maj. Gen. Wm. T. Sherman today wrote U.S. Grant concerning the status of a boy who had been arrested within the Union lines:

I inclose you a letter sent me by Maj. Watts, agent for the exchange of prisoners in Vicksburg, asking that we return a prisoner captured on Deer Creek. This prisoner is a large boy, dressed in a kind of uniform, found with a rifle which he attempted to conceal, and was confused in his statements, at one time admitting himself to be a soldier and again denying it. With your consent I will send the boy home, as from the scare of his mother I think he will give us no further trouble.

### April 7 (Tuesday)

Secy. of War Edwin M. Stanton wired P.H. Watson, his assistant in Washington, concerning some smallpox cases:

I am informed that twenty-five prisoners having the smallpox are now at Locust Point in a railroad station there, having been brought there from places where they were confined, and are to be sent to Ft. Monroe. I think it is outrageous that the commissary-general of prisoners should allow infected persons to travel through the States and be introduced to our posts. You will please see the commissary-general of prisoners and consult with Gens. Halleck, Meigs and Hitchcock as to what shall be done with them, and inform the commissary-general of prisoners that I shall expect him to investigate the facts and see who is responsible for such acts if my information be correct.

Following the above, Col. Hoffman wired Lt. Col. J.L. Donaldson at Baltimore for more information on the status of the patients.

### April 8 (Wednesday)

Col. Hoffman today wired P.H. Watson, Asst. Secy. of War in Washington, concerning the smallpox patients near Baltimore:

Ten cases among the prisoners and one of the guards have been reported.... These cases were provided for without delay at the Marine Hospital....

    It appears ... that on leaving the camp the examination of the sick was intrusted to the rebel surgeon who was attending on the prisoners and he suffered nine slight cases to be brought with the well men. These are probably the cases which developed themselves on the way, for unless the infection was very strong it could not be so fully developed in the time required to make the journey.... These cases came from Camp Douglas, Chicago.

### April 11 (Saturday)

At Nashville, Tenn., Union Col. Abel D. Streight took a mule-mounted force of 1700 to begin a raid into Georgia.

The Quartermaster at Baltimore, J.L. Donaldson, wired Col. Wm. Hoffman that prisoners were arriving in large bodies at the railroad station without prior notice of their coming. This caused problems in the prisoners standing around in the station awaiting transportation to the point where they were to be housed or to further transportation. To further add to the confusion, nine prisoners with typhoid fever were left at the station unattended and no indication of where they came from could be found. The sick prisoners were sent to the Marine Hospital.

### April 16 (Thursday)

Col. Abel D. Streight and his Union force moved into northern Alabama. Confederate Gen. Nathan B. Forrest would soon be on Streight's trail.

### April 18 (Saturday)

As spring neared, the availability of food in Richmond increased. However, since the prisoners' food was also obtained from the local markets, and the prisoner population was increasing, the people of the city saw little difference. Some, like Jones, believed that food was being kept from the market to increase, or maintain, the price.

Jones, John B., Rebel War Clerk, Confederate War Dept., Richmond, Va.:

Bacon fell today from $2 to $1.50 per pound, and butter from $3.50 to $3.25; potatoes are $16 per bushel. And yet they say there is no scarcity in the country. Such supplies are hoarded and hidden to extort high prices from the destitute. An intelligent gentleman from North Carolina told me, today, that food was never more abundant in his state; nevertheless, the extortioners are demanding there very high prices.

### April 26 (Sunday)

From Tuscumbia, Ala., Col. Abel D. Streight's cavalry launched their raid into Georgia and headed for Rome.

### April 30 (Thursday)

In Georgia, Col. Abel D. Streight's men fought at Day's Gap, Crooked Creek, and Hog Mountain. Their days were numbered however; Forrest was coming up rapidly.

### May 1 (Friday)

Streight's cavalry skirmished at Blountsville and the area of Big Warrior River, Ala., deep into Confederate territory.

In Richmond, a Joint Resolution of the Confederate Congress was passed concerning the treatment of former slaves who were recaptured by the Confederate forces and the status of the Union officers commanding or serving with former slaves.

4. That every white person being a commissioned officer or acting as such who during the present war shall command negroes or mulattoes in arms against the Confederate States or who shall arm, train, organize or prepare negroes or mulattoes for military service against the Confederate States or who shall voluntarily aid negroes or mulattoes in any military enterprise, attack or conflict in such service shall be deemed as inciting servile insurrection, and shall if captured be put to death or be otherwise punished at the discretion of the court.

7. All negroes and mulattoes who shall be engaged in war or be taken in arms against the Confederate States or shall give aid or comfort to the enemies of the Confederate States shall when captured in the Confederate States be delivered to the authorities of the State or States in which they shall be captured to be dealt with according to the present or future law of such State or States.

The Army of the Potomac, with 70,000 men, crossed the fords today and began the Battle of Chancellorsville. Lee left Jubal Early and 10,000 Confederates facing Maj. Gen. Sedgwick's 40,000, and with 47,000 men turned to face Hooker.

The Army of the Potomac moved rapidly forward and then that afternoon Hooker stunned his own officers *and* Lee by withdrawing into a small area near Chancellorsville. "Fighting Joe" Hooker went on the defensive.

Lee and Jackson talked well into the night in a conference which resulted in Jackson taking 26,000 of the 47,000 available forces around the Confederate left flank to attack Hooker's right flank.

### May 2 (Saturday)

Trouble was catching up with the Federal raiders under Col. Abel D. Streight; heavier fighting took place at Blount's Plantation, at Black Creek, and near Centre, Ala. So far, Streight's losses had been minimal, but his mules and men were tiring.

At Chancellorsville, Jackson reached the Orange Turnpike late in the afternoon and at 6 P.M. opened the assault against the unsuspecting Federals' right flank. On the Federal left flank, Lee opened fire against Darius Couch's Second Corps troops to draw attention from Jackson. The Union right flank fell back in panic and rolled up like a carpet. Few of the units fought well, most fleeing back towards the main body of the army at Chancellorsville, many being captured.

In the twilight, Jackson and some of his staff were riding in front of the Confederate lines when they were mistaken for Federals and fired upon by their own troops. Jackson was struck twice in the left arm and once through the palm of the right hand. He was taken to a nearby field hospital, where his arm was amputated later that evening. Command of Jackson's Corps went to Stuart.

Tonight, Hooker ordered Sedgwick to assault Lee from the rear, which brought on the Second Battle of Fredericksburg.

### May 3 (Sunday)

The odds finally went against Col. Abel D. Streight and his band of merry raiders today when Gen. Nathan B. Forrest caught up with him near Cedar Bluff, Ala. The Confederate force was outnumbered 3 to 1 by the Federals, but with his usual audacity, Forrest bluffed his way through the action and Streight surrendered his entire command. The enlisted personnel would be assigned to prison camps in Richmond and other points. Streight would be incarcerated at Libby Prison in Richmond. On February 3, 1864, Streight, and several others, would escape from Libby.

With the dawn, Stuart's artillery, now on a low hill called Hazel Grove, shelled the Federal emplacements. A shell struck Hooker's headquarters and falling debris struck him on the head, temporarily disabling him. Hooker ordered a retreat. Nearer Fredericksburg, Sedgwick twice attacked Marye's Heights and finally drove Early off, but with tremendous Union casualties. Lee, using some of the troops poised to assault Hooker's new position, turned and stopped Sedgwick at Salem Church late in the afternoon.

### May 4 (Monday)

The Battle of Chancellorsville ended today after three days of bloody fighting. The Federal losses were put at 1606 killed, 9762 wounded, and 5919 missing, presumed captured. This was from an estimated force of 133,868. Confederates present on the battlefield were estimated at 60,000. Of these, 1665 were killed, 9081 wounded, and 2018 captured. The South lost a greater proportion of the forces engaged.

Late this day, the cleanup of the battlefield began. Hooker prepared to withdraw across the river, leaving his dead, and many of the wounded, behind. The Federal prisoners were gathered and prepared to begin their trek south to Richmond. On both sides, the wounded were placed in any wagon available and their ride of torture began to the hospitals at Aquia Creek and Richmond.

### May 6 (Wednesday)

Col. Hoffman wrote to Surgeon Simpson, Medical Director, Eighth Army Corps, at Baltimore, concerning his expenditures for the hospital at Camp Parole. Hoffman pointed out that Simpson had spent $995 during the month of April. Among the purchases were 12 barrels of ale and 1 barrel of whiskey. With only 122 patients in the hospital, Hoffman thought the expenditure a trifle extravagant.

### May 14 (Thursday)

Gen. N.B. Forrest still had Col. Abel D. Streight's officers under guard in Alabama, not having forwarded them as yet. In keeping with President Davis's proclamation of last December which stated that any Union officer captured could be tried by the state in which the capture was made for "inciting the slaves to insurrection," Gov. Shorter of Alabama demanded that Streight and his officers be turned over to the State of Alabama for trial. The turnover was not effected.

## May 15 (Friday)

Lt. Col. Wm. H. Ludlow, Union Agent for Exchange, notified Secy. of War Stanton today that the men of Col. Abel Streight's command, captured in Georgia on May 3, had been released at City Point, Va. The officers were not among those released.

Jones, John B., Rebel War Clerk, Confederate War Dept., Richmond, Va.:

Gen. Schenck (Federal) has notified Gen. W.E. Jones that our men taken dressed in Federal uniform will not be treated as prisoners of war, but will be tried and punished as spies, etc. The President directed the Secretary of War today to require Gen. Lee to send an order to the commander of the Federal army, that accouterments and clothing will be deemed subjects of capture, and if our men are treated differently than prisoners of war, when taken, we will retaliate on the prisoners in our possession....

## May 16 (Saturday)

It seems that two "notorious prostitutes" were sent to City Point, Va., with the citizen prisoners from Old Capitol Prison in Washington. Lt. Col. Wm. H. Ludlow, Union Agent for Exchange, received a letter from Robert Ould, Confederate Agent for Exchange, concerning these "ladies":

Sir: I send back to you two strumpets who were landed at this place yesterday in company with honorable and virtuous women. If after arriving here they had behaved themselves I should have stood the transaction, though with hard thoughts. A state of war even does not allow any outrage to be perpetrated upon the sanctity of a pure woman's character and last of all where a flag of truce is the vehicle.... If I did not believe you were imposed upon I would be justified in taking this matter as a personal affront. These women since their arrival at City Point have descended to a depth of infamy that I hardly thought could be reached by the sex. They have delighted themselves with the foulest billingsgate that ever disgraced a fish-woman, courting prostitution at every turn and making themselves loud-mouthed in their denunciation of everything cherished and beloved by our people. Their conduct for one night has been so outrageous as to attract the attention of the press and engage the gossip of the streets. Though I cannot charge myself with blame in the affair I feel a deep sense of mortification that so infamous a proceeding should have had the countenance of the purity of a flag of truce.

## May 17 (Sunday)

Yesterday, the Battle of Champion Hill, Miss., was fought. By midafternoon, the hill had changed hands three times, and the Confederates had had enough. They began their withdrawal towards Vicksburg and the bridge crossing the Big Black River. The Confederates had lost about 3850 men at Champion's Hill as opposed to the loss of 2440 Union.

Today, Confederates under Lt. Gen. John C. Pemberton had their backs to the Big Black River and they faced Grant's Union troops with misgivings. Grant attacked, and Pemberton retreated across the bridge and burned it. Grant, stopped temporarily, watched as Pemberton went into Vicksburg—minus about 1700 prisoners. Starting with about 23,000 men, in two days Pemberton had lost nearly 5550, about 30 percent of his force.

## May 19 (Tuesday)

At Vicksburg, Grant made his first assault on the entrenchments in a quick rush he hoped would gain a quick victory. The Union forces were repulsed and the Union fleet of mortarboats began their deadly barrage, supported by the gunboats on the flanks of the city.

## May 21 (Thursday)

Col. Wm. Hoffman wrote Secy. of War Edwin Stanton today in response to an unfavorable Sanitary Commission report concerning conditions at the Camp Douglas, Ill., hospital:

In July last,... the hospital at Camp Douglas was in a very fair condition. Ample provisions had been made of bedding, including sheets and pillow cases and all other necessary articles, but the general sanitary condition of the camp was very bad in consequence of its unfavorable location, being on flat, low ground with very little drainage, and in part owing to the want of proper attention to the police by the garrison. I made a full report ... and recommended a system of sewerage which was thought would remedy much of the evil complained of.... When the prisoners left the camp in September my control over it ceased.

In the latter part of January between 3000 and 4000 prisoners of war arrived at the camp with some 800 under medical treatment. The smallpox prevailed at the camp and it soon spread among the prisoners....

On the 20th of April I made a report ... urging that immediate steps should be taken to improve the sanitary condition of Camp Douglas by the introduction of the system of sewerage recommended a year ago, and on the 12th instant I again called attention to this subject.

When there are such frequent changes of commanders and medical officers as there have been at Camp Douglas it is almost impossible to have instructions properly carried out. There is no responsibility and before neglects can be traced to anyone he is relieved from duty.

## May 23 (Saturday)

Our humble diarist in Richmond, John B. Jones, was not too good with numbers, but he was great with rumors and misinformation.

Jones, John B., Rebel War Clerk, Confederate War Dept., Richmond, Va.:

Now for the prisoners. Today the last lot taken by Hooker arrived by flag-of-truce boat, making in all just 2700. We have already sent off 7000 prisoners taken from him, and 1000 are yet to go. Our killed, wounded, and missing amount to but little over 8000. Hooker's killed and wounded are admitted by the Northern papers to be 20,000, and some say his entire loss was fully 40,000. So much for his march over the Rappahannock and his flight back again. If he is not satisfied, Lee will try him again.

## May 26 (Tuesday)

Clement L. Vallandigham, of Ohio, had been sentenced to two years in a military prison for treason. His sentence had been commuted by President Lincoln to banishment to the Confederacy. Today, he arrived at the Confederate lines outside Murfreesboro, Tenn., and was told to head south. He was to find that the Confederates didn't want him either.

## June 2 (Tuesday)

Vallandigham, former prisoner in Ohio, who had previously been sent south from Murfreesboro,

Tenn., from the Union lines, was now sent to Wilmington, N.C., by President Davis, where the Ohioan was held as an "alien enemy."

## June 3 (Wednesday)

Today, the Gettysburg campaign began when Lee's long gray columns quit their camps and began the trek to the Shenandoah Valley, where they would turn north for Pennsylvania. Two days later, unaware of when Lee had left, Hooker, at Fredericksburg, was trying to find out where Lee's army had gone. His Federal cavalry probed the crossings at Franklin's Crossing and Deep Run only to find them screened with pickets from A.P. Hill's Corps.

On June 9, at Beverly and Kelly's Ford on the Rappahannock west of Fredericksburg, Union cavalry galloped across the fords, driving in the Confederate pickets, bent on a "seek-and-destroy" mission to prevent a feared raid by Stuart on Washington. Stuart, at Brandy Station, was caught by surprise, but rapidly engaged the Union cavalry in the largest cavalry battle ever fought on the North American continent. Almost 20,000 horsemen, evenly divided, swirled and clashed at Stevenburg and Fleetwood Hill for about eight hours. The Confederates held the ground at the end of the day, but it was a close thing indeed.

## June 10 (Wednesday)

Today, Hooker finally found out the direction in which Lee was headed, but thought he should go to Richmond. Lincoln told him that the target was Lee's army, not the Confederate capital.

One group of Confederate prisoners would not make it to their Union prison camp. Being transported to Ft. Delaware on the steamer *Maple Leaf*, they overpowered the guards, captured the ship and forced it to land below Cape Henry, Va., where they escaped.

## June 12 (Friday)

The Army of Northern Virginia, led by Ewell's corps, poured through the Blue Ridge Mountains of Virginia today, headed towards Winchester and the Potomac crossings. Hooker was slow to leave Falmouth, just now starting to move.

The next day, Ewell's corps, still leading Lee's army northwest, was at Winchester, where they drove in the Union pickets and moved on to occupy Berryville. Hooker finally started his blue columns north by northwest from Falmouth, Va., about three days behind Lee.

### June 14 (Sunday)

Lt. Col. William H. Ludlow, Federal Agent for Exchange of Prisoners, had requested a copy of the recent act of the Confederate Congress "to determine officially what disposition under the act was proposed to be made of officers and men captured in arms and who had been duly mustered into the service of the United States, and also that the issues thereby presented could be fully understood and promptly met." Col. Ludlow continued his letter to Robert Ould, Confederate Agent for Exchange:

Sections 4, 5, 6, and 7 of this act propose a gross and inexcusable breach of the cartel both in letter and spirit. Upon reference to the cartel you will find no mention whatever of what was to be the color of prisoners of war. It was unnecessary to make any such mention, for before the establishment of this cartel and before one single negro or mulatto was mustered into the U.S. service you had them organized in arms in Louisiana. You had Indians and half-breed negroes and Indians organized in arms under Albert Pike in Arkansas. Subsequently negroes were captured on the battlefield at Antietam and delivered as prisoners of war at Aiken's Landing to the Confederate authorities, and receipted for and counted in exchange. And more recently the Confederate legislature of Tennessee have passed an act forcing into their military service (I quote literally) all male free persons of color between the ages of fifteen and fifty, or such number as may be necessary, who may be sound in body and capable of actual service; and they further enacted that in the event a sufficient number of free persons of color to meet the wants of the State shall not tender their services, then the Governor is empowered through the sheriffs of different counties to impress such persons until the required amount is obtained.

But it is needless to argue the question. You have not a foot of ground to stand upon in making the proposed discrimination among our captured officers and men. I protest against it as a violation of the cartel, of the laws and usages of war, and of your own practices under them.

Passing events will clearly show the impractica-

bility in executing the act referred to. In case, however, the attempt is made to execute it I now give you formal notice that the United States Government will throw its protection around all its officers and men without regard to color, and will promptly retaliate for all cases violating the cartel or the laws and usages of war.

### June 15 (Monday)

In the lower Shenandoah Valley, about 1 o'clock this morning Gen. Milroy started his Union troops towards Harpers Ferry only to run into Gen. Edward Johnson's Confederate division at Stephenson's Depot about 4 miles up the road. A brisk fight ensued in which some of Milroy's men got away, but not many. The Confederates captured over 4000 men and tons of supplies and equipment. Gen. Rodes crossed the Potomac with three brigades of Ewell's corps into Maryland at Williamsport, and the invasion was on.

The following day, Lee's columns were strung out along western Virginia and into Maryland. Hooker finally reached Fairfax C.H., about 20 miles from the capital, and between Lee and Washington.

### June 20 (Saturday)

At the conflux of the Cahaba and Alabama Rivers in central Alabama, the first capital of the state was located in the town of Cahaba, prior to 1819. The location offered several advantages, not the least of which was its abundant water. Many natural springs dotted the area which provided good, clean water for human use. During the development of the town several large warehouses were built along the riverfront of the Alabama River and these were confiscated for use by the Confederate government. The largest of these measured 193 feet in length and was 116 feet wide and enclosed nearly 22,000 feet. Most of the warehouse was without a roof, work being stopped before the building was completed. On this date, Confederate Capt. H.A.M. Henderson wrote a letter to Confederate Secretary of War Seddon requesting permission to recruit local troops to be used as prison guards at Cahaba. Shortly thereafter, the prison came into being.

To increase security, a platform was built around the 14-foot-high outside walls at a height to permit the guards to view the inside of the prison. Inside the compound, wooden bunks were built several tiers high to accommodate 432 men, providing about 52 square feet per person. No bedding or straw was provided during its entire occupation by the prisoners. The unlucky ones slept on the ground. Water was provided from a natural spring located about 200 yards outside the prison. The water flowed through an open ditch through the town, under the wall on the west side and then across to the four-holer outhouse located on the east side of the warehouse building, and from there into the Alabama River. During its course to and through the prison, the water was subject to pollution from washtub water, trash, garbage, and other foreign objects. By the time it reached the prison where the prisoners had access to it, the water was seriously polluted. Only one fireplace was located in the larger building, wholly insufficient for the use of so many men. To compensate, open fires were built in the compound yard, causing serious smoke problems in the warehouse. Despite its shortcomings, the prison would be later commended for its cleanliness and healthy living conditions when compared to other prisons.

The seesaw fortunes of war in the Shenandoah Valley had a direct effect on the amount and type of rations available for the Confederate Army around Richmond, as well as for the civilian population of the city. Lee and the Army of Northern Virginia were on the way to Gettysburg, having liberated the lower end of the Valley and sent supplies on to Richmond. War Clerk Jones recorded:

Jones, John B., Rebel War Clerk, Confederate War Dept., Richmond, Va.:

The operations of Gen. Lee have relieved the depot here, which was nearly empty. Since the capture of Winchester and Martinsburg, only about 1500 bushels of corn are sent to the army daily, whereas 5000 were sent before, and there were rarely more than a day's supply on hand.

### June 22 (Monday)

In Richmond the food supply on the market was very short. Again, it was the transportation system that was at fault. Considering that the food for the prisoners in Libby and on Belle Isle came from the market and the prisoners had to compete with the civil population, the prisoners came up short.

Jones, John B., Rebel War Clerk, Confederate War Dept., Richmond, Va.:

It is a difficult matter to subsist in this city now. Beef is $1 and bacon $1.65 per pound, and just at this time there are but few vegetables. Old potatoes are gone, and the new have not yet come. A single cabbage, merely the leaves, no head, sells for a dollar, and this suffices not for a dinner for my family.

### June 24 (Wednesday)

Jones, John B., Rebel War Clerk, Confederate War Dept., Richmond, Va.:

The first installment of Winchester prisoners reached the city yesterday, 1600 in number, and there are over 4000 more on the way. So much for Milroy's 2000 or 3000!

At the Potomac crossings near Harpers Ferry, Longstreet and A.P. Hill began moving into Maryland. There was a short, brisk skirmish in the vicinity of the old Antietam battlefield.

### June 26 (Friday)

Today, Confederate Gen. Jubal Early passed through Gettysburg, Pa., (for the first time) on his way to York, Pa. Gov. Curtin of Pennsylvania called for 60,000 volunteers to serve for 90 days to repel the invaders.

The next day, in Washington, Lincoln relieved the commander of the Army of the Potomac on the eve of battle. "Fighting" Joe Hooker was relieved by Maj. Gen. George Gordon Meade, USA, who was assigned commander of the Army of the Potomac.

Longstreet and A.P. Hill were at Chambersburg, Pa., and Early was at York, with other Confederate units near Harrisburg. Stuart's cavalry were still in Virginia, skirmishing near Fairfax C.H.

### June 28 (Sunday)

About 7 A.M., Gen. Meade received word that he was to relieve Hooker in command of the Army of the Potomac. Meade now had over 100,000 men in his command scattered widely between the Potomac and points south, and Frederick, Md. In Pennsylvania, Lee, on the morning of the 29th, started to concentrate his forces at Cashtown Gap, recalling Gen. Jubal Early from York and Ewell from Carlisle.

In Maryland, Meade wasted no time in ordering the Army of the Potomac towards Gettysburg. Gen. Buford's cavalrymen were at Emmitsburg, Md.

### June 30 (Tuesday)

In Pennsylvania, Early's men left York for Cashtown to join Lee, and Gen. Meade ordered Gen. Reynolds to occupy Emmitsburg. Buford's Union cavalry was scouting the area looking for Lee's main force. They were about to find it.

### July 1 (Wednesday)

Today at a little crossroads town in Pennsylvania the Union and Confederate armies began a three-day battle that would have dire consequences for the South. Lee, whose strength was about 70,000 men, engaged nearly 94,000 Federals, but the commitments were piecemeal. Not all the Federals were up and in position when the fighting began, but were fed into the fight as they arrived. At the end of this day, the lines would be fairly drawn.

### July 2 (Thursday)

The second day of the Battle of Gettysburg, the fighting lasted well into the evening, not stopping until about 10 P.M. So far, no decisive blow had been struck. Lee had tried both of the Federal flanks and could turn neither.

### July 3 (Friday)

The final day at Gettysburg saw Lee attacking the middle of the Union line with Pickett's and Pettigrew's divisions leading the charge. The charge failed and the troops withdrew. At the end of the day, the Union had lost 3155 killed, 14,529 wounded, and 5365 missing, mostly prisoners. The South lost 2952 killed, 12,709 wounded (many of whom would die on the retreat), and 5150 missing (again, mostly prisoners). Lee would plan his withdrawal this night.

Morning in Vicksburg saw white flags of truce appear on the defenses of the city. Gen. Pemberton had finally bowed to a superior force and six weeks of siege after nearly a year of Union operations against him. The two generals, Grant and Pemberton, met under an oak tree to discuss the terms of surrender which would take place on the Fourth of July.

### July 4 (Saturday)

Today about 29,500 Confederates under Gen. John Pemberton surrendered to Gen. Grant at Vicksburg, laying down their arms and marching out of the battered city. Grant watched the flag-raising at the Court House as on the riverfront the boats shrilled their whistles. The Mississippi River was now open save for Port Hudson, which would not hold out much longer. The prisoners were retained in their old organizational formations and the business of paroling them got under way as rapidly as possible.

In Pennsylvania, Lee had decided to retreat to Virginia. Late in the afternoon, in a heavy downpour, the wagons filled with wounded began their agonizing journey south, going ever so slowly. The wounded had days of riding in springless wagons before they could reach safety and proper care. Many would not make it, but would be buried along the road. Long columns of prisoners preceded the wounded, heading for the Potomac fords and Richmond.

Back at Gettysburg, the Confederate prisoners were marched to Westminster, placed on railcars and sent to Ft. Delaware, Johnson's Island, and elsewhere for incarceration.

### July 5 (Sunday)

In the west, Sherman was driving his forces towards Jackson, Miss., and Gen. Joseph Johnston's Confederate army.

The Federal gunboats continued to batter Port Hudson below Vicksburg.

The following day, in Indiana, the Knights of the Golden Circle, a Copperhead organization, seized guns and ammunition at the depot at Huntington.

### July 7 (Tuesday)

In Kentucky, John Hunt Morgan was on the prowl again. This trip he would go into Indiana and Ohio to spread panic. Today, he obtained a new recruit.

Stanfield, N.B., 1st Ky. Cavalry, Marion Co., Ky.:

In June 1863, I was at home on furlough, just before Morgan's command went through. We lived about five miles from Brandenburg, and on the 7th of July I went in town with a brother. I was sitting in the office at the hotel about ten o'clock, when some one shouted: "Here come the boys!" They were coming down Main Street, on the riverside, so as to surround the town and capture any Federals who might be in the place. The latter must have learned their intentions, for they all skipped. Going to the door of the hotel, I saw the boys coming. It was Taylor's Company, including several of the Meade County boys. Capt. Sam Taylor stayed at our home part of the time while raising his company. He asked me to go to the wharf and hail the first passing boat, and I readily assented. We all went down to the wharf boat, however, the boys concealing themselves on either side of the door and behind trees on the river bank. The first boat coming along was the *John T. McCombs*. I got where I could be seen, and hailed her. I had on a white linen suit and waved a white flag. She landed by the wharf boat and our boys jumped aboard and took possession. The passengers all got off laughing. In a short time we could see the *Alice Dean*, a Yankee boat, coming up the river. Our boys pulled off down the river towards Mockport, and, save myself, not a soul could be seen. I hailed her and she stopped. We got the *Alice Dean* by steering up beside her, some of the boys jumping on board. Very little resistance was made. There were several Yankees on board, going home on furlough, and we paroled them. About six o'clock that evening the advance came, and that night we began crossing the river.

## July 8 (Wednesday)

When the news of Vicksburg's surrender reached Port Hudson, it seemed the last straw. Gen. Franklin Gardner, commanding the garrison, asked Union Gen. Nathaniel Banks for surrender terms and then surrendered after six weeks of siege. Gardner surrendered about 7000 men and the Mississippi River was open all the way to the sea. The Confederate enlisted men were paroled and sent home as early as possible.

The paroles given the Confederates at Vicksburg and Port Hudson would become game pieces in the struggle to match man-for-man exchanges in the months to come.

Morgan and his cavalry raiders crossed the Ohio River at Cumming's Ferry and Brandenburg, Ky., and entered southern Indiana. It was hoped that the Copperhead movement, reasonably strong in Indiana and Ohio, would provide support to Morgan. This did not occur.

Stanfield, N.B., 1st Ky. Cavalry, with Morgan in southern Indiana:

By ten o'clock on the 8th we were in Indiana. We turned the *John T. McCombs* loose and set the *Alice Dean* on fire. She sunk near Mockport, one and one-half miles below.

Jones, John B., Rebel War Clerk, Confederate War Dept., Richmond, Va.:

Our loss is estimated at 10,000. Between 3000 and 4000 of our wounded are arriving here tonight. Every preparation is being made to receive them.

Gen. Scales and Pender have arrived here wounded, this evening. Gens. Armistead, Barksdale, Garnett, and Kemper are reported killed. Gens. Jones, Heath, Anderson, Pettigrew, Jenkins, Hampton, and Hood are reported wounded....

The hills around Gettysburg are said to be covered with the dead and wounded of the Yankee Army of the Potomac....

But the absence of dispatches from Gen. Lee himself is beginning to create distrust, and doubts of decisive success at Gettysburg. His couriers may have been captured, or he may be delaying to announce something else he has in contemplation....

But alas! we have sad tidings from the West. Gen Johnston telegraphs from Jackson, Miss., that Vicksburg capitulated on the 4th inst. This is a terrible blow, and has produced much despondency.

## July 9 (Thursday)

Confederate Morgan, loose in southern Indiana, was raiding near Croydon, looting homes and businesses. The raid continued moving east for several more days.

Stanfield, N.B., 1st Ky. Cavalry, with Morgan in southern Indiana:

We moved on to Croydon and took the place, capturing one good piece of artillery and four hundred or five hundred prisoners.

Jones, John B., Rebel War Clerk, Confederate War Dept., Richmond, Va.:

The sad tidings from Vicksburg have been confirmed by subsequent accounts. The number of men fit for duty on the day of capitulation was only a little upwards of 7000. Flour was selling at $400 per barrel!...

The fall of Vicksburg, alone, does not make this the darkest day of the war, as it is undoubtedly. The news from Lee's army is appalling. After the battle of Friday, the accounts from Martinsburg now state, he fell back towards Hagerstown, followed by the enemy, fighting but little on the way. Instead of 40,000 we have only 4000 prisoners. How many we have lost we know not.

### July 10 (Friday)

Morgan's raiders, leaving Croydon, Ind., went towards New Salem and then in the direction of southern Ohio. Morgan would capture many home guards and civilians whom he would parole, illegally, and these paroles would later become a basis for declaring prisoners exchanged by the Southern Agent for Exchange, Robert Ould.

Stanfield, N.B., 1st Ky. Cavalry, with Morgan in southern Indiana:

The next place we struck was Salem, on the Albany and Indianapolis Railroad. We captured the town and about five hundred home guards.

Jones, John B., Rebel War Clerk, Confederate War Dept., Richmond, Va.:

Early this morning a dispatch was received from Gen. Beauregard that the enemy attacked the forts in Charleston harbor, and subsequently, that they were landing troops on Morris Island....

... A dispatch from an officer at Martinsburg, stating that Gen. Lee was still at Hagerstown awaiting his ammunition ... which, however, had not arrived at the Potomac. That all the prisoners (number not stated) except those paroled, were at the river. That *nothing was known of the enemy*....

... We lost twelve general officers in the fall of Vicksburg—one lieutenant general, four major generals, and seven brigadiers.

### July 11 (Saturday)

Stanfield, N.B., 1st Ky. Cavalry, with Morgan in southern Indiana:

We moved on and came to Seymour, a small place where the O. & M. Railroad crosses the J., M. & I. We tore up the tracks and got all the information we could by wire.

The next day, the 12th, Morgan was at Vernon, Ind., with his cavalry troopers straggled all along his route of march as they fell out with broken-down horses and were captured by the aroused Hoosiers. The prisoners were sent to Camp Morton in Indianapolis.

Stanfield, N.B., 1st Ky. Cavalry, with Morgan in southern Indiana:

On the 12th we went near Cincinnati, on the Cincinnati and Indianapolis Railroad. We cut the wire and sent a message to Burnside for reinforcements, our object being to find out how strong his forces were. He replied that he did not have men to spare.

### July 13 (Monday)

Morgan left Indiana and crossed into southern Ohio at Harrison, moving for Hamilton and Cincinnati, where Federal authorities declared martial law.

Stanfield, N.B., 1st Ky. Cavalry, with Morgan in southern Ohio:

The next day at ten o'clock we were seventy-five miles from Cincinnati. We were blockaded and bushwhacked from the start, for the Yankees in all parts were after us. They cut down trees across the roads and did everything they could to stop and to capture us. It is estimated that there were at least one hundred thousand men after us. We would have made the trip to Richmond if the river had not risen. Adam Johnson and seven hundred men got over safely, but portions of the command were captured at different places.

Jones, John B., Rebel War Clerk, Confederate War Dept., Richmond, Va.:

The *Enquirer* says the President has got a letter from Gen. Lee (why not give it to the people?) stating that his operations in Pennsylvania and Maryland have been successful and satisfactory, and that we have now some 15,000 to 18,000 prisoners, besides the 4000 or 5000 paroled. Nonsense!

... It has been officially ascertained that Pemberton surrendered, with Vicksburg, 22,000 men! He has lost, during the year, not less than 40,000!

### July 14 (Tuesday)

Jones, John B., Rebel War Clerk, Confederate War Dept., Richmond, Va.:

Today we have tidings of the fall of Port Hudson, on the Mississippi River, our last stronghold there. I suppose some 10,000 or 12,000 of our men had to surrender, unconditionally. Thus the army of Gen. Pemberton, first and last, some 50,000 strong, has been completely destroyed....

... We have nothing authentic from Gen. Lee; but long trains of the slightly wounded arrived yesterday and today.

### July 15 (Wednesday)

During John Hunt Morgan's raid into southern Ohio, many of the captured Confederates were taken to Camp Chase, Ohio, for incarceration. The first one to arrive was Pvt. Jacob Hix. The ride so far had allowed for very little sleep and Hix fell asleep in the saddle, the horse wandering along the road. After several miles, the horse wandered up a country lane and stopped. Hix awoke, startled to see no troops around him. He kept on and finally entered the hamlet of Richmond, Ohio, about 50 miles south of Columbus. The villagers were startled to see a live Rebel wandering around and a mad search was made for shotguns and rifles. Hix surrendered and was taken to Chillicothe, where he was delivered to the Provost Marshal, who took him to Camp Chase.

### July 16 (Thursday)

Jones, John B., Rebel War Clerk, Confederate War Dept., Richmond, Va.:

The United States agent of exchange has sent a notice to our agent that the negroes we capture from them in battle must be exchanged as other soldiers are, according to the cartel, which said nothing about color; and if the act of Congress in relation to such

soldiers be executed, the United States would retaliate to the utmost extremity.

The idea of placing enemy prisoners of war "under fire" of their own guns originated on this date in Charleston, S.C., when Col. John L. Branch wrote Confederate Gen. Thomas Jordan:

General: It has been suggested by my brother, Mr. D.W. Branch, that the difficulty of holding that portion of Morris Island now in the possession of the enemy (after we shall have retaken it) might be gotten over by establishing a camp there for holding under heavy guard all Yankee prisoners, officers and privates, until it can be strongly fortified.

These prisoners to be exposed during our operations.

### July 17 (Friday)

Jones, John B., Rebel War Clerk, Confederate War Dept., Richmond, Va.:

At last we have the authentic announcement that Gen. Lee has recrossed the Potomac!...

Meantime we are in a half-starving condition. I have lost twenty pounds, and my wife and children are emaciated to some extent. Still, I hear no murmuring.

Today, for the second time, ten dollars in Confederate notes are given for one in gold; and no doubt, under our recent disasters, the depreciation will increase.

### July 18 (Saturday)

Confederate Gen. Thomas Jordan, at Charleston, S.C., replied to Col. J.L. Branch, CSA, about his brother's suggestion concerning placing prisoners of war under fire:

Colonel: I have to acknowledge the receipt of your communication of the 16th instant proposing that the portion of Morris Island now occupied by the enemy after it shall have been retaken might be held and fortified by exposing our prisoners to the enemy's fire.

In reply the commanding general directs me to say that it is not considered in accordance with the usages of war to use our prisoners as a means of defense or protection.

In Ohio, the chase after John Hunt Morgan was coming to a close. His weary and saddle-sore men were riding slower and slower as they passed through Pomeroy and Chester, Ohio, attempting to make it to Bluffington, where they hoped to cross into Kentucky. A Federal force guarding the crossing blocked the escape and Morgan had to wait until dawn.

Daylight of the 19th found Morgan's raiders embroiled in a stiff fight with Union forces and gunboats guarding the crossing. The U.S.S. *Moose* and steamer *Allegheny Belle* repeatedly prevented Morgan from crossing the river. Caught from behind by militia and Federal troops, he lost about 700 captured and 120 killed, but he escaped with the remaining 400 and turned north and east towards Pennsylvania. The prisoners were loaded on steamers and sent to prisons in Indiana and Illinois.

### July 20 (Monday)

Having eluded capture yesterday with about 400 of his men, Morgan ran into another Union force at Hockingport, Ohio, before turning away from the Ohio River.

Stanfield, N.B., 1st Ky. Cavalry, prisoner, Camp Morton, Indianapolis, Ind.:

I fell into the hands of the enemy at Chesi, O., on July 20. Most of the men, however, were captured at Bluffington's Island.

We were taken on boats to Cincinnati; then in boxcars to Camp Morton, where we were kept until September 13.

Rumor and speculation were the usual replacements for hard facts in Richmond following almost any battle. Seldom did the rumors get things correctly.

Jones, John B., Rebel War Clerk, Confederate War Dept., Richmond, Va.:

A letter from Lee's army says we lost 10,000 in the recent battle, killed, wounded, and prisoners. We took 11,000 prisoners and 11 guns.

### July 22 (Wednesday)

In Charleston, S.C., Gov. M.L. Bonham wrote Gen. P.G.T. Beauregard, commanding the area, concerning the capture of Negro troops in Union uniform on James Island, S.C.

Sir: I am informed that on the 11th instant, on James Island, certain "negro slaves" of different Confederate States were captured in armed insurrection against the lawful authority of the State of South Carolina, and associated with them were a number of armed free negroes from the Federal State of Massachusetts; and that on the night of the 18th instant there were captured "in arms" on Morris Island certain other negro slaves of different Confederate States, and also certain other armed free negroes of Federal States, and also certain commissioned officers of the United States "found serving in company with armed slaves in insurrection against the authority of South Carolina."

By proclamation of the President of the 23d of December, 1862, among other things, it was ordered "that all negro slaves captured in arms be at once delivered over to the executive authorities of the respective States to which they belong to be dealt with according to the laws of the said States." Also "that the like orders be executed in all cases with respect to all commissioned officers of the United States when found serving in company with armed slaves in insurrection against the authorities of the different States of this Confederacy." The observance and enforcement of the above orders by the officers of the C.S. Army is required by an order from the office of the Adjutant and Inspector General of the 24th of December, 1862.

No action having been as yet taken on your part, so far as I am informed, to carry into effect the above orders, I deem it my duty to the State to call your attention to the matter and ask that you will turn over to me the said commissioned officers and slaves to be dealt with according to the laws of this State.

The expression in the order as to turning over slaves in arms, namely, "to the executive authorities of the respective States to which they belong," was used by the President under the supposition, I presume, that the slaves would be found in insurrection in the States to which they belong and that he could but mean that they are to be turned over to the executive authorities of those States in which the offense might be committed. But if you should differ from me in this opinion I then request that you will retain them here till the question shall be decided by the President and till my demand for their delivery to me can be made according to law on the Governors of the States to which they respectively belong.

The point as to free negroes is for the present reserved till I can correspond directly with the War Department as to their disposition, and I request that they also be retained.

The letter was forwarded to Richmond for resolution. On a third indorsement, J.A. Campbell, Assistant Secy. of War, noted that "The question presented in this ... is whether persons of color belonging to the Army of the United States and captured by the Confederate troops are to be surrendered to the State authorities of the State in which the capture was made when there is no testimony to show that these persons had been slaves in that State. The ground on which the claim of the State rests is not apprehended."

The fall of Vicksburg had cut the supply line from the Confederate states west of the Mississippi River, and the occupation of most of the western part of Mississippi had further depleted the area of supply. Tennessee had been long gone as a provider and parts of northern Alabama had also come under Federal control. This caused a very tight squeeze on the supplies available to both the Army of Northern Virginia and to the troops in North Carolina. If the ration to the active soldier is reduced, the ration is also reduced for the prisoner of war even further— not too bright a prospect for the Federals in Libby Prison, Belle Isle, Cahaba, and other prisons.

Jones, John B., Rebel War Clerk, Confederate War Dept., Richmond, Va.:

Col. Northrop, Commissary-General, sends in a paper today saying that only a quarter of a pound of meat per day can be given the soldiers, except when marching, and then only half a pound. He says no more can be derived from the trans-Mississippi country, nor from the State of Mississippi, or Tennessee, and parts of Georgia and Alabama; and if more than the amount he receives be given the soldiers, the negroes will have to go without any. He adds, however, that the peasants of Europe rarely have any meat, and in Hindostan, never.

### July 23 (Thursday)

Gov. Bonham of South Carolina today wrote the

Hon. James A. Seddon, Secy. of War in Richmond, concerning the status of the free Negroes captured on Morris and James Islands a few days before.

Sir: I have the honor to submit to you a copy of my demand, under General Orders, No. 3, dated December 24, 1862, containing the proclamation of President Davis, upon Gen. Beauregard for certain negro slaves and commissioned officers in company with them captured in arms on James and Morris Islands on the 11th and 18th instant.

I now beg leave to call your attention to the free negroes who were captured at the same time. By an act of our assembly of 1805 (5 Stat.,6) it is enacted that—

*Every person or persons who shall or may be, either directly or indirectly, concerned or connected with any slave or slaves in a state of actual insurrection within the State, or who shall in any manner or to any extent excite, counsel, advise, induce, aid, comfort, or assist any slave or slaves to raise or to attempt to raise an insurrection within this State by furnishing them with any written or other passport, with arms or ammunition, or munitions of war, or knowing of their assembling for any purpose tending to treason or insurrection, shall afford to them shelter or protection or shall permit his, her, or their house or houses to be resorted to by any slave or slaves for any purpose tending to treason or insurrection as aforesaid, shall, on conviction thereof in any court having jurisdiction thereof, by confession in open court or by the testimony of his witnesses, be adjudged guilty of treason against the State and suffer death.*

You will perceive by my letter to Gen. Beauregard that there were "slaves in insurrection" and that the free negroes "were concerned and connected with those slaves in a state of insurrection," and are therefore amenable to this law. I cannot suppose the mere fact that these free negroes were under the flag and clothed in the uniform of the United States will protect them from the operation of the State laws on the subject of insurrection.

I therefore respectfully request that these free negroes be turned over to me to be dealt with under the laws of this State.

Morgan's tired, saddle-weary force was almost caught again at Rockville, Ohio, but, again, he slipped away after losing a few men and horses.

## July 24 (Friday)

The immensity of the problem of supplying the armies during the war is indicated by the entry of John Jones on this date.

Jones, John B., Rebel War Clerk, Confederate War Dept., Richmond, Va.:

A letter from the Commissary-General to Gen. Lee states that we have but 1,800,000 pounds of bacon at Atlanta, and 500,000 pounds in this city, which is less than 30 days' rations for Bragg's and Lee's armies. He says all attempts to get bacon from Europe have failed, and he fears they will fail, and hence, if the ration be not reduced to ¼ pound we shall soon have no meat on hand. Gen. Lee says he cannot be responsible if the soldiers fail for want of food.

Morgan was again forced into another skirmish, which further weakened his force by loss of men, horses and ammunition. This one occurred near Athens, Ohio. Morgan was moving north and east.

The next day, John Hunt Morgan was finally run to ground near the Pennsylvania line, at Salineville, Ohio, where he and his spent command of 364 officers and men surrendered. Morgan and the officers were sent to the state prison at Columbus and the enlisted men to prison camps. He would escape from prison on November 27.

## July 27 (Monday)

The *Ohio State Journal* of Columbus, Ohio, contained an editorial about the capture of Gen. John H. Morgan and his raiders:

The career of the great Rebel raider is ended. He and his whole force are now in Gen. Shackelford's possession. Morgan surrendered unconditionally at three o'clock yesterday (Sunday) afternoon. All honor is due the gallant and hardy boys who have finally captured the reckless rider of Rebeldom. Morgan and his command will doubtless be brought to Camp Chase.

The *Journal* was wrong about Morgan's destination. He, and several of his men, were taken to the Ohio State Penitentiary for incarceration, where much controversy would be aroused over the treatment of Morgan and his men on their arrival. They were, of course, searched and all money taken from

them. It was rumored in the South that their beards and heads were shaved as a retaliatory measure.

## July 31 (Friday)

General Orders, No. 252, this date, published by the Federal War Department, contained an Executive Order of President Lincoln, dated July 30, concerning the treatment of Union soldiers and the possible retaliation for mistreatment:

It is the duty of every Government to give protection to its citizens, of whatsoever class, color, or condition, and especially to those who are duly organized as soldiers in the public service. The law of nations and the usages and customs of war, as carried on by civilized powers, permit no distinction as to color in the treatment of prisoners of war as public enemies. To sell or enslave any captured person on account of his color and for no offense against the laws of war is a relapse into barbarism and a crime against the civilization of the age.

The Government of the United States will give the same protection to all its soldiers; and if the enemy shall sell or enslave any one because of his color, the offense shall be punished by retaliation upon the enemy's prisoners in our possession.

It is therefore ordered that for every soldier of the United States killed in violation of the laws of war a rebel soldier shall be executed, and for every one enslaved by the enemy or sold into slavery a rebel soldier shall be placed at hard labor on public works and continued at such labor until the other shall be released and receive the treatment due to a prisoner of war.

## August 1 (Saturday)

Montgomery, J.J., Lowry's Scouts, Confederate escapee, returned to Mississippi:

At Enterprise, Miss., in August 1863, I was discharged from the army, not being able to serve longer in the infantry. On returning to Tennessee, I found the Federals burning houses, stealing horses, and committing other depredations. It did not take me long to get a cavalry outfit, and I was soon at it again.

## August 2 (Sunday)

Jones, John B., Rebel War Clerk, Confederate War Dept., Richmond, Va.:

The exchange of prisoners is practically resumed;

the Federal boat delivering yesterday 750 of our sick and wounded; and we returned 600 of their sick and wounded.

## August 3 (Monday)

The heavy campaigning of 1863, especially the invasion of the North in June and July, discouraged many of the Confederate troops. They could see no end to the fighting, and they felt they would be better off home, so they deserted in large numbers.

Jones, John B., Rebel War Clerk, Confederate War Dept., Richmond, Va.:

Mr. W.H. Locke, living on the James River, at the Cement and Lime Works, writes that more than a thousand deserters from Lee's army have crossed at that place within the last fortnight. This is awful; and they are mainly North Carolinians.

## August 8 (Saturday)

The earlier battles of the war took a terrible toll upon the Confederate manpower pool and that pool took a major shock at Gettysburg, Pa., during the July 1 to 3 battle. The Confederate government this month adopted a policy of recruiting Union prisoners, military and civilian alike, to take an *oath of neutrality*. This permitted their release from prison and their employment as craftsmen and artisans in desperately needed skills in Southern manufacture. In general, these former prisoners conducted themselves well in their parole.

## August 12 (Wednesday)

Jones, John B., Rebel War Clerk, Confederate War Dept., Richmond, Va.:

Col. Northrop, Commissary-General, is still urging a diminution of rations, and as our soldiers taken by the enemy fare badly in the North, and as the enemy make a point of destroying all the crops they can when they invade us, he proposes, in retaliation, to stop meat rations altogether to prisoners in our hands, and give them instead oat gruel, cornmeal gruel, and pea soup, soft hominy, and bread. This the Secretary will not agree to, because the law says they shall have the same as our troops.

## August 16 (Sunday)

Rosecrans, citing a need to resupply his army, had remained in the vicinity of Tullahoma, Tenn., for six weeks. Today he finally moved towards Chattanooga about the same time that Burnside left Louisville for eastern Tennessee.

By the 21st, Rosecrans's Army of the Cumberland had reached the Tennessee River at Chattanooga, where Bragg awaited. Bragg was reluctant to go on the offensive, since he had only 40,000 effectives, according to him, and Rosecrans had nearly 60,000, with Burnside coming down with about 30,000 more.

## August 31 (Monday)

Following the heavy fighting of the early summer, the desertion rate was alarming in the Army of Northern Virginia. Many of the deserters from North Carolina had fled into the mountains in the western part of that state, and there they defied all authority.

Jones, John B., Rebel War Clerk, Confederate War Dept., Richmond, Va.:

Gov. Vance writes that large bodies of deserters in the western counties of North Carolina are organized, with arms, and threaten to raise the Union flag at the court-house of Wilkes County on next court-day.

## September 1 (Tuesday)

In September 1862, the remaining prisoners at Camp Morton, Indianapolis, Ind., had been removed and sent to other locations. The camp lay largely idle except as a minor training ground for recruited regiments. The Official Records show that in July 1863, an initial input of 111 prisoners, soon followed by 1165, mostly from the surrender of Vicksburg, brought the camp back into the fold of prison camps. Prisoner population would grow to 3060 by the end of August, and again be depleted to 1601 by the end of September.

## September 3 (Thursday)

When Vicksburg fell, some 28,000 prisoners were paroled and sent home "to see the wife and kids" for 15 to 30 days. Many had not returned to the control of the Confederate Army as yet, and some would never return. Robert Ould, the

Confederate Agent for Exchange in Richmond, had declared a number of the men paroled at Vicksburg to be already exchanged and available for further service. This did not agree with the Northern viewpoint, since the exchange had to be mutually agreed upon by both parties of the cartel. The Union's position was that these Southern troops had not been exchanged and therefore could not legally be used in combat. Some of these same troops would be recaptured at Chattanooga, Tenn., in the near future.

### September 8 (Tuesday)

In Richmond, diarist Jones today could be sold almost anything if he truly believed his entry for this day. Most likely he would receive somewhat of an argument from the inmates at Belle Isle, Libby, Salisbury, and Cahaba prisons.

Jones, John B., Rebel War Clerk, Confederate War Dept., Richmond, Va.:

A report on the condition of the military prisons, sent in today, shows that there is no typhoid fever, or many cases of other diseases, among the prisoners of war. Everything is kept in cleanliness about them, and they have abundance of food, wholesome and palatable. The prisoners themselves admit these facts, and denounce their own government for the treatment alleged to be inflicted on our men confined at Ft. Delaware and other places.

### September 9 (Wednesday)

Yesterday the Chickamauga Campaign opened, with Rosecrans probing towards Bragg in the vicinity of Chattanooga, Tenn. Outflanked, Bragg evacuated Chattanooga without a struggle. Rosecrans's Army of the Cumberland immediately occupied the city. Rosecrans's troops were stretched over forty miles and had to be consolidated before they would be in any shape for battle.

Dodson, W.C., Pvt., 51st Alabama Cavalry, captured, McLemore's Cove, Ga.:

I was captured on the 9th of September, 1863, in McLemore's Cove, by Gen. Negley's escort, in what the General referred to in his official report as a "gallant charge against a superior force of the enemy."

The "superior force," however, consisted of only three, two of whom rode safely out, carrying one of the escort with them. Naturally, I was a much disappointed chap when I was brought up, "all standing," but soon recovered myself sufficiently to remind my captors that everything they had captured, except myself, was only their own property recovered—horse, saddle, bridle, blanket, gun, cartridge box, and belt—being a part of what our command (Wheeler's) had captured at LaVergne a few months before. This fact was communicated to Gen. Negley when I was carried back to his august presence at a near-by cross roads. The General asked me the usual questions—viz., was I not conscripted, was I not half starved, was I not tired of fighting, etc. When I entered an empathic negative to all these, he said he thought it would be good policy for "a rat to leave a sinking ship." I must have greatly disgusted him when I replied that I was one rat that was going down with the ship.

Leaving the General, I was carried back to my captor's quarters. Supper was over, but a bountiful meal was soon improvised for me, with apologies for it not being better and the explanation that had they known I was coming they "would have waited supper" for me. These were gentlemen.... One of them wanted one of my spurs (I had lost the other in the horse race so recently indulged in), and I very cheerfully handed it to him. But he refused to take it as a gift, and gave me the first greenback I ever possessed.

I remained with these people, or rather the rear guard, for several days, and could not have been treated with more courteous consideration. I was at this time the only prisoner, with the exception of a creature who said he was a "deserter from the Sixth Georgia Regiment." In a cowardly effort to gain favor with the enemy, he claimed that he was conscripted, was starved, was forced to fight, etc. Naturally the Federals had no respect for such a man and treated him with but little less contempt than I did; while they continued to call me "pet Rebel," and seemed glad to talk with me, notwithstanding we never agreed on a single proposition concerning the war.

There being for several days only two prisoners, we were naturally thrown together, but I persistently refused to associate with the deserter—to eat or sleep with him. The commissary respected my feelings, and issued my rations separately, remarking each time: "Now, Johnny, when you eat that up come back and get some more."

I had no blanket (having left mine under my saddle), and the first night I determined to sit up by the fire. A good-natured teamster asked me why I didn't go to bed. I told him that I had no blanket, and could not afford to sleep with that ———— deserter. "Well, Johnny," said the teamster, "durn him, you needn't sleep with him! Come here to my wagon, and I will lend you a blanket."...

I could mention many other pleasant incidents connected with my stay with these brave men on the front, and could enumerate many acts of kindness from officers and privates. I truly wish there was no other side to the picture, but there is. Soon other prisoners came in, and we were sent back to Stevenson. Here we received a bogus parole ... and were sent back by rail and soon turned over to some home guards, who succeeded in making life almost a h———— to us....

I remained six months at Camp Chase, but the policy of starvation did not commence until afterwards, though nearly every other species of petty tyranny was practiced.... Here, to those of us who were nearest naked, were issued Federal uniforms which had probably been condemned. The tails of the coats were cut off, as were the legs of the pants. Some were of light and some of dark blue cloth, and to those who drew light-blue garments, dark-blue pieces were issued. To the credit of the men, be it said, they declined to patch the clothes so as to appear like convicts, as was intended.

From Camp Chase we were transferred to Rock Island. It was in the dead of winter, and, as many of us were without blankets, we suffered intensely. Here again we encountered the home guards, and they displayed their bravery by forcing us to lie flat on the bottom of boxcars, threatening to shoot the first man who raised his hand or head. On this trip some of the boys escaped, but I had not the nerve to attempt it, for fear of freezing, as the snow was nearly two feet deep on a level.

At Rock Island the era of starvation was inaugurated, and for over twelve months my hunger was never appeased. Even in my dreams I was tantalized by visions of bountiful repasts of things good to eat. Rations for the day were issued each morning, and it was the custom to make but one meal and fast till the

next morning. Saturday rations were issued for two days, and it was not uncommon for the men to eat all at once and do without until Monday. Here we were guarded by negroes—insolent and overbearing, as is characteristic of the race when clothed with authority over those who had once been their masters. Here two of our boys were shot by the guard, who had accepted a bribe to allow them to escape; and it was not unusual to see in the early morning the corpse of one of our comrades lying where he had been shot during the night. Here,... smallpox broke out and aided chronic diarrhea to carry thousands to their graves. I suffered from both, and escaped death from the smallpox only because I determined not to die, though I know I saw others die who were not as ill as I. I escaped death from diarrhea by being sent to the hospital, where, it gives me pleasure to state, an honest effort was made, apparently at least, to alleviate suffering.

Our dog-eating experience was probably much the same as in other prisons; but I must confess that my stomach was not equal to a meal of this kind, though I did taste of a little yellow mice.

### September 13 (Sunday)

Stanfield, N.B., 1st Ky. Cavalry, prisoner, Camp Douglas, Chicago:

Some of us were then conveyed to Camp Douglas, some to Johnson's Island, and others to Camp Chase. It was very hard for us. Our food consisted of one-half pint of bean soup, one-half pound of beef, one pone of bread or pint of meal. This scanty ration was to last for a day. We had very little fire—one stove to one hundred and eighty men—and the weather was very cold....

### September 17 (Thursday)

In Georgia, Rosecrans concentrated his troops in the vicinity of Lee and Gordon's Mills on the Chickamauga Creek some 12 miles south of Chattanooga. The positions taken placed Crittenden at Gordon's Mill, Gen. Thomas to his right (farther south), and Gen. Alexander McCook on the right flank, near Pond Springs, Ga.

Bragg missed his chance to attack the isolated Federal units and beat them piecemeal, and now had to deal with an entire army. Bragg's intent was to turn Rosecrans's left flank and cut off the Union retreat to Chattanooga. Rosecrans understood the tactic and moved to counter it.

### September 18 (Friday)

Gen. John B. Hood, with three brigades of Longstreet's corps from the Army of Northern Virginia arrived at Bragg's location in Georgia this morning. Bragg, wasting no time, sent Bushrod Johnson's division and Forrest's cavalry across West Chickamauga Creek from Ringgold with a part of Longstreet's corps. Heavy fighting broke out with Rosecrans's cavalry.

### September 19 (Saturday)

Rosecrans and Bragg stumbled towards each other at Chickamauga in Georgia, neither knowing where the other's lines were. The fighting became general, and by 2 P.M. or so the entire three-mile front was engaged. Bragg, attempting to cut the lines to Chattanooga, couldn't make any progress, and casualties were heavy on both sides. As darkness settled, the fighting ceased, and the troops were out looking for the wounded, for this was to be a cold night.

On Chesapeake Bay, Acting Masters John Yates Beall and Edward McGuire, CSN, captured the schooner *Alliance* with a cargo of sutler's stores bound for Norfolk. Beall's two-ship fleet, containing the sloops *Raven* and *Swan*, was lightly manned and relied on the element of surprise for success.

### September 20 (Sunday)

The second, and last, day of the battle of Chickamauga was fought with fury, until both sides were exhausted. Rosecrans left the field and returned to Chattanooga, where his army would be penned up until late November. The North entered the battle with about 58,000 effectives. Of these, 1657 were killed, 9756 were wounded, and 4757 were missing, mostly prisoners. The weight was on the side of the Confederates, who had about 66,000 engaged. They suffered 2312 killed, 14,674 wounded, and 1468 missing. The wounded were transferred to hospitals in Georgia and Alabama for treatment. The Federal prisoners were sent to Richmond, and then on to Salisbury, N.C.

### September 21 (Monday)

Confederate raiders Beall and McGuire continued their actions today, seizing the schooner *J.J. Houseman*, adding this ship to their captured fleet.

At Chickamauga, Ga., Union Gen. George Thomas moved back to Chattanooga at dark after determining that Bragg was not going to attack the Federal force.

### September 22 (Tuesday)

On this night, Acting Masters Beall and McGuire took two more schooners, the *Samuel Persall* and *Alexandria*. Saving only the *Alliance*, Beall cast all the other boats adrift in the Wachapreague Inlet and attempted to run the blockade. The *Alliance*, being chased by the U.S.S. *Thomas Freeborn*, ran aground under fire at Milford Haven and was burned early on the morning of the 23rd. Beall and McGuire escaped and returned to Richmond.

### October 2 (Friday)

Jones, John B., Rebel War Clerk, Confederate War Dept., Richmond, Va.:

Our 5000 prisoners taken at the battle of Chickamauga have arrived in this city, and it is ascertained that more are on the way hither. Gen. Bragg said he had 5000 besides the wounded, and as none of the wounded have arrived, more must have been taken since his dispatch.

### October 3 (Saturday)

Confederate Gen. Joseph Wheeler continued his raids through Tennessee, harassing the Union supply lines and generally creating chaos. In the vicinity of Cainsville, Tenn., J.K. Womack, a member of Wheeler's cavalry, was captured during a skirmish. The prisoners were initially taken to Murfreesboro and placed in the city jail, being moved later to the penitentiary in Nashville, where they remained until about October 28.

### October 6 (Tuesday)

Jones, John B., Rebel War Clerk, Confederate War Dept., Richmond, Va.:

Gen. Bragg also gives timely notice to the Commissary-General that the supplies at Atlanta will suffice for but a few weeks longer. This, Commissary-General Northrop took in high dudgeon, indorsing on the paper that there was no necessity for such a message to him; that Bragg knew very well that every effort had been and would be made to subsist the army; that when he evacuated Tennessee, the great source of supplies was abandoned. In short, the only hope of obtaining ample supplies was for Gen. Bragg to recover Tennessee and drive Rosecrans out of the country.

## October 9 (Friday)

In northern Virginia, Lee, on the move, crossed the Rapidan and moved north trying to get around Meade's right flank and to threaten Washington. Meade, alerted, took action to cover his flank.

Our friend in Richmond, John B. Jones, ever one to carp about other people taking advantage of the system, seems to have had no qualms about taking food that should have gone to the prisoners at Libby or Belle Isle.

Jones, John B., Rebel War Clerk, Confederate War Dept., Richmond, Va.:

Capt. Warner, who feeds the prisoners of war, and who is my good "friend in need," sent me yesterday 20 odd pounds of bacon sides at the government price. This is not exactly according to law and order, but the government loses nothing, and my family have a substitute for butter.

## October 10 (Saturday)

Montgomery, J.J., Lowry's Scouts, Confederate prisoner, recaptured, Camp Morton, Ind.:

In October 1863, the Yankees caught me by surprise. I reported as belonging to a command, in order to save my neck. They took me to jail at Columbia, Tenn., and from there to the penitentiary at Nashville. I refused to take the oath, and was sent to Louisville, then to Indianapolis, Ind.

My treatment at the other prisons was bad enough, but nothing to compare with Camp Morton. I was first stripped and searched, and everything they found of value was taken from me. Our barracks were the stables built and used for horses. They were made of inch plank standing on end, the cracks partly covered with narrow strips. There was no floor but

the ground, and the rooms were from sixty to eighty feet long, each containing two wood stoves. The sergeant who called our roll would sometimes amuse himself by shooting along our line and by beating sick prisoners over the head with his saber. We called him "Bloody H———." I often ate my day's rations at one meal, and have seen men crying for something to eat. I saw men pull up their sleeves and run their hands down into the hospital slop barrels in search of meat, cabbage stalks, etc., which were eaten. I determined to leave the place or die in the attempt, as death threatened if I stayed. Having escaped once, I believed I could do so again.

In Richmond, Robert Ould, Confederate Agent for Exchange, notified Lt. Col. N.G. Watts, CSA, in Mobile, Ala., that all the prisoners taken at Port Hudson were declared free to return to duty because *neither government recognized the parole.* The latter was pure fabrication on the part of Ould. He used a subterfuge based on the original cartel of July 22, 1862. In that cartel the agreed-upon sites for exchange of prisoners was City Point, Va., and Vicksburg, Miss. The cartel further stated *that if either site was rendered impossible for use, another site would be selected.* Since the fall of Vicksburg rendered that site untenable for exchange, Mobile, Ala., was selected as the next alternate, and the prisoners who were paroled were sent there.

Ould, in his interpretation, used the reasoning that since the Federals did not use Vicksburg, the paroles were not valid. On November 28, Col. Watts, by direction of Lt. Gen. Kirby Smith in Shreveport, La., directed that all prisoners from Port Hudson would report to duty at once.

## October 13 (Tuesday)

Meade, now in the vicinity of Manassas and Centreville, was closely followed by Lee, who was picking up several prisoners from the skirmishing and cavalry action.

The next day, in the vicinity of Bristoe Station, Va., Meade was hit by A.P. Hill's Confederates, but the blow was weak and did little damage. Lee and Meade, for once evenly matched, looked for openings to exploit, but could find none. Meade was losing a lot of cavalry in skirmishes, mostly captured.

After several days of scrabbling around, Lee grew

tired of trying to outflank Meade and withdrew towards Warrenton and the Rappahannock River, thus ending campaigning until Nov. 7.

On the 17th, Grant was given command of the forces around Chattanooga, relieving Rosecrans.

Stanfield, N.B., 1st Ky. Cavalry, prisoner, Camp Douglas, Chicago:

They finally raised the barracks four feet from the ground. They would march us out in the coldest weather, keep us out for half a day, and occasionally shoot into us for tunneling. Several were killed in this way. Again, they would make us stand stiff-kneed, with our hands on the ground, as long as we could endure it. Lights were not allowed.

Brig. Gen. Gilman Marston, commanding the prison at Point Lookout, Md., had requested that monies be made available for the construction of barracks at that site for housing the Confederate prisoners. On this date, Col. William Hoffman, Federal Commissary-General of Prisoners, notified Gen. Marston:

Your plans and estimates for barracks at Point Lookout have been submitted to the Secretary of War for his approval, but he declines at this time to order the barracks constructed. It will, therefore, be necessary to have on hand a supply of tents to meet any unexpected arrival of prisoners, and I have, therefore, to request you will make requisition for sufficient tents, with what you have on hand, to accommodate 10,000 prisoners. Kitchens will also have to be provided, but these may be built with the prison fund. Locate them in such a way that if hereafter barracks are erected they will be in convenient position.

The refusal to construct the barracks at Point Lookout on the part of the Federal government would result in untold suffering on the part of the Confederate prisoners who would occupy the camp.

On this same date, Col. Hoffman also notified Col. C.V. De Land, commanding the prison at Camp Douglas, Ill., that Secretary Stanton would not approve the *reconstruction* of barracks at that location, which had burned the previous winter. Hoffman indicated that plans were being made to transfer about 1000 prisoners to the new depot at Rock Island, Ill. The monthly returns for the following months do not support this happening.

Lt. Col. William S. Pierson, commanding the prison at Johnson's Island, Ohio, informed Col. Hoffman of the recent escape attempts at that location:

You mention that you heard that three prisoners attempted an escape by sawing off the pickets, and that if I think best, to board up on the inside. Those men could have sawed a hole through plank as well as what they did. They would have had more difficulty to get in the saw, it is true, unless they had an augur. I shall put up more lamps. There must be lamps enough so that the sentinels can see, however stormy and dark. It was a very stormy and dark night. It does not do to rely on hearing at all, as the noise of the waves overcomes every other. The prisoners have exhibited much enterprise of late in the attempts to get out. They have tried digging under ground from sinks; also from quarters, commencing under the buildings. None have been successful and I hope none will be.

Lt. Col. Pierson also notified Col. Hoffman that smallpox had been brought to Johnson's Island by incoming prisoners three times; twice from the prison at Alton, Ill. The disease was causing somewhat of a panic among the prisoners, even though those sick were confined to the pesthouse.

### October 18 (Sunday)

It seemed too bad that Jones hadn't toured the entire prison in Richmond to learn more about the real conditions in those facilities.

Jones, John B., Rebel War Clerk, Confederate War Dept., Richmond, Va.:

Capt. Warner took me in his buggy this morning to the military prisons. He did not lead me into the crowded rooms above, where he said I would be in danger of vermin, but exhibited his cooking apparatus, etc.—which was ample and cleanly. Everywhere I saw the captives peeping through the bars; they occupy quite a number of large buildings—warehouses—and some exhibited vengeful countenances. They have half a pound of beef per day, and plenty of good bread and water—besides vegetables and other matters furnished by themselves. Several new furnaces are in process of erection, and most of the laborers are Federal prisoners, who agree to work (for their own convenience) and are paid for it the usual wages. There are baths to the prisons; and the conduits for venting, etc. have cost some $10,000. Today the weather is as warm as summer, and no doubt the prisoners sigh for the open air (although all the buildings are well ventilated), and their distant homes in the West—most of them being from the field of Chickamauga.

### October 22 (Thursday)

Thomas, D.C., Texas Cavalry, prisoner, north Mississippi:

I was captured in North Mississippi by the Seventh Illinois Cavalry, October 22, 1863, together with an old friend named R.L. Robinson (and several others whom I did not know), who was at the time a paroled Vicksburg prisoner, but they refused to recognize his parole papers. Soon after my capture the command was ordered on a march....

The cold October rain gave me a pretext, and I put on my Mexican blanket and concealed my money as best I could. About midnight we reached a country church and took shelter for the night. Robinson and I were permitted to lie down in the pulpit, where we spent the night whispering our plans of escape to avoid the winter in a Northern prison.... The next morning Serg. Porter told me that he had heard that a thief had stolen my spurs, and that he had recovered my property, at the same time offering to return them, but I requested him to accept them as a present. He thanked me, and offered to pay me for them, but I refused the money. Long after this, while a prisoner at Ft. Delaware, I learned by letter that my spurs had been recovered at Ft. Pillow when Forrest captured the place. I suppose that Porter was killed there.

### October 23 (Friday)

Thomas, D.C., Texas Cavalry, prisoner, western Tennessee:

That evening we arrived at Collierville, a town of tents, as we had burned the place about a week before. Joe Dewey invited me to take supper at his table, apologizing for a "short meal," and said that he had received some fine butter from home a few days before, and would have some for supper "if you fellers had not smoked us out." After supper Dewey invited me to walk with him through the camp, and

I gladly accepted. He said that if I would promise not to attempt to escape he would not take any arms with him. I made the promise for that walk, but told him candidly that when we returned my promise would be null and void, as I should certainly try to make my escape if an opportunity offered afterward.... At the sutler's tent he handed me a good cigar, the first I had seen since crossing the Mississippi. On our return I was incarcerated in a log pen which had been improvised for a guardhouse. Soon after we lay down Joe disappeared, and a drunken brute in Federal uniform stumbled in and fell down on me. He cursed and abused me, saying that he recognized me, that I was a bushwacker, and that I should have attention in the morning, as he would report me. This did not soothe me to a refreshing slumber, for the latter part of his charge was true. The guards finally pulled him out of the pen and drove him off.

At Chattanooga, Tenn., Grant arrived to take command in person. The plan to open the "Cracker Line" was approved.

Thomas, D.C., Texas Cavalry, prisoner, Memphis, Tenn.:

Next morning I was taken to headquarters; but the commanding officer, after questioning me for a few minutes, ordered me taken back to the guardhouse.

That evening all of the prisoners were placed on board the train and carried to Memphis. At the entrance of the Irving Block we were saluted with the cry of "fresh fish" by about one hundred unfortunates who had preceded us. We were searched and robbed. About dusk we were arranged in columns, and two filthy negroes, each with a tin bucket, came in. One handed each of us a fat cracker, and the other would gig up a small piece of fat meat with a sharp stick and push it off to us with his thumb.

### October 26 (Monday)

Brig. Gen. Gilman Marston, commanding the prison at Point Lookout, Md., notified Col. William Hoffman, Federal Commissary-General of Prisoners, that:

Among every lot of prisoners sent from Ft. Delaware to this point there have been cases of smallpox. There were twenty-six in the last lot. So many cases create alarm here among the troops and the citizen employes of the Government. I trust no more will be sent here.

The Federal Surgeon-General directed that no additional prisoners be transferred from Ft. Delaware until the smallpox had abated.

### October 28 (Wednesday)

Womack, J.K., Wheeler's Cavalry, CSA, prisoner, Camp Morton, Ind.:

…sent from there [Murfreesboro] to the penitentiary in Nashville, thence to the barracks in Louisville, and finally to Camp Morton…. That den of misery a little north of Indianapolis … was constructed as a fairground. Temporary stables for horses were erected in long rows. These were converted into barracks for Confederate prisoners.

There was not a bunk in the division, so our bed during that winter was an oilcloth spread upon the earth in the aisle of these barracks. Those who had preceded us were in much want. They were dirty, pale, emaciated, ragged, and lousy. Only a few had a change of clothing. We slept in our clothing every night to keep from freezing. There were two hundred and fifty prisoners in No. 7, and about four thousand in the prison. Those who had occasion to be up at night walked upon us unavoidably, as we slept in the only outlet. We were often spit upon at night by comrades who had colds.

Camp life as a Confederate soldier was hard, but prison life in Camp Morton was harder. Daily rations were eaten immediately upon being issued. We were supplied with one loaf of bread and one small piece of beef, and nothing more. It happened occasionally that we would draw this about eight o'clock in the morning, and then not get any more until the following day, late in the evening. When this was the case, we became so hungry that we would stand and look for the wagons to come through the gates with our bread. Sometimes, by stealth, we would pick up potato peelings thrown out from the cook rooms, roll them into balls, and cook and eat them with a relish. The beef bones were [broken] into small pieces, boiled in clear water, the grease dipped off and poured into a saucer, and sold as bone butter at ten cents a half cake. Crawfish were caught in the ditches, boiled, their pinchers pulled off when hot, and then converted into most excellent soup. A sutler's dog, killed and barbecued, furnished food that we relished.

Every man who was able to walk was required to fall in line for roll call about sunrise each morning. The Yankee sergeant who called the roll for our division was named Fiffer. I never heard a kind word fall from his lips. He was about grown and really a demon in human flesh. I have seen him walk through our barracks with a heavy stick in his hand, striking right and left on the heads faces, backs, or stomachs of the poor, starving prisoners, as though they were so many reptiles, crying out: "This is the way you whip your negroes."…

Death had thinned our ranks so much during the first winter that we had a bunk the next. We were packed in like sardines on our sides in spoon fashion. When one became tired he would cry out, "Turn!" when all would turn from right to left or left to right. We existed in this condition, with the thermometer below zero, in open stables without door shutters, hungry, and shivering with cold, having only one stove for two hundred fifty men. How good a piece of corn bread from home would have been at that time!

### November 2 (Monday)

On this date, Pvt. Eliab Hickman, Co. E, 92nd Ohio Volunteer Infantry, was detailed as a Division teamster by order of Gen. Baird, 3rd Div. Commander. He would remain in this duty until he was captured on November 6, 1864, near Cassville, Ga.

### November 6 (Friday)

Ransom, John, QM Sgt., 9th Michigan Cavalry, Rogersville, east Tenn.:

The rebel citizens got up a dance at one of the public houses in the village, and invited all the union officers. This was the evening of Nov. 5th. Nearly all the officers attended and were away from the command nearly all night and many were away all night. We were encamped in a bend of the Holston River. It was a dark rainy night and the river rose rapidly before morning. The dance was a ruse to get our officers away from their command. At break of day the pickets were drove in by rebel cavalry, and orders were immediately received from [the] commanding officer to get wagon train out on the road in ten minutes. The quartermaster had been to the dance and had not returned, consequently it devolved upon me to see to the wagon train, which I did, and in probably ten minutes the whole seventy-six mule army wagons were in a line on the main road, while companies were forming into line and getting ready to fight. Rebels had us completely surrounded and soon began to fire volley after volley into our disorganized ranks. Not one officer in five was present; Gen. commanding and staff as soon as they realized our danger, started for the river, swam across and got away. We had a small company of artillery with us commanded by a lieutenant. The lieutenant in the absence of other officers, assumed command of the two regiments, and right gallantly did he do service. Kept forming his men for the better protection of his wagon train, while the rebels were shifting around from one point to another, and all the time sending volley after volley into our ranks. Our men did well, and had there been plenty of officers and ammunition, we might have gained the day. After ten hours fighting we were obliged to surrender after having lost in killed over a hundred, and three or four times that number in wounded. After surrendering we were drawn up into line, counted off and hurriedly marched away south. By eight o'clock at night had probably marched ten miles, and encamped until morning.

At the Federal prison located on Point Lookout, Md., scurvy seemed to be prevalent among the prisoners. Brig. Gen. Gilman Marston, commanding the prison, wrote Col. William Hoffman, Federal Commissary-General of Prisoners:

The surgeon in charge of the rebel camp informs me that most of the prisoners are afflicted with scurvy, and he advises that vegetables be furnished them. I have thought it might be advisable to purchase a schooner load of beets, carrots, turnips, cabbages, and the like and pay for the same out of the fund arising from the savings from food rations. It would probably not add to the actual cost of their food.

Considering the poor diet already furnished the prisoners—usually a reduction of the same as that issued Union troops, which was bad enough—it is not surprising that scurvy was not more prevalent.

### November 7 (Saturday)

On June 18, 1861, Bartlett Yancey Malone, born January 22, 1839, enlisted in Co. H, 6th North Carolina Infantry, CSA, and began his military service for the Confederacy. He began a diary on January 1, 1862, and continued entries until March 5,

1865. On this November day, he was engaged in action near Rappahannock Bridge, Va., when part of his unit was cut off and forced to surrender. At the time of his surrender, he had advanced to the rank of Sergeant.

Malone, B.Y., Sgt., Co. H, 6th N.C. Infantry, CSA, captured at Rappahannock Bridge, Va.:

The 7th about 2 o'clock in the eavning orders came to fall in with armes in a moment that the enemy was advancen. Then we was doubbelquicked down to the river (which was about 5 miles) and crost and formed a line of battel in our works and the yanks was playing on ous with thir Artillery & thir skirmishers a fyting into ous as we formed fyring was kept up then with the Skirmishers untell dark. And about dark the yanks charged on the Louisianna Bregain which was clost to the Bridg and broke thir lines and got to the Bridge we was then cutoff and had to Surender; was then taken back to the rear and staid thir untell next morning.

Ransom, John, QM Sgt., 9th Michigan Cavalry, en route to Bristol, Va.:

An hour before daylight we were up and on the march towards Bristol, Va., that being the nearest railroad station. We were cavalrymen, and marching on foot made us very lame, and we could hardly hobble along. Were very well fed on corn bread and bacon.

Jones, John B., Rebel War Clerk, Confederate War Dept., Richmond, Va.:

Night before last some of the prisoners on Belle Isle (we have some 13,000 altogether in and near the city) were overheard by the guard to say they must escape immediately, or else it would be too late, as cannon were to be planted around them. Our authorities took the alarm, increasing the guard, did plant cannon so as to rake them in every direction in the event of their breaking out of their prison bounds. It is suspected that this was a preconcerted affair, as a full division of the enemy has been sent to Newport News, probably to co-operate with the prisoners. Any attempt now must fail, unless, indeed, there should be a large number of Union sympathizers in the city to assist them.

Several weeks ago it was predicted in the Northern papers that Richmond would be taken in some mysterious manner, and that there was a plan for the prisoners of war to seize it by a *coup de main*, may be probable. But the scheme is impracticable.

### November 8 (Sunday)

Malone, B.Y., Sgt., Co. H, 6th N.C. Infantry, CSA, prisoner, Washington, D.C.:

The morning of the 8th we was marched back to Warrenton Junction and got on the cars and about day next morning we got to Washington we then staid in Washington until 3 o'clock in the eavning of the 8th [9th] then was marched down to the Warf and put on the Stemer *John Brooks* and got to Point Lookout about one O'clock on the eavning of the 10th day of November 1863.... Our rations at Point Lookout was 5 crackers and a cup of coffee for Breakfast. And for dinner a small ration of meat 2 crackers three Potatoes and a cup of Soup. Supper we have non. We pay a dollar for 8 crackers or a chew of tobacco for a cracker.... All the wood we get to burn at Point Lookout is one sholder tirn of pine brush every other day for ten or 16 men to every tent.

Ransom, John, QM Sgt., 9th Michigan Cavalry, en route to Richmond, Va.:

Reached Bristol, Va., Nov. 8th and were soon aboard cattle cars en route for the rebel capital.... After we were captured everything was taken away from us, blankets, overcoats, and in many cases our boots and shoes. I had on a new pair of boots, which by muddying them over had escaped the rebel eyes thus far, as being a good pair. As our blankets had been taken away from us we suffered considerably from cold.... The cars ran very slow, and being crowded for room the journey to Richmond was very tedious.

Thomas, D.C., Texas Cavalry, prisoner, up the Mississippi River:

Ten or fifteen days later we were marched down to the Mississippi River and onto the boiler-deck of an old steamboat, and a strong guard was placed in the cabin. The old boat backed out, groaned, puffed, and in a few minutes we were going up the great Mississippi, away from home and friends, we knew not where, because *they* said we were in rebellion.

It was a glorious evening—clear, calm, and just cool enough to be pleasant. The sun was setting in splendor, but no one can imagine my feelings. My brain was racked trying to devise some means of escape. About dusk the cry was raised, "The yawl is gone!" and immediately a hundred Yankees were on hurricane-deck with guns in hand. I looked down the river, and could see the little boat floating, but no person was visible in it. After it was well out of gunshot a man raised up, grasped the paddles, and struck out for the Arkansas shore. We learned that our lucky comrade was a young man who had been married but a few days when he was captured, and was now landing near the residence of his young wife.

### November 9 (Monday)

Col. William Hoffman, Federal Commissary-General of Prisoners, replied to Brig. Gen. Marston's request of November 6 concerning the purchase of vegetables for the Confederate prisoners to prevent scurvy. Col. Hoffman agreed that the vegetables were necessary, and that their purchase should be out of the "prisoners fund." Hoffman then expounded the view of a *parsimonious* bureaucracy by stating that *"By the use of vegetables the savings of other parts of the ration will be increased, so that the cost will be to some extent refunded...."* Hoffman further said that *"As the prisoners are bountifully supplied with provisions, I do not think it well to permit them to receive boxes of eatables from their friends"* [italics added].

There were probably 10,000 prisoners at Point Lookout who would have contested Hoffman's concept of "bountiful" when it applied to their rations.

### November 11 (Wednesday)

Jones, John B., Rebel War Clerk, Confederate War Dept., Richmond, Va.:

Capt. Warner, who feeds the 13,000 prisoners here, when he has the means of doing so, says Col. Northrop, the Commissary, does not respond to his requisitions for meat. He fears the prisoners will take or destroy the city, and talks of sending his family out of it.

### November 13 (Friday)

The winter of 1863–64 was a starving time for the Army of Northern Virginia, much worse than the previous winter. Gone now were the "bread baskets" of Tennessee and the trans-Mississippi regions. Lee, in camp south of the Rapidan River, was in bad shape.

Jones, John B., Rebel War Clerk, Confederate War Dept., Richmond, Va.:

Gen. Lee dispatched the President, yesterday, as follows:

Orange C.H., Nov 12th.—For the last five days we have only received three pounds of corn per horse, from Richmond, per day. We depend on Richmond for corn. At this rate, the horses will die, and cannot do hard work. The enemy is very active, and we must be prepared for hard work any day.—R.E. Lee.

On the back of which the President endorsed: "Have the forage sent up in preference to anything else. The necessity is so absolute as to call for every possible exertion.—Jefferson Davis."

Perhaps this may rouse the department. Horse starving in the midst of cornfields ready for gathering! Alas, what mismanagement!

Ransom, John, QM Sgt., 9th Michigan Cavalry, Belle Isle Prison, Richmond, Va.:

Arrived on the morning of Nov. 13th, seven days after capture, at the south end of the "long bridge," ordered out of the cars and into line, counted off and started for Belle Isle. Said island is in the James River, probably covers ten or twelve acres, and is right across from Richmond. The river between Richmond and the island is probably a third or half a mile. The "long bridge" is near the lower part of the island. It is a cold, bleak piece of ground and the winter winds have free sweep from up the river. Before noon we were turned into the pen which is merely enclosed by a ditch and the dirt taken from the ditch thrown up on the outside, making a sort of breastwork. The ditch serves as a dead line, and no prisoners must go near the ditch. The prison is in command of a Lt. Bossieux, a rather young and gallant looking sort of fellow. Is a born Southerner, talking so much like a negro that you would think he was one, if you could hear him talk and not see him. He has two rebel sergeants to act as his assistants, Sergt. Hight and Sergt. Marks. These two men are very cruel, as is also the Lieutenant when angered. Outside the pen is a bake house, made of boards, the rebel tents for the accommodation of the officers and guard, and a hospital also of tent cloth. Running from the pen is a lane enclosed by high boards going to the water's edge. At night this is closed up by a gate at the pen, and thrown open in the morning. About half of the six thousand prisoners here have tents while the rest sleep and live out of doors.

## November 14 (Saturday)

Stanfield, N.B., 1st Ky. Cavalry, prisoner, Camp Douglas, Chicago:

They put those of us who had tried to escape to ourselves, and built a plank fence between the two camps, so that we could not see across. They had a horse made of joists, with legs twelve feet high, which they called "Morgan's horse." They would make us sit on this for a long time in the cold. When our people sent us anything to eat, they kept it until it was not fit to eat. They cut our clothing to pieces, hunting for money.

Jones, John B., Rebel War Clerk, Confederate War Dept., Richmond, Va.:

Another letter from Brig. Gen. Meredith, Fortress Monroe, was received today, with a report of an agent on the condition of the prisoners at Ft. Delaware. By this report it appears our men get meat three times a day—coffee, tea, molasses, chicken soup, fried mush, etc. But it is not stated *how much* they get. The agent says they confess themselves satisfied. Clothing, it would appear, is also issued them, and they have comfortable sleeping beds, etc. He says several of our surgeons propose taking the oath of allegiance, first resigning, provided they are permitted to visit their families. Gen. M. asks for a similar report of the rations, etc. served the Federal prisoners here, with an avowed purpose of retaliation, provided the accounts of their conditions are true. I know not what response will be made; but our surgeon-general recommends an inspection and report. They are getting sweet potatoes now, and generally they get bread and beef daily, when our Commissary-General Northrop has them. But sometimes they have little or no meat for a day or so at a time—and occasionally they have bread only once a day. It is difficult to feed them, and I hope they will be exchanged soon. But Northrop says our own soldiers must soon learn to do without meat; and but few of us have little prospect of getting enough to eat this winter. My family had a fine dinner today—the only one for months.

## November 15 (Sunday)

Acting Master John Yates Beall, CSN, raiding on the Chesapeake Bay, became the focus of a large search after his destruction of several lighthouses on Maryland's Eastern Shore. The search terminated with his capture on this day. Beall and his crew were taken to Ft. McHenry, Md., and charged with piracy. This was later reduced to a prisoner-of-war status, and he was exchanged in May 1864.

Thomas, D.C., Texas Cavalry, prisoner, Alton, Ill.:

A few days later we arrived at Alton, Ill. We were marched into the inside of the outer wall of the old penitentiary building, and were taken up a stairway, one by one, thoroughly searched, and again systematically robbed. While waiting for my name to be called, Dr. J.R. Riley came to a gate in a partition wall and looked through at me. I inquired of the sentinel stationed at the gate if I could speak to a friend. In a gruff voice he answered, "No!" but at the same time looked off in another direction, which encouraged me to take my chances. I stepped up to Dr. Riley, shook hands with him, and placed a five-dollar gold piece in his hand. He whispered to me to try to avoid the hospital, and, if possible to avoid vaccination, saying that they were using poisonous virus.

My name was soon called, and I ascended the stairway, entered the search room, and was ordered to take off my coat, boots, pants, etc., was well searched, my gray jacket thrown on the filthy floor and the buttons cut off, taking out a piece of cloth about the size of a twenty-five cent piece with each button. I was then ordered down another flight of stairs, and instructed to go to the hospital and be vaccinated. At the foot of the stairway I discovered a narrow, dark alley at right angles, and without knowing what the result would be, I sprang into the dark. After groping my way for perhaps a hundred feet, I saw light, and, stepping out I found myself among about twelve hundred fellow prisoners. So there I was, more than a thousand miles from home, surrounded by stone walls forty feet high, in a cold latitude with but little clothing or bedding, guarded by bitter enemies, with but little prospect of ever again seeing the land of Dixie. And for what? Because I had dared to defend my home and Southland when invaded by enemies.

## November 19 (Thursday)

On this date, one of the most eloquent and brief speeches every delivered was given at Gettysburg, Pa., by President Abraham Lincoln at the dedication of the Soldiers' National Cemetery.

## November 20 (Friday)

Thomas, D.C., Texas Cavalry, prisoner, Alton, Ill.:

The winter was unusually severe, even for this climate, and our supply of provisions, coal, and wood was very limited. I was soon prostrated with a severe fever, and when Dr. Riley visited me he pronounced it a distinct case of smallpox, and told me that it was his imperative duty to report it to the authorities, and that I would be sent to the smallpox island. Imagine my feelings. The Mississippi River was now frozen over, so that wagons loaded with green wood and drawn by six mules were constantly crossing on the ice. Soon after Dr. Riley pronounced mine a case of smallpox two men placed me on a litter and carried me to the river's edge, where I was rolled onto a sled and drawn over the ice to the island, where I was again placed on a litter, carried into a tent and rolled off onto the ground. I told Dr. Gray, a Confederate prisoner on detail service, that I was a special friend of Dr. Riley, and requested that I be furnished with a bed. Dr. Gray inquired of a nurse if he could furnish me a place to lie down. The nurse replied that a man had just died, and that as soon as he was removed I could have his place.

This smallpox island was in the Mississippi River, between the Missouri and Illinois shores, and the hospitals were cloth tents. After waiting for some time I was carried into the tent and tumbled off onto the dead man's bunk, the nurse remarking: "They have sent some dead men over here for us to bury."

On the bunk were two pairs of blankets: one pair to lie on, and the other to cover with. A nurse approached, and asked how many blankets I had. I replied that I had three pairs, but that one was my private property, that I had brought with me. With an oath he snatched my blankets, remarking that I was entitled to but two pairs of blankets, and should have no more. I was as weak as a child and had a burning fever, but my anathemas dumfounded him, and without a word he laid my blankets on another bunk and left the tent. A convalescent prisoner named Lane was a witness to what had occurred, and when the nurse left the tent he brought my blankets and spread them over me, and said that a detail had been over that day from the prison and had washed and hung out to dry some blankets, and that as soon as it grew dark I should have another pair. He was true to his promise, and also took the socks off my feet, washed and dried them, and did all in his power to render me more comfortable. That night a nurse came round and placed on my bunk a tin cup filled with a white fluid, which he said was milk. There was also a hard lump of boiled cornmeal in the cup. This he called mush. Being thirsty, I drank the white fluid, but did not know how to manage the lump, as I had no spoon. My good friend, Robinson, hearing through a returned convalescent of my condition, bribed a passing guard, and sent me a spoon and an apple. That night a man called for a nurse to come with a light, saying that a man was on him in his bunk. When the nurse came the delirious man had gotten off the bunk and was sitting on the ground at the foot of it dead. All day and all night, day after day, night after night, the groans and prayers of the poor, suffering prisoners could be heard piteously begging for water or for some trivial attention from the cold-hearted nurses.

## November 21 (Saturday)

At Chattanooga, Tenn., Grant was gearing up for an offensive. Sherman was moving towards the right flank of the Confederate line via Brown's Ferry to hit the line at the north end of Missionary Ridge. Joseph Hooker was to move his men via Lookout Valley to strike the left end of the line. Rainy, sloppy weather delayed some movements.

Jones, John B., Rebel War Clerk, Confederate War Dept., Richmond, Va.:

Every night robberies of poultry, salt meats, and even of cows and hogs are occurring. Many are desperate.

... We are a shabby-looking people now—gaunt, and many in rags. But there is food enough, and cloth enough, if we had a Roman Dictator to order an equitable distribution.

## November 22 (Sunday)

Bragg, on Missionary Ridge, detached Simon Buckner's command to go to Knoxville, Tenn., to assist Longstreet's operations against Burnside. Bragg was unaware of the movement of Sherman's blue columns.

## November 23 (Monday)

The question as to whether prisoners held in Federal camps could receive clothing or other articles from their families and other sympathizers had been debated for some time. The same problem existed in the Confederate camps as regards the Union prisoners. One of the major problems, of course, was that the prisoner might use some of the clothing to disguise himself as a civilian and escape. Today, Col. William Hoffman, Federal Commissary-General of Prisoners, notified Brig. Gen. Gilman Marston, commanding at Point Lookout, Md., that "hereafter prisoners of war may be permitted to receive clothing or other articles only from members of their immediate family. Contributions by disloyal friends or sympathizers for the general benefit of prisoners must not be received."

Jones, John B., Rebel War Clerk, Confederate War Dept., Richmond, Va.:

Everywhere the people are clamorous against the sweeping impressments of crops, horses, etc. And at the same time we have accounts of corn, and hay, and potatoes rotting at various depots! Such is the management of the bureaus.

Ransom, John, QM Sgt., 9th Michigan Cavalry, Belle Isle Prison, Richmond, Va.:

Having a few dollars of good Yankee money which I have hoarded since my capture, have purchased a large blank book and intend as long as I am a prisoner of war in this Confederacy, to note down from day to day as occasion may occur, events as they happen, treatment, ups and downs generally. It will serve to pass away the time and may be interesting at some future time to read over.

Near Chattanooga, Tenn., Gen. George H. Thomas, the "Rock of Chickamauga," moved his blue lines out towards Orchard Knob, an elevation about a mile in front of Missionary Ridge. Maj. Gen. Philip Sheridan and Brig. Gen. T.J. Wood captured the Knob with little trouble and few casualties. Everyone settled down for the night.

## November 24 (Tuesday)

Early this morning, Hooker drove three blue divisions against the base of Lookout Mountain and soon was climbing the heights. At the end of the day, the mountain was in Federal hands. Sherman, meanwhile, thought he had captured Billy Goat Hill, an area he believed to be part of Missionary Ridge, but it turned out to be an area north of his objective. By the end of the day the Confederates were aware of the main objective—Missionary Ridge.

Ransom, John, QM Sgt., 9th Michigan Cavalry, Belle Isle Prison, Richmond, Va.:

Very cold weather. Four or five men chilled to death last night. A large portion of the prisoners who have been in confinement any length of time are reduced to almost skeletons from continued hunger, exposure and filth. Having some money just indulged in an extra ration of corn bread for which I paid twenty cents in Yankee script, equal to two dollars Confederate money, and should say by the crowd collected around that such a sight was an unusual occurrence.... We received for today's food half a pint of rice soup and one-quarter of a pound loaf of corn bread. The bread is made from the poorest meal, coarse, sour and musty; would make poor feed for swine at home. The rice is nothing more than boiled in river water with no seasoning whatever, not even salt, but for all that it tasted nice.... No wood tonight and it is very cold. The nights are long and are made hideous by the moans of suffering wretches.

## November 25 (Wednesday)

Grant sent Sherman against the north end of Missionary Ridge and Hooker was to swing wide, seize Rossville Gap and try to cut off the retreat route of the Confederates. George Thomas was to watch the middle of the line. Sherman ran into trouble and the going was heavy until mid- to late afternoon. At that time, Grant sent Thomas forward a little, just to break the pressure on the end of the line. The blue-clad infantry in Thomas's four divisions had different thoughts about this. They hit the base of the ridge at full tilt and kept going up, driving the surprised Rebels ahead of them or bypassing them to gain the top. The result was a clear Federal victory and a big bag of Confederate prisoners. The chase began towards Graysville and Ringgold, Ga.

Ransom, John, QM Sgt., 9th Michigan Cavalry, Belle Isle Prison, Richmond, Va.:

Hendryx is in a very good tent with some nine or ten others and is now trying to get men into the already crowded shelter. They say I can have the first vacancy and as it is impossible for a dozen to remain together long without losing some by sickness, my chances will be good in a few days.... Food again at four o'clock. In place of soup received about four ounces of salt horse, as we call it.

## November 26 (Thursday)

In Virginia, Meade nudged Lee in the area of the Rapidan River, creating a flurry of activity in the Army of Northern Virginia's camps. There would be some fighting in the vicinity of Mine Run for the next few days.

In Washington, Col. William Hoffman, Federal Commissary-General of Prisoners, planned for the return of sick and wounded Union prisoners. Hoffman notified Surgeon A.M. Clark:

You will proceed immediately to Fortress Monroe, Va., with a view to consult with Brig. Gen. S.A. Meredith, commissioner for the exchange of prisoners, in relation to making suitable provision on the flag of truce boat for the reception of sick Federal prisoners of war who may be delivered from time to time at City Point. Sufficient bedding should always be upon the boat when such deliveries are to be made, with a proper supply of such food as prisoners in their condition require, and ample accommodations for cooking. The boat should be prepared to deliver them at Annapolis and notice should be given to Col. Waite, commanding in that city, of the time of their arrival so that everything may be prepared for their reception in the general hospital or the hospital at Camp Parole.

Ransom, John, QM Sgt., 9th Michigan Cavalry, Belle Isle Prison, Richmond, Va.:

Are getting food twice today; old prisoners say it is fully a third more than they have been getting. Hardly understand how we could live on much less. A Michigan man (could not learn his name) while at work a few moments ago on the outside with a squad of detailed yankees repairing a part of the embankment which recent rains had washed away, stepped upon the wall to give orders to his men when one of the guards shot him through the head, killing him instantly. Lt. Bossieux, commander of the prison, having heard the shot, came to learn the cause. He told the guard he ought to be more careful and not shoot those who were on parole and doing fatigue duty, and ordered the body carried to the dead house.

Fredrick N. Knapp, Associate Secretary of the U.S. Sanitary Commission in Washington, today forwarded a copy of an inspection report, dated November 13, on Point Lookout, Md., to Col. William Hoffman, Federal Commissary-General of Prisoners. The report indicates a rather grim picture of the life of the prisoners in the hospital and prison at that location.

The accommodations here were much better than I expected to find them and much more comfortable, yet they had by no means the best of care. The hospital was situated in the southern part of the encampment and was composed of eighteen hospital tents, complete, arranged two together, end to end, and placed in two rows, a broad street intervening, with the cook and dining tent on the eastern end and facing the street. In these tents there were 100 patients, and all were lying on mattresses with at least one blanket for covering. Eight of their own men were detailed to take care of them, and although they were enlisted men, yet six were graduates from some medical school and the other two had been students. Four were graduates from the University of the City of New York; one of the school at New Orleans; one from the eclectic school, Cincinnati, and the other two were students in the University of Pennsylvania, seceders. Still, little or no attention did they give to their sick comrades, and, except in giving the necessary food and medicine, they scarcely even visited them. There is either a lack of sympathy or else indolence enters largely into their composition, and I am inclined to believe it is the latter, for, with the accommodations at their command, with good beds and shelter for the sick, if they had one particle of pride they could render them much more comfortable, especially as regards cleanliness. As it is, they are in a filthy condition; faces and hands apparently strangers to soap and water and hair seemingly uncombed for weeks.

No attention was given to the separating of different diseases. Wounded and erysipelas, fever and diarrhea, were lying side by side. (The wounded were two that were shot while trying to escape; two were killed.) Their being no stoves in the hospital, the men complain greatly of cold, and I must admit that for the poor emaciated creatures suffering from diarrhea a single blanket is not sufficient; yet as I told them, they had plenty of bricks and plenty of men; they could build fireplaces. One tent only had a board floor. Chronic diarrhea is the most prevalent disease, yet they have mild cases of remittent fever and some erysipelas. Mortality, none, for when any cases assume a dangerous character they are immediately removed to the general hospital, and they generally remove from twenty to thirty per day on an average, leaving in camp hospital eighty sick.

The dispensary is a poor apology for one, having little or nothing but a few empty bottles. Not a particle of oil or salts, in fact, a cathartic of no kind. About half a dram of opium, half pound of sulphether, half pound of simple cerate, and a few other things constitute the whole supply. Here also was shown the want of discipline and cleanliness; everything covered with dust, and what few articles they had were exposed to the air and placed indiscriminately along the counter and in the most perfect confusion; were going to arrange the bottles, &c. The books were extremely well kept, neat and cleanly, and each day's report was copied in the report book as soon as returned from the surgeon in charge.

The rations are very good, both in quantity and quality; amply sufficient for any sick man; but there are exceptional cases where they need something more delicate than the regular army ration. But the majority are perfectly well satisfied, and very little complaint is made in this particular. I will here give the quantities they received in full, half, and low diet:

Full diet: Dinner—beef or pork, 4 ounces; potatoes, 4 ounces; hardtack, 3 ounces. Breakfast and tea—coffee or tea, 1 pint; rice, 2 gills; molasses, 1 ounce; hardtack, 3 ounces.

Half diet: Dinner—meat 2 ounces; potatoes, 3 ounces; hardtack, 2 ounces. Breakfast and tea—coffee or tea, 1 pint; rice, 1 gill; molasses, half an ounce; hardtack, 2 ounces.

Low diet: Dinner—no meat; potatoes, 2 ounces; hardtack, 1 ounce. Breakfast and tea—coffee or tea, 1 pint; rice, 1 gill; molasses, half an ounce; hardtack, 1 ounce.

Soup and soft bread is also given at least once a week. The cooking is done by their own men, and heard no complaint in this quarter, except they were poorly supplied with cooking utensils and were very much in want of tin cups, knives and forks. The patients were required generally to eat with their fingers. They had a large cooking stove, but they complained it was not sufficient for their purpose, as it kept them at work nearly all the time; the very reason that it should not be changed or another given them. The cooks' tent and stove were dirty (the peculiar characteristic), and the tent where the nurses and attendants dined was in the same plight although I am glad to say the table from which they ate was scoured and looked very clean, as also the plates and cups.

The grounds around the hospital have not, according to looks, been policed for a very long time. Filth is gradually accumulating, and the sinks are not at all thought of, requiring a little extra exertion to walk to them. They void their excrement in the most convenient place to them, regardless of the comfort of others.

The surgeon in charge of this hospital and of the whole rebel encampment is Dr. Bunton, assistant surgeon Second New Hampshire Volunteers, assisted by Drs. Russell and Walton, acting assistant surgeons, the latter gentlemen having just entered upon their duties. I think a great amount of the misery experienced in the hospital and throughout the camp might be obviated if a little more energy was displayed by the surgeon in charge. There is lack of system and want of discipline, neither of which (with all due respect to the doctor) do I think he is possessed of. The assistants saw what was needed and were determined to entirely renovate and change the whole condition and aspect. If done, much suffering might be alleviated and less sickness would ensue.

It is in the quarters that we have the most complaint and suffering. Men of all ages and classes, descriptions and hues, with various colored clothing, all huddled together, forming a motley crew, which to be appreciated must be seen, and what the pen fails to describe the imagination must depict; yet I will endeavor to convey their exact condition, &c.,

and give as accurate description as possible.

They are ragged and dirty and very thinly clad; that is, the very great majority. Occasionally you will find one the fortunate possessor of an overcoat, either a citizen's or the light blue ones used by our infantry, and these serve as coverings for the rags beneath. Others, again, are well supplied as regards underclothing, especially those who are from Baltimore, being sent to them by friends. But the great mass are in a pitiable condition, destitute of nearly everything, which, with their filthy condition, makes them really objects of commiseration. Some are without shirts, or what were once shirts are now hanging in shreds from their shoulders. In others the entire back or front will be gone, while again in some you will see a futile attempt at patching. Their clothing is of all kinds and hues—the gray, butternut, the red of our zouaves and the light and dark blue of our infantry, all in a dilapidated condition.

Of their shelter there can be no possible complaint, for they all have good tents, such as wall, hospital, Sibley, wedge, shelter, hospital and wall tent flies. Majority are in the wedge tent. Average in a hospital tent, from 15 to 18 men; in wall tent, from 10 to 12; in shelter tent, 3; in Sibley tent, from 13 to 14.... The shelter tents, only a very few are excavated and boarded at the sides, and almost every tent throughout the camp has a fireplace and chimney built of brick made by them from the soil (which is clay) and sun baked. In a few of the Sibleys holes are dug, fire built, and covered at the top. Generally the tents are filled with smoke. Although they have fireplaces wood is not issued to them, but they are allowed to go out in squads every day and gather such as may be found in the woods where trees have been cut down, but they are not allowed to cut down others. There are instances where they have completely dug around the root of a stump and taken all; for it is impossible in this way for them to get enough to keep them warm, and as they are poorly supplied with blankets they must have suffered severely from the cold, more so where they are, for it is a very bleak place.

On visiting the quarters, found them crowded around a few coals in their respective tents, some having good blankets thrown across the shoulders, others pieces of carpet, others a gum blanket, others a piece of oilcloth commonly used for the covering of the tables. Generally they have one blanket to three men, but a great many are entirely without. A great many of the tents have been pitched over old sinks lightly covered. Complaints have been made, but nothing has been done to change them. The interior of the tents are in keeping with the inmates, filthy; pieces of cracker, meat, ashes, &c., are strewn around the tent, and in which they will lie. In preference to sitting on a stool they will sit upon the ground, and I even heard their own men say that they never saw such a dirty set in their lives, fully convincing me that it is their element, and they roll into it as a hog will wallow in the mire.

Concerning the rations, I heard a great deal of complaint that they did not get enough to eat. They wanted more meat. What they did get they spoke of in the highest terms. On questioning some of them which they would prefer an increase of the rations or blankets, all concluded that they could get along with the ration if they could get blankets. On being shown a ration, I do not think they receive half the amount of meat they are entitled to, but with the crackers, &c., given they cannot suffer at all from hunger. The ration to the well man is, pork, 3 ounces; salt or beef, 4 ounces; hardtack, 10 ounces; coffee, 1 pint; a day's ration. Soup is also given once a week; potatoes and beans every five days; soft bread once a week, and fresh meat had been issued to them once a week up to two weeks ago, when from some cause unable to find out it was stopped. Others, again, did not find fault with the ration, but the cooking; that it was not done well, and there ought to be changes made, &c., so visited the kitchens and dining-rooms. These are in the northwest corner of the camp and composed of six wooden buildings, 160 feet in length, with twenty feet off for the kitchen. Only five of the buildings are in use. The kitchen arrangements are very good, each one containing four cauldrons, and in one five, each cauldron capable of containing from fifty to sixty gallons. Here the rations were cooked, and was told that they served the meat ration all at dinner, not being enough to make two meals, and they were thus enabled to give them one good meal a day. Breakfast and supper they relied upon hardtack, tea or coffee; and, as I said before, there is no likelihood of their starving. The dining-room contains three tables, and each house feeds 1529 men, 500 at a time. Seem to be well supplied with all necessary articles, both for kitchen and dining-room. Will make allowance for the condition of the kitchen, as

they were just through serving dinner, and were making preparations for cleaning up. Yet there was evidence of a want of care and cleanliness. Still, I found them in a much better condition than I expected. There was such a vast difference that I did not notice as much the number of bones thrown from kitchen on the outside. Still there were some.

The sick in quarters average from 160 to 200. Prevailing disease, scurvy. Yet a great many are troubled with the diarrhea, and as they gradually grow worse are admitted to the hospital to be sent to the general hospital. These men who are sick in quarters and who are unable to eat the ration given them have instead, vinegar, 3 ounces; potatoes, 5; rice, 1 gill; molasses, 1 gill; one day's rations. Each man cooks for himself. They are troubled greatly with the itch, and it is spreading throughout the camp, and until sulphur was sent them by the commission they had nothing for it. They have abundance of water in the camp, notwithstanding several of the wells are unfit for use. The waters of those not in use are strongly impregnated with iron and will stain white clothing yellow or light brown. Outside of these there is an abundance of good water, and no excuse whatever for being otherwise than cleanly, but they seem to abhor soap and water. At least their appearance so indicates.

A great many are employing their time making brick and have now a great quantity on hand. Others employ themselves in making rings, chains, seals, &c., from bone and gutta percha, and notwithstanding the complaint that they do not get enough to eat, you will find them on the main street, which they call The Change, gambling both for money and rations. They have games at cards, keno, sweat cloth, &c. Also on this street they do their trading, hardtack for tobacco and tobacco for hardtack. It is here that you will find them in crowds, sitting or kneeling in the dirt, eagerly watching the different games, and see them arise dissatisfied at having lost their day's rations, and while thus engaged they are unmindful of the cold. The size of the encampment is a little over 1000 feet square, or about 16 acres, the whole surrounded by a board fence twelve feet high, with a platform on the outside for the sentinel, sufficiently high for him to look within the inclosure. With so many men and no one to take charge of them, it is not at all to be wondered at that the camp is in any but a desirable condition. The sinks, which should have special consideration, especially in a camp of this size, and where so many men are congregated, are entirely neglected, and it is a perfect mystery that there is not more sickness than they have, and God knows they have enough, for they live, eat, and sleep in their own filth. Sinks have been prepared for them, but little or no attention is paid to them, unless they should be in close proximity when they desire to answer the calls of nature. The holes dug in getting out clay for bricks are used as sinks. You will find them by the side and in front of their tents, in various portions of the encampment, and are the receptacles of their filth. Refuse matter from the tents or what not right under their very noses, yet they heed them not. Others, again, have no particular place, but will void their excrement anywhere on the surface that is most convenient to them, heedless of the convenience of others.

Have no drainage around the tents, but there has been an attempt to drain the streets. Ditches were dug, but they are worse than useless, constantly filled with water, and afford another place to throw filth. With this state of affairs and so many men (by the by, over 1300 more came in the camp on the afternoon of November 10, making nearly 10,000 men) the camp would soon become in an impassable condition. The men themselves complain and hope that some severe punishment, even shooting, will be the penalty to any one who will so outrage decency and lose respect due themselves. Some of the sinks are filled and not been covered and not a particle of chloride of lime has been used in the encampment for a long time. After stating the above facts, giving the condition of the camp and its inmates, some might say that it is not our fault that they are in this condition. As far as clothing, it is not; but it is our fault when they neglect to enforce those sanitary rules which keep camps and inmates in a cleanly condition and this [way] try to prevent disease. It is our fault when the officer in command fails to place in charge some one of good executive ability, capable of giving commands and seeing that they are enforced, one who will have the camp regularly policed and severely punish any offender of the sanitary rules. It is beneficial otherwise, for it will give employment to a certain number of men every day.

As regards medicine and clothing, they are sadly in want of both, and would suggest that the commission send them, place them in the hands of Mr.

Fairchild, and I know they will be judiciously distributed. I know that they are our enemies, and bitter ones, and what we give them they will use against us, but now they are within our power and are suffering. Have no doubt that to compare their situation with that of our men words would hardly be adequate to express our indignation. I merely gave this suggestion because I think you would be doing right and it might prove beneficial to us.

### November 27 (Friday)

To provide the sentries at the various Federal prisons with more firepower, Col. William Hoffman, Federal Commissary-General of Prisoners, today directed that revolvers and ammunition be issued to each of the prison camp guards.

Col. Hoffman also reviewed the report of Frederick N. Knapp, U.S. Sanitary Commission, which was sent to him yesterday. Hoffman notified the commander of Point Lookout, Md., Brig. Gen. Marston, that quantities of inferior clothing was available for issue to the prisoners immediately when the requirements were known. Marston was requested to provide the requirement to Washington at the earliest possible time. Hoffman doubted the accuracy of Knapp's ration description. Actually, the prisoners' accounts of the rations made the situation far worse than Knapp indicated.

Col. Hoffman addressed another problem—that of transferring prisoners from one camp to another by railroad. Today, Hoffman tweaked the nose of Col. C. Thomas, Acting Quartermaster-General, by calling his attention to the fact that in a recent transfer of about 150 rebel officers, arrangements were made to get them to the train at 6:30 A.M. only to find that no cars were available for their use. In another case, 60 prisoners were put into two boxcars at Louisville to be sent to Indianapolis. Loaded at 8 P.M. in cars without lights, there was a three-hour delay along the line, during which time 3 prisoners escaped.

Ransom, John, QM Sgt., 9th Michigan Cavalry, Belle Isle Prison, Richmond, Va.:

Stormy and disagreeable weather. From fifteen to twenty and twenty-five die every day and are buried just outside the prison with no coffins—nothing but canvas wrapped around them. Eight sticks of four-foot wood given every squad of one hundred men today, and when split up and divided it amounted to nothing towards warming a person. Two or three can put their wood together and boil a little coffee made from bread crusts. The sick are taken out every morning and either sent over to the city or kept in the hospital just outside the prison and on the island. None are admitted unless carried out in blankets and so far gone there is not much chance of recovery. Medical attendance is scarce.

At Columbus, Ohio, John Hunt Morgan and several of his officers escaped from the Ohio State Penitentiary, and made their way to the South. Much speculation as to exactly how the escape was effected would appear in newspapers and journals for years, even into the 20th century.

### November 28 (Saturday)

For weeks there has been an outcry in the North about the lack of exchange of prisoners and a rash of reports of the treatment being received by the Union troops in Southern prisons. The problem was not simple in its form and certainly not in its solution. Maj. Gen. E.A. Hitchcock of the Adjutant-General's office in Washington prepared an article to be released to the *New York Times* outlining the problem on the exchange. Excerpts are shown below:

The public appears to be in need of information on the subject of the exchange of prisoners of war. The condition of our men held as prisoners of war in Richmond, the extreme sufferings to which they have been subjected, contrary to the usages of war and the dictates of humanity, have naturally aroused the sympathies of our people, and the question is asked by many, Why are they not exchanged?

I propose to furnish you a statement of facts....

On the 16th of January of the present year Col. Ludlow,... as the agent of exchange under the cartel which was published in September 1862, addressed me a letter, forwarding a copy of the Richmond *Enquirer* of the 15th of that month containing a message to the rebel Congress from Jefferson Davis referring to the proclamation of the President of the United States, dated the 1st of January.... The denunciatory character of Mr. Davis's message leveled against the proclamation of the President ... will be remembered by most of your readers at this time.

One passage ... very clearly indicates the policy

then determined upon in the South...

*So far as regards the action of this Government on such criminals as may attempt its execution (referring to the proclamation of the President of the United States), I confine myself to informing you that I shall, unless in your wisdom you deem some other course more expedient, deliver to the several State authorities all commissioned officers of the United States that may hereafter be captured by our forces in any of the States embraced in the proclamation that they may be dealt with in accordance with the laws of those States providing for the punishment of criminals engaged in exciting servile insurrection.*

...the threatening character of Mr. Davis's declared purpose, as set out in his message, it has been thrown entirely into the shade by subsequent events....

... When the Congress of the United States proceeded to authorize by law the employment of colored troops for the suppression of the rebellion there was, throughout the whole length and breadth of the South, one universal cry of real or well-affected indignation, accompanied with the wildest threats of vengeance against such officers as might be captured with colored troops; while the colored soldiers themselves, it was everywhere declared, should be either "returned or sold into slavery."...

What has actually been done up to the present time in the South in obedience to this spirit of vengeance so openly declared it may be impossible to determine in detail ... but ... in no single instance has the smallest evidence come to light tending to show that any officer connected with colored troops has been captured alive and held in the South as a prisoner of war; nor has any colored man employed as a soldier of the United States been captured in the South and accounted for as a prisoner of war. To any reasonable man this glaring fact might be sufficient to show the fell purposes of the rebel authorities to countenance, if they have not directly ordered, the destruction of this class of troops whenever and wherever they unhappily fall into their power....

... When the rebel agent of exchange offers, as he has done, to exchange all the prisoners of war in his hands against all that we have in our hands, the surplus to remain on parole, it would manifest the most stupid blindness on our part to imagine for one moment that he has ever intended to include colored troops as subject to exchange....

... Only a few weeks since a proposition was

*William Hoffman (on steps), Federal Commissary-General of prisoners*

*The hanging of Henry Wirz, Washington, D.C., 1865*

*Rock Island Prison, Rock Island, Ill.*

A

*Confederate prisoners at Belle Plain, near Fredericksburg, Va.*

*Old Capitol Prison, Washington, D.C.*

*The burnt district of Richmond, Va., 1865*

John Henry Winder, pictured before the war
in Union uniform

(Above). Eliab Hickman,
before his imprisonment at
Andersonville

A hospital railway car

C

*19th Iowa Regt. officers after their release*

*Belle Isle Prison, Richmond, Va.*

*Roper Hospital, Charleston, S.C.*

*Camp Douglas, Chicago, Ill.*

*Confederate military prison, Salisbury, N.C.*

*Another photo of the 19th Iowa Regt. officers*

E

*Libby Prison, Richmond, Va.*

**Elmira Prison Camp.**

*Elmira Prison Camp, Elmira, N.Y.*

*Confederate prisoners at Belle Plain, Va.*

*Castle Pinckney, used as a prison in Charleston Harbor*

*Ruins of the Circular Church, Charleston, S.C., 1865*

*Castle Thunder, Richmond, Va.*

G

*Stockade on Morris Island, S.C., used to house the "Immortal 600"*

*Sketch of Andersonville Prison, Ga.*

*Stereopticon view of the house in Charleston, S.C., where Federal officers were confined while under Union fire*

made from our side that all chaplains held as prisoners of war should be mutually released, irrespective of numbers, on either side. The rebel agent, Mr. Ould, professed to accept this proposition "cordially," upon which we sent to the South all we had of that class of noncombatants in good faith and received from the South about one half the number belonging to us, supposing this was all they had in custody; but, as I now learn ... a chaplain belonging to a Massachusetts colored regiment upon being captured was heavily ironed and sent to a prison in Columbia, S.C., where he has been held in violation of Mr. Ould's "cordial" acceptance.... Within the past few days, upon a formal application made by Gen. Meredith at my instance to learn the history of two men who were reported to be and are believed to be officers of the Federal Army said to be in the hands of the enemy, Mr. Ould furnished to Gen. Meredith what purported to be the proceedings of a civil court in the State of Virginia, the testimony in the cases not being furnished, by which it appeared that the two men had been sentenced to a penitentiary for a term of years on a charge of negro stealing....

I suppose it unnecessary to proceed further into detail to show to the satisfaction of every one who is willing to accept the truth that the practice of the South has been and is entirely in keeping with the spirit of Mr. Davis's message to the rebel Congress ... and I hold it to be certain that while they will keep from the light as much as possible their barbarous practices they will pursue them inexorably unless they can be made to feel that the national power is the strongest....

It has been supposed, even in many parts of the North, that the proposition of Mr. Ould of the 20th of October for an exchange of prisoners is fair and ought to be accepted, but it does not appear to be considered that Mr. Ould has not proposed to yield to us a certain number of prisoners of war and receive a like number in return, which would be a most happy consummation that would be at once accepted by this Government. But his proposition is that we shall deliver to him all of the prisoners in our possession, amounting now to about 40,000 men, and receive in return about 13,000 men, leaving about 27,000 men who might, for a few days, be considered on parole ... and then what would Mr. Ould do with those men?

Judging by what he has actually done, he would undoubtedly assume to discharge those men from all obligations under their parole and put them into the field to fight against nation[al] troops ... the very troops who gallantly captured those men upon bloody battlefields within the past few months.

To show the extreme probability of this ... Gen. Meredith, officially communicated to me, that he (Mr. Ould) would "proceed to make declarations of exchanges whenever he conscientiously felt the right to do so, for the purpose of putting men into the field," thus openly setting aside the cartel ... in favor of his individual sense of right, which sense of right in Mr. Ould is so obtuse and wild as to justify him in making use of a "tabular statement" of alleged captures, principally in the Western States, amounting to over 18,000 men, a considerable portion of whom were undoubtedly captured by guerrilla parties and were not soldiers, but for the most part peaceable citizens of the country.... And this class of persons Mr. Ould expects us to accept in exchange for rebel troops, captured mostly at Vicksburg, who, having been paroled in the South, were "declared" exchanged by Mr. Ould without any conference or understanding with our agent, in violation of the provisions of the cartel....

It must be borne in mind that the cartel was virtually abrogated by the message of Mr. Davis; not, indeed, as to its binding character upon the South, for Mr. Davis had no power under the laws of war to abrogate the provisions of that instrument, but his declared purposes, in violation of the cartel, would have fully justified the United States Government in declaring its provisions null and void, while at the same time the Government has been at liberty to require its observance on the part of the South....

Mr. Ould is a mere agent under the cartel and has no powers beyond those recognized in the cartel for the execution of its provisions, yet he has recently assumed to decide an important question by which he undertook to liberate from the obligations of their parole the whole of the prisoners, some 6000 or 7000, captured by Gen. Banks at Port Hudson and paroled by Gen. Banks under a special agreement with the rebel commander....

The cartel for the exchange of prisoners provided for two places for their delivery, to whit, City Point, on the James River, and Vicksburg, on the Mississippi; but it provided also that when either of these places should become unavailable by the exigencies of war for the delivery of prisoners other points might be "agreed upon" by the commanders in the field.... Vicksburg having fallen into the hands of Gen. Grant, had by that exigency become unavailable for the delivery of captured rebel soldiers, and when subsequently Gen. Banks came into possession of several thousand prisoners by the unconditional surrender of Port Hudson he made an agreement with the rebel Gen. Gardner, their commander, to deliver his prisoners on parole at Mobile, and did so.

Mr. Ould, without any proper authority whatever, assumed to write a letter on the 10th of October last, a copy of which he has not furnished us, but which has been published in a Richmond newspaper, in which he attempts to release all of those prisoners from obligations under their parole, because, as he undertakes to decide, they were not delivered at places named in the cartel.... In the meantime, however, it cannot be doubted that the body of men in question have been put into the field....

... I have received an official report ... that Gen. Meredith, for the purpose of withdrawing our suffering prisoners from Richmond, distinctly proposed to Mr. Ould that he would send him 12,000 or more Confederate prisoners, as many as he might hold of our men, and receive in return our prisoners held in the South, which proposition Mr. Ould refused to accept, but said that he would agree to a general exchange, the effect of which undoubtedly would be to cancel the excess of prisoners in our hands by a delivery of about 40,000 for about 13,000; to leave the rebel authorities the entire disposition of such colored troops and their white officers as they might capture....

We consider at this time the rebel authorities owe us upon the exchange list more than all the prisoners of war they now hold as equivalent for the prisoners paroled by Gens. Grant and Banks; and even already the question has come up from ... Chattanooga as to what shall be done with a body of the enemy who, having been paroled as prisoners of war at Vicksburg, have been recaptured in arms at Chattanooga without having been properly exchanged.

Ransom, John, QM Sgt., 9th Michigan Cavalry, Belle Isle Prison, Richmond, Va.:

Very cold and men suffer terribly with hardly any clothing on some of them. A man taken outside today, bucked and gagged for talking with a guard; a severe punishment for this very cold weather.

## November 30 (Monday)

Jones, John B., Rebel War Clerk, Confederate War Dept., Richmond, Va.:

Capt. Warner has sold me two pieces of bacon again, out of his own smokehouse, at $1 per pound, while it is selling in the market at $3.50 per pound—and he has given us another bushel of sweet potatoes. Had it not been for this kind friend, my little revenue would not have sufficed for subsistence.

## December 1 (Tuesday)

Ransom, John, QM Sgt., 9th Michigan Cavalry, Belle Isle Prison, Richmond, Va.:

With no news concerning the great subject—exchange of prisoners. Very hungry and am not having a good time of it. Take it all around I begin to wish I had stayed at home and was at the *Jackson Citizen* office pulling the old press. Dream continually night about something good to eat.... Have succeeded in getting into the tent with Hendryx. One of the mess has been sent over to Richmond Hospital leaving a vacancy which I am to fill.... Gen. Neil Dow today came over from Libby Prison on parole of honor to help issue some clothing that has arrived for Belle Isle prisoners from the Sanitary Commission at the North.... A man froze to death last night where I slept. The body lay until nearly dark before it was removed.

## December 2 (Wednesday)

Ransom, John, QM Sgt., 9th Michigan Cavalry, Belle Isle Prison, Richmond, Va.:

Pleasant weather and favorable for prisoners. At about nine in the morning the work of hunting for vermin commences, and all over camp sit the poor starved wretches, nearly stripped, engaged in picking off and killing the big gray backs. The ground is fairly alive with them, and it requires continual labor to keep from being eaten up alive by them. I just saw a man shot. He was called down to the bank by the guard, and as he leaned over to do some trading another guard close by shot him through the side and it is said mortally wounded him.... The wounded man was taken to the hospital and has since died.... Food twice today; buggy bean soup and a very small allowance of corn bread. Hungry all the time.

## December 3 (Thursday)

Ransom, John, QM Sgt., 9th Michigan Cavalry, Belle Isle Prison, Richmond, Va.:

Gen. Dow is still issuing clothing, but the rebels get more than our men do of it. Guards nearly all dressed in Yankee uniforms. In our mess we have established regulations, and any one not conforming with the rules is to be turned out of the tent. Must take plenty of exercise, keep clean, free as circumstances will permit of vermin, drink no water until it has been boiled, which process purifies and makes it more healthy, are not to allow ourselves to get despondent, and must talk, laugh and make as light of our affairs as possible. Sure death for a person to give up and lose all ambition. Received a spoonful of salt today for the first time since I came here.

## December 4 (Friday)

At Point Lookout, Md., Brig. Gen. Gilman Marston, commander of the prison, is highly incensed at the report of Mr. Frederick Knapp, U.S. Sanitary Commission, that was sent to Col. William Hoffman, Federal Commissary-General of Prisoners, on November 27th. His reply to the report is shown briefly:

Of the report I have to remark that one more disingenuous and false could not well have been made. It is surprising that the commission should employ agents so stupid or dishonest as the author of this report.

You know the number of prisoners here and the monthly savings from their rations, and of course do not require to be told that the statements respecting their rations are erroneous in every particular....

For the month of November the allowance per man was 13.3 ounces of bread, 8.1 ounces of meats, of vegetables and molasses the full ration; a pint of coffee on the days when soup is served and on other days a quart.

The statement that two men had been killed by the guard is simply untrue. No one has been killed by the guard or by any one else since the camp was established....

Every bed in the hospital is supplied with two blankets. There is a laundry for cleansing the clothing of sick men and the hospital is abundantly supplied with wash basins, towels and soap....

The surgeon has all the table furniture he desires, and the supply is ample. For the use of the sick the surgeon has had farina, cornstarch, meal, soft crackers, fruit, beef extract, wine, jelly, and cordials.... Wounded men are alone in one tent, erysipelas patients alone in another.... Frequent inspections are made and coats, pants, shirts, shoes, and blankets issued as health and decency require. According to the report the camp is a little over 1000 feet square and contains sixteen acres. A child ten years old who did not know and could not find out that a plat of ground 1000 feet square contained over twenty-three acres would not be regarded as a very surprising genius.

The sinks for use by day are without the encampment and over the waters of the Chesapeake, and they have been so from the beginning. For use at night boxes have been provided, which at reveille are removed to the bay and cleansed. This has been done since the date of the report. The camp is policed every day. The drainage is not good, and will not be until some genius equally as brilliant as the author of this report in question discovers a method of causing water to flow as readily from a level surface not much elevated above the surrounding seas.

The prisoners are treated as prisoners of war ought to be by a civilized people, and they and their friends are content. They have shelter, clothing, and wholesome food sufficient to insure vigorous health. They have an abundance of fresh water in the camp and daily access to the waters of the bay. That they are a dirty, lousy set is true enough, but having afforded them every facility for cleanliness the duty of the Government in this regard as respects well men is accomplished.

Now, colonel, come and inspect the camp yourself or send some one, a soldier or army surgeon, who knows what camp life is and who has sufficient ability to apprehend the facts and integrity enough to state them.

Ransom, John, QM Sgt., 9th Michigan Cavalry, Belle Isle Prison, Richmond, Va.:

Rather colder than yesterday; a great many sick and dying off rapidly. Rebel guards are more strict than usual, and one risks his life by speaking to them at all. Wrote a letter home today.... We call our establishment the "Astor House of Belle Isle." There are so many worse off than we are that we are very well contented and enjoy ourselves after a fashion.

In the west the problem of exchanging officers who served in Negro regiments was being somewhat solved by the local commanders, Gen. Richard Taylor, CSA, and Maj. Gen. W.B. Franklin, USA. Taylor agreed to shut his eyes to the official Confederate policy of not exchanging this category of officer for the time being. He notified Franklin that "he has no prisoners who are officers of Negro regiments. He expresses willingness to exchange officers and men, officer for officer and man for man, without acknowledging the principle that officers of Negro regiments are subject to exchange or without saying anything about it."

Thomas, D.C., Texas Cavalry, prisoner, Alton, Ill.:

After some two weeks ten or fifteen of us were pronounced sufficiently recovered to return to prison, and each of us was furnished with a pair of old blue pants with a large hole cut in the seat and an old army overcoat with the tail bobbed off in an unshapely manner. These garments, which they compelled us to wear, they called the "Jeff Davis uniform."

The sun had shown out for several days, and the ice on the river was beginning to thaw. We were marched across the river, a distance of about a mile, sinking into the mush ice up to the top of our shoes at every step, and when we reached the city and were again incarcerated in the old penitentiary my feet were wet, half-frozen, and a ring of ice around each ankle. Why this trip did not kill us all is more than I can explain....

### December 5 (Saturday)

Edwin M. Stanton, Union Secy. of War, forwarded a report prepared by Maj. Gen. Henry W. Halleck, General-in-Chief of the Union Army, on the status of Confederate prisoners now held by the Union:

In the operations that have been alluded to, prisoners of war to the number of about 13,000 have fallen into the hands of the enemy and are now held by them. From the commencement of the rebellion until the War Department came into my charge there was no cartel or formal exchange of prisoners; but at an early period afterward a just and reasonable cartel was made between Maj. Gen. Dix and the rebel Gen. Hill, which, until recently, was faithfully acted upon by both parties. Exchanges under that cartel are now stopped, mainly for the following reasons:

First. At Vicksburg over 30,000 rebel prisoners fell into our hands, and over 5000 more at Port Hudson. These prisoners were paroled and suffered to return to their homes until exchanged pursuant to the terms of the cartel. But the rebel agent, in violation of the cartel, declared the Vicksburg prisoners exchanged; and, without being exchanged, the Port Hudson prisoners he, without just cause, and in open violation of the cartel, declared released from their parole. These prisoners were returned to their ranks, and a portion of them were found fighting at Chattanooga and again captured. For this breach of faith, unexampled in civilized warfare, the only apology or excuse was that an equal number of prisoners had been captured by the enemy. But, on calling for specifications in regard to these alleged prisoners, it was found that a considerable number represented as prisoners were not soldiers, but were noncombatants—citizens of towns and villages, farmers, travelers, and others in civil life, not captured in battle, but taken at their homes, on their farms, or on the highway, by John Morgan and other rebel raiders, who put them under a sham parole. To balance these men against rebel soldiers taken on the field would be relieving the enemy from the pressure of war and enable him to protract the contest to indefinite duration.

Second. When the Government commenced organizing colored troops the rebel leader, Davis, by solemn and official proclamation, announced that the colored troops and their white officers, if captured, would not be recognized as prisoners of war, but would be given up for punishment by the State authorities.

These proceedings of the rebel authorities were met by the earnest remonstrance and protest of this Government, without effect. The offers of our commissioner to exchange man for man and officer for officer, or to receive and provide for our own soldiers, under the solemn guarantee that they should not go into the field until duly exchanged, were rejected. In the meantime well authenticated statements show that our troops held as prisoners of war were deprived of shelter, clothing, and food, and some have perished from exposure and famine. This savage barbarity could only have been practiced in the hope that this Government would be compelled, by sympathy for the suffering endured by our troops, to yield to the proposition of exchanging all the prisoners of war on both sides, paroling the excess not actually exchanged; the effect to which operation would be to enable the rebels to put into the field a new army 40,000 strong, forcing the paroled prisoners into the ranks without exchange as was done with those paroled at Vicksburg and Port Hudson, and also to leave in the hands of the rebels the colored soldiers and officers, who are not regarded by them as prisoners of war, and therefore not entitled to the benefit of the proposed exchange.

Ransom, John, QM Sgt., 9th Michigan Cavalry, Belle Isle Prison, Richmond, Va.:

Cold and raw weather with no wood. Men are too weak to walk nights to keep warm, sink down and chill to death. At least a dozen were carried out this morning feet foremost.

Gov. David Tod, of Ohio, a little red-faced about John Hunt Morgan escaping from the Ohio State Penitentiary, notified Secy. of War Stanton that two of the captains that escaped with Morgan had been recaptured near Louisville, Ky. They had reached Louisville by train after waiting in a cornfield for nearly forty-eight hours. The recaptured officers refused to provide any information on Morgan.

### December 6 (Sunday)

Ransom, John, QM Sgt., 9th Michigan Cavalry, Belle Isle Prison, Richmond, Va.:

One month a prisoner today—longer than any year of my life before. Hope I am not to see another month in the Confederacy. A great deal of stealing going on among the men. There are organized bands of raiders who do pretty much as they please. A ration of bread is often of more consequence than a man's life. Have received food but once today; very cold; at least one hundred men limping around with frozen feet, and some of them crying like little children. Am at work on the outside today; go out at nine in the morning and return at four in the afternoon, and by right smart figuring carry in much extra food for tent mates, enough to give all hands a good square meal.

### December 7 (Monday)

At Ft. Monroe, Va., Maj. Gen. Benjamin F. Butler, commanding the Department of Virginia and North Carolina, learned of an epidemic of smallpox among the Federal prisoners at Belle Isle in Richmond and farther west in Lynchburg, Va. Butler took action and communicated with Robert Ould, Confederate Commissioner of Exchange in Richmond:

Sir: I have been informed that the smallpox has unfortunately broken out among the prisoners of war now in the hands of the Confederate authorities, both at Belle Isle and at Lynchburg.

Anxious from obvious humane considerations to prevent the spread of this terrible disorder, I have taken leave to forward for their use, by Maj. Mulford, assistant agent of exchange, in behalf of the United States, a package of vaccine matter sufficient, as my medical director informs me, to vaccinate six thousand persons. May I ask that it shall be applied under the direction of the proper medical officer to the use intended.

Being uncertain how far I can interfere as a matter of official duty, I beg you to consider this note either official or unofficial as may best serve the purposes of alleviating the distresses of these unfortunate men....

No formal receipt is needed; a note acknowledging the receipt of this being all that can be desired.

If more vaccine matter is necessary, it will be furnished....

### December 8 (Tuesday)

Ransom, John, QM Sgt., 9th Michigan Cavalry, Belle Isle Prison, Richmond, Va.:

The men all turned out of the enclosure and are being squadded over. A very stormy and cold day; called out before breakfast and nearly dark before again sent inside. Very muddy and the men have suffered terribly, stand up all day in the cold drizzling rain, with no chance for exercise and many barefooted. I counted nine or ten who went out in the morning not able to get back at night; three of the number being dead.

Thomas, D.C., Texas Cavalry, prisoner, Alton, Ill.:

A few days later I was stricken with pneumonia, followed by flux, and although that eminent physician and true friend of mine, Dr. Riley, gave me every attention, he despaired of saving my life, and my messmates were permitted, one by one, to visit me and to look on me, as they supposed, for the last time in life. I well knew that Dr. Riley had lost hope, and requested him to administer a powerful stimulant, which he did, to gratify what he supposed my last wish. The stimulant had the desired effect, and I was soon asleep. When I awoke Dr. Riley was standing by me with a smiling countenance. He inquired if I wished the stimulant repeated, and when I answered in the negative he told me to try to sleep and that I would soon be up again.

### December 9 (Wednesday)

Following the shipment of the smallpox vaccine matter to Confederate authorities two days previously, Maj. Gen. Benj. F. Butler today received a response from Robert Ould, Confederate Commissioner of Exchange:

Sir: The package of vaccine matter has been received and will be faithfully devoted to the purposes indicated in your letter. Permit me in response to the friendly tone of your letter to assure you that it is my most anxious desire and will be my constant effort to do everything in my power to alleviate the miseries that spring out of this terrible war.

Ransom, John, QM Sgt., 9th Michigan Cavalry, Belle Isle Prison, Richmond, Va.:

Rumors that one thousand go off today to our lines and the same number every day until all are removed. It was not believed until a few moments ago the Lieutenant stepped upon the bank and said that in less than a week we would all be home again, and such a cheering among us; every man who could yell had his mouth stretched.... All in good spirits and we talk of the good dinners we will get on the road home. Food twice today and a little salt.

### December 10 (Thursday)

Ransom, John, QM Sgt., 9th Michigan Cavalry, Belle Isle Prison, Richmond, Va.:

Instead of prisoners going away five hundred more have come, which makes it very crowded. Some are still confident we will go away soon, but I place no reliance on rebel reports.... A priest in the camp distributing tracts. Men told him to bring bread; they want no tracts. Exchange news has died away, and more despondent than ever. I today got hold of a Richmond *Enquirer* which spoke of bread riots in the city, women running around the streets and yelling, "Peace or bread!"

### December 11 (Friday)

Ransom, John, QM Sgt., 9th Michigan Cavalry, Belle Isle Prison, Richmond, Va.:

Was on guard last night over the clothing outside. Lt. Bossieux asked Corp. McCarten and myself to eat supper with him last night, which we were very glad to do. Henry, the negro servant, said to the lieutenant after we had got through eating: "I golly, masser, don't nebber ask dem boys to eat with us again, dey eat us clean gone"; and so we did eat everything on the table and looked for more.

### December 12 (Saturday)

Ransom, John, QM Sgt., 9th Michigan Cavalry, Belle Isle Prison, Richmond, Va.:

At just daylight I got up and was walking around the prison to see if any Michigan men had died through the night, and was just in time to see a young fellow come out of his tent nearly naked and deliberately walk up the steps that lead over the bank. Just as he got on the top the guard fired; sending a ball through his brain, and the poor fellow fell dead in the ditch. He had been sick for a number of days and was burning up with fever, and no doubt deranged at the time.... His name was Perry McMichael, and he was from Minnesota.

### December 13 (Sunday)

Ransom, John, QM Sgt., 9th Michigan Cavalry, Belle Isle Prison, Richmond, Va.:

The officers come over from Richmond every day or two, and make a showing of issuing clothing. The work goes on slowly, and it would seem that if clothing was ever needed and ought to be issued, it is now; yet the officers seem to want to nurse the job and make it last as long as possible.... The death rate increases from day to day. A little Cincinnati soldier died today. Was captured same time as myself.... I have many talks with the rebels, and am quite a privileged character. By so doing am able to do much for the boys inside, and there are good boys in there...

Thomas, D.C., Texas Cavalry, prisoner, Alton, Ill.:

When I was well enough to return to my mess I learned that a roll was being made up of those who had recovered from smallpox, and that they would be sent somewhere, but we could not learn where. At all events, they were to leave Alton; and, although I was very weak, I determined to try to have my name enrolled, and at least start away from that abominable old penitentiary. Dr. Riley tried to prevail on me to remain, and informed me that he had the promise of a position as medical director on the smallpox island; that if I would remain he would secure me a position as superintendent of gardening on the island, and that we two could certainly make our escape and go to Canada. The prospect was tempting, but I did not believe that I could live there until spring, and determined to leave, although I did not know where I was going or what would be my fate. The Doctor carried out his program, made his escape, and, under an assumed name, wrote to me from Canada. My name was enrolled, and on February 29, 1864, with the assistance of friends, I boarded the train, and was soon whirling over the prairies of Illinois.

A day or two later we learned our destination was Ft. Delaware, and that it was simply a hell on earth, a statement which I afterward learned was literally true.

Thomas, and his fellow travellers, arrived at Ft. Delaware on March 5, 1864, after six days of travel in boxcars without any sanitary accommodations, little to eat, and few facilities for warming. Thomas was not released from Ft. Delaware until June 1865. He returned to Texas, studied law, and became a judge in Lampasas, Tex.

### December 16 (Wednesday)

Malone, B.Y., Sgt., Co. H, 6th N.C. Infantry, CSA, prisoner, Point Lookout, Md.:

...a Yankey Captain shot his Pistel among our men and wounded 5 of them since one has died—he shot them for crowding arond the gate. The captain's naim that shot was Sids.

### December 17 (Thursday)

Ransom, John, QM Sgt., 9th Michigan Cavalry, Belle Isle Prison, Richmond, Va.:

I have plenty to eat. Go outside every day whether clothing is issued or not.... Officers stay on the island only two or three hours, and clothe four or five hundred men, when they could just as well do

three or four times as much. It is comical the notes that come in some of the good warm woolen stockings. These have evidently been knit by the good mothers, wives and sisters at the North, and some of the romantic sort have written letters and placed inside, asking the receiver to let them know about himself, his name, etc,

### December 18 (Friday)

Ransom, John, QM Sgt., 9th Michigan Cavalry, Belle Isle Prison, Richmond, Va.:

Today as a squad was drawn up in front of us, waiting for clothing, I saw an Irishman in the ranks who looked familiar. Looked at him for some time and finally thought I recognized in him an old neighbor of mine in Jackson, Michigan; one Jimmy Devers, a whole souled and comical genius as ever it was my fortune to meet. Went up to him and asked what regiment he belonged to; said he belonged to the 23d [19th ?] Indiana, at which I could not believe it was my old acquaintance. Went back to my work. Pretty soon he said to me: "Ain't you Johnny Ransom?" And then I knew I was right. He had lived in Jackson, but had enlisted in an Indiana regiment. Well, we were glad to see one another and you may just bet that Jimmy got as good a suit of clothes as ever he had in our lines. Jimmy is a case; was captured on the 1st day of July at the Gettysburg battle, and is consequently an old prisoner. Is very tough and hardy.

### December 20 (Sunday)

Ransom, John, QM Sgt., 9th Michigan Cavalry, Belle Isle Prison, Richmond, Va.:

James River frozen nearly over, and rebels say it has not been so cold for years as at the present time. There are hundreds with frozen feet, ears, hands &c., and laying all over the prison; the suffering is terrible.... Got a letter from home, everybody is well. They say keep up a good heart and we will be exchanged before many weeks.

### December 21 (Monday)

Ransom, John, QM Sgt., 9th Michigan Cavalry, Belle Isle Prison, Richmond, Va.:

Still cold. Have enough to eat myself, but am one of a thousand. The scurvy is appearing among some of the men, and is an awful disease—caused by want of vegetable diet, acids, &c. Two smallpox cases taken to the hospital today. A sutler has been established on the island and sells at the following rates: poor brown sugar, $8 per pound; butter, $11; cheese, $10; sour milk $3 per quart and the only article I buy; eggs, $10 per dozen; oysters, $6 per quart and the cheapest food in market.

War Clerk Jones, in Richmond, wrote that "Such is the scarcity of provisions, that rats and mice have mostly disappeared, and the cats can hardly be kept off the table."

## December 22 (Tuesday)

At Salisbury, N.C., Brig. Gen. John H. Winder, Confederate Commissary-General of Prisoners, telegraphed James A. Seddon, Confederate Secy. of War in Richmond that three Union officers had been selected "to undergo hard labor during the war in the penitentiary at Salisbury, N.C., for a like number of our own officers confined in the penitentiary at Alton, Ill."

Ransom, John, QM Sgt., 9th Michigan Cavalry, Belle Isle Prison, Richmond, Va.:

A large mail came this morning, but nothing for me. A man who gets a letter is besieged with questions, and a crowd gathers around to learn the news.... Rations smaller than usual, and Lt. Bossieux says that it is either exchange or starve with us prisoners sure, as they have not the food to give us.... Lots of Sanitary [Commission] stores sent on to the island for us, but as yet none have been issued, the rebels (officers in particular), getting fat on what rightfully belongs to us.

## December 23 (Wednesday)

Ransom, John, QM Sgt., 9th Michigan Cavalry, Belle Isle Prison, Richmond, Va.:

Almost Christmas and we are planning for a Christmas dinner. Very cold.... A woman found among us—a prisoner of war. Some one who knew the secret informed Lt. Bossieux and he immediately had her taken outside, when she told him the whole story—how she had "followed her lover a soldiering" in disguise, and being of a romantic turn, enjoyed it hugely until the funny part was done away with, and Madame Collier, from East Ten-

nessee, found herself in durance vile; nothing to do but make the best of it and conceal her sex if possible, hoping for a release, which, however, did not come in the shape she wished. The lieutenant has sent her over to Richmond to be cared for and she is to be sent north by the first flag of truce boat. She tells of another female being among us, but as yet she has not been found out.

## December 24 (Thursday)

Ransom, John, QM Sgt., 9th Michigan Cavalry, Belle Isle Prison, Richmond, Va.:

Must hang up my stocking tonight for habit's sake if nothing else. I am enjoying splendid health, and prison life agrees with me. Wrote home today.

## December 25 (Friday)

This Christmas will long be remembered by a group of 502 Confederate prisoners who were repatriated at City Point, Va. The gesture was made by Maj. Gen. Benj. F. Butler, commanding at Ft. Monroe, Va., for the prisoners formally at Point Lookout, Md. Butler, having recently inspected that prison camp, decided to send south those prisoners who were, borderline, either too ill or handicapped for further military service. He addresses the matter to Robert Ould, Confederate Commissioner of Exchange:

Sir: I send by Maj. Mulford, assistant commissioner of exchange, (502) five hundred and two prisoners of war, from the confederate army, from Point Lookout—all I believe, serviceable men, and substantially those longest there in confinement.

I offer them for delivery at City Point, upon condition of receiving the same number of men held by your authorities as prisoners of war,... leaving all questions of difference ... in abeyance.

I have made personal examination of the condition of the prisoners of war of the confederate army, now in prison at Point Lookout, and beg leave to assure you that they are as well cared for, and in as good health, and as well fed, as the soldiers in our army....

I do not mean to say that their ration is as large as our regularly issued ration, because of their state of entire inactivity; but it is in every respect of the same quality as those issued to the men generally....

I have made this examination, and this statement to you, in order that you may be able to satisfy the friends of the prisoners, who may be disturbed by the unfounded reports of ill treatment and cruelty suffered by the prisoners at Point Lookout, in like manner as our people are excited by what I hope are like groundless stories of ill usage and starvation suffered by our soldiers in your hands.

I find there some of the wounded from Gettysburg, and some that have been sick that are convalescent, and some so far disabled by sickness that while they may be sent forward for exchange, they will probably be of no further service in the field.

Men without arms and legs, and debilitated by sickness, are certainly unfit to bear the necessary hardships incident to a condition of prisoners of war; besides, they encumber our hospitals.

As, upon examination, I did not think it proper to order them into the prisoners' camp, with wounds freshly healed, and health hardly restored, and as perhaps the hope of seeing their friends might have a beneficial influence upon their health, therefore I suggest that in the next transport I send up as many of these as are entirely able to bear the exposures of traveling, without probable danger to their health, and that in exchange you will return to me an equal number of our soldiers that may be in like condition. As it may be inconvenient and prejudicial to their health to transship these invalids, on either side, I will have them put upon a separate boat, upon which there shall be nothing but provisions for them, and will direct that that boat be put at your disposal at City Point, to carry them immediately to Richmond, and bring back those that you shall give in exchange.

Ransom, John, QM Sgt., 9th Michigan Cavalry, Belle Isle Prison, Richmond, Va.:

Christmas. One year ago today first went into camp at Coldwater, little dreaming what changes a year would bring.... We had our good things for supper instead of dinner, and it was a big thing, consisting of corn bread and butter, oysters, coffee, beef, crackers, cheese, &c.; all we could possibly eat or do away with, and costing the snug little sum of $200 Confederate money, or $20 in greenbacks. Lay awake long before daylight listening to the bells. As they rang out Christmas good morning I imagined they

were in Jackson, Michigan, my old home, and from the spires of the old Presbyterian and Episcopal churches. Little do they think as they are saying their Merry Christmases and enjoying themselves so much, of the hunger and starving here.

Jones, John B., Rebel War Clerk, Confederate War Dept., Richmond:

It is a sad Christmas; cold, and threatening snow. My two youngest children, however, have decked the parlor with evergreens, crosses, stars, etc. They have a cedar Christmas-tree, but it is not burdened. Candy is held at $8 per pound. My two sons rose at 5 A.M. and repaired to the canal to meet their sister Anne, who has been teaching Latin and French in the country; but she was not among the passengers, and this has cast a shade of disappointment over the family. A few pistols and crackers are fired by the boys in the streets—and only a few.

Malone, B.Y., Sgt., Co. H, 6th N.C. Infantry, CSA, prisoner, Point Lookout, Md.:

The 25th was Christmas day and it was clear and cool and I was boath coal and hungry all day onley got a peace of Bread and cup of coffee for Breakfast and a small Slice of Meat and a cup of Soop and five Crackers for Dinner and Supper I had non.

### December 26 (Saturday)

Ransom, John, QM Sgt., 9th Michigan Cavalry, Belle Isle Prison, Richmond, Va.:

Extra quantity of wood. Rebels all drunk and very domineering. Punish for the smallest kind of excuse. Some men tunneled out of the pen but were retaken and were made to crawl back through the same hole they went out of and the lieutenant kept hitting them with a board as they went down and then ran back and forward from one hole to the other and as they stuck up their heads would hit them with a club, keeping them at it for nearly an hour.

### December 27 (Sunday)

Ransom, John, QM Sgt., 9th Michigan Cavalry, Belle Isle Prison, Richmond, Va.:

Col. Sanderson and Col. Boyd came over this morning in a great hurry and began to issue clothing very fast saying an exchange had been agreed upon and they wanted to get rid of it before we all went away. Pretty soon the news got inside and the greatest cheering, yelling, shaking of hands and congratulating one another took place. Just before dinner five hundred were taken out, counted and sent away.... Some of the outside went and the rest go tomorrow. It is a sure thing.... Extra ration of food and wood tonight and am anxiously waiting for the morrow.

### December 28 (Monday)

Ransom, John, QM Sgt., 9th Michigan Cavalry, Belle Isle Prison, Richmond, Va.:

For some reason or other no more being taken away and more despondent than ever. Very cold.

### December 29 (Tuesday)

Ransom, John, QM Sgt., 9th Michigan Cavalry, Belle Isle Prison, Richmond, Va.:

Nearly as cold weather as I ever saw at the North. All the supplies brought by hand over the long bridge owing to the river being frozen over and not strong enough to hold up. Rebel officers all drunk during the holidays. Snow an inch deep.

At Richmond, War Clerk Jones reported, "Mr. Ould, agent of exchange, has sent down some 500 prisoners, in exchange for a like number sent up by the enemy. But he has been instructed by the President not to hold correspondence with Gen. Butler, called 'the Beast,' who is in command at Fortress Monroe."

### December 30 (Wednesday)

Ransom, John, QM Sgt., 9th Michigan Cavalry, Belle Isle Prison, Richmond, Va.:

No rations issued yesterday to any of the prisoners and a third of all here are on the very point of starvation. Lt. Bossieux sympathizes with us in word but says it is impossible to help it as they have not the food for us. This is perhaps true as regards edibles but there is no excuse for our receiving small supplies of wood. They could give us plenty of shelter, plenty of wood and conveniences we do not now get if they felt so disposed.

### December 31 (Thursday)

Malone, B.Y., Sgt., Co. H, 6th N.C. Infantry, CSA, prisoner, Point Lookout, Md.:

The 31st which was the last day of 63 was a raney day. And maby I will never live to see the last day of 64. And thairfour I will try and do better than I have.

Ransom, John, QM Sgt., 9th Michigan Cavalry, Belle Isle Prison, Richmond, Va.:

Still very cold and no news encouraging. Rebels very strict. One prisoner found a brother among the guards who had been living in the south for a good many years and lately conscripted into the Confederate army. New Year's eve. Man wounded by the guard shooting, and ball broke his leg. Might better have shot him dead for he will surely die. Raw rice and corn bread issued today in small quantities. Richmond *Enquirer* spoke of the five hundred who left here day before yesterday and they have reached Washington.

The situation of the prisoners, North and South, was as muddied as it could get. Although the cartel was in effect, the South, with its political actions, had made it almost inoperative. This caused many administrative problems for the two governments, but not nearly the problems it caused for the prisoners. Both sides were guilty of abuse of prisoners, both intentionally and unintentionally. Both sides were doing stupid things that caused suffering among the prisoners. It seemed unfortunate that a former prisoner could not have become an Agent for Exchange. Perhaps the next year would be better.

# 1864

The war entered its fourth year and no end seemed in sight. The eastern armies were lying quietly in Virginia, one nearly starving, the other merely dormant. In the west, Grant had control of the situation in Tennessee, and the area farther west was fairly quiet. In the prison camps, life continued to be hard, the weather being extremely cold and disagreeable. Two of the more infamous camps, Andersonville and Elmira, had not, as yet, come into being. The battle over the exchange of prisoners continued.

## January 1 (Friday)

War Clerk Jones in Richmond reported that flour was now $150 per barrel. His friend, Capt. Warner, who was involved with feeding the prisoners in the area, sold Jones two bushels of meal at $5 per bushel. A good deal. The market price was $16 per bushel. But did the grain come from the prisoners' rations?

Ransom, John, QM Sgt., 9th Michigan Cavalry, Belle Isle Prison, Richmond, Va.:

A great time this morning wishing one another a Happy New Year. Robinson bought on the outside a dozen apples and gave us all a treat. Nothing but corn bread to eat and very poor quality. Dr. F.L. Lewis, Vet. Surg. 9th Mich. Cavalry, came in today; was captured at Dandridge, East Tennessee, where our regiment had a severe engagement. Tells me all the news.... Thinks we will be exchanged before many weeks.

Malone, B.Y., Sgt., Co. H, 6th N.C. Infantry, CSA, prisoner, Point Lookout, Md.:

I spent the first day of January 64 at Point Lookout, Md. The morning was plesant but towards evening the air changed and the nite was very coal. was so coal that five of our men froze to death befour morning. We all suffered a great deal with coal and hunger too of our men was hungry today that they caught a Rat and cooked him and eat it. Thir names was Sergt. N.W. Hester & I.E. Covington.

## January 2 (Saturday)

Col. Adrian R. Root, commander of Camp Parole, Md., wrote Col. Wm. Hoffman that the clothing in which the last group of prisoners wore from Richmond was "although comparatively new and in good condition, was filled with vermin to such an extent that it was considered best to reclothe the men entirely." Col. Root had the clothes boxed up and asked if they should be sent back to Richmond for reuse. Hoffman told him to at least get them cleaned first.

Ransom, John, QM Sgt., 9th Michigan Cavalry, Belle Isle Prison, Richmond, Va.:

Rebel congress about to meet, and the people of Richmond demand through the papers that the prisoners confined here be removed immediately, as there is hardly enough for themselves to eat, aside from feeding us "Northern Hirelings." Hear of bread riots and lots of trouble across the river. A big fire last night in the vicinity of Libby Prison.

### January 3 (Sunday)

At Camp Morton, Ind., Col. A.A. Stevens had received a shipment of clothing for the prisoners in his charge which he immediately distributed because of the extremely cold weather. He then submitted duplicate requisitions, with an explanation that many of the prisoners were nearly naked when they arrived.

Ransom, John, QM Sgt., 9th Michigan Cavalry, Belle Isle Prison, Richmond, Va.:

Received a letter from Michigan. Not quite so cold, but disagreeable weather. Nine men bucked and gagged at one time on the outside, two of them for stealing sour beans from a swill-barrel. They would get permission to pass through the gate to see the lieutenant, and instead, would walk around the cook-house to some barrels containing swill, scoop up their hats full and then run inside; but they were caught, and are suffering a hard punishment for it.

### January 4 (Monday)

Maj. Gen. S.A. Hurlbut, USA, commanding Six-teenth Army Corps, Memphis, Tenn., received a let-ter from Maj. Gen. Nathan B. Forrest concerning the exchange of prisoners. Forrest suggested an alter-native meeting place, which would reduce the fatigue of the prisoners. He then went on to say:

George M. Robertson, who is reported in your list of officers as second lieutenant Company B, McDonald's battalion, is not and never was an officer. He is a pri-vate, a deserter and a thief. In order to get him will give a man for him. He has represented himself falsely, as also have others on the same list belonging to Twelfth Tennessee Cavalry. They were men sent out to gather up absentees from the army and from their commands, but never were commissioned officers.

Ransom, John, QM Sgt., 9th Michigan Cavalry, Belle Isle Prison, Richmond, Va.:

Some ladies visited the island to see us blue coats, and laughed very much at our condition; thought it so comical and ludicrous the way the prisoners crowded the bank next the cook house, looking over at the piles of bread, and compared us to wild men, and hungry dogs. A chicken belonging to the lieu-tenant flew up on the bank and was snatched off in short order, and to pay for it we are not to receive a

mouthful of food today, making five or six thousand suffer for one man catching a little chicken.

### January 5 (Tuesday)

Ransom, John, QM Sgt., 9th Michigan Cavalry, Belle Isle Prison, Richmond, Va.:

Succeeded in getting Dr. Lewis into our tent; is rather under the weather, owing to exposure and hardship. Jimmy Devers spends the evenings with us and we have funny times talking over better days—and are nearly talked out.... We offer a reward for a good new story.

### January 6 (Wednesday)

Ransom, John, QM Sgt., 9th Michigan Cavalry, Belle Isle Prison, Richmond, Va.:

Some of the paroled Yankees on the outside curse and treat the inside prisoners more cruel (when they have a chance,) than the rebels themselves. Blass, a Spaniard, who has been a prisoner over a year and refuses to be exchanged, is the lieutenant's right hand man. He tied up a man a few days ago for some mis-demeanor and whipped him. He is afraid to come inside, knowing he would lose his life in a jiffy.

Malone, B.Y., Sgt., Co. H, 6th N.C. Infantry, CSA, prisoner, Point Lookout, Md.:

The 6th was coal and cloudy and we had 9 men die at the Hospital today. Our beds at this plaice is com-posed of Sea feathers that is we geather the small stones from the Bay and lye on them...

### January 7 (Thursday)

In Richmond, John B. Jones, Rebel War Clerk, recorded the arrival of Confederate Gen. John Hunt Morgan in the city to the delight of a host of admir-ers. This was Morgan's first visit since his escape from the Ohio Penitentiary last November.

Ransom, John, QM Sgt., 9th Michigan Cavalry, Belle Isle Prison, Richmond, Va.:

Rainy, cold and disagreeable weather.... A good deal of raiding is going on among the men. One Capt. Moseby commands a band of cut-throats who do nearly as they please, cheating robbing and knocking down—operating principally upon new prisoners who are unacquainted with prison life. Moseby is named after the rebel guerrilla, his real name being something else. He is from New York City, and is a regular bummer.

At Columbus, Ohio, Surgeon A.M. Clark, newly assigned Medical Inspector for Col. Hoffman's prison camps, reported that the condition of the camp was good except for the quarters of the 88th Ohio Volunteers. Upon inspection, Surgeon Clark found four cases of varioloid had recently occurred, the last case on the morning of his visit. The local surgeon, young and inexperienced, had not reported the cases to the commanding officer of the post. Clark took immediate remedial action.

### January 8 (Friday)

In Richmond, Gen. John H. Morgan dutifully received the congratulations of a host of admirers today. The Governor advertised a reception in Morgan's honor for this evening.

Ransom, John, QM Sgt., 9th Michigan Cavalry, Belle Isle Prison, Richmond, Va.:

All taken outside today to be squadded over—an all day job and nothing to eat. The men being in hundreds and some dying off every day, leave vacancies in the squads of as many as die out of them, and in order to keep them filled up have to be squadded over every few days, thereby saving rations. Richmond papers are much alarmed for fear of a break among the prisoners...

### January 9 (Saturday)

Col. Hoffman today wrote Brig. Gen. W.W. Orme, commanding Camp Douglas, Ill., concerning a case of fraud involving the rations furnished by local contractors. Hoffman directed immediate investigation of the fraud and stated that while the subcontractor may have been the one guilty of fraud, the prime contractor would be held accountable to the government for the action and would be required to reimburse the government for rations not provided, but for which they had been billed. Not much change in the operations of some government contractors since then.

In a follow-up, on February 20th, Col. Hoffman notified Brig. Gen. Orme that Messrs. Fowler & Co., the prime contractor furnishing the provisions in question, would be required to make good in money the deficiencies in beef, soap, and molasses, at a rate to be determined by Gen. Orme. The money collected was to be paid to the post or prison fund for use by the prisoners. In addition, Col. C.V. De Land, First Michigan Sharpshooters, the officer responsible for supervising the contracts, would be brought before a court-martial for trial. *Sometimes there was justice!*

Ransom, John, QM Sgt., 9th Michigan Cavalry, Belle Isle Prison, Richmond, Va.:

A signal light suspended over the island all last night for some reason.... One of the raiders went through a man who lay near the bank and started to run after robbing him. A guard who saw the whole affair shot the villain dead and was applauded by all who knew of the affair. Fifteen or twenty carried out this morning dead and thirty or forty nearly so in blankets.

### January 10 (Sunday)

From Ft. Delaware, Del., came welcome news. The smallpox epidemic had abated. In two weeks the number inflicted had dropped from 178 to only 84. No new cases had been reported.

Stanfield, N.B., 1st Ky. Cavalry, prisoner, Camp Douglas, Chicago, Ill.:

Our men died from diseases, including smallpox, and from cold and starvation. In 1864 there were about fifteen thousand prisoners in Camp Douglas, and about three thousand died during the nineteen months I was there. I was in the hospital for four months with a crippled leg. This hospital was in their camp, and had only four guards, while there were none around their camp. Upon recovering, I was made nurse in the hospital, and, with McDervett, the ward master, and Bob Vandever, of the First Missouri, planned escape. We decided to make a hole in the floor of the closet under the stairway, and crawl to the steps in front of the building, then tunnel under the fence, a distance of about fifteen feet. We kept the hole in the closet floor covered with clothing for the laundry. After preparations were complete, we waited until a dark, rainy night.

In North Carolina, Gov. Zebulon Vance took some matters into his own hands, according to John B. Jones, in Richmond:

Letters from Gov. Vance received today show that he has been making extensive arrangements to clothe and subsist North Carolina troops. His agents have purchased abroad some 40,000 blankets, as many shoes, bacon, etc., most of which is now at Bermuda and Nassau. He has also purchased an interest in several steamers; but, it appears, a recent regulation of the Confederate States Government forbids the import and export of goods except, almost exclusively, for the government itself. The governor desires to know if his State is to be put on the same footing with private speculators.

He also demands some thousands of bales of cotton, loaned the government—and which the government cannot now replace at Wilmington—and his complaints against the government are bitter.

### January 11 (Monday)

Surgeon A.M. Clark, Col. Hoffman's man on the road, today submitted a report on the conditions at Johnson's Island, Ohio:

Prison quarters ... are, with but one or two exceptions, filthy, the prisoners policing or not ... left to the caprice of the prisoners themselves. The kitchens are filthy, with all their utensils, and the ground around the outer doors covered with filth and slops frozen to the depth of several inches. The grounds show no evidence of having been policed for a long time. Sinks ... are in a filthy condition.... The principal cause urged by the prisoners for their filthy condition is the scarcity of water, caused by the freezing of the pumps.... This excuse, however, will not hold good, for there is no difficulty in obtaining a sufficient supply of water from the lake. Ventilation ... there is an utter absence of ventilation in all the quarters, and to this fact, together with that of their being generally overheated and almost constantly crowded ... is attributable the great majority of the cases of disease which occur among the prisoners. Hospital ... the kitchen ... though small can be made to answer its purpose. It is under the charge of a Confederate major, whom the surgeon in charge states to be a competent cook.... Statistics—the total number of prisoners during the month of December 1863 was 2625. Number of sick reported, 219; deaths, 18.

Jones, John B., Rebel War Clerk, Confederate War Dept., Richmond, Va.:

Gen. E.S. [W.E.] Jones has captured several hundred of the enemy in Southwest Virginia, and Moseby's men are picking them up by the score in Northern Virginia.

Ransom, John, QM Sgt., 9th Michigan Cavalry, Belle Isle Prison, Richmond, Va.:

A steady rain for twenty-four hours, and have not been dry during the time.... As I came inside tonight with some bread in my haversack some fellows who were on the watch pitched into me and gobbled my saved up rations. I don't care for myself for I have been to supper, but the boys in the tent will have to go without anything to eat for this night.

### January 12 (Tuesday)

At Ft. Monroe, Va., Maj. Gen. Benjamin F. Butler had been appointed as the Agent for Exchange for the Union, an appointment which was violently objected to by President Davis of the Confederacy, who had branded Butler "an outlaw," and many other names. Robert Ould, Confederate Agent for Exchange, had written a letter to Maj. Gen. E.A. Hitchcock in Washington saying that the South would not accept Butler in the assigned role. Today, Butler responded to Ould:

Sir: Your note addressed to Maj. Gen. Hitchcock, in relation to the appointment by the Government of the United States of a commissioner of exchange, is returned.

This Government claims and exercises the power of appointing its own agents to represent its interests, irrespective of any supposed sanction by the Confederate authorities.

No right of declaration of outlawry by those authorities of any officer or soldier of the United States can be admitted or for a moment regarded by the Government of the United States, as it certainly will not be by the persons upon whom such intimidation is attempted.

I am instructed to renew the offer, leaving all other questions in abeyance, to exchange man for man and officer for officer of equal rank actually held in custody by either party, until all prisoners of war so held are thus exchanged.

Ransom, John, QM Sgt., 9th Michigan Cavalry, Belle Isle Prison, Richmond, Va.:

James River very high. A continual roar in our ears caused by the water falling over the cataract just above the island. Rebels fired a large shell over the prison to scare us.

### January 14 (Thursday)

On this date, Brig. Gen. John Hunt Morgan, recently escaped from the Ohio State Penitentiary, wrote a report to James A. Seddon, Confederate Secy. of War, concerning his treatment while incarcerated. In his report, he stated that "I and sixty-nine of my officers were carried to Columbus, Ohio, where we were scrubbed, our hair cut very close, and our beards shaved. We were then locked up in cells, where we remained for two days in solitary confinement.... Our treatment was in all respects that of felons, except that we were not habited in the convict dress." Previous reports in the South had indicated that their heads had been shaved.

Stanfield, N.B., 1st Ky. Cavalry, escaped from Camp Douglas, Chicago, Ill.:

After getting out, we separated. I went twenty miles that night. Next day I overtook a wagon and asked the driver to let me ride. I talked animatedly about farming to keep him from talking about the war.

### January 15 (Friday)

Confederate Capt. E. Pliny Bryan, in Charleston, S.C., had been directed to investigate the condition of the U.S. Colored prisoners being held in that city. He wrote his report to Gen. Thomas Jordan, Chief of Staff, today:

I had a conversation with H.P. Estelle, an inmate of the institution, and one apparently well versed in its operations. He stated that the prisoners' rations a day consisted of one pound of rice flour or cornmeal, half an ounce of salt, half an ounce of soap, one pound of beef. On an average of two weeks, the prisoners lose about three rations of their meat in some way; many get only three-quarters of a pound of beef. This is practiced on those who submit, or are afraid to assert their rights. He has seen the commissary send pieces of meat away

from the prison by his servant; has bought rice and salt from Colquit, a prisoner. Colquit and one other prisoner weigh rations and act the part of stewards. Estelle said the jailer and turnkey sell things to the prisoners in copartnership. Three small loaves of bread for $1; a plug of common tobacco for $3; and other things at exorbitant prices. He says two-thirds of the men are without blankets; half without a change of clothing; consequently the prison is full of vermin.

I went among the Federal prisoners; they had no blankets; they get one meal in twenty-four hours.... The negroes look as if they were poorly fed. I asked one if he got enought to eat; he said he did by working about the office, but the others did not.... As a prison the arrangements are shocking.... I do respectfully suggest that the prisoners should have at least straw for beds, and that their rations be cooked and given to them at regular hours. The Yankee prisoners told me that they did not get their food some days until 3 o'clock.

Ransom, John, QM Sgt., 9th Michigan Cavalry, Belle Isle Prison, Richmond, Va.:

Lt. Bossieux lost his dog. Some Yanks snatched him into a tent and ate him up. Bossieux very mad and is anxious to know who the guilty ones are.... Seems pretty rough when a man will eat a dog, but such is the case.

Stanfield, N.B., 1st Ky. Cavalry, recaptured, Camp Douglas, Chicago, Ill.:

At ten o'clock next night I was in Michigan City, and boarded the train for New Albany, Ind. I got off about six miles from the city and made my way to Leavenworth. After crossing the Ohio, I was recaptured near Owensboro, Ky., and was taken back to Camp Douglas. I was paroled on March 15, 1865, and waited in Chicago for money from home.

N.B. Stanfield returned to Marion County, Ky., where he lived for the remainder of his life, still carrying the scars from Camp Douglas.

### January 18 (Monday)

On the 13th, a person reported to be Pvt. Samuel Jones, Co. B, Fifth Ohio Volunteers, was hanged by men of Maj. Gen. George Pickett's command in retaliation for an act by men of Brig. Gen. Wild's command during a recent raid in North Carolina.

The body was taken down and buried by local people and the Federal authorities notified. Investigation found that the person was actually Pvt. Samuel Jordan, Co. D, Fifth U.S. Colored Troops, captured in North Carolina and taken from among the prisoners in Richmond for the purpose of the retaliation.

The retaliation was for the trial and hanging of one Pvt. Daniel Bright, a deserter from Co. L, Sixty-second Georgia Regiment, who was carrying on robbery and pillage in the counties of Camden and Pasquotank, North Carolina. Gen. Wild, to preclude retaliation, took into custody as hostages Mrs. Munden and Mrs. Weeks, who he stated he would hang if necessary. On January 27, Maj. Gen. Butler got into the act.

Ransom, John, QM Sgt., 9th Michigan Cavalry, Belle Isle Prison, Richmond, Va.:

> Too much exertion to even write in my diary.... Some mail today but nothing for me.... Am still outside most every day. Geo. Hendryx at work in the cook house cooking rations for the prisoners. Comes down where I am every day and hands me something to take inside for the boys.

### January 20 (Wednesday)

At Camp Chase, Ohio, there had been a series of prisoner shootings over a period of time, and Col. Hoffman was investigating the circumstances. Col. Wm. Wallace, commanding at Camp Chase, provided Hoffman with information on some of the cases:

> On December 19, 1863, Pvt. F. Allen, a sentinel, ordered the persons in mess No. 10, prison 1, to extinguish their lights between the hours of 10 P.M. and midnight. After repeated calls, which were clearly heard by other sentries, he fired his rifle into the building, wounding a prisoner in the arm. Several days later, while the arm was being amputated, the prisoner died. The lesson was needed in that the prisoners had been disobeying the sentries' orders before.
>
> ... On November 5, 1863, Pvt. H. Wilson, a sentinel, ordered a man who was approaching the wall to halt and return to his barracks, this at about 10 P.M. The call was distinctly heard by the Officer of the Day who was inspecting the guard and others at some distance.
>
> ...The inmates in the western part of prison No. 3

had been digging tunnels and had been frequently warned about keeping the lights on after tattoo had been sounded. On the night of November 16, 1863, the lights of mess 49 were still lit at about 11 P.M. Pvt. John White, a sentinel, called loudly several times to extinguish the light and was not heeded. His call was loud enough to be heard across the compound by another sentinel. He fired into the building killing one prisoner instantly. The lights are now put out on time.

Ransom, John, QM Sgt., 9th Michigan Cavalry, Belle Isle Prison, Richmond, Va.:

> Rebel officers over today inspecting us Yanks. Some of the worst looking Arabs in shape of officers I ever saw.... McCarten is, as his name would indicate, an Irishman, and his home is Louisville, Ky. Is a shoemaker by trade. He is also a Mason, and I am going to write down wherein the fact of his being a Mason has brought good into the camp today. The boys feeling rather more hungry than usual were rather despondent, when the corporal [McCarten] gets up and says: "Boys, I'll go and get something to eat." Went out of the tent and in twenty minutes came back with three or four pounds of bacon and two loaves of corn bread.... Told us then that he was a Mason, as also was the lieutenant in charge, from whom the food came. We decided then and there that the first opportunity that presented itself we would join the Masons.

### January 21 (Thursday)

The day before this, Gen. Robert E. Lee had written a letter to Brig. Gen. J.D. Imboden concerning a matter of law:

> I have been informed that you have in arrest a citizen of Hardy County named Michael Yoakum, who is charged with outrages committed upon the persons and property of some of our citizens of that county, and that you propose trying him before a court-martial. I am also informed that a writ of *habeas corpus* has been sued out by Yoakum, to which you have made return claiming jurisdiction over the case. You have the power to afford immediate protection to our citizens against threatened or attempted violence, but where an offense has been committed by one not in the military service of the United States or our own you have no jurisdiction to try the offender by a court-martial. You

can arrest and deliver him to the civil authorities, who alone are competent to try him. If the facts of this case be such as I have represented them above I desire that you will surrender the accused to the civil authorities, in obedience to the writ, to be disposed of by the court having jurisdiction.

Jones, John B., Rebel War Clerk, Confederate War Dept., Richmond, Va.:

The prisoners here have been six days without meat; and Capt. Warner has been ordered by the Quartermaster-General to purchase supplies for them, relying no longer on the Commissary-General.

### January 22 (Friday)

Maj. Gen. Rosecrans, former commander at Chattanooga, was assigned as commander of the troops in Missouri, relieving Maj. Gen. Schofield, who was shifted to the Department of the Ohio. In Arkansas, Isaac Murphy, a new pro-Northern provisional governor was inaugurated.

Malone, B.Y., Sgt., Co. H, 6th N.C. Infantry, CSA, prisoner, Point Lookout, Md.:

The 22th day of January 64 was a very pritty day And it was my birth day which maid me 25 years of age I spent the day at Point Lookout. Md. And I feasted on Crackers and Coffee The last two weeks of January was beautyfull weather

### January 24 (Sunday)

Ransom, John, QM Sgt., 9th Michigan Cavalry, Belle Isle Prison, Richmond, Va.:

We are all troubled with heart-burn, sour stomach, &c. Drink weak lye made from ashes for it.... Good deal of gambling going on among prisoners. Chuck-a-luck is the favorite game. You lay your ration of bread down on a figure on a board, and a fellow with a dice-box shakes it up a little, throws out the dice, and your bread is gone. Don't understand the game myself. That's all I ever saw of the game. Lay down the bread and it's gone.... Some men are very filthy, which makes it disagreeable for those of more cleanly habits. I believe that many, very many, who now die, would live if they adopted

the rules that our mess has, and lived up to them. It is the only way to get along.

### January 25 (Monday)

In Richmond, the North had an unwilling ally in the person of Henry Stuart Foote, Congressman from Tennessee. Foote, among other things, was pro-exchange and antigovernment. Foote, born in Fauquier County, Va., in 1804, and transplanted first to Mississippi where, in 1851, he defeated Jefferson Davis in the governor's race and then to Tennessee, which was largely pro-Union. The people of Tennessee still elected him to the Confederate Congress in the fall of 1861. His outspoken criticism of the Davis Administration made him unpopular and a source of irritation to nearly everyone. He consistently voted against any and all war measures, including conscription and the suspension of *habeas corpus*, and selected as his favorite target Commissary-General Northrop. His temper caused two physical confrontations with Northrop that led to blows.

Jones, John B., Rebel War Clerk, Confederate War Dept., Richmond, Va.:

I noticed today, eight slaughtered deer in one shop; and they are seen hanging at the doors in every street. The price is $3 per pound. Wild turkies, geese, ducks, partridges, etc. are also exposed for sale, at enormous prices, and may mitigate the famine now upon us. The war has caused an enormous increase in wild game. But ammunition is difficult to be obtained. I see some perch, chubb, and other fish, but all are selling at famine prices.

### January 26 (Tuesday)

In Richmond, there were fears about the prisoners of war and their possible reactions to the lack of rations, and, as War Clerk Jones recorded, Henry Foote was after Northrop again:

The prisoners on Belle Isle (8000) have had no meat for eleven days. The Secretary says the Commissary-General informs him that they fare as well as our armies, and so he refused the commissary (Capt. Warner) of the prisoners a permit to buy and bring to the city cattle he might be able to find. An outbreak of the prisoners is apprehended: and if they were to rise, it is feared some of the inhabitants of the city would join them for they too, have no meat—many of them—or bread either. They believe the famine is owing to the imbecility, or worse, of the government. A riot would be a dangerous occurrence now: the city battalion would not fire on the people—and if they did, the army might break up, and avenge their slaughtered kindred. It is perilous time. The President receives visitors tonight; and, for the first time, I think I will go.

Mr. Foote, yesterday, offered a resolution that the Commissary-General ought to be removed; which was defeated by a decided vote, twenty in the affirmative. Twenty he relied on failed him. Letters from all quarters denounce the Commissary-General and his agents.

Ransom, John, QM Sgt., 9th Michigan Cavalry, Belle Isle Prison, Richmond, Va.:

Ninety-two squads of prisoners confined on less than six acres of ground—one hundred in a squad, making nine thousand and two hundred altogether. The lice are getting the upper hand of us. The ground is literally covered with them. Bean soup today and is made from the following recipe, (don't know from what cook book, some new edition): Beans are very wormy and musty. Hard work finding a bean without from two to three bugs in it. They are put into a large caldron kettle of river water and boiled for a couple of hours. No seasoning, not even salt put into them. It is then taken out and brought inside. Six pails full for each squad—about a pint per man, and not over a pint of beans in each bucket. The water is hardly colored and I could see clear through to the bottom and count every bean in the pail.

### January 27 (Wednesday)

Maj. Gen. Benj. F. Butler, Commanding Department of Virginia and North Carolina, today wrote Col. James W. Hinton, Commanding North Carolina State Forces, concerning his position on the hanging of two private soldiers, one each, North and South.:

Your letter per flag of truce of date January 15 was received, inclosing a copy of a letter of Brig. Gen. Wild to John T. Elliott, captain of guerrillas. I am glad of an opportunity to state to you the exact policy which I propose to pursue in carrying on the war now raging between the Confederate authorities and my Government, because upon that subject there seems to be a wide misunderstanding. Perhaps the easiest way to elucidate it will be an explicit statement of what I *do not mean to do* [italics added].

First then, I do not mean to conduct the war like some fishwoman in Billingsgate by calling hard names, such as "brute," "beast," &c.

Second. I do not mean to carry it on by any futile proclamations of outlawry against any officer or soldier duly authorized and commissioned for doing his duty.

Third. I do not mean to carry it on by threatening when I am beaten to take to the woods and organize guerrilla forces.

Fourth. I do not propose to carry it on unless my troops will obey my orders, and if they do not while I am in command of them I shall not afford them protection.

Again, I do mean to carry on this war according to the rules of civilized warfare as between alien countries.

To apply, then, this principle to the case you mention of the action of Gen. Wild. Gen. Wild found Daniel Bright, a deserter from the Sixty-second Georgia Regiment, carrying on robbery and pillage in the peaceable counties of Camden and Pasquotank. He was further informed and believed that being such a deserter he and his company had refused to obey any order emanating from you or the Governor of North Carolina, because you had frequently ordered the squad of which he had pretended to be one across the Chowan River, and they had refused to obey. These facts appeared to the court-martial before which Daniel Bright was tried, and, in my judgment, brought him within the strict meaning of the word "guerrilla."...

If Elliott and his men had refused to obey your orders and to march as they were directed, but remained in a peaceable county against the will of the inhabitants, plundering and burning as they were doing, and as we were informed they were doing, they also deserve a like fate as Daniel Bright by every rule of civilized warfare....

Gen. Wild's threat was only against "guerrillas," and these are men coming within the description which I have given, and you can easily determine for yourself whether your regiment as organized does come within that description. If not, they may fear nothing worse than imprisonment. If they do, it will be more convenient for them not to get into our hands.

Ransom, John, QM Sgt., 9th Michigan Cavalry, Belle Isle Prison, Richmond, Va.:

More prisoners came today and say there is to be no general exchange during the war, and we are to be sent off to Georgia immediately. Stormy and disagreeable weather and everybody down-hearted.

At Andersonville, Ga., a prison camp was being built and would not open for some weeks yet. Capt. R.B. Winder, Asst. Quartermaster, was trying to get things organized for the grand opening. Today, he wrote Col. Harris at Macon, Ga., looking for detail men to drive beef cattle from southwestern Georgia and Florida to the camp for consumption by the prisoners.

### January 28 (Thursday)

The Rev. J. Johns, Bishop of the Protestant Episcopal Church in Virginia, wrote the Federal Secy. of War, Edwin Stanton, today about a public relations problem. It seems that the Rev. Johns frequently visited the Federal prisoners at the prisons in Richmond and inquired about the health and comfort of these unfortunate men. Often the results were not what was expected. In one case, the Reverend had visited Surgeon Goldsborough, a Federal prisoner, several times, each time performing for the prisoner some act to increase the prisoner's comfort. Finally, Goldsborough had been exchanged as a surgeon and returned to the North upon the urging of the Reverend. When he arrived in the United States he then "began to utter the grossest misrepresentations as to the treatment to which his fellow prisoners and himself had been subjected." He even boasted that his statements helped stimulate the retaliation of the Federal government for the treatment of prisoners.

Ransom, John, QM Sgt., 9th Michigan Cavalry, Belle Isle Prison, Richmond, Va.:

No officers over from Libby for a few days past. Nearly all the clothing issued. A few days more will close up the clothing business, and then probably all the outsiders will be sent inside; and for fear such will be the case we have decided upon tomorrow night for the escape (which I have not said much about in

my diary). The nights are dark and cloudy. Messrs. Mustard and Hendryx both sleep outside now, and I must arrange to, both tonight and tomorrow night. I have been two weeks trying to get a map of Va., and have at last succeeded. A negro brought it to me from the city. It has cost over thirty dollars Confederate money—at the North would have cost twenty-five cents. I would not take for it, unless I could get another one, a thousand dollars in gold. We are well rigged, have some food saved up to take along; in good health and determined to get away. Lt. Bossieux suspects, and today took the pains to say in our hearing that he knew an escape among the outsiders was in view, and as sure as there was a God in heaven if we tried it and got caught, and we surely would be, he would first shoot all he could before catching us, and the balance would be tied up and whipped every day until he got tired, as long as we lived. We must expect trouble. It does not change us in the least; if anything, makes us the more determined to get away. Tonight we are to start, and I will write down the plans we have, running the risk of the rebels getting hold of it. At a few moments past eleven and before midnight the guard will let us cross his beat and go to the water's edge. We all have rebel clothing which we will wear, furnished partly by a negro, and partly by the guard who helps us off. We take the quartermaster's boat which we unlock, and having been furnished the countersign give it to the picket who will pretend that he thinks we are rebel guards going over to the city, in case we are caught, which will screen him in a measure. Having passed him, we get into the boat and row across the river, give the countersign to the guards on the other side of the river, and talk with them a little, being ourselves posted on general information regarding the place. To quiet their suspicions if they have any, we then start up into the town and when out of sight of the guards take a turn to the left, and go straight to the Richmond jail; taking care to avoid patrols &c. We will then meet with a negro who will guide us ten miles up the river, and then leave us in charge of friendly blacks who will keep us through the next day and at night pilot us further along towards our lines. If possible, I shall steal a rebel flag, which is kept nights in the lieutenant's tent, and a few other relics, to take along with me. The big bell in Richmond strikes six, and we close our diary, hoping never to look upon it again until we return to free our fellow prisoners, with the glorious army of the

North. Now we leave our diary to finish preparations for the flight for freedom. May God aid us in this land of tyranny, where we have met nothing but suffering. Good bye, Belle Isle and Prison. Hail! Freedom, Home Friends, and the Grand Army of the Old Flag! What is in store for us in the future?

### February 1 (Monday)

The Federal Congress today reinstituted the rank of Lieutenant General for the military forces. Grant, the hero of Vicksburg and Chattanooga was the intended recipient of the rank.

In Danville, Va., the Confederate government had established a prison stockade outside of the town and placed the prison hospital in the middle of town. The residents of the town were very concerned about this situation. Yesterday, they wrote the Confederate Secy. of War, James A. Seddon:

Your petitioners, the mayor and common council of Danville, would respectfully represent that we deem it our imperative duty earnestly to petition for the removal of the Yankee prisoners located among us to some other place, or at least outside the limits of the corporation of Danville. The reasons for this application, which are embodied in this petition are explained by the certificates hereto annexed.

The hospitals of the prisoners and sick are located in the very heart of the town, and are not all in one place, but scattered in the most public and business places, so as to infect the whole atmosphere of the town with smallpox and fever now raging within the limits of the corporation. Your petitioners fear mostly the increase of the number of cases of fever and the virulence of the same.

The stench from the hospitals even now (in winter) is almost insupportable, and is offensive at the distance of several hundred yards. We are advised by our medical advisers, the board of health, that they believe the great number of cases of fever now in Danville proceeds from the cause above indicated. Your petitioners believe that no police regulations, however efficient, can remove the evil from which they apprehend so much mischief, particularly in the summer months. The filth of the neighborhood of the hospitals runs down in small sluggish branches that run nearly through the breadth of the town, and it is permitted to remain until a rain partially

removes it, the most of it finding a permanent lodgment in the drains. The town has no waterworks to cleanse its streets.

### February 2 (Tuesday)

In Calhoun, McMinn County, Tenn., three men had been arrested by the Federal military authorities to be held as hostages for the treatment of one Jesse R. Blackburn, a citizen of the county who had been arrested in November by the Confederate military as a bushwhacker and for harboring bushwhackers. Blackburn had supposedly been taken to Richmond.

What caused all this ruckus was hogs. It seemed that one John Dunn, an agent for the Confederate States, came to Blackburn's house to impress some hogs belonging to Blackburn and his son-in-law, Thomas A. Cass. Cass and Blackburn disagreed with Dunn's authority to take the hogs and an altercation resulted. Dunn insisted on taking the hogs, so Cass left, without the knowledge of Blackburn, collected a couple of friends and came back, intercepted Dunn, fired into Dunn's party, and freed the hogs. Blackburn was not present and had no knowledge of the action until he was arrested for being a bushwhacker.

Now, the three men arrested and held as hostages asked President Davis to free Blackburn so they could be free to go home. The letter, sent via the Union chain of command, was first forwarded to Washington to Maj. Gen. E.A. Hitchcock (15 days), who then sent it to the War Department (another 8 days), where it was forwarded by Brig. Gen. E.R.S. Canby to Maj. Gen. Butler (another 9 days), in Ft. Monroe, who, in turn, sent it to Robert Ould in Richmond, who sent it to President Davis for action (another 8 days). Forty days had elapsed before Davis saw the letter. The hogs had probably long gone for sausage by then.

### February 3 (Wednesday)

Ten months previously two correspondents of the *New York Tribune*, A.D. Richardson and Junius Henri Browne, were captured while attempting to run past the city of Vicksburg, Miss., in a tugboat. Today they arrived at the Confederate prison at Salisbury, N.C. They became celebrities of a sort because of the efforts to obtain their release. The Confederate government had no great love for the

*Tribune*, believing it was a major factor in creating dissention before the war began. Richardson estimated that upon his arrival at Salisbury there were in excess of 500 prisoners in the facility. These included a number of Confederate convicts, some Yankee deserters, about 20 Union Naval personnel, three Union officers being held as hostages, and about 150 *civilian* prisoners.

In the west, Sherman marched with 26,000 men to wreck the railroads of Mississippi and disrupt the flow of food to the Confederate armies in the east. His cavalry arm, 7600 under Gen. William Sooy Smith, was late in arriving for the campaign. Facing Sherman and Smith were about 20,000 widely scattered Confederate troops under Lt. Gen. Leonidas Polk.

### February 5 (Friday)

Two days previously, Capt. R.B. Winder, Asst. Quartermaster at Andersonville, Ga., wrote Maj. A.M. Allen at Columbus, Ga., concerning rations for the expected prisoners:

I shall soon have the Yankee prisoners at this post, and as I am instructed by the Quartermaster-General, first, to call upon the nearest commissary for supplies, I now write to know in what quantities you can supply me beyond the possibility of failure. In regard to corn and meal, I can relieve you of the trouble in that matter, as I can draw that in sufficient supply from the quartermaster's department, but I shall want beef, meat, flour, sugar, molasses, rice, soap, candles, &c. You can give me meat or beef as you please; sugar I shall only want for hospital purposes, and shall not require a large quantity of flour. I shall have 10,000 prisoners at this post, and you can easily calculate what I shall require. Mr. Harrold cannot begin to furnish me with one half what I shall need. The beef which you turn over to me I do not want stripped of the tallow, as I intend to manufacture candles at this place. All beef which has been heretofore sent me by Mr. Harrold, he has (so he says) taken out the tallow by your orders.

After picking up McPherson's corps near Champion's Hill, Sherman pushed on towards Jackson, Miss., fighting a series of little battles on the way with Confederate cavalry.

Ransom, John, QM Sgt., 9th Michigan Cavalry, Belle Isle Prison, Richmond, Va.:

Have been reading over the last few pages on my diary. It sounds well, but the rebel flag still floats over Belle Isle. Our escapade was a grand fizzle, and all hands have been punished in more ways than one in the last few days. Bossieux suspected something going on among us and had us secretly watched, and long before we had made a move towards fulfilling our projected plans we were thrown into a guard house on the island; next morning taken out of it, and underwent a severe cross-questioning. He found our rebel clothing, food we had packed, found the lock to the boat broke, and numerous other signs of an abandonment. Well, the result has been that we were bucked and gagged twice a day for an hour each time, and for four hours each of us carried a big stick of wood up and down in front of the gate, a guard to prick us with his bayonet if we walked too slow to suit him. Then Hendryx has been strung up by the thumbs. Nights we have been thrown into a damp, cold guard house to shiver all night. Every day now for six days we have walked with our sticks of wood so many hours per day, and last night were turned inside with all the prisoners to stay; Bossieux says, till we *rot*, he can place no dependence on us.

### February 6 (Saturday)

Sherman's force left Jackson for Meridian, Miss., his initial destination.

Ransom, John, QM Sgt., 9th Michigan Cavalry, Belle Isle Prison, Richmond, Va.:

We have to laugh over our trials and tribulations. Where we had plenty a week ago, plenty of exercise, and many favors, we are now right where we were at first, faring just as the rest, with no favors shown us. It's all right, we can stand it just as well as the rest. We have never belittled ourselves in the least in our dealings with the rebels. Bossieux told us himself, as we came inside, that he didn't blame us in the least for trying to get away, but he was obliged to punish us for the attempt. Hendryx says that he will be out again in three days.

### February 7 (Sunday)

Gen. Pickett, unable to capture New Bern, N.C., fell back towards Richmond, where an alarm had been given, later proved false, that Gen. Ben Butler's troops were approaching the city from the Peninsula. Preparations were made to send the "home guards" from Richmond in addition to the regular Confederate troops in the city to positions of defense at Drewry's Bluff. The citizens feared that with the troops gone, the Union prisoners, about 12,000, would escape.

Jones, John B., Rebel War Clerk, Confederate War Dept., Richmond, Va.:

We have good news from the Rappahannock. It is said Gen. Rosser yesterday captured several hundred prisoners, 1200 beeves, 350 mules, wagons of stores, etc. etc.

Nevertheless, there is some uneasiness felt in the city, there being nearly 12,000 prisoners here, and all the veteran troops of Gen. Elzey's division are being sent to North Carolina.

### February 8 (Monday)

In Richmond, Va., the Speaker of the Virginia House of Delegates today sent President Davis a copy of resolutions passed by the House concerning the exchange of prisoners. In many, many words, the message, essentially, was that the Confederate Government (in the person of Jefferson Davis) should get off its high horse about the fact that Maj. Gen. Benjamin F. Butler had been appointed as Federal Agent for Exchange and get on with the business of exchanging prisoners. The past actions of Gen. Butler should be set aside in the interest of humanity in getting the prisoners back into their respective countries.

On the 12th, the Richmond *Examiner* ran an article in which it criticized the House of Delegates for its action in the strongest terms:

Some extremes of abasement there are to which our Government will not degrade this Confederacy. For example, we shall be slow to believe that it would ever ask an officer bearing a Confederate commission—let us say Judge Ould—to meet on terms of equality and to treat about exchange of prisoners with a negro colonel of a Massachusetts regiment. If

President Lincoln should signify that he is ready to permit a new negotiation to be entered upon, with a view to exchange, provided we send our commissioner to settle the terms with Frederick Douglass or with Col. Pompey, on the part of the other belligerent, we presume that our Executive would decline....

But the Legislature of Virginia is not of our opinion. There is no depth of degradation, it is said, that they are not willing and eager to plunge us into ... requesting him to accept, as Federal agent for exchange, not even the mulatto Frederick, or the wretched runaway slave Pompey, but a person whom the President has officially proclaimed "a felon deserving of capital punishment"—"an outlaw or common enemy of mankind," a criminal who wherever he shall be caught, "is to be executed by hanging."...

But what do our unhappy legislators imagine we shall gain if we commit this filthy action? We are not offered, even on this condition, a renewal of the exchange on the terms of the cartel. The enemy only say to us, accept Butler without conditions, and he will tell you then what we are going to do to you. If we accept him that is only the first step. We can refuse nothing after that ignominious concession.... To hold our own recovered runaway slaves as prisoners of war, to receive a negro officer as Butler's lieutenant on the flag of truce boat, and account with him for the prisoners—there is nothing of all this that Lincoln may not exact and ought not to exact if he finds us compliant enough to negotiate with the felon.... The intention is to compel us to certify to our own disgrace. Yankee ingenuity will exhaust itself in the invention of ever new and more humiliating conditions, and there will be no end of it until we all consent to crawl to the footstool of Lincoln with handcuffs on our hands and ropes around our necks.

John Ransom, in Belle Isle prison, had his dates confused. The entry for February 8, 1864, was actually for Sunday, February 7, 1864.

Ransom, John, QM Sgt., 9th Michigan Cavalry, Belle Isle Prison, Richmond, Va.:

Congress still in session over in the city and we watch the papers eagerly for something relative to us. The Holy Sabbath day and the church bells ringing for morning service. Don't think I shall attend this morning; it is such a long, long walk and then I look so bad.... A man stabbed a few minutes ago by his tent mate, killing him instantly. They had all along been the best friends until a dispute arose, and one of them drew a knife and killed his comrade. Strong talk of lynching the murderer.

### February 9 (Tuesday)

In one of the most spectacular escapades of the war, Col. Thomas E. Rose of Pennsylvania led 109 Federal officers, including the elusive Col. Abel D. Streight, who had been captured by Forrest, in an escape through a tunnel out of Libby Prison in Richmond. Eventually, 48 were recaptured, two drowned, and the remaining 59, including Col. Streight, made it back to Union lines.

Ransom, John, QM Sgt., 9th Michigan Cavalry, Belle Isle Prison, Richmond, Va.:

Great news this morning. A raid is being made on Richmond by Kilpatrick, Rebels manning their forts in sight of us. All are at work, women, children, in fact everybody who can shovel. No cars running over the big bridge. Double guards placed over us and the greatest activity prevails among them.... All business is suspended in Richmond; no papers issued, and everybody with their guns or working utensils.... A portion of the congress came over this afternoon to take a look at us, among whom were Davis, Benjamin and Howell Cobb. They are a substantial looking set of men and of the regular southern cut. The broad rim hats, gold-headed canes and aristocratic toss of the head.... A band accompanied them and played the "Bonnie Blue Flag," which was hissed and groaned at by the Yankees, and in return a thousand voices sang "Yankee Doodle," very much to their discomfiture.

### February 10 (Wednesday)

A day earlier, Federal Brig. Gen. I.N. Palmer in New Bern, N.C., wrote Maj. Gen. George Pickett, Commanding Confederate troops in North Carolina, concerning some medical personnel who had been captured:

A few days since, while the forces under your command were in front of this place, I sent a medical officer with some ambulances to the smallpox hospital, near which some of your forces had arrived, with a flag, for the sole purpose of bringing away the

unfortunate occupants of the building, as in case of an attack on my lines they would certainly be in great danger of having their house burned over their heads. Besides, I had no desire to see the loathsome disease spread among your own forces, and it was proper that you should be put on your guard as to the nature of the hospital.

The medical officer who went on this humane errand was instructed, of course, to explain these matters to any of your forces that he might meet, and he doubtless did so. He was, however, seized and carried away as a prisoner, with the ambulances and drivers.

... I respectfully request you do what I feel certain I would do myself under the circumstances— that is, return the surgeon and the drivers to me. The ambulances with the horses I say nothing of, for they are too trifling for me to mention.

On the 17th, Gen. Pickett replied to Palmer indicating that "The case was duly and immediately reported to me by Maj. Read, C.S. Army, who took charge of the medical officer and party. They came with no flag of truce and therefore could not be recognized; in addition, the surgeon, by his inquiries, conversation, and observation, had learned too much to render his return desirable." Pickett agreed to forward the letter to Richmond and recommend the release of the men.

Ransom, John, QM Sgt., 9th Michigan Cavalry, Belle Isle Prison, Richmond, Va.:

The hospital signal lights suspended over the island all night in order to direct the batteries where to aim their pieces in case of an outbreak which is greatly feared.... Reported that there are six hundred muskets secreted among the prisoners and citizens very much alarmed and afraid of us.... It is impossible for me to sleep...

### February 11 (Thursday)

Surgeon A.M. Clark, Col. Hoffman's travelling medical inspector, visited Rock Island prison yesterday and wrote a report to Hoffman indicating:

I find that there has been much remissness on the part of the medical officers of the prison in not taking proper measures to prevent the spread of smallpox. In some cases the proper steps have been suggested but not urged with sufficient energy. On my arrival I found some thirty-eight cases of the disease, and some of these in an advanced stage, lying among their fellows in the prison barracks. This is inexcusable. The fact had not been reported to the commanding officer by the surgeon in charge. That officer should, however, have been acquainted with the fact through his provost-marshal, and should have directed their immediate removal, even without the request of the surgeon.

Ransom, John, QM Sgt., 9th Michigan Cavalry, Belle Isle Prison, Richmond, Va.:

Cold and pleasant. A good deal of fighting going on among us—a discontented set of beings; just like so many hungry wolves penned up together.... A number of Yankees have been taken out on parole of honor to work building breastworks etc., but a very few will go and it is considered a great crime among us to work for them.

Montgomery, J.J., Lowry's Scouts, Confederate prisoner, escaped from Camp Morton, Ind.:

I succeeded [in escaping] by digging a tunnel. About 4:30 A.M., February 11, 1864, W.B. Bell, of Charlotte, Tenn., and John Branch, of Culleoka, Tenn., escaped with me in that way. Branch left us near the prison, and said that he was going to Canada, which he did. Bell urged that he and I go to the depot and take the first train for Canada. I favored going to the best hotel in the city, but I yielded to Bell, as he was much the older. I was to go into the depot about fifteen steps in front of him, and if either one was captured the other was not to know him. I passed the guard all right, but when Bell came to him I heard the guard say: "Hallo, old man! when did you get out?" Bell replied: "Nothing wrong with me, sir; nothing wrong." I then turned towards the side entrance to depart, and on looking around I saw a man from Arkansas, wearing a Confederate overcoat with cape coming towards me. I shook my head at him and turned to go out. As I reached the door the guard hallooed: "Halt!" I looked back over my shoulder and saw that he had the man from Arkansas. Not having any further business there, I left the depot, having seen two captured up to six o'clock A.M. Having no overcoat, and the weather being cold, I soon found a Jew clothing store, where I bought a coat,

handkerchief, and gloves, which made me look a little more respectable, having had the dirt scraped off my face in a barber shop.

Being now alone, I went to the Depot Hotel and registered under my assumed name, and went back to the fire, where two Yankee sergeants and one corporal were sitting. When the bell rang for breakfast I went with them, and we all ate at the same table. About nine o'clock I walked over to the depot. There were no guards nor any one else to be seen. On my return one of the sergeants asked me if I had heard about a lot of prisoners escaping the night before, and told me that they had caught some of them. I replied that they ought to have caught every one of them and hung them. These Yankees were going to Evansville; so was I. We missed connection at Terre Haute, and spent the night at the same hotel.

There seems to be some difference of opinion between J.J. Montgomery and J.T. Branch as to who did what and when. Branch's version follows:

Branch, J.T., Co. G., Ninth Tenn. Cavalry, escaped from Camp Morton, Ind.:

After the surrender of Donelson Tuesday morning, as Mr. Montgomery says, we took "deck passage," not knowing our destination. We went to Cairo; then up the river to Alton, Ill. There we were loaded into boxcars and run to Springfield, where we were taken to Camp Douglas, Chicago, where I remained for some three months.... On the night of June 1, W.P. Renfro, of my company, and I decided we would go to Dixie. We paid the guard $7.50 to "look the other way" while we went over the fence. We made it on foot back to Middle Tennessee, which we reached about the 1st of July. My regiment still being in prison, I enlisted in Company G, Ninth Tennessee Cavalry, and served with it until November 9, 1863, when I was again captured. This time I was taken to Camp Morton, arriving there on the 6th day of December. The next morning I met J.J. Montgomery. Both having made our escape from Camp Douglas, we pledged each other our assistance in getting out of Morton.

In the latter part of January, 1865 [1864], ten of us conceived the idea of digging a tunnel to make our escape. Our party was: J.B. Morgan, Columbus Gillian, Jim Gillian, Reuben Branch, and myself, of Tennessee; a Mr. Hill and Tom Moore of Mississippi;

Sebastian Schwartz, of Louisiana; Mr. Kilgore and Mr. Burnett, of Texas. We together planned the scheme and dug the tunnel, and we only had to do with it.

We began in the north end of Division 5, in the bunk occupied by J.B. Morgan, commencing on the night of February 8, and completed it in three nights. The first night we packed the dirt taken from the tunnel in our bunk, preparations for which had previously been made by boxing up the front side of the bunk, so the dirt would not be observed. Our excuse to the guard for planking this up was that the men occupying the bunks directly over ours—the bunks being made three tiers high—were continually getting our blankets muddy in climbing to their bunks. The second night we piled the dirt in the topmost bunk, just across the hall from ours, and the third night, having made our calculations to get through in time to leave that night, we scattered it anywhere.

Between 3 and 4 o'clock on the morning of the 11th we dug through to the outside, a distance of thirty-three feet from the mouth. In compliance with my promise to Montgomery, I notified him on the night we commenced the tunnel to be ready at any hour. He wanted to know how we were going out, and persisted in my telling him; but as we ten had solemnly pledged ourselves to reveal the plan to no one, I of course refused; but the others had given their consent to bringing Montgomery out with us when the tunnel should be completed. Montgomery was located in another division at the far end of the prison from us and across a little stream running through the grounds, which we had named the "Potomac."

On the evening of the 10th I went to Montgomery and told him I was going to leave that night. He again wanted to know how we were going out—whether over the wall or under it. I again refused to tell him, as I was obligated not to do so, but simply said to him: "I am going, so be ready." I told him to come to our barracks and remain, but not to come to my end of the division, and to let me know just where to find him at the proper time, and he said he would be at the first bunk below stove No. 3 in Division 5. He then told me he had a friend and bunk mate named Bell whom he wished to bring out with him, to which I assented. About half past four o'clock I went for Montgomery, and found him and Bell waiting at the appointed place. Montgomery here again asked me how I was going out, and I told him to come on and I would show him

the way. When we reached the mouth of the tunnel I said to him, "John, here's the hole"; and this was the first he knew of how we were going out. I started through, with Montgomery and Bell following. The rest of my crowd, except Burnett, who had backed out at the last moment, had already gone through.

Mr. Montgomery is again mistaken about my telling him I was going to Canada, for I had no money and no clothes, except the regulation suit of gray jeans. I did sometime afterwards, in September, when the big draft was called for, go over to Canada, and remained there until April, 1865.

The ten who planned and dug the tunnel—all except Burnett—made their escape, the majority of them coming South, and most of them reentered the army. Two of them—Schwartz and Tom Gillian—were killed just before the surrender....

My reason for writing this is that justice may be done to the brave dead who did this work. Should any of the statements herein be doubted, Mr. Morgan and Mr. Gillian will both confirm what I have written.

### February 12 (Friday)

Ransom, John, QM Sgt., 9th Michigan Cavalry, Belle Isle Prison, Richmond, Va.:

Lt. Bossieux has sent a squad of men from the island composed of runaways over to Castle Thunder to remain during the war as hostages, among whom were our friends Myers and Mustard. I never expect to see them again.

Montgomery, J.J., Lowry's Scouts, Confederate prisoner, escaped from Camp Morton, Ind.:

Arriving at Evansville the next day, we all stopped at the Washington Hotel. After two days waiting for a boat to Nashville, I succeeded, and on the fourth day after leaving Evansville I arrived in the Rock City.

### February 13 (Saturday)

Surgeon A.M. Clark visited Rock Island, Ill., prison and today wrote a report to Col. William Hoffman:

Rock Island Barracks are situated near the center in length and on the northern side of the island. The prison barracks are 84 in number, each intended to accommodate 120 men. They are arranged in blocks of 7 each, fronting on streets 100 feet wide, with 2 main avenues 130 feet wide, intersecting the camp in the center. The sinks are placed 4 in each street running north and south. The barracks have each 2 ridge ventilators and 12 windows, with 2 doors. These would afford abundantly sufficient ventilation were it not for the difficulty in having the windows kept open, and in view of that difficulty I have suggested that the ridge ventilation be carried the full length of the barracks. This can be done by prison labor and at trifling expense. Each barracks is 100 by 22 feet by 12 feet in dimensions. Eighteen feet in length is partitioned off for a kitchen, which is furnished with a 40-gallon caldron and the requisite kitchen and table furniture. The barracks are sufficiently heated by two coal stoves in each. The bedding is well aired each day, and the police and discipline, as well as the general condition of the men, is admirable. Here, however, commendation must cease.

The camp grounds are poorly policed. Some excuse exists for this in view of the very severe weather of late, the lack of transportation and the lack of drainage. A feeble attempt has been made to drain the camp, which is, however, entirely inadequate to its purpose. Near the southwest corner of the prison inclosure is a small marsh which receives the surface drainage of the adjacent portion of the island and into it the camp drain empties.... On the northern shore of the island, at the northwest corner of the inclosure, is placed a steam pump which forces the water through a 3-inch wooden supply pipe into four cisterns, two outside the inclosure for the use of the garrison, and two inside for the use of the prisoners. There is also an artesian well of 9-inch bore and 125-feet depth just inside the west gate of the prison. The present location of the waterworks is such as to render the river on the north side of the island useless to the prison for all purposes of drainage....

The smallpox hospital is located on the south shore of the island, directly opposite the prison, and at present consists of 3 barracks, each 129 by 22 by 12 feet in dimensions and accommodating 42 beds in each, and 2 small dwelling houses, unfit for any use at all, except for kitchens or wash-houses.... There are now over 100 cases of smallpox within the prison inclosure, and it is of the utmost importance that they should be removed as rapidly as possible.

Ransom, John, QM Sgt., 9th Michigan Cavalry, Belle Isle Prison, Richmond, Va.:

Very cold. The rebels are again settling down and getting over their scare. Not much to eat now and the men are more disheartened than ever. A rebel preacher delivered us a sermon of two hours length from a dry-goods box. He was listened to attentively and made the remark before closing that he didn't know as he was doing any good talking to us. It was like casting pearls before swine and he would close his remarks, to which a Yankee told him he might have stopped long ago if he had wanted to; no one would have made any objections. Was told that six hundred are to start for Georgia today and subsequently six hundred every day until all are removed from Richmond.

## February 14 (Sunday)

In the west, Sherman entered Meridian, Miss., today after a march of almost 140 miles from Vicksburg. Gen. Polk continued to withdraw his troops in the face of an overwhelmingly superior force. Sherman took a night off to rest his men.

Ransom, John, QM Sgt., 9th Michigan Cavalry, Belle Isle Prison, Richmond, Va.:

Six hundred sent away today, some say to our lines while others think to Georgia. Rebels say to our lines, and that a general exchange has been agreed upon. Great excitement among the men. EVENING—Lt. Bossieux called me outside just before night and told me he was called upon to furnish some hostages to be sent to Charleston to be kept during the war, and had decided to send Hendryx and myself, with some others.... Have succeeded in buying a pair of shoes, which, although about four sizes too large, are much better than none.... Six hundred sent away this afternoon under a very strong guard, which does not look like an exchange.

Malone, B.Y., Sgt., Co. H, 6th N.C. Infantry, CSA, prisoner, Point Lookout, Md.:

The 14th of Feb was a pritty day And the Yankes Sirched the Prison Camp the Rebels was all sent out side under gard. And then they sirched and taken evry mans Blanket that had more than one. And taken evry other little trick that the Rebels had. They found too Boats that the Rebs had maid.

375 Officers arived at Point Lookout from Jonstan Isle the 14th of Feb. The Yankey papers say that they are having a Gun maid that weighs 115,000 lbs. 21 ft. long carries a Ball that weighs 1000 lbs. and a shell that weighs 700 lbs.

### February 16 (Tuesday)

Beginning yesterday morning after a good night's rest, Sherman turned 10,000 of his troops loose on Meridian, Miss., where they proceeded to take apart railroads, warehouses, shops, supply depots, arsenals, offices, cantonments, hotels (and nearly everything else) in a five-day binge of destruction. The Confederates were concerned that Sherman was headed for Mobile, Ala., only about 150 road miles away. Resistance from Polk's small force was negligible.

Montgomery, J.J., Lowry's Scouts, escaped Confederate prisoner, Nashville, Tenn.:

A friend of mine sent for Misses Kizzie Henderson and Annie Menifee (later Mrs. Paul). They were heroines without fear, for when they heard that I had escaped from prison and wanted to leave the city for the South they lost no time in going after a pass, although it was snowing hard.

### February 17 (Wednesday)

At Pt. Hudson, La., Brig. Gen. George L. Andrews wrote Brig. Gen. Wirt Adams, commanding C.S. Forces in the area, about an incident that had occurred on August 3, 1863:

...in an affair at Jackson, La., between the Confederate forces under Gen. [Col.] Logan and a detachment of U.S. troops, mostly colored men, several of said colored troops were taken prisoners, and it was then reported that some of them were shot by the Confederate soldiers after capture.

A communication on the subject was sent from the undersigned to Gen. Logan, to which he (Gen. Logan) replied, denying that any such acts had been committed under his authority. For want of direct and positive evidence of the commission of the acts referred to, the matter for the time was allowed to rest. Recently, however, a citizen of Jackson has made the statement under oath that the day after the affair at Jackson

he saw Lt. Shattuck, of Scott's Confederate Cavalry, dismount from his horse and deliberately shoot dead a wounded U.S. Colored soldier then lying wounded on the ground; also, that he heard Lt. Shattuck say that he had shot thirteen negro soldiers that day, and that they took no prisoners. There was no fighting on the day referred to; also that he saw Confederate soldiers taking other negro soldiers outside of town, as they said, to shoot them, and that he saw their bodies afterward on the ground, not forming any part of the battlefield, but a mile and a half distant therefrom, and in the direction in which the negro soldiers were taken for the avowed purpose of shooting them.

There is also much additional testimony corroborating the foregoing statement. I cannot longer doubt that U.S. Colored soldiers captured by the C.S. forces have been deliberately murdered after capture. I am further directed to inquire of you whether such acts are or have been permitted by your officers or other authorities? If such acts are permitted, I have to inform you that prompt retaliation will take place on the prisoners in our possession. If such acts are unauthorized, I must demand the punishment of the perpetrators.

Ransom, John, QM Sgt., 9th Michigan Cavalry, Belle Isle Prison, Richmond, Va.:

Still on the island. Another squad taken out yesterday. It will not be our turn to go for some days, even if six hundred are taken out every day. Have not been sent for as hostages yet. Hendryx and myself have decided to flank out and go with the next that go, no matter where their destination may be.

Federal prisoners of war began filing into a new prison camp near Americus, Ga., today. The camp, named Camp Sumter, would become infamous as Andersonville Prison. Many of the prisoners from Belle Isle in Richmond were transferred to this location to ease the crowding in Richmond.

Jones, John B., Rebel War Clerk, Confederate War Dept., Richmond, Va.:

We are now sending 400 Federal prisoners to Georgia daily; and I hope we shall have more food in the city when they are all gone.

Montgomery, J.J., Lowry's Scouts, escaped Confederate prisoner, Giles County, Tenn.:

On their return they had one, which read: "Miss Henderson, sister, and driver." I was the "driver." We had to show the pass three times going out. I bade them good-bye twelve miles from the city. I then started South on foot, going from one skirt of timber to another, avoiding all roads, and going into Giles County.

### February 20 (Saturday)

At Andersonville, Ga., Capt. R.B. Winder, Asst. Quartermaster, wired Maj. P.W. White, his commissary agent, that he had only received 10,000 pounds of the bacon he had ordered because the agent at Americus only had about 5000 pounds on hand. Winder indicated that the prisoners were due in shortly and he had not adequate food for them. This would be a constant problem.

In Mississippi, Sherman, having destroyed Meridian, turned his army back towards Vicksburg. In no hurry, the army moved at a leisurely pace, destroying the railroad as far north as Lauderdale as it went. When the Yanks hit the west side of town, the Confederates immediately started rebuilding the railroads.

Ransom, John, QM Sgt., 9th Michigan Cavalry, Belle Isle Prison, Richmond, Va.:

All sorts of rumors afloat, but still we stay here. Strange officers come over and look at us. Bossieux away considerable, and something evidently up. Anything for a change. My health is good, and tough as a bear.

### February 21 (Sunday)

War Clerk Jones reported on a situation where several hundred dollars per month was being taken by the persons responsible for forwarding mail through the "flag-of-truce" system, the difference between the actual cost of the postage (3 cents), and what was enclosed for the postage (often 5 to 10 cents) being kept by the mail handler as a "perk":

There is war between Gen. Winder and Mr. Ould, agent for exchange of prisoners, about the custody and distribution of prisoners, Federal and Confederate. It appears that parents, etc., writing to our prisoners in the enemy's country, for want of three-cent stamps, are in the habit of inclosing five- or

ten-cent pieces, and the perquisites of the office amounts to several hundred dollars per month— and the struggle is really between the clerks in the two offices. A Mr. Higgens, from Maryland, is in Winder's office, and has got the general to propose to the Secretary that he shall have the exclusive handling of the letters; but Mr. Ould, it appears, detected a letter, of an alleged treasonable character, on its way to the enemy's country, written by Mr. Higgens, and reported it to the Secretary. But as the Secretary was much absorbed, and as Winder will indorse Higgens, it is doubtful how the contest for the perquisites will terminate.

### February 22 (Monday)

Maj. Gen. Benj. F. Butler, at Ft. Monroe, wrote Col. Hoffman concerning the movement of food boxes to the prisoners in the South:

In the course of the negotiations for the supplying of comforts to our prisoners this state of facts has obtained:

First. That the rebel authorities received all provisions from whatever source sent to the prisoners. Then, because of accusations of the late commissioner of exchange, Gen. Meredith, published in the newspapers, that these provisions were embezzled for sustenance for Gen. Lee's army, they refused to receive any boxes either from our Government or from State governments. Then, because the Sanitary Commission and various benevolent individuals indulged their patriotism by labeling their boxes "To our starving soldiers in Richmond," "To our brave defenders in Libby Prison," the rebel authorities refused to receive all boxes sent to our prisoners. At my intercession, however, Mr. Ould, the Confederate commissioner, agreed to receive boxes from private sources, *i.e.*, from the friends and families of our prisoners. But after the 500 prisoners were exchanged from Point Lookout and reported that by your order boxes of provisions and clothing were not delivered to Confederate prisoners there, true, Ould refused, owing to a cry arising from the newspapers at Richmond that he was furnishing our prisoners with their boxes, while the Confederate prisoners were deprived of their boxes, to permit any boxes to be sent to our men under his charge unless I would assure him that the Confederate prisoners under my charge received their boxes, and as I had long since been taught, "Do as you would be done by," this seemed to me eminently just, and I therefore gave an order to Gen. Marston that the boxes containing nothing contraband or hurtful sent from private sources might be delivered to the prisoners and informed Mr. Ould by the last flag of truce boat of that fact, and received his assurance through the assistant agent of exchange that the boxes sent by friends of our prisoners should be delivered to them.

Montgomery, J.J., Lowry's Scouts, escaped Confederate prisoner, Giles County, Tenn.:

I could not go home, but sent word, and got some clothes. I then got hold of a little mule branded "U.S.," which I rode bareback to the Tennessee River, sixty miles, through a cold, drizzling rain.

### February 23 (Tuesday)

Capt. R.B. Winder, Asst. Quartermaster at Andersonville, Ga., wrote Capt. Brotherton about a shipment of meat:

When I was in Savannah I suggested to Maj. Locke, chief purchasing commissary for this State, that I would gladly feed any offal [indicating the organ meat such as hearts, livers, etc., not intestines] from the slaughter-houses in Albany that could not readily be kept on hand or forwarded to the army to the prisoners at his post, thereby saving that much provision to the Government, but never dreamed of paying $2 apiece for the luxury of beef tongues for them or $1 for shanks, or 50 cents per pound for shank meat and pickled hearts.... I regret that any misunderstanding about prices should have taken place, but will assure you that Mr. Pickett entirely misunderstood his instructions in purchasing at any such prices. Of course I shall not want any more.

Ransom, John, QM Sgt., 9th Michigan Cavalry, Belle Isle Prison, Richmond, Va.:

None have been taken away from the island for a number of days. Have heard that a box came for me, and is over in Richmond. Hope the rebel that eats the contents of that box will get choked to death.... Rebels are trying to get recruits from among us for their one-horse Confederacy. Believe that one or two have deserted our ranks and gone over. Bad luck to them.

### February 24 (Wednesday)

In Richmond, Braxton Bragg was appointed, effectively, chief of staff of the Confederate forces by Jeff Davis. Bragg had lost much of the confidence of the people by his defeat at Missionary Ridge and his never-ending battles with his generals.

Malone, B.Y., Sgt., Co. H, 6th N.C. Infantry, CSA, prisoner, Point Lookout, Md.:

The 24th was a beautifull day And too of the Rebs got kild the nite of the 24th attempting to get away: We was garded at Point Lookout by the second fifth and twelfth Newhampshire Regiments untell the 25th of Feb: And then the 26th N.C. Negro Regiment was plaised gard over ous

Ransom, John, QM Sgt., 9th Michigan Cavalry, Pemberton Bldg., Richmond, Va.:

We are confined on the third floor of the building, which is a large tobacco warehouse. Was removed from the island yesterday.... Was not sorry to bid adieu to Belle Isle. Were searched last night but our mess has lost nothing, owing to the following process we have of fooling them: One of the four manages to be in the front part of the crowd and is searched first, and is then put on the floor underneath and we let our traps down through a crack in the floor to him, and when our turn comes we have nothing about us worth taking away. The men are so ravenous when the rations were brought in, that the boxes of bread and tubs of poor meat were raided upon before dividing, and consequently some had nothing to eat at all, while others had plenty. Our mess did not get a mouthful and have had nothing to eat since yesterday afternoon, and it is now nearly dark. The lice are very thick. You can see them all over the floors, walls, &c., in fact everything literally covered with them; they seem much larger than the stock on Belle Isle and a different species.

### February 25 (Thursday)

Ransom, John, QM Sgt., 9th Michigan Cavalry, Pemberton Bldg., Richmond, Va.:

We divide the night up into four watches and take turns standing guard while the other three sleep, to protect ourselves from Capt. Moseby's gang of robbers. We are all armed with iron slats pulled off the window casings. They are afraid to pitch in to us, as we are a stout crowd and would fight well for our worldly goods. We expect to take it before long. They are eying us rather sharp, and I guess will make an attack tonight. Very long days and more lonesome than when on the island. Got rations today, and the allowance did not half satisfy our hunger.

## February 26 (Friday)

Sherman was honing his troop conservation skills during the Meridian campaign, which was nearly complete. With only 21 killed, 68 wounded, and 81 missing, his force had destroyed the city of Meridian, about 115 miles of railroad track, 61 bridges, and 20 locomotives (nearly impossible to replace). The march had totalled between 360 and 450 miles.

Ransom, John, QM Sgt., 9th Michigan Cavalry, Pemberton Bldg., Richmond, Va.:

Rather cold, almost spring. Guards unusually strict. Hendryx was standing near the window, and I close by him, looking at the high, ten-story tobacco building, when the guard fired at us. The ball just grazed Hendryx's head and lodged in the ceiling above; all we could do to prevent Hendryx throwing a brick at the guard.

## February 27 (Saturday)

Robert Ould, Confederate Agent for Exchange, wrote Secy. of War James A. Seddon on this date:

I have just returned from City Point.... Maj. Mulford assures me upon his own personal knowledge that Gen. Butler is in favor of a general exchange and release of prisoners, and further, that he is entirely satisfied of his ability to consummate the same. He distinctly declares that he is authorized to say so. Maj. Mulford never yet has deceived me and I am very much inclined to believe what he says. Butler has evidently set his heart, for some reason or other, on securing the release of the Yankee prisoners. He would hate a failure in that direction after recognition more than a refusal to recognize him.... I think that upon an interview with him as commanding general at Ft. Monroe I could get a distinct written agreement from him for a general exchange. The difficulty occurring to my mind about that arrangement is that he might require some pledge as to slaves. If

he is now recognized as an agent I am quite sure I can avoid that difficulty. The flag of truce boat remains at City Point to await your decision. The subject is environed with so many difficulties that I hesitate to pronounce any judgment in the premises.

Ransom, John, QM Sgt., 9th Michigan Cavalry, Pemberton Bldg., Richmond, Va.:

Organizing the militia; hauling artillery past the prison. Have a good view of all that is going on. Bought a compass from one of the guards for seven dollars, greenbacks; worth half a dollar at home. It is already rumored among the men that we have a compass, a map of Virginia, a preparation to put on our feet to prevent dogs from tracking us, and we are looked up to as if we were sons of Irish lords in disguise, and are quite noted personages. Cold last night, and we suffer much in not having blankets enough to keep us warm. The walls are cold and damp, making it disagreeable, and the stench nearly makes us sick. It is impossible for a person to imagine prison life until he has seen and realized it.... Time passes more drearily.... Were all searched again today but still keep my diary.... A man shot for putting his head out of the window.... We are nearly opposite and not more than twenty rods from Libby Prison, which is a large tobacco warehouse.... Hendryx had a fight with the raiders—got licked.

## February 28 (Sunday)

Gen. Judson Kilpatrick led a force of 3500 Federal cavalry south on a raid to crash through the weakened defenses of Richmond and free the Union prisoners there. He crossed the Rapidan early in the morning accompanied by Col. Ulric Dahlgren.

Brig. Gen. George A. Custer also began a raid in the vicinity of Albemarle County, Va., as a diversionary tactic.

Ransom, John, QM Sgt., 9th Michigan Cavalry, Pemberton Bldg., Richmond, Va.:

Had the honor (?) of seeing Jefferson Davis again and part of his congress today. They visited Libby and we were allowed to look out of the windows to see them as they passed in and out of the building. Strut around like chickens with frozen feet.... Have no more exalted opinion of them than before.

Jones, John B., Rebel War Clerk, Confederate War Dept., Richmond, Va.:

Yesterday the Secretary ordered Col. Northrop to allow full rations of meal to the engineer corps; today he returns the order, saying: "There is not sufficient transportation for full rations to the troops in the field."

Last night the Secretary sent for Mr. Ould, exchange agent, and it is thought an exchange of prisoners will be effected, and with Butler.

### February 29 (Monday)

Kilpatrick's cavalry hurried south from the Rapidan towards Richmond, the force splitting, sending 500 men under Col. Ulric Dahlgren to Goochland C.H., the remainder staying with Kilpatrick. Richmond, alerted as to the intent of the raid, was taking defensive measures to counter the attack.

Ransom, John, QM Sgt., 9th Michigan Cavalry, Pemberton Bldg., Richmond, Va.:

Excitement among the Johnnies—flying around as if the Yankee army were threatening Richmond. Cannot learn what the commotion is, but hope it is something that will benefit us. LATER—The occasion of the excitement among the rebels is that Dahlgren is making a raid on Richmond, acting in conjunction with Kilpatrick, for the purpose of liberating prisoners. We are heavily guarded and not allowed to look out of the windows...

Montgomery, J.J., Lowry's Scouts, escaped Confederate prisoner, Tenn.:

I had to ford the river about one mile into McKennon's Island after dark, where I stayed the night...

### March 1 (Tuesday)

The Federal cavalry raid led by Gen. Kilpatrick which started on February 28th was now within a few miles of Richmond. The "home guard" in the city was alerted and was out to defend the city in the entrenchments to the north. Kilpatrick, thinking the works too heavy to carry, turned east towards Chickahominy and the Peninsula in a driving rain. Col. Ulric Dahlgren, riding strapped to the saddle, had gone more westerly to Goochland C.H., and was within two miles of the city at nightfall. Faced with stiff resistance from Gen. Custis Lee, Dahlgren realized that the raid had failed and attempted to escape with his men.

Quartermaster Sgt. John Ransom, being held in the Pemberton Building next to Libby Prison, made an entry in his diary for *February 30*. The context of the entry would place it for this date, March 1.

Ransom, John, QM Sgt., 9th Michigan Cavalry, Pemberton Bldg., Richmond, Va.:

Rebels in hot water all night and considerably agitated. Imagined we could hear firing during the night. This morning small squads of tired-out Union soldiers marched by our prison under guard, evidently captured through the night. Look as if they was completely played out. Go straggling by sometimes not more than half a dozen at a time. Would give something to hear the news.

Montgomery, J.J., Lowry's Scouts, escaped Confederate prisoner, Tenn.:

...so on the morning of March 1, 1864, I was once more a free man in Dixie's land, something the worse by wear from my ride. I rested two months in North Alabama. In May I recrossed [the Tennessee River] in a skiff, about dark, and walked back to Giles County, where I was soon mounted, and returned to North Alabama with a complete outfit of everything the U.S. government issued to its cavalry.

Malone, B.Y., Sgt., Co. H, 6th N.C. Infantry, CSA, prisoner, Point Lookout, Md.:

The first day of March was coal and raney: And our Company was examined on the Oath question evry man was taken in the House one at a time and examiond: the questions asked me was this: Do you wish to take the Oath and join the U.S. Armey or Navy: or work at government work or on Brestworks or Do you wish to take a Parole and go to your home if it be insied of our lines or do you wish to go South I told I wished to go South: He then asked me my name County State Company & Regiment The 2d two thousen Rebels left Point Lookout Md. for Dixie:

Brig. Gen. A. Schoepf, commanding Ft. Delaware, Del., informed Col. Hoffman today that smallpox had entirely disappeared from Pea Patch Island. Schoepf was preparing for 4000 more prisoners.

### March 2 (Wednesday)

In Washington, the Congress approved the

appointment of U.S. Grant as Lieutenant General of the U.S. Army.

East of Richmond, Gen. Fitzhugh Lee's cavalry pursued the remnants of Judson Kilpatrick's cavalrymen through the night and into the morning. Kilpatrick headed on to a junction with Gen. Ben Butler's men on the Peninsula.

Col. Ulric Dahlgren (son of Rear Admiral John Dahlgren), who had already lost a leg in the action at Boonsboro, Md., had insisted on being one of the leaders of a cavalry raid against Richmond. His force of about 500 men was sent on a separate part of the raid to Goochland C.H., where it reached a point to within two miles of the city. Realizing the raid had failed, Dahlgren swung east, hotly pursued by Fitzhugh Lee's cavalry. An ambush at Mantapike Hill between King and Queen C.H. and King William C.H. trapped Col. Dahlgren and his remaining men, and Dahlgren was killed in the action; about 100 of his men were captured by a force of Confederate infantry and cavalry. A few escaped to the U.S.S. *Morse*, positioned on the York River near Brick House Farm. Admiral Dahlgren, hearing of his son's death, wrote in his diary, "How busy is death—oh, how busy indeed!"

As a result of the raid, which was an attempt to release the prisoners in Richmond, the fear of the prisoners getting loose in Richmond caused much panic and concern. War Clerk Jones recorded the effect of this fear:

Last night, when it was supposed probable that the prisoners of war at Libby might attempt to break out, Gen. Winder ordered that a large amount of powder be placed under the building, with instructions to blow them up, if the attempt were made. He was persuaded, however, to consult the Secretary of War first, and get his approbation. The Secretary would give no such order, but said the prisoners must not be permitted to escape under any circumstances, which was considered sanction enough. Capt. ―― ―― obtained an order for, and procured several hundred pounds of gunpowder, which were placed in readiness. Whether the prisoners were advised of this I know not; but I told Capt. ――― it could not be justifiable to spring such a mine in the absence of their knowledge of the fate awaiting them, in the event of their attempt to break out,—because such prisoners are not to be condemned for striving

to regain their liberty. Indeed, it is the *duty* of a prisoner of war to escape if he can.

Ransom, John, QM Sgt., 9th Michigan Cavalry, Pemberton Bldg., Richmond, Va.:

The food we get here is poor, water very good, weather outside admirable, vermin still under control and the Astor House Mess flourishing. We are all in good health with the exception of Dr. Lewis, who is ailing.... Have become quite interested in a young soldier boy from Ohio named Bill Havens. Is sick with some kind of fever and is thoroughly bad off. Was tenderly brought up and well educated I should judge. Says he ran away from home to become a drummer. Has been wounded twice, in numerous engagements, now a prisoner of war and sick. Will try and keep track of him. Every nationality is here represented and from every branch of service, and from all parts of the world.

### March 3 (Thursday)

Maj. Gen. Benj. F. Butler, at Ft. Monroe, Va., wrote Robert Ould, Confederate Agent for Exchange, in Richmond, about a problem in North Carolina, where Maj. Gen. George Pickett was threatening retaliation for the proposed execution of a Confederate soldier:

I inclose you copies of the correspondence, so far as received, between Gen. Peck and Gen. Pickett, and instructions to Gen. Peck from myself, in regard to the execution of certain men in North Carolina enlisted in the U.S. Service.

I desire to ask your especial attention to the threat of Gen. Pickett that he will hang ten men for any retaliation that may be made by Gen. Peck for the murder of men in the U.S. Army. If that threat had been made in answer to a claim that deserters from an army situated as is yours were not liable to be executed upon capture if found in arms in our ranks, it might have been possibly justified under the laws of war; but even then the question of the right of executing such persons is still worthy of careful consideration and discussion. True, Gen. Pickett having deserted his own flag and the Army of the United States on the 25th of June, 1861, would probably know what should be the fate of a deserter found in arms against his Government; but the question will be whether he would be permitted to allow his own personal feelings to prevail in a matter of so grave importance to his brother officers and soldiers now in our hands.

*I beg you, however, to observe that this threat was in answer to a claim that a negro soldier enlisted in the Army of the United States, and under the protection of its Government, should not be wantonly murdered simply because that, while in the field and in the course of military operations, he, in pursuance of his duties as a soldier, shot a colonel of the Confederate Army while he was building a pontoon bridge—a meritorious act on the part of the soldier, and one because of which, under no rule of civilized warfare, should a hair of his head be injured....*

*But the question which I desire to submit for authoritative decision on the part of those who you represent is, whether a soldier of the United States who is duly enlisted and has not deserted from your army, and who has committed no act which could be construed as crime—save acts of hostility in the field against the Confederate armies, whatever may be the color or complexion of that soldier—is to be regarded by your authorities as a prisoner of war, and, as such, entitled to the rights and immunities of such condition....* [italics added]

Ransom, John, QM Sgt., 9th Michigan Cavalry, Pemberton Bldg., Richmond, Va.:

The ham given us today was rotten, with those nameless little white things crawling around through it. Promptly threw it out of the window and was scolded for it by a fellow prisoner who wanted it himself. Shall never become hungry enough to eat poor meat.

### March 4 (Friday)

Ransom, John, QM Sgt., 9th Michigan Cavalry, Pemberton Bldg., Richmond, Va.:

And now we are getting ready to move somewhere, the Lord only knows where. One good thing about their old prisons, we are always ready for a change.... My boy Havens has fever and chills. Is rather better today. It is said we move tonight. Minnesota Indians confined here, and a number of sailors and marines.

### March 6 (Sunday)

In Richmond, the clerks, walking wounded, old men, and anyone else who could walk, crawl, or totter, had been called out to defend the city against Kilpatrick's abortive raid. War Clerk Jones had been railing against the government offices being staffed with able-bodied young men while the army went in need of recruits. He believed that all such men, except his son, of course, should be in the army.

Col. W. Pinkney Shingler, CSA, wrote Brig. Gen. Hunton, Holombe Legion, on this date about a singular problem:

I send up four negro soldiers captured by Lt. Hume on the advance of the enemy from Williamsburg. In a conversation with Gen. Elzey's assistant adjutant-general some months since in the presence of Gen. E., I think, it was suggested and sanctioned by Gen. E. that *the best disposition of such soldiers was to sell them and give the proceeds to the command capturing them.* [italics added] If such a proceeding is admissible you will allow the guard with the prisoners to proceed with them to Richmond, as they are instructed what to do with them, or you can let the guard go with them to Gen. E. in case you do not feel authorized to act in the matter. I have directed Lt. Hume not to report any more such captures to me.

### March 7th (Monday)

Ransom, John, QM Sgt., 9th Michigan Cavalry, en route south from Richmond, Va.:

We were roused from our gentle slumbers during the night, counted off and marched to the cars, loaded into them, which had evidently just had some cattle as occupants. Started southward to some portion of Georgia, as a guard told us. Passed through Petersburg, and other towns which I could not learn the names of. Cars ran very slow, and being crowded, we are very uncomfortable—and hungry. Before leaving Richmond hardtack was issued to us in good quantity for the Confederacy. Have not much chance to write. Bought some boiled sweet potatoes of the guard, which are boss. The country we pass through is a miserable one. Guards watch us close to see that none escape, and occasionally a Yank is shot, but not in our car. Seems as if we did not run over thirty or forty miles per day. Stop for hours on side tracks, waiting for other trains to pass us.

### March 8 (Tuesday)

Today, U.S. Grant arrived in Washington, D.C., to take command of all U.S. armies.

Ransom, John, QM Sgt., 9th Michigan Cavalry, en route south from Richmond, Va.:

Were unloaded last night and given a chance to straighten our limbs. Stayed all night in the woods, side of the track, under a heavy guard. Don't know where we are, as guards are very reticent.

### March 9 (Wednesday)

U.S. Grant was commissioned Lieutenant General on this date, being officially handed the commission by President Lincoln in the presence of the Cabinet. Later, Grant and Lincoln held private conversations before Grant left for the Army of the Potomac and a visit to Maj. Gen. Meade.

Col. Hoffman had problems with the railroad, which he outlined for Quartermaster-General Montgomery C. Meigs:

By your instructions of the 5th of January passenger cars were to be furnished. They were to be well supplied with water and lights, and the time was to be not over forty-eight hours. The officer in charge of the party reports that at Pittsburgh they were put on freight cars which were inadequately supplied with water and lights, and that the travel was from eight and a half to seventeen miles per hour. He does not report the time of arrival at Baltimore, but as they did not leave there till the morning of the 13th, having left Sandusky on the 10th of February, they were probably some twenty hours behind time. The commander of the guard reported that the transporting of the prisoners in the freight cars and the slow rate of travel gave them great facilities for making their escape, which a number availed themselves of. Having no means of communication with the engineer it was impossible for him to stop the train when escapes were made. I report these facts in order that if the contract by the railroad company was not complied with it may be made to forfeit some part or all of their compensation...

Jones, John B., Rebel War Clerk, Confederate War Dept., Richmond, Va.:

This is the famine month. Prices of every commodity in the market—up, up, up. Bacon, $10 to $15 per pound; meal, $50 per bushel. But the market-houses are deserted, the meat stalls all closed, only here and there a cart, offering turnips, cabbages, parsnips, carrots, etc., at outrageous prices. However, the superabundant paper money is beginning to flow into the Treasury, and that reflex of the financial tide may produce salutary results a few weeks hence.

### March 10 (Thursday)

Grant visited Gen. Meade at the latter's headquarters for a talk that concerned the state of the Army of the Potomac and their working command relationship. Grant would stay in the field with Meade during the coming campaign.

Jones, John B., Rebel War Clerk, Confederate War Dept., Richmond, Va.:

Maj. Griswold is at variance with Gen. Winder, who has relieved him as Provost Marshal, and ordered him to Americus, Ga., to be second in command of the prisons...

Ransom, John, QM Sgt., 9th Michigan Cavalry, en route south from Richmond, Va.:

Still traveling, and unload nights to sleep by the track. Rebel citizens and women improve every opportunity to see live Yankees. Are fed passably well. Lewis feeling poorly. Watch a chance to escape but find none.

### March 13 (Sunday)

At Andersonville, Ga., Capt. R.B. Winder, Asst. Quartermaster, was trying to get construction done on some necessary buildings for the prison administration. Being out in the wilderness and away from the usual facilities for such things as lumber, everything seemed to be at least twice as difficult. Today he wrote Maj. A.M. Allen, the commissary officer.

I will have your building put up with pleasure, and am already putting up the logs, but I cannot get lumber sufficient to do my own work, and told you when you were here that you must furnish you own materials, and I am even willing to pay for them, but not at the price of $100 per thousand, which was the price that Capt. Armstrong informed me he could purchase lumber at. Harold is purchasing lumber and has authority, too, to impress same, at least he so informed me this morning. If you have this authority come at once and impress the lumber.

Ransom, John, QM Sgt., 9th Michigan Cavalry, en route south from Richmond, Va.:

Ran very slow through the night, and are in the vicinity of Macon, Ga. Will reach our prison tonight. Received a pone of corn bread apiece weighing about two pounds, which is liberal on their part. Two more days such riding as this would kill me. The lice are fairly eating us up alive, having no chance to rid ourselves of them since leaving Richmond.

Yesterday Grant had returned to Washington only long enough to catch a train to Nashville, where he had an appointment with Sherman, who was to be the commander of the western armies. Maj. Gen. Halleck, at his own request, was relieved as General-in-Chief and named Chief of Staff to Grant; Grant was assigned command of *all* the armies; Sherman was named as Grant's replacement in the west. McPherson moved into Sherman's vacated billet as commander of the Army of the Tennessee.

Surgeon A.M. Clark, Hoffman's speedy Medical Inspector, had gone to Nashville, Tenn., to inspect things there. Today he reported to Hoffman:

...report of inspection of the penitentiary and several hospitals at this post where prisoners of war are detained. Prisoners on arriving from the front are placed in the east wing and main building of the State penitentiary, but are rarely detained at this post for more than twenty-four hours, being as quickly as practicable transferred to Louisville, Ky., unless sufficiently ill to require hospital treatment. One difficulty obtains here, which I have not met with elsewhere. The penitentiary is used as a general guardhouse for the district, all prisoners being crowded in together without distinction of class, excepting that the west wing is devoted to civil prisoners only.... The cooking arrangements are somewhat contracted, yet are sufficient for their purpose, prisoners being furnished with cooked rations during their stay. The cooking is done by contrabands. No prison fund is established, rations being only drawn for prisoners as they arrive and for one day at a time. The sinks are in the prison yard, and are altogether inadequate in accommodation, and in a miserable state of police. The sink consists of one box, about 12 by 3 by 3 feet in dimensions, with four half casks for use as urinals. These are supposed

to be cleaned daily, but such is by no means the case. I found them full to overflowing and exceedingly offensive....

... March 12 I found 64 prisoners, 56 of whom were prisoners of war, sick in U.S. Army General Hospital No. 1, in charge of Surg. C.W. Hornor, U.S. Volunteers.... The patients are clean, well clad, and well cared for, and the ward and furniture in good order and police.... Every prisoner is vaccinated on his entrance into the hospital.... This hospital is located on the public square and consists of two large warehouses not at all well adapted to this purpose.... I would suggest that a distinct prison hospital be organized at this post.

## March 14 (Monday)

The South had problems everywhere with a high mortality rate among prisoners in its charge. Even with the transportation of prisoners from Richmond to the other prisons like Andersonville and Salisbury, a major problem still existed in the hospitals.

Confederate Gen. Braxton Bragg, now acting as a senior advisor to Jefferson Davis, directed that Surgeon T.G. Richardson conduct an inspection of the prison hospital facilities in Richmond. On this date Surgeon Richardson forwarded his report to Gen. Bragg:

The buildings are three in number, each of brick, three stories above ground. One is situated at the corner of Twenty-fifth and Carey streets, one at the corner of Main and Twenty-sixth streets, and the other at the corner of Franklin and Twenty-fifth streets. The last two seem to be well adapted for the purpose designed, being well ventilated and easily kept clean; but the first, possessing neither of these conditions, is wholly unsuitable.

The three buildings can accommodate comfortably about five hundred (500) patients, allowing eight hundred (800) cubic feet per man.

On the 11th instant, there were present in hospital 1127 sick and wounded. The wards contain, therefore, more than twice the number patients prescribed by orders; and such is their crowded condition that in some instances two patients were found on a single bunk.

The evil consequences of this state of affairs are clearly manifested in the severe mortality exhibited by the reports of the surgeon in charge:

Ratio of deaths per 1000 in January 1864          188
Ratio of deaths per 1000 in February          240
Number of deaths in March, to date
  (eleven days)          244

Stated in another form, the average number of deaths per day during the month of January was 10; the average ... of February, 18; the average ... of March to date, 22; on the day previous to that of inspection, the number was 26.

The ratio, it will be observed, is rapidly increasing; and, compared with that of the hospital for our own sick and wounded, the mortality in which for the same period did not in any case exceed 20 per 1000, and in some did not reach 10 per thousand, is truly frightful.... In the month of February, of 337 cases of diarrhea admitted, 265 were fatal, a result ascribed, in part, by the medical officer, to the want of flour—cornmeal alone being furnished.

Of typhoid fever cases admitted during the three months preceding March 1st, $64\frac{1}{2}$ percent. proved fatal.

Dr. Wilkins, the surgeon in charge until very recently,... made to the proper authorities a report dated November 21, 1863, setting forth the capacity of the hospital buildings, and the overcrowded state of his wards, and urging the necessity for further accommodations; but it seems that his request was not complied with. He again, in a communication dated December 16, 1863, called attention to the same subject; but so far as it appears, with no effect. He further reports ... that the medical purveyor does not furnish a sufficiency of medicines, and that the commissary does not provide for the sick requiring its use.

The kitchen and laundries of two of the buildings are tolerably well arranged, and well attended to. The latrines are badly located, but well cared for. From the crowded condition of the wards it is impossible to preserve them from offensive effluvia....

The ward at Libby Prison appropriated to sick and wounded federal officers is also objectionable, being on the ground floor and not well ventilated; but the mortality has been very slight, owing in a measure ... to the fact that the patients generally have the means and privilege of purchasing better diet than can be furnished by the commissary. There are 40 sick in this ward, which is its full capacity.

The bedding of the hospital is, in the main, good, and, considering the limited facilities, well taken care of. The books and records are neatly kept.

Ransom, John, QM Sgt., 9th Michigan Cavalry, Andersonville Prison, Ga.:

Arrived at our destination at last and a dismal hole it is, too. We got off the cars at two o'clock this morning in a cold rain, and were marched into our pen between strong guard carrying lighted pine knots to prevent our crawling off in the dark. I could hardly walk have been cramped up so long, and feel as if I was a hundred years old. Have stood up ever since we came from the cars, and [am] shivering with the cold. The rain has wet us to the skin and we are worn out and miserable. Nothing to eat today, and another dismal night just setting in.

### March 15 (Tuesday)

At Andersonville, Capt. R.B. Winder, Asst. Quartermaster, still had problems getting building materials to complete the support buildings for the post. He also had another problem. The isolated location of the prison meant that *all* workers had to subsist at the location because there was no other place to live or eat. Before the ground rules were changed on where rations were to be obtained, Winder had furnished rations, at cost, to the workers through the Quartermaster Dept. However, recently, the control of rations had been given to the Commissary Dept. and he no longer had control. The local Commissary Officer, Maj. Allen, was somewhat of a stuffed shirt and not too cooperative.

Jones, John B., Rebel War Clerk, Confederate War Dept., Richmond, Va.:

By the correspondence of the department, I saw today that 35,000 bushels of corn left North Carolina nearly a week ago for Lee's army, and about the same time 400,000 pounds of bacon was in readiness to be shipped from Augusta, Ga. At short rations, that would furnish bread and meat for the army several weeks.

Ransom, John, QM Sgt., 9th Michigan Cavalry, Andersonville Prison, Ga.:

At about midnight I could stand up no longer, and lay

down in the mud and water. Could hardly get up. Shall get food this morning, and after eating shall feel better. There is a good deal to write about here, but I must postpone it until some future time, for I can hardly hold a pencil now. LATER—Have drawn some rations which consisted of nearly a quart of cornmeal, half a pound of beef, and some salt. This is splendid. I have just partaken of a delicious repast and feel like a different person. Dr. Lewis is discouraged and thinks he cannot live long in such a place as this.

### March 16 (Wednesday)

Ransom, John, QM Sgt., 9th Michigan Cavalry, Andersonville Prison, Ga.:

The prison is not yet entirely completed. One side is yet open, and through the opening two pieces of artillery are pointed. About 1800 Yankees are here now. Col. Piersons commands the prison, and rides in and talks with the men. Is quite sociable, and says we are all to be exchanged in a few weeks. He was informed that such talk would not go down any longer. We had been fooled enough, and paid no attention to what they told us. Our mess is gradually settling down. Have picked out our ground, rolled some big logs together, and are trying to make ourselves comfortable. I am in the best of spirits, and will live with them for some time to come if they will only give me one quarter enough to eat, and they are doing it now, and am in my glory. Weather cleared up and very cold nights. We put on all our clothes nights and take them off day-times. The men do most of their sleeping through the day, and shiver through the long nights.

### March 17 (Thursday)

Grant arrived in Nashville and took time to formally assume command of all the armies of the United States. Then he and Sherman boarded a train for Cincinnati, Ohio, to do their planning in private. Sherman would recall forever the details of what happened in that room—the plan to skin the Confederacy alive.

Ransom, John, QM Sgt., 9th Michigan Cavalry, Andersonville Prison, Ga.:

Get almost enough to eat, such as it is, but don't

get it regularly; sometimes in the morning, and sometimes in the afternoon. Six hundred more prisoners came last night, and from Belle Isle, Va., our old home. Andersonville is situated on two hillsides, with a small stream of swampy water running through the center, and on both sides of the stream is a piece of swamp with two or three acres in it. We have plenty of wood now, but it will not last long. They will undoubtedly furnish us with wood from the outside, when it is burned up on the inside. A very unhealthy climate. A good many are being poisoned by poisonous roots, and there is a thick green scum on the water. All who drink freely are made sick, and their faces swell up so they cannot see.

### March 18 (Friday)

Maj. Gen. Benj. F. Butler suggested that the officers of Morgan's command still in the Ohio State Penitentiary be transferred to Point Lookout for public relations purposes. Secy. of War Stanton, hearing a rumor that Morgan was planning another raid, decided to leave them securely locked up.

Ransom, John, QM Sgt., 9th Michigan Cavalry, Andersonville Prison, Ga.:

There are about fifteen acres of ground enclosed in the stockade and we have the freedom of the whole ground. Plenty of room, but they are filling it up. Six hundred new men coming each day from Richmond. Guards are perched upon top of the stockade; are very strict, and today one man was shot for approaching too near the wall. A little warm today. Found W.B. Rowe, from Jackson, Mich.; he is well and talks encouraging. We have no shelter of any kind whatever. Eighteen or twenty die per day. Cold and damp nights. The dew wet things through completely, and by morning all nearly chilled. Wood getting scarce. On the outside it is a regular wilderness of pines. Railroad a mile off and can just see the cars go by, which is the only sign of civilization in sight. Rebels all the while at work making the prison stronger. Very poor meal, and not so much today as formerly. My young friend Billy Havens was sent to the hospital about the time we left Richmond. Shall be glad to hear of his recovery.

### March 19 (Saturday)

Ransom, John, QM Sgt., 9th Michigan Cavalry, Andersonville Prison, Ga.:

A good deal of fighting going on among us. A large number of sailors and marines are confined with us, and they are a quarrelsome set. I have a very sore hand, caused by cutting a hole through the car trying to get out. I have to write with my left hand. It is going to be an awful place during the summer months here, and thousands will die no doubt.

### March 21 (Monday)

Ransom, John, QM Sgt., 9th Michigan Cavalry, Andersonville Prison, Ga.:

Prison gradually filling up with forlorn looking creatures. Wood is being burned up gradually. Have taken in my old acquaintance and a member of my own company "A" 9th Mich. Cavalry, Wm. B. Rowe. Sergt. Rowe is a tall, straight, dark complexioned man, about thirty-five years old. He was captured while carrying dispatches from Knoxville to Gen. Burnside. Has been a prisoner two or three months, and was in Pemberton Building until sent here. He is a tough, abled-bodied man. Every day I find new Michigan men, some of them old acquaintances.

Jones, John B., Rebel War Clerk, Confederate War Dept., Richmond, Va.:

Yesterday another thousand prisoners were brought up by the flag of truce boat. A large company of both sexes welcomed them in the Capitol Square, whither some baskets of food were sent by those who had some patriotism with their abundance. The President made them a comforting speech, alluding to their toils, bravery, and sufferings in captivity; and promised them, after a brief respite, that they should be in the field again.

### March 23 (Wednesday)

The Medical Director of the hospitals in Richmond requested reports from the various medical officers in the area concerning the state of the command's health. This included the prison camps. As a part of this report, Surgeon G. Wm. Semple, on Belle Isle, Richmond, Va., reported on the condition of the prison as of March 6th:

Into the camp containing an area sufficient for the accommodation of about 3000 men have been crowded for many months past from 6000 to 10,000 prisoners. To prevent escapes they have not been allowed to visit the sinks at night. Thus deposits of excrement have been made in the streets and small vacant places between the tents. The streets are so greatly crowded during the day as greatly to interfere with the working police parties, so that nearly the whole day is consumed by them in the imperfect removal of the filthy accumulations of the night. The whole surface of the camp has thus been saturated with putrid animal matter. Surrounded by such circumstances the prisoners have been totally careless of personal cleanliness.

The rations now consist entirely of bread, rice, and peas or beans. The bread is made of cornmeal, unsifted or bolted. Not separating the bran from the meal tends greatly to cause and continue the two diseases (diarrhea and dysentery) most prevalent among the prisoners. Many of them are badly clad and destitute of blankets, having sold the articles lately furnished them by their Government. Under these circumstances, though they have been furnished with fuel, there has been great suffering from cold during the unusually cold weather of January and February, to which the brutal conduct of the prisoners in expelling their comrades from their tents at night has greatly added.

To the crowded and necessarily filthy condition of the camp, the absence of personal cleanliness of the prisoners, the meager rations, and the effects of the cold may be added the depressing effect of long continued confinement without employment, mental or physical, and with little hope of an early termination of the imprisonment, which together make up sufficient sum of causes to account for the report during the month of February of a sufficient number of cases to amount to one fourth the average number of prisoners in the camp. The diseases have been such, consisting principally of typhoid fever, diarrhea, dysentery, and catarrh and the diseases of the respiratory organs, as might be expected to result from the causes stated. But great as is this amount of disease, it is not greater than the average sickness among the U.S. troops in the field on the Atlantic coast, as reported by one of their own surgeons.

Much difficulty has been experienced in procuring the regular attendance of the sick at sick call.

Patients have been brought out on litters, unable to walk and greatly emaciated, who have never before attended sick call, and several deaths have occurred in camp without the prisoners having been seen by or reported to a medical officer, the sergeants in charge of squads alleging that they could not attend regularly to the duty of bringing the sick up to sick-call, because of the necessity of at the same time drawing and distributing rations. A sergeant has been selected from each squad to attend to this duty alone, and it is hoped that a more regular attendance of the sick at sick-call will thus be secured.

There is not space enough in the camp to establish as large a temporary hospital as desired, but five hospital tents have been pitched, which afford the means of treating temporarily the sick ordered to general hospital when prevented by the rising of the river or ice or the nonattendance of ambulances from being sent.

The overcrowding of the camp is now being rapidly reduced by transfers and exchange of prisoners. The number of prisoners being sufficiently reduced, the irregularities of the surface of the camp are to be filled up and the ditches and drains cleaned out. I have recommended to the commanding officer, and shall urge it most strongly on his attention, to have a sufficient number of sinks dug within the camp [down] to water, which rises within a few feet of the surface. In consequence of vaccination having been so generally practiced among the prisoners previous to their capture, it has been found impracticable to continue to propagate vaccination among them. But varioloid, which has prevailed to some extent, seems to attack indiscriminately those who have been vaccinated early in life and those recently vaccinated. The reports show a great diminution in the number of variola and varioloid cases, giving ground to hope they will soon cease.

To the report from Surgeon Semple, a report from Surgeon John Wilkins, General Hospital No. 21, Richmond, dated March 7th, was appended:

...to submit the following report of the deaths, diseases, and conditions of the patients received into this hospital: The daily list of deaths is regulated by the number admitted each day from Belle Isle. During the past month twenty-five cases died before they had been in the hospital twenty-four hours. Is is so common an occurrence for the patients from Belle

Isle to be speechless or delirious and unable to give their names, &c., that I have requested the surgeon in charge, in addition to the list forwarded by the conductor of the ambulances, to pin their names, companies and regiments of desperate cases on the lapel of their coats. The majority of cases die of chronic diarrhea. During the past month 337 cases suffering with this disease were admitted. The deaths from this disease during the month sum up to 265. Of typhoid fever cases for the last month 64.5 per cent. have died; from diarrhea 59.7 per cent. The commissary department for five weeks has not been able to furnish me with flour. The meal furnished in lieu thereof is ground with the husk and will produce diarrhea. I have ordered it to be sifted, but it is ground too fine to separate the husk from the meal.

The medical purveyor does not furnish the hospital with sufficient quantity of medicines. I made a requisition on the 1st of March, which has not been filled as yet. I would be most happy to receive suggestions from you in the treatment of diarrhea. I believe the medical officers have tried all known and approved remedies for the disease. In the case of other diseases, as pneumonia, &c., they generally occur in constitutions already enfeebled by diarrhea, and are generally in the second stage when admitted. In conclusion, the prominent character of all cases is emaciation.

Ransom, John, QM Sgt., 9th Michigan Cavalry, Andersonville Prison, Ga.:

Stockade all up, and we are penned in. Our mess is out of filthy lucre—otherwise, busted. Sold my overcoat to a guard, and for luxuries we are eating that up. My blanket keeps us all warm. There are two more in our mess. Daytimes the large spread is stretched three or four feet high on four sticks, and keeps off the sun, and at night taken down for a cover.

### March 24 (Thursday)

Gen. Samuel Cooper, Adjutant-Gen. of the Confederate Army, received a report from Branchville, S.C., concerning the movement of prisoners:

...make the following report: Number of Federal prisoners receipted for up to March 20, 6488; number escaped, 12; number died, 2; number left sick on the way, 117.

Six escaped February 27 between Macon and

Millen, Ga., during the night, by a hole cut in the end of the car. There was no light in the car, the train not being supplied with lights. Their names were not obtained. Six escaped March 20, near Windsor Station, South Carolina Railroad, at night, through a hole in the floor of the car, the train not being supplied with lights....

One died March 15 at a wood station near Macon, Ga., and was buried there, no receipt being taken for the corpse. One died March 26 at Macon, Ga. The names of the two dead are unknown.

... Fifteen convalescents, whose names were not obtained, were removed from Augusta to Andersonville, Ga., on the last trip.

Ransom, John, QM Sgt., 9th Michigan Cavalry, Andersonville Prison, Ga.:

Digging a tunnel to get out of this place. Prison getting filthy. Prisoners somewhat to blame for it. Good many are dying, and they are those who take no care of themselves, drink poor water, etc.

## March 25 (Friday)

John Ransom states that Capt. Wirz came to Andersonville today. The *OR* indicates that he was assigned to the post on March 27.

Ransom, John, QM Sgt., 9th Michigan Cavalry, Andersonville Prison, Ga.:

Lt. Piersons is no longer in command of the prison, but instead a Capt. Wirtz. Came inside today and looked us over. Is not a very prepossessing looking chap. Is about thirty-five or forty years old, rather tall, and a little stoop shouldered; skin has a pale, white livered look, with thin lips. Has a sneering sort of cast of countenance. Makes a fellow feel as if he would like to go up and boot him. Should judge he was a Swede, or some such countryman. Hendryx thinks he could make it warm for him in short order if he only had a chance. Wirtz wears considerable jewelry on his person—long watch chain, something that looks like a diamond for a pin in his shirt, and wears patent leather boots or shoes. I asked him if he didn't think we would be exchanged soon. He said: Oh, yes, we would be exchanged soon. Somehow or other this assurance don't elate us much; perhaps it was his manner when saying it. Andersonville is going to be a rather bad place as it grows warmer. Several sick with fevers and sores.

## March 26 (Saturday)

Ransom, John, QM Sgt., 9th Michigan Cavalry, Andersonville Prison, Ga.:

Well, well, my birthday came six days ago, and how old do you think I am? Let me see. Appearances would seem to indicate that I am thirty or thereabouts, but as I was born on the 20th day of March, 1843, I must now be just twenty-one years of age, this being the year 1864. Of age and six days over. I thought that when a man became of age he generally became free and his own master as well. If this ain't a burlesque on that old time-honored custom, then carry me out—but not feet foremost.

Sgt. Bartlett Yancey Malone of the 6th N.C. Infantry, confined at Point Lookout, Md., recorded the departure of Confederate prisoners for exchange—600 left on the 3rd and another boatload on the 16th. The cutoff on exchange had not yet taken effect. Malone went to work in the cook house yesterday.

## March 27 (Sunday)

Capt. Henry Wirz, having returned from convalescing in Europe, was today assigned to the Confederate prison at Andersonville, Ga.

Ransom, John, QM Sgt., 9th Michigan Cavalry, Andersonville Prison, Ga.:

We have issued to us once each day about a pint of beans, or more properly peas, (full of bugs), and three-quarters of a pint of meal, and nearly every day a piece of bacon the size of your two fingers, probably three or four ounces. This is very good rations taken in comparison to what I have received before. The pine which we use in cooking is pitch pine, and a black smoke arises from it; consequently we are black as negroes. Prison gradually filling from day to day, and situation rather more unhealthy. Occasionally a squad comes in who have been lately captured, and they tell of our battles, sometimes victorious and sometimes otherwise. Sometimes we are hopeful and sometimes the reverse. Take all the exercise we can, drink no water, and try to get along. It is a sad sight to see the men die so fast. New prisoners die the quickest and are buried in the near vicinity, we are told in trenches without coffins. Sometimes we have visitors of citizens and women who come to look at us. There is sympathy in some of their faces and in some a lack of it. A dead line composed of slats of boards runs around on the inside of the wall, about twelve or fourteen feet from the wall, and we are not allowed to go near it on pain of being shot by a guard.

### March 28 (Monday)

The situation of exchange regarding Negro soldiers in the U.S. forces had remained at a stalemate for months. The South, ignoring the problem as much as possible, and obfuscating what could not be ignored, tried a new tactic. In a letter to Secy. of War Stanton, Maj. Gen. E.A. Hitchcock explained the new twist:

The rebel authorities have virtually been countenanced in holding colored troops as excepted from the terms of exchange; for, while they decline to entertain any questions by which such troops are to be recognized as entitled to the privileges of soldiers in conformity with express orders from the rebel Government, they enter upon a cartel under a mere declaration that they hold no colored men belonging to "*organizations*," [italics added] by which they have been permitted to set out the principle that they will not entertain any proposition which would require them to treat colored troops as soldiers.

Ransom, John, QM Sgt., 9th Michigan Cavalry, Andersonville Prison, Ga.:

We are squadded over today, and rations about to come in. It's a sickly dirty place. Seems as if the sun was not over a mile high, and has a particular grudge against us. Wirtz comes inside and has began to be very insolent. Is constantly watching for tunnels. He is a brute. We call him the "Flying Dutchman." Came across Sergt. Bullock, of my regiment, whom I last saw on Belle Isle. From a fat, chubby young fellow, he is a perfect wreck. Lost his voice and can hardly speak aloud; nothing but skin and bone, and black and ragged. Never saw such a change in a human being. Cannot possibly live, I don't think; still he is plucky and hates to die. Goes all around enquiring for news, and the least encouraging cheers him up. Capt. Moseby, of the raiders, is in the same squad with me. He is quite an intelligent fellow and often talks with us. We lend him our boiling cup which he returns with thanks.

### March 29 (Tuesday)

Ransom, John, QM Sgt., 9th Michigan Cavalry, Andersonville Prison, Ga.:

Raiders getting more bold as the situation grows worse. Often rob a man now of all he has, in public, making no attempt at concealment. In sticking up for the weaker party, our mess gets into trouble nearly every day, and particularly Hendryx, who will fight any time.

The Confederate prison at Cahaba, Ala., had increased in population sufficiently to require more guards. The local newspapers reported that orders had been given to increase the guard strength because all Federal prisoners in the Department were to be confined there. The prison had far outgrown its designed population of 432 prisoners, now containing over 660 men.

### March 30 (Wednesday)

William Walker Ward was born at Ward's Crossroads, Tenn., on October 5, 1825. He was raised in rural Smith County, Tenn., obtaining the usual elementary education and then attending law school at Cumberland University in Lebanon, Tenn., graduating in 1851. During the 1850s he practised law in Smith County and served one term in the state legislature.

During the events leading to the war, Ward, and many of his fellow Tennesseeans, were not in favor of secession from the Union. After South Carolina fired on Ft. Sumter and began the conflict, Lincoln called for volunteers to put down the rebellion. Ward did not believe that the Federal government had a right to *force* the seceding states to remain in the Union, and so he enlisted in Company B, 7th Tennessee Infantry, of the Confederate Army. His initial service was with "Stonewall" Jackson in western Virginia, and during the Romney campaign. In February 1862, the regiment moved to Manassas, Va. In early May 1862, the regiment moved to Richmond to take part in the Peninsula campaign. Ward, however, was discharged for medical reasons on May 19, 1862, and was sent back to Tennessee.

In August 1862, John Hunt Morgan was recruiting for his cavalry in the area of Smith County, Tenn., and Ward enlisted. Rapidly progressing from

First Sgt. to Captain, Ward was permitted to form his own company, which he organized at Hartsville, Tenn., on August 27, 1862, and it became part of the 15th Tennessee Battalion. When merged with the battalion, Ward was elected Lieutenant Colonel.

On December 23, 1862, William W. Ward married Elizabeth Hughes Rucks. He was to see little of his bride for the next two years. This was also the date of his promotion to Colonel and his assignment to regimental command. The regimental designation was shortly changed to the 9th Tennessee from the 15th.

Ward participated in Morgan's raids into Kentucky, Indiana, and Ohio, during 1863, but his luck ran out when he was captured attempting to cross the Ohio River at Bluffington Island, Ohio. He was first taken to the Cincinnati jail, where he spent two days, and then he was transferred to Johnson Island, near Erie, Pa. He remained at Johnson Island for only four days before being moved to the state prison in Columbus, Ohio.

On November 27, 1863, Morgan and six of his men escaped from the prison in Columbus, two being recaptured shortly. Morgan made his way back to Tennessee. Ward remained in the Ohio prison until March 1864, when he was moved to Ft. Delaware, arriving there on March 28, 1864.

Ward, William W., Col., 9th Tenn. Cavalry, prisoner, Ft. Delaware, Del.:

By the kindness of Gen. Schoeph, Cols. Morgan, Tucker, Coleman and myself were paroled to the Island. Yesterday was a beautiful day. Today is the most blustry rainy day I ever experienced. We form into a mess, Bennett Griffin Ellis Harper & myself. Live pretty well.

Ransom, John, QM Sgt., 9th Michigan Cavalry, Andersonville Prison, Ga.:

The gate opens every little while letting some poor victims into this terrible place, which is already much worse than Belle Isle. Seems as if our government is at fault in not providing some way to get us out of here. The hot weather months must kill us all outright. Feel myself at times sick and feverish with no strength seemingly. Dr. Lewis worries, worries, all the day long, and it's all we can do to keep him from giving up entirely. Sergt. Rowe takes things as they

come in dogged silence. Looks like a caged lion. Hendryx sputters around, scolding away, &c.

### March 31 (Thursday)

Surgeon R.H. Whitfield, assigned to the Confederate Prison at Cahaba, Ala., was not happy with the conditions at the prison, which, at this time, held 660 men. He was seriously concerned about the pollution of the water supply caused by the

washing of the hands, feet, faces, and heads of soldiers, citizens, and negroes, buckets, tubs, and spittoons of groceries, offices and hospital, hogs, dogs, cows, and horses, and filth of all kinds from the streets and other sources.

Whitfield's report further stated that only a portion of the warehouse was covered, the remaining space, approximately 1600 square feet, being left open. He further complained that only one wheelbarrow was available for the prisoners' use to haul trash and garbage from the compound. This resulted in heaps of trash which added to the already crowded conditions and posed an additional health hazard. No improvements resulted from the report of Surgeon Whitfield.

Ward, William W., Col., 9th Tenn. Cavalry, prisoner, Ft. Delaware, Del.:

Gen. A. Scoepf ordered Coleman (Col. C), Col. R.C. Morgan & Col. Tucker and myself to his quarters and paroled us to the Island. Gen. M. Jeff Thompson Gen. Vance and the Cols of our command form a mess, and live very well. We give a negro woman $7.00 per week for cooking, $10.00 for washing.

### April 1 (Friday)

Ransom, John, QM Sgt., 9th Michigan Cavalry, Andersonville Prison, Ga.:

This is an April Fool sure. Saw a fellow today from our regiment, named Casey. Says I was reported dead at the regiment, which is cheerful. Perhaps it is just as well though, for them to anticipate the event a few months. Often hear the guards shoot and hear of men being killed. Am not ambitious to go near them. Have completely lost my desire to be on the outside working for extra rations. Prefer to stick it out where I am than to have anything to do with them. They are an ungodly crew, and should have the warmest corner in that place we sometimes hear mentioned.

## April 2 (Saturday)

Ransom, John, QM Sgt., 9th Michigan Cavalry, Andersonville Prison, Ga.:

James Robins, an Indiana soldier, is in our close proximity. Was wounded and taken prisoner not long since. Wound, which is in the thigh, is in a terrible condition, and gangrene setting in. Although he was carried to the gate today, was refused admission to the hospital or medical attendance. Rebels say they have no medicine for us. Robins has been telling me about himself and family at home, and his case is only one of a great many good substantial men of families who must die in Southern prisons, as victims to mismanagement. The poorer the Confederacy, and the meaner they are, the more need that our government should get us away from here, and not put objectionable men at the head of exchange to prevent our being sent home or back to our commands.

## April 3 (Sunday)

Ransom, John, QM Sgt., 9th Michigan Cavalry, Andersonville Prison, Ga.:

We have stopped wondering at suffering or being surprised at anything. Can't do the subject justice and so don't try. Walk around camp every morning looking for acquaintances, the sick, &c. Can see a dozen most any morning laying around dead. A great many are terribly afflicted with diarrhea, and scurvy begins to take hold of some. Scurvy is a bad disease, and taken in connection with the former is sure death. Some have dropsy as well as scurvy, and the swollen limbs and body are sad to see. To think that these victims have people at home, mothers, wives and sisters, who are thinking of them and would do much for them if they had the chance, little dreaming of their condition.

Ward, William W., Col., 9th Tenn. Cavalry, prisoner, Ft. Delaware, Del.:

Spent the forenoon in reading and went to the barracks to hear Dr. Handy, a political prisoner from Portsmouth preach. The first sermon I have heard for about 12 months. The Dr. is a good old man & a good preacher.

## April 4 (Monday)

Jones, John B., Rebel War Clerk, Confederate War Dept., Richmond, Va.:

Mr. Ould and Capt. Hatch, agents of exchange (of prisoners), have returned from a conference with Gen. Butler, at Fortress Monroe, and it is announced that arrangements have been made for an immediate resumption of the exchange of prisoners on the old footing. Thus has the government abandoned the ground so proudly assumed—of nonintercourse with Butler, and the press is firing away at it for negotiating with the "Beast" and outlaw. But our men in captivity are in favor of a speedy exchange, no matter with whom the agreement is made.

Ransom, John, QM Sgt., 9th Michigan Cavalry, Andersonville Prison, Ga.:

Same old story—coming in and being carried out; all have a feeling of lassitude which prevents much exertion. Have been digging a tunnel for a day or two with a dozen others who are in the secret. It's hard work. A number of tunnels have been discovered. The water now is very warm and sickening.

## April 5 (Tuesday)

Ransom, John, QM Sgt., 9th Michigan Cavalry, Andersonville Prison, Ga.:

Dr. Lewis talks about nothing except his family. Is the bluest mortal here, and worries himself sick, let alone causes sufficient for that purpose. Is poorly adapted for hardships. For reading we have the "Pilgrim's Progress," donated to me by some one when on Belle Isle.... "Scotty," a marine, just now is edifying our mess with his saltwater yarns, and they are tough ones.

Malone, B.Y., Sgt., Co. H, 6th N.C. Infantry, CSA, prisoner, Point Lookout, Md.:

The 5th was a very bad day it raind hard snowed and the wind blew the Bay was so high that it overflowed part of the Camp. Some men had to leave thir tents and moove up to the Cook house: There was some men in camp who had been going about of nits and cutting tents and sliping mens Knapsacks Hats Boots and Sumetimes, would get Some money They cut into ours and got money and cloathen all amounting to about one hundred dollars: One nite the Negros was on gard and caught them they was then plaised under gard and made ware a Barrel Shirt (and march) up and down the Streets with large letters on them the letters was this Tent Cutters

### April 6 (Wednesday)

Ransom, John, QM Sgt., 9th Michigan Cavalry, Andersonville Prison, Ga.:

The slightest news about exchange is told from one to the other, and gains every time repeated, until finally it's grand good news and sure exchange immediately. The weak ones feed upon these reports and struggle along from day to day. One hour they are all hope and expectation and the next hour as bad the other way. The worst looking scalawags perched upon the stockade as guards, from boys just large enough to handle a gun, to old men who ought to have been dead years ago for the good of their country. Some prisoners nearly naked, the majority in rags and daily becoming more destitute. My clothes are good and kept clean, health fair although very poor in flesh. Man killed at the dead line.

Ward, William W., Col., 9th Tenn. Cavalry, prisoner, Ft. Delaware, Del.:

A very pleasant day. Bet a bottle of Whiskey with Col. Morgan that we would not be exchanged by the 25th Inst. to be paid after our exchange. Wrote a letter to my wife at night. Cols Duke, Morgan, Coleman Tucker & myself and Capts Gibson & C.H. Morgan are within one room. We all get on pritty well.

### April 7 (Thursday)

Ransom, John, QM Sgt., 9th Michigan Cavalry, Andersonville Prison, Ga.:

Capt. Wirtz prowls around the stockade with a rebel escort of guards, looking for tunnels. Is very suspicious of amateur wells which some have dug for water. It is useless to speak to him about our condition, as he will give us no satisfaction whatever. Says it is good enough for us ———— Yankees.... Prison is all the time being made stronger, more guards coming and artillery looking at us rather unpleasantly from many directions. Think it impossible for any to get away here, so far from our lines. The men are not able to withstand the hardships attendant upon an escape, still fully one-half of all here are constantly on

the alert for chances to get away.... Weather is getting warmer, water warmer and nastier, food worse and less in quantities, and more prisoners coming nearly every day.

Ward, William W., Col., 9th Tenn. Cavalry, prisoner, Ft. Delaware, Del.:

Arose early. Most delightful morning. Capt Gibson & myself walked to the sutlers. He ordered a pair of fine Cavalry boots from Philadelphia, we then walked to the shore & looked out on the Bay and across to Dela. City. It is about one & a quarter miles to the city. We can see it much plainer this morning than we have been able to do heretofore. After breakfast we all went to the Barracks and found the officers in fine spirits and doing very well. Had a chat this morning with Dr. Handy. Brogden is playing chess with Col. Duke. He is quit[e] a nice, kind and intelligent gentleman. He carried a ring over to a political prisoner yesterday and had my wife's name cut on it. One Mr. Long, a political prisoner, cut the name & would not charge me anything for it. I am under obligation to Long & Brogden both for their kindness and also to Col. Morgan, who gave me the ring. I will send it in my next letter to my wife. I walked a long walk this evening to our new quarters. Do not like them much.

### April 8 (Friday)

Ransom, John, QM Sgt., 9th Michigan Cavalry, Andersonville Prison, Ga.:

We are digging with an old fire shovel at our tunnel. The shovel is a prize; we also use half of canteens, pieces of boards, &c. It's laborious work. A dozen are engaged in it. Like going into a grave to go into a tunnel. Soil light and liable to cave in. Take turns in digging. Waste dirt carried to the stream in small quantities and thrown in. Not much faith in the enterprise, but work with the rest as a sort of duty. Raiders acting fearful.

### April 9 (Saturday)

At Culpeper C.H., Va., U.S. Grant issued his famous campaign order to Maj. Gen. George G. Meade, stating that Lee's army was Meade's objective: "Wherever Lee goes, there you will go also." Grant intended to grab Lee by the nose and not let go.

Ransom, John, QM Sgt., 9th Michigan Cavalry, Andersonville Prison, Ga.:

See here Mr. Confederacy, this is going a little too far. You have no business to kill us off at this rate. About thirty or forty die daily. They have rigged up an excuse for a hospital on the outside, where the sick are taken. Admit none though who can walk or help themselves in any way. Some of our men are detailed to help as nurses, but in a majority of cases those who go out on parole of honor are cut-throats and robbers, who abuse a sick prisoner. Still, there are exceptions to this rule. We hear stories of Capt. Wirtz's cruelty in punishing the men, but I hardly credit all the stories. More prisoners today.... Scurvy and dropsy taking hold of the men. Many are blind as soon as it becomes night, and it is called moon blind. Caused, I suppose, by sleeping with the moon shining in the face.

### April 10 (Sunday)

Ransom, John, QM Sgt., 9th Michigan Cavalry, Andersonville Prison, Ga.:

Getting warmer and warmer. Can see the trees swaying back and forth on the outside, but inside not a breath of fresh air. Our wood is all gone, and we are now digging up stumps and roots for fuel to cook with. Some of the first prisoners here have passable huts made of logs, sticks, pieces of blankets, &c. Room about all taken up in here now. Rations not so large.... Rations have settled down to less than a pint of meal per day, with occasionally a few peas, or an apology for a piece of bacon, for each man. Should judge that they have hounds on the outside to catch runaways, from the noise. Wirtz don't come in as much as formerly. The men make it uncomfortable for him.

### April 11 (Monday)

Ransom, John, QM Sgt., 9th Michigan Cavalry, Andersonville Prison, Ga.:

Dr. Lewis is very bad off with the scurvy and diarrhea. We don't think he can stand it much longer, but make out to him that he will stick it through.... As many as 12,000 men here now, and crowded for room. Death rate is in the neighborhood of eighty per day.... A very heavy dew nights, which is almost a rain. Rebels very domineering. Many are tunneling to get out. Our tunnel has been abandoned, as the location was not practicable. Yank shot today near our quarters. Approached too near the dead line. Many of the men have dug down through the sand and reached water, but is poor; no better than out of the creek.

Jones, John B., Rebel War Clerk, Confederate War Dept., Richmond, Va.:

The FAMINE is still advancing, and his gaunt proportions loom up daily, as he approaches with gigantic strides. The rich speculators, however, and the officers of influence stationed here, who have secured the favor of the Express Company, get enough to eat.... The pigeons of my neighbor have disappeared. Every day we have accounts of robberies, the preceding night, of cows, pigs, bacon, flour—and even the setting hens are taken from their nests!

### April 12 (Tuesday)

About 50 miles from Memphis, Tenn., Ft. Pillow had been used for some time to protect a small trading post located nearby. On this night, about 1500 of Gen. Nathan Bedford Forrest's troopers struck against 557 defenders. Although the cavalry was driven back by the guns of the gunboat U.S.S. *New Era*, the Confederates mounted an all-out assault by midafternoon and the fort was quickly overrun after its commander, Maj. William F. Bradford, refused to surrender. There was, and still is, over 125 years later, controversy over just how many men surrendered and when. Southern accounts say that about 231 Federals were killed and 100 wounded before the surrender. Federal accounts state that the surrender occurred almost immediately, without many casualties. Investigation showed that Forrest's men killed nearly 350 of the Union troops at the fort, including most of the 262 Negro troops stationed there. Forrest himself, in a later report to his commander, stated, "We busted the fort at ninerclock and scatered the niggers. The men is a cillanem in the woods."

Ransom, John, QM Sgt., 9th Michigan Cavalry, Andersonville Prison, Ga.:

Another beautiful but warm day with no news. Insects of all descriptions making their appearance, such as lizards, a worm four or five inches long, fleas, maggots, &c. There is so much filth about the camp that it is terrible trying to live here. New prisoners are made sick the first hours of their arrival by the stench which pervades the prison.... No visitors come near us any more. Everybody sick, almost, with scurvy— an awful disease. New cases every day. I am afraid some contagious disease will get among us, and if so every man will die.... New prisoners coming in and are shocked at the sights.

Malone, B.Y., Sgt., Co. H, 6th N.C. Infantry, CSA, prisoner, Point Lookout, Md.:

The 12th the 3d Maryland Negro Regiment was plaised on gard around the Prison Camp: When the Negrows first come on gard they wore thir knapsacks and when they was put on poast they puled them off and laid them down at the end of thir lines And Some of our men stole too of them: And when the Negro found it was gone he sais to the next one on post Efrum-Efrum: tell that other Negrow up dar that the white folks has stold my knapsack a redy: The other one sais they have stold mine too but I want caring for the knapsack all I hate about it is loosing Sophys Garotipe. One day too of them was on poast in the Streets and met up at the end of thir lines and comenced fooling with thir Guns what they cauld plaing bayonets they had thir guns cocked preseantly one of thir guns went of and shot the other one threw the brest he fell dead: the other one sais: Jim, Jim get up from dar you are not hurt your just trying to fool me:

### April 13 (Wednesday)

Ransom, John, QM Sgt., 9th Michigan Cavalry, Andersonville Prison, Ga.:

Jack Shannon, from Ann Arbor, died this morning. The raiders are the stronger party now, and do as they please; and we are in nearly as much danger now from our own men as from the rebels.... During the night some one stole my jacket. Have traded off all superfluous clothes, and with the loss of jacket have only pants, shirt, shoes, (no stockings,) and hat; yet I am well dressed in comparison with some others, many have nothing but an old pair of pants which reach, perhaps, to the knees, and perhaps not. Hendryx has two shirts and should be mobbed. I do quite a business trading rations, making soup for the

sick ones, taking in payment their raw food which they cannot eat. Get many a snack by so doing.

### April 14 (Thursday)

Ransom, John, QM Sgt., 9th Michigan Cavalry, Andersonville Prison, Ga.:

At least twenty fights among our own men this forenoon. It beats all what a snarling crowd we are getting to be. The men are perfectly reckless, and had just as soon have their necks broken by fighting as anything else. New onions in camp. Very small, and sell for $2 a bunch of four or five. Van Tassel, a Pennsylvanian, is about to die. Many give me parting injunctions relative to their families, in case I should live through. Have half a dozen photographs of dead men's wives, with addresses on the back of them. Seems to be pretty generally conceded that if any get through, I will.... Signs of scurvy about my person. Still adhere to our sanitary rules. Lewis anxious to get to the hospital. Will die anyway shortly, whether there or here.

### April 15 (Friday)

Ransom, John, QM Sgt., 9th Michigan Cavalry, Andersonville Prison, Ga.:

The hospital is a tough place to be in, from all accounts, the detailed Yankees as soon as they get a little authority are certain to use it for all it is worth. In some cases before a man is fairly dead, he is stripped of everything, coat, pants, shirt, finger rings (if he has any), and everything of value taken away. These the nurses trade to the guards.... The sick now, or a portion of them, are huddled up in one corner of the prison, to get as bad as they can before being admitted to the outside hospital. Every day I visit it, and come away sick at heart that human beings should be thus treated.

### April 17 (Sunday)

Lt. Gen. U.S. Grant ordered that no further prisoner exchanges would be permitted until the Confederates balanced Federal releases—in other words, one-for-one. He further directed that "no distinction whatever be made in the exchange between white and colored prisoners."

Conley, Capt., 101st Penna. Volunteers, Plymouth, N.C.:

The spring of 1864 found the 101st Regiment, to which I had the honor to belong, forming part of the garrison of Plymouth, N.C. Our garrison consisted of the 85th N.Y., 16th Conn., 101st and 103rd Pa., two companies of the 2nd N.C. Union, one company of the 12th N.Y. Cavalry, and the [unit designation unreadable] Mass. Heavy Artillery, numbering in all about 2000 men.

About 4 P.M. on Sunday the 17th of April the garrison was suddenly startled by heavy firing in the picket line. The company of cavalry went out and had just disappeared in the woods in front of the town when another heavy volley was heard and soon they again appeared, supporting on his horse one of the Lieutenants, severely wounded. They reported they had found the enemy in force.

At the first volley, all our works were manned and the attack awaited. Very soon they planted several batteries just in the edge of the woods in front of us and commenced to shell us. From that time, the fight was on.

### April 18 (Monday)

The Confederate attack that began the day before was continued today on the garrison at Plymouth, N.C. The Union Army steamer *Bombshell* was sunk during the engagement, but by late evening the advance of the Confederates had been halted. The two Union gunboats U.S.S. *Southfield* and *Miami* supported the defense of the garrison. Lt. Commander Flusser reported that the Confederate ram C.S.S. *Albemarle* would be down at Plymouth tomorrow.

### April 19 (Tuesday)

At 3:30 in the morning the Confederate ram C.S.S. *Albemarle* attacked the Union gunboats U.S.S. *Southfield* and *Miami*, which had been lashed together for protection and concentration of firepower, at Plymouth, N.C. As the ironclad approached, Lt. Commander Flusser headed the two wooden ships directly at the *Albemarle*, firing as they went. The Confederate ram struck the *Southfield* a blow which "tore a hole clear through to the boiler" and the captain of the ram, Commander Cooke, said that his ship plunged ten feet into the side of the wooden gunboat. As the *Southfield* was released after the ram pulled back, the replacement

for Flusser, who had been killed during the engagement, had the cables cut that held the two ships together and continued firing into the *Albemarle*. Once the ram was free and turned her attention to the *Miami*, the *Southfield* turned and headed downriver in company with the steamer U.S.S. *Ceres* and the tinclad *Whitehead*. The *Albemarle* was left in possession of the sound.

Conley, Capt., 101st Penna. Volunteers, Plymouth, N.C.:

...just before daylight, the Rebel ironclad ram *Albemarle*, which had been built up the river at Rainbow Bluffs, came down and in a very short engagement with our wooden vessels, sunk the *Southfield*, one of the largest, while the others retreated down the river, leaving the *Albemarle* in undisputed possession of the river. We were now entirely surrounded.

At Point Lookout, Md., a prisoner had been shot by one of the Negro sentries during the night. William H. Laird, Sergeant-Maj. of the Camp, reported in his deposition:

I respectfully submit a report of the shooting case near my tent last night, and beg leave to express the hope that the case will be investigated and steps taken to preserve us against the vindictiveness of certain of the colored troops who guard us.... About two months ago Capt. Patterson ordered that each company should have a tub, to be used at night for sink purposes, and I obtained one for my tent and those standing near it. This tub has been used almost every night since it has been there, and is put out conspicuously in front expressly to prevent accident. Last night when the man who was shot came out of his camp tent the guard was just in front of it, and, I imagine, must have seen the man preparing to sit down, for between the man's coming out of the tent and being shot the guard did not walk more than twenty or thirty paces. The man had scarcely sat down when, without a word, the guard turned and fired. The animus of the guard is manifest from his having two bullets in his gun.... Both the conduct and conversation of the colored men evidence that there is a sort of rivalry among them to distinguish themselves by shooting some of us.

### April 20 (Wednesday)

Facing an overwhelming Confederate force, and

with no protection from the gunboats, the Federal garrison at Plymouth, N.C., surrendered at 10 A.M..

Conley, Capt., 101st Penna. Volunteers, prisoner of war, Plymouth, N.C.:

On Wednesday morning, just before daybreak, an assault was made on our left, supported by the gunboat. They broke our lines and got in our rear. After much desperate hand-to-hand fighting, the last of the garrison surrendered about 9 A.M. The troops attacking us were Hooke's [Maj. Gen. Robert F. Hoke, CSA] division, some 12,000 to 15,000 strong.

After our capture we were marched to Hamilton, about 25 or 30 miles above them. When we were about to leave there, the 17th N.C., which was stationed near them, was marched out along the road, where they halted, opened ranks, and faced inward. The prisoners were then required to form in two ranks and march through. This, we soon learned, was done to pick out the "Buffaloes" as they called them; that is, North Carolinians who had either deserted from their own regiment, or were known to them to be deserters, or who had fled to avoid the general conscription.

As we passed through, they picked out five or six. I shall never forget the look of hopeless despair depicted on the countenances of those when thus picked out. But most of them escaped unrecognized. I afterwards learned that all of those arrested were court martialed and executed.

For about three months previous to the capture, by order of the Commanding General, I had been placed in command of the recruiting parties at the post. This included the two companies of the 2nd N.C. This brought me in close touch with them, they being under my command during the engagement. Consequently, my sympathy went out to them, but I was powerless to help them.

From Hamilton we marched to Tarboro where we took the cars, crowding 50 of us in one boxcar. In this way we passed through Wilmington, Charleston, Savannah, Macon, Ga., and from there to Andersonville. All the way we were known as the "Plymouth Pilgrims."

## April 23 (Saturday)

Ward, William W., Col., 9th Tenn. Cavalry, prisoner, Ft. Delaware, Del.:

Morning quite pleasant.... Considerable stir with our crowd preparing to have pictures taken. Have mine taken, order ½ doz. John L. Gihon, Photographic Art Galleries, 1024 Chestnut Street Philadelphia Pa. is the artist. Paid $2½ to the Artist.

## April 24 (Sunday)

Gen. Samuel Cooper, Adjutant-General of the Confederate Army, ordered that all prisoners currently interned at Cahaba, Ala., be transferred to Andersonville Prison.

## April 26 (Tuesday)

Ransom, John, QM Sgt., 9th Michigan Cavalry, Andersonville Prison, Ga.:

Ten days since I wrote in my diary.... On the 21st the tunnel was opened and two fellows belonging to a Massachusetts regiment escaped to the outside. Hendryx and myself next went out. The night was very dark. Came up out of the ground away on the outside of the guard. We crawled along to gain the woods, and get by some pickets, and when forty or fifty rods from the stockade a shot was fired at someone coming out of the hole. We immediately jumped up and ran for dear life.... It was almost daylight and away we went. Found I could not run far and we slowed up, knowing we would be caught, but hoping to get to some house and get something to eat first. Found I was all broke up for any exertion. In an hour we had traveled perhaps three miles, were all covered with mud, and scratched up. I had fell, too, in getting over some logs, and it seemed to me broken all the ribs in my body. Just as it was coming light in the east we heard the dogs after us. We expected it, and so armed ourselves with clubs and sat down on a log. In a few moments the hounds came up with us and began smelling of us. Pretty soon five mounted rebels arrived on the scene of action. They laughed to think we expected to get away. Started us back towards our charnel pen. Dogs did not offer to bite us, but guards told us that if we had offered resistance or started to run they would have torn us. Arrived at the prison and after waiting an hour Capt. Wirtz interviewed us. After cussing us a few minutes we were put in the chain gang, where we remained two days. This was not fine, but contrary to expectation not so bad after all. We had more to eat than when inside, and we had shade to lay in, and although my ankles were made very sore, do not regret my escapade.

### April 27 (Wednesday)

Ransom, John, QM Sgt., 9th Michigan Cavalry, Andersonville Prison, Ga.:

Well, I was out from under rebel guard for an hour or so anyway. Hurt my side though, and caught a little cold.... Have given up the idea of escaping. Think if Hendryx had been alone he would have gotten away. Is tougher than I am. A man caught stealing from one of his comrades and stabbed with a knife and killed.... The occurrence was not an unusual one.

Ward, William W., Col., 9th Tenn. Cavalry, prisoner, Ft. Delaware, Del.:

Morning clear and pleasant. My head has gotten easy and I feel pretty well.... Went to the Barracks. Found all well there and in good spirits. Had news in the papers confirmatory of that we have heretofore had in reference to the Red River, or Pleasant Hill or Cane River affair. Seeming to establish the fact that our forces gained quite a victory there. Captured many, perhaps 6000, prisoners and killed & wounded many more. Also establishing the fact of Plymouth being in our hands with a capture of 1600 prisoners, 25 pieces artilery many stores &. Gen Wessel was in command there & Hauk [Hoke] in Command of our forces.

### April 29 (Friday)

Ward, William W., Col., 9th Tenn. Cavalry, prisoner, Ft. Delaware, Del.:

Morning pleasant and bright not quite so cool.... Saw two most handsome ladies in the fort who desired to show themselves as sympathisers with us. One pretty little curly-haired one nodded and laughed & spoke & did many little cute things to draw attention. I would like to know her name, but do not.

### April 30 (Saturday)

Sgt. Bartlett Yancey Malone, of the 6th N.C. Inf., confined at Point Lookout, Md., recorded the shooting of a prisoner by a Negro sentinel on April 18th. The prisoner was wounded, but evidently survived. Three days later, on the 21st, another sentinel shot into a tent, wounding two prisoners. On the 27th, several sick Confederate prisoners were sent south for exchange. Malone also recorded the suicide of one of the Negro guards on the 29th—he blew the top of his head off with his musket.

Ransom, John, QM Sgt., 9th Michigan Cavalry, Andersonville Prison, Ga.:

Very small rations given to us now. Not more than one quarter what we want to eat and that of the poorest quality. Splendid weather, but too warm; occasional rains.

Conley, Capt., 101st Penna. Volunteers, prisoner, Andersonville, Ga.:

The first carload of us, in which were all of the officers, reached Andersonville on Saturday, April 30, just ten days after our capture. Here we had a chance to view the Andersonville prison, of which so much has been written. We were halted near the railroad and here the commissioned officers and enlisted men were separated. The latter we saw marched into the stockade. At that time the prison was comparatively new and its horrors had not yet become known. The notorious Capt. Wirz was in command of the prison and the manner in which he would curse the prisoners, if any seemed to fail to promptly obey his commands, revealed the true character of the man.

### May 1 (Sunday)

Ransom, John, QM Sgt., 9th Michigan Cavalry, Andersonville Prison, Ga.:

Warm.... Last evening 700 of the 85th New York arrived here. They were taken at Plymouth, NC, with 1400 others, making 2100 in all. The balance are on the road to this place. Wrote a letter home today. Have not heard from the North for over six months. Dying off very fast.

Conley, Capt., 101st Penna. Volunteers, prisoner, Camp Oglethorpe, Macon, Ga.:

The commissioned officers, about 100 number, were kept under guard at an old church that stood near the railroad station until the next morning. Then we were again put on the cars and taken back to Macon where an officer's prison named Camp Oglethorpe was established, we being the first prisoners in it. On our way back to Macon, it being Sunday, there were large crowds at every station waiting to see the "Plymouth Pilgrims."

At Savannah our guards were changed. A company of the 1st Georgia, under command of Capt. Davenport, taking charge of us. In that company was a big, burly Irishman, very full of Irish wit, and we soon learned, had no sympathy for the Rebel cause. While on the way from Andersonville, one of the prisoners unfortunately lost his hat, it being carried out of the car window by a blast of wind. When the Irishman learned of it he said to the prisoner, "Never mind, I'll get you a hat." At the next stopping place a large crowd was waiting to see us and not far from our car door stood a man with a pretty good hat on his head. Just as the train commenced to move, our Irishman called and beckoned to him to come to the side door of the boxcar. Apparently without any suspicion, the citizen came right up to him. Then the Irish guard, bending his body forward as if to speak to him, suddenly lifted his hat from his head and threw it back to the prisoner who had lost his. This was so unexpected that the man just stood, apparently in a dazed condition, until the train passed away.

During the afternoon we reached Macon where we were marched to the fairgrounds, and a few tents furnished us, and a heavy guard placed around us. Within a few days the Rebels commenced to build a stockade in part of the fairgrounds near where we were. We had been there about three weeks before the stockade was completed; then the officers from Libby prison were brought in and put into it, and the same evening we were moved in.

## May 2 (Monday)

Ransom, John, QM Sgt., 9th Michigan Cavalry, Andersonville Prison, Ga.:

A crazy man was shot dead by the guard an hour ago. The guard dropped a piece of bread on the inside of the stockade, and the fellow went inside the dead line to get it and was killed. The bread wagon was raided upon as soon as it drove inside today and all the bread stolen, for which offense no more will be issued today.

## May 3 (Tuesday)

In Washington, the Adjutant-General of the

Army issued General Orders No. 190, which in Section 127, page 4, contained the following:

The principle being recognized that medical officers and chaplains should not be held as prisoners of war, all medical officers and chaplains so held by the United States will be immediately and unconditionally discharged.

The transfer of all prisoners, except those too sick to travel, to Andersonville Prison from Cahaba, Ala., had been completed. The Alabama prison supposedly was to be closed.

Ransom, John, QM Sgt., 9th Michigan Cavalry, Andersonville Prison, Ga.:

A rebel battery came today on the cars, and is being posted around the stockade.... Over 19,000 confined here now, and the death rate ninety or one hundred [per day].

Near Brandy Station, Va., Grant instructed Meade to move the Army of the Potomac out of winter quarters and to cross the Rapidan River on the morning of the 4th. The new offensive was set to go.

## May 4 (Wednesday)

In the early minutes of this day, near Brandy Station, Va., the Army of the Potomac bestirred itself and moved across the Rapidan River, headed for the Wilderness crossroads. Grant's army had nearly 122,000 present for duty against Lee's 66,000. Grant moved around Lee's right, forcing Lee to move from Orange C.H. and the Gordonsville area to meet him. Gen. Richard Ewell led the way towards the Wilderness, with A.P. Hill and Longstreet following.

Yesterday in Washington, President Lincoln directed L.E. Chittenden to go to Annapolis, Md., to the Parole Camp to determine if the rumors of the conditions of the returning prisoners of war were true. Today, Chittenden reported back to Lincoln that the rumors were not only true, but that the poor physical condition of the prisoners was worse than at first believed.

Ransom, John, QM Sgt., 9th Michigan Cavalry, Andersonville Prison, Ga.:

Good weather. Gen. Howell Cobb and staff came among us today, and inspected the prison. Wirtz accompanied them pointing out and explaining matters. Gen. Winder, who has charge of all prisoners of war in the South, is here, but has not been inside.... Three men out of every hundred allowed to go out after wood under a strong guard.

### May 5 (Thursday)

At the Wilderness in Virginia, Meade's Army of the Potomac collided with Lee's Army of Northern Virginia in the tangled wooded area south of the Rapidan. By noon they were locked in full-scale combat. Unlike previous contestants with Lee, Grant would not commit his forces piecemeal—Lee would have to fight the whole army. At the close of the day, both armies lay on their arms and awaited tomorrow.

Henry S. White was born in New York in 1828, the son of a blacksmith. After serving as an apprentice to his father for a time, he decided to become a minister in the Methodist Church. He was graduated from the Methodist Biblical Institute in New Hampshire in 1851 at the age of 23, and assumed his duties as a minister. In January 1863, he was the pastor of a Methodist Episcopal Church in Providence, R.I., when he appointed as chaplain of the Rhode Island Regiment Heavy Artillery, which was then based in the vicinity of New Bern, N.C. White joined the regiment in North Carolina shortly after his appointment. Nothing beyond routine occurred for several months until the Confederate government decided to relieve the pressure on its coastal cities and launched an offensive in the region of New Bern. The winter remained calm, however. With the coming of spring the offensive again became active, until Grant moved the Army of the Potomac across the Rapidan River in Virginia and began his drive on Richmond. Lee then recalled most of the troops engaged in North Carolina and the offensive in that area ground to a halt, except for cavalry action.

A day ago, the 4th of May, Chaplain White left New Bern and rode to Croatan Station, N.C., where a small force of the regiment was based. He rode the eleven miles without incident and spent the day with the men, delivering mail and distributing tracts. He spent the night within the fort and during this time the Union troops were informed that Con-

federate cavalry was in the vicinity and in considerable strength. These reports were initially discounted, but verification was made shortly and the Union defenders, numbering only about 50, were attacked by a force of about 1600 Confederate cavalry. Chaplain White's ordeal began on this date.

White, H.S., Chaplain, R.I. Regt. Heavy Artillery, Croatan Station, N.C.:

Capt. Aigan gave orders for the tents to be struck, water and food to be taken inside the work, and all preparation made for defense.... The drawbridge was removed, gate shut, and all took shelter in the fort. The fort was a small irregular earthwork, with only one six-pound brass gun beside the muskets of the men for defense.... The preparations had not long been completed when the enemy made his appearance on the Railroad nearly a mile distant between us and Newbern. They came down towards us rapidly.... Presently we saw skirmishers cross the Railroad to the right, and not long after a brisk fire was opened upon us from an old house and the adjacent woods. We at once returned the fire with the piece and the muskets.... The piece became so hot that it was almost impossible to work it; the water began to give out, and the cartridges began to take fire when put in the mouth of the piece.... At half past two o'clock a white flag was seen coming down the Railroad; firing ceased on both sides. Capt. Aigan went out to meet it and asked what was wanted, if it was a mere show to enable him to get a better position.... The surrender of the fort was demanded. Capt. Aigan replied that he could not surrender the fort. He was then informed that it would be reduced.... As he came back he saw what he suspected, that the enemy had taken advantage of the truce. As soon as the firing ceased, some sixteen hundred men arose from their sheltered positions and came out into sight.... Capt. Aigan called Lt. Durfee and myself together and informed us of the result of the interview, and asked our opinion. We at once indorsed his position.... The only course left was to surrender the fort, provided we could get such conditions as we deemed honorable. A white flag was then raised by us, and soon the one that came from the enemy returned.... Capt. Aigan met Col. Falk of Dearing's Brigade of Cavalry under truce, and agreed to surrender the fort....

When we were ready, Capt. Aigan gave the

order for the men to fall in, and they took their muskets and prepared to evacuate the works. With music, and all the pomp our little handful of nearly fifty men could give, we marched out. Sixteen hundred men, partly mounted, and others on foot, surrounded us.... Firing ceased about half-past two P.M., and we turned and marched from the fort under guard shortly after four o'clock.... We were marched about one mile along the railroad towards Newbern, where we remained till about sundown. The woods and country about was full of rebels. Some were foraging, some cooking, and other burning the railroad and other property.... Just as the sun passed from sight, we were ordered to fall in.... A guard of cavalry took charge of us.... Six miles to Evan's Mill for the first march.... Tired and weary with fighting and marching, we were turned into the old blockhouse, and amid filth and dirt found a place for repose. Of course we got no supper.

Ransom, John, QM Sgt., 9th Michigan Cavalry, Andersonville Prison, Ga.:

Cold nights and warm days. Very unhealthy, such extremes. Smallpox cases carried out, and much alarm felt lest it should spread.

## May 6 (Friday)

In the Wilderness, the early dawn hours found the Federals ready, and they took up the advance and collided heavily with the Rebels. Longstreet made a flank attack that set the Federals back, but temporarily. Longstreet was severely wounded and then evacuated. Late in the afternoon Lee tried again, only to be stopped short of the Union lines.

At darkness the fighting abated, but slowly. The next question then to be settled was: In which direction would the Yankees move? Would they recross the river as they had done before, or would they move on towards Richmond? Casualties were heavy for the North—nearly 17,700 killed, wounded, or missing. The Rebels fared better—somewhere around 7500.

Abbott, A.O., 1st Lt., 1st N.Y. Dragoons, Battle of the Wilderness, Va.:

My brigade broke camp from the base of Pony Mountain, near Culpeper, Va., on the morning of the 5th of May; took the Stevensburg Road, and

encamped at night three miles from Germania Ford. The infantry had preceded us, and, as is always the case at the commencement of a spring campaign, the roads were strewn with blankets, overcoats, knapsacks, etc., cast off by the soldiers to lighten their load....

We crossed the Rapidan at Ely's Ford by fording, the pontoons being used by the infantry and artillery; took the old Chancellorsville Road, and picketed it for three miles beyond Chancellorsville. As we passed over the battlefield, I could see very plainly the marks of the terrible struggle of last year. The tops of the trees looked as though they had been measured and trimmed by a skillful hand, while their trunks and limbs were scarred and broken. But little of the *debris* of the battle remained on the ground, it having been picked up and carried off by the inhabitants of the vicinity last year, for the benefit of the Rebel government, who made a practice of sending out agents to collect all such spoils from the inhabitants. This I learned from one of the residents near Ely's Ford.

During the long night in the blockhouse at Evan's Mill, the Union prisoners got little rest. The accommodations, to say the least, were less than desirable.

White, H.S., Chaplain, R.I. Regt. Heavy Artillery, prisoner of war in North Carolina:

During the morning, one of the servants brought us food. It was on a common breakfast plate, and consisted of scraps of pork rind and pieces of corn bread, gathered from the table of the rebels. Capt. Aigan took it, and turning to me, said, "Here, chaplain, take this and give it to the men," refusing to take any himself. I broke the bread into pieces, not so large as my thumb, and gave it out. Not two thirds of the men got even a crumb. I turned to the servant and said, "Go and get these men some food. We fought all day yesterday and marched last night, and are to march today, and we need some breakfast." He scraped a little closer and brought us another plate full of smaller pieces. The men joked a little about the generous hospitality of the Southern chivalry, and we fell in, and about nine in the morning marched away. As the column moved we saw the foragers coming from the farmhouses with bags of good things, and sides of bacon strung on poles borne on the shoulders of the soldiers.... For twenty miles back we saw but little evidence of cultivation; the houses were burned and the plantations abandoned.... After a weary march... we came... to Pollocksville, N.C. Twas about sundown. We were stationed in a field, and took quarters on the fresh green grass.... About ten o'clock we were furnished rations. The captives were about sixty in number. We drew about three pecks of unsifted cornmeal and some bacon. Not two ounces of bacon for a man. No other article was given us. We sent to a camp near and borrowed a skillet, and mixing the meal with water, attempted to make bread. We had no salt. Nearly two hours were consumed in baking ten cakes by the camp fire. We cut each cake into six parts and gave one to each man. The cakes were about eight inches across and an inch and a quarter thick. They were not sufficiently cooked, and I gave mine to a soldier, as two days had not made me hungry. The bacon I ate raw.

Ransom, John, QM Sgt., 9th Michigan Cavalry, Andersonville Prison, Ga.:

Six months a prisoner today. Longer than any six years of my previous life.... There are about eighty-five or ninety dying now per day, as near as I can find out. Of course there are stories to the effect that a hundred and fifty and two hundred die each day, but such is not the case.... Nearly every day someone is killed for some trifling offense, by the guards. Rather better food today than usual.

### May 7 (Saturday)

Early into the first hour of this day the Army of the Potomac waited for a sign that would decide its immediate future. That sign would come from the actions of the small, bearded man with three stars on his shoulders. The fires were burning bright behind the lines as the units collected themselves and recounted what had happened to them that day. Suddenly, it seemed, long blue columns were moving across their rear to the southeast—not towards the fords across the Rapidan, but towards Richmond. Grant had made his decision. He now had Lee's nose and was not going to let go for forty-eight long weeks. The army was jubilant; for the first time they were not turning tail and quitting. Lee, realizing that Grant was headed for Spotsylvania C.H., sent cavalry to cut trees to delay the Union advance while he went there to prepare the defenses.

At Dalton, Ga., Sherman started his campaign to capture Atlanta. Dalton was the site of Gen. Joseph Johnston's winter camp for the Army of Tennessee. Sherman moved his men out of their camps and lunged directly for the Rebel lines. The Confederates held a good defensive position on and along a high ridge that they had been improving all winter. Now there were few gaps in the line. Sherman's army of nearly 100,000 was divided into three armies facing Johnston's 60,000.

Johnston's position on the high ridge was found to be too strong for a frontal attack, so Sherman began what would be a pattern for him all the way to the sea—outflank 'em.

Abbott, A.O., 1st Lt., 1st N.Y. Dragoons, Battle of the Wilderness, Va.:

We had no fighting to do until Saturday, being kept on picket on the Fredericksburg Road. On that day we were ordered, at 12 M., to Todd's Tavern. The weather was intensely hot, and the clouds of dust through which we rode almost suffocated us. After a halt of a few moments at Todd's Tavern were ordered out on the Spottsylvania Road to discover the position and movements of the Rebels; soon found they were advancing down the road, supported by two brigades of dismounted cavalry, intending, no doubt, to drive us from our possession of the roads leading to Richmond.... We at once opened on them with our "seven shooters," and sent their skirmish line tumbling back to their supports. As we charged up a little rise of ground, we at once discovered them entrenched behind some bushes that hid them from our view. We held our position in their front till they brought down five times our numbers, when they made a dash on our line, and, just as our support was coming in sight, "scooped out" six officers and about forty men. I was in a thick piece of underbrush, closely watching matters in my front, when I head a shouting behind me, and, as I turned round, a Rebel captain confronted me, and, presenting a loaded revolver at my breast, said, "Do you surrender?" Looking him calmly in the face, after a moment's reflection, I replied with a smile, "Of course I do. I don't see any sight for anything else right here." "Give me up your sabre, then." I did so, and then the captain ordered two men to take me to the rear on the double-quick.

"Come out of them boots," said one, as soon as he saw that I had a pair of good ones. "Give up them boots." "I want them ar boots." "You 'Yank,' leave them boots." "You d——d son of a ————, take them boots off, or I'll blow your brains out," as he prepared to fulfill his threat.... I kept my boots ... but had to appeal to an officer to save them. After the boot question had been settled, they turned their attention to arms, and found I had a belt and pistol, which they then took from me. They marched me back about half a mile, where I found Lts. West and Lewis, of my regiment, and soon after we were joined by Capt. Britton, also, 1st New York Dragoons, Capt. Carpenter and Lt. Hazel, of the 6th Pennsylvania. We were tired completely out, had had nothing to eat since breakfast, and no immediate prospect of getting anything for some time, and were nearly sunstruck. While sitting by a tree, an officer rode up to Lt. West, and, without saying a word, reached down and snatched a good new hat from off his (West's) head, put it on his own, and replaced it by an old worn-out cap, which was so small it could with difficulty be kept upon his head at all, and then left....

We had not remained there long before we could see that the tide of battle had turned, and that our gallant boys were driving them. Back they came pell-mell, horses, artillery, and ambulances, drivers and skulkers, crying out, "The Yankees are coming—the Yankees are coming;" and *we* said, "Let them come, for *we* are not afraid of them."...

They marched us back, with their train and lead horses, till nearly dark, when we went on ahead to Spottsylvania Court-house, about five miles from the battlefield.... We arrived ... soon after dark, and, after some delay in trying to find us quarters, they turned us out into an old orchard, backed us up against a board fence, put a guard around us, and told us we would stay there all night. We asked the sergeant of the guard who had us in charge for something to eat, as we had had nothing since breakfast; but he very politely informed us that "they could not get enough to eat for themselves," consequently could not divide with prisoners.

The night was cold and damp, and, as we had no blankets or extra clothing, the guards built us a small fire out of rails...

White, H.S., Chaplain, R.I. Regt. Heavy Artillery, prisoner of war in North Carolina:

We expected to have a chance in the morning to cook the rest of our meal and get a good breakfast, but at a quarter before five we were ordered to fall in, and without breakfast or dinner we were marched forty miles. The men carried the meal for a while, and then threw the bag into a baggage wagon, and we never saw it afterwards. We were urged forward for several miles at almost double quick.... The day was one of the warmest I ever saw. We were put in the rear of the artillery train. The wheels of more than one hundred guns, with caissons and attending wagons, cut up the sandy roads, and it was like marching in a newly ploughed field. We had gone on many miles, and the men were showing the effect of the treatment.... When the men began to show symptoms of exhaustion and got behind, the guards would raise their carbines and order them to "close up," as no one alive would be left behind.... O the horrors of that dreadful march!... Hour after hour went by of the hottest day, mile after mile of that sandy road.... It was a forced march. Endurance began to fail. The men began to fall. I appealed to the Captain to allow us to go more slowly.... He at length halted the column and gave them rest and water. From this time our men were frequently halted, and then we pushed on. About ten o'clock we reached Kinston jail, where we were turned in behind the bars, and the rusty iron door was locked upon us.... A man acquainted with the course we took said we marched forty miles that day.... We had not been in Kinston jail long before they brought us hard bread and raw bacon. Dark and filthy was the place, but we were so exhausted that hunger alone kept us awake till we could take some food, and we were soon lost in profound slumber.

### May 8 (Sunday)

As the Union army approached Spottsylvania C.H., they found the Confederates already there and entrenched. The Rebels had won the footrace, at least this time. The Union troops waded into the Rebels, only to find that the Rebels were in strong defensive positions and couldn't be shaken. A new attack was made—this failed also—and darkness brought an end to the fighting and both sides formed new lines.

Grant sent Sheridan to go around Lee and disrupt the Confederate rail communications and to keep Stuart off Grant's back. A.P. Hill became ill and was replaced by Jubal Early temporarily. This left Lee without two of his steady corps commanders—Hill and Longstreet.

In Georgia, Sherman was working on the flank of Joe Johnston.

Capt. Henry Wirz, now at Andersonville, Ga., and assigned as the commandant of the *prison*, not the *post*, wrote Maj. Thomas P. Turner, CSA, on this date:

Major:... I was assigned to the command of the prison by Col. A.W. Persons, the commandant of the post, on the 27th of March, 1864, having reported to him for duty by order of Gen. J.H. Winder, commanding C.S. military prisons. I found the prison in bad condition, owing to the want of tools, such as axes, spades, and lumber to erect proper buildings. The first commandant of the post, Capt. W.S. Winder, and his successor, Col. A.W. Persons, had left nothing untried to supply th[ese] so important articles. Only two weeks ago I received axes, spades, &c., from Columbus, Ga.; went to work cutting ditches, &c. I hope to have everything in the interior of the prison completed in two weeks. The bakery, which could not be completed from want of lumber, is now in operation. The necessity of enlarging the stockade is unavoidable, and I shall commence as soon as I can gather a sufficient number of negroes.

I would respectfully ask you to present to the authorities at Richmond the impediments thrown in my way by having hospitals inside of the prison.

| | |
|---|---|
| Number of prisoners on the 1st day of April | 7160 |
| Received up to today, from various points | 5787 |
| Received up to today, recaptured | 7 |
| Total | 12,954 |
| Number of dead from the 1st of April to 8th of May | 728 |
| Number escaped from the 1st of April to 8th of May | 13 |
| Total on hand | 12,213 |

I consequently lost six prisoners. I would also call your attention to the danger of having our present guard forces withdrawn and their places supplied by the reserve forces of Gov. Brown.

In conclusion, allow me to make a few remarks concerning myself. I am here in a very unpleasant position, growing out of the rank which I now hold, and suggest the propriety of being promoted. Having the full control of the prison, and consequently of the daily prison guard, the orders which I have to give are very often not obeyed with the promptness the occasion requires, and I am of the opinion that it emanates from the reluctance of obeying an officer who holds the same rank as they do. My duties are manifold and require all my time in daytime and very often part of the night, and I would most respectfully ask that two commissioned officers (lieutenants) would be assigned to me for duty.

Abbott, A.O., 1st Lt., 1st N.Y. Dragoons, en route to Libby Prison, Richmond, Va.:

We started at daylight for Guinea's Station, twenty miles distant, without a mouthful of breakfast or anything to appease our hunger, having been up to that time twenty-four hours without food. As the sun came up, the day began to be very hot; and, being cavalrymen, we were not much accustomed to marching on foot, our feet soon got sore and we tired out, so that the latter part of the distance we could not march over half a mile without stopping to rest. The guard marched us *very* fast, would not even allow us to stop at the creeks long enough to wash our faces. We reached the railroad about 12 o'clock, so much exhausted we could not sit up, but threw ourselves upon the ground while the sergeant went to get us some rations. After a few moments' rest we were ordered on board the train. Soon after the Sergeant came back and told us that, as it was Sunday, he could get nothing for us, but that when the train arrived at Hanover Junction rations would be put on board for us, and our wants would then be supplied.

The train left Guinea's Station at 2 P.M. for Richmond, but no rations did we see at Hanover. As we passed Ashland Station, a number of *ladies* (I suppose they called themselves such) came up to the train with delicacies for their sick and wounded, and, although we told them how long we had been without food, yet not one of them deigned to give us a particle, but made up faces at us, called us "Yankee thieves," murderers, scoundrels, etc.; and one, more bitter that the others, threw a handful of water in our faces saying, "Take that, you miserable wretches."...

We arrived in Richmond about 4:30 P.M., just as the churches were out. The streets will filled with people whose countenances betokened anxious hearts in regard to the terrible struggle that was then going on in the Wilderness.... They marched us first to Gen. Winder's office, detained us a few moments while a gaping crowd satisfied their curiosity, and then we passed on through some of the principal streets of the city.... After a walk of a mile or more we came up before a large three-story brick building, dark and frowning, and from the corner of which hung an old weather-beaten sign, "Libby & Son, Ship-chandlers." All at once I comprehended the fact that this was the *in*famous "Libby Prison," and we were to be confined in it as prisoners of war.

White, H.S., Chaplain, R.I. Regt. Heavy Artillery, prisoner of war, Kinston, N.C.:

It was late in the morning of the Holy Sabbath before we awoke. Among the first sounds I remember was the scolding of our men. I soon learned that we had been treated to another specimen of Southern nobleness. On retiring, the men put some of their things, such as hats, shoes, coats, etc. in the recesses of the windows. It was warm, and the windows were open. The guards were stationed outside, a few feet from the jail, and so of course no one but those they permitted to approach could come near. They meanly stole these things from the men. Our canteens were of tin, and so large that they could not be drawn through the square formed by the iron bars. The men then were without these articles, as they could not be replaced. Complaint was made to the officers about it, but they did not seem to care. Nothing came back to us. The morning light revealed to us more perfectly the character of our quarters. We were in the space between the cells and the outer wall of the jail, a kind of entry and passage way, filthy with dirt, tobacco and refuse matter of the prison; rats, mice, cockroaches, and visitors more minute and annoying.... We went with a guard to a house nearby, and which was evidently the property of a well-to-do family. They treated us kindly. They were rebels, and no mistake....

During the morning the privates, a few at a time, were allowed to go to the street pump not far off, to wash. The boys, negroes, and curious of the town, gathered to look upon us as a kind of show. The jeers and insulting remarks were endured as best as we could bear them.... The prison quarters were changed during the day, and we were removed to the Court House, where we had plenty of room.... Towards night I held service among our own men.

Ransom, John, QM Sgt., 9th Michigan Cavalry, Andersonville Prison, Ga.:

Awful warm and more sickly. About 3500 have died since I came here, which is a good many, come to think of it—cooked rations of bread today. We get a quarter of a loaf of bread, weighing about six ounces, and four or five ounces of pork.... There is nothing the matter with me now but lack of food. The scurvy symptoms which appeared a few weeks ago have all gone.

## May 9 (Monday)

Grant and Lee were still faced off at Spotsylvania C.H., sizing each other up and adjusting lines. Burnside moved up closer with his Ninth Corps. Sheridan, drawing Stuart off, began a sixteen-day run around Lee and towards Richmond.

In Georgia, Sherman couldn't find an easy way around Johnston, so he stopped to think about it.

The ambulance trains of wounded ground their long, weary way towards the field hospitals, and the long lines of prisoners began their trek to the land of depression.

Abbott, A.O., 1st Lt., 1st N.Y. Dragoons, Libby Prison, Richmond, Va.:

As soon as we were inside the prison the officers were separated from the enlisted men, and we were not permitted after that to be near enough to hold any conversation with them. We were then marched into the office of the prison, where were registered our names, rank, company, and regiment, when and where captured.... We were then taken into the hall in the rear of the prison, and were politely requested to give up all United States money we had in our possession. If we gave it up voluntarily they would keep it for us, and perhaps we might get it again, and perhaps not. If they searched and found it upon us, they would confiscate it. We gave it up at once.... The sergeant then led the way, and we followed to the third story of the building, and, taking us to the northeast corner of the upper west room, told us "that place would be our quarters for the present." We then asked him for some rations, as it had been thirty-six hours since we had eaten anything. He politely informed us "that it was past prison ration hours, and we would have to wait till next day." He then left us "alone in our glory."...

We had expected to find in prison some of the conveniences of a soldier's camp life, but we were sadly mistaken. We found not, in all the prison, a bunk, table, blankets, conveniences for eating, or any thing of the kind. Bare walls and a wet floor greeted us whichever way we looked....

The prison stands on such ground that it has three stories front and four in the rear. It is about 130 feet in length and 100 in width, built of brick, and contains six rooms, each 40 x 100 feet. The partitions are of brick, two feet thick. The lower west room is partitioned off and used for offices to the prison. The lower middle room was furnished with stoves, and was used for a kitchen. In one corner of this kitchen was a room or cell, in which were confined "Gen. Kilpatrick's raiders."

The lower east room was the prison hospital. The sashes from all the windows had been removed, and [replaced] by grates made of one-inch rods of iron, passing through three cross-bars, two and a half by three-fourth inches; the whole firmly imbedded in the walls. A flight of stairs led from each room to the one above, but at night those leading to the lower story were taken down, and sentinels were stationed to prevent any attempt to escape that way. A hydrant in each room supplied us with water from the river, and an apology for a bathtub was placed in each for our use....

Our rations while in "Libby" consisted of corn bread, beans, or cow pease, or, in lieu thereof, rice and bacon. The bread was made of unsifted meal mixed with water, without salt, and baked in cards of twelve loaves; each loaf being two and a half inches square by two inches thick, a single loaf constituting a ration. The beans were small, red or black, a little larger than a pea, with a tough skin, a strong bitter taste, emitting a flavor very much like an old blue dye-tub. It was almost impossible for one to eat them *at first*, but hunger soon brought us to it. Those we got while in "Libby" were generally filled with black bugs which had eaten out the inside and then died. It was not an uncommon thing to see the

pail of soup they brought up to us with the top spotted over with their cooked carcasses. When we got bacon, it was strong, rancid, and maggoty, and we received about two ounces a day.... We were put upon half rations as soon as we arrived, and before we left were reduced to quarter rations.... We were very hungry all the time,

## May 10 (Tuesday)

At Spotsylvania C.H., Va., the Army of the Potomac assaulted the Confederate "mule shoe" positions late in the afternoon, with a very heavy attack being made at about 6 P.M. which temporarily breached the Confederate line, then fell back.

Sheridan and Stuart skirmished along the North Anna River near Beaver Dam Station, with Sheridan now within 20 miles of Richmond, tearing up track on the Virginia Central Railroad. Stuart took a position between Sheridan and Richmond at a place called Yellow Tavern.

Sherman ordered a general movement around the Confederate left to Resaca. So far there had been little contact with the Confederates, mostly skirmishes. Few prisoners had been taken by either side.

Ransom, John, QM Sgt., 9th Michigan Cavalry, Andersonville Prison, Ga.:

Capt. Wirtz very domineering and abusive. Is afraid to come into camp any more. There are a thousand men in here who would willingly die if they could kill him first. Certainly the worst man I ever saw. New prisoners coming in every day with good clothes, blankets, &c., and occasionally with considerable money. These are victims for the raiders who pitch into them for plunder. Very serious fights occur.

## May 11 (Wednesday)

Sheridan had reached the little crossroads called Yellow Tavern about 6 miles north of Richmond when he was attacked by J.E.B. Stuart's cavalry. In the swirling, dusty melee that ensued, a dismounted Federal cavalryman shot Stuart as he rode past, mortally wounding the Rebel. Stuart was evacuated and then taken to Richmond for treatment.

At Spotsylvania C.H., Grant and Lee still were still faced-off and it was Grant's move. Lee could not afford to attack the larger army and hope to survive.

He could not stand the casualties.

In Georgia, Sherman ordered a swing towards Resaca to the southeast and behind the Confederate army, now at Rocky Face and Buzzard Roost; Sherman was unwilling to waste Union men on a frontal assault.

White, H.S., Chaplain, R.I. Regt. Heavy Artillery, prisoner of war, Wilmington, N.C.:

On Wednesday, May the 11th,... at 8 A.M. we were marched to the depot.... We left, and slowly by rail went to Goldsboro.... The negroes came about with pies to sell, and thinking we might get a palatable morsel, we sent out a dollar for one. It was a crust of about the thickness of pasteboard, filled with sweet potato paste. It was not exceedingly tempting.... We remained here a few hours and began to see specimens of the natives. The men were all soldiers. The women showed the prevalence of caste. Some dressed richly, but most were dressed in the most untidy manner. Many of them had a stick protruding from the mouth several inches. These persons were chewing snuff.... Leaving Goldsboro, N.C., we proceeded south on the Wilmington and Weldon Railroad, reaching Wilmington just before dark.... We had our rations of hard bread and raw bacon, but it did not, somehow, produce the right impression on the inner man, and we thought to get something better. We knew that the blockade runners came in here pretty freely, and hoped to get a good lunch at least. Asking the lieutenant for permission to go for supper, he sent us under guard to the restaurant in the depot close by.... We found that several blockade runners had just come in. One brought several thousand pounds of bacon, and others brought various stores, and of course they were jubilant and hopeful. The South would win....

Returning to our company we found many had gone to bed.... About midnight we were ordered to fall in, and crossed the Cape Fear River on a steam ferryboat.

### May 12 (Thursday)

At Spotsylvania C.H., Va., Grant's Federals charged Lee's prepared lines in one of the costliest battles of the war. The "Bloody Angle" claimed about 6800 Union and 5000 Confederate casualties in killed and wounded alone. Another 4000 Confederates were captured, a loss that was far greater

for the South, because of the attrition—these veterans could not be replaced easily, while the North had seemingly endless manpower. Grant may have been accused of butchery in the Northern papers, but Lee had nearly 10,000 fewer men in his army than he had had seven days previously.

Sheridan, moving towards the James and Ben Butler's army, had to fight nearly every mile of the way. Butler was still stuck at City Point and Bermuda Hundred, contained by Beauregard.

The fabled "Cavalier," J.E.B. Stuart was dead, having succumbed to the wounds he had received at Yellow Tavern on the 11th of May.

In Georgia, Sherman's troops had flanked the Confederates, passed Snake Creek Gap, and were approaching Resaca and Johnston's army, which had moved from Dalton.

Chaplain White got a rare glimpse of the Wilmington port during his transfer to the south bank of the Cape Fear River. Much traffic, mostly northbound, was evident on the ferries.

White, H.S., Chaplain, R.I. Regt. Heavy Artillery, prisoner of war, Augusta, Ga.:

Here we met large numbers of troops from Charleston hastening north towards Richmond. They were turbulent, saucy, ragged and homely.... We saw the effects of the great fire that broke out at the place a few days before, and just after the Plymouth prisoners passed through on their way South.... Here we were thrust into baggage cars so thick that we could not lay down, and on the Wilmington and Marietta Railroad departed for Florence. The locomotives were old and rusty. The cars had been broken and patched. The rails were worn and poor. We could not go ten miles an hour. Our train broke down and detained us for several hours....

... Making no delay at Florence, we continued our journey to Kingsville. The old rickety cars, in spite of all their care, smashed up again, and it took us ten hours to gather up the fragments and get under way again.... From Kingsville we passed on to Branchville, on the South Carolina Railroad running from Charleston to Atlanta, Ga., and on this went west to Hamburgh, on the Savannah River. Crossing the river we entered the fine town of Augusta.... We remained here only a few hours.... From Augusta we went to Millen, on the Central

Georgia Railroad, and thence west to Macon.... We remained at Macon but a short time as we went west, although the officers soon returned there. Leaving Macon in the morning [May 14th], we went sixty miles to the southwest, to that famous and ever-to-be-remembered Andersonville. On the map it is marked Americus.

Ward, William W., Col., 9th Tenn. Cav., prisoner, Ft. Delaware, Del.:

Morning dark gloomy and desperately uninviting. I spent a bad night owing to a discussion before bedtime, in my room. I come nearer having the blues this morning than at any time since my imprisonment. But I will not be dejected, my soul shall not be cast down nor troubled within me. I have a dear loving wife to live for and for her I will live and for her sake I'll be cheerful & grow fat and lively preparatory to my meeting her—God bless her!

Ransom, John, QM Sgt., 9th Michigan Cavalry, Andersonville Prison, Ga.:

Received a few limes from George Hendryx, who again went out to work on the outside last night.... Patrols also looking among the prisoners for deserters. A lame man, for telling of a tunnel, was pounded almost to death last night, and this morning they were chasing him to administer more punishment, when he ran inside the dead line claiming protection of the guard. The guard didn't protect worth a cent, but shot him through the head.... More rumors of hard fighting around Richmond. Grant getting the best of it I reckon.

## May 13 (Friday)

Grant, failing to break Lee's lines at Spotsylvania C.H., moved around to the Union (his own) left and put Warren's corps in the lead, maneuvering to the southeast. This sidestepping movement would characterize the campaign. In all this fighting, the numbers of Confederate prisoners was increasing rapidly. These were sent to a large holding area at Belle Plain near Fredericksburg, Va. At one time, more than 5000 prisoners were held at that site.

At Resaca, Joe Johnston's army took up positions and awaited Sherman's arrival.

The Confederate prison at Cahaba, Ala., became a receiving point and collection station for Federal prisoners. The prisoners thus collected were held for a period of time and then transferred to Andersonville.

Ransom, John, QM Sgt., 9th Michigan Cavalry, Andersonville Prison, Ga.:

Rainy morning. We are guarded by an Alabama regiment, who are about to leave for the front. Georgia militia to take their places.... Carpenter is now sick with scurvy, and I am beginning to get the same disease hold of me again. Battese cut my hair which was about a foot long. Gay old cut. Many have long hair, which, being never combed, is matted together and full of vermin. With sunken eyes, blackened countenances from pitch pine smoke, rags and disease, the men look sickening. The air reeks with nastiness, and it is a wonder that we live at all.

## May 14 (Saturday)

In Virginia, Grant had sidestepped a short distance to the southeast on the far side of the Ni River, only to find that Lee had countered him. In Georgia, Sherman arrived at Resaca and immediately ordered probing attacks on the flanks of Johnston's positions.

Today, E.D. Townsend notified Col. Hoffman, Federal Commissary-General of Prisoners, that "there are quite a number of barracks at Elmira, N.Y., which are not occupied, and are fit to hold rebel prisoners."

White, H.S., Chaplain, R.I. Regt. Heavy Artillery, prisoner of war, Andersonville, Ga.:

Andersonville is a station on the Southwestern and Georgia Railroad, sixty miles to the southwest of Macon, Ga. There is no town or settlement of the least importance. A small wooden church, never completed, and less than a dozen houses in sight. I arrived here at 1:30 P.M.... Immediately on our arrival we were ordered out of the cars and formed in line, and turned over to the commandant of the prison. Here I saw that long-to-be-remembered scamp, Capt. Wurtz, who was in charge of the Union prisoners of war at that post. He is a lean, tall, rough, coarse-looking German. He swears incessantly, and curses most cruelly. While the men were being turned over to him he began to curse them....

The captain, lieutenant and myself he would not receive, and we were sent to the church nearby, and remained with the guard that came with us. The men were marched down towards the stockade, a short distance from the depot and in clear view, and I saw them to speak to them no more. It was a sad farewell....

... You remember how large and liberal were the supplies sent to the Sanitary Commission, and by friends to the prisoners at Libby Prison, Richmond, last winter; you also remember the complaints made by our officers that the rebels stole much, and gave them but little. Our men told us that two hundred and seventy-five of these boxes were brought down to Andersonville for the use of the officers and the garrison. Our informant was a good and truthful man, and was employed in a position to know, as the contents of the boxes were used to supply the table at which he ate, after the officers had finished. He said he thought we had as good a right to it as anyone, and so brought us coffee, sugar, bread, and a cake of fine soap sent by some northern wife or mother, to husband or son in prison.

I visited Dr. Johnson and asked him many questions about our men. Their want and destitution he admitted, and also said that they were unable to give them what was needed for their health. He said if stores were sent him he would see that they were faithfully distributed. The use made of the boxes in their hands at that time did not exactly look like doing all that honest-minded men could do for our men.

## May 15 (Sunday)

At Resaca, Ga., Sherman again decided that Johnston's positions were too strong for a frontal assault and started another flanking movement. Johnston, afraid of being outflanked, evacuated his positions during the night, burning the railroad bridge over the Oostenaula and withdrawing towards Calhoun and Adairsville. Some few prisoners were taken for the pens at Cahaba and Salisbury.

White, H.S., Chaplain, R.I. Regt. Heavy Artillery, prisoner of war, Andersonville, Ga.:

As I was at the depot on the day of our departure for Macon ... the sun came down upon us on the platform so intensely, that I asked permission to go into the commissary building, that was part of the long building used for railroad and other purposes. The men that were issuing rations allowed us to come in, and we sat down upon some sacks quite out of the way.

... Presently the officer in command came in and saw us there, and with rude oaths drove us brutally out. Even the officer in charge of us was annoyed, and took us round the building so as to allow us to sit in the shade. I saw a short distance from where I was a large heap of boxes. I arose and sauntered out towards them, and found them to be the identical ones described to me by the Union soldiers. They were of all sizes, from twelve to twenty inches square, and even larger. They had on them the red labels and prints of the northern express companies. There were directed with paint to colonels, majors, captains, and lieutenants, *Libby Prison, Richmond, Va.* Half of them were out doors, and the rest in a storeroom of the building. Many of the boxes were empty. Others seemed not to be opened as yet. Some were opened and examined, and the contents found spoiled, and the box was left opened and partly emptied. In the room and on the ground, the rubbish from these boxes, consisting of loaves of mouldy bread, cords of biscuits and loaves of cake, cooked fowls, hams, all kinds of rotten fruit, dried fruit, all covered with mould; papers of flour, sugar and garments spoiled by being in contact with things that had spoiled in consequence of not being delivered promptly, was nearly knee-deep. The glass was broken in the window through which I saw the ruin in the room. Nice woolen shirts, such as are called sutlers' shirts (being usually supplied by sutlers), coats, pants, hats and caps, and shoes taken from these boxes, were on the persons of commissary and quartermasters' sergeants, and those employed about the depot.

As near as I could judge, no attempt was made to stop or conceal the plunder. This wholesale and shameful stealing I had read and heard about, but it seemed far off, and I thought perhaps it might be a little overstated; but when I came to look upon it with my own eyes, in broad day,... how could I help cursing that hellish and unearthly Confederacy, in the name of my God....

The officers of the three regiments of guards and the officers of the prison had joined and gathered up a grand ball. I should as soon think of having a band of negro minstrels perform the funeral service of a bishop. Men in that Andersonville stockade were starving and dying in their hands, and under their treatment, by the score and hundred, and yet they could gather the ladies of the whole region, obtain a band, and have a drunken revel.... The ladies that danced I presume were all white, but many of the dusky shades, and of several varieties, were all about us. The band was composed of negroes that were by no means black. They played well. The Andersonville prison, or, as the men call it, the "slaughter pen," seems to be looked upon by the Southern women as a kind of grand show, and on Sabbaths the trains from each direction come loaded down with the curious and the scoffer. They come and gather on the high grounds that overlook the stockade, and watch the inmates....

At 11 o'clock... we were ordered aboard the train, and in company with soldiers and women we started for the officers' prison of Macon, sixty miles from Andersonville.... My position with my brother officers was on the rear platform of the last car in the train. The cars were crowded, and we chose this position for the opportunity it gave to study the country, people, buildings, crops, etc. The stores at the crossroads were everywhere abandoned. We seldom saw a man who was not a soldier. Negroes and women were numerous. The only things growing were corn, with army beans planted between the hills of corn. The amount of land under cultivation, compared with the fields lying waste and growing up in weeds and brush was small. There was no cotton growing. The chief fruit was the peach. Some of these orchards were several miles long, and as wide as we could see. The fruit is much inferior, both in size and quality, to the New Jersey fruit.... Wild hogs and cattle were to be seen here and there roaming at will through the forests.... In the large towns there are some good buildings, and occasionally we see a fine house, but you would not see one once in ten miles in the country. You look on the map and you will see the names of towns along the railroads, but there are not half of these towns that have five longhouses apiece, in sight of the water tank and wood yard. The locomotives all burn wood, and you will see several slaves at each station preparing the wood, which is done with the axe. The water is pumped up into the tanks by mules, with a rude gearing prepared for the purpose.... It was late afternoon when we reached Macon.... Our place of confinement was the Fair Ground, a mile or so from the town.... For the present my travels were over...

Ward, William W., Col., 9th Tenn. Cavalry, prisoner, Ft. Delaware, Del.:

When I awoke this morning heavy peals of rolling thunder seemed to be playing the reveille of the world. It is raining a little this morning and a heavy rain seems to have fallen last night. Day pretty pleasant without rain. Bad news all day. Lee & A P Hill are wounded & J.E.B. Stuart and Longstreet are dead. Lee's retreat converted into a rout and Grant picking up prisoners by the thousands after having taken Gen. Ed. Johnson & his whole division and a large portion of Early's division or brigade. All this and much more in dispatches to Gen Dix N.Y. over Secty Staunton's own name. I do not believe the half of it.

Ransom, John, QM Sgt., 9th Michigan Cavalry, Andersonville Prison, Ga.:

Sabbath day and hot. Would give anything for some shade to lay in. Even this luxury is denied us, and we are obliged to crawl around more dead than alive. Rumors that Sherman is marching towards Atlanta, and that place threatened. Kilpatrick said to be moving towards us for the purpose of effecting our release.

### May 16 (Monday)

White, H.S., Chaplain, R.I. Regt. Heavy Artillery, prisoner of war, Camp Oglethorpe, Macon, Ga.:

On Monday,... we drew our rations, and commenced prison life in camp. Here we drew flour, meal and bacon, and were quite elated. I was kindly invited by Capt. Mackey to mess with him, and as he had plenty of money, and was allowed to send into town by the guards for extras, we got along finely.... A gallon of molasses cost twenty-five dollars. A Dutch bake kettle, holding some two gallons, cost thirty-five dollars. When the Plymouth officers first came to Macon, the ladies came and brought small gifts and books, and showed us much sympathy. This class of Union sympathizers soon became known, and were watched and ordered off. I have seen ladies come and walk up and down just beyond the beat of the sentinel, with bundles under their shawls, seeking a chance to slip them in, but being baffled by the vigilance of the guards, with downcast and sorrowful face would walk away. These persons were either Union people or had friends in Northern prisons, and gave to us, hoping others would do the same for their friends.

The stockade just in sight was rapidly approaching completion. One day we saw a column of the roughest looking men pass us towards the stockade. They were the captives from the Libby Prison, Richmond, Va. Towards night our company was turned into the stockade with them. A new class of suffering was before me. The men were old prisoners, and pale and haggard. They were ragged, and some partly naked. They were filthy, and covered with vermin. Prison life makes men hard, selfish and rough.... The stockade was an enclosure of nearly three acres, surrounded by a strong board fence some sixteen feet high. On the outside, some four feet from the top, a platform, some three feet wide, with a railing, ran entirely round the stockade. On this platform the guards were posted. On the inside, some twelve or fifteen feet from the stockade fence, was a small picket fence. This was the dead line.... At the west end of the enclosure was a small brook and the sink. The fence was so built that the stream came in, and for some sixty feet, ran within the enclosure. Some twenty feet of this stream before it entered the sink was used for bathing and washing clothes. As much filth from some manufactories just above found its way into the sink; it was not used for drinking or cooking. Several tubs were set in the slope of ground at the roots of an old tree, and they were filled by a spring in the bank. A well at the other end of the enclosure also furnished us with water. As a thousand men were to be supplied, we found the supply entirely inadequate to the demand....

... The shelter of the place consisted of two buildings formerly used at the County and State fairs. One was nearly a hundred feet long and some thirty-five feet wide, having a floor. The other was an old stable used for cattle and swine, and very filthy. The one with floor was used for a hospital for the accommodation of the more feeble, and the other for the field and staff, together with the general officers. There were a few pine and oak trees in the prison that afforded some shelter from the sun. Some three or four hundred found quarters in these buildings, the others crouched down wherever they chose to. Many had no shelter from the burning sun, the rain,

or the night air. After a while some boards were furnished and some poles and rude roofs could be erected, that helped to keep off the sun and storms. There were no sides, ends or floors, and of course the shelter was but partial. These sheds were for only a part, and large numbers found quarters in the open air.

Our food was much inferior to that given us when in the field outside. We drew several days' rations at a time. Less than a quart of unsifted cornmeal, with about two ounces of bacon, a tablespoonful of rice, about the same quantity of beans, a spoonful of salt, and sometimes instead of bacon we got two or three spoonfuls of molasses.... The rice and beans were issued but a few times. The bacon was often rotten and full of worms.... A ration of wood was a small stick each day. This was split with the squad axe, which was issued to us each morning and taken out at night.... The utensils for cooking were few. For a hundred men eight small skillets, several tin pans, and six or eight tin kettles comprised the total furnished us.... A few bricks were furnished us, and we put them together so as to put the skillet on them and build a fire beneath.... For some twenty dollars a pound we could obtain soda. By allowing the dough to stand awhile it would become sour, and by adding soda it would sweeten and cause to rise, and often we would get a loaf of good bread....

As the unsifted meal made coarse and quite indigestible bread, we had to resort to some expedient to sift it. When I entered the Confederacy I had a tin canteen. This we threw into the fire and melted the halves apart, and took one for a plate and the other we punched full of holes with a sharp bit of iron, and made of it quite a respectable sieve. At one time this was the only sieve in prison so far as I knew, and it was set at work early and kept well at it till dark. Presently a lady in Macon sent in a piece of wire cloth some fifteen inches square, which was fitted with a frame and did the work much better. Each man must do his own cooking. Some took hold quite handy, and others seemed to view the operation with some modest measure of disgust. Often four or five would club together and take turns cooking. When a new captive would arrive we would invite him to dine. The first day would pass pretty well. The second he would begin to look around, make inquiries, and look over his rations. The third day the starch would be pretty well taken out, and off would come the coat, and you would seem him experimenting with his Indian dough. To some men it seemed almost like breaking the bones to bend them, but they had to come down. Some had not much genius for cooking, and would do it poorly, and soon became sick....

Our sink was composed of planks resting on some scantlings thrown across the ditch through which the brook ran, and as there was no seat many a poor weak fellow would fall. The deadline was near, and if a man staggered he was in danger of being shot. The whole place was excessively filthy, and soon became alive with vermin. No one could escape.... We used to watch the trains of cars as they passed near us, and could read in the loads of wounded and the movement of troops something of what was going on.

Ransom, John, QM Sgt., 9th Michigan Cavalry, Andersonville Prison, Ga.:

Two men got away during the night and were brought back before noon. (Was going to say before dinner.) The men were torn by the dogs, and one of them full of buckshot. A funny way of escape has just been discovered by Wirtz. A man pretends to be dead and is carried out on a stretcher and left with the row of dead. As soon as it gets dark, Mr. Dead-man jumps up and runs.... An examination now takes place by the surgeon before being permitted out from under guard.

## May 17 (Tuesday)

Leaving Calhoun, Ga., Joe Johnston's Army of Tennessee briefly delayed the Union forces at Adairsville with Gen. George Thomas in front and McPherson and Schofield coming around both flanks. Johnston hurried his retreat to escape the box.

Ransom, John, QM Sgt., 9th Michigan Cavalry, Andersonville Prison, Ga.:

Had a funny dream last night. Thought the rebels were so hard up for mules that they hitched up a couple of grayback lice to draw in the bread.... Some prisoners came today who were captured near Dalton, and report the place in our possession, and the rebels driven six miles this side.... Nineteen thousand confined here now and dying at the rate of ninety per day.... Fine weather but very warm. The sandy soil fairly alive with vermin. If this place is so bad at this time of the year, what must it be like in July, August and September? Every man will die, in my estimation.

## May 19 (Thursday)

Lee, to find out if Grant was moving to the Confederate right, sent Richard Ewell to demonstrate against the Union line at Spottsylvania C.H., which brought on a severe fight that lasted most of the day, again accomplishing nothing except more casualties. Grant was moving towards the Po River to the southeast. For the several battles which made up the whole of Spottsylvania, the Federals lost about 17,500 out of nearly 110,000. The South's losses were never accurately recorded, but could be estimated roughly at 6000 from a total engaged of about 50,000. Grant could afford the loss, Lee could not.

Col. William Hoffman, Federal Commissary-General of Prisoners, wrote Secy. of War Stanton today about a suggestion to reduce the cost of feeding the Confederate prisoners in his care. He would reduce the ration size issued to the prisoners. Simple method, great gains, hungry prisoners. Hoffman explained it this way:

Sir:... Suggest that the ration as now issued to prisoners of war may be considerably reduced without depriving them of the food necessary to keep them in health, and I respectfully recommend that hereafter the ration be composed as follows, viz: Hard bread, 14 ounces, or 16 ounces soft bread; cornmeal, 16 ounces; beef, 14 ounces; pork or bacon, 10 ounces; beans, 6 quarts per 100 men, or rice, 8 pounds per 100 men; sugar 12 pounds per 100 men; coffee, 5 pounds ground or 7 pounds raw per 100 men, or tea, 1 pound per 100 men; soap, 4 pounds per 100 men; salt, 2 quarts per 100 men; vinegar, 3 quarts per 100 men; molasses, 1 quart per 100 men; potatoes, 15 pounds per 100 men. I also recommend that ration of sugar and coffee, as above fixed, be issued only every other day.

Hoffman also wrote to Stanton concerning the barracks at Elmira, N.Y. On June 12, 1862, Hoffman had directed that Capt. H.M. Lazelle, one of his aides, inspect the camp at Elmira for a possible "depot for prisoners." On June 25, 1862, Lazelle reported on the capacity of the camp(s) and their condition. Because of the buildup of Confederate prisoners caused by Grant's offensive in Virginia, the prison population at Point Lookout, Md., had reached overflow stage and more room was needed immediately. Pointing out the space problem to Stanton, Hoffman wrote:

I respectfully suggest that one set of the barracks at Elmira may be appropriated to this purpose. I am informed there are barracks there available which have, by crowding, received 12,000 volunteers. By fencing them in at a cost of about $2000 they may be relied on to receive 8000 or possibly 10,000 prisoners. They can be shipped directly from Belle Plain, on steamers already ordered for the purpose, to New York, and thence by railroad to Elmira...

Also on this date, Hoffman wired Lt. Col. S. Eastman at Elmira that he would receive instructions to set apart the barracks on the Chemung River for use as a "depot for prisoners." He instructed Eastman to begin construction of a stockade fence to enclose sufficient space to house 10,000 prisoners. Eastman, for some strange reason, kept working towards a goal of only 5000 prisoners. This would cause many problems almost immediately.

Ransom, John, QM Sgt., 9th Michigan Cavalry, Andersonville Prison, Ga.:

Nearly twenty thousand men confined here now. New ones coming every day. Rations *very* small and *very* poor. The meal that the bread is made out of is ground, seemingly, cob and all, and it scourges the men fearfully. Things getting continually worse. Hundreds of cases of dropsy. Men puff out of human shape and are perfectly horrible to look at. Philo Lewis died today. Could not have weighed at the time of his death more than ninety pounds, and was originally a large man, weighing not less than one hundred and seventy.

## May 20 (Friday)

In Georgia, Johnston passed through Cartersville, crossed the Etowah River and took up strong defensive positions at Allatoona Pass. Schofield's corps followed closely through Cartersville, almost entering before the rebels were clear.

White, H.S., Chaplain, R.I. Regt. Heavy Artillery, prisoner of war, Macon, Ga.:

I had not been more than a day or two in the stockade at Macon before Maj. Bates, a fine and noble Christian officer, spoke to me about holding service, and we arranged for an evening sermon that week. I did intend to preach, but not feeling well, Chaplain

Dixon changed work with me and preached the sermon, while I conducted the opening service. Our meeting was held at the end of an old building erected for a store and show room at the fairs held on the grounds. One of the shutters resting on the steps and an old bench made our pulpit. Several had soldiers' hymn books, and the singing was good. I read a chapter and offered prayer. In my devotions I asked God to "bless the President of these United States, his cabinet, the Congress, the army and navy."... Chaplain Dixon preached a good and appropriate sermon, and we retired to rest.... The next day I think it was, one of the general officers in the prison said to me as he was passing, "Chaplain, the rebel authorities did not like your sermon the other night." I replied, "General, it was not me that preached, it was Chaplain Dixon." "Well, your prayer, then," said he, "it was you who gave the offense, by praying for the President of the United States."... a feverish expectation went on a few days, till one evening when it devolved on me to preach and on Bro. Dixon to offer the opening prayer. All were gathered close about as I stepped on the platform and read the first hymn. As I closed and turned about to hand the hymn book to Bro. Dixon, Capt. Tabb, Commandant of the prison, stepped upon the platform and said, saluting me, "Chaplain, I have come to say that we cannot allow you to pray for the President of the United States and the success of your army and defeat of ours, as you have done." Chaplain Dixon arose and stepped upon the platform just by his side, and among the audience was the most perfect silence. The guards were within hearing with muskets at the soldiers, stopped walking their beats on the top of the stockade and listened. The gunners stood to their post beside the twelve-pound brass Napoleon that was trained upon the place where we stood.... This was a new, and I felt quite delicate, position.

I thought it best to take the Captain only on a single point and replied, "Captain, do I understand you to command me as Chaplain in the United States Army, acting in my official capacity among our own officers, not to pray for the President of the United States?" "Yes," said he, "I command you not to do it."... "Very well," said I, "you give me a written order to that effect and I will obey it. But, Captain, are you aware what kind of an order this is that you are giving me? It strikes me as very strange indeed. Your chaplains in our prisons pray loud and long for Jeff. Davis and the Confederate States, and no one cares a thing for it, and now you come and attempt to interfere with our consciences and our prayers before God."...

"If we were out in the city and interfered with your people it would be different, but what little comfort we can get from our devotion it is not right or manly to deprive us of.... As long as we do not interfere with your prison discipline we have a right to preach, pray, lecture on temperance, spiritualism, God, or no God, play ball, pitch quoit, wrestle or any other thing that may amuse or interest us."... By this time, as you may imagine, I had become decidedly interested in my subject, and ... was proceeding to introduce sundry other reasons why he should mind his own business, and leave us alone, when he said, "I permit you, I permit you," repeating it with kind and feeling earnestness. I thanked him and saluting each other we parted, he retiring into the building, and I turned and again announced the hymn, which was sung with a will.

Ransom, John, QM Sgt., 9th Michigan Cavalry, Andersonville Prison, Ga.:

Hendryx sent me in today from the outside a dozen small onions and some green tea. No person, on suddenly being lifted from the lowest depths of misery to peace and plenty, and all that money could buy, could feel more joyous or grateful than myself for those things.

## May 21 (Saturday)

Even more than two weeks after the Battle of the Wilderness, the wounded soldiers, both North and South, were still not completely sorted out and back to their own army. Grant had arranged with Lee, or so they both thought, to have some of the Federal wounded at "Old Wilderness Tavern" picked up by a train of Federal ambulances and accompanying medical personnel. Asst. Surgeon Edward De W. Breneman took the train of ambulances to pick up the wounded prisoners and came back empty. He wrote his report to Brig. Gen. John A. Rawlins, Grant's Chief of Staff:

I this morning proceeded to the "Old Wilderness Tavern" with twenty-five ambulances under flag of truce. The major commanding the forces at that

point declined receiving any communications, under instructions from his superiors, unless addressed to Gen. Robert E. Lee, and I returned with empty ambulances.

Supplies were sent to the wounded yesterday, of whom more than 600 remain in the hands of the enemy at different points.... They are represented to be comfortably situated. The major commanding the Confederate forces stated that Gen. Lee would be notified that I appeared today, while I agreed to meet again under flag of truce tomorrow at 12 o'clock at the "Old Wilderness."

Ward, William W., Col., 9th Tenn. Cavalry, prisoner, Ft. Delaware, Del.:

No letter. A little annoyed as I certainly ought to have one. News still very good. Lee's address to his army. Very encouraging. Our Paroles were taken away from us today by order, as Gen. Shoepf says, of the War Department at Washington. We are not permitted to go out of the house except with a guard. In other respects our privileges are the same. I am not at all sorry that mine was taken away. Day very pleasant. Mr. Somebody's school of young ladies was down at the fort today. Some with school girl vanity and want of experience acting rather imprudently. That highly, adorning quality of a lady, Modesty, is much more sparingly dispensed among the northern than southern ladies. The most Yankee women I have seen are "tom boys." Would not like to have one for a wife.

## May 22 (Sunday)

In Virginia, the Confederates reached Hanover Junction, just north of Richmond, only a short time before Grant's columns arrived from Guiney's Station. Another lost race.

Johnston's Army of Tennessee, located near Allatoona on the Chattanooga-Atlanta railroad, was in fairly strong defensive positions. Sherman again moved around Johnston's left flank, going towards Dallas, Ga.

Ransom, John, QM Sgt., 9th Michigan Cavalry, Andersonville Prison, Ga.:

Am now a gallant washer-man. Battese, the Minnesota Indian, learn't me in the way of his occupation, made me a wash board by cutting creases in a piece of board, and I am fully installed. We have a sign out, made by myself on a piece of shingle: "WASHING." We get small pieces of bread for our labors, some of the sick cannot eat their bread, and not being able to keep clean, give us a job. Make probably a pound of bread two or three days in the week.... Have many applications for admission to the firm, and may enlarge the business.

### May 24 (Tuesday)

Yesterday, Sherman moved his entire army across the Etowah River and headed towards Dallas, Ga.; Johnston, having little choice with his left flank, turned again, moved towards that same location via New Hope Church, which was even closer to Atlanta. This would lengthen Sherman's supply line and contract Johnston's, which was based in Atlanta.

On the North Anna River near Hanover Junction, Va., the Army of the Potomac was divided into three parts by the bend in the North Anna River and Lee's protruding line.

Yesterday, the 23rd, Lt. Col. Eastman, Elmira, N.Y., wrote Col. Wm. Hoffman that the barracks set aside for use as prisoner-of-war billets were those designated Nos. 1 and 3, which were located about 2 miles from the other barracks. Eastman reported that the stockade fence, 12 feet high, would be completed in about ten days. It was requested that no prisoners be sent until Eastman indicated that the facility was ready to receive them.

Ransom, John, QM Sgt., 9th Michigan Cavalry, Andersonville Prison, Ga.:

Sherman coming this way, so said, towards Atlanta. It is thought the cavalry will make a break for us, but even if they do they cannot get us north. We are equal to no exertion. Men busy today killing swallows that fly low; partly for amusement, but more particularly for food they furnish. Are eaten raw before hardly dead. No, thank you, I will take no swallow.

### May 25 (Wednesday)

In a raging thunderstorm, Hooker's corps, at New Hope Church, Ga., drove against Hood's corps along Pumpkin Vine Creek.

Ransom, John, QM Sgt., 9th Michigan Cavalry, Andersonville Prison, Ga.:

One thousand new prisoners came today from near Petersburg, Va. They give us encouraging news as to the termination of the spring campaign.... Getting warmer after the rain. Our squad has a very good well, and about one quarter water enough, of something a trifle better than swamp water. Man killed by the raiders near where we slept. Head all pounded to pieces with a club. Murders an every day occurrence.

### May 26 (Thursday)

In Virginia, Grant decided not to attack Lee's position at North Anna, so he began movement towards Hanovertown, south and east around Lee's right flank.

Ransom, John, QM Sgt., 9th Michigan Cavalry, Andersonville Prison, Ga.:

For the last three days I have had nearly enough to eat, such as it is. My washing business gives me extra food. Have taken in a partner, and the firm now is Battese, Ransom & Co. Think of taking in more partners, making Battese president, appointing vice-presidents, secretaries, &c. We charge a ration of bread for admittance. Sand makes a very good soap. If we could get hold of a razor and open a barber shop in connection, our fortunes would be made.... Molasses given us today, from two to four spoonfuls apiece, which is indeed a treat. Anything sweet or sour, or in the vegetable line, is the making of us....

Jones, John B., Rebel War Clerk, Confederate War Dept., Richmond, Va.:

Gen. Bragg did a good thing yesterday, even while Senator Orr was denouncing him. He relieved Gen. Winder from duty here, and assigned him to Goldsborough, N.C. Now if the rogues and cut-throats he persisted in having about him be likewise dismissed, the Republic is safe!

### May 27 (Friday)

Sheridan's cavalry moved into Hanovertown, Va., south of the Pamunkey River, passed through the town and scouted the area south for Confederates. Lee, outflanked again, began moving to get between Grant and Richmond.

In the vicinity of New Hope Church, Ga., Otis O. Howard's corps attacked and was repulsed at

Pickett's Mill. Howard took heavy losses in wounded and captured.

Ransom, John, QM Sgt., 9th Michigan Cavalry, Andersonville Prison, Ga.:

We twist up pieces of tin, stovepipe, &c., for dishes. A favorite and common dish is half of a canteen. Our spoons are made of wood. Hardly one man in ten has a dish of any kind to put his rations of soup or molasses in, and often old shoes, dirty caps and the like are brought into requisition. Notwithstanding my prosperity in business the scurvy is taking right hold of me.... Fresh beef given us today, but in very small quantities with no wood or salt to put it into proper shape.

## May 28 (Saturday)

In Virginia, Lee hastily moved south and east, trying desperately to get back in front of Grant's army. Lee finally made it to a line covering the crossings of the Tolopotomoy, ten miles northeast of Richmond. Grant's forces crossed at Hanovertown with heavy cavalry contact on the Pamunkey and Totopotomoy rivers.

In Georgia, the Confederates under Hardee added to the casualty toll, taking heavy casualties when Johnston ordered a reconnaissance in force against McPherson near Dallas, Ga.

Ransom, John, QM Sgt., 9th Michigan Cavalry, Andersonville Prison, Ga.:

No more news.... My mouth getting sore from scurvy and teeth loose. New prisoners coming in every day and death rate increasing. I don't seem to get hardened to the situation and am shuddering all the time at the sights. Rainy weather.

## May 29 (Sunday)

In Virginia, Lee, along the Tolopotomoy, prepared his lines. Grant, moving up, could see little opposition.

At Good Hope Church and Dallas, Ga., Johnston opened his artillery against McPherson's army, doing little damage to the Union troops.

Ransom, John, QM Sgt., 9th Michigan Cavalry, Andersonville Prison, Ga.:

Nearly a thousand just came in. Would seem to me that the rebels are victorious in their battles. New men are perfectly thunderstruck at the hole they have got into. A great many give right up and die in a few weeks, and some in a week. My limbs are badly swollen with scurvy and dropsy combined. Mouth also very sore. Battese digs for roots, which he steeps up and I drink.

## May 30 (Monday)

At Rock Island, Ill., the prisoners who volunteered for work were being used to construct a sewer and waterworks. The prisoners working were skilled blasters, masons, tenders, etc., who followed these trades prior to entering the Confederate service. The prisoners expected some compensation for their labor, expecting to be able to buy "extras" such as tobacco, fruit, etc., with the money. Normal skilled labor from the civilian force would receive pay of about $1.50 or $1.75 per day for their labor. The camp commandant suggested that they be paid $0.40 per day for a full ten-hour day. On June 7, Col. William Hoffman, Federal Commissary-General of Prisoners, approved a wage rate of $0.10 per day. The princely sum of one cent per hour! How generous! On June 10, the Union Secy. of War, Edwin Stanton, approved the wage rate and provided that prisoners "so laboring have full rations."

Ransom, John, QM Sgt., 9th Michigan Cavalry, Andersonville Prison, Ga.:

Another thousand came today and from the eastern army. Prison crowded. Men who came are from Siegel's corps in the Shenandoah Valley.... Charlie Hudson, from some part of Ohio, took his canteen an hour ago and went to the swamp for water. He has not returned for the very good reason that he was shot while reaching up under the dead line to get the freshest water. Some one has pulled the body out of the water on to dry land, where it will stay until tomorrow.

Also at Andersonville, Ga., Capt. Richard B. Winder, Assistant Quartermaster for the prison, was having difficulty getting a shoe factory started in which the prisoners would be employed. Winder sent a progress report to Richmond:

...the present condition of progress made by me in

organizing and establishing the shoe factory. A few days prior to my departure from this I had sent Mr. Smoot, a person furnished me by Maj. Cunningham, at Atlanta, as superintendent of the factory, on business connected with it. He informed me by letter that during his absence he had been conscribed, and that he is now with Maj. Cunningham, who had succeeded in procuring his release. A few days since, and shortly after my return here, a Mr. McMullen reported to me by letter from Maj. Dillard, at Columbus. I have sent him off in search of such tools as are needed. What success he may meet with I am unable to say. The principal difficulty I now see and now have to contend [with] is the scarcity of upper leather. I have up to this time succeeded in obtaining a quantity sufficient to last only for three days for fifty operatives. It would not answer to commence on so small a quantity. Next in importance are shoe pegs. I find difficulty in procuring enough required. Permit me to suggest that within ten miles of this, at a place called Americus, there are two tanneries, I think, under the control of the Government. Their capacity, I have been informed, are sufficient to contribute quite largely to the requirements of this factory. A very short distance from this, the savings of transportation, and their position so contiguous, would warrant my getting from them the materials so far as they could supply my wants. It will not answer to commence operations until every branch of the department was properly furnished both with tools and stock, a sufficient quantity of the latter being particularly required; without, the work men would be idle in a very few days.

## May 31 (Tuesday)

Sgt. Bartlett Yancey Malone of the 6th N.C. Infantry, confined at Point Lookout, Md., recorded during the month of May the departure of 600 prisoners for the South. In the early part of the month, the campaign in central Virginia had begun with Grant crossing the Rapidan and colliding with Lee in the Wilderness. The results of the fighting were immediately apparent at Point Lookout by the influx of Confederate prisoners. Malone recorded the arrival of 100 on May 13th from the Petersburg area; 40 more on the 15th captured by Maj. Gen. Ben Butler's army; 1000 on the 17th from the Wilderness; 400 more on the 18th from the Wilderness; and an additional 400 on the 28th. Business in prisoners was brisk.

Abbott, A.O., 1st Lt., 1st N.Y. Dragoons, Richmond, Va. to Macon, Ga.:

On the morning of the 31st of May we were aroused at 5 o'clock by the sergeant, and ordered to get ready to go South at once. We had barely time to roll up our blankets when the drum sounded, and we were ordered to fall in and march downstairs in single file. As we passed out the front door of the middle room we each received half a loaf of corn bread, and a slice of bacon one fourth of an inch thick and one and one half inch square, for a day's ration.

I had been an inmate of "Libby" but three weeks, yet when my feet struck the pavement I nearly fell, and many of those who had been confined there six or eight months could scarcely stand when they first reached the ground.

... There were at this time but sixty-two officers in Libby, and one of these, who was too sick to accompany us, was left behind and sent to the hospital.

While waiting for orders to march, they brought up in the rear of our column 700 enlisted men, who were to go on the same train with us. They marched us over the James River to Manchester, and halted us alongside of the Danville Railroad, made up a train of boxcars and loaded us in, putting forty enlisted men in a car; but to the officers they were a little more generous, giving us two cars. They were very filthy, and had no seats or anything for us to sit on, yet we got along very comfortably. Before we left we could hear the dull, heavy thunder of Grant's guns, and knew he was not far from the city; and we interpreted the move as one to place us in a safer prison.... We had an opportunity to see some of the enlisted men who had spent the winter on Belle Isle. They looked as though they had had a hard time to live, for they were pale and sickly looking, and very many of them, from long suffering with the chronic diarrhoea, were so weak that they could scarcely walk.

The weather was intensely hot, and the guards would allow but one of the car doors open at a time; so these poor, and many of them sick men, had to ride for twelve hours suffering for the pure air of heaven; but this was only the beginning of sorrows.

... We soon found that traveling on a Rebel railroad was very different from what it would be on one in our Northern States. Their rolling stock was nearly worn out, the rails broken, splintered, and battered, the ties rotten, and, altogether, it was a dangerous matter to ride at all upon them, to say nothing of speed.... Their fastest trains were limited to twelve miles per hour....

During this ride we suffered for water, for the day was intensely hot.... The stations along this route are not villages such as you find on our Northern roads, but consist of five or six houses dignified with a name high-sounding enough for a corporation. The depots are small, unpainted buildings, with but few conveniences and much dilapidation.

... The country through which we passed was very poor, the cultivated portions of it being planted to corn by the negroes.... The negroes were the power that supplied the Rebel armies with food...

At Rock Island, Ill., Commandant Col. A.J. Johnson, wrote Col. William Hoffman, Federal Commissary-General of Prisoners:

I have just returned from a careful inspection of the prison. I find the police and everything in excellent condition. The grounds outside the prison inclosure are being improved as fast as practicable. Received Friday morning 179 prisoners from Little Rock, per steamer, via St. Louis; Saturday, 331 from Louisville by rail; all very dirty and badly clothed. Health of the Louisville squad, good; of the Little Rock squad, bad. A few cases of measles among the sick.

### June 1 (Wednesday)

At Cold Harbor, Va., near Richmond, the fighting began after everyone got done moving around. The next few days would lengthen the casualty lists and add to the prisons immeasurably.

In Georgia, the Federal cavalry under Stoneman occupied the pass at Allatoona, providing Sherman with his rail link to Chattanooga and ensuring that his supply line would be open.

In Washington, by the authority of the Secy. of War, the ration allowance for prisoners of war was reduced from that equivalent to a United States soldier serving in the field. This was a direct violation of the cartel governing the treatment of prisoners as it was agreed upon in September 1862. The difference between the ration shown below and that for an active soldier constituted the "savings" and this amount would be used to form the "prison fund." The new ration was announced to be the following amounts:

| | |
|---|---|
| Pork or bacon (in lieu of fresh beef) | 10 oz. |
| Fresh beef | 14 oz. |
| Flour or soft bread | 16 oz. |
| Hard bread (in lieu of flour or soft bread) | 14 oz. |
| Cornmeal (in lieu of flour or bread) | 16 oz. |
| Beans or peas (per 100 rations) | 12.5 lbs. |
| Or rice or hominy (per 100 rations) | 8 lbs. |
| Soap (per 100 rations) | 4 lbs. |
| Vinegar (per 100 rations) | 3 qts. |
| Salt (per 100 rations) | 3.75 lbs. |
| Potatoes (per 100 rations) | 15 lbs. |

Considering that, in most Federal prison camps, the prisoners were fed in a central location(s), the economy of scale obtained would permit better food preparation than in the Confederate prison camps, where the raw rations were issued to the prisoners for their own preparation. Issuing a tablespoon of beans to a prisoner who has not the means to prepare the food properly is, in fact, reducing the value of the ration considerably. This does not relieve the fact that the cartel was violated unilaterally.

In Chicago, Col. B.J. Sweet, commanding the prison at Camp Douglas, reported the renovation of the camp complete. The grounds had been thoroughly policed and drained. The old barracks were moved and placed on blocks four feet above the ground to prevent burrowing. There were now 32 barracks ninety feet long and one 70 feet long with a 20-foot kitchen. Each barrack would accommodate 165 prisoners. Additional room was available for barracks to increase the capacity to about 12,000 prisoners. Returns for this month showed a prisoner strength of 5277. Peak occupancy was at the end of December 1864, when prisoner strength was reported at 11,702.

Abbott, A.O., 1st Lt., 1st N.Y. Dragoons, Richmond, Va., to Macon, Ga.:

We arrived at Danville about one o'clock the next morning. We were not allowed to leave the train until seven, when we were marched to another train in waiting to take us to Greensboro', North Carolina. After we were on board they issued us half a loaf of corn bread warm from the oven, and a small piece of cooked bacon, in quality much better than any we had ever received at Libby....

Danville ... had at this time a population of about five thousand. It had increased in numbers since the war, many of the refugees from Northern Virginia coming here with their families to escape the immediate horrors of the battlefield. It had several government hospitals, and at times Federal prisoners have been confined here....

The road connecting Danville with Greensboro' is a new one, built in 1863–64, by the Rebel government, and we were among the first that went over it. The train did not make over eight miles per hour....

We arrived at Greensboro' about 1 o'clock P.M., and were ordered from the train and marched to a little grove to rest and wait for a train to be made up for us. As soon as we were bivouacked there began a sharp business in trading. Some of the inhabitants came around with something to eat.... Watches, knives, rings, jewelry, pocket-books, any thing that could be spared, was sold for rations. We paid for onions five dollars per half dozen, scallions at that; bacon, four dollars per pound; crackers, homemade, two dollars per dozen; biscuit, three dollars and fifty cents per dozen....

Night came, and, there being no prospect of a train, we composed ourselves to rest. About eleven o'clock we were aroused, to take the train at one....

Ransom, John, QM Sgt., 9th Michigan Cavalry, Andersonville Prison, Ga.:

Prisoners come daily. E.P. Sanders, Rowe and myself carried our old friend Dr. Lewis to the hospital. He was immediately admitted and we came away feeling very sad, knowing he would not live but a short time.

Confederate Gen. Samuel Jones telegraphed Gen. Braxton Bragg in Richmond concerning the movement of Federal prisoners into Charleston, where they would be placed under fire from the Federal guns on Morris Island.

The enemy continue their bombardment of the city with increased vigor, damaging private property and endangering the lives of women and children. I can take care of a party, say fifty Yankee prisoners. Can you not send me that number, including a general? Seymour will do, and other officers of high rank, to be confined in parts of the city still occupied by citizens, but under the enemy's fire.

This action, which would have far-reaching effect, was the first by either North or South to use prisoners of war as hostages-under-fire for leverage to gain advantage.

### June 2 (Thursday)

The second day at Cold Harbor. Nothing seemed to be working right for Grant. Problems in troop placement, ammunition resupply, and a very tired army compounded normal situations and caused the delay of the attack until 5 P.M., and then again until morning.

In Georgia, Sherman moved northeast towards the railroad that linked Atlanta and Chattanooga. The Rebels dug in further along the New Hope Church line with skirmishing at Acworth and Raccoon Bottom.

Abbott, A.O., 1st Lt., 1st N.Y. Dragoons, Richmond, Va., to Macon, Ga.:

After some delay we were marched to the cars, and halted before an old rickety thing with two large holes in the bottom, and ordered to embark. About forty succeeded in getting into the car, when the lieutenant in charge of us was told that the car was full. He said it was *not*, and more should ride there. Ten or twelve more were crowded in, when it was declared that no more *could* ride there. The lieutenant then ordered in two of his guards, and told them to use their muskets in driving the men back, *for the whole sixty-one must and should ride in that car*, no matter what the consequences might be. After a good deal of swearing on his part,... the whole sixty-one *were* crowded into the car; but for more than one quarter of us to sit down at the same time was out of the question.... Finally ... the lieutenant gave permission for four of the officers to ride on top of the car, thus leaving room for the guard, and in that packed, suffocating condition, we were to ride to Charlotte, N.C. We finally started from Greensboro' about two o'clock the next morning, ran about ten miles, then came to a dead stand. The engine was unable to draw us. It was uncoupled and started off to get up steam, and after an hour returned, and we went on at the rate of about eight miles per hour.

A drenching storm came on during the night, which, though uncomfortable to those on the outside, seemed to cool the atmosphere, and make it more tolerable to us inside. This morning we found ourselves passing through a low, flat country, but little cultivated, and at nine o'clock crossed the Yadkin River, and arrived at Salisbury, N.C....

We left Salisbury at 12M., passing through a wet, marshy section of country, interspersed with pine groves. After we left Salisbury, Lt. Gay allowed six or eight more to ride on the top of each car. At one of the stopping places, permission was given to four enlisted men to climb to the top. Three of them had succeeded in reaching it safely; the fourth one was a sickly, weakly boy, hardly able to walk. The lieutenant, in company with a guard, was watching him, when the whistle blew, the train started. Instead of leaving him to make his way up alone, as he was likely to succeed in doing, he at once ordered the guard to shoot him, which he did. The poor fellow dropped upon the track, and the cars passed over him. We received no rations till dark that night, being thirty-six hours with nothing to eat.

We arrived at Charlotte about four o'clock in the midst of a rainstorm; but we were very glad to get out of the packed cars, for we felt almost dead. We were marched to a little grove, and waited patiently for our rations till dark, when we received, for two days, four hardtacks, four inches by six, made of bran and middlings, black, mouldy, and rotten, and one fourth of a pound of bacon.

We made sure of *one* full meal, that is certain, and then lay down on the wet ground to sleep.

### June 3 (Friday)

It was 4:30 A.M. at Cold Harbor when the attack started with a charge all along the line. The Confederates, having had two days to prepare, were well fortified. The Federal lines were enfiladed and the slaughter was terrible. The Federal losses, killed and wounded, were about 5000 in one hour. Nearly 50,000 troops were in the assault out of a strength of about 117,000. The South lost about 1500 from a strength of some 60,000. Around noon the attack was called off and Grant started to move to the left again.

At Richmond, as a result of the fighting at Cold Harbor, John B. Jones, Rebel War Clerk, reported, "About 800 prisoners were marched into the city this afternoon, and it is believed many more are on the way." As the fighting went on, the prisoner

count on both sides would increase—and no exchanges were being made.

Federal cavalry entered Acworth, Ga., as Sherman again outflanked Gen. Joe Johnston near New Hope Church.

Abbott, A.O., 1st Lt., 1st N.Y. Dragoons, Richmond, Va., to Macon, Ga.:

My chum and I each had a blanket, so we slept comfortably, till about half past two the next morning, when it began to rain very hard. It awoke us, and we discussed the question as to what we had better do, but finally concluded to *let it rain*, and sleep what we could. We covered our heads, and finally awoke at daylight, to find ourselves wet to the skin, and four inches of water in the centre of the bed; but we found no fault with that, for we were used to rough weather.

We started soon after daylight for Columbia, the capital of South Carolina.... We had anticipated seeing much of the spirit of hatred manifested towards us in our passage through this state, but we were most happily disappointed. At no point along our route had we found the people so willing to attend to all our wants as they were in this. At almost every station we found white people or negroes with snacks to sell, at moderate prices to what some had obliged us to pay.... The people seemed more anxious to obtain "greenbacks" than any we had seen before....

During this day's travel we passed through some very pleasant little villages, Chester and Winnsboro' being the principal ones.... We reached Columbia at dark, and changed cars again, but from bad to worse. The car to which we were transferred had been used for transporting cattle and mules, and had not been cleaned out. The guards were dirty, lousy, and abusive, and the air was damp and thick. We had but one door open, and that was filled by the guards, and orders were issued to *allow no one to leave the car under any circumstances whatever*. Many of the officers were sick with diarrhoea, and we were literally packed into the car. All of these things made the night one of horror, long to be remembered by us all.

Ransom, John, QM Sgt., 9th Michigan Cavalry, Andersonville Prison, Ga.:

...now some negro prisoners brought inside. They belong to the 54th Massachusetts. Came with white prisoners. Many of the negroes wounded, as, indeed,

there are wounded among all who come here now....
Hot and wet.

## June 4 (Saturday)

In Georgia, Gen. Joe Johnston moved his troops in a rainstorm from the area around New Hope Church to the vicinity of Pine Mountain.

Ransom, John, QM Sgt., 9th Michigan Cavalry, Andersonville Prison, Ga.:

Have not been dry for many days. Raining continually. Some men take occasion while out after wood, to overpower the guard and take to the pines. Not yet been brought back. *Very* small rations of poor molasses, corn bread and bug soup.

Abbott, A.O., 1st Lt., 1st N.Y. Dragoons, Richmond, Va., to Macon, Ga.:

Morning found us at Branchville, the junction of the South Carolina Railroad with the Charleston branch. It consists of one very good house, used as a depot and hotel, three or four others much inferior, and the usual number of negro huts. As we passed on towards Augusta, the country began to look better, and more cultivated....

The day was quite pleasant, and passed off without much occurring worthy of record except that some of the privates jumped from the train while it was running, and the guards would shoot at them, but did not hurt one of them. We finally arrived at Augusta, Georgia, about 4 o'clock P.M., so tired and hungry we could scarcely stand up. As soon as we crossed the river we were ordered to leave the cars and were placed in an old cotton shed to remain till the next day.... We were turned over to Capt. Bradford, son of ex-Gov. Bradford, Maryland, provost marshal of the city.... A citizen guard was placed around us and we were marched to our quarters.

The people flocked around to see the Yankees, and we had reason to believe that some of them were disposed to do us all the good they could. A hose was at once attached to a hydrant nearby, and plenty of water was furnished up, of which we availed ourselves immediately, taking the first wash we had had since leaving Libby Prison. They then brought in to us sufficient ration of hard bread and bacon, of splendid quality, to which we did ample justice. The enlisted men had the same issued to them. Supper

over, we lay down, and had a good night's rest.

## June 5 (Sunday)

In the Shenandoah Valley of Virginia, Union Gen. David Hunter moved his forces towards Staunton, Va., forcing the Confederates into battle at Piedmont. The Confederate forces, under W.E. "Grumble" Jones, were defeated, Jones was killed, and Hunter's troops the next day looted Staunton. The Confederates lost about 1600 men, 1000 of whom were taken as prisoners.

In Georgia, Johnston placed his troops on the line near Marietta, while Sherman shifted closer to the railroad.

The South was at variance with Davis's Executive Order of December 23, 1862, concerning white Union officers who commanded Negro troops.(The order required the officers to be turned over to the various Confederate states for punishment.) Instead, the white officers were placed in the same category as the Negro troops, not recognizing their rank as officers. At Macon, Ga., Capt. George C. Gibbs, commanding the prison, wrote CSA Adjutant-Gen. Samuel Cooper that:

The Yankee major of a negro regiment who was captured at the battle of Ocean Pond, Fla., is, and I think very properly, confined with the negro prisoners at Andersonville. I would like to obtain permission to send to the same place Lt. J.O. Ladd, of Company E, Thirty-fifth U.S. Negro Regiment, who is now a prisoner here, and who was also captured in Florida on board steamer *Columbine*.

Abbott, A.O., 1st Lt., 1st N.Y. Dragoons, Richmond, Va., to Macon, Ga.:

Sabbath morning dawned upon us bright and beautiful, yet we were still prisoners of war.... About nine o'clock visitors commenced flocking around the shed, peeping through the cracks at us, and watching all our movements; yet they treated us with a kind of respect....

At 12 M. they issued us another day's rations of hard bread and meat, and then marched us into the street, where a large crowd was waiting to see us; but, after standing a little while, we were sent back again, and remained till 5 P.M., when we were marched to the depot in a most drenching shower, while the enlisted men remained behind, to come up on

Monday. They furnished us with two large, clean, nice boxcars, and the guard put in seats for us, a luxury we had not enjoyed before since we started.... This was, by far, the most pleasant part of our journey.

### June 6 (Monday)

Ransom, John, QM Sgt., 9th Michigan Cavalry, Andersonville Prison, Ga.:

Eight months a prisoner today. A lifetime has been crowded into these eight months. No rations at all. Am now a haircutter. Have *hired* the shears.... Wirtz comes inside no more, in fact, very few rebels. The place is too bad for them.

Abbott, A.O., 1st Lt., 1st N.Y. Dragoons, arriving at Camp Oglethorpe, Macon, Ga.:

Monday morning, at nine o'clock, found us at Macon, Ga., our point of destination. As we came in sight of the prison stockade my heart sunk within me, for it seemed like being buried alive to go inside of it; but there was no relief, and here we were at the office, waiting for the calling of the roll.... In squads of five we were marched through the gate, inside the stockade, where we were at once greeted with cries of "Fresh fish!"...

This prison, or stockade, was built in May, 1864, and was located three quarters of a mile east of the city, on what was known as the old Fair Ground. It embraced two acres and seven-eighths inside of the "deadline," by actual measurement. It was surrounded, or inclosed rather, by a stockade built of boards, twelve feet high, and so tight we could not look through the cracks even....

The Rebel authorities pretended to furnish materials for the building of quarters, but at no time while in Macon were there less than 200 officers without any shelter at all.... As fast as the Rebels furnished the materials, sheds were erected, from seventy-five to one hundred feet long by twenty feet broad, ends and sides left open for two reasons, viz., we could not get the lumber to close them up, and we needed the air. Many dug holes in the ground under the large building, and lived there, getting along tolerably well except when it rained....

It no doubt would have amused our friends at home could they have seen the straits to which we were often put for something to draw our rations *in*. We could not do without them; we were obliged to draw them that we might have something to live on, but what to draw them *in* was an important question. One came with a bag made from one of the legs of his drawers (and his only pair at that) for his cornmeal; another had a coat-sleeve lining for rice, a stocking for salt, a chip for soft soap, his hat for beans; while another, who has been robbed before getting into prison, is obliged to take his only remaining shirt to put *his* rations in....

They issued to each squad of 100 five iron skillets with covers; fifteen iron skillets without covers; ten tin pails or buckets, holding about six quarts each; ten small tin pans for mixing our meal in; five wooden pails or buckets.

As for any thing to eat with, such as plates, knives and forks, etc., I have never known of their issuing anything of the kind.... "Borrow and lend" was one of the first and principal rules of our prison life.

Col. William Hoffman, Federal Commissary-General of Prisoners, today directed the commander of the prison at Point Lookout, Md., to erect the wooden shelters necessary within the prison hospital to care for the Confederate prisoners. Col. Hoffman also requested information on the shooting of prisoners on March 20, which incident had not been previously reported.

Effective this date, prisoners at Johnson's Island, Ohio, were not to be permitted visitors except by permission from the War Department or from Col. William Hoffman.

Maj. Gen. Howell Cobb, commanding the Georgia Reserves at Macon, wrote Secy. of War James A. Seddon in Richmond concerning the prisoner exchange:

I venture to address you on another subject which I am well aware has engaged much of your attention and is full of embarrassment. I allude to the question of exchange of prisoners. I need not say to you that the number accumulating in Georgia is not only eating up our subsistence, but are withdrawing for their safekeeping a large force from the field and from agricultural interests. To get clear of them is only second in importance to getting back our men now in Yankee prisons. I have no idea that I can make any new suggestions to you on these points, but I wish to say that the country will sustain the President in any arrangement he wishes that will bring about an exchange that does not yield two points: First. We must get all our prisoners back when the enemy have got theirs. Second. *We cannot consent to regard our slaves as prisoners of war when captured in the enemy's army.* All else our people will sustain the President in doing what he thinks best that will result in an exchange.

... *Nor do our people object to the exchange of negro prisoners (not slaves).* I do not know the points of difficulty in resuming the exchange, but so deeply impressed have I been for some time that if possible the exchange should be resumed. [italics added]

In response to Cobb's letter, Seddon, on June 13, expressed his opinion that "On the two points as to which you comment I agree with you entirely. I doubt, however, whether the exchange of negroes at all for our soldiers would be tolerated. As to the white officers serving with negro troops, we ought never to be inconvenienced with such prisoners."

Seddon did not elaborate on what should be done with the officer prisoners that caused such inconvenience.

At Andersonville, Capt. Henry Wirz was doing his best to get things organized and operating, fighting tremendous odds:

The bread which is issued to prisoners is of such an inferior quality, consisting fully of one sixth of husk, that it is almost unfit for use and increasing dysentery and other bowel complaints. I would wish that the commissary of the post be notified to have the meal bolted or some other contrivance arranged to sift the meal before issuing. If the meal, such as it is now, was sifted the bread rations would fall short fully one-quarter of a pound.

There is a great deficiency of buckets. Rations of rice, beans, vinegar, and molasses cannot be issued to prisoners for want of buckets, at least 8000 men in the stockade being without anything of the sort. If my information is correct, any number of buckets can be got from Columbus, Ga., if the quartermaster of the post would make the requisition for the same.

## June 7 (Tuesday)

At the prison in Camp Ford, Tex., the senior officer prisoners wrote to the local U.S. commanders, through Confederate Gen. E. Kirby Smith, requesting clothing for the prisoners at that location. Both soldiers and sailors were confined at the prison. Many of the men had been captives for a period of seventeen months and were practically naked. Clothing for 1662 soldiers was requested. For the naval personnel, sufficient clothing for 205 men was requested. These men were from the crews of the four naval vessels *Morning Light, Velocity, Clifton,* and *Sachem,* some of whom had been in prison for 17 months.

Ransom, John, QM Sgt., 9th Michigan Cavalry, Andersonville Prison, Ga.:

Heard today that Hendryx had been arrested and in irons for inciting a conspiracy. Not much alarmed for him. He will come out all right. Still rainy.... Nearly all the old prisoners who were captured with me are dead. Don't know of over 50 or 60 alive out of 800.

Abbott, A.O., 1st Lt., 1st N.Y. Dragoons, prisoner at Camp Oglethorpe, Macon, Ga.:

Our rations at this time consisted of the following articles, issued once in five days, viz: Seven pints coarse cornmeal; one half pint sorghum; one seventh pound of maggoty, rancid bacon; two tablespoonsful of beans (black and wormy) or rice; two tablespoonsful of salt. The cooking utensils were not sufficient for our use, and we were obliged to wait one for the other. It was often ten o'clock before we could get breakfast, for want of something to cook it in.

For bread, we would mix our meal with water and a little salt, and, putting it in a skillet with a cover on, build a little fire under and on top of it, and in about twenty or thirty minutes you had what was called a "pone"—not very good, yet eatable to us. Of our beans we made soup, putting in a little meat when we had any. For variety we would make mush, or, instead of pone, bake the dough as griddle cakes.... The bacon was maggoty more or less, and had been preserved in ashes in lieu of salt. At home we would not consider it fit to eat.

For wood, a detail of two from each mess of twenty was allowed to go out, *under guard,* to the woodpile, and bring in all they could at one time for their mess, and this was for twenty-four hours. They issued, each morning at nine o'clock, at the gate, something they called *axes,* and spades, with orders to have them returned at six in the evening upon penalty of being deprived of them the next day.... The axes resembled two iron wedges put together, with a hole through them, and a straight stick in them for a helve. The steel is not over half an inch deep, and invariably breaks off after two or three days' use....

For water we had a fine spring in the centre of the camp, and in July they dug three wells, and put in wooden pumps, which supplied us with abundance of water. A little brook ran through the rear of the camp, in which we used to bathe and do our washing.... While we were engaged in the work, the most common plan was to go without till our garments got dry again; here it was not an uncommon sight to see officers around the camp *minus* some *very necessary* articles of clothing.... We went barefooted during the summer, and those who had drawers wore them in place of pants during the hot weather.

In Richmond, John B. Jones, Rebel War Clerk, recognized the tenacity with which Grant was holding on to Lee's army, preventing it from gaining an advantage by maneuver. Today Jones recorded that:

A man from New Kent County, coming through the lines, reports that Gen. Grant was quite drunk yesterday, and said he would try Lee once more, and if he failed to defeat him, "the Confederacy might go to hell." It must have been some other general.

### June 8 (Wednesday)

In Charleston, S.C., the Federal sick and wounded in the hospitals were being transferred to Andersonville. This move could constitute a death sentence.

Ransom, John, QM Sgt., 9th Michigan Cavalry, Andersonville Prison, Ga.:

More new prisoners. There are now over 23,000 confined here, and the death rate 100 to 130 per day, and I believe more than that. Rations worse.

### June 9 (Thursday)

In Georgia, Sherman was about to move against Johnston at Pine Mountain.

Lincoln, notified of his nomination by the Republican convention for a second term as President, immediately called for a constitutional amendment to abolish slavery.

At Cold Harbor, Grant ordered the building of

fortifications to cover his movement to the left towards Petersburg.

At Andersonville, Ga., Capt. Wirz had discovered a plot whereby the outside prisoners would overcome the guards and free those in the stockade.

In Washington, Secy. of War Edwin M. Stanton complained to Maj. Gen. Benjamin F. Butler (who was in Bermuda Hundred) that he had not been receiving his Richmond, Va., newspapers and inquired as to why Maj. Mulford had not forwarded them. Butler replied:

Communication through flag of truce is cut off— firstly, because of a communication by myself to Commissioner Ould making inquiry whether negro soldiers should be treated as prisoners of war if captured. Secondly, sent up for wounded prisoners, which they refused to deliver, I having refused to deliver well ones until that question is definitely settled. This was in obedience to my instructions from the lieutenant-general. Maj. Mulford, you will see, therefore, is not in fault.

The selection of Federal prisoners to be sent to Charleston, S.C., from Macon, Ga., to be placed in the line of fire within the city fell upon Maj. Gen. Howell Cobb of the Georgia Reserves on this day. He was directed by CSA Adjutant-Gen. Samuel Cooper:

Gen. Winder has been ordered to Andersonville to command the cantonment of prisoners there. Gen. S. Jones, at Charleston, asks for fifty officers of rank, Federal prisoners, to be sent to him at Charleston for special use in Charleston during the siege. The President approves the application, and you are desired to select [from] among them as far as practicable such as have served near Charleston and send the number without delay to Gen. Jones under a suitable guard.

### June 10 (Friday)

In Mississippi, at Brice's Cross Roads, south of Corinth, Union Brig. Gen. Sam D. Sturgis finally found Forrest. In the following fracas, the Federals lost their artillery, over 170 wagons with supplies and over 1500 prisoners to a much inferior force— Sturgis with 8000, Forrest with only about 3500. The prisoners would add to the population of Macon and Andersonville prisons.

At Cold Harbor, Grant prepared to march towards the James River crossings. In the Valley,

Hunter readied his columns to head for Lexington, preparatory to crossing the Blue Ridge and attacking Lynchburg, opposed by Breckinridge.

At Rock Island Barracks, Rock Island, Ill., the camp commander, Col. A.J. Johnson, was directed to place all Confederate prisoners who had expressed a desire to take the oath of allegiance and enter the U.S. Naval service in separate barracks pending their transfer to another location.

Col. William Hoffman, Federal Commissary-General of Prisoners, wrote Brig. Gen. Joseph T. Copeland, commander of the prison at Alton, Ill., of:

...the receipt of your letter ... in relation to the employment of Sisters of Charity at the prison hospital....

As you will perceive by my letters to Col. Sweet the employment of these sisters has not been authorized by me, and as their services can be obtained only on unusual conditions, viz., the renting and furnishing a house for them and the hire of a servant, their continued employment at the hospital is not approved....

If there is an absolute necessity that female nurses should be employed, please report the number required, the services they are to perform, and the compensation they should receive.

I am under the impression that the Sisters of Charity take advantage of their position to carry information from and to prisoners which is contraband, and if this is so they cannot under any circumstances be employed at the hospital.

At Andersonville, Wirz sent most of the conspirators inside the stockade and then posted a notice to the effect that canister would be fired from the artillery located around the prison if the escape attempt were carried forward. The escape conspiracy came to nothing. George Hendryx, Ransom's friend and fellow prisoner, managed to escape during the excitement.

Also at Andersonville, Capt. R.B. Winder sent a request to the Confederate Quartermaster-General in Richmond:

I would respectfully state that I am in great need of some sheet iron to make some baking-pans to cook bread for prisoners of war and cannot get along at all without it. I can have the pans made at the post, if I could only get the iron and wire, much cheaper that they could be purchased. Tin is entirely too expensive and it burns out in a few weeks. I have

tried everywhere in Georgia to get this iron, but cannot succeed in finding any.... I have built two large bakeries and am now constructing a third. We have 22,000 prisoners here and are now extending the stockade, inclosing two more acres of ground....

Ten bunches, twenty-four in bunch, sheet iron, thirty inches by ten, sixteenth inch, or as near this width and thickness as possible. Two coils No. 8 wire.

Please answer me by telegraph in regard to this matter

It would appear that not everyone in Andersonville was ignoring the needs of the prisoners.

Abbott, A.O., 1st Lt., 1st N.Y. Dragoons, prisoner at Camp Oglethorpe, Macon, Ga.:

The 10th of June fifty officers were sent to Charleston, including all the general and field officers down to about one half of the majors. It was surmised that they were to be exchanged, and we all hoped it was to be so....

About this time, some of the other squad, who had been occupying the old "shell," had so far completed their quarters as to move in, and squad 12 was ordered to take their places. We had no lumber to build bunks, so we made sand-hills for a bed, by piling up a bed of sand a foot high, four feet wide, and six feet long. By this means we kept out of the water when it rained...

Gen. John H. Morgan, raiding again in Kentucky, sent the 9th Tenn. Cav. into Sterling, Ky., to roust up the Union troops there. As the fighting swirled around the streets of the town, Pvt. James P. Gold of Co. D and several of his comrades were captured. When the fighting abated, the prisoners were hurried off to Lexington, Ky., where they were held for forwarding.

### June 11 (Saturday)

At Salisbury, N.C., a problem arose which probably had no precedent. Capt. G.W. Alexander, CSA, commanding the post, asked for guidance:

Sir: About twelve months ago several Yankee deserters desired to take the oath of neutrality. The oath was administered, the prisoners were released, and allowed to go to work; they procured employment near this place; their conduct so far has been unexceptional. The enrolling officer has recently conscripted them. They claim protection from the Government in virture of this oath. If the Government releases a man, he pledging himself to remain neutral, I do not think it just to force him to break the oath which we have voluntarily offered him. The matter rests in abeyance, awaiting your decision.

No information on the decision is available.

Abbott, A.O., 1st Lt., 1st N.Y. Dragoons, prisoner at Camp Oglethorpe, Macon, Ga.:

Time would not drag so heavily on a prisoner's hands if he had something to busy himself about; but we had so little to do, and so little to take up our time in the way of reading matter, studies, etc., that the days were long and wearisome. There were, however, classes in German, French, Logic, Rhetoric, Butler's Analogy, and in some of the higher mathematics.

For meetings, we usually had preaching on the Sabbath by one of the chaplains present, at 11 A.M. and 7 P.M. The forenoon services were usually held under the large tree on the west side of the old building that was near the east line of the camp.

## June 12 (Sunday)

Pulling out of the Cold Harbor lines at dark, Grant sent the troops racing to the previously selected James River crossing sites at Windmill Point and Wilcox's Landing bridges and south to a position near Petersburg within record time.

Today, the first Federal prisoners arrived in Charleston, S.C., to be used as hostages-under-fire by the Confederates.

Ransom, John, QM Sgt., 9th Michigan Cavalry, Andersonville Prison, Ga.:

Rained every day so far this month. A portion of the camp is a mud hole, and the men are obliged to lay down in it. Ft. Pillow prisoners tell some hard stories against the Confederacy at the treatment they received after their capture. They came here nearly *starved to death*, and a good many were wounded after their surrender.

## June 13 (Monday)

In Virginia, Lee finally got the drift of the movement of the Army of the Potomac from Cold Harbor and began to shift his troops rapidly to cover Richmond.

Ransom, John, QM Sgt., 9th Michigan Cavalry, Andersonville Prison, Ga.:

It is now as hot and sultry as it was ever my lot to witness.... Today saw a man with a bullet hole in his head over an inch deep, and you could look down in it and see maggots squirming around at the bottom. Such things are terrible, but of common occurrence.... Flies by the thousand millions.

## June 14 (Tuesday)

At Pine Mountain, Ga., Lt. Gen. Leonidas Polk, along with Gens. Johnston and Hardee, were watching the Federal movements in front of Pine Mountain when Polk was shot by a Federal cannon. The shot struck him in the chest, killing him instantly. His remains were evacuated from the battle area and sent to Atlanta.

Today, the Charleston *Mercury* printed an article listing the Federal prisoners of war that had arrived two days previously to be held within the city of Charleston and placed under the fire of the Federal guns. The beginning of the article would indicate that the arrival and use of the prisoners was known for some time—hardly a "spur-of-the-moment" action.

For some time past it has been known that a batch of Yankee prisoners, comprising the highest in rank now in our hands, were soon to be brought hither to share the pleasures of the bombardment. They accordingly arrived on Sunday. We give a list of their names and rank:

Brig. Gens. Seymour, Wessells, Scammon, Shaler, and Heckman; Cols. I.G. Grover, I.R. Hawkins, W. Harriman, T.F. Lehmann, O.H. La Grange, H.C. Lee, R. White, H.C. Bolinger, H.L. Brown, E.L. Dana, and E. Fardella; Lt. Cols. E.L. Hayes, H.B. Hunter, T.H. Higinbotham, G.C. Joslin, W.E. McMackin, D. Miles, W.C. Maxwell, J.D. Mayhew, S. Moffitt, E. Olcott, J.J. Polsley, A.F. Rodgers, J.H. Burnham, C.B. Baldwin, W.G.

Bartholomew, W.R. Cook, C.J. Dickerson, J.F. Fellows, G.A. Frambes, W.H. Glenn, J.P. Spofford, J.W. Stewart, A.W. Taylor, and W.P. Lasselle; Majs. C.H. Beeres, W.F. Baker, E.N. Bates, J.E. Clark, D.A. Carpenter, W. Crandall, H.D. Grant, J. Hill, and J.H. Johnson.

These prisoners we understand will be furnished with comfortable quarters in that portion of the city most exposed to the enemy's fire. The commanding officer on Morris Island will be duly notified of the fact of their presence in the shelled district, and if his batteries still continue their wanton and barbarous work it will be at the peril of the captive officers.

This destroys the myth that the Confederate "Immortal 600" were the first to be deployed as hostages-under-fire.

### June 15 (Wednesday)

At Folly Island, S.C., Union Brig. Gen. A. Schimmelfennig wrote Maj. Gen. J.G. Foster's Assistant Adjutant-General concerning the Federal prisoners being held inside Charleston. Gen. Schimmelfennig believed that the threat was bluster on the part of Gen. Jones:

Yesterday evening I received, by flag of truce, a letter from Gen. Jones to the major-general commanding department, a letter from Gen. Ripley to myself, which I respectfully annex, and several private letters by the same means. My only answer to Gen. Ripley, until orders from the major-general commanding are received, has been and will be a continuation of the usual fire on the city, with a constant change of direction, to avoid, if possible, the design of the enemy to bring their prisoners under our fire....

Charleston must be considered a place "of arms." It contains a large arsenal, military foundries, &c., and has already furnished three ironclads to the enemy. It is our duty to destroy these resources. In reference to the women and children of the bombarded city, I therefore can only say the same situation occurs whenever a weak and strong party are at war, and the practice of exposing prisoners of war to the fire of the attacking force is as old as the fact that weak and wicked parties must fall under the blows of justice. I may be allowed here to state that the act which the enemy has now committed he has threatened ever since the first shell exploded in the city, over nine

months ago, and it is therefore fair to suppose some special reason now exists for the fulfillment of his threat, although I can find no reason other than his desperate situation.... I also think that the United States can furnish as large a number of Confederate generals and field officers as they can procure of ours. From the fact of the enemy's being so anxious for an immediate reply I am led to believe the whole thing a ruse, or at least only a threat not yet carried out.

Ward, William W., Col., 9th Tenn. Cavalry, prisoner, Ft. Delaware, Del.:

Morning pleasant. Had the headache all night & all this day. Did not get out of bed long at a time.

Ransom, John, QM Sgt., 9th Michigan Cavalry, Andersonville Prison, Ga.:

I am sick: just able to drag around. My teeth are loose, mouth sore, with gums grown down in some places lower than the teeth and bloody, legs swollen up with dropsy and on the road to the trenches.... Lice by the fourteen hundred thousand and million infest Andersonville.

### June 16 (Thursday)

At Hilton Head, S.C., Maj. Gen. J.G. Foster, USA, wrote Maj. Gen. Samuel Jones, CSA, in Charleston, S.C., regarding the placement of Federal prisoners of war within the city of Charleston as a means to deter the bombardment of the city. *The letter of June 13 was the first communication received by the Federal military authorities that the Confederates had moved prisoners into Charleston:*

General: I have to acknowledge the receipt this day of your communication of the 13th instant, informing me that 5 generals and 45 field officers of the U.S. Army, prisoners of war, have been sent to Charleston for safekeeping; that they have been turned over by you to Brig. Gen. Ripley, with instructions to see that they are provided with quarters in a part of the city occupied by noncombatants, the majority of which latter, you state, are women and children. You add that you deem it proper to inform me that it is a part of the city which has been for many months exposed to the fire of our guns.

Many months since, Maj. Gen. Gillmore, U.S. Army, notified Gen. Beauregard, then commanding at Charleston, that the city would be bombarded.

This notice was given that noncombatants might be removed and thus women and children be spared from harm. Gen. Beauregard, in a communication to Gen. Gillmore, dated August 22, 1863, informed him that the noncombatant population of Charleston would be removed with all possible celerity. That women and children have been since retained by you in a part of the city which has been for many months exposed to fire is a matter decided by your own sense of humanity. I must, however, protest against your action in thus placing defenseless prisoners of war in a position exposed to constant bombardment. It is an indefensible act of cruelty, and can be designed only to prevent the continuance of our fire upon Charleston. That city is a depot for military supplies. It contains not merely arsenals but also foundries and factories for the manufacture of munitions of war.... To destroy these means of continuing the war is therefore our object and duty. You seek to defeat this effort, not by means known to honorable warfare, but by placing unarmed and helpless prisoners under our fire.

I have forwarded your communications to the President, with the request that he will place in my custody an equal number of prisoners of like grades, to be kept by me in positions exposed to the fire of your guns so long as you continue the course stated in your communication.

Col. William W. Ward, 9th Tenn. Cavalry, was currently a prisoner at Ft. Delaware, Del., and would become one of the prisoners sent to Hilton Head to be placed under fire of the Confederate guns. At this point, he was blissfully unaware of his future role.

Ward, William W., Col., 9th Tenn. Cavalry, prisoner, Ft. Delaware, Del.:

Morning dark & warm. Am some better though not well yet. Write a not[e] to Capt Bennett this morning in answer to one rec. from him yesterday. Get worse in the evening.

### June 17 (Friday)

Ward, William W., Col., 9th Tenn. Cavalry, prisoner, Ft. Delaware, Del.:

Very sick. Dr. calls & leaves a prescription which is filled in the evening. Am very sick all day with severe headaches & fever. Recd. a good letter from my father. Helps me some.

Ransom, John, QM Sgt., 9th Michigan Cavalry, Andersonville Prison, Ga.:

Must nurse my writing material. A New York *Herald* in camp, which says an exchange will commence the 7th of July. Gen. Winder is on a visit to Andersonville.... Chas. Humphrey, of Massachusetts, who has been in our hundred for months, has gone crazy; wanders about entirely naked, and not even a cap on his head. Many of the prisoners are crazy...

### June 18 (Saturday)

At the Gratiot St. Prison in St. Louis, Mo., between the hours of 9 and 10 A.M., some prisoners exercising in the yard seized an axe from the kitchen and broke the lock on a gate leading into an alley. Some of the Rebel prisoners disarmed the guard from behind and several scattered in all directions. Troops from the Tenth Kansas Infantry were sent after them and they were joined by other Union troops in the area. After a wild scramble over backyard fences, through sheds and outbuildings, and down alleys, two of the escapees were killed and three wounded. The remainder were recaptured and returned to prison.

Ransom, John, QM Sgt., 9th Michigan Cavalry, Andersonville Prison, Ga.:

Have now written two large books full; have another at hand.... Dying off as usual—more in numbers each day as the summer advances. Rebels say that they don't begin to have hot weather down here until about August. Well, it is plain to me that all will die. Old prisoners have stood it as long as they can, and are dropping off fast, while the new ones go anyhow. Someone stole my cap during the night. A dead neighbor furnished me with another, however.

Ward, William W., Col., 9th Tenn. Cavalry, prisoner, Ft. Delaware, Del.:

Still very sick. My medicine operates finely. Hope to be up soon. I am taking Rhubarb & Magnesia & Quinine pills. Receive my photographs, 9 in number. Twelve months ago today I bid my dear, darling Bette good by. How long the year has been. Heaven permitting I will never spend another away from her. I had rather live retired from the world, unknown to all save a few honest neighbors & my kinspeople & be with her all the while than to live away from her & write my name high upon the scroll of fame. I am better this evening.

### June 19 (Sunday)

In the west, Maj. Szymanski, Confederate Agent for Exchange, received a letter from Capt. De Witt Clinton, USA, concerning the exchange of prisoners in the trans-Mississippi area. Capt. Clinton informed Szymanski that Col. C.C. Wright, 160th N.Y. Vol., was appointed agent for exchange under the cartel. Clinton then wrote Wright:

The articles of that cartel, so far as applicable, will be adopted, with the understanding expressed that they shall apply to all troops in the service of the United States. The officers and men of colored regiments to receive the same treatment, be entitled to the same privileges, and be exchanged in the same manner as other troops, without exception or distinction of any kind. The same rule will apply to civilians in the service without regard to color, who are to be exchanged in accordance with the provisions of article 3 of the cartel.

The same sticking point existed that had been preventing the exchange since December 1862. The South would not budge from its position on former slaves.

Ward, William W., Col., 9th Tenn. Cavalry, prisoner, Ft. Delaware, Del.:

Morning bright or rather foggy & pleasant. I am much better. Get up in the evening and sit up several hours. Eat a little toast & coffee for breakfast. The first of anything to eat since Thursday morning. Attempt to write to my dear wife but can not as I am too nervous. Sit up until night. Go down to supper. Continue to improve.

At Louisville, Ky., a group of prisoners were received at the military prison that had been captured during Morgan's last raid through Kentucky. Among the prisoners was Pvt. James P. Gold, Co. D, 9th Tenn. Cav., Col. William W. Ward's regiment, who had been captured at Mt. Sterling. Gold would be held here but a few days.

### June 20 (Monday)

From Andersonville, Ga., Brig. Gen. John H. Winder, in desperate need of guards for the prison, telegraphed Gen. Braxton Bragg in Richmond:

Upon assuming command I ordered measures to bring in every man not with his regiment. Whether they can be brought in or not I can not tell. Even were [the guard] all present, the force is entirely inadequate to guard 24,000 prisoners, daily increasing. Gen. Cobb can not give me a man. Measles and whooping cough prevailing in command.

Chief Surgeon Isaiah H. White, at Andersonville, reported:

The report of sick and wounded for the month of April exhibits a ratio per 1000 of mean strength, 306.1 cases treated, and 57.6 deaths. May, 640.33 cases treated, and 47.3 deaths.

The daily ratio per 1000 of mean strength for the twenty days of present month has been $1\frac{5}{7}$ deaths, which taken as an average for the thirty days would make 51.4 deaths per 1000 of mean strength for month of June.

The morning report of C.S. prison shows: Remaining in hospital, 1022; in quarters, 2665; deaths, 40; strength of command, 23,911.

The number of medical officers on duty at the prison is inadequate to perform the duties required of them. There are in all twelve, seven of whom attend sick-call and five on duty at hospital; of this number five are employed by contract. I would suggest that the medical force be increased by ten additional officers.

Ransom, John, QM Sgt., 9th Michigan Cavalry, Andersonville Prison, Ga.:

All the mess slowly but none the less surely succumbing to the diseases incident here. We are not what you may call hungry. I have actually felt the pangs of hunger more when I was a boy going home from school to dinner. But we are sick and faint and all broken down, feverish, &c. It is starvation and disease and exposure that is doing it. Our stomachs have been so abused by the stuff called bread and soups, that they are diseased. The bread is coarse and musty. Believe that half in camp would die now if given rich food to eat.

## June 21 (Tuesday)

In Virginia, the lines around Petersburg were being defined. While much skirmishing, and some heavy fighting, would occur here, it would be mostly a war of attrition against Lee.

In Georgia, Sherman would press his attack against Johnston, gobbling up prisoners and playing Grant's game of attrition.

In Washington, Quartermaster-General M.C. Meigs received a letter, dated yesterday, from the U.S. Sanitary Commission requesting information on the treatment of prisoners in the South as well as the North. The request was forwarded to Col. William Hoffman, Federal Commissary-General of Prisoners, for action. The questions asked were: First. What are the rations furnished by the United States Government to the Rebel prisoners, their quality and quantity? Second. Does the United States Government supply them with needful clothing and blankets? Third. Does the United States Government or its officials deprive them of fire in their prisons during the season when fires are needed, as in the late fall, winter, and early spring? Fourth. Are any of them denied shelter, by day or night, during the inclement and cold season? Fifth. Have orders at any time been issued to shoot the prisoners who may be at the windows or near them in their rooms? Have any ever been shot or shot at thus? Sixth. What provisions does our Government make for the care and treatment of wounded and sick Rebel prisoners (or is it similar to that made for our own men)? Seventh. Did Gen. Butler in the early part of this year offer exchange of prisoners, man for man, of those confined at Point Lookout or elsewhere?

To reply to the above questions, Col. Hoffman would require some fancy footwork—or some real imagination. The Confederate authorities, if they were queried on the same subjects, would require even more imagination in their replies.

At Macon, Ga., Capt. W.M. Hammond wrote an inspection report to Gen. Braxton Bragg, CSA, in Richmond:

Gen. Jones being absent, I proceeded on receipt of your telegram of 15th instant to inspect prison depot at Andersonville. Number of prisoners at depot on 20th instant was 23,951. The guard, commanded at present by Col. J.H. Fannin, First Georgia Reserves, consist of four regiments State reserves, a detachment from Fifty-fifth Georgia Volunteers, and Dyke's Florida battery, the aggregate effective strength being 1588. The reserve troops are poorly instructed and without discipline. The prison camp is surrounded by a stockade seventeen feet high, and covers an area of sixteen acres and a half, only twelve acres of which can be occupied. It is crowded, filthy, and insecure. An additon now being made will give ample room. Rations issued to prisoners the same in quality and quantity as those issued to the guard. Average rate of mortality during present month has been thirty-six per diem. The guard should be strengthened by the addition of at least 1500 men. Additional surgeons and 150 hospital tents are immediately needed.

Ransom, John, QM Sgt., 9th Michigan Cavalry, Andersonville Prison, Ga.:

I am a fair writer, and am besieged by men to write letters to the rebel officers praying for release, and I do it, knowing it will do no good, but to please the sufferers. Some of these letters are directed to Capt. Wirtz, some to Gen. Winder, Jeff Davis and other officers. As dictated by them some would bring tears to a stone. One goes on to say he has been a prisoner of war over a year, has a wife and three children destitute, how much he thinks of them, is dying with disease, etc., etc. All kinds of stories are narrated, and handed to the first rebel who comes within reach. Of course they are never heard from. It's pitiful to see the poor wretches who think their letters will get them out, watch the gate from day to day, and always [are] disappointed. Someone has much to answer for.

In New Orleans, Maj. Gen. E.R.S. Canby, USA, had been dealing with Gen. E. Kirby Smith, CSA, on the exchange of prisoners in Louisiana. A major sticking point was still unresolved on this matter. The Confederate government, as a policy, did not consider the Union Negro troops, *and the white officers who commanded them*, in the same category as other troops. Gen. Canby had informed Gen. Smith that "all negotiations shall be conducted under the recognized and expressed understanding that the conditions of the cartel of July 22, 1862, shall apply to all troops in the service of the United States; that officers and men of colored regiments shall receive the same treatment, be entitled to the same privileges, and be exchanged in the same manner as other troops, and that the third article of the cartel shall apply to all conditions without distinction...."

At Andersonville, Ga., Brig. Gen. John H. Winder, Confederate Commissary-General of Prisoners, wired Gen. Samuel Cooper, in Richmond, that urgent consideration must be given to the establishment of a new prison, because the Andersonville site was overflowing. Union Springs, Ala., was suggested.

### June 22 (Wednesday)

Maj. Gen. Samuel Jones, CSA, commanding at Charleston, S.C., wrote Maj. Gen. J.G. Foster, USA, commanding U.S. forces near Charleston, to explain the problems associated with the bombardment of Charleston by giving a little of the background of the situation:

It may be well that we should understand correctly the circumstances under which the fire on this city was commenced and has been continued. You, I think, seem to be under some apprehension in regard to the matter. First, you inaccurately assume that before opening fire on this city Maj. Gen. Gillmore, in accordance with the usages of civilized warfare, notified Gen. Beauregard of his intention, in order "that noncombatants might be removed, and thus women and children be spared from harm." Secondly, you evidently mistake the object of the bombardment. On the 21st of August last a letter without signature was sent from Maj. Gen. Gillmore's headquarters to Gen. Beauregard, informing him that unless certain extraordinary conditions were complied with, or if no reply was thereto was received within "four hours" after the delivery of the letter at Battery Wagner for transmission to Charleston, fire would be opened on the city from batteries already established. Gen. Beauregard received that letter after 11 o'clock at night, and two hours later, when this city was in profound repose, Maj. Gen. Gillmore opened fire on it and threw a number of the most destructive projectiles ever before used amidst the sleeping and unarmed population. If Maj. Gen. Gillmore only desired to go through the barren form of giving notice of his intention, without allowing the noncombatants time to withdraw, he would have accomplished that useless end if in his haste and eagerness to begin his wicked work he had not forgotten to sign so important a letter. The time allowed

was four hours from the delivery of the letter at Battery Wagner for transmission to Gen. Beauregard's headquarters, five miles distant. Maj. Gen. Gillmore knew very well that in the ordinary course of transmission all the time allowed would elapse before he could receive a reply to his demand, and he knew quite as well that it was impossible in the brief space of time allowed to remove the noncombatants of a large and populous city. It is clear, therefore, that due time was not allowed and that the object of the notification was not "that noncombatants might be removed."...

He proposed to fire on the city of Charleston to enforce the surrender of Morris Island and Ft. Sumter. His language admits of no doubt. The price of refusal to comply with his demands was the threatened destruction of the city of Charleston.... The shells have been thrown at random, at any and all hours, day and night, falling promiscuously in the heart of the city, at all points remote from each other, and from the works you mention....

... The object of your fire may legitimately be judged of by its effects. It has never suspended for an instant the labor on or in any military or naval work, factory, foundry, arsenal, or depot of supplies; it has never killed or wounded, so far as I can learn, a soldier or a laborer engaged thereon; but it has damaged a number of private houses in the heart of the city, and killed and wounded some noncombatants. Indeed, it seems that, with the exception of an old man, an octogenarian, killed whilst quietly sitting by his fire at night, the only persons killed have been women and children.... From 24th of August to the 27th of October not a shot or shell was thrown into the city.... On the 27th of October, after an interval of more than two months, without a word of warning, he again opened fire, and threw a few shells into the city—just enough to frighten, irritate, and kill a few noncombatants, but not enough to produce any military result, and then ceased firing for three weeks. On the 17th of November he again opened and continued very slow fire. It was apparent that the fire was especially directed at churches during the hours of public worship.

Christmas day, 1863,... was ushered in by Maj. Gen. Gillmore with a fire more than tenfold heavier and more continuous than usual. These facts ... show conclusively that the object of the fire was not what you allege, and they show, besides, that it has been conducted in a spirit of mere malice and cruelty....

To this city, thus circumstanced, the prisoners of war referred to in my letter of the 13th instant have been sent for safekeeping. You assert this to be an act of indefensible cruelty, unknown to honorable warfare.... It is not true that the prisoners of war now in this city are treated with any cruelty. They are in a large city, not besieged, but partially blockaded by land and naval batteries, from five to ten miles distant. They are provided with commodious and comfortable quarters, remote from all military and naval works, or any object on which you may legitimately fire, and they are treated with all consideration due to prisoners of war. They are surrounded by citizens of all classes and conditions, and it cannot be regarded as an act of cruelty to place them in the immediate neighborhood of the houses occupied by our wives and children.... You regard that treatment as justifying you in asking your Government to place in your custody an equal number of prisoners of like grade, to be kept by you in positions exposed to the fire of my guns. We direct our fire only on your batteries, shipping, and troops. If you will direct your guns only on the works that you distinctly specify as the objects of your fire, or on any object in which an honorable foe may legitimately fire, the prisoners of war and their neighbors, noncombatants, women and children, among whom they live, will be in no danger whatever from the effects of your shot. If the C.S. officers, prisoners of war, shall be placed by you as you indicate, I have to ask that you will, as promptly and minutely as I have done, inform me when and where they are placed and how treated.

Abbott, A.O., 1st Lt., 1st N.Y. Dragoons, prisoner at Camp Oglethorpe, Macon, Ga.:

On the 22d we were visited by a Catholic priest, who had been at Andersonville, and had seen our men there. The story he told of their sufferings touched every heart, and we each inquired, "Can not something be done for them by the officers?"... The plan advised was that a committee should be appointed, who should address the Rebel Secretary of War upon the subject, asking permission for five of the officers to be paroled to visit Andersonville and other prisons, and then be permitted to go through to Wash-

ington and report the facts to our government.... The address was signed by only a small minority, and was finally sent out to the Rebel authorities, and that was the last we ever heard of it.

Again today, Col. Wm. Hoffman wired Lt. Col. S. Eastman at Elmira, "In establishing the fence it is advisable, if practicable, to inclose the ground enough to accommodate in barracks and tents 10,000 prisoners." The number 10,000 kept coming up, but Eastman wasn't listening.

### June 23 (Thursday)

The military facility at Salisbury, N.C., was not only a prison for Federals, it also contained several civilian and military prisoners of the Confederacy. Other work was done here as well, even providing 6000 horseshoes per month to the Army. On this day, an inspection report of the prison and facility at Salisbury by Lt. Col. Archer Anderson, CSA, was sent to Gen. Braxton Bragg, CSA, in Richmond:

The guard consists of three companies of about 200 men for duty.... These companies have been recently largely recruited by the enlistment of boys between seventeen and eighteen years old.... The men are pretty well drilled as companies but not at all as a battalion.... Clothing and shoes good; arms indifferent and ill kept....

There are twenty-three sentry posts. The prison wards are kept as clean as they can be in the absence of proper water-closets, which are being built, and with so many inmates. They are very much crowded with 132 men in a room 60 by 40 feet. There are now in confinement 550 persons, consisting of soldiers working out their sentences, political prisoners, deserters from the enemy, and prisoners of war. Since the establishment of the prison 3802 persons have been confined in it, of whom 1176 have been treated in hospital and 77 have died. The kitchen seems to be well arranged. Ration—eighteen ounces of flour and one-third pound of meat, with rice, beans, and salt. The prisoners have never been a day without meat....

... Employees—one clerk, one transportation agent, one messenger, one shipping agent, one wagon-master, one head mechanic, twelve carpenters, three blacksmiths, one harnessmaker, one wheelright (all exempts or detailed upon certificate of physical disability or for mechanical skill), and twenty-six negroes. This force is employed to building a wayside hospital at Salisbury and a forage house at Concord....

Since March 1 the following stores have been collected and shipped and issued ... 290,127 pounds of bacon, 5944 barrels flour, 300,629 pounds meal. Capt. Brenizer, in charge of the ordnance works, was absent. He has thirty-five conscripts (amongst them one clerk and one superintendent) either detailed or with applications pending. These works are engaged in making 10-pounder Parrott shell and horseshoes; of the latter the product is 6000 a month.

Ransom, John, QM Sgt., 9th Michigan Cavalry, Andersonville Prison, Ga.:

My coverlid nobly does duty, protecting us from the sun's hot rays by day and the heavy dews at night. Have no doubt but it has saved my life many times. Never have heard anything from Hendryx since his escape. Either got away to our lines or shot.... Much fighting. Men will fight as long as they can stand up. A father fights his own son not ten rods from us. Hardly any are strong enough to do much damage except the raiders, who get enough to eat and are in better condition than the rest.... Does not seem to me as if any can stand it. After all it's hard killing a man. Can stand most anything.

The fight at Brice's Crossroads, Miss., on June 10, 1864, yielded more Union prisoners for the Confederate camps. This date, several of the officers captured by Forrest at the Crossroads arrived at Camp Oglethorpe.

Abbott, A.O., 1st Lt., 1st N.Y. Dragoons, prisoner at Camp Oglethorpe, Macon, Ga.:

Some officers arrived from Sturgis's command, captured by Forrest in Mississippi. They had been robbed of everything, clothing, money, watches, rings, diaries, and even the photographs of their friends at home.... They were destitute indeed.

Little time had been lost since Maj. Gen. Foster notified Washington that the Confederate authorities had moved Federal prisoners into Charleston, S.C., and placed them under the fire of the Federal guns from Morris Island. In Washington, Maj. E.N. Strong had been given the task of conducting Con-

federate prisoners from Ft. Delaware, Del., to Hilton Head, S.C., to be turned over to Foster. These prisoners were to be used to retaliate against the South for using Federal prisoners in Charleston as hostages-under-fire. Among the list of prisoners, which included two major generals, three brigadier generals, fifteen colonels, fourteen lieutenant colonels, and seventeen majors, was Col. William W. Ward of Tennessee.

### June 24 (Friday)

Gov. M.L. Bonham, of South Carolina, got a little testy about his prerogatives regarding the disposition of captured former slaves. Today he blasted the Confederate Secy. of War, J.A. Seddon:

Dear Sir: I have recently seen in the Richmond papers two notices that certain slaves recently captured from the enemy by our troops will be delivered to their owners upon application to certain officers who have them in charge.

If there have been any regulations adopted since the provision by Congress in 1863, that they should be delivered to the Governors of the States where captured, they have escaped my notice, and if there have been any regulations, orders of the War Department, acts, or resolutions of Congress on this subject since the period above referred to, be so good as to order me a copy furnished.

Ransom, John, QM Sgt., 9th Michigan Cavalry, Andersonville Prison, Ga.:

Almost July 1st, when Jimmy Devers will have been a prisoner of war one year. Unless relief comes very soon he will die. I have read in my earlier years about prisoners in the revolutionary war, and other wars. It sounded noble and heroic to be a prisoner of war, and accounts of their adventures were quite romantic; but the romance has been knocked out of the prisoner of war business, higher than a kite. It's a fraud.... Take exercise every morning and evening, when it is almost impossible for me to walk. Walk all over before the sun comes up, drink of Battese's medicine made of roots, keep clear of vermin, talk and even laugh, and if I do die, it will not be through neglect.

Ward, William W., Col., 9th Tenn. Cavalry, prisoner, Ft. Delaware, Del.:

Morning very warm.... The list comes. My name

among others to go to Charleston, Cols Duke Morgan Tucker & myself, Maj Steel Webber & High of our old crowd go. Gens Archer Stuart Thompson (Brgds.), Johnson & Gardner Maj Gens go. Those who are to go to Charleston come up to our quarters. All the rest of our Mess & the crowd who were in the Fort go to the barracks.... Every thing is pcl mcl this evening.

On this date, Pvt. James P. Gold, Co. D, 9th Tenn. Cavalry, who had been captured at Mt. Sterling, Ky., then taken to Louisville Military Prison, arrived at Rock Island Prison, Ill. He would remain at Rock Island, refusing the oath of allegiance, until his parole on March 6, 1865, when he was sent to be exchanged.

### June 25 (Saturday)

At Ft. Monroe, Va., Maj. Gen. Benjamin F. Butler, USA, was still trying to unravel the knot of getting the South to exchange the Negro soldiers who were captured after joining the Federal army. Today, he notified Maj. Mulford, Agent for Exchange, that:

Mr. Ould having refused to allow the flag-of-truce boats to go up the river I have no way of sending the rebel surgeons except through our lines, and I don't think that is safe. They know too much. Ould desires us to agree upon a new place to make our exchanges, but refuses to answer officially what will be done with colored soldiers. Therefore I have cut off all exchange and flag-of-truce communciations.

Ransom, John, QM Sgt., 9th Michigan Cavalry, Andersonville Prison, Ga.:

Another lead pencil wore down to less than an inch in length, and must skirmish around for another one. New men bring in writing material and pencils. Today saw a New York *Herald* of date June 11th, nothing in it about exchange, however.... Our guards are composed of the lowest element of the South—poor white trash. Very ignorant, much more so than the negro. Some of them act as if they never saw a gun before. The rebel adjutant does quite a business selling vegetables to those of the prisoners who have money, and has established a sutler stand not far from our mess. Hub Dakin, an old acquaintance, is a sort of clerk and can get enough to eat thereby. Hot! Hot! Raiders kill someone now every day. No restraint in the least. Men who were no doubt

respectable at home, are now the worst villains in the world. One of them was sneaking about our quarters during the night, and Sanders knocked him about ten feet with a board. Some one of us must keep awake all the time...

Ward, William W., Col., 9th Tenn. Cavalry, prisoner, Ft. Delaware, Del.:

Morning very warm—Up early & quite a stir around the building.... It is said that all our command with several hundred other officers arrived here today from Point Lookout. I asked permission to see Lieut Ruck but heard nothing from my application. We are kept in considerable suspense all day. The transport not ariving.... Day passed of[f] very unpleasantly with the heat, the suspense & the desperate headache which I had.

The heavy fighting around northern Georgia where Sherman was advancing on Atlanta resulted in a steady influx of Federal prisoners both at Andersonville, Ga., and at Cahaba, Ala. The Cahaba prison now contained over 2000 prisoners, reducing the space per man to about 10 square feet.

At this time, fearing a cavalry raid to free the prisoners at Andersonville, the Confederate government in Richmond ordered Brig. Gen. John H. Winder to select another site for those prisoners that could be moved from Andersonville. The new site was to be either Cahaba or Union Springs, Ala. Winder's site surveyor, Capt. C.E. Dyke, looked only at Union Springs and did not visit Cahaba. Union Springs, Dyke reported, had limited water supplies and he recommended another site—Silver Run—which was located about 20 miles south of Columbus, Ga., had plenty of water, and was next to the railroad line. Winder recommended movement to Silver Run in his report to Richmond, which he telegraphed on July 7.

### June 26 (Sunday)

Ward, William W., Col., 9th Tenn. Cavalry, prisoner, Ft. Delaware, Del.:

Morning very hot. Sergeant Polzer announces the arrival of the Transport. I hastily write a note to Mrs. Ward. Purchase two common indifferent calico shirts at $2 each. Am now in readiness for my departure to be ordered.

Ransom, John, QM Sgt., 9th Michigan Cavalry, Andersonville Prison, Ga.:

They die now like sheep—fully a hundred each day. New prisoners come inside in squads of hundreds, and in a few weeks are *all dead*. The change is too great and sudden for them. Old prisoners stand it best. Found a Jackson, Michigan man, who says I am reported dead there. Am not, however, and may appear to them yet.

## June 27 (Monday)

Ransom, John, QM Sgt., 9th Michigan Cavalry, Andersonville Prison, Ga.:

Raiders going on worse than ever before. A perfect pandemonium. Something must be done, and that quickly. There is danger from disease, without being killed by raiders. Any moment fifty or a hundred of them are liable to pounce upon our mess, knock right and left and take the very clothing off our backs. No one is safe from them.... The farther advanced the summer, the death rate increases, until they die off by scores. I walk around to see friends of a few days ago and am told "dead."... Some of the most horrible sights that can possibly be, are common everyday occurrences.

Abbott, A.O., 1st Lt., 1st N.Y. Dragoons, prisoner at Camp Oglethorpe, Macon, Ga.:

The 27th was a day of considerable excitement among us.... The evening before, five of the officers had made a plan to escape by crawling under the stockade at the point where the little brook ran under it. It was a dark night, and several trees shaded that corner, which facilitated operations. The first had succeeded ... but the second one was less fortunate, and, in passing out, made a little noise which attracted the attention of the guard, who at once fired in that direction, but hurt no one.

The long roll was at once sounded in the Rebel camps, the men turned out under arms, the artillery manned, and everything put in order to quell a general outbreak.... Very soon we heard the howling of the dogs, which were brought down to the place on the outside of the stockade and started on the trail, and, after about an hour, they succeeded in treeing—not a Yank, but a veritable *coon*. They were finally obliged to give up the chase till daylight.... Roll-call came on, and

we soon found out there was something terrible on the minds of the authorities of the prison.... They searched for tunnels. After three hours close searching, they succeeded in finding *three*.

At Hilton Head, S.C., Capt. W.L.M. Burger, Assistant Adjutant-General, notified Brig. Gen. A. Schimmelfennig, USA:

General: I am directed by the major-general commanding to inform you that his application to the General-in-Chief for rebel officers, prisoners of war, for the purpose of awarding them similar treatment as is being received by our prisoners in Charleston, has been granted. Thirty-five field and general officers are now en route for this place, and their arrival is hourly expected. The general directs that quarters for their accommodation be erected, and in the following places: One in Ft. Putnam, one in Chatfield, one in Strong, and, if convenient and you think advisable, one between Putnam and Chatfield, each capable of accommodating 12 or 15 officers. The chief quartermaster has been directed to supply the necessary men and material for their construction.

Ward, William W., Col., 9th Tenn. Cavalry, at sea, en route to Charleston, S.C.:

Morning bright & pleasant. Sea swelling pretty smartly. Some sick. I am not except the headache. It is better. Pass Fortress Monroe at 7 o'clock this morning. See nothing of interest today. Get not much sea sick. Have the headache. A shower came up in the evening which cooled the air very much.

## June 28 (Tuesday)

Ransom, John, QM Sgt., 9th Michigan Cavalry, Andersonville Prison, Ga.:

It seems to me as if three times as many as ever before are now going off, still I am told that about one hundred and thirty die per day. The reason it seems worse, is because no sick are being taken out now, and they all die here instead of at the hospital. Can see the dead wagon loaded up with twenty or thirty bodies at a time, two lengths, just like four-foot wood is loaded on to a wagon at the North, and away they go to the graveyard on a trot. Perhaps one or two will fall off and get run over. No attention is paid to that; they are picked up on the road back for more.... Many entirely naked.

Ward, William W., Col., 9th Tenn. Cavalry, at sea, en route to Charleston, S.C.:

Morning very rough. Most of our men rather sick. Passed Cape Hatteras in the night. Also pass a blockading vessel off the co[a]st of North Carolina. Day cool & calmed off in the evening. Have to lay in my bunk all day. Have eat nothing since I've been on board. Lay in my bunk & think of my dear wife & the trouble this trip of mine will bring on her.

### June 29 (Wednesday)

Ransom, John, QM Sgt., 9th Michigan Cavalry, Andersonville Prison, Ga.:

Capt. Wirtz sent inside a guard of fifteen or twenty to arrest and take out quite a number of prisoners. They had the names and would go right to their quarters and take them. Some tell-tale traitor has been informing on them, for attempting to escape or something. Wirtz punishes very hard now; so much worse than a few months ago. Has numerous instruments of torture just outside the gate. Sores afflict us now, and the Lord only knows what next.... Have had no meat now for ten days; nothing but one-third of a loaf of corn bread and half a pint of cow peas for each man, each day. Wood is entirely gone, and occasionally squads allowed to go and get some under guard.

Ward, William W., Col., 9th Tenn. Cavalry, at sea, arrival at Charleston, S.C.:

Morning very pleasant & quit[e] calm. Move in sight of Morris Island & the blockading fleet off Charlston at 9 o'clock A.M. We are now there while a blockader is approaching us and I am stretched on my back looking at her approach & trying to write while our ship, or boat, rolls from side to side. The Blockader comes up, passes around us & asks several questions which were answered & the[n] waddled off back to the fleet. Remain in sight of land along down the coast of S.C. Meet a steam boat at 1 P.M. with Gen Foster on board. Maj Strong goes on board with papers &c., returns. We each go our way. The boat with Gen. Foster was bound for Stono River. A few miles farther we find a small schooner anchored & put one of the men off our vessel on her & piloted her on in our wake. We continue in sight of land &

it now appears on our left as well as the right. We arrive at Hilton Head at 5 P.M. and anchor. Find many vessels of many kinds here. At dark we moved up under the guns, (72) of *Wabash*. Anchor all night.

### June 30 (Thursday)

Sgt. Bartlett Yancey Malone of the 6th N.C. Infantry, confined at Point Lookout, Md., recorded during June the arrival of more than 1100 prisoners from the fighting between Grant and Lee. He also recorded on the 4th that "We had Beef and Potato Soop for dinner the Yanks are not a going to give us no more Coffee and Sugar from this on."

At Andersonville, Ga., the prisoners who terrorized and robbed the other prisoners were about to have their rope shortened. Some discussion had been held and the Confederate prison authorities now issued General Order 57, dated today, which provided for a prisoner-sponsored court to be held to hear the charges brought against the marauders. William S. Winder, son of Brig. Gen. John S. Winder, signed the order as Assistant Adjutant-General. The order provided for:

A gang of evil-disposed persons among the prisoners of war at this post having banded themselves together for the purpose of assaulting, murdering, and robbing their fellow prisoners and having already committed all these deeds, it becomes necessary to adopt measures to protect the lives and property of the prisoners against the acts of these men, and, in order that this may be accomplished, the well-disposed prisoners may and they are authorized to establish a court among themselves for the trial and punishment of all such offenders.

II. On such trials the charges will be distinctly made with specifications setting forth time and place, a copy of which will be furnished the accused.

III. The whole proceedings will be properly kept in writing, all the testimony fairly written out as nearly in the words of the witnesses as possible.

IV. The proceedings, findings, and sentence in each case will be sent to the commanding officer for record, and if found in order and proper, the sentence will be ordered for execution.

In essence, a proper military court-martial would be conducted and recorded. Fair enough.

Ransom, John, QM Sgt., 9th Michigan Cavalry, Andersonville Prison, Ga.:

A new prisoner fainted away on his entrance to Andersonville and is now crazy, a raving maniac.... My pants are the worse for wear from repeated washings, my shirt sleeveless and feet stockingless; have a red cap without any front piece; shoes by some hocus-pocus are not mates, one considerably larger than the other. Wonder what they would think if I should suddenly appear on the streets in Jackson in this garb.... Strong talk of forming a police force to put down raiders and to enforce order. If successful it will prove of great benefit.

Ward, William W., Col., 9th Tenn. Cavalry, at anchor, off Hilton Head, S.C.:

Morning bright & hot. Rest at ease until about 10 o'clock when it is stated that Gen. Foster has arrived. Rumor this morning that the *Alabama* is not far off. Rumor now is (1 o'clock P.M. the Gen has not arrived. Polser inquires if we will have some Chowder made of Clams (Clam Chowder). We take it and find it pritty good not so good however as sisters.

Quartermaster-General M.C. Meigs, Washington, was notified today that the prison at Elmira, N.Y., was ready for occupancy. Eight acres of land had been enclosed with a 12-foot-high fence and hospital tent accommodations had been prepared for 200 patients.

Col. Hoffman immediately notified the commander at Point Lookout to send 2000 prisoners to Elmira, N.Y., on the next available transportation.

## July 1 (Friday)

In the Shenandoah Valley of Virginia, Jubal Early's Confederates were on the move towards Harpers Ferry and meeting little, or no, opposition.

Maj. Gen. Samuel Jones, CSA, commanding at Charleston, S.C., wrote a letter to Maj. Gen. J.G. Foster, commanding Union forces in the area, in which he enclosed a letter signed by five Union brigadier generals being held inside Charleston. The enclosure requested that action be taken to exchange the prisoners now held by both factions to relieve the suffering among all prisoners. Jones concurred with this sentiment and made an officer available empowered to discuss terms of exchange.

In response, Gen. Foster requested definitive

information on the placement of the prisoners under fire; if they, in fact, had been placed under fire; and what manner of accommodations they had been receiving. Foster requested a reply to the latter to be written by one of the prisoners.

Ward, William W., Col., 9th Tenn. Cavalry, at anchor, off Hilton Head, S.C.:

Morning passed in calm anxiety & uncertainty. In the afternoon we were ordered into the hold of an old sail vessel where the temperature is about 120. It is almost intolerable. Capt Young will not let but two to remain on deck at a time. Had to pay the stuart on the *M. A. Boadman* 50$ for a little coffee & little butter & one dish of soup worth in all about 10$ —

Ransom, John, QM Sgt., 9th Michigan Cavalry, Andersonville Prison, Ga.:

Matters must approach a crisis pretty soon with the raiders. It is said that even the rebels are scared and think they will have no prisoners, should an exchange ever occur.

Malone, B.Y., Sgt., Co. H, 6th N.C. Infantry, CSA, prisoner, Point Lookout, Md.:

The first day of July 1861 I left home And the first day of July 1862 I was in the fight of Malvin Hill And the first day of July 1863 I was in the fight at Gettersburg And today whitch is the first day of July 1864 I am at Point Lookout Md. It is very plesant today We had pical Pork for breakfast this morning and for dinner we will have Been Soop.

## July 2 (Saturday)

Early's gray columns reached Winchester, Va., and some of his men were near Harpers Ferry and at Bolivar Heights driving in the Federal pickets. In Virginia, the fighting around the lines at Petersburg was becoming almost routine. In Georgia, Joe Johnston moved his entire line back to keep from being outflanked, again.

Brig. Gen. John H. Winder, CSA, reported to Gen. Samuel Cooper, Adjutant-General, CSA, that during the month of June 1864, Camp Sumter (Andersonville) prison camp had:

Begun the month with 17,415 prisoners in the camp, with an additional 1039 in the hospital.

During the month, 9143 prisoners were received, and 44 escapees were recaptured.

A total of 1203 died during the month, an average of more than 40 per day.

Forty-seven escaped during the month.

Twenty-three were sent off to various places.

June ended with a total of 25,012 prisoners in camp and 1355 in the prison hospital.

Ransom, John, QM Sgt., 9th Michigan Cavalry, Andersonville Prison, Ga.:

Have taken to rubbing my limbs, which are gradually become more dropsical. Badly swollen. One of my teeth came out a few days ago, and all are loose. Mouth very sore. Battese says: "We get away yet."... Probably one hundred negroes are here. Not so tough as the whites. Dead line being fixed up by the rebels. Got down in some places. Bought a piece of soap, first I have seen in many months. Swamp now in frightful condition from the filth of camp. Vermin and raiders have the best of it. Capt. Moseby still leads the villains.

Ward, William W., Col., 9th Tenn. Cavalry, at anchor, off Hilton Head, S.C.:

Weather very warm, particulary in this hole. Write to my wife & to Capt Bennett. Send the letters out by Capt Young. Had a bad headache in the evening, slept out on deck. Very pleasant.

### July 3 (Sunday)

Fighting flared again at Big Shanty and Sweetwater Bridge in Georgia, as Sherman marched past Kennesaw Mountain towards Johnston's new line at Smyrna.

At Ft. Delaware, Del., Brig. Gen. A. Schoepf, commander of the prison, received a communication from Col. William Hoffman, Federal Commissary-General of Prisoners, stating that, on the certificate of the surgeon in charge, quantities of sugar and tea could be purchased for the sick if the current ration was not considered sufficient. Hoffman further stated that "the Commissary-General of Subsistence will order a small supply of desiccated vegetables to be sent to the commander" for use in preventing scurvy among the prisoners. Had the prisoners known this, they would probably have held a mass escape. These desiccated vegetables,

commonly referred to among the Union troops as "decimated vegetables," were usually greeted with howls of protest from their recipients.

Severe food shortages inflicted the civil and military population of Petersburg and Richmond due to the fighting around Petersburg, where the railheads are located. The *Petersburg Express* proposed that the Yankee prisoners be fed solely on bread and water rather than starve the Confederate population in the two cities.

Ransom, John, QM Sgt., 9th Michigan Cavalry, Andersonville Prison, Ga.:

Three hundred and fifty new men from West Virginia were turned into this summer resort this morning. They brought good news as to successful termination of the war, and they also caused war after coming among us. As usual the raiders proceeded to rob them of their valuables and a fight occurred in which hundreds were engaged. The cutthroats came out ahead. Complaints were made to Capt. Wirtz that this thing would be tolerated no longer, that these raiders must be put down or the men would rise in their might and break away if assistance was not given with which to preserve order. Wirtz flew around as if he had never thought of it before, issued an order to the effect that no more food would be given us until the leaders were arrested and taken outside for trial.... Hundreds that have before been neutral and noncommittal are now joining the police force. Captains are appointed to take charge of the squads which have been furnished with clubs by Wirtz. As I write, this middle of the afternoon, the battle rages. The police go right to raider headquarters, knock right and left and make their arrests. Sometimes the police are whipped and have to retreat, but they rally their forces and again make a charge in which they are successful. Can lay in our shade and see the trouble go on. Must be killing some by the shouting. The raiders fight for their very life, and are only taken after being thoroughly whipped. The stockade is loaded with guards who are fearful of a break. I wish I could describe the scene today. A number killed. After each arrest a great cheering takes place. NIGHT—Thirty or forty of the worst characters in camp have been taken outside, and still a good work goes on. No food today and don't want any. A big strapping fellow called Lumber Jim heads the police. Grand old Michael Hoare is at the front and goes for a raider as quick as he would a rebel.... The orderly prisoners are feeling jolly.

Ward, William W., Col., 9th Tenn. Cavalry, at anchor, off Hilton Head, S.C.:

Morning more pleasant, particularly to me as I was out all night. Vesals all in their sunday rigs, Blue Jack Flags, Pendants &c. Sailors with white shirts with large blue collars, S[t]aid out all day. Better.

Federal prisoners were being scooped up near Harpers Ferry by Jubal Early's Confederates and headed south up the Shenandoah Valley and eventual imprisonment. Sigel withdrew into Maryland Hights.

In Georgia, Gen. Joseph E. Johnston had set a new defensive line along Nickajack Creek. Sherman was approaching after leaving Kennesaw Mountain and coming through Marietta, Ga. Trickles of prisoners from both sides continued to mount.

### July 4 (Monday)

Near Harpers Ferry, Gen. Early's troops, on their way to Washington for a visit, skirmished with the Federals at Patterson's Creek Bridge, South Branch Bridge, and other points along the Potomac. Washington was becoming more nervous.

The expedition up the Stono River near Charleston disembarked Federal troops to capture shore batteries of artillery after the gunners had been chased away by naval gunfire. The ships continued upriver.

In Georgia, McPherson's Federals, on Sherman's right flank, were closer to Atlanta than was Confederate Joe Johnston. Johnston pulled back, yet again, to prepared positions on the Chattahoochee River.

Three days previously, Maj. Gen. Samuel Jones, CSA, commanding at Charleston, S.C., sent a letter to the Adjutant-General of Maj. Gen. J.G. Foster's command which enclosed a letter from the Federal generals being held in Charleston under Union fire from Morris Island. The prisoners' letter requested that action be taken to exchange the prisoners rather than keep them in peril of bombardment. Jones, in his letter, seconded the motion on exchange.

Today, Gen. Foster replied to Jones:

I fully reciprocate your desire for an exchange of prisoners, but before any steps can be taken to effect it, it will be necessary for you to withdraw from exposure to our fire those officers now confined in Charleston. I have not yet placed your prisoners in a similar position of exposure.

Ransom, John, QM Sgt., 9th Michigan Cavalry, Andersonville Prison, Ga.:

The men taken outside yesterday are under rebel guard and will be punished. The men are thoroughly aroused, and now that the matter has been taken in hand, it will be followed up to the letter. Other arrests are being made today, and occasionally a big fight. Little Terry, whom they could not find yesterday, was today taken. Had been hiding in an old well, or hole in the ground.... The writer hereof does no fighting, being on the sick list. The excitement of looking on is most too much for me.... Capt. Moseby is one of the arrested ones. His right name is Collins and he has been in our hundred all the time since leaving Richmond. Has got a good long neck to stretch.... It is said that a court will be formed of our own men to try the raiders. Any way, so they are punished. All have killed men, and they themselves should be killed. When arrested, the police had hard work to prevent their being lynched. Police more thoroughly organized all the time. An extra amount of food this P.M. and police get extra rations, and three out of our mess is doing pretty well, as they are all willing to divide.... Rebel flags at half mast for some of their great men. Just heard that the trial of raiders will begin tomorrow.

Ward, William W., Col., 9th Tenn. Cavalry, at anchor, off Hilton Head, S.C.:

Slept out again last night. Very warm this morning. A salute of 21 guns was fired by the *Wabash* this morning. Maj. Strong came aboard yesterday, for no other purpose but to tantelise us with the statement that the news of Gen Boreguard's capture with 15,000 men had been confirmed. I do not believe it. A salute of 21 guns at 12 & the same at 6 P.M. It rained a hard shower & quite a squall this afternoon. It has cooled the atmosphere vastly.

### July 5 (Tuesday)

Sherman, with his right flank on the Chattahoochee River near Atlanta, pressed Joe Johnston closely. In southwest Tennessee, at LaGrange, yet another Federal force left in search of the elusive Nathan Bedford Forrest, this time under the command of Maj. Gen. Andrew Jackson Smith.

Jubal Early started his Confederates across the Potomac today at Shepherdstown, W.Va., abandoning the idea of taking Harpers Ferry. He did, however, leave a force there to contain Sigel's Federals.

Ransom, John, QM Sgt., 9th Michigan Cavalry, Andersonville Prison, Ga.:

Court is in session outside and raiders being tried by our own men. Wirtz has done one good thing, but it's a question whether he is entitled to any credit, as he had to be threatened with a break before he would assist us. Rations again today. I am quite bad off with my diseases, but still there are so many thousands so much worse off that I do not complain much, or try not to however.

## July 6 (Wednesday)

At Shepherdstown, W.Va., Early's gray columns finally were all across the Potomac. Some had already reached Hagerstown, Md., where $20,000 in "ransom" was extracted from the citizens of that town in retribution for the damage done in the Shenandoah Valley.

Ransom, John, QM Sgt., 9th Michigan Cavalry, Andersonville Prison, Ga.:

Boiling hot, camp reeking with filth, and no sanitary privileges; men dying off over a hundred and forty per day. Stockade enlarged, taking in eight or ten more acres, giving us more room, and stumps to dig up for wood to cook with. Mike Hoare is in good health; not so Jimmy Devers. Jimmy has now been a prisoner over a year, and poor boy, will probably die soon. Have more mementoes than I can carry, from those who have died, to be given to their friends at home. At least a dozen have given me letters, pictures &c., to take North. Hope I shan't have to turn them over to someone else.

On this date 399 Confederate prisoners arrived at Elmira, N.Y., and were incarcerated in the new prison. One had escaped en route.

## July 7 (Thursday)

At Hilton Head, S.C., Maj. Gen. J.G. Foster requested a reading from Maj. Gen. Henry W. Halleck in Washington on the possibility of exchanging the Confederate prisoners now being held in retaliation for those held in Charleston as hostages-under-fire.

In Washington, the panic prevailed among the faint-hearted as visions of Early's men arriving at the capital caused consternation. Federal troops and militia assembled at Baltimore and the arrival of one division of the Sixth Army Corps from the Army of the Potomac helped settle things down for a while. Early was approaching from the west, his long gray columns eating dust.

In Georgia, Sherman and Johnston were still skirmishing and picking up prisoners here and there for the prison pens. Johnston had retreated to the Chattahoochee and a new defensive line.

Ransom, John, QM Sgt., 9th Michigan Cavalry, Andersonville Prison, Ga.:

The court was gotten up by our own men and from our own men; Judge, jury, counsel, &c. Had a fair trial, and were even defended, but to no purpose. It is reported that six have been sentenced to be hung, while a good many others are condemned to lighter punishment, such as setting in the stocks, strung up by the thumbs, thumb screws, head hanging, etc. The court has been severe, but just. Mike goes out tomorrow to take some part in the court proceedings. The prison seems a different place altogether; still, dread disease is here, and mowing down good and true men. Would seem to me that three or four hundred die each day, though officially but one hundred and forty odd is told. About twenty-seven thousand, I believe, are here now in all. No new ones for a few days. Rebel visitors, who look at us from a distance. It is said the stench keeps all away who have no business here and can keep away. Washing business good. Am negotiating for a pair of pants. Dislike fearfully to wear dead men's clothes, and haven't to any great extent.

## July 8 (Friday)

In Maryland, along the Monocacy River, Federal Gen. Lew Wallace was gathering what troops were available to face Early's veteran Confederates. At best, it was a pickup force of odds and ends. The 3d Div., Sixth Corps, Army of the Potomac, was shaking itself and boarding railroad cars after its arrival in Baltimore, and getting ready to march on Early.

Johnston, in Georgia, was outflanked again when Schofield crossed the Chattahoochee River on Johnston's right flank.

Ransom, John, QM Sgt., 9th Michigan Cavalry, Andersonville Prison, Ga.:

Oh, how hot, and oh, how miserable. The news that six have been sentenced to be hanged is true, and one of them is Moseby. The camp is thoroughly under the control of the police now, and it is a heavenly boon. Of course there is some stealing and robbery, but not as before. Swan, of our mess, is sick with scurvy. I am gradually swelling up and growing weaker.... Over a hundred and fifty dying per day now, and twenty-six thousand in camp. Guards shoot now very often. Boys, as guards, are the most cruel.... The swamp now is fearful, water perfectly reeking with prison offal and poison. Still men drink it and die. Rumors that the six will be hung inside. Bread today and it is so coarse as to do more hurt than good to a majority of the prisoners. The place still gets worse.... Having formed a habit of going to sleep as soon as the air got cooled off and before fairly dark, I wake up at two or three o'clock and stay awake. I then take in all the horrors of the situation. Thousands are groaning, moaning and crying, with no bustle of the daytime to drown it. Guards every half hour call out the time and post, and there is often a shot to make one shiver as if with the ague.... Have taken to building air castles of late, on being exchanged. Getting loony, I guess, same as all the rest.

### July 9 (Saturday)

At Monocacy, Md., the 6000-man scrub squad of Gen. Lew Wallace met the 10,000 veterans of Jubal Early in a battle that cost the Confederates about 700 casualties and the Federals almost 2000, 1200 of whom were captured. Wallace withdrew the remainder of his force towards Baltimore.

Brig. Gen. John H. Winder, currently at Andersonville, Ga., telegraphed Gen. Samuel S. Cooper, CSA Adjutant-General, in Richmond, about his problems with guard personnel at the prison:

Send me the officers I have asked for. I have not officers enough for the duty. The guard is raw and dissatisfied. I must have assistance of more officers. Send me the detectives I have asked for. There is treason going on around us, even to depositing arms in the adjacent counties to arm the prisoners.

... Twelve of the reserves deserted last night with arms, and I cannot depend upon them.

Ransom, John, QM Sgt., 9th Michigan Cavalry, Andersonville Prison, Ga.:

Battese brought me some onions, and if they ain't good then no matter; also a sweet potato. One half of the men here would get well if they only had something in the vegetable line to eat, or acids. Scurvy is about the most loathsome disease, and when dropsy takes hold with the scurvy, it is terrible. I have both diseases but keep them in check, and it only grows worse slowly. My legs are swollen, but the cords are not contracted much, and I can still walk very well.... I still do a little washing, but more particularly haircutting, which is easier work. You should see one of my haircuts. Nobby! Old prisoners have hair a foot long or more, and my business is to cut it off, which I do without regards to anything except to get it off.... Some stole Battese's washboard and he is mad; is looking for it—may bust up the business. Think Hub Dakin will give me a board to make another one. Sanders owns the jackknife, of this mess, and he don't like to lend it either; borrow it to carve on roots for pipes.

### July 10 (Sunday)

Around Washington, Early moved on towards the city, a little more slowly this time. Grant sent another two divisions from the Sixth Corps from City Point, Va., by steamer to Washington.

Back up around Harpers Ferry, Sigel became a little braver and sent his men out to gather up several hundred Confederates left there to contain the Federals and to guard the escape route. These prisoners were sent first into Pennsylvania and then to Point Lookout, Md. Some would later be sent to Elmira, N.Y.

Ransom, John, QM Sgt., 9th Michigan Cavalry, Andersonville Prison, Ga.:

Have bought of a new prisoner quite a large (thick I mean) blank book so as to continue my diary.

Although it's a tedious and tiresome task, am determined to keep it up. Don't know of another man in
prison who is doing likewise. Wish I had the gift of
description that I might describe this place.... At
Belle Isle we had good water and plenty of it, and I
believe it depends more upon water than food as
regards health. We also had good pure air from up
the James River. Here we have the very worst kind of
water. Nothing can be worse or nastier than the
stream drizzling its way through this camp. And for
air to breathe, it is what arises from this foul place.
On all four sides of us are high walls and tall trees,
and there is apparently no wind or breeze to blow
away the stench, and we are obliged to breathe and
live in it. Dead bodies lay around all day in the broil-
ing sun, by the dozen and even hundreds, and we
must suffer and live in this atmosphere. It's too horrible for me to describe in fitting language.

### July 11 (Monday)

In Silver Spring, Md., Gen. Jubal Early's Confederates burned the home of Postmaster General Blair
and threatened the forts surrounding the city. Early
ordered an assault for tomorrow.

Meanwhile, at the Washington 6th Street
wharves, steamers carrying the veterans of the Sixth
Army Corps, Army of the Potomac, unloaded
troops such as the city had never seen. These were
not the nattily dressed soldiers normally seen around
town looking as if they had stepped from a band-
box, these men were lean, dirty, somewhat ragged,
and handled their muskets as if they knew exactly
what to do with them. They came off the steamers
and formed long lines and struck off across the city
with a swinging stride that had eaten up the miles
on many a long and dusty road from Petersburg to
Gettysburg. These were Grant's veterans of Cold
Harbor, the Wilderness, and the Chickahominy,
and were not men to be trifled with. Some straggling occurred when a soldier would make the occasional stop for a cold beer in a bar and then run to
catch up again. Old Jubal Early, watching developments, spotted a long, low cloud of dust which indicated troops moving. But what troops? When they
got to within range, Early could see they were not
wearing the linen dusters and high-peaked caps of
the local troops. These men wore the kepis such as
he had encountered two days previously when he

tangled with men from the Sixth Corps west of the
city. To compound Early's problem, soldiers of the
Nineteenth Corps who had been en route from
Louisiana as reinforcements for Grant, arrived shortly after dark and unloaded, heading for the western
defenses of the city.

At Ft. Stevens, Md., Lincoln and his wife paid a
visit. They witnessed Early's approach before the
Union soldiers ordered them away because of the
danger. Lincoln seemed more curious than worried.

Ransom, John, QM Sgt., 9th Michigan Cavalry,
Andersonville Prison, Ga.:

This morning lumber was brought into the prison by
the rebels, and near the gate a *gallows* erected for the
purpose of executing the six condemned Yankees. At
about ten o'clock they were brought inside by Capt.
Wirtz and some guards, and delivered over to the
police force. Capt. Wirtz then said a few words about
their having been tried by our own men and for us to
do as we chose with them, that he washed his hands
of the whole matter, or words to that effect.... I have
learned by enquiry, their names, which are as follows:
John Sarsfield, 144th New York; William Collins,
alias "Moseby," Co. D, 88th Pennsylvania; Charles
Curtiss, Battery A, 5th Rhode Island Artillery; Pat
Delaney, Co. E, 83d Pennsylvania; A. Munn, U.S.
Navy, and W.R. Rickson of the U.S. Navy. After
Wirtz made his speech he withdrew his guards, leaving the condemned at the mercy of 28,000 enraged
prisoners who had all been more or less wronged by
these men. Their hands were tied behind them, and
one by one they mounted the scaffold. Curtiss, who
was last, a big stout fellow, managed to get his hands
loose and broke away and ran through the crowd and
down towards the swamp. It was yelled out that he
had a knife in his hand, and so a path was made for
him. He reached the swamp and plunged in, trying
to get over on the other side, presumably among his
friends. It being very warm he overexerted himself,
and when in the middle or thereabouts, collapsed and
could go no farther. The police started after him,
waded in and helped him out. He pleaded for water
and it was given him. Then led back to the scaffold
and helped to mount up. All were given a chance to
talk. Munn, a good looking fellow in marine dress,
said he came into the prison months before perfectly
honest, and as innocent of crime as any fellow in it.

Starvation, with evil companions, had made him what he was. He spoke of his mother and sisters in New York, that he cared nothing as far as he himself was concerned, but the news that would be carried home to his people made him want to curse God he had ever been born. Delaney said he would rather be hung than live here as the most of us lived, on their allowance of rations. If allowed to steal could get enough to eat, but as that was stopped had rather hang. Bid all good-bye. Said his name was not Delaney and that no one knew who he really was, therefore his friends would never know his fate, his Andersonville history dying with him.... The excited crowd began to be impatient for the "show" to commence as they termed it.... While the men were talking they were interrupted by all kinds of questions and charges made by the crowd, such as "don't lay it on too thick, you villain,"... "less talk and more hanging,"... At about eleven o'clock they were all blindfolded, hands and feet tied, told to get ready, nooses adjusted and the plank knocked from under. Moseby's rope broke and he fell to the ground, with blood spurting from his ears, mouth and nose. As they were lifting him back to the swinging-off place he revived and begged for his life, but no use, was soon dangling with the rest, and died very hard. Munn died easily, as also did Delaney, all the rest died hard and particularly Sarsfield, who drew his knees nearly to his chin and then straightened them out with a jerk, the veins in his neck swelling out as if they would burst. It was an awful sight to see, still a necessity.... All during the hanging scene the stockade was covered with rebels, who were fearful a break would be made if the raiders should try and rescue them. Many citizens too were congregated on the outside in favorable positions for seeing.... Wirtz stood on a high platform in plain sight of the execution and says we are a hard crowd to kill our own men. After hanging for half an hour or so the six bodies were taken down and carried outside.... Rebel negroes came inside and began to take down the scaffold; prisoners took hold to help them and resulted in its all being carried off to different parts of the prison to be used for kindling wood, and the rebels get none of it back and are mad. The ropes even have been gobbled up, and I suppose sometime may be exhibited at the north as mementoes of today's proceedings.

At Elmira, N.Y., another 249 Confederate prisoners arrived from Point Lookout, Md.

## July 12 (Tuesday)

This morning, Jubal Early had second thoughts about beginning an assault on the Washington forts, especially now that some "real" soldiers were there. He started pulling his troops away from Washington, leaving the skirmishers to mask the withdrawal. He was pursued by the Federals.

Ransom, John, QM Sgt., 9th Michigan Cavalry, Andersonville Prison, Ga.:

Good order has prevailed since the hanging. The men have settled right down to the business of dying, with no interruption.... Not less than one hundred and sixty die each twenty-four hours. Probably one-fourth or one-third of these die inside the stockade, the balance in the hospital outside. All day and up to four o'clock P.M., the dead are being gathered up and carried to the south gate and placed in a row inside the dead line. As the bodies are stripped of their clothing in most cases as soon as the breath leaves, and in some cases before, the row of dead presents a sickening appearance. Legs drawn up and in all shapes. They are black from pitch pine smoke and laying in the sun. Some of them lay there for twenty hours or more, and by that time are in a horrible condition. At four o'clock a four or six mule wagon comes up to the gate and twenty or thirty bodies are loaded on to the wagon and they are carted off to be put in trenches, one hundred in each trench, in the cemetery, which is eighty or a hundred rods away.

An additional 600 Confederate prisoners arrived at Elmira, N.Y., from Point Lookout, Md., which brought the total to about 1250.

## July 13 (Wednesday)

On the 7th of July, Maj. Gen. J.G. Foster, USA, requested that Maj. Gen. Samuel Jones, CSA, commanding the area of Charleston, S.C., release the medical officers currently being held by the Confederates in accordance with "well-established custom." Jones, not knowing what the "custom" was, responded that he would investigate and if the "custom" was still in usage, he would comply. The cartel of July 1862 did not specifically mention the release of medical doctors and chaplains without parole or officer-for-officer exchange. This practice was agreed upon, and begun as a separate agreement between the warring factions.

Brig. Gen. John H. Winder, in charge of all Confederate prisons in the South, again urged Richmond to approve Silver Run, Ala., as the site for the relocation of prisoners from Andersonville. His recommendation would be repeated on July 16.

Ransom, John, QM Sgt., 9th Michigan Cavalry, Andersonville Prison, Ga.:

Can see in the distance the cars go poking along by this station, with wheezing old engines, snorting along. As soon as night comes a great many are blind, caused by sleeping in the open air, with moon shining in the face. Many holes are dug and excavations made in camp. Near our quarters is a well about five or six feet deep, and the poor blind fellows fall into this pit hole.... Half of the prisoners have no settled place for sleeping, wander and lay down wherever they can find room.... One prisoner made some buttons here for his little boy at home, and gave them to me to deliver, as he was about to die. Have them sewed on to my pants for safekeeping.

Malone, B.Y., Sgt., Co. H, 6th N.C. Infantry, CSA, prisoner, Point Lookout, Md.:

The 13th day of July, 13 of our men died at the Hospital and it was reported that Gen. Ewel was a fiting at Washington and that our Cavalry was in 4 miles of this plaice. The Yanks was hurried up sent in all Detailes at 2 o'clock in the eavning and run thir Artilry out in frunt of the Block house and plaised it in position...

The following day, the 14th, Malone recorded that 500 of his fellow Rebels had taken the oath of allegiance and had left the prison.

Sherman prepared to move across the Chattahoochee and around the north side of Atlanta. Jubal Early crossed the Potomac at Leesburg, Va., and consolidated his troops.

### July 14 (Thursday)

Yesterday in northern Mississippi, Gen. Andrew Jackson Smith's Federal column moved nearer to Tupelo, as the Confederates pursued. Fighting was wild for a period of time at Camargo Cross Roads, as the Confederates moved in for the attack against over 14,000 Federals. Smith took up a strong position on a low ridge east of Harrisburg and awaited results.

Today, Maj. Gen. Andrew Jackson Smith's Federal force near Tupelo, Miss., repeatedly repulsed Confederate assaults with heavy Rebel casualties. Smith had nearly 14,000 men, only losing 674 by all causes, less than 5 percent, while the Confederate losses were about 1350 out of about 9500, nearly sixteen percent.

At White's Ford near Leesburg, Va., Jubal Early's Confederate force was back across the Potomac, but it was a near thing. Gen. Horatio Wright's Federals were at Poolesville, Md., just east of the crossing. Wright did not pursue into Virginia.

Ransom, John, QM Sgt., 9th Michigan Cavalry, Andersonville Prison, Ga.:

We have been too busy with the raiders of late to manufacture any exchange news, and now all hands are at work trying to see who can tell the biggest yarns.... Rumors of midsummer battles with Union troops victorious. It's "bite dog, bite bear," with most of us prisoners; we don't care which licks, what we want is to get out of this pen. Of course we all care and want our side to win, but it's tough on patriotism. A court is now held every day and offenders punished, principally by buck and gagging, for misdemeanors. The hanging had done worlds of good, still there is much stealing going on yet, but in a sly way, not openly. Hold my own as regards health.

Col. Ward had been sick for the past several days and he lumped his diary entries for the period 9 through 14 July into one entry:

Ward, William W., Col., 9th Tenn. Cavalry, at anchor, off Hilton Head, S.C.:

We lay at the same point on the same desperate disagreeable old boat, the "Dragon", during all the above days, without any change. Most awful suspense and a most horrible condition. If our Government does not retaliate for our treatment here there is not retaliation in it. I have been too sick to write all the time imbraced in the above note—Am much better today. Feel pretty well all day.

At Washington, Surgeon C.T. Alexander wrote Col. William Hoffman, Federal Commissary-General of Prisoners, concerning a recently completed inspection of the prison at Elmira, N.Y.:

Colonel:... I inspected the camp for prisoners of war recently established at Elmira, N.Y. The camp at present is in good condition. Your attention is respectfully called to the sinks. Some being placed upon a slough, at present stagnant, others over vaults, they may soon become offensive and a source of disease. The remedy suggested is either to bring water from the city of Elmira and construct new sinks with suitable drainage, or to cause the river near which the camp is situated to communicate with the slough, thereby producing a running stream through the camp. Upon the cost of the first method and the practicability of the second the commanding officer was requested to inform you without delay, sending at the same time a plan of the camp, that all might be readily understood.

The barracks for the prisoners will accommodate 5000, and there is room sufficient in the inclosure to pitch tents for from 3000 to 5000 more.... At present there is no proper hospital organization. The surgeon in charge of the hospitals for the troops at Elmira visits daily the prisoners' camp. He had as an assistant to look especially after the prisoners a young man, lately a medical cadet, recently contracted with, and not a suitable person to organize or control a hospital such as will be needed. I found the sick, fortunately but few, in no way suitably provided for except as for shelter; diet not suitable; some without bedsacks; blankets scarce. Your attention is called to the immediate necessity of a competent surgeon to take charge. After consulting with the commanding officer, a site was chosen for a hospital and directions given that a laundry and three pavilion wards should be immediately built, one to be so divided as to make suitable apartments for administrative duties. A building formerly used as a carpenter shop is so situated as to be serviceable as kitchen and mess-room, and is to be altered as such. The cost per ward will be about $500. I also stated to the commanding officer the necessity of having a requisition made for supplies for hospital of 300 beds.

### July 15 (Friday)

In Mississippi, Maj. Gen. A.J. Smith kept his Federals waiting for another Confederate attack until midafternoon, then he pulled up stakes and headed back to Tennessee, closely followed, and attacked, by Nathan Bedford Forrest's cavalry.

Ransom, John, QM Sgt., 9th Michigan Cavalry, Andersonville Prison, Ga.:

Blank cartridges were this morning fired over the camp by the artillery, and immediately the greatest commotion outside. It seems that the signal in case a break is made, is cannon firing. And this was to show us how quick they could rally and get into shape. In less time than it takes me to write it, all were at their posts and in condition to open up and kill nine-tenths of all here. Sweltering hot. Dying off one hundred and fifty-five each day. There are twenty-eight thousand confined here now.

Ward, William W., Col., 9th Tenn. Cavalry, at anchor, off Hilton Head, S.C.:

Day pretty pleasant. Condition not changed. Great excitement as to what wil be done with us. Do not partake much in the wrangle. Am a little unwell today, but not much so.

Gen. Braxton Bragg, acting as an advisor to President Davis, settled the question of the relocation of prisoners from Andersonville by stopping all transfers to Florence, S.C., and points east and then directed that Cahaba be the new prisoner depot. However, things did not work out quite that way. No prisoners were sent to Cahaba and they continued going to Florence and Charleston, S.C. Cahaba remained as a collection depot for prisoners, and shortly 3000 men were crowded in the old warehouse. Some improvements were made. Additional rough wood bunks were added to bring the total to around 600 beds, still with no bedding of any sort. The water no longer ran through an open ditch; wooden pipes carried the water to the prison, where it was stored in three sunken barrels. The water, however, was very high in sulfur and distasteful.

### July 16 (Saturday)

Ward, William W., Col., 9th Tenn. Cavalry, at anchor, off Hilton Head, S.C.:

Crowding around with more enthusiasm than reason—We have on board some of the most ultre fanatics. I mean men who are credulous to a fault, rush to conclusions without reason or rather against it & most obstinately persist in assertions. No news.

Ransom, John, QM Sgt., 9th Michigan Cavalry, Andersonville Prison, Ga.:

Well, who ever supposed that it could be any hotter; but today is more so than yesterday, and yesterday more than the day before.... Just like a bake oven. The rabbit mules that draw in the rations look as if they didn't get much more to eat than we do. Driven with one rope line, and harness patched up with ropes, strings, &c. Fit representation of the Confederacy. Not much like U.S. Army teams. A joke on the rebel adjutant has happened. Some one broke into the shanty and tied the two or three sleeping there, and carried off all the goods. Tennessee Bill (a fellow captured with me) had charge of the affair, and is in disgrace with the adjutant on account of it. Every one is glad of the robbery. Probably there was not ten dollars worth of things in there, but they asked outrageous prices for everything. Adjt. very mad, but no good. Is a small, sputtering sort of fellow.

### July 17 (Sunday)

In Georgia, probably one of the worst mistakes made by the Confederate high command was made today when it assigned John Bell Hood to lead the troops that had been so carefully hoarded by Gen. Joseph E. Johnston. By the end of the year, this army would cease to effectively exist, having been battered and spent against the Federals around Atlanta, Franklin, and Nashville.

Ransom, John, QM Sgt., 9th Michigan Cavalry, Andersonville Prison, Ga.:

Cords contracting in my legs and very difficult for me to walk—after going a little ways have to stop and rest and am faint. Am urged by some to go to the hospital but don't like to do it.... Many old prisoners are dropping off now this fearful hot weather; knew that July and August would thin us out; cannot keep track of them in my disabled condition.... Succeeded in getting four small onions about as large as hickory nuts, tops and all for two dollars Confederate money.... It is said that two or three onions or a sweet potato eaten raw daily will cure the scurvy. What a shame that such things are denied us, being so plent[iful] the world over. Never appreciated such things before but shall hereafter. Am talking as if I expected to get home again. I do.

### July 18 (Monday)

Capt. Richard B. Winder, CSA, son of Brig. Gen. John H. Winder, was assigned as Post Quartermaster at Andersonville, Ga., and was having a very difficult time in getting money with which to run the prison. Today, he wired Maj. W.L. Bailey:

I am so seriously in need of funds that I do not know what I shall do. For God's sake send me $100,000 for prisoners of war and $75,000 for pay of officers and troops stationed here. You can put in my estimates, and if you only knew what trouble I was in here for the want of funds I know you would do your very best to send me at once above amounts. I have only had $75,000 since 1st of April.

Capt. Winder's desperation was apparent and near panic. The local authorities had no means of impressing food or materials for use at the prison and had no monies for which to pay for anything required.

Ransom, John, QM Sgt., 9th Michigan Cavalry, Andersonville Prison, Ga.:

Time slowly dragging itself along. Cut some wretches's hair most every day. Have a sign out "Hair Cutting," as well as "Washing," and by the way, Battese has a new washboard made from a piece of the scaffold lumber.... Death rate more than ever, reported one hundred and sixty-five per day; said by some to be more than that, but 165 is about the figure.... Jimmy Devers most dead and begs us to take him to the hospital and guess will have to. Every morning the sick are carried to the gate in blankets and on stretchers, and the worst cases admitted to the hospital. Probably out of five or six hundred half are admitted. Do not think any lives after being taken there; are past all human aid. Four out of every five prefer to stay inside and die with their friends rather than go to the hospital. Hard stories reach us of the treatment of the sick out there and I am sorry to say the cruelty emanates from our own men who act as nurses. These deadbeats and bummer nurses are the same bounty jumpers the U.S. authorities have had so much trouble with. Do not mean to say that all the nurses are of that class but a great many of them are.

Ward, William W., Col., 9th Tenn. Cavalry, at anchor, off Hilton Head, S.C.:

Day pleasant and passed off as usual. This old ship is a bore to me now. Various reports are afloat in reference to when we will move, where we will go to & what will be done with us.

In response to a query, Brig. Gen. John H. Winder wired Gen. Samuel Cooper in Richmond that "The prison at Macon is not secure and will take great expense and labor to make it so. It is within a few hundred yards of three important railroad depots and very large workshops, which escaped prisoners might and probably would burn. It is in a large town, which renders an inefficient guard more inefficient. It is in an unhealthy locality, to which our troops ought not be exposed."

The handling of crews from the blockade runners of other nations was a different situation from that of blockade runners from the South. The Southern crews were to be treated as prisoners of war, while foreign national crews were to be released. This was defined very clearly to Secy. of War Stanton by the Union Secy. of the Navy, Gideon Welles:

Sir: The Department understands that some of the officers and crew of the steamer *Pevensey*, which was run ashore and destroyed near Beaufort, N.C., while endeavoring to run the blockade, have been sent to Point Lookout for imprisonment. They claim to be British subjects, and if they are really such, their transfer to Point Lookout was made under the misconstruction of the Department's orders respecting the disposing of blockade runners. Bona fide neutral subjects captured in neutral vessels violating the blockade are not subject to treatment as prisoners of war. I will thank you, therefore, to give directions for the immediate release of those of the officers and crew of the *Pevensey* as well as of any other neutral blockade-running vessels that have been sent to Point Lookout for imprisonment, and are foreign subjects.

### July 19 (Tuesday)

For many days the almost constant skirmishing between Early's Confederates and the Federals in the Shenandoah Valley had taken many bites from both forces in the way of prisoners. Early, however, had the long-term problem: he could not get replacements easily.

Ransom, John, QM Sgt., 9th Michigan Cavalry, Andersonville Prison, Ga.:

There is no such thing as delicacy here. Nine out of ten would as soon eat with a corpse for a table as any other way. In the middle of last night I was awakened by being kicked by a dying man. He was soon dead. In his struggles he had floundered clear into our bed. Got up and moved the body off a few feet, and again went to sleep to dream of the hideous sights. I can never get used to it as some do. Often wake most scared to death, and shuddering from head to foot. Almost dread to go to sleep on this account. I am getting worse and worse, and prison ditto.

### July 20 (Wednesday)

North of Atlanta, Ga., Gen. Hood sent about 20,000 troops in against the same number of Federals under Maj. Gen. George H. Thomas. At the end of the scrap, Thomas had lost about 10 percent of his force, but Hood had lost nearly 25 percent of his Confederates, and he had no replacements. The prison holding pens were full that night.

### July 21 (Thursday)

Ransom, John, QM Sgt., 9th Michigan Cavalry, Andersonville Prison, Ga.:

...rebels are still fortifying.... Hear that Kilpatrick is making a raid for this place. Troops (rebel) are arriving here by every train to defend it. Nothing but corn bread issued now and I cannot eat it any more.

### July 22 (Friday)

The battle of Atlanta took place this date, when the Confederate force of Gen. Hardee attempted to outflank the Union force under Gen. James B. McPherson. Each side lost a Major General during the battle: W.H.T. Walker for the South, and McPherson for the North. The South gained about 1700 more prisoners from the 3722 casualties suffered by the North out of about 20,000 engaged. Confederate losses amounted to nearly 25 percent—7000 to 10,000 out of a force of about 40,000. Devastating for Hood's army.

Capt. Morris H. Church, commanding a guard transferring prisoners from Point Lookout, Md., to the new prison site at Elmira, N.Y., had a problem which he explained to his Commanding Officer, Lt. Col. S. Eastman at Elmira:

Sir: As officer in command of guard in charge of prisoners of war from Point Lookout, Md., I have to report that we left on Steamer *Crescent* with a guard of 125 men and 3 commissioned officers and 833 prisoners on the eve of July 12. Arrived at New York at 3 P.M. July 14, and disembarked at Jersey City at 4 A.M. of the 15th.

Left Jersey City at 6 o'clock via Erie Railway, and at 3 P.M. came in collision with a coal train near Shohola, Pa., causing a complete wreck of the train and killing 14 of the guard and 40 of the prisoners instantly, and mortally wounding 3 of the guard and 93 prisoners.

Nearly all of the guard were either killed or wounded, and immediately I caused the reserve to be posted around the wreck and prisoners to prevent escape.

The wounded were extracted as soon as possible and taken to Shohola, where every attention was rendered by the citizens and guard.

The wounded all being cared for, the dead were buried in the immediate vicinity of the accident, and each grave properly designated. The prisoners were removed to Shohola, where we remained until 11 A.M. July 16, when we proceeded on our way, arriving at Elmira at 9:30 P.M.

Many of the prisoners killed were so disfigured that it was impossible to recognize them, and five escaping whose names are unknown, I am unable to give a correct list of killed.

Ward, William W., Col., 9th Tenn. Cavalry, at anchor, off Hilton Head, S.C.:

Morning warm & a little rainy. Raised the anchors this morning & was towed up near the *Wabash* again. Got some tainted bacon this morning, refused by the soldiers—The first meat we have had in three days—If it were not for what we purchase we could not live.

Ransom, John, QM Sgt., 9th Michigan Cavalry, Andersonville Prison, Ga.:

A petition is gotten up signed by all the sergeants in the prison, to be sent to Washington, D.C., *begging* to be released. Capt. Wirtz has consented to let three

representatives go for that purpose. Rough that it should be necessary for us to *beg* to be protected by our government.

### July 24 (Sunday)

In the Shenandoah Valley of Virginia, Early took on Gen. George Crook's Federals at the Second Battle of Kernstown and chased Crook down the valley, gathering prisoners along the way. Tomorrow they would fight again at Bunker Hill, W. Va.

Maj. E.A. Scovill, commander of the prison at Johnson's Island, Ohio, reported a total of 2406 prisoners confined on this date. Forty-seven had reported sick since the last report, and no deaths were reported for the past week. Good news for a change.

### July 25 (Monday)

Brig. Gen. John H. Winder, at Andersonville, Ga., was visited by one L.B. Lowe, of Selma, Ala., today at the prison. Mr. Lowe had received permission from the Confederate Secy. of War, James A. Seddon, to recruit workmen from the prison population to work in an iron rolling mill at Selma. Winder reports that Lowe had, in fact, recruited some workmen and asked Seddon if they should be released since Winder did not think this a good policy. On the 26th, tomorrow, Seddon replied that the prisoners to be used were to be paroled for this purpose. This was one of several instances where the Confederacy used volunteer Federal prisoners as a part of the labor force.

Ransom, John, QM Sgt., 9th Michigan Cavalry, Andersonville Prison, Ga.:

Am myself much worse, and cannot walk, and with difficulty stand up. Legs drawn up like a triangle, mouth in terrible shape, and dropsy worse than all. A few more days. At my earnest solicitation was carried to the gate this morning, to be admitted to the hospital. Lay in the sun for some hours to be examined, and finally my turn came and I tried to stand up, but was so excited I fainted away. When I came to myself I lay along with the row of dead on the outside. Raised up and asked a rebel for a drink of water, and he said: "Here, you Yank, if you ain't dead, get inside there!" And with his help was put inside again. Told a man to go to our mess and tell them to come to the gate, and pretty soon Battese and Sanders came and carried me back to our quarters; and here I am, completely played out. Battese flying around to buy me something to eat. Can't write much more.

The distribution of food throughout the South became more critical as the war progressed. The rolling stock, aged in most cases in 1861, was falling apart and replacements were scarce or nonexistent. This problem affected all people in the South, even prisoners of war. At Andersonville, Ga., Brig. Gen. John H. Winder telegraphed Gen. Samuel S. Cooper, Adjutant-General of the Confederate Army:

There are 29,400 prisoners, 2650 troops, 500 negroes and other laborers and not a ration at the post. There is great danger in this state of things. I have ordered that at least ten days' rations should be kept on hand, but it has never been done.

Gen. Winder eventually saw the reply that was provided by the Confederate Commissary-General Northrop and probably blew his stack. He had been on the outs with the Commissary-General for some time—hard feelings going all the way back to Winder's stint as Provost Marshal of Richmond—and the climate had not improved much. The fact that Winder had no rations did not deter this bureaucrat from standing on his prerogatives:

The relation which subsists between commissaries of posts and the commanding officers thereof, so far as relates to the subsistence of prisoners of war, is quite different from their duties connected with troops. In the former relation the commanding officer of the post has nothing to do with the person employed in feeding the prisoners; if he thinks the prisoners are likely to rebel on account of food he should state the case to the Commissary-General.

A reference to the acts approved May 21, 1861, and February 17, 1864, is conclusive.

Prisoners, either soldiers or sailors, were first turned over to the Quartermaster-General to be kept in custody and fed by him and his subordinates under direction of the Secretary of War.

Now the latter part of these duties are by law devolved on the Commissary-General. If Gen. Winder has the custody of the prisoners of war he is so far a subordinate of the Quartermaster-General. The Commissary-General claims to control every-

thing relating to subsisting them through his subordinates. If the commanding officer of the post thinks anything about supplies is going wrong, it is his duty to report his views to the Commissary-General. Gen. Winder has no right to give any orders on the subject according to my understanding of the laws, and practice hitherto, when the Quartermaster-General had charge of the prisoners' subsistence and the Commissary-General furnished the stores.

The supplies for the prisoners are furnished by the district commissary, Second District of Georgia, who has long been under orders to send stores for the Army of Virginia as fast as possible hither.

Had Gen. Winder's orders for ten days' rations for over 32,000 men to be kept ahead been complied with, I should have countermanded it to the district commissary. The reasons against such accumulation are greater than before. The West Point Railroad is cut. Fifteen or twenty days will be required to repair it if we succeed in keeping it open; hence the support of the Army of Tennessee is on Georgia, which must still furnish Virginia with stores. Alabama had previously supplied the former army with corn, while the troops on the waters of the Atlantic drew from Georgia and South Carolina.

Meanwhile we have no money either to buy or impress provisions. See my paper of July 2 instant. Gen. Winder thinks the prisoners should have ten days' ahead, while the army may be restricted in a day's ration. And during this campaign around Richmond, with all the roads cut, a deficiency below what was here could have been critical.

### July 26 (Tuesday)

In the area of Atlanta, Ga., Union Gen. George Stoneman led his cavalry towards Macon, Ga., and the prison pen holding the Union officers in captivity. News of the activity of Sherman's army was reaching Chaplain White at Macon, who eagerly awaited some rescue action.

### July 27 (Wednesday)

Federal Gen. Stoneman's cavalry, raiding towards Macon, Ga., was meeting resistance from the Confederates between Atlanta and Macon, not much progress being made the first day into the raid.

At the Confederate prison near Macon, the prison authorities were getting nervous and the removal of many of the officer prisoners was ordered.

White, H.S., Chaplain, R.I. Regt. Heavy Artillery, prisoner of war, Camp Oglethorpe, Macon, Ga.:

One day near the close of July, an order was posted for six hundred of the officers to get ready to leave. The camp was full of joy. The rebels gave us to understand that it was for exchange. All were eager to go. With my good wishes they left us. What became of them for some time was not known to us. Capt. Aigan and Lt. Durfee left with the others, and I was left alone.

Abbott, A.O., 1st Lt., 1st N.Y. Dragoons, prisoner at Camp Oglethorpe, Macon, Ga.:

On the morning of the 27th of July, Lt. Davis at roll-call notified the first division to be ready to move to Charleston at 5 P.M. It was a busy time till that hour. Clothes were washed, pones baked, haversacks made ready and filled for *emergencies* [to escape].... After sleeping on the ground till 3 A.M. the next morning, were marched to the train, and at four o'clock started for Charleston *via* Savannah. This was the last we saw of them till we joined them, seven weeks after, at Charleston.

Conley, Capt., 101st Penna. Volunteers, prisoner, en route to Charleston, S.C.:

We remained there until the evening of the 27th of July when six hundred of us were taken out and put on board a train of freight cars and taken to Charleston, S.C. to be placed under the fire of our own guns on Morris Island.

Ransom, John, QM Sgt., 9th Michigan Cavalry, Andersonville Prison, Ga.:

Sweltering hot. No worse than yesterday. Said that two hundred die now each day. Rowe very bad and Sanders getting so. Swan dead, Gordon dead, Jack Withers dead, Scotty dead, a large Irishman who has been near us a long time is dead. These and scores of others died yesterday and day before. Hub Dakin came to see me and brought an onion. He is just able to crawl around himself.

### July 28 (Thursday)

With his cavalry raiding in all directions, Sherman sent Union Gen. O.O. Howard and the Army of the Tennessee towards Ezra Church, south and west of Atlanta. Confederate John B. Hood sent Gens.

Stephen D. Lee and A.P. Stewart to stop Howard. The result, after a battle that lasted from early afternoon to dark, was about 600 Federal losses and an estimated 5000 losses for the Confederacy. Hood could ill afford such losses and withdrew into Atlanta.

Abbott, A.O., 1st Lt., 1st N.Y. Dragoons, prisoner, en route from Macon to Savannah, Ga.:

The next morning we received a re-enforcement of 111 officers, captured both from Sherman's and Grant's army. Those from Sherman informed us that Hardee's great victory of the 22d was a dear one to the Rebels; that he had been unable to maintain his position, and was obliged to fall back to his former one.... On the 28th 600 more left, being marched to the cars at 3 A.M. the 29th.

White, H.S., Chaplain, R.I. Regt. Heavy Artillery, prisoner of war, Camp Oglethorpe, Macon, Ga.:

Two days after, another six hundred prisoners arrived. Another hour passed as we were being counted out and rolls prepared. They marched us to the cars and took us off for the night. I suppose they did not wish the citizens of Macon to see such a crowd as we were. The train consisted of boxcars full of filth and vermin. We reached Gordon, a station on the Central Georgia Railroad at the junction of the road from Milledgeville, about eight o'clock in the morning. The day was charming; the railway accommodations here were quite extensive and well arranged, and several trains met here. There were several good buildings, and in one was a "Wayside Home," a kind of free hospital and retreat for soldiers. Just as our train came up, about a dozen ladies came sailing out from the wayside home and moved down towards the train. We had not seen many ladies in the South. These were neatly attired, in light dresses, and with flowers in their hair they presented a most charming appearance, as with a plate in each hand, on which was a cup of coffee, a sandwich, some cold meat and bread, and a piece of cake, they came gaily sailing down towards us. I was in the front car. The guards with muskets sat in the doors of the cars, three in each door, and we were crowded in behind them.

Just as the group of ladies came close to the first car, one of the guards said, "These are Yanks." The first lady and leading spirit of the group halted as sudden as though she had been shot, and turning up that pretty nose of hers, said in that tone and style so natural to the daughters of the sunny South, "O! I thought they were some of our people," and turning upon her heel marched off with an air of ineffable disdain that some of my readers can better imagine than my pen describe. In a few moments we were hurried away.... Gen. Stoneman with his cavalry...struck the road at this point. At least it was shortly after, and finding how near he came to obtaining us, I presume his good nature was not particularly improved, and after the most approved method he proceeded to mix things somewhat. As track and train and building went up in smoke, or were "fixed," in my mind's eye, I see those fair damsels with raven locks and flashing eye, taking a beeline for the wilderness. Perhaps it is a little naughty in me, but I have often thought that I would have called it square with her if I could have stood about a hundred rods from those smoking ruins, and as they swept past me have said, "Ladies, have you seen anything of 'our people' around here?"

Admiral Dahlgren notified Gen. Foster at Hilton Head, S.C., that the gunboat *Wabash* would depart that area, leaving the Confederate prisoners aboard another ship without protection. The Confederate prison ship was towed under the guns of the *New Hampshire*.

Ward, William W., Col., 9th Tenn. Cavalry, at anchor, off Hilton Head, S.C.:

Weather warm—Today the *Wabash* left here. We were to[w]ed around under the guns of another boat.

Ransom, John, QM Sgt., 9th Michigan Cavalry, Andersonville Prison, Ga.:

Taken a step forward towards the trenches since yesterday, and am worse. Had a wash all over this morning. Battese took me to the creek; carries me without any trouble.

In Washington, Col. Hoffman, Federal Commissary-General of Prisoners, informed Quartermaster-General M.C. Meigs that the 60,000 prisoners of war on hand will require, for one-third of them, coats, pants, shirts, socks, shoes, and blankets. Hoffman suggests that 35,000 sets of inferior clothing that were

unclaimed at the hospitals be issued to the prisoners.

On this day also, Hoffman authorized the commander of the Elmira, N.Y., prison to lease a half-acre lot in the Woodlawn Cemetery for use as a burying ground for Confederate prisoners. The hire of a grave digger at $40/month was also authorized at Elmira. This man would become very busy.

### July 29 (Friday)

Today, Maj. Gen. J.G. Foster, USA, notified Maj. Gen. Samuel Jones, CSA, that the Union Secy. of War had authorized a special prisoner exchange at Charleston. Foster sent Maj. Anderson to arrange the time and place of the exchange. This was a major break from past policy on prisoner exchange. This would not prevent the Confederates from replacing the exchanged prisoners with more from Camp Oglethorpe and Andersonville.

Conley, Capt., 101st Penna. Volunteers, prisoner, Charleston, S.C.:

We reached Charleston on the morning of the 29th and were marched to the jail and jail yard for about two weeks when we were offered the use of two hospitals, the Roper and Marine, if we would give our paroles not to escape while in these hospitals. We were so uncomfortable in the jail and jail yard that we believed that any change would be an improvement. So we consented to give our paroles and were moved into the two hospitals, I, with most of the comrades of our regiment, going to the Marine Hospital. Here we were a little more comfortable. Here we spent the latter part of August, all of September, and [a] few of the first days of October.

While here, the yellow fever became epidemic in Charleston. The Rebel officer who was in command of the prison, as well as several of the guards, died with the disease, but strange as it may seem, we did not have a single case of it in our prison. This was probably due to the sanitation that we carried on in our prison.

While in Charleston the rations issued to us for ten days at a time were just about sufficient to last us five days. Those of us who had money bought enough to supply us the balance of the time. The principal rations issued were cornmeal, rice and black beans (called them "Cow Peas"). These were of very inferior quality and would not be eaten by persons who had anything else to eat.

Abbott, A.O., 1st Lt., 1st N.Y. Dragoons, prisoner, arrival at Savannah, Ga.:

Several embraced the opportunity to get *under* instead of *into* the cars, and thus managed to escape. Many of us had determined to escape while running from Savannah to Charleston, and we were quite busy cutting holes with saw-knives in the bottoms of the cars. As we reached the road leading to Charleston ... we were run into Savannah....

As we arrived in the city, a crowd collected around the train to see the "Yankee prisoners," the majority of whom were colored people.... We were escorted by a company of the City Battalion to the old United States Marine Hospital, and turned loose into the yard.

White, H.S., Chaplain, R.I. Regt. Heavy Artillery, prisoner of war, Savannah, Ga.:

About five o'clock in the afternoon of July 29 the train reached Savannah, Ga. The train stopped in the street and we were ordered out of the cars and formed in line. This took some time. Multitudes gathered about us of both sexes and all shades. Just at my right in a large elegant brick mansion, a lady threw up the window and shook out that detestable emblem of all meanness, a rebel flag....

We were marched into a stockade, built on the brick wall or fence surrounding the yard of the Marine hospital. It rained that night. Obtaining a board, I propped it up and slept well on it, being above the running water. The majority were less fortunate, and slept or laid in the slush and mud. Chaplain Dixon came with me, and we remained here about one month. The food was better and more abundant than at any place I was at. The hospital building was shut out from us by the stockade and deadline built across that end of the yard. The sick for a long time could obtain no attention or medicine. At last a small tent was pitched in the yard for them, but not a thing put in it for comfort, not a straw. The surgeons of our army that were held acted nobly, and did all that could be done, but having no remedies they could give but partial aid. After a time, small tents were issued to the prisoners, which helped to keep off the rain and sun. Sometime after our arrival the hospital building was opened to our sick.

Ransom, John, QM Sgt., 9th Michigan Cavalry, Andersonville Prison, Ga.:

Alive and kicking. Drank some soured water made from meal and water.

Ward, William W., Col., 9th Tenn. Cavalry, at anchor, off Hilton Head, S.C.:

Morning pleasant.... Great news & much blowing about our exchange—Some say that Capt. McWilliams says we are already exchanged and that the officers at Charleston will be down in a day or tomorrow. I do not believe any of the reports; only the one that we will be sent to Morris Island & put under fire for a while.

### July 30 (Saturday)

In the lines at Petersburg, Va., a tunnel 510 feet long had been dug under the siege lines at Petersburg by the Federals and the galleries packed with gunpowder. At about 4:45 A.M. the powder was exploded, which dug a hole 170 feet long, nearly 80 feet wide, and thirty feet deep in the Confederate entrenchments. About 280 Confederate soldiers died, never knowing what happened to cause their demise. The assault began immediately thereafter and by about 8:30 A.M. there were nearly 15,000 Union troops in the cratered area. Confederate Gen. Mahone's troops contained the Federals and around 2 P.M. the Federals pulled back. It cost 4000 Union killed, wounded and missing to about 1500 Confederates.

Abbott, A.O., 1st Lt., 1st N.Y. Dragoons, prisoner, Savannah, Ga.:

The next morning they brought us in some small "A" tents, issuing sixteen to ninety-six men. These we pitched in regular streets, first cutting them open to the peak, that we might spread them wider and make them cover six of us comfortably. They also issued to each squad of 100 a large iron pot, holding sixteen gallons, for washing purposes; eight tin kettles or pails, holding twelve quarts each, for cooking; eleven small iron skillets for baking our bread in and frying our meat; sixteen tin pans, each holding six quarts, for mixing our meal in; four wooden buckets or pails, two axes, and two hatchets.

For rations they issued to us daily one pound of

fresh beef five days of the week, one half pound of bacon the other two days; one quart of cornmeal; one pint of rice; one fourth of a gill of vinegar; one teaspoonful of salt, and a small piece of hard soap. The rations were of very fair quality, and, had the bread been anything but corn, we would have got along tolerably well....

We were guarded by the 1st Georgia Regulars, Col. Wayne commanding. The officers of his regiment were gentlemanly, and uniformly treated us with respect.

### July 31 (Sunday)

Capt. Henry Wirz, commander of Camp Sumter (Andersonville) prison camp, reported that during the month of July, 1864, the prison had:

Begun the month with 25,005 prisoners in the camp, with an additional 1362 in the hospital.

Total beginning, 26,367.

During the month, 7064 prisoners were received, and 12 escapees were recaptured.

A total of 1742 died during the month, an average of more than 56 per day.

Twenty escaped during the month.

Three were sent off to various places.

July ended with a total of 29,998 prisoners in camp and 1680 in the prison hospital.

Grand total of prisoners, 31,678.

On Johnson's Island, Sandusky, Ohio, Maj. E.A. Scovill reported:

The want of lime is severely felt. The extremely hot weather of the present week has affected the drains and sinks, and with all possible attention they could not be kept from smelling badly.... There has been great trouble again this last week with the pumps. They broke down again, making it necessary to let the prisoners out to the bay to get a supply of water. Two more pumps would be an improvement.

Ward, William W., Col., 9th Tenn. Cavalry, at anchor, off Hilton Head, S.C.:

Had a heavy gale & rain last night.... Capt McWilliams brings a few letters aboard and assures us the negotiations for our exchange have been completed & that we will leave here on exchange next Wednesday. Great excitement.

### August 1 (Monday)

Gen. Jubal Early's cavalry under command of McCausland burned Chambersburg, Penna., and returned to Hancock, Md., across the Potomac from Berkeley Springs, W.Va. With Averell's cavalry hot on their trail, the Confederates headed towards Cumberland, Md., upriver.

At City Point, Va., Grant sent to the Valley the one man in whom he had faith to do the job—Maj. Gen. Philip Sheridan. Sheridan was appointed commander of the Army of the Shenandoah and sent to Washington by the first boat. His job was to rid the Valley of Jubal Early once and for all.

Ransom, John, QM Sgt., 9th Michigan Cavalry, Andersonville Prison, Ga.:

Just about the same. My Indian friend says: "We all get away."

### August 2 (Tuesday)

Ransom, John, QM Sgt., 9th Michigan Cavalry, Andersonville Prison, Ga.:

Two hundred and twenty die each day. No more news of exchange.

Abbott, A.O., 1st Lt., 1st N.Y. Dragoons, prisoner, Savannah, Ga.:

The 2d of August brought some hope to our discouraged hearts; for on that day went out from us, to be sent through the lines, two chaplains and seven surgeons, and we read it as an omen of good to us, saying that the government wishes to get out of the way all the noncombatants, the sick and wounded, and then would commence the general work.

As soon as the chaplains were notified that they were to leave the next morning, a desire was manifested by many to have religious services once more before they went away. Accordingly, word was circulated through the camp that there would be preaching by one of the chaplains at dark on the green.

The appointed hour came, and with it a large attendance of the officers, for it was a lovely evening....

Chaplain Dixon preached from Luke XV, 25: "Lord help me." The text was short, and so was the sermon.... Chaplain White followed him in exhortation, bringing out some most beautiful thoughts drawn from our situation and circumstances....

They were expected to leave at four o'clock in the morning, and were on hand, as were many of their special friends, to see them off; but the provost guard, which was to go with them to the railroad, was delayed till after the train had gone, consequently they did not get off till five o'clock in the afternoon.

Ward, William W., Col., 9th Tenn. Cavalry, en route to Charleston, S.C.:

Much excitement & anxiety all day.... We thank God to leave the *Dragoon* & go aboard the *Cosmopolitan*, a fine steamer and leave the harbor at 10 P.M. Get supper on board at 50 cts. each. Have a nice stateroom & spent a pleasant night, eating at a table with a cloth, though I regret to say not much else on it & sleep in a pleasant bed with sheets, though not very clean.

### August 3 (Wednesday)

Confederate Gen. McCausland was back across the Potomac and had rejoined Early. Lincoln, unhappy with events in the Valley, told Grant that something had to be done immediately.

The commander of the prison at Elmira, N.Y., in his report of this date stated that "At Barracks, No. 1, there are 200 colored drafted men and substitutes, organized into two companies, armed and equipped, doing guard duty there." This is the first indication seen of *drafted* Negro soldiers.

Ransom, John, QM Sgt., 9th Michigan Cavalry, Andersonville Prison, Ga.:

Had some good soup, and feel better. All is done for me that can be done by my friends. Rowe and Sanders in almost as bad a condition as myself. Just about where I was two or three weeks ago.

Ward, William W., Col., 9th Tenn. Cavalry, exchanged, Charleston, S.C.:

In Charlston harbor. Have not looked around yet. Fine Morning. See the five small houses scattered over the head of Morris Island which were erected for our occupancy. They look not at all inviting as there is not a sprig of vegetation near them. All white sand around. We are in sight [of] old Ft. Sumpter and see the enemy shelling it from Cummings point of Morris Island. Point where we were to have gone.

At 10 o'clock our old rusty-looking shell of a steamboat arived along side the *Cosmopolitan*. Our steamer is named the *Chesterfield* & a hard-looking boat it is—We came unto the Warf amid the deafning cheers of the gallant soldiers in the different batteries. We passed Sillivens Island. It is well defended. Old Ft. Sumpter looks as though it is nearly done for. It can afford to fall now for like a noble heroe its glory is full. Revd. Mr. Gadsden (C.P.) presented on behalf of the ladies of the Soldiers Relief Association a beautiful wreath of flowers. Gen [Edward] Johnson recd. it on the part of the officers in a brief speech which had no merit but brevity & earnestness. The Gen. is a much better fighter than he is talker. Gen. Jeff Thompson also made a few remarks. It was a glorious opening for a fine speech, but poorly filled. I was introduced to the Rev. Porter of [blank] street who carred Lt. Col. Swingly & myself home with him. He is as nice a man & [as] good a Christian apparently as I have met with in a long, long time.... Have a good plain dinner though cheap which illustrates how cheaply a family can live and at the same time live well. All in all this has been a glorious day.

Col. William W. Ward was now back in Confederate hands. He eventually returned to his unit and served in the southwestern part of Virginia for the remainder of the war. His last diary entry was on April 6, 1865. He returned home, not having seen his wife for two years. He died in 1871 in Tennessee, aged 46.

In Maryland, Maj. Gen. "Black Dave" Hunter, USA, had issued orders for the arrest of civilians in the town of Frederick following the raid earlier in the month. Lincoln, hearing of this order, directed Edwin Stanton, Secy. of War, to suspend the order and find out what the problem was that caused the arrests. Stanton issued the necessary directives.

In Kentucky, Charles Buford, currently in Scott County, wrote his wife this date concerning events in that area:

Dear Wife: I wrote you five or six days ago. Since then, we have had startling events here. On last Thursday two Confed. prisoners were executed (shot to death) at Georgetown, in retaliation for a Union citizen killed on Eagle Creek in Scott. Six or eight prisoners have been shot in different places recently on similar grounds. Thus innocent men suffer for the guilty, [and] as was to be expected, retaliatory murders follow. Eight or ten Fed. soldiers were shot the other day at Owenton, and several at Williamstown, among them a Provost Marshall. It seems that all the horrors of the strife in Mo. are to be reproduced here. What it will end in, God only knows. Guerrilla bands hold many of hill Counties in the State—are very bold—defying the Federals—and making raids into the most populous counties—as Woodford, Shelby, Nelson, Scott, &c. Two hundred Bushwhackers rode deliberately through Georgetown the other day. It is said as many as 2000 are organized in Owen, and defy all the Fed. soldiers to drive them out. This is a terrible state of things, and I fear the recent course of Genl. Burbridge will only aggravate the end. A few days since he sent off to Louisville dozens perhaps hundreds of the most influential democratic citizens. About 15 or 20 that I know were sent from Scott. Many more from Fayette. John Payne, Ron Payne, Dr. Rankins, Dr. Hall, Billy Graves & [others] were of the number. No examination was made, but they were taken with an hour's notice. From Fayette, W. McGaw and family, James Grinsted & some of them were taken off under distressing circumstances. W. McGaw had to take her dying grandchild. Another family were hurried off leaving dead and dying children to the mercies of neighbors. It is said that Parson Dudley (the old Dr.'s son) and Mike Wickliff were among the proscribed, but they with others got secret intelligence and escaped. They were Union men and claim to be so still. The farce of a General Election was held on Monday last and some think these arrests were made in view of that, but I hardly believe this, for Judge Duvall's name was ordered stricken from the list of candidates, and this obviated the necessity of expelling voters. What the real motive is, or was, nobody knows. It seems to me, if those in command wanted to produce the most frightful disorder, they could not have hit upon a surer plan. But enough of such things.

When I wrote last I had just had an attack of Cholera and thought I was about gone but was mistaken. My old neighbors on Friday last got up a Burgoo, at which I was to meet all my old friends. I attended and spent a delightful day with them. They gave me a most cordial meeting. I could not but be moved by the seeming warmth of their friendship. A good many came from Lexington, and many more would have come but for their arrest on that day. From the Burgoo I went of course to W. Gaines

where I remained two days, in that time visiting with G. Johnson, W. Robers and W. Tom Payne. They are all well, but Mrs. G. is a very distressed woman for her young son (only 16) had just run off to the Confederate Army.... On Sunday while making this visit, I was attacked with Dysentery or Flux and immediately came back to Mary's. I have been under treatment by Aham since, and am glad to tell you, that all the bad symptoms have disappeared, and with prudence in diet, I shall be entirely well in a few days.

## August 4 (Thursday)

Maj. Gen. J.G. Foster, commanding the Department of the South at Hilton Head, S.C., wrote Maj. Gen. H.W. Halleck, Chief of Staff, in Washington on this day that:

General: The information given by our prisoners of war, now liberated, and by deserters, also by the late rebel papers, represent that our soldiers now prisoners at Andersonville, Ga., are destitute of comforts and necessaries, and are rapidly dying. The number of deaths per day varies, according to reports, from 30 to 70. I do not know what the wishes of the Government may be, but if it desire[s] that our imprisoned soldiers may be exchanged, so as to relieve them from their distress, I can easily have the matter arranged with the Confederate authorities so as to effect an exchange here. The exchange can be made by way of the Savannah River, and we can easily arrange to guard any number of prisoners on our islands here, and to supply them at least as bountifully as our men are supplied that are in the hands of the enemy.

I think the Confederate authorities are very desirous to have an exchange effected, both of officers and of men. The insecure position in which our prisoners have been confined probably causes this desire. They have already been obliged to remove our officers from Macon, and 600 of them have already arrived in Charleston and the others are to follow; this from its being the only secure place and the hope that it may induce to a still further exchange.

I shall notify Maj. Gen. Samuel Jones that no more exchanges will be made through Charleston Harbor, and that if any are authorized by the Government they will be made by the Savannah River. The effect of this is to induce them to remove our officers from Charleston to Savannah, so that our fire may be continued on the city without risk of hurting our friends. I have, however, taken pains to ascertain where our prisoners were confined so as to direct the fire to other parts.

### August 5 (Friday)

Today, at about 6 A.M., Admiral Farragut took 18 ships, including four monitors, against the defenses of Mobile Bay. The fighting was fierce and deadly. At about 10 A.M., the white flag on the Confederate ships went up and the battle was over.

Ransom, John, QM Sgt., 9th Michigan Cavalry, Andersonville Prison, Ga.:

Severe storm. Could die in two hours if I wanted to, but don't.

Abbott, A.O., 1st Lt., 1st N.Y. Dragoons, prisoner, Savannah, Ga.:

The 5th of August brought us the glorious intelligence of the defeat of Hood and the occupation of Atlanta by our forces. It seemed too good to be true, yet we all hoped it might be.... When the news was confirmed, we felt glorious over it for several days.

### August 6 (Saturday)

In Georgia, Sherman was trying to cut the railroads south of Atlanta, finally outflanking the Confederate line, forcing it to fall back.

On the Potomac, Early's men were back in Virginia, south of the river, but things were due to change shortly. Sheridan was coming.

Malone, B.Y., Sgt., Co. H, 6th N.C. Infantry, CSA, prisoner, Point Lookout, Md.:

The 6th of the month there rose a thunder cloud early in the morning and raind very hard: there was whirlwind just out sid of the Prison on the point it blew the Comasary house and Shop down and seven other buildings it distroyed a good deal wounded four sentinels broak ones leg There was but littel wind inside of the Prison.

### August 8 (Monday)

After a severe bombardment the day before, at ten A.M. Col. Charles D. Anderson, CSA, surrendered the garrison of Ft. Gaines, in Mobile Harbor.

Abbott, A.O., 1st Lt., 1st N.Y. Dragoons, prisoner, Savannah, Ga.:

About this time there was considerable sickness, and the authorities concluded to fill up the open sink we had been using and make us a new one. For this purpose they sent in one day fourteen of their colored people, seven men and seven women, to do this work. They were all barefooted, ragged, and dirty, and to our Northern eyes the women looked sadly out of place. Among them was a boy so white, and his hair so straight, we had a dispute as to his being a slave, but, upon asking the guard, he told us he was owned there in the city. He could not have been one-sixteenth colored, and yet they told us he was a "*slave*"—a "nigger." As I turned away in disgust from the scene, I could but think of the *boasted* morality of the South. They affect great horror at the idea of negro equality; they are very much afraid of the North's embracing the doctrine of miscegenation, and yet they have the fruit of it right in their midst—not, not *that*, but the fruit of concubinage, practiced from year to year by those who claim to be first in society.

### August 9 (Tuesday)

On this date, the records show that 33,006 prisoners were lodged in the Confederate prison at Andersonville, Ga., the peak number for that facility.

### August 12 (Friday)

Ransom, John, QM Sgt., 9th Michigan Cavalry, Andersonville Prison, Ga.:

Warm. Warm. Warm. If I only had some shade to lay in, and a glass of lemonade.

### August 13 (Saturday)

At Berryville, Va., fighting broke out between Sheridan's Federals and Early's Rebel forces as Sheridan moved up the Valley towards Cedar Creek.

Ransom, John, QM Sgt., 9th Michigan Cavalry, Andersonville Prison, Ga.:

A nice spring of cold water has broken out in camp, enough to furnish nearly all here with drinking water. God has not forgotten us. Battese brings it to me to drink.

## August 15 (Monday)

In the Valley, Sheridan withdrew from the area of Cedar Creek and headed back towards Winchester, giving up his advance until he could get his logistics worked out.

In Georgia, Sherman moved slowly to the southeast below Atlanta and its railroads. Joe Wheeler's Confederate cavalry raided the supply line on the railroads in Tennessee, sending prisoners to Andersonville and Macon.

Abbott, A.O., 1st Lt., 1st N.Y. Dragoons, prisoner, Savannah, Ga.:

Day after day passed, long, wearisome, tedious, bringing us little news, and no prospect of exhange. Sherman had indeed taken Atlanta; Stoneman had made his "*raid*," and had been captured, and Grant was thundering before Richmond and Petersburg. Our prison life grew more and more intolerable from day to day, and yet there was no prospect of anything better in store for us at present, and we could only "while the hours away" in sleep, play, or harrowing thoughts of our situation. *Oh, this turning the mind loose on itself* is what makes prison life so terrible. Could the mind be kept active; had we had books, papers, or had we known what was going on outside of us, we would not have suffered as much as we did. "Oh for a change," said many, and soon it came.

## August 17 (Wednesday)

The Acting Consul of Prussia at Charleston, S.C., requested that several hundred foreigners desired to leave the State of Georgia, and indeed the Confederate States of America, because the Governor of Georgia was making them eligible to be drafted into the State Militia. Maj. Gen. J.G. Foster, at Hilton Head, S.C., referred the problem to Washington for decision.

Lt. Col. Stewart L. Woodford, 127th N.Y. Volunteers, had been selected by Maj. Gen. J.G. Foster to travel to the prisoner exchange point and become acquainted with the process preparatory to becoming the exchange agent. Several positive actions, and reactions, were reported by Col. Woodford:

It was agreed between Maj. Lay and myself that all surgeons and chaplains who might be captured by either army in this department should be released as

soon as their profession should be ascertained....

... I asked Maj. Lay what authority he had in regard to the future exchange of prisoners, and he replied that he was empowered to exchange, man for man and rank for rank, as many prisoners of war as we would deliver to him in this department....

... I am fully satisfied that an exchange of our officers now confined at Charleston, Savannah, and Macon can be effected, as also of many of our soldiers who are confined and suffering at Andersonville, Ga. The privates received by me yesterday unite in describing the condition of their late comrades at Andersonville as being pitiful in the extreme. They state that they are but half fed, that they are naked, suffering, sick and dying. They beg the Government to at least exchange as many of their number as possible, and thus save them from further agony. In their prayer I respectfully concur.

Ransom, John, QM Sgt., 9th Michigan Cavalry, Andersonville Prison, Ga.:

Hanging on yet. A good many more than two hundred and twenty-five die now in twenty-four hours. Messes that have stopped near us are all dead.

Lt. Col. S. Eastman, commander at Elmira, N.Y., wrote Col. Wm. Hoffman in Washington about the pond at Elmira:

Report to you that the pond inside of the prisoners' camp at Barracks, No. 3, has become very offensive, and may occasion sickness unless the evil is remedied very shortly. The only remedy for this is to dig a ditch from the pond to the river so that the water will run freely through it. I have given orders to have a survey made. The ditch will have to be about one mile in length. The only objection to this is that a freshet might do some damage to the land through which the ditch will run, and the owners would call upon the United States for that. They have, however, no objection to having the ditch dug. I respectfully request that you will give instructions in regard to this with as little delay as possible, for if this work is to be done, it should be done immediately.... The sinks are removed from the pond, and large vaults have been dug in place of them.

Lt. Col. Eastman's letter had an attachment in the form of a letter to him (Eastman) from his camp surgeon, E.F. Sanger:

I carefully examined the pond inside the enclosure of Barracks No. 3, and the sources of the disgusting odors therein. The trouble does not seem to arise altogether from the decayed matter which has been thrown in, but from the daily accumulation. The drainage of the camp is into this pond or pool of standing water, and one large sink used by the prisoners stands directly over the pond which receives its fecal matter hourly. The new sinks will be completed in a day or two, when one of the sources of miasma will be removed, but this does not remedy another very important cause. Seven thousand men will pass 2600 gallons of urine daily, which is highly loaded with nitrogenous material. A portion is absorbed by the earth, still a large amount decomposes on the top of the earth or runs into the pond to purify. Again, without constant care and watching, more or less of the garbage or its washing finds its way into the pond....

I see no remedy which will effectually remove the odor or improve the sanitary condition of the prisoners than passing a current of water through the pond to carry off all the effects.

### August 20 (Saturday)

Sheridan and Early were doing a "Virginia reel" in the Valley, skirmishing around Berryville, Opequon Creek, and other points. At Petersburg, Warren and the Fifth Corps still held the Weldon Railroad south of the city.

Ransom, John, QM Sgt., 9th Michigan Cavalry, Andersonville Prison, Ga.:

Some say three hundred now die each day. No more new men coming. Reported that Wirtz is dead.

Benson, P.H., prisoner, Hilton Head, S.C.:

Of the party removed from the island [Johnson's] with me, numbering about six hundred, we were taken to Point Lookout, Md., for the ostensible purpose of exchange, as there was a great clamor at that time in the North to exchange the prisoners, and a small batch were sent through on exchange. The other two-thirds, on our arrival at the [City] Point, were placed in the hospital building, and had very comfortable quarters. We were fed at mess hall on convalescents' rations, though but few of us were or had been sick. However, we did very well on the food. We were kept in the building until hostilities between Lee and Grant began, when we were moved out and placed in tents to make room for the wounded.

We remained in tents until warm weather, and were sent to Ft. Delaware, and there I remained until about August 20, 1864, when about six hundred of us were taken on a steamer to Morris Island, S.C., off the bar of Charleston Harbor. After being on the vessel twenty-seven days, we were landed on the island and put in a stockade of about an acre in extent, on a direct line between our Ft. Moultrie and Ft. Anderson, occupied by the Federals, so the shells fired from one at the other passed directly over our heads unless they fell short, and seventeen of them fell short, but none of us were hurt by them. We were kept in this place for forty days. Our rations were prepared by the Yankees, and given in tin cups. We received twice a day one-half pint of mush well seasoned with worms, and about two ounces of bacon. One of our party, being of an inquiring turn of mind, counted the worms in his half pint of mush. He said he got seventy-two, and seeing that he was losing too much of his grub, quit and ate the balance. I never doubted his figures.

After forty days, we were loaded on two schooners, and towed to Ft. Pulaski, Ga., and placed in the casements of the fort, and were kept there until a few days after the presidential election in 1864. Then were sent to Hilton Head, S.C. I was of this party.

Upon arrival there we were put in two buildings arranged after the manner of a livery stable, with stalls on either side of the building, dignified as "cells." In each were two bunks, one above the other, accommodating four occupants. There was a table running the entire length of the building in the center, with benches on either side. We were told by our captors that the Confederates were starving the prisoners at Andersonville, and that we were to receive the same treatment in retaliation. Our rations were then issued, each man drawing ten days' rations at one time. When divided into ten parts it consisted of about ten ounces of cornmeal, fully one-half of which could crawl, four ounces of flour, three cucumber pickles, and a tablespoonful of salt. Those who were able to live on this diet were kept on it forty days. About twenty-five percent died, and another twenty-five percent were crippled from black scurvy, and after the forty days were out they added to our rations four ounces of pork and four ounces of Irish potatoes, and we lived on this twenty-seven days.

It was then decided to exchange us, and we were sent to Charleston.

On boarding the vessel we found our Ft. Pulaski comrades, whom we learned had gone through just what we had. Before leaving Hiltonhead news came that Charleston had been captured. We were then ordered to City Point for exchange, and when we arrived at Fortress Monroe it was learned that Richmond was also captured, so we were sent to Ft. Delaware, where we remained until the end. I left prison June 15, 1865, got transportation home, and in six days was with my family, from whom I had heard nothing for twelve months.

## August 21 (Sunday)

The surgeon at Elmira, N.Y., notified Col. Wm. Hoffman, Federal Commissary-General of Prisoners, that scurvy was now prevalent among the prisoners. Anti-scorbutics and fresh vegetables were ordered for the prisoners.

Also at Elmira, Lt. Col. S. Eastman, commanding, wrote Col. Wm. Hoffman concerning the stagnant pond of water inside the enclosure of the camp:

…forward you a copy of the survey made for the purpose of digging a ditch to let in water from the Chemung River to the pond inside the prisoners' camp. The only survey necessary to be made was to ascertain the elevation of the river above the pond and the depth that the ditch should be dug.

The length of the ditch would be 5960 feet, the average depth about 6 feet, though for a short distance it will be 7 feet. The soil is very light and easily dug. It will run through four farms, and two of the owners will not consent to have the work done for the reason, they say, that the next freshet will ruin all their land lying between the ditch and river. Probably it would change the course of the river and make islands of these lands, which are very valuable. Should heavy rains come on shortly this work would not be required, for the springs would then be full, as well as the river, and sufficient water would flow through the pond to keep it pure and sweet. The effusive smell of the pond has been occasioned more from the sinks than the drought. These sinks have all been removed and large, deep vaults have been dug which do not communicate with the pond excepting the little that sinks through the soil. This pond can be drained, or

nearly so, by digging a small ditch to the river below it, but the surgeon is of the opinion that this would not answer. To let water into this camp from the city waterworks would be expensive and of no use at this season, for, owing to the want of rain, these waterworks cannot supply the inhabitants with water.

The length of pipe to be laid to bring the water to the prisoners' camp will be about one mile and the cost about $5000. The camp is now well supplied with excellent well water for cooking and drinking and the river supplies for washing and bathing. There are seven wells completed and a pump in each. Two more are to be made. These wells require to be dug only from 15 to 22 feet in depth.

An abrupt halt to prisoner exchanges in the Hilton Head area came today when Lt. Gen. Ulysses S. Grant, Commander of all Union Armies, wired Secy. of War Edwin Stanton from City Point, Va.:

Please inform Maj. Gen. J.G. Foster that in no circumstances will he be authorized to make exchange of prisoners of war. Exchanges simply re-enforce the enemy at once, whilst we do not get the benefit of those received for two or three months, and lose the majority entirely. I telegraph this from just hearing that some 500 or 600 more prisoners had been sent to Maj. Gen. Foster.

## August 22 (Monday)

Secy. of War Edwin Stanton today approved the entry of aliens fleeing the draft in Georgia through Federal lines as requested on August 17. The Acting Consul of Prussia was so notified.

There seemed to be a problem with camp followers and others of the like around the camps on Hilton Head, S.C. The problem became so bad that General Order No. 122 was issued this date that directed:

The number of idle persons, of both sexes, found loitering around the camps and posts of the Districts of Beaufort and Hilton Head is subversive of good order and military discipline, and is a fruitful source of vice and disease.

The provost-marshals of these districts are therefore directed to arrest all such persons, either white or black, within the military lines of their respective districts, and to place them on police, sanitary, or such other duty as the commanding officer of the district may direct. The provost-marshals will also report all colored persons arrested under this order to the superintendent of contrabands, and will hold them subject to his orders.

It would appear that the dens of iniquity were going to be out of business, at least temporarily.

### August 23 (Tuesday)

Ft. Morgan, the last bastion at Mobile Bay, surrendered today after two weeks of heavy naval bombardment.

The location of the camp for the 600 prisoners coming in from the Northern prison camps was being finalized at Hilton Head, S.C. Maj. Gen. J.G. Foster wanted the camp to be between Ft. Strong and Battery Putnam. However, if this was not a suitable location, it could be placed anywhere, so long as it would not be in immediate danger of attack and could be defended easily.

### August 24 (Wednesday)

On this date, Maj. John H. Gee, CSA, was assigned as the commandant of the Confederate Prison at Salisbury, N.C. A medical professional, he administered to the Union prisoners' physical needs as well as controlling their movements. Although the prison had been designed for only 2500 prisoners, by November it would contain in excess of 9000 and would be plagued by many problems. One major problem was the "chain of command" at the prison. Gee was not the ranking officer among the Confederates at the prison, and those who outranked him often refused to obey his directives, being jealous of their prerogatives. The result was chaos. This problem was eventually brought to the attention of Brig. Gen. John H. Winder, Commissary-General of Prisoners, who held an inspection of the facility in December 1864, resulting in the appointment of Brig. Gen. Bradley Johnson as commandant. This problem, of course, did nothing to alleviate the problems and sufferings of the Union prisoners.

Ransom, John, QM Sgt., 9th Michigan Cavalry, Andersonville Prison, Ga.:

Had some soup. Not particularly worse, but Rowe is, and Sanders also.

### August 25 (Thursday)

In the Valley, Sheridan remained inside his fortifications at Halltown, while Early reentered Maryland at Williamsport.

In Georgia, Sherman sent his blue columns to cut off the area south and east along the south side of Atlanta towards Jonesborough, intending to isolate Atlanta completely.

At Hilton Head, S.C., Maj. Gen. J.G. Foster had inquired of Maj. Gen. Samuel Jones, commanding the Confederate force at Charleston, if medical and other supplies, such as clothing, food, etc., could be sent to the Union prisoners at Andersonville, Ga. This request was responded to on this date by Gen. Jones:

General: I received your letter of the 21st instant yesterday. The U.S. soldiers, prisoners of war at Andersonville, Ga., are in no way whatever under my control, and I therefore cannot undertake to deliver to them the sanitary stores you desire to send without the sanction of the officer having charge of the prisoners. I have referred the matter to him, and feel quite sure that he will not hesitate to allow the stores to be sent to them. I cannot permit any prisoner to take charge of the stores and act as quartermaster to distribute them, but if the officer having charge of the prisoners will permit them to be delivered I will designate an officer to receive and receipt to the proper officer of your command for them, and hold him to as strict accountability for their proper delivery as though they were stores belonging to my Government.

I will communicate with you further on this subject when I receive a reply from the office to whom I have referred your request.

Gen. Jones was at least cooperative in the endeavor. Everyone was trying his best to solve the problem, snarled in red tape.

John Ransom's brother, George W. Ransom, was stationed with the Union forces on Hilton Head, south of Charleston, S.C. Not quite believing the reports of John's death, George wrote a series of letters, one about every two weeks, to John and directed them to the prisoner-of-war mail drop. Today, John received one of his brother's letters.

Ransom, John, QM Sgt., 9th Michigan Cavalry, Andersonville Prison, Ga.:

In my exuberance of joy must write a few lines. Received a letter from my brother, George W. Ransom, from Hilton Head. Contained only a few words.

## August 26 (Friday)

Surgeon E.F. Sanger at Elmira, N.Y., reported to the Assistant Adjutant-General on the health of the prisoners.

I examined in person the prisoners at the barracks, 9300 in number, and found 793 cases of scurvy. I observed that the prisoners more recently from Point Lookout were more exempt from scurvy than the old ones. We may account for this either from the fact that our recent captures were from home guards, unaccustomed to the exposure and privations of a soldier's life, or from better diet at Point Lookout. I am inclined to believe it is partly from both. The prisoners at this station have prisoner's rations, with the addition of two rations per week of mixed vegetables. Scurvy has been on the increase. It would seem, therefore, that an increase in quantity and variety of antiscorbutics was called for to improve the standard of health and prevent an increase of scurvy. The scurvy existing does not arise from any sanitary neglect, if we except the sinks, which cannot be remedied without authority from Washington. I find it will be impossible to furnish antiscorbutics from the hospital fund for so large a number. It would require $300 per month for a single ration of potatoes daily for the scurvy cases. Our fund amounts to about $500 and we are drawing upon it largely at present to feed hospital patients. Without change of diet we may reasonably expect an increase of scurvy. I would therefore suggest an extra issue of one ration per week of potatoes, cabbage, or onions to the prisoners for the present, and a daily issue to the scurvy cases. As soon as our straw comes we shall have accommodations for 400 patients in hospital.

Ransom, John, QM Sgt., 9th Michigan Cavalry, Andersonville Prison, Ga.:

Still am writing. The letter from my brother had done good and cheered me up. Eyesight very poor and writing tires me. Battese sticks by; such disinterested friendship is rare. Prison at its worst.

Maj. Gen. J.G. Foster, commanding the Dept. of the South, wrote Rear-Admiral J.A. Dahlgren, commanding South Atlantic Blockading Squadron:

600 Rebel officers arrived here yesterday for the purpose of being placed under fire on Morris Island. I propose to take them up tomorrow morning between daylight and 10 o'clock. As the steamer on which they are confined is very much crowded I would respectfully request that you send one of your fleet with prison ship as a convoy.

## August 27 (Saturday)

One of the major problems confronting prisoner exchange between North and South was the status of the Negro who had enlisted in the Union army. The South still considered such personnel slaves, the North considered them soldiers. Much publicity was given by the South on what they considered the North's refusal to exchange prisoners, blaming the Union for much of the suffering caused by such delays. Maj. Gen. Benjamin F. Butler, from Bermuda Hundred, wrote the Hon. Robert Ould, Confederate Commissioner for Exchange:

Sir: Your note to Maj. Mulford, assistant agent of exchange, under date of 10th of August, has been referred to me.

You therein state that Maj. Mulford has several times proposed to exchange prisoners respectively held by the two belligerents, officer for officer, and man for man, and that "the offer has also been made by other officials having charge of matters connected with the exchange of prisoners," and that "this proposal has been heretofore declined by the Confederate authorities;" that you now consent to the above proposition, and agree to deliver to you (Maj. Mulford) the prisoners held in captivity by the Confederate authorities, provided you agree to deliver an equal number of officers and men. As equal numbers are delivered from time to time they will be declared exchanged. This proposal is made with the understanding that the officers and men on both sides who have been longest in captivity will be first delivered, where it is practicable.

*From a slight ambiguity in your phraseology, but more, perhaps, from the antecedent action of your authorities, and because of your acceptance of it, I am in doubt whether you have stated the proposition with entire accuracy.*

It is true, a proposition was made both by Maj. Mulford and myself, as agent of exchange, to exchange all prisoners of war taken by either belligerent party.... *It was made by me as early as the first of the winter of 1863–64, and has not been accepted.* In May last I forwarded to you a note desiring to know whether the Confederate authorities intended to treat colored soldiers of the U.S. Army as prisoners of war. To that inquiry no answer has yet been made. *To avoid all possible misapprehension or mistake hereafter as to your offer now, will you say now whether you mean by "prisoners held in captivity" colored men, duly enrolled and mustered into the service of the United States, who have been captured by the Confederate forces, and if your authorities are willing to exchange all soldiers so mustered into the U.S. Army, whether colored or otherwise, and the officers commanding them, man for man, officer for officer?*

At an interview which was held between yourself and the agent of exchange on the part of the United States, at Ft. Monroe, in March last, *you will do me the favor to remember the principal discussion turned upon this very point, you, on behalf of the Confederate Government, claiming the right to hold all negroes who had heretofore been slaves and not emancipated by their masters, enrolled and mustered into the service of the United States, when captured by your forces, not as prisoners of war, but, upon capture, to be turned over to their supposed masters or claimants, whoever they might be, to be held by them as slaves.*

By the advertisements in your newspapers, calling upon masters to come forward and claim these men so captured, I suppose that your authorities still adhere to that claim... and the officers in command of such soldiers, in the language of a supposed act of the Confederate States, are to be turned over to the Governors of States, upon requisitions, for the purpose of being punished by the laws of such States for acts done in war in the armies of the United States....

I am reciting these public acts from memory, and will be pardoned for not giving the exact words, although I believe I do not vary the substance and effect. These declarations on the part of those whom you represent yet remain unrepealed, unannulled, unrevoked, and must therefore be still supposed to be authoritative. By your acceptance of our proposition, is the Government of the United States to understand that these several claims, enactments, and proclaimed declarations are to be given up, set aside, revoked, and held for naught by the Confederate authorities, and that you are ready and willing to exchange, man for man, those colored soldiers of the United States, duly mustered and enrolled as such, who have heretofore been claimed as slaves by the Confederate States, as well as white soldiers?...

I unite with you most cordially, sir, in desiring a speedy settlement of all these questions, in view of the great suffering endured by our prisoners in the hands of your authorities, of which you so feelingly speak. Let me ask, in view of that suffering, why you have delayed eight months to answer a proposition which, by now accepting, you admit to be right, just, and humane, allowing that suffering to continue so long? One cannot help thinking, even at the risk of being deemed uncharitable, that the benevolent sympathies of the Confederate authorities have been lately stirred by the depleted condition of their armies, and a desire to get into the field, to affect the present campaign, the hale, hearty, and well-fed prisoners held by the United States, in exchange for the half-starved, sick, emaciated, and unserviceable soldiers of the United States now languishing in your prisons. The events of this war, if we did not know it before, have taught us that it is not the Northern portion of the American people alone who know how to drive sharp bargains.

The wrongs, indignities, and privations suffered by our soldiers would move me to consent to anything to procure their exchange, except to barter away the honor and faith of the Government of the United States, which has been so solemnly pledged to the colored soldiers in its ranks.

Consistently with national faith and justice we cannot relinquish this position. With your authorities it is a question of property merely. It seems to address itself to you in this form: Will you suffer your soldier, captured in fighting your battles, to be in confinement for months rather than release him by giving for him that which you call a piece of property, and which we are willing to accept as a man?

*You certainly appear to place less value upon your soldier than you do upon your negro.* I assure you, much as we of the North are accused of loving property, our citizens would have no difficulty in yielding up any piece of property they have in exchange for one of their brothers or sons languishing in your prisons. [italics added]

Ransom, John, QM Sgt., 9th Michigan Cavalry, Andersonville Prison, Ga.:

Have now written nearly through three large books, and still at it. The diary am confident will reach my people if I don't. There are many here who are interested and will see that it goes North.

### August 28 (Sunday)

In Georgia, Maj. Gen. George Thomas's Army of the Cumberland reached the Atlanta and West Point Railroad at Red Oak, where some heavy fighting occurred. Otis O. Howard's Army of the Tennessee was on the same railroad near Fairburn, and Schofield's Army of the Ohio was at nearby Mount Gilead Church. Slocum's Twentieth Corps manned the Union lines immediately around Atlanta. The city was almost sealed off.

In the Shenandoah Valley, Sheridan came out of his fortifications at Halltown, and advanced towards Charles Town, W.Va.

The prison for Confederate prisoners at Elmira, N.Y., which opened only last month already had over 10,000 inmates, and this did not count the guard and other administrative staff. The planning for the coming winter is under consideration, as is the solving of the problem of feeding this large number of prisoners. Lt. Col. S. Eastman, commanding the prison at Elmira, today reported to Col. William Hoffman, Federal Commissary-General of Prisoners, that:

…the mess room and kitchen for prisoners of war at this depot is too small to accommodate 10,000 men. The present mess room will seat from 1600 to 1800, and it requires from two to three hours to feed 10,000. By erecting another mess room and kitchen to accommodate from 1000 to 1200 they can be fed in half that time. A mess room should also be made for the hospital. The surgeon has applied for it. There is a kitchen attached to the hospital, and will be ready for use as soon as the stoves are put in, which will be done in two or three days. Three wards for the sick have been completed, and a washhouse. Three more wards are being built as fast as lumber can be obtained. When they are all up they will be insufficient for the number of sick now on the sick list.

I have also turned over to the surgeon in charge

four barracks for hospital purposes. I would also request to be informed if any arrangement is to be made for winter quarters for the prisoners of war, and the troops now guarding them, who are in tents. If so, it should be commenced immediately, owing to the difficulty of obtaining lumber at this point. If temporary barracks are not to be erected I should recommend that Sibley tents be supplied in lieu of the common tent now used.

An inspection of Elmira prison by Capt. B. Munger, aside from Col. Eastman's comments, showed other problems:

To report the police of this camp good; quarters good, with the exception of wards 24 to 30 inclusive. Ward 32 is overcrowded and the building unfit for quarters; guardhouse, good; mess house, filthy; hospitals, very good. The two wards, Nos. 2 and 4, which were cleaned for patients on Tuesday last are not occupied for want of straw.

The administration of the various prisons and their inspection on a regular basis was a major command problem, North and South. The North had the advantage in this in that more manpower was available, transportation was better to get around to the prisons, and facilities were better built and maintained.

Today, 1st Lt. J.W. Davidson, described by his colonel as "a very energetic and efficient officer," submitted his inspection report of the prison at Camp Morton, Indianapolis, Ind.:

The quarters occupied by the prisoners are and have been kept in as good condition as quarters built as they are can be kept, but it is impossible to keep them in a perfect state of cleanliness for the reason that they are built low and on the ground, making a ground floor, which, by being constantly in use as they are by the filthiest set of men in the world, becomes perfectly saturated with saliva and other nuisance that is constantly being committed, and is damp all the time, especially in wet weather; and there being no undercurrent ventilation, there is an offensive odor constantly arising from the floor, which must eventually, from constantly inhaling it, cause more or less sickness; and to remedy this, the buildings should be raised at least two feet from the ground and good substantial floors put in them. They can then be thoroughly cleansed by washing the floor every day, if necessary, and the ventilation from beneath will be perfected and drive all foul air from the building; and another benefit derived will be the preventing of the prisoners from escaping by tunneling, which they are continually trying to do.

The kitchens are in good condition and are kept clean. The prisoners get their rations cooked in good order from the kitchens in messes of from ten to twenty men each. The grounds have been undergoing a thorough policing every day; ditches are being renewed and deepened, making the drainage as perfect as the locality of the camp will permit. The enlargement of the grounds is progressing as rapidly as possible and will soon be completed. The sinks that have just been adopted have not been in use long enough to determine their success, but in my opinion they will not be as efficient as the large sink which has been in use for the last two months by all the men in camp except those in the hospital, and the camp is now clearer of nuisance and stench than it has ever been, and the sanitary condition of the whole camp is being improved generally.

The bedding and general condition of the prisoners will require to make them comfortable for the coming winter as follows: 530 woolen blankets, 835 pairs of trousers, 1250 pair of shoes, 850 shirts, 350 coats. The majority of the prisoners confined in this camp are of the poorer class of the inhabitants of the Confederacy, and cannot obtain the means for supplying themselves with the necessary clothing and bedding to keep them from suffering. The rations that are being furnished daily to the prisoners in this camp by the commissary of subsistence at this post are in compliance with the circular issued by the Commissary-General of Prisoners June 1, 1864. The rations of soap, I have found, is not more than is required, owing to the water that has to be used for washing being of such a nature as to require a large quantity to enable them to keep themselves and their clothing clean.

The hospitals under charge of Surg. Charles J. Kipp, U.S. Army, are kept in as good condition as they can be, but unless more buildings are built for hospital purposes soon, new tents will have to be drawn to replace the old ones that are now in use, for I find they will soon be unfit for that purpose as many of them will not turn the rain at present.

## August 29 (Monday)

White, H.S., Chaplain, R.I. Regt. Heavy Artillery, prisoner of war, Savannah, Ga.:

I spent nearly a month in the stockade at Savannah. From time to time we held service. Sometimes we had preaching, and sometimes social meetings. In every place I tried to obtain a Bible; I could get none. I wrote letters to the Methodist preachers wherever I was, inviting them to call, or at least, send me a Bible. No one ever called, and I got no Bible. At one time, in answer to my request, I received a few papers and tracts published by the Church South. They were bitter and hard on the North. Many of the most earnest and bitter were Southern Methodists....

The rebels put up a small building for a kind of sutler's shop, and to put rations in, as they were brought into the stockade. The work was done by negro carpenters.... The sink for the prison was a trench dug across one end of the yard; but becoming so loathsome, other arrangements were eventually made. The slaves were sent to fill in the old trench. The most of the number were women and girls. The overseer seemed to have no shame about sending women to perform such a task. Most of the slaves were partly white. Their arms were naked and their lower limbs partly exposed. They seemed to be healthy and happy....

One afternoon it was announced in prison that the chaplains and surgeons would go next morning to be exchanged. We were much elated.... The next morning at half past three we were all ready to go. No call was made for us.

## August 30 (Tuesday)

The West Point-Atlanta rail link fell into Union hands when Sherman's bluecoats occupied the line and continued their advance towards Jonesborough. That left only the Atlanta-Macon rail link. Hood, in a vain attempt to stop Sherman, sent Gen. Hardee with two corps, his led by Pat Cleburne, and Hood's now commanded by S.D. Lee, to head Sherman off. Even with Sherman's armies separated, the combined strength of Cleburne and Lee could not successfully assail Howard's Army of the Tennessee.

White, H.S., Chaplain, R.I. Regt. Heavy Artillery, prisoner of war, Charleston, S.C.:

Next morning we were sent from Savannah.... Our party consisted of nine, two chaplains and seven surgeons. We expected to meet a party from Charleston, and with them go through the lines to Hilton Head. On we went to Charleston, and hope began to droop. In the car was a Confederate soldier, a kind-looking old man, sitting just behind me. At one time I looked around, and he was eating his lunch. He had a roasted sweet potato. He gave me a piece, and also a bit of bread and meat. It would be useless to attempt to tell how that potato tasted. It was not much the lack of quantity, as it was the *kind* of food.

Not far from noon, we entered Charleston. The cars stopped out of town and we were marched in. A few negroes sat with a few vegetables to sell by the sides of the streets. The negroes looked kindly upon us. The Irish and German women seemed to pity us. The Southern women made us feel like throwing brickbats. The stores were mostly closed. The grass was rank, and a few cows were feeding. Here and there we saw a pig....

We were sent to a house on Broad Street used for the noncombatants' prison. We passed the Work House and Roper Hospital, Marine Hospital, and Jail in which the officers were confined under fire. Just as we were passing, a fine shell exploded in the air, just above our heads. We were put in a building perhaps one hundred rods off from the Roper Hospital. We had plenty of room and a chance to bathe in the bathhouse near our quarters. Here we got flour and fresh beef. Obtaining money, we secured some sweet potatoes and tomatoes. We purchased some rice. The ever-present and ever-kind negro again helped us, and we lived in some little comfort.

The city looked a ruin. No men were to be seen, save here and there an old man. Negroes were passing to and fro to their work on the fortifications. Soldiers in small numbers could be seen, and a few officers were gallanting with the ladies. They used to come and gaze, as children go to Barnum's.

Perhaps the deep interest connected with our stay at Charleston arose from our being placed under fire.

## August 31 (Wednesday)

Around Atlanta, Schofield's Army of the Ohio cut the last rail link to Atlanta when the Macon-Atlanta line was crossed between Jonesborough and Atlanta.

Hood sent Hardee to attack Otis O. Howard's Army of the Tennessee near Jonesborough. The Confederate attack was not pressed vigorously, and it failed, the Southern losses heavy. With most of the Confederates south of the city trying to keep the rail lines open, Sherman told Slocum to try and enter the city, if possible. Prisoners from the Confederate army were being sent back to Chattanooga and then to Indiana and Illinois for incarceration.

Capt. Henry Wirz, commander of Camp Sumter (Andersonville) prison camp, reported that during the month of August, 1864, the prison had:

Begun the month with 29,985 prisoners in the camp, with an additional 1693 in the hospital.

Beginning total, 31,367 prisoners.

During the month, 3078 prisoners were received, and 4 escapees were recaptured.

A total of 2993 died during the month, an average of more than 96 per day.

Thirty escaped during the month.

Twenty-three were sent off to various places, and 21 were exchanged.

August ended with a total of 29,473 prisoners in camp and 2220 in the prison hospital.

Grand total of prisoners, 31,693.

Records indicate that over 33,000 prisoners were present on August 9—the peak for the Andersonville prison. John Ransom entered in his diary that the death rate was much higher than that reported by Wirz for the month—August 3, 220; August 17, 225; August 20, 300. A wide variance from the average of 96 per day as reported by Wirz.

## September 1 (Thursday)

Atlanta was evacuated and the munitions dumps and railroad yards were blown up by Hood's retreating Confederates. Fires broke out in the area of the explosions and little was done to extinguish them in the surrounding area. Hood had failed gloriously in his task of holding one of the south's most important rail terminals.

Confederate Gen. S.D. Lee's corps started back towards Atlanta and was held up at Rough and Ready by Hood. Hardee's corps took on Howard's army and elements from both Thomas's army and Schofield's Army of the Ohio, not an easy task.

The Battle of Jonesborough started about noon and within a reasonably short period of time the Federals had shattered two Rebel brigades, even though other Confederates held their ground. At dark Hardee pulled back to Lovejoy's Station to join with Hood and the remainder of the Army of Tennessee. At the end of the second day, the Confederate army was mauled, and the prison pens were full of Confederates.

Ransom, John, QM Sgt., 9th Michigan Cavalry, Andersonville Prison, Ga.:

Sanders taken outside to butcher cattle. Is sick but goes all the same. Mike sick and no longer a policeman. Still rumors of exchange.

### September 2 (Friday)

From Atlanta, Sherman wired President Lincoln: "Atlanta is ours, and fairly won!" Lincoln could have received no better present at this time. It confirmed his faith in his commanders and showed the doubters in the North that the war could be won.

Southeast of Atlanta, Hood was regrouping around Lovejoy's Station with the tattered remains of the Army of Tennessee, and Maj. Gen. Slocum's corps entered the city.

There was skirmishing at Darkesville and Bunker Hill in the Valley. Lee, feeling the shortage of troops at Petersburg, pressured Jubal Early to return the troops loaned from the Army of Northern Virginia.

Malone, B.Y., Sgt., Co. H, 6th N.C. Infantry, CSA, prisoner, Point Lookout, Md.:

The 2d day this is and our Rations gets no better we get half a loaf of Bread a day a smal slice of Pork or Beef or Sault Beef for Breakfast for Dinner a cup of Been Soup and Supper we get none. Mr. A. Morgan of South Carolina has a vacon Cook House which he has bin teaching School in evry Sience last Spring he is a Christian man he preaches evry Sunday and has prayers evry morning befoaur School we have a Preacher to evry Division in the Camp Mr. Carrol preaches to our Divi which is the 8th.

### September 3 (Saturday)

Sherman, in Atlanta, began planning for the next step. Hood, at Lovejoy's Station, southeast of the city, regrouped, pulling the scattered remnants of units together.

Sheridan was moving up the Valley Pike with his now-enlarged army. Early, in response to Lee's direction, detached Kershaw's division from his army to send it back to Petersburg. However, en route, Kershaw's division accidentally ran into a corps of Sheridan's army, which caused Early to rethink his decision about sending Kershaw back to Lee.

Ransom, John, QM Sgt., 9th Michigan Cavalry, Andersonville Prison, Ga.:

Trade of my rations for some little luxury and manage to get up quite a soup. LATER—Sanders sent in to us a quite large piece of fresh beef and a little salt; another Godsend.

### September 4 (Sunday)

In Greeneville, Tenn., Federal cavalry surprised Gen. John H. Morgan's command headquarters, capturing most of the staff and killing Morgan. Much celebrating was done in eastern Tennessee when the news was spread. Many a Federal commander in Kentucky and Tennessee breathed easier with the "raider" gone.

### September 5 (Monday)

Ransom, John, QM Sgt., 9th Michigan Cavalry, Andersonville Prison, Ga.:

The nice spring of cold water still flows and furnishes drinking water for all; police guard it night and day so to be taken away only in small quantities. Three hundred said to be dying off each day.

Malone, B.Y., Sgt., Co. H, 6th N.C. Infantry, CSA, prisoner, Point Lookout, Md.:

This is the 5th day of the month and we are going to have Been Soup with onions in it today for dinner we will have Potatoes and Onions boath tomorrow the Dr had them sent in here for rebs to se if they would not stop Scirvy

### September 6 (Tuesday)

In a report to Maj. Gen. Halleck, Chief of Staff, in Washington, Maj. Gen. J.G. Foster, commanding at Hilton Head, S.C., indicated that the exchange of the surgeons and chaplains had been completed.

Maj. Gen. Samuel Jones, commanding the Confederate forces at Charleston, also returned two enlisted men who were tricked into being captured—Jones took a dim view of the trick. Jones had not, as of this date, replied to the request about sending sanitary supplies to the Union prisoners at Andersonville—this being because he had no reply from the officer in charge of that facility.

Ransom, John, QM Sgt., 9th Michigan Cavalry, Andersonville Prison, Ga.:

Hurrah! Hurrah! Hurrah! Can't holler except on paper. Good news. Seven detachments ordered to be ready to go at a moment's notice. LATER—*All who cannot walk must stay behind.* If left behind shall die in twenty-four hours. Battese says *I shall go.* LATER—Seven detachments are going out of the gate; all the sick are left behind. Ours is the tenth detachment and will go tomorrow so said. The greatest excitement; men wild with joy. Am worried fearful that I cannot go, but Battese says I shall.

Malone, B.Y., Sgt., Co. H, 6th N.C. Infantry, CSA, prisoner, Point Lookout, Md.:

My health is very good today which is the 6th of Sept. 64. But I cannot tell how long it will remain so. for it is raning and very coal today And I have not got eney Shoes

## September 7 (Wednesday)

In Atlanta, Sherman took a rather unpopular stand and ordered the evacuation of the city—everyone other than his army was to leave. This included some 1600 people comprising about 446 families who left, abandoning their possessions and homes in the city. The Mayor of Atlanta, Gen. Hood, and everyone else who could reach Sherman protested, to no avail. Sherman said he would have enough trouble feeding his own troops and would not feed the civilians.

Ransom, John, QM Sgt., 9th Michigan Cavalry, Andersonville Prison, Ga.:

Anxiously waiting the expected summons. Rebels say as soon as transportation comes, and so a car whistle is music to our ears. Hope is a good medicine and am sitting up and have been trying to stand up but

can't do it; legs too crooked and with every attempt get faint. Men laugh at the idea of my going, as the rebels are very particular not to let any sick go, still Battese says I am going. MOST DARK—Rebels say we go during the night when transportation comes. Battese grinned when this news came and can't get his face straightened out again.

## September 10 (Saturday)

Maj. Gen. Samuel Jones, commanding at Charleston, S.C., wrote Maj. Gen. J.G. Foster at Hilton Head concerning the prisoners on Morris Island:

General: I have reason to believe that a number of C.S. officers, prisoners of war, are at present confined in a stockade on Morris Island, between and very near Batteries Gregg and Wagner. I have respectfully to ask if such is the case, and, if so, what shelter is provided for them, and if they receive in all respects, save location, the treatment accorded to prisoners of war among civilized nations?

I make this inquiry because I believe you are retaliating on those officers for a supposed disregard of the usages of civilized warfare in the treatment extended to U.S. officers, prisoners of war, now in this city. Those officers are comfortably housed and receive the treatment due prisoners of war, and I will repeat what I have before had occasion to say to you, that I shall greatly deplore any necessity you may force on me to direct any change in their treatment. If by the 15th instant I receive no reply, I shall be justified in the conclusion that my supposition is correct and act accordingly.

White, H.S., Chaplain, R.I. Regt. Heavy Artillery, prisoner of war, Charleston, S.C.:

On Friday, June 10,... five generals, eleven colonels, twenty-five lieutenant colonels and nine majors ... were placed in the shell district at Charleston. The object was to compel our men not to shell the city. When our government was about to put a like number of their officers under fire, the rebels said, "Let us exchange them," and they did so.

On Wednesday, July 27, another order came, and six hundred went.... They went under fire. In a few days three or four hundred more were brought into the city, and early in September the six hundred at Savannah were added, making not far from sixteen hundred in all. The four buildings ... stand on four sides of a square; and if shells came into the city, they would stand a chance to strike here. Our forces soon learned the location, and aimed not to hit the buildings; but Charleston is not a large town, and the wind, or an unequal charge of powder, or a random aim in the night would send the shells in rather close proximity....

... I have seen hundreds of shells by night and by day thrown near us and explode just by or above us. One passed so near as to set a man whirling. Another tore the sleeve of an officer's coat. One passed down through the building and struck a table around which several were just going to eat some corn bread, and spoiled the ration. A man was taking his comfort on a bench, when a shell struck one end of it, and sent him sprawling. But from first to last not a drop of blood was drawn on a Union officer. They hit *other people*....

Sometime in September about six hundred rebel officers were put under fire on Morris Island. The enemy asked Gen. Foster to exchange them, but he would not. A few days before I left Charleston, the yellow fever broke out, and some cases were reported on the next street to our prison, and shortly after I was released, all the officers were removed to Columbia, S.C.

### September 12 (Monday)

The "Virginia reel" being played in the Shenandoah Valley by Sheridan and Early took a break, much to the dismay of both Lincoln and Grant. Sheridan didn't seem to be able to get things moving.

Abbott, A.O., 1st Lt., 1st N.Y. Dragoons, prisoner, Savannah, Ga.:

"Pack up and be ready to *move* tomorrow morning at five o'clock," was an order that came in to us Monday evening, September 12th....

The most of the night was spent in cooking our cornmeal and meat, and getting ready to go at the appointed hour.

### September 13 (Tuesday)

The wheels of the bureaucracy ground slowly—at times hardly moving—but they did grind. The prisoners at Andersonville would be allowed to receive the sanitary supplies offered by the U.S. Government. Maj. Gen. Samuel Jones, commanding at Charleston, designated Charleston harbor as the transfer point, as opposed to the Savannah River, as had been requested by the Union.

Abbott, A.O., 1st Lt., 1st N.Y. Dragoons, prisoner, Charleston, S.C.:

We left the yard at 5:15 A.M., the 13th instant, and were marched to the same place where we had left the cars two months before; and, after waiting three quarters of an hour, a train of freight cars was backed down to us, and we were ordered on board, forty being assigned to each car. These cars were old and filthy, and had been used for transporting coal, the bottoms of the cars being covered with about two inches of the dust. I asked one of the Rebel officers for a broom to sweep it out, when he replied, "The Confederacy were not able to furnish brooms to sweep cars for Yankee prisoners"; so into the dirt we had to go, and make the best of it....

It is one hundred and four miles from Savannah to Charleston. The railroad runs through a low, flat, marshy country, being built much of the way on trestlework from eight to twelve feet high. The only station of any importance is Pocotaligo, about midway between the two places, and within eleven miles of our lines. Had it been in the night when we passed it, many would have escaped by jumping from the train; but, as it was daylight, they were prevented.

As we neared the city, we could see some of the fortifications on the land side; yet they were empty, and, for the most part, without guns. In crossing the Cooper River, we could see Castle Pinckney in the distance, and, for the first time since we left Richmond, could hear the fire of our own guns. As we entered the city, about 2:30 P.M., the streets were fairly crowded by the negroes, with a slight mixture of the whites....

We left the train, and were marched a mile and a half up "Coming Street," beneath a boiling sun, to the city jail yard, the grand receptacle for all the Federal prisoners who arrive in Charleston. I think it was the nastiest, dirtiest, filthiest, lousiest place I ever was in. At the time we arrived, they had just removed several hundred of our enlisted men who had come from Andersonville. The ground was literally covered with *lice*. The next morning after my arrival there I killed over fifty on my shirt alone, and my case was not an isolated one.

The yard embraced about an acre. It is built of brick, and consists of two parts.... The wing is of an octagon shape, extending out towards the centre of the yard, having the same height as the other. A tower forty feet high rises from the centre of the octagon part, and in this they confined their worst criminals. While we were there, the negro soldiers of the 54th and 55th Massachusetts were confined there....

For quarters, about one third had no shelter at all. Those who had used "A" tents, pitched "flat on the ground."... We could get but little fresh air, for the walls were twelve feet high; and when we did, it was a whirling breeze, which raised the dirt and filth from the ground, at times almost suffocating us....

We were forty-eight hours there before we received anything to eat, and, when the rations *did* come in, we had neither wood nor utensils with which to cook...

## September 15 (Thursday)

Ransom, John, QM Sgt., 9th Michigan Cavalry, Marine Hospital, Savannah, Ga.:

A great change has taken place since I last wrote in my diary. Am in heaven now compared with the past. At about midnight, September 7th, our detachment was ordered outside at Andersonville, and Battese picked me up and carried me to the gate. The men were being let outside in ranks of four, and counted as they went out. They were very strict about letting none to go but the well ones, or those who could walk. The rebel adjutant stood upon a box by the gate, watching very close. Pitch pine knots were burning in the near vicinity to give light. As it came our turn to go Battese got me in the middle of the rank, stood me up as well as I could stand, and with himself on one side and Sergt. Rowe on the other began pushing our way through the gate. Could not help myself a particle, and was so faint that I hardly knew what was going on. As we were going through the gate the adjutant yells out: "Here, here! hold on there, that man can't go, hold on there!" and Battese crowding right along outside. The adjutant struck over the heads of the men and tried to stop us, but my noble Indian friend kept straight ahead, hallooing: "He all right, he well, he go!" And so I got outside, [the] adjutant having too

much to look after to follow me. After we were outside, I was carried to the railroad in the same coverlid which I fooled the rebel out of when captured, and which I presume has saved my life a dozen times. We were crowded very thick into boxcars. I was nearly dead, and hardly knew where we were or what was going on. We were two days in getting to Savannah. Arrived early in the morning. The railroads here run in the middle of very wide, handsome streets. We were unloaded, I should judge, near the middle of the city. The men as they were unloaded fell into line and were marched away. Battese got me out of the car, and laid me on the pavement. They then obliged him to go with the rest, leaving me; would not let him take me. I lay there until noon with four or five others, without any guard. Three or four times negro servants came to us from houses nearby, and gave us water, milk and food. With much difficulty I could set up, but was completely helpless. A little after noon a wagon came and *toted* us to a temporary hospital in the outskirts of the city, and near a prison pen they had just built for the well ones. Where I was taken it was merely an open piece of ground, having wall tents erected and a line of guards around it. I was put into a tent and lay on the coverlid. That night some gruel was given to me, and a nurse whom I had seen in Andersonville looked in, and my name was taken. The next morning, September 10th, I woke up and went to move my hands, and could not do it; could not move either limb so much as an inch. Could move my head with difficulty. Seemed to be paralyzed, but in no pain whatever. After a few hours a physician came to my tent, examined and gave me medicine, also left medicine, and one of the nurses fed me some soup or gruel. By night I could move my hands. Lay awake considerable through the night thinking. Was happy as a clam in high tide. Seemed so nice to be under a nice clean tent, and there was such a cool pure air. The surroundings were so much better that I thought now would be a good time to die, and I didn't care one way or the other. Next morning the doctor came, and with him Sergt. Winn. Sergt. Winn I had a little acquaintance with at Andersonville. Doctor said I was terribly reduced, but he thought I would improve. Told them to wash me. A nurse came and washed me, and Winn brought me a white cotton shirt, and an old but clean pair of pants; my old clothing, which was in rags, was taken away. Two or three times during the day I had gruel of some kind. I don't know what. Medicine was given me by the nurses. By night I could move my feet and legs a little. The cords in my feet and legs were contracted so, of course, that I couldn't straighten myself out. Kept thinking to myself, "Am I really away from that place Andersonville?" It seem[ed] too good to be true. On the morning of the 12th, ambulances moved all to the Marine Hospital, or rather an orchard in same yard with Marine Hospital, where thirty or forty nice new tents have been put up, with bunks about two feet from the ground, inside. Was put into a tent. By this time could move my arms considerable. We were given vinegar weakened with water, and also salt in it. Had medicine. My legs began to get moveable more each day, also my arms, and today I am laying on my stomach and writing in my diary. Mike Hoare is also in this hospital. One of my tentmates is a man named Land, who is a printer, same as myself. I hear that Wm. B. Rowe is here also, but haven't seen him.

Malone, B.Y., Sgt., Co. H, 6th N.C. Infantry, CSA, prisoner, Point Lookout, Md.:

The 15th of Sept was a beautyfull day And a general Stir among the Rebs the Dr. was getting up a load of Convalesant men to Send to Dixie. You could See men going to the Hospital to be examinond Some on Crushes and Some was not able to walk and would be Swinging a round others necks graging a long

They got a load of five hundred and Sent them out of the Prison we Surpose they will leave the 15th for Dixie...

Abbott, A.O., 1st Lt., 1st N.Y. Dragoons, prisoner, Charleston, S.C.:

After inflicting upon prisoners this kind of treatment several days, it was the custom of the Rebels to come in and offer *better* quarters to any who would take a parole not to escape or to hold communication with anyone outside of the guard in which they might be placed.

We learned that nearly all the officers who had preceded us to Charleston were thus paroled, and were quartered in the Marine and Roper Hospitals. I gladly availed myself of the opportunity of getting out of the jail yard, and was sent, with fifty others, to Roper Hospital....

After signing ... we were marched under guard

to Roper Hospital, where we found 300 of those who were sent on the first train from Macon. From them we learned that over 70 of the officers escaped on the way down, but the majority of them had been recaptured by *dogs* and *citizens*.

We were glad to meet our old friends, and they, in turn, greeted us warmly. The place seemed "a paradise," compared to the jail yard.

### September 16 (Friday)

At Charles Town, W.Va., Sheridan and Grant met to discuss the situation in the Valley. Sheridan had just learned that Kershaw's division and Crenshaw's artillery battalion had departed for Petersburg and Richmond, weakening the Confederate forces.

Abbott, A.O., 1st Lt., 1st N.Y. Dragoons, prisoner, Charleston, S.C.:

Roper Hospital was founded by the gentleman whose name it bears, who gave it a munificent donation.... It is built of brick, plastered over, and marked; thus giving it the appearance of brown stone. The main building is seventy-eight feet front by sixty feet deep, and four stories high.

On both sides, east and west, are wings, each one hundred feet long by fifty feet deep, and three stories high. On each corner is a tower rising fifteen or twenty feet above the roof, adding beauty as well as strength to the structure. In each wing and on each floor are three large rooms, nearly the size of the wings, which, I conclude, were the rooms containing the beds. The main part of the building has smaller rooms for the dispensary, offices, living rooms, etc. The whole was lighted by a very poor quality of gas, which we were permitted to use till nine o'clock in the evening.

The grounds around the building were quite pleasant, particularly the front yard. It was tastefully laid out, and filled with flowers and shrubbery; and as we were permitted the freedom of the yard, we enjoyed them very much. The backyard was filthy and unhealthy. It used to be policed every day, but they would neglect to carry out the filth, leaving it lying in piles for two or three days at a time, till the very atmosphere became impregnated with the poisonous vapors. But the greatest nuisance was the sink. They allowed the vault to become filled up, and then it ran over, standing in pools in the yard, and no effort was made by them to remedy the evil, and this it remained while we were there. It is no wonder we had the yellow fever among us before we left the city....

A well of brackish water supplied us in part, and the balance we drew from two or three old cisterns; and when *they* failed, we went outside under guard to a street pump. The last two weeks we were there we were much troubled for want of water, for the pump to the well gave out, and the cisterns were dry.

The cooking was done in the backyard with such utensils as we could find around the building, or had managed to buy or steal from the Rebels.

Lt. Roach, of the 49th New York Volunteers, formerly of Rochester, did us great service. He was a coppersmith, and succeeded in picking up a few old tools, some old stovepipe, and pieces of iron, from which he made several kettles, frying pans, dishes, etc., for many of the officers. Pieces of old iron were found around the hospital which served for griddles, upon which we baked pancakes. We also built several brick ovens in which we did our bread baking.

... *Rations* were small in quantity, and rather poor in quality. They were issued for ten days at a time, and consisted of flour, three pints; cornmeal, two and one third quarts; rice, two quarts; beans, three pints (black, and full of bugs); meat, either four ounces of fresh beef, or two ounces of bacon daily, or, in lieu thereof, one gill sorghum. In addition to our rations, the authorities allowed the market women to come up to the sidewalk, that we might purchase from them vegetables, fruit, etc., for our comfort.

### September 17 (Saturday)

Jubal Early moved down the Valley towards Martinsburg and the Baltimore and Ohio Railroad, which had been repaired after his last track-bending party. Early started with about 12,000 men against Sheridan's nearly 40,000.

Ransom, John, QM Sgt., 9th Michigan Cavalry, Marine Hospital, Savannah, Ga.:

Four in each tent. A nurse raises me up, sitting posture, and there I stay for hours, dozing and talking away. Whiskey given us in very small quantities, probably half a teaspoonful in half a glass of some-

thing. I don't know what. Actually makes me drunk. I am in no pain whatever.

### September 18 (Sunday)

In the Valley, Jubal Early sent part of his small force from Bunker Hill north to Martinsburg, where it drove in the Federal cavalry and then Early pulled back to Bunker Hill. Sheridan ordered Averill's cavalry division to advance up the Valley Pike, while the rest of his army prepared to march west from Berryville.

Jones, John B., Rebel War Clerk, Confederate War Dept., Richmond, Va.:

We have intelligence of another brilliant feat of Gen. Wade Hampton. Day before yesterday he got in the rear of the enemy, and drove off 2500 beeves and 400 prisoners. This will furnish fresh meat rations for Lee's army during a portion of the fall campaign. I shall get some shanks, perhaps; and the prisoners of war will have meat rations.

Abbott, A.O., 1st Lt., 1st N.Y. Dragoons, prisoner, Charleston, S.C.:

The firing upon the city was continued daily, except when the flag-of-truce boat went down the bay.

The shells usually came over at intervals of thirty minutes, but when a fire broke out they would open three or four *extra* guns, and send them as often as one every five minutes. One Saturday afternoon a fire broke out nearly opposite the workhouse, when they commenced shelling it; and so direct was their aim that twice they burst their shells in the midst of the burning buildings. The negroes informed us that it was a common practice of Gen. Gilmore's, and that he had entirely destroyed one of the fire engines by bursting a shell inside of it, and the firemen were afraid to go to the sites of the fires for fear of being killed by his shells.

From the attic window of the "Roper Hospital" we could look down the bay towards "Morris Island," and could see the flash of our guns in the clear evenings; could trace the course of the shell as it left the mouth of the gun, climbing up, higher, still higher, till it reached the zenith. Then we heard the report of the gun, and would for the first time, hear the sharp, shrill shriek of the shell cutting its way through the air, and could trace it still farther by its own light, as it gradually descended the other arc of its circle; nearer, and still nearer it came. Now it is right over our heads; it gives out its lightning flash; the danger is past. The report soon follows, and we hear the pieces rattle among the brick walls and wooden tenements beyond us.

### September 19 (Monday)

In the Valley, Sheridan sent 40,000 troops against Early's 12,000, north of Winchester, Va. The main force of Sheridan's infantry drove west, guided by the Winchester-Leesburg road, and hit the Confederates hard. During the fighting, Confederate Gen. Robert E. Rodes was mortally wounded. About 4:30, Sheridan ordered another advance and Early withdrew up the Valley. Federal casualties were about 10 percent—4000 out of 40,000. Confederate losses were heavier in percentages—nearly 26 percent—3921 out of about 18,000. Early retreated with a much weakened force, but with a bag of prisoners.

Near Sandusky, Ohio, the iron side-wheeler gunboat U.S.S. *Michigan*, Commander J.C. Carter, was assigned to guard the Confederate prisoners held at Johnson's Island.

Acting Master John Yates Beall, CSA, had spent several months in Canada in 1862 and had conceived the idea of capturing a ship on Lake Erie, swooping down on the *Michigan* and releasing the prisoners on Johnson's Island. Maj. Charles H. Cole, CSA, a secret agent in the Lake Erie region, was assigned the role of gaining the confidence of the Union personnel aboard the *Michigan* and at the prison camp. Maj. Cole's actions were described:

Cole, one of John Morgan's men, a man of great brilliancy, polished manners, utmost coolness, and dauntless courage, was to have charge of the expedition. When all was in readiness, he went to Sandusky City, opposite Johnson's Island, where he could be in easy communication with Capt. Beall, who had gone to Canada. Maj. Cole was supplied abundantly with means, and passed as a very wealthy Philadelphian, heir to immense estates. He entertained lavishly, won the regard of prominent men of all parties, and by his winning ways ingratiated himself with all classes, civil and military.

He became intimate with the officers of the *Michigan*, who invited him to visit them, and showed him over the ship, and allowed him to go

onto the island and converse freely with the prisoners. He entertained the officers in splendid style, and used to have long confidential talks with the engineer of the vessel.

On the evening set for the capture he had invited the officers of the *Michigan* to a supper at his hotel. They were there to be drugged, so as to incapacitate them for duty.

Capt. Beall's part was to secure and man a vessel, and to be near enough that when the officers were in the midst of their entertainment, he could, at a given signal, steam up beside the warship and suddenly board her, taking possession of her in the name of the Confederate States. Then Maj. Cole would take command, and they would carry out the remainder of the plan.

On this day, Bennet G. Burley, who had been under Capt. Beall in his privateering ventures on the Chesapeake Bay, went aboard the steamboat *Philo Parsons*, at Detroit, taking passage to Sandusky City. She was a boat of 220 tons burden, plying regularly between the two cities. He arranged for her to touch at Sandwich and Amherstburg, small Canadian villages, to take on some friends of his.

Capt. Beall and two companions got on at Sandwich, and at Amherstburg sixteen men came aboard with an old trunk tied with rope which contained grappling hooks and hatchets. At the time there were eighty other passengers aboard the *Philo Parsons*.

About 4 P.M., just as the boat was leaving Kelly's Island, five miles north of Sandusky City, Capt. Beall put a pistol to the head of the helmsman, and giving a signal, his men gathered around him with hatchets and grappling hooks, taking possession of the *Philo Parsons* in the name of the Confederate States. There was no resistance, the Confederate flag was hoisted, and the passengers and crew were landed at Middle Bass Island.

While at Middle Bass Island, the *Philo Parsons* was approached by the screw steamer *Island Queen*, which Beall boarded and captured. On board the *Philo Parsons* were about thirty Federal soldiers whom Beall paroled. Beall then put the crew and passengers ashore and scuttled the *Island Queen* after setting her afire. The *Philo Parsons* then headed for Sandusky.

Beall placed his ship in position to board the *Michigan* and waited for the signal. No signal was ever given. Maj. Cole had been discovered and arrested and the entire plot had fallen apart. Beall was all in favor of going ahead with the plan, believing that the Federals were unaware of his presence. The majority of his crew felt differently. Only three of his crew agreed to try the scheme, the remainder opted to run for it. Beall returned the ship to Sandwich, Canada, where it was scuttled and the crew scattered. Beall went eastward with a few of his loyal men.

There were several versions of the events of this day, one of which was presented by Dr. J.S. Riley, of Bloomfield, Tex., in 1901:

I was a prisoner of war at Alton, Ill., in the year 1864, and escaped in June of that year to Canada. I there became acquainted with Beall. I understood that he and Booth were college mates at the University of Virginia, and that they were sworn friends.... We joined a company of eighteen men (secretly) in Canada; went to Sandusky and arranged for the capture of the war steamer *Michigan* (the only warship the United States was allowed on the Lakes as per treaty with Great Britain). Preliminaries now being fully arranged, we dressed as first-class gentlemen, armed ourselves with six-shooters and Bowies, concealed in an old trunk. On a beautiful Sunday morning we boarded the steamer *Philo Parsons* at Sarney, Canada, and sailed for Sandusky as passengers. After dinner we went into our room and put on our arms. Beall, commanding, assigned his lieutenants to their duties. I had been assigned to surgeon's duty, but was ordered to capture the engineer. Beall himself went to the captain of the ship. We captured the ship, made prisoners of the crew, and went towards our destination (Johnson's Island); but we had a Judas aboard, and where we stopped after dark to take on fuel, he escaped in the darkness, gave information which defeated our enterprise, and we were compelled to return to Canada after having been compelled to take and sink another schooner, the *Island Queen*.

We talked the matter over on our retreat to Canada. We landed at the place of our embarkation, and scuttled our ship. Myself and fourteen of our crew went to Halifax, and Beall and his chief lieutenant returned to New York, where they were subsequently arrested, and tried for treason, convicted and hanged. Pending their imprisonment, J. Wilkes Booth, as the special friend of Beall, went before President Lincoln and implored and besought him to spare his friend, and that he be spared his life. Lincoln promised him that he would spare Beall's life if convicted. This satisfied Booth, and he conveyed the fact to Beall in his prison. Hence Beall was not alarmed for his life. He believed it was safe, and Booth remained easy; otherwise he would have used all his great powers to have released his friend from his prison and death. When Stanton and Seward found that Lincoln had promised to pardon Beall in the event of his conviction, they besought him to let the law do its worst, and with his promise to Booth, Lincoln yielded to Stanton and Seward, and did not inform Booth of his change of heart, and Booth rested easy until after the execution at Governor's Island. Then overwhelmed with grief and disappointment, he swore in his wrath that he would take the life of Lincoln if it cost him his own, and engaged two others, one to assassinate Stanton, and the other to assassinate Seward. They all three boarded at Mrs. Surratt's house, although she was in ignorance of the plot. She was hanged for being accessory to it before the fact. The night of the assassination it was planned that at the same hour and minute Lincoln, Stanton, and Seward should suffer death. Booth succeeded, Stanton's assassin made no attempt, and Seward escaped with a slight wound on the neck. These are facts as told to me, not as a party to plot, but owing to my connection with the raid on Lake Erie.

The reason Booth killed President Lincoln was conjectured upon for decades after, and, in fact, the reason is still a matter of controversy. H.B. Baylor, of Cumberland, Md., wrote in the *Confederate Veteran* of 1901 that he knew Beall's mother, and, although he did not have *direct* knowledge of the fact, she is *supposed* to have claimed to have visited Lincoln, accompanied by Booth, to plead for her son's life. Lincoln supposedly told her that Beall would not die by hanging, but when she returned home she received a telegram saying that Beall was dead. Then Booth killed Lincoln.

To further confuse things in this controversy, a Maj. John W. Tench, CSA, wrote in 1901 that Beall was captured in an attempted raid on St. Alban's prison, the idea being to release several Confederate soldiers there. He supposedly was in uniform at the time, which would make his activities legal—at least not liable for trial as a spy. This story has no credence. It is just another of those made of whole cloth to add to the confusion.

Who really knows? The times in which they lived were very dramatic, and the stuff legends were made of was often conjecture that took on reality.

### September 20 (Tuesday)

In the Valley, Sheridan's troops drove Early's retreating columns through Middletown and finally stopped when the Confederates were south of Strasburg on Fisher's Hill.

Abbott, A.O., 1st Lt., 1st N.Y. Dragoons, prisoner, Charleston, S.C.:

> While here, we received the most mail, and, I think, enjoyed the best mail facilities of any place we had occupied while in prison, except Richmond. Several loads of boxes were also received, in tolerably good condition, much to the joy of those to whom they belonged. The authorities also allowed us to have as many of the morning papers as we chose by paying twenty-five cents for them, which we very gladly did—a privilege we had not enjoyed since we had been in Rebeldom. About the 20th of September, we learned from them that Sherman and Hood were trying to effect terms of exchange for all the officers who had been captured since the army started in the spring.

### September 22 (Thursday)

Yesterday, in the Valley at Strasburg, Sheridan advanced on Early's fortifications. There was fighting at Fisher's Hill and at Front Royal. In the morning, Sheridan sent Crook with one of the Federal corps around the left flank of the Confederates to a position of attack.

Today, late in the afternoon, Crook's Federals came charging over the Rebel entrenchments, attacking the Rebel rear and flank. The Union troops in front attacked at the same time across the Tumbling Run ravine and up Fisher's Hill. During the melee, Confederate Lt. Col. Alexander Swift Pendleton, called "Sandie," was wounded in the abdomen and died a short time later. The Union bluecoats chased the Confederates for four miles up the Valley before Early could get his lines together. Early lost 1235 men from his steadily diminishing force.

In Atlanta, Ga., Maj. Gen. William T. Sherman offered to provide clothing, etc. to the prisoners at Andersonville if Gen. John B. Hood, CSA, would permit this to be done:

> General: My latest authentic information from Andersonville is to the 12th, and from what I learn our prisoners of war confined there are being removed to Savannah, Charleston, Millen, [and] need many articles which we possess in superfluity, and can easily supply, with your consent and assistance, such as shirts, drawers, socks, shoes, soap, candles, combs, scissors, &c. If you will permit me to send a train of wagons with a single officer, to go along under flag of truce, I will send down to Lovejoy's or Palmetto a train of wagons loaded exclusively with 10,000 or 15,000 of each of these articles, and a due proportion of soap, candles, &c., under such other restrictions as you may think prudent to name. I would like my officer to go along to issue these things, but will have no hesitation in sending them if you will simply promise to have them carried to the places where our prisoners are and have them fairly distributed.

On September 27th, Hood responded in the affirmative. Sherman wrote Hood again on the 29th stating that he had ordered the supplies from St. Louis and they were expected in a few days. Sherman further stated that he would provide the requisite paperwork for the transaction. Not everyone was hardhearted.

### September 23 (Friday)

White, H.S., Chaplain, R.I. Regt. Heavy Artillery, exchanged and homeward bound:

> The deep and thrilling joy that inspired us as we were ordered to fall in on the morning of the twenty-third of September can hardly be appreciated by one that has not for months been a prisoner in the hands of such scamps as Jeff. Davis and Company.... As we lay on the wharf waiting to embark, I sauntered a little to one side, where I saw a curious little steamer used for exploding torpedoes under ships. She was perhaps thirty feet long, cigar-shaped, and was entered from the top side. Extending in front were two long iron arms which were securely bolted to a pole, some ten or fifteen feet long, and on the end of the pole was an iron to which the torpedoes were fastened. The pole had been broken in some service, and she was being refitted.
>
> We went on board the rebel steamer *Celt*, at

Chinn's wharf.... About eight o'clock in the morning of Sept. 23, we were finally off. The day was fine.... Presently a large, elegant steamer from the southeast shot rapidly through the fleet, and sweeping a graceful circle came along side, and we were soon locked together. 'Twas the United States transport steamer *Delaware*. A large elegant ship, clean, and everything in perfect trim. The *Celt* was a mean, little patched-up, half-painted one-horse affair, and I felt almost ashamed to be exchanged from the deck of such a scrawny ship. The neatly dressed soldiers on the *Delaware* looked sweet enough to kiss.... Col. Woodford, that Christian gentleman, stood at the end of the plank and took us each by the hand and gave us a cordial and hearty welcome.... Presently the business of the truce was concluded, the boxes, bales and barrels in vast quantities put on board the *Celt* for the prisoners, and we parted; she to go back to her den, and we to move off to get into God's land among his people.

We reached Hilton Head soon after dark, and in a few days left for New York and home. So far as I know, out of the fifty men who were captured with me, about forty-one have died.

Chaplain Henry S. White returned home for a period before rejoining his unit in North Carolina on November 9, 1864. After his discharge, he returned to the ministry and spent many years serving churches throughout the country. In 1883, while in Detroit, he retired. He died in that city in 1916.

Abbott, A.O., 1st Lt., 1st N.Y. Dragoons, prisoner, Charleston, S.C.:

The 23d, an order came for about 150 to be ready to move in the morning. It was a joyous time for those who were to go, and we all hoped it was only the commencement of a "general exchange" soon to take place...

Ransom, John, QM Sgt., 9th Michigan Cavalry, Marine Hospital, Savannah, Ga.:

Shall write anyway; have to watch nurses and rebels or will lose my diary. Vinegar reduced I drink and it is good; crave after acids and salt. Mouth appears to be actually sorer than ever before, but whether it is worse or not can't say. Sergt. Winn says the Doctor says that I must be very careful if I want to get well. How in the old Harry can I be careful? They are the ones that had better be careful and give me the right medicine and food. Gruel made out of a dish cloth to eat.

## September 24 (Saturday)

In the Valley, Sheridan turned his men to burning crops, barns, and anything else usable to the Confederacy while he slowly advanced up the Valley towards Early. Early had a shortage of everything, but mostly men, and nothing was in sight.

In Richmond, the supply of tents and lumber was becoming more critical. The prisoners on Belle Isle needed permanent sheds built and replacement tents before the coming winter. The Quartermaster at Richmond said neither were available for the use of the prisoners. All available tents were required for the wounded in the Valley following Lt. Gen. Early's disastrous campaign.

## September 25 (Sunday)

Sheridan's army moved towards Staunton and Waynesborough, Va., destroying everything in its path. Early was forced back to Brown's Gap in the Blue Ridge, near Waynesborough.

The pace of prisoner exchange was picking up, especially among the sick and wounded. At 11 A.M. on this date, Maj. Gen. Benj. F. Butler, at Bermuda Hundred, wrote to Col. Wm. Hoffman, Federal Commissary-General of Prisoners:

Maj. Mulford leaves City Point this morning with 600 officers and soldiers, mostly disabled, except in case of special exchange. There are at least 600 more at and about Richmond for another load. Please get ready 600 of disabled Confederates, either at Point Lookout or Ft. Delaware, preferably the latter, for return trip. Nearly 30 died out of 500 in the last load. Instruct the surgeons to send none who are in that condition. The occurrence does not speak well either for the Government or its officials. The rebel commissioner of exchange agrees to deliver us at Ft. Pulaski all of the sick in Georgia by the 10th of next month, to the number of at least 5000. I am preparing transportation for 5000 disabled Confederates to be carried down by the same transport that brings ours up. Please assemble them from the various camps and hospitals to points where they can be reached by the boats, and notify me.

At 8:30 P.M. this date, Gen. Butler further instructed Col. Hoffman:

I have made arrangements with Mr. Ould to give me at least 5000 of our sick men in Georgia and South Carolina and take what equivalent we may have. I have offered to take them at Ft. Pulaski, as an act of humanity, because I think that railroading through the Confederacy with such accommodations as they would get would bring many of them to their death. He will receive on the Mississippi or its tributaries, at such points as may be agreed upon, all the sick we may have at the Western camps, and will be glad to do it for the same reason.

 After the boatload up the river we may as well send our balance down with the same transportation to Ft. Pulaski. Please advise.

Ransom, John, QM Sgt., 9th Michigan Cavalry, Marine Hospital, Savannah, Ga.:

Can eat better—or drink rather; some rebel general dead and buried with honors outside. Had another wash and general clean up; ocean breezes severe for invalids.... Food principally arrowroot; have a little whiskey. Sleep a great deal of the time.... Everything clean here, but then any place is clean after summering in Andersonville.

In Elmira, N.Y., the weekly inspection was again completed by Capt. B. Munger. His report was forwarded this date to Col. Wm. Hoffman:

Some clothing is received daily from the friends of the prisoners, but there is still great destitution. The weather is cold for the season, and those in tents especially suffer. There are no stoves in quarters or hospital. About 500 are sick in hospital and about 100 in quarters who are fit subjects for, and should receive, hospital treatment. Those sick in quarters are fed on the ordinary prison ration, nothwithstanding an order has been issued to treat them as in hospital. During the past week there have been 112 deaths, reaching one day 29. There seems little doubt numbers have died both in quarters and hospital for want of proper food.

Capt. Munger's report was endorsed by Col. B.F. Tracy, commanding Elmira Depot, and forwarded to Col. Hoffman:

Forwarded to the Commissary-General of Prisoners with the following remarks:

Drainage of camp is not good. There is a pond of stagnant water in the center, which renders camp unhealthy. This can be remedied by bringing water from the river through the camp. This being done, with more perfect drainage, there is no reason why the camp should not be healthy. Many men are in tents without floors or blankets. Barracks should be erected instead of tents. Hospital accommodations insufficient at present. New wards are being built. Hospital mess rooms to accommodate about 200 patients much needed. Police of hospital good, except sinks; an offensive smell enters the tents from these. I doubt whether, with present mode of construction, this could be prevented. Scurvy prevails to a great extent. Few if any vegetables have been recently issued. Greater efforts should be made to prevent scurvy.

For the period September 19 to 25, 1864, Capt. Henry Wirz reported an average of nearly 10,600 prisoners at Andersonville. Of these, an average of almost 2000 were in hospital. An average of 185 died each day.

### September 26 (Monday)

In the Valley, Sheridan began his pullback after his cavalry had clashed with Early's around Port Republic, Weyer's Cave, and other points on the Valley Pike.

Ransom, John, QM Sgt., 9th Michigan Cavalry, Marine Hospital, Savannah, Ga.:

Am really getting better and hopeful. Battese has the two first books of my diary; would like to see him.... Quite a number die here not having the constitution to rally. This is the first hospital I was ever in. My old coverlid was washed and fumigated the first day in hospital. Am given very little to eat five or six times a day; washed with real soap, an improvement on sand.... A discussion on the subject has set me down as weighing about ninety-five; I think about one hundred and five or ten pounds; weighed when captured one hundred and seventy-eight; boarding with the Confederacy does not agree with me. The swelling about my body has all but left me.

### September 27 (Tuesday)

Maj. Gen. J.G. Foster, at Hilton Head, S.C., wrote Maj. Gen. Samuel Jones, commanding the

Confederate forces at Charleston, that he had been informed that yellow fever existed at that time in Charleston and also in Savannah. Foster notified Jones that no civilians who had heretofore received permits to enter the Union lines would be accepted until after November 1.

### September 28 (Wednesday)

Ransom, John, QM Sgt., 9th Michigan Cavalry, Marine Hospital, Savannah, Ga.:

Sent word to Battese by a convalescent who is being sent to the large prison, that I am getting well. Would like to see him. Am feeling better. Good many Union men in Savannah. Three hundred sick here, with all kinds of diseases—gangrene, dropsy, scurvy, typhoid and other fevers, diarrhea, &c. Good care taken of me.

### September 29 (Thursday)

In the Valley, Sheridan's troops and Early's Rebels engaged at Waynesborough, Va., with light contact.

At Elmira, N.Y., Col. B.F. Tracy, commanding the Prison Depot, received explicit instructions from Col. Wm. Hoffman, Federal Commissary-General of Prisoners, concerning the movement of sick prisoners of war to be sent South for exchange.

All the invalid prisoners of war in your charge who will not be fit for service within sixty days will be in a few days sent South for delivery to the rebel authorities, and, as directed in my telegram of yesterday, you will immediately prepare duplicate parole-rolls to accompany them and an ordinary roll for this office. None will be sent who wish to remain and take the oath of allegiance, and none who are too feeble to endure the journey. Have a careful inspection of the prisoners made by medical officers to select those who shall be transferred. Detail to accompany them a medical officer or two, if necessary, with as many attendants and nurses, taken from the well prisoners, as may be required, and have them organized into companies of convenient size, so that all may receive proper attention.

You will send suitable guard under a field officer in charge of the prisoners, and give instructions in writing as to the service to be performed. The guard and prisoners will be furnished with cooked rations for two days. Require transportation of the quarter-master's department to Baltimore, and see that the cars are of a suitable character and well provided with lights and water. Direct the commanding officer not to give a certificate for the transportation unless the contract is fully complied with. The quartermaster at Baltimore will be directed to provide transportation to Point Lookout. Furnish the commanding officer with a list of all moneys placed in his hands belonging to prisoners, which list, with the money, will be delivered to the rebel officer who receives them.

One of the parole-rolls, with the officer's receipt, will be returned through you to this office as evidence of the delivery. On arriving at Point Lookout the officer in charge will report to the commanding officer, Brig. Gen. Barnes, and, if relieved from charge of the prisoners, he will turn over to the relieving officer the rolls, money, &c., taking a receipt therefrom.

P.S. Report by telegram to the quartermaster at Baltimore, Lt. Col. C.W. Thomas, and to this office the time at which the prisoners will leave at least twenty-four hours before their departure.

Ransom, John, QM Sgt., 9th Michigan Cavalry, Marine Hospital, Savannah, Ga.:

Yes, I am better, but poor and weak. Feeling hungry now, and can take nourishment quite often. Mike Hoare calls to see me. He is thinking of escape.... Sweet potatoes for sale. Like to see such things, but cannot eat them.... It is said the Yankees can throw shell into Savannah from their gunboats down the river. Sgt. Winn comes to see me and cheers me up. Winn is a sutler as well as nurse, that is, he buys eatables from the guards and other rebels, and sells to our men. Number of marines and sailors in the building adjoining our hospital; also some Yankee officers sick. Winn makes quite a little money. They have soap here to wash with.

On this date, Confederate Gen. Sam Jones at Charleston, S.C., wired Gen. Samuel Cooper in Richmond:

I have sent an officer to Columbia to endeavor to procure a place of confinement for Federal officers, prisoners, and will send all prisoners from here as soon as possible; the enlisted men all to Florence. The prevalence of yellow fever as an epidemic makes this necessary precaution. I recommend that a few acclimated troops be sent here for duty in the city. The Twenty-seventh South Carolina regiment or some New Orleans troops would be desirable.

On September 23rd, Abbott and his fellow prisoners had been notified that 150 of them were to be ready to move shortly. Their hopes rose dramatically, only to be unrealized.

Abbott, A.O., 1st Lt., 1st N.Y. Dragoons, prisoner, Charleston, S.C.:

Our expectations were increased by an order received the 29th for all of the naval officers to be sent to Richmond for "exchange." Oh how anxiously we watched the papers to see something that would give us further hope in the matter, and perhaps settle the question! But we watched and waited in vain, and soon our feelings sank back into the old state, thus to remain till somebody started a plausible rumor which would arouse them again.

I can not forebear transcribing a few thoughts from my journal, written at this time in my little room in the attic. Whether my predictions have proved true, the public must judge.

I stand by the little window in the attic of Roper Hospital, and look out upon the "burnt district" of this city. It is desolation indeed. The bare, broken walls of the ruined houses remain as monuments to the graves of a once thriving business portion of the city. The streets and thoroughfares are deserted, and tall, rank weeds have grown up in their places. As far as I can see, no improvements have taken place since the fire. It seems as though the curse of God was resting on the place to prevent its being rebuilt. It gives me an unpleasant feeling to look upon so much destruction; yet above all this comes the reflection that it is, in fact, but *justice* to this city of sin.

## September 30 (Friday)

Ransom, John, QM Sgt., 9th Michigan Cavalry, Marine Hospital, Savannah, Ga.:

Am decidedly better and getting quite an appetite but can get nothing but broth, gruel, &c. Mouth very bad. Two or three teeth have come out, and can't eat any hard food anyway. They give me quinine, at least I think it is quinine. Good many visitors come here to see the sick, and they look like Union people. Savannah is a fine place from all accounts of it.... Nurses are

mostly marines who have been sick and are convalescent. As a class they are good fellows, but some are rough ones. Are very profane. The cords in my legs loosening up a little. Whiskey and water given me today, also weakened vinegar and salt. Am all the time getting better. LATER—My faithful friend came to see me today. Was awful glad to see him. He is well. A guard came with him. Battese is quite a curiosity among the Savannah rebels. Is a very large, broad-shouldered Indian, rather ignorant, but full of common sense and very kindhearted. Is allowed many favors.

## October 1 (Saturday)

Forrest was in middle Tennessee and northern Alabama cutting communications and capturing blockhouses, his main purpose was to make enough trouble to get Sherman to pull out of Georgia. Hood's Army of Tennessee, a mere shadow of its former self, was moving around and to the south of Sherman, headed for northwest Georgia to get on Sherman's rail link with Chattanooga.

Today, about 1000 former Andersonville prisoners, who had been moved to Charleston, S.C., and herded into the fairgrounds on September 12th, were moved to Florence, S.C., to a new stockade that had been prepared for them. The move from Andersonville was supposed to have been for exchange; however, Grant's new policy forbade the exchange on the grounds that it would help the South solve its manpower problems. The prisoners remained at Florence until December 15, 1864.

Ransom, John, QM Sgt., 9th Michigan Cavalry, Marine Hospital, Savannah, Ga.:

A prisoner of war nearly a year. Have stood and went through the very worst kind of treatment. Am getting ravenously hungry, but they won't give me much to eat. Even Mike won't give me anything. Says the doctors forbid. Well, I suppose it is so.... A dozen or twenty die in the twenty-four hours.... A high garden wall surrounds us. Wall is made of stone.

## October 2 (Sunday)

Hood's Army of Tennessee reached Sherman's rail link with Chattanooga at Big Shanty and the Kennesaw Water Tank in Georgia, and started tearing up the track of the Western & Atlantic Railroad and interrupted service.

Ransom, John, QM Sgt., 9th Michigan Cavalry, Marine Hospital, Savannah, Ga.:

Coming cool weather and it braces me right up. Sailors are going away to be exchanged. Ate some sweet potato today, and it beats everything how I am gaining. Drink lots of gruel, and the more I drink the more I want.... Am crazy for anything, no matter what. Could eat a mule's ear. Eat rice and vegetable soup.... Have washed all over and feel fifty per cent better. Just a-jumping towards convalescence.

### October 3 (Monday)

With Hood's Confederate Army of Tennessee astraddle the railroad linking Atlanta and Chattanooga and tearing up more track, Sherman was finally forced to pay some attention to both Hood and Forrest. He began to send troops from Atlanta to cope with the problem.

Col. William Hoffman wrote Col. B.F. Tracy, commanding at Elmira, N.Y., about getting some shelters built:

You will order the erection of shed barracks for the prisoners of war at the Elmira depot. The lumber will be purchased with the prison fund, and as far as practicable the work will be done by the prisoners, selecting in preference, when they have the capacity, those who have desired to take the oath of allegiance.

You will require your quartermaster to make the purchases, direct the work, and pay the workmen, as if it were done under the direction of his department, but rendering the accounts as for other expenditures of the prison fund.

A building 100 feet long and 22 feet broad will accommodate 120 men and give a room at the end of 20 by 22 feet for a kitchen. The elevation from the floor should be nine feet, and the floor should be high enough from the ground to prevent burrowing, with a view to escape, without detection.... Place the bunks in three tiers.... It will probably be necessary to employ an experienced carpenter to superintend the work

Hoffman also on this day wrote Col. A.A. Stevens at Camp Morton, Ind., concerning his latest status report. It also provided Col. Stevens with a classic chewing-out:

Your weekly reports of the condition of the camp are duly received, but they do not cover the case.

Many improvements are spoken of as necessary, but nothing is said of any steps taken to meet these necessities. If you can make the improvements without reference to this office, why is it not done? Or, if it is requisite to submit plans and estimates, let it be done without delay.

Lt. Davidson in his report of the 18th ultimo, says, "many of the prisoners being entirely destitute of blankets and almost destitute of clothing, &c." This report is referred by you without comment, and if this state of things exists it shows great neglect. Paragraph 12 of the circular of April 20 provides for supplying prisoners with clothing, and you should always have a sufficient supply on hand. Send in your requisitions immediately.

On the 14th ultimo I instructed you as to the extension of the hospital, but your report makes no allusion to the work.

I do not know whether you have made the improvements on the old barracks estimated for in your letter of August 16, 1864. If you have not, let them be made at once. If more barracks are required for the winter, submit a plan of them with an estimate of the cost.

Vague suggestions of what is required or recommendations without details are of no value.

Acknowledge the receipt of the letter by telegram and make the required reports at once.

Ransom, John, QM Sgt., 9th Michigan Cavalry, Marine Hospital, Savannah, Ga.:

The hospital is crowded now with sick; about thirty die now each day. Men who walked away from Andersonville and come to get treatment, are too far gone to rally, and die.... I am better where I am for a few weeks yet.... Gnaw onion, raw sweet potato. Battese here, will stay all day and go back tonight. Says he is going with marines to be exchanged.... Says he will come to see me after I get home to Michigan.

### October 4 (Tuesday)

Sgt. Bartlett Yancey Malone of the 6th N.C. Infantry, confined at Point Lookout, Md., seemed to be in pretty fair shape. His health was holding out so far. Between September 26th and 27th a total of more than 1300 prisoners were added to the list at Point Lookout, most of them belonging to Confederate Gen. Jubal Early's command in the Shenandoah Valley. Today, 100 more prisoners arrived, bringing the total to somewhere over 10,000. This was down from nearly 15,000 last summer, many of them sent to Elmira, N.Y.

Ransom, John, QM Sgt., 9th Michigan Cavalry, Marine Hospital, Savannah, Ga.:

Am now living splendid; vegetable diet is driving off the scurvy and dropsy, in fact the dropsy has dropped out but the effect remains.... Heard that all the prisoners are going to be sent to Millen, Ga. Wrote a few lines directed to my father in Michigan. Am now given more food but not much at a time.... Battese on his last visit to me left the first two books of my diary which he had in his possession. There is no doubt but he has saved my life, although he will take no credit for it. It is said all were moved from Andersonville to different points; ten thousand went to Florence, ten thousand to Charleston and ten thousand to Savannah; but the dead stay there and will for all time to come. What a terrible place and what a narrow escape I had of it. Seems to me that fifteen thousand died while I was there; an army almost and as many men as inhabit a city of fifty thousand population.

Sherman finally took full note of the situation near Big Shanty and Acworth, Georgia. He left one corps to hold Atlanta and took the rest up the rail line to discuss the situation with Hood.

## October 5 (Wednesday)

Today a small Union force showed the world what guts and determination could do in the face of the enemy. Hood's Army of Tennessee was attacking the Union troops at Allatoona Pass, where Brig. Gen. John M. Corse refused to surrender to Confederate Maj. Gen. S.G. French. To the southeast, from atop Kennesaw Mountain, Sherman watched the smoke of battle around Allatoona 18 miles away. The Confederates assaulted the Union garrison, resulting in high casualties on both sides. The Union lost 706 out of about 2000, the Confederates lost 799 out of about the same number. French received a report, later proved erroneous, that Maj. Gen. Jacob D. Cox was moving a Union force to relieve Corse, pulled up stakes and left, leaving the field to Corse.

Abbott, A.O., 1st Lt., 1st N.Y. Dragoons, prisoner, off to Columbia, S.C.:

"Be ready to move to Columbia, the capital, in an hour," said Capt. Mobly to us the morning of the 5th of October, while we were all busily engaged in getting breakfast. It was not altogether unexpected.... The reason of this move the Rebels did not condescend to inform us, but we supposed the principal one was, to remove us from under the fire of Gen. Gilmore's guns. Perhaps the breaking out of the yellow fever among us had something to do with it. All the officials told us we should be much better off in Columbia than Charleston; the old story of improvement, often told, less often realized.

We "packed up" and waited in the front yard till eight, when the gates were opened, and we marched into the road or street, with guards on either side. Just before we left, the Irish and negro washerwomen came flocking to the fence with the bundles of clothes that had been given them to wash, many of them only the night before. They had been put into the washtub, only to be wrung out and returned to their owners, wet and still unwashed. Quite a number were as unfortunate as your humble servant, who sent out his only whole and best shirt to be washed, anxiously waiting its return, that he might indulge in the luxury of a *clean* one. Vain hope! No shirt returned to him, and he was obliged to go to the capital of the chivalrous State of South Carolina with only the *remnant* of a six-dollar sutler's piece of flannel by that name.

Having been moved several times before, we had learned wisdom thereby; and hence we determined to leave nothing that would add to our comfort in a new camp that we could possibly carry. As we stood in the street, we formed the most motley-looking crowd I have ever seen. Boxes packed with remnants of dishes, and rags tied up with an old piece of rope, a stick thrust through, and the whole borne on the shoulders of two. Chairs, pails, satchels, packs of blankets and brooms, old arch doors, griddles, benches, pieces of boards, kettles, pans and cups, were all taken along with us. Dressed as we were, blue, gray, red, white, and, in fact, a mixture of many colors, we looked more like the inmates of some county poorhouse or insane asylum than United States military officers.

As we passed the Marine Hospital we were joined

by 100 more. We soon entered upon King Street, the "Broadway" of Charleston, and as we passed along up its now-deserted walks, we could see some of the fruits of secession. Tall grass and rank weeds were growing untrodden in its midst and alongside its walks. Block after block we passed that was *entirely* closed; many, with only door opened, revealing scantily filled shelves and empty showcases....

When we reached the cars we were nearly exhausted, for the day was intensely hot. Embarked again in boxcars, but were situated very comfortably, for we were not very much crowded. Just before we started, Gen. Gilmore sent over his compliments in the shape of a thirty-pound shell, which struck in a field near us without bursting. We gave it three hearty cheers. The whistle blowed, and on we went towards Columbia. Passed through a very poor section of country, and arrived at Branchville at 6 P.M.; prepared to rest as best we could, and finally arrived at Columbia at 1 A.M.

Conley, Capt., 101st Penna. Volunteers, escape en route to Columbia, S.C.:

On the morning of the 5th of October we received orders to be ready to leave the prison in one hour. We at once began to make such preparations as were necessary. My own preparations consisted of doing up my blanket and overcoat and our few cooking utensils, after which I bought a small loaf of bread, a little salt, and corked them up tightly to secure them against wet so as to be ready in case we should see a chance to escape.

About ten o'clock between four and five hundred of us were marched out of the prison and through the city to the Charleston & Branchville R.R. depot. Here we found a train of freight cars awaiting us. After about one hour's delay (during which time we discovered that there were some Union men even in Charleston) we were ordered aboard the cars. After all the cars were filled, there were still about seventy-five to one hundred prisoners unprovided for, among whom was the writer. We were at once ordered to get on top of the cars, and having done so, distributed ourselves along on the different cars. The car that I was on was about the middle of the train. About eleven o'clock the train pulled out. In addition to the guards inside the cars, a guard was placed on top of each car.

As soon as we were under way, Capt. F.B. Daw-son of Co. F, 1st Lt. W.C. Davidson of Co. C of our regiment, and I decided to escape en route if any opportunity was offered. We soon noticed that the guard on our car took his position at the front end of the car to guard the steps, or ladder leading up, and the one on the car in the rear of ours took his position at the rear end of his car for the same purpose, thus leaving the rear end of our car and the front of the one in the rear of us unguarded. We therefore took our position at the rear end of our car so as to be as far from the guards as possible. Nothing worthy of note occurred during the day. About sunset we passed Branchville, taking the road towards Columbia, which point we now became satisfied was our destination.

After dark the train made several stops but always in small towns where there were always crowds of curious people around to see the "Yanks." About 10 o'clock we crossed the Congaree river and about a half hour later the train stopped at a water tank where there were woods on both sides of the road. Believing this to be our opportunity, we quickly put our plan into execution. Placing a hand on each car, we let ourselves down until one foot reached the coupling, then stepping quietly down and as quietly lying down on the outside of the track, we followed each other as quickly as possible, Capt. Dawson lying down on the left side of the track and Lt. Davidson and myself on the right side. I lay with my face down, my head towards the rear of the train, being shielded from view by the projecting body of the car, about half of my body resting on the ends of the ties, and supporting myself on my left hand and knee.

It was a moment of great suspense. Minutes seemed lengthened into hours. We knew that if discovered, the guards would fire on us and one, or more, of us might be instantly killed. At last the whistle blew and the train began to move slowly. Two guards were sitting in each side door of each car and as they passed I could have touched their feet.

Just as the last car passed, I noticed a light and turning my head I took in the situation at a glance. The rear car was a passenger car. The rear door was open and a lantern hung over it. On the rear platform stood a guard just in the act of bringing his musket to his face. I saw that I was the target. At the same instant, I heard my two comrades running into the woods on the left side of the road, they having noticed the light sooner than I did. I saw at a glance that it would be unwise of me to attempt to run; and acting with quickness of thought, I made a sudden movement sidewise, placing myself off the ends of the ties. The report of the musket seemed to be simultaneous with my movement, and I felt the dead thud of the ball as it appeared to strike the ground under me. At the same time I was conscious of a slight burning sensation on the outside of my right hip joint. I lay perfectly still, watching the train to see if it would stop, intending if it did to spring up and run into the woods; but this I knew would be attended with some danger, as I could see two guards on the rear end of the rear car and any movement of mine would be likely to draw their fire. But the train moved on and I lay still until it had gotten far enough away so that the light would not reveal my movements. I then rose and followed in the direction I had heard my comrades running.

After getting some distance from the road, my comrades still being in advance of me, I called to them and they waited for me. The first question they asked me was whether I was wounded; and I answered, "very slightly, if at all." We then retired a little farther from the road and stopped to lay plans and to determine our route. We were now in a country entirely new to us, and with nothing more than a general knowledge of the geography of the country; knowing nothing of its woods and streams. The first thing to be determined was what direction we would take. To the coast was little more than a hundred miles; but we did not believe it at all a feasible route. Up through S.C. and the mountains of N.C. and Tenn. we knew was a long and hard route to travel but we believed that it promised better results, so we determined to try that route.

Our next thought was to find a road leading in the direction we wished to go. For this purpose we started through the woods fearing to show ourselves along the railroad. For between three and four hours we wandered through woods, fields and swamps. The night was dark and cloudy and we soon lost all idea of direction. Thus we became painfully conscious of our unfitness for such an undertaking. Insufficient food and lack of exercise while in prison had so enervated us that fatigue soon overtook us. We decided to lie down and take a little rest until break of day, so that we could take our bearings.

Ransom, John, QM Sgt., 9th Michigan Cavalry, Marine Hospital, Savannah, Ga.:

All in Andersonville will remember Daly, who used to drive the bread wagon into that place. He came to Savannah with us and was in this hospital; a few days ago he went away with some sailors to be exchanged. Soon after leaving Savannah he fell off the cars and was killed, and a few hours after leaving here was brought back and buried; it is said he had been drinking.... It's wonderful the noticeable change of air here from that at Andersonville—wonder that any lived a month inhaling the poison.... Have a disagreeable task to perform—that of going to see the relatives of fifteen or twenty who died and deliver messages. Rebel surgeons act as if the war was most over, and not like very bad enemies. Fresh beef issued to those able to eat it, which is not me; can chew nothing hard, in fact cannot chew at all.

### October 6 (Thursday)

The Confederate officers being held as prisoners on Morris Island, S.C., were about to get their latrine facilities updated. Directions were given to the colonel in charge of the prisoners to

make requisition at once on the quartermaster's department for a sufficient amount of lumber to build proper sinks for the use of the rebel officers.... These sinks should be inside of the deadline, and the vault dug to such a depth that will not be rendered offensive. I am directed to inform you that the brigadier-general commanding is not desirous that the prisoners should be employed to empty their sink tubs, our own officers in the hands of the rebel authorities not being subjected to this indignity.... If upon investigation you find that the plan would be impracticable, on account of water coming up too high, or in any other way objectionable, you will please report the fact to these headquarters.

Conley, Capt., 101st Penna. Volunteers, escaped prisoner, near Columbia, S.C.:

At daybreak we started out again and travelled until nearly sunrise but without better success. We then stopped for the day under a large oak tree just in the edge of the swamp. We had spent between four and five hours in a fruitless effort to find a road; the only result was great fatigue. Here we spent the day, each of us having a part of a small loaf of bread, which we ate not knowing where we would get the next. An examination that morning showed that one ball, two buckshot and several small shot had passed through the skirt of my coat, and one buckshot and two fine shot had passed through my trousers, just grazing the skin.

Abbott, A.O., 1st Lt., 1st N.Y. Dragoons, prisoner, Columbia, S.C.:

Were kept in the cars until daylight, when we disembarked, and found a train, both before and behind us, loaded with officers. Thus we were all together again as we were at Macon. Soon after we disembarked, a Capt. Semple, in whose charge we now were, rode into our midst, and gave orders that all the baggage should be made ready to be transported in wagons to camp. "Bully for Columbia," said we, "may this state of things continue for many days." For once, we began to hope we had changed for the better. Our baggage loaded, we sat down to wait for orders. No breakfast, and nothing to eat. Ten, eleven, twelve, one, and two o'clock came and passed, and still we were there. The hot sun poured down upon us; we had no shade. Some of the officers got uneasy, and began to explore. Near us they found a cellar filled with bacon, but they could not reach it. Found a long pole, drove a nail into the end for a hook, and went fishing. Met with decided success, judging from the bacon that I saw in the hands of the officers; but, alas! the game was discovered, and the issue of bacon from that time was *stopped*.

At four o'clock an order came for us to move, but it was only to the other side of the depot, to get into a yard for safer keeping. An attempt was made to purchase bread, and, in part, succeeded. By sending little boys after it, we could get it for fifty cents a loaf; but as soon as it came to the knowledge of Capt. Semple, he ordered it stopped, and appointed a sutler, who soon came down with a load, and asked seventy-five cents. This started a proposition to "raid" him, which so frightened the poor fellow that he sold for anything the prisoners were inclined to pay; but it was a dear job for us, for when they got us in their power again we had to atone for our temerity.

A guard was placed around us, and, without anything to eat or promise of any, we were told we would remain there all night, and perhaps longer. We had no wood. Many had no rations, no money, and were very hungry. *Wait* was the word, and must

be the act. A few, who had a little meal, made an attack on the fence, got a little wood, and made mush. About five o'clock it began to rain, a regular South Carolina shower, and continued until about eleven that evening. Not one of us had a particle of shelter, and were consequently drenched to the skin. The night turned cold, and, without fires, it was anything but agreeable. But it was no use to repine; so, in the midst of the rain, a number of us collected together at the point nearest the depot, and sung, lustily, "Rally round the Flag," "The Star-Spangled Banner," "Red, White, and Blue," and other patriotic pieces, for the benefit of a crowd of our "sesech" friends, who had gathered in the building opposite to look upon "the hated Yankee prisoners." For once, at least, Columbia had loyal men and patriotic singing in her midst.

As the rain continued, the ground was flooded, till, in some places, it was ankle deep. Sleep and rest were out of the question, as we were obliged to walk to keep warm.

## October 7 (Friday)

Abbott, A.O., 1st Lt., 1st N.Y. Dragoons, prisoner, Columbia, S.C.:

Morning dawned at last, revealing two hideous-looking cannon that had been planted near us during the night.... While waiting here, a Lt. Parker was brought in, who had escaped from the train on its way from Charleston to Columbia. He had been recaptured, with others, by the "blood-hounds." He was badly torn by them, and was so weak he could scarcely stand up. He was taken to the hospital that night, where he died the next day from his wounds—*a sacrifice to Southern chivalry.*

While we were thus waiting, Capt. Semple came among us, and asked us to take a "parole" not to escape, same as we had in Charleston, representing that he had a fine camp for us about two miles from the city; that we should have the largest freedom that could possibly be allowed; should be supplied with good comfortable tents for shelter; should have enlisted men to do our cooking for us....

When asked if all these things should be ours now, he answered that they had not got the things quite ready, but they would have them in a few days. "We wait till we see the advantages of a parole before we take it," said we *all.*

About eight o'clock we were marched out on the Augusta Road, across the Saluda River, about two miles from the city, on the top of a hill overlooking the valley. Around an old worn-out cornfield, partially covered with second growth pines, had been cut a space for a guard-line. Here were posted their lines of sentinels, and into this we were turned to make ourselves as comfortable as we could. This was the *good place* that had been provided for us, and not to escape from which, we were asked to give our parole of honor.

... They turned us out, like so many cattle, into an old worn-out field containing about half a dozen little pine trees six inches in diameter, without a foot of board, or a piece of canvas for shelter; without a spade, an ax, a shovel, a cooking utensil, or anything to make or keep ourselves comfortable. The wood, water, and sink were all outside of the guard-line the first two weeks we were there. If a man wanted to get something to eat, and wished a pail of water, he could go and stand by the guard-line opposite the place, and when his turn came out of 1200, could go and get his bucket filled.... It was not an uncommon sight to see 100 standing in line at each of the places named, waiting their turn.

As soon as we were on the spot, Capt. Semple came to the senior officer of the prisoners, Col. Huey, 8th Pennsylvania Cavalry, and informed him that he had one hundred wall-tents in the city, which he would send up *at once* for the use of the prisoners ... and that "they would do the best they could for us." This last was a stereotyped phrase which we heard from every Rebel official with whom we had to do. Although we should have known better, we concluded to wait a few days before we tried to build much of a house.

Ransom, John, QM Sgt., 9th Michigan Cavalry, Marine Hospital, Savannah, Ga.:

Haven't time to write much; busy eating. Mouth getting better, cords in my legs loosening up. Battese has not gone; was here today and got a square meal. Don't think I have heretofore mentioned the fact that I have two small gold rings, which have been treasured carefully all during my imprisonment.... Have worn them part of the time and part of the time they have been secreted about my clothes. Yankee rings are in great demand by the guards; crave delicacies and vegetables so that think I may be pardoned for letting them go

now, and as Mike says he can get a bushel of sweet potatoes for them, have told him to make the trade, and he says will do it. Sweet potatoes sliced up and put in a dish and cooked with a piece of beef and seasoned, make a delicious soup. There are grayback lice in the hospital, just enough for company's sake—should feel lonesome without them.

Conley, Capt., 101st Penna. Volunteers, escaped prisoner, near Columbia, S.C.:

The day was cloudy and during the afternoon it commenced to rain, and as night approached it rained very heavy. We learned, by the sound of passing trains, during the day that we were near the railroad. We decided that we would follow the railroad until we could find a wagon road. We therefore moved out in sight of the road before dark where we waited until about nine o'clock when we started out in the direction of Columbia. We followed the railroad about five miles when we found a wagon road that seemed to run in the same general direction as the railroad; this we followed until nearly morning when we turned to our left to find a hiding place for the day. At the point where we left the road there was an abandoned field in the left of the road, but we could see at a short distance what looked like timber, but on reaching that place we found that it was only a grown-up fencerow, beyond which there seemed to be a large abandoned field. As we passed through we came to a narrow ledge that was covered with small gravel, with scarcely a spear of grass. As it was raining some, we believed that we would leave less scent in the gravel than on the grass, should they get bloodhounds on the track. We therefore followed this ledge as far as we could and then turned in to the timber. Being thoroughly wet, we built up a fire and then built beside it a little booth covered with pine boughs. We had nothing to eat except a few ears of ripe corn that we had taken from a field during the night. We ate some of it now and tried to parch some, but having no facilities for parching, did not succeed well. Two of us now lay down at a time to sleep while the other kept watch and kept up the fire.

### October 8 (Saturday)

Ransom, John, QM Sgt., 9th Michigan Cavalry, Marine Hospital, Savannah, Ga.:

Talk of Millen, about ninety miles from here. Mike

will trade off the rings tonight. Owe Sergt. Winn $12 for onions and sweet potatoes, Confederate money however; a dollar Confed. is only ten cents in money.... It is said that Savannah will be in our hands in less than two months.... Union army victorious everywhere. Going on twelve months a prisoner of war. Don't want to be exchanged now; could not stand the journey home; just want to be let alone one month and then home and friends. Saw myself in a looking glass for the first time in ten months and am the worst looking specimen—don't want to go home in twelve years unless I look different from this; almost inclined to disown myself. Pitch pine smoke is getting peeled off; need skinning. Eyesight improving with other troubles. Can't begin to read a newspaper and with difficulty write a little at a time. Can hear big guns every morning from down the river; it is said to be Yankee gunboats bidding the city of Savannah "good morning."

Conley, Capt., 101st Penna. Volunteers, escaped prisoner, near Columbia, S.C.:

About two o'clock P.M. we were startled by the baying of hounds in the distance, and from the sound felt very sure that they were bloodhounds. We soon became convinced that they were following the road we had travelled. Soon we found that they had left the wood, at or about the point we did and were coming towards us. We each selected a tree to climb in case they came to us, determined to make no fresh tracks. But we soon discovered that they had lost the trail at about the place where we entered the gravelly ledge and were circling to find it again. We could hear the voices of the men on horseback who followed them, and once caught sight of one of them through the timber; but after spending some time in a fruitless effort, gave it up and withdrew, very greatly to our relief.

We decided that it would not be prudent to go back to the road at the point we left, but rather to strike it farther up; for which purpose we started a little before dark, travelling through the woods, and just as it was getting dark we reached the road. We now started out at a brisk walk and had proceeded not more than one hundred and fifty or two hundred yards when we were suddenly startled by the bay of a hound in the road about five or six rods in the rear of us. Our first thought was that they had been watching for us and now found us; but looking around, saw only one

hound and he stood off and barked. Picking up a piece of a limb at the side of the road, I threw it at him, when he ran away. Looking back along the road to a point near where we had entered we saw some men with a pine torch. We became satisfied that they were only hunters with their hunting dog.

Passing on a short distance, we came to a large plantation and just after we entered the lane leading through it, we were again startled by being unexpectedly addressed, "Good ev'nin', ge'men." Looking up we discovered a colored man. We responded "Good Evening," and walked on. This we afterwards learned was a great mistake. We should have made ourselves known to him, sought information and something to eat. Our reasons for not doing so were that we had been mislead while in Charleston by their daily papers which were almost daily boasting of the faithfulness of their servants and reporting frequent captures of "Yankee prisoners" by their servants. This we afterward became satisfied was simply done to mislead the prisoners held by them. But on account of these frequent reports, our purpose was to trust no none but to forage for living, fearing that here in the very heart of South Carolina, the hotbed of secession, the slaves might not understand the issues.

But, after travelling briskly for several miles, began to fear that we were getting too near Columbia. Not being able to learn how far we were from it, we took a road leading to the left. We had not gone far when we saw a fire near the road and as we came nearer, saw several colored men around the fire; but still fearing to make ourselves known to them, we passed quietly by, unnoticed by them. After following the road for a few miles, it ended at a large plantation. It being nearly morning, we sought a hiding place for the day which we found in the woods near the above-named plantation. A little reconnaissance that morning showed that we were quite near the Congaree River. We were now suffering the pangs of hunger, having found nothing to eat but corn, and it did not satisfy our hunger. As we lay there that day, a large flock of wild turkeys came picking along through the woods quite near to us. How we did wish for one of them! But we had no means of killing any. As soon as they saw us, one of them sounded the alarm and they disappeared.

Thinking that we could save distance by leaving the road, taking a shortcut across fields and through woods, and thus striking the main road two or three miles further on, we took our bearing by the north star and after a hard tramp through wet grass and weeds, through briers and swamps, we reached the main road as calculated. Soon after reaching it, we found a fingerboard which told us that we were yet eight miles from Columbia. We travelled on to within about three miles of Columbia, where we again sought a hiding place and built up a little fire.

## October 9 (Sunday)

At Tom's Brook, Va., near Fisher's Hill, the Union cavalry of Gen. A.T.A. Torbet was sent against the Confederates who had been harassing Sheridan's troops. Custer's and Wesley Merritt's divisions attacked and drove the Confederate cavalry of Thomas L. Rosser and L.L. Lomax for several miles back up the Valley, capturing 300 prisoners.

Conley, Capt., 101st Penna. Volunteers, escaped prisoner, near Columbia, S.C.:

This was Sunday morning, October 9th and our fourth day out and still nothing to eat except ripe corn. We began to discover that corn did not agree with us. Our stomachs seemed to revolt. Our strength was giving away, but we were not discouraged. We rested quietly that day until near ten o'clock in the evening when we again took to the road and travelled on until we reached the suburbs of Columbia, when we made a detour to the right, passing through the outskirts of the city, sometimes through outer streets and again through lots. While passing through what appeared to be a pasture lot, we noticed a light in the lot next to us. Carefully approaching the fence, I discovered an officer's tent and in the background I noticed a number of other tents, but dark. Evidently there were several companies encamping here. Once, while passing through a lot finding it difficult travelling on account of the briers and weeds, we decided to risk an outer street with only here and there a house. As we approached it and were about to cross the fence that separated the lot from the street, a musket was discharged in front of a house about a hundred yards to our right and in the direction we wished to go. We did not know why it was fired, but we did know that we did not want to pass that house. Consequently, we quietly retreated and made our way through the out lots notwithstanding the briers.

Ransom, John, QM Sgt., 9th Michigan Cavalry, Marine Hospital, Savannah, Ga.:

The reason we have not been exchanged is because if the exchange is made it will put all the men held by the Union forces right into the rebel army, while the Union prisoners of war held by the rebels are in no condition to do service; that would seem to me to be a very poor reason.... A rebel M.D., by name Pendelton, or some such name, says if I am not careful will have a relapse, and is rather inclined to scold; says I get along all together too fast, and tells the nurse and Mike and Land, that I must not eat but little at a time and then only such food as he may direct, and if I don't do as he says, will put me in the main building away from my friends. Says it is suicide the way some act after a long imprisonment. Well, suppose he is right and I must go slow. Names of Yankee officers marked on the tents that have occupied them as prisoner of war before us.

## October 10 (Monday)

An inspector of prisons reported to the commander of the prison at Rock Island, Ill., today that "the streets and avenues, by constant policing, are clean and free from all filth. The buildings, being well ventilated, are in a healthy condition. The kitchens are in excellent order. The clothing and bedding of the prisoners, by frequent washings and airing, are clean and comfortable."

Ransom, John, QM Sgt., 9th Michigan Cavalry, Marine Hospital, Savannah, Ga.:

Mike traded off the gold rings for three pecks of sweet potatoes and half a dozen onions; am in clover. Make a nice soup out of beef, potato, bread, onion and salt; can trade a sweet potato for most anything. Mike does the cooking and I do the eating; he won't eat my potatoes, some others do though and without my permission. 'Tis ever thus, wealth brings care and trouble. Battese came today to see me and gave him some sweet potatoes. He is going away soon, the rebels have promised to send him with next batch of sailors; is a favorite with the rebels.... Set now at the door of the tent on a soapbox; beautiful shade trees all over the place. Am in the 5th Ward, tent No. 12; coverlid still does me good service. Many die here but not from lack of attention or medicine. They haven't the vitality to rally after their sufferings at Andersonville. Sisters of Charity go from tent to tent looking after men of their own religion; also citizens come among us. Wheat bread we have quite often and is donated by citizens. Guards walk on the outside of the wall and only half a dozen or so on the inside, two being on the gate.... Should judge the place was some fine private residence before being transformed into the Marine Hospital. Have good water. What little hair I have is coming off; probably go home bald-headed.

Conley, Capt., 101st Penna. Volunteers, escaped prisoner, near Columbia, S.C.:

About two o'clock in the morning we reached a railroad that appeared to run in the direction we wished to go. We started out along it, being anxious to get away from the city as soon as possible. We had not gone far until we discovered that it was leading nearer due north than we wished to go, but we travelled along it until we found a wagon road that led very nearly in the same direction. We followed it for some time, when feeling very much fatigued, and believing that we were at a safe distance from the city we sought a hiding place for the day, when we again built a fire. My comrades both said that they could go no farther without something to eat. We could no longer eat any of the corn as it produced nausea. It now became clear to us that a crisis was at hand and the only hope left us was the slaves. We had made every possible effort to secure something else to eat but without success. The number of dogs about every plantation prevented us from making a very thorough search about or near the buildings. We had strong misgivings about trusting the slaves, but it was our last hope. It happened that our hiding place was near a large plantation. I spent a large part of the day lying along a fence surrounding the plantation in the hope of getting a chance to interview one of the slaves, but notwithstanding I could see a score or more of them at work in the fields, yet they were too far away for me to speak to them. But I carefully noted the lay of the buildings and the means of approach to the slaves' cabins. I saw that by going along a lane that led in from the side of the plantation nearest us, that I could reach the slaves' quarter first.

I then went back to our fire and waited until after dark when I started in this lane. When I got to

within eight or ten rods of the nearest cabin, I heard voices in that direction. Crossing over the fence to my left, I approached with great caution. When I got within three or four rods of them, I saw that they were slaves sitting on the fence busily engaged in conversation. When I got a little nearer, I saw one of them sitting several feet nearer me than the rest, who seemed to be listening to the conversation that was going on. They were all facing the road. I carefully approached the one nearest me, and laying my hand on his shoulder, I whispered in his ear, "Come down the lane; I want to talk to you." I again retreated and he got down off the fence and walked down the lane several rods when he stopped. I now approached him, giving him my hand, and said to him, "Can I trust you as a friend?" He replied, "Yes, sah, I 'spect you can." I then said, "Are you a friend of the Yankees?" His cautious reply was, "Well, sah, I 'spect I'se a friend to most everybody's." I then said, "Can I trust you that you will not expose me?", to which he replied, "Yes, sah, you can do dat." I then told him that I was an escaped Yankee prisoner. At this he seemed to brighten up, and replied, "I's a friend of de Yankees." I then asked him if he could get me something to eat. His reply was, "I'se got nuffin' but I'll go and bring de oberseer down, I 'spect he can give you something." I said, "Ah, but he's a white man, isn't he?" He replied, "No, sah, we's got a cullud oberseer here." "And he's all right?" I asked. To which he replied, "Yes, sah, he's all right." I then told him that I would wait until he brought him.

In a few minutes he returned with the overseer who told me that he could supply my wants. I then informed him that I had two comrades who were in the woods a short distance away. He told me to meet him at the head of the lane in an hour. I returned to my comrades and reported success. I remained by our fire until time to meet our overseer, when I went to the end of the lane and waited. Soon he and the other one I had just interviewed put in an appearance with baskets on their arms. I piloted them to where my comrades were. He took out of one basket a crock of rice boiled with slices of fat bacon. The other basket was a bountiful supply of corn bread. He had with him three spoons with which we attacked the crock of rice and bacon, which held at least a gallon, and in a very short time the crock was empty. I thought that was one of the most delicious dishes I had ever tasted. As I ate it, I seemed to feel new blood coursing through my veins and my wasted strength returning to me. The bacon was old and I think very strong, but our famished condition caused us to think it very delicious. We now attacked the corn bread, and I believe, could have eaten all of it, but feared to do so and decided to keep some for the next day.

The next thing was to secure all the information we could. In this we were fortunate as the overseer (who informed us that his name was Wade) was a slave of a good deal more than the average intelligence. He had been raised near Knoxville, Tenn., and had been over the route two or three times in his life and was therefore able to give us a pretty good idea of the route. We then inquired as to whether we would find the slaves friendly to us, and he assured us that we were safe with any of the field hands, but to avoid the house servants, as they were generally pets of their masters. He informed us that we were 4½ miles from Columbia, but that we had taken the wrong road at Columbia. The railroad that we started on led to Charlotte, N.C., and we then were about three miles off the road we should have taken, and said that he would send one of the boys along to pilot us across the country to the right road. We did not regret our mistake in roads. Indeed, we were inclined to believe that our mistake was providential as it led us to such a valuable friend. After many thanks to our kind friend, the colored overseer, for his homely but generous hospitality, we started with our man.

As we were going along we asked whether there was a chance to get any sweet potatoes. "Oh, yes," he answered, "there is a nice patch just ahead of us. When we come to it I will get you some." When we reached it he got over the fence and dug us as many as we could carry. We had but one haversack with us. We filled it and our handkerchiefs, putting our corn bread in our pockets. Reaching the road we were to travel, we bade our guide good-bye and proceeded on our way traveling about fifteen miles. During the night we ate all of our corn bread and yet our hunger was not satisfied. Indeed our appetites appeared to be insatiable. We felt that we were not only regaining our strength, but having found friends that we could trust, our prospects for success were greatly brightened. This was the greatest distance we had made in any one night since our escape. We had just been feeling our way; but with the information we now

had, we were able to proceed without loss of time.

## October 11 (Tuesday)

Conley, Capt., 101st Penna. Volunteers, escaped prisoner, near Columbia, S.C.:

In the morning, as usual, we sought a safe hiding place in the woods, and built up a fire and feasted that day on roasted sweet potatoes. That evening we secured a little corn bread and a few sweet potatoes from a slave and that night passed through a village of Monticello and traveled until time to turn in and secure a hiding place without any incident worthy of note. As usual, we built a fire and roasted and ate our sweet potatoes, after which, leaving my comrades by the fire, I cautiously approached the road and took my position behind a thick clump of bushes about 25 or 30 feet from the road hoping that some slave would pass with whom I might make arrangements for something to eat and thus save delay at night.

I had lain there for an hour or more when I heard the tramp of horses but could not see them until they were quite near me. I then discovered it was a company of rebel cavalry passing. They were walking their horses slowly and as I watched them through the bushes, I could see their faces quite plainly and hear their conversation; and I feared that if they should look in my direction they might see me, but they passed without looking towards me. After waiting for some time longer without seeing a slave, I returned to my comrades.

A little later in the day as we lay by our fire, two hunters with dogs passed through the woods about twenty rods from us. We lay perfectly still and they passed without seeing us. As evening approached we found ourselves entirely out of provisions and quite hungry. That evening we started out and tried at every plantation we came to but failed to get anything to eat. The trouble at nearly every plantation was that the slaves' rations were issued to them every morning, and by night it was all eaten. We found all of the slaves friendly and anxious to see us, but had nothing to give us. After trying at three or four plantations without success, I asked one of the slaves at the last plantation at which we stopped whether he could tell me of any place where we could get something. He told me that about five miles ahead at Col. Fenner's plantation they had a colored overseer and that there were no white folks living on the plantation; that if we would stop there we could get plenty to eat.

### October 12 (Wednesday)

Ransom, John, QM Sgt., 9th Michigan Cavalry, Marine Hospital, Savannah, Ga.:

Still getting better fast, and doctor says too fast. Now do nearly all the diary writing. Hardly seems possible that our own Yankee gunboats are so near us, so near that we can hear them fire off their guns, but such is the case. Reports have it that the Johnny Rebels are about worsted. Has been a hard war and a cruel one. Mike does all the cooking now, although an invalid. He trades sweet potato for vinegar, which tastes the best of anything, also have other things suitable for the sick, and this morning had an egg. My gold rings will put me in good health again. All the time medicine, that is, three or four times a day; and sores on my body healing up now for the first time. Mouth, which was one mass of black bloody swellings on the inside, is now white and inflammation gone, teeth however, loose, and have lost four through scurvy, having come out themselves. My eyes, which had been trying to get in out of sight, are now coming out again and look more respectable. Battese was taken prisoner with eighteen other Indians; they all died but one beside himself.

Conley, Capt., 101st Penna. Volunteers, escaped prisoner, near Columbia, S.C.:

We had met one colored overseer, and were anxious to meet more, so receiving careful directions from him we reached the place about two o'clock in the morning, and, being very much fatigued, decided to lie down until morning. Securing a good hiding place, we built a fire and lay down and slept until daybreak. About sunrise I saw two slaves coming through the woods; I walked out and met them and after telling them who I was, I asked them for something to eat. They replied that they did not have anything, but that the overseer had gone with the wagons to the cornfield and that they were taking a shortcut through the woods and when they got there they would send the overseer to us.

In about half an hour we saw a tall, fine looking colored man, apparently between fifty and sixty years of age, approaching through the woods. I walked out so as to attract his attention, when he hastened to me, exclaiming as he approached us, "De boys done tole me dar was some Yankees up hyar. Now, is you r'al Yankees?" On being assured that we were the genuine article, he said, "God bress you, I never seed no Yankees before. When de boys done tole me dar was some Yankees up hyar, I come right up. Bress de Lord, I never 'spected to see no Yankees down hyar." He seemed so overjoyed and had so many questions to ask us about the progress of the war, and the prospects for emancipation of the slaves, and all about "Marse Lincum" that he spent more than an hour, when a sudden thought struck him, and he exclaimed, "Bress de Lord, I forgot to ask you if you had any breakfuss." We told him that we had not and had but little to eat yesterday, but as the forenoon was now well advanced, we would wait until dinner, as we were accustomed to fasting. To which he replied, "I'll go and bring Uncle Friday up and den I'll go and get your dinner. I'll get you a good dinner. I'se got plenty. I rans dis plantation, God bress you."

He left us and soon returned with another colored man, apparently about his own age, who he introduced to us as "Uncle Friday," who, we learned, was a kind of sub or assistant overseer. Uncle Friday, like the overseer, had an unlimited number of questions to ask about "Marse Lincum" and the emancipation Proclamation and what were the prospects for their becoming free. He, like the overseer, was intensely interested in securing their freedom. We assured him, from our own knowledge of the inside of the Confederacy, that the war was drawing to a close and that inside of one year he would be a free man. At which the old man seemed to go into a state of ecstacy. He made what seemed to me to be quite a high leap into the air, cracked his heels together, and exclaimed, "I'se an old man, but if de war'll give me my freedom, I can s'port me and de ole woman yet, God bress you." He talked with us until nearly noon, seeming to be anxious to learn all about the progress of the war, and all he could about the Yankees. Among the things he asked was it true that "Marse Lincum was a nigger." When told that he was a white man, he said, "Our folks all says dat he is a nigger." Having with us a greenback with the vignette of Lincoln, we showed it to him. He looked at it for a long time and then said, "He looks like a mighty good man."

About noon he started to the house for dinner

and soon after we saw the overseer coming with a large basket on each arm. As he set the basket down, he said, "I'se got you a good dinner. I got it all myself." He then took out a nice clean tablecloth and spread it on the ground. Next he took out plates, knives and forks and spoons which he arranged nicely. Then came the dinner which consisted of a large dish of chicken potpie, hot biscuit, butter, syrup, milk, etc. It was such a feast as we had not enjoyed for many months. And the way that dinner disappeared must have given our colored friend a high opinion of his proficiency in the culinary art. I had always been fond of chicken pie, but it seemed to me that I had never eaten any quite as fine as that, and how delicious those biscuits tasted! Well, we ate until satisfied for the first time since our escape and yet there was some left.

After dinner all the colored men in the place came to see us and some of them spent nearly all of the afternoon with us. They were all intensely interested in securing their freedoms, and had many questions to ask, and in return for the information we gave them, we learned much of the life of the slaves.

A number of colored women came out to see us, but none of them would venture nearer than four or five rods although we assured them that we would not harm them. Some of the young slaves were greatly attracted by our uniforms and proposed trading for them. Both my comrades showed a willingness to trade at which several of them went to their cabins and brought out their best suits, which were of grey material but good substantial goods. Capt. Dawson and Lt. Davidson soon struck bargains with two of them. My own uniform was pretty well worn, and beside, I being tall and rather slender, it would not fit one of them. The one with whom Capt. Dawson traded was a fine looking young slave. When he put on the Captain's dress coat and buttoned it up, it fit him very nicely, and he appeared very proud of it. He then said to the Captain, "Captain, I'll tell you what I want dis for. I'se gwine to get married, and I want dis for a weddin' suit. I tell you dat'll make a mighty fine weddin' suit."

They urged us to stop with them for several days but we were anxious to push on so as to get through the mountains before winter. But we were afterwards satisfied that we would have lost nothing by doing so. That evening the overseer furnished us with a good supply of biscuits and corn bread, and when we

were ready to start, the overseer, Uncle Friday, and several of their men accompanied us for two or three miles. After giving us valuable information about our route and how to avoid danger, they bid us good-bye with many a hearty "God bress you." And, as we proceeded on our journey, we realized as we had never done before, the truth of the old maxim, "A friend in need is a friend indeed."

### October 13 (Thursday)

In the Valley there was skirmishing around Cedar Creek as the Confederates probed from their old lines at Fisher's Hill against Sheridan's troops astraddle the Valley Pike.

The Medical Director at Baltimore, Md., Surgeon J. Simpson, wrote Col. Hoffman, Federal Commissary-General of Prisoners, today about prisoners arriving in that city. These were the prisoners from Elmira, N.Y., whom Hoffman had sent instructions relating to the shipment of on September 29th.

A train of over 1200 rebel prisoners arrived in this city today from Elmira, en route for City Point. The officer in charge reporting to me that many of the prisoners were exceedingly ill and that five had died on the road, I made a personal inspection of the men and found a number unable to bear the journey. I directed that they should be admitted to the West Hospital, and gave Surgeon Chapel instructions to examine those on board the boat. As soon as a report from Surgeon Campbell, who continued the inspection, is received I will forward it, with a full report of the case to you. The physical condition of many of these men was distressing in the extreme, and they should never have been permitted to leave Elmira.

The instructions given to Surgeon A. Chapel by the Medical Director at Baltimore were explicit as to the extent of his duty:

You will receive such sick and wounded rebels into the hospital under your charge as may be sent you by Surg. C.F.H. Campbell, U.S. Volunteers, from those now *in transitu* through this city from Elmira, N.Y., and receipt for them on the customary rolls to Maj. E.A. Roberts, in charge of the squad. As it is possible that some cases might have been overlooked you will visit the steamer on which the prisoners are embarking for exchange, and admit to the hospital under your charge such as humanity requires should be taken care of. You will report to this office in the morning the number thus received.

Conley, Capt., 101st Penna. Volunteers, escaped prisoner, north of Columbia, S.C.:

We were becoming anxious to cross Broad river as soon as we could, as following the east bank was leading us too much north and out of the direction we wished to go. The overseer advised us not to attempt to cross the river until we reached the place where the Columbia & Spartanburg R.R. crosses the river, saying that we could not cross on the bridge as it was guarded, but that there was a ferry close by the bridge that was run by a slave; that we should hunt him up and he would take us across at night. A good night's travel brought us within one mile of the bridge, which is forty-five miles above Columbia. Finding a hiding place, we built a fire, and here spent the day. We were now beginning to suffer very greatly with sore feet, having become blistered the first few nights that we were out. Indeed, we had constant suffering while traveling although we had started out the evening before with a good supply of provisions yet, by evening it had all been eaten. Our appetites seemed to be insatiable.

When evening approached it was arranged that I should go back to a plantation that we had passed that morning and Lt. Davidson should go to one nearby in another direction. We had the double purpose of securing information about the slave that was in charge of the ferry, and also of securing some provisions. When we started out it was just after dark. Just as I approached the road, I heard footsteps coming from the direction of the bridge. Stepping behind a tree beside the road, I waited to see who was coming. As he approached, I saw that he was a colored man. Stepping out, I said to him, "Good evening, sir. Will you please step to the side of the road? I want to talk to you." At this he seemed to become alarmed and commenced to back away from me, saying as he did so, "Well sah, if you's got anything to say to me, say it heah, sah." Seeing his alarm, I said, "I am a Yankee." He exclaimed, "Is you?" and without a moment's hesitation he hastened into the woods. When we had gotten a safe distance from the road, I explained to him that I was an escaped Yankee prisoner, and had two comrades with me, that we wanted to cross the river at this point, and asked him

whether he knew the colored man that attended the ferry at the river. His answer was, "Well, sah, I'se de nigger what runs de ferry." I expressed my gratification at being so fortunate to meet him and asked him whether he could take us across tonight. He said that he could not as he was compelled to report to "Ol' Marse" at once, but that he could put us across at four o'clock in the morning. He then said, "You can cross on the R.R. bridge." "But, is it not guarded?", I asked. He replied, "No, the only guard there is a man who lives in a house at the end of the bridge, who has de care of de bridge, but he goes to bed about ten o'clock." That settled, I asked about something to eat. He said, "Well sah, we had no co'n meal dis mo'ning when I left, but Ole Marse said he 'spected to get some today, and if he did, I will bake you a good big pone." I then asked him if he had any sweet potatoes. Answering that he had, I then told him if he did not have the cornmeal to get us some sweet potatoes. He then told me to come to the cotton gin which stood some distance from the house and wait for him. Soon after he left me, Lt. Dawson returned unsuccessful. We did as he said and waited until nearly ten o'clock before he put in an appearance, but when he did come he had a "Great big pone" and a good supply of sweet potatoes. After partaking of our supper, and securing all the information we could from our kind host, with thanks for his kindness, we bade him good-bye, and advanced to within a few rods of the bridge when we stopped and made a careful reconnoiter, and finding the coast clear, we stepped on the trestle work of the bridge; stepping from tie to tie we made our way across. We judged that the bridge and trestle work to be about a quarter of a mile in length. We felt greatly relieved at being safely across this, the only large stream we would have to cross before reaching the mountains.

## October 14 (Friday)

About two miles from Columbia, S.C., 1200 Union officer prisoners had been living in an open field without any shelter for a week. The Confederate officer in charge, Capt. Semple, had promised to send 100 wall tents to the field a week previously, but nothing arrived. Lt. Abbott continued his recording of the ordeal.

Today, Surgeon A. Chapel, Baltimore, Md., reported to Surgeon J. Simpson, Medical Director,

Baltimore, on his inspection of the rebel prisoners en route to City Point from Elmira, N.Y.:

I went on board the steamer loaded with prisoners of war last evening ... and examined the worst cases. I found at least forty cases that should not have been sent on such a journey, most of whom were in a very feeble and emaciated condition, but as my hospital had been more than filled by those sent by Surgeon Campbell, and they were all very anxious to continue the journey with their comrades, I thought it better not to remove them. I found no medical officer, hospital steward, or nurse aboard the boat with the worst cases. Someone, in my opinion, is greatly censurable for sending such cases away from camp even for exchange.

Surgeon C.F.H. Campbell, Asst. Medical Inspector, at Baltimore, had inspected the prisoners on the train which had come from Elmira, N.Y., on the afternoon of October 13th and today submitted his report to Surgeon Simpson, Medical Director, in Baltimore:

I yesterday proceeded to inspect the physical condition of the rebel prisoners then in transit through this city from Elmira, N.Y., to City Point, Va., for exchange. The train was composed of over 1200 men, from which number I selected sixty men as totally unfit to travel and sent to general hospital. These men were debilitated from long sickness to such a degree that it was necessary to carry them in the arms of attendants from the cars to the ambulances, and one man died in the act of being thus transferred. Such men should not have been sent from Elmira. If they were inspected before leaving that place in accordance with orders it was most carelessly done, reflecting severely on the medical officers engaged in that duty and is alike disgraceful to all concerned. The effect produced upon the public by such marked displays of inefficiency or neglect of duty cannot fail to be most injurious to our cause both at home and abroad. Five men had died on the train on the road to this city from utter prostration and debility, their appearance after death bearing evidence of this fact. Thus it will be seen six men have died from the number sent, and if the above selection of men had not been made and sent to general hospital many more deaths would have been added to this number ere they reached City Point.

Surgeon Simpson, Medical Director at Baltimore, forwarded the reports from the other Surgeons to Col. William Hoffman, Federal Commissary-General of Prisoners, in Washington. With the reports he stated that "The condition of these men was pitiable in the extreme and evinces criminal neglect and inhumanity on the part of the medical officers making the selection of men to be transferred."

Abbott, A.O., 1st Lt., 1st N.Y. Dragoons, prisoner, Columbia, S.C.:

A week passed, and seeing no prospect of being furnished with the promised tents, and feeling the need of some kind of shelter, made, as best we could of the pine brush, *shanties*, which, though uncomfortable, seemed better than to lie on the open ground.

About this time we had a cold storm of two weeks duration, raining nearly every day. We were almost entirely destitute of blankets or overcoats. Our other clothing was poor, and very thin, consisting of a pair of pants, often nothing but cotton at that, perhaps made from an old commissary meal-sack; a ragged shirt, or *none at all,* and a coat with the lining torn out, buttons sold off, and patched with many colors; a pair of boots or shoes, mended with straps, strings, cloth, anything; if we had socks, they were patched from top to toe with various-colored cloth. Through all of this the wind would sweep with a vengeance that kept us shivering from morning till night, and from night till morning. Our little brush houses were no protection from the storm; our clothing was little better; we had little wood, and could get but a small quantity, and that of second-growth pine; we were camped on the top of a hill, where the wind had a fair sweep at us, and taking all of these things together, we were about as uncomfortable as we could be.

The ladies at home, "God bless them," did us a kindness which we shall never forget. Through the Sanitary Commission, they sent us several boxes of goods, originally designed, no doubt, for a hospital, yet nonetheless acceptable. Upon opening the boxes, we found shirts, drawers, towels, pocket-handkerchiefs, a few hospital gowns, bedsacks, and several quilts. These were judiciously divided among us, giving to each one a towel, a handkerchief, and either a shirt or a pair of drawers, *but not both,* else someone would have to go without....

Soon after this the Christian Commission sent us a valuable donation in the shape of a box of reading matter, books, papers,... something that would help to pass a lonely hour.

Conley, Capt., 101st Penna. Volunteers, escaped prisoner, above Columbia, S.C.:

We now continued on our course towards Spartanburg until nearly morning without any incident worthy of note. As usual we built a fire and rested during the day. About ten o'clock that night we started again and after traveling a short distance, we stopped at a plantation to look for something to eat. I cautiously approached one of the slave's cabins, opened the door, stepped inside and closed the door before I spoke. This we did so as not to attract the attention of the dogs, of which there were usually several about each plantation. Waking up a slave, he gave me a small piece of corn bread, which he brought outside of the house where we sat under a peach tree. I got out my pocket book and gave him a dollar in Confederate money, after which I asked him if he could get me any sweet potatoes. Saying that he could, we started to the sweet potato patch which was some distance from the house. After digging me what we wanted, I again reached for my pocket book, intending to give him another dollar, when to my surprise I found that it was gone. We hunted through the potato patch, and then along the path we had come, and under the peach tree, but could not find it. In the pocket book was one twenty dollar greenback besides some Confederate money. This left me without one cent of money.

After traveling two or three miles, and in the meantime passing through a small village, the name of which we did not know, we noticed a bright fire burning beside the road in front of us. This brought us to a sudden halt. The road at this place led through heavy timber, but a fence ran along the right-hand side. After carefully viewing the situation, we believed it would be next to impossible for us to pass around through the woods without losing our bearings as the night was tolerably dark. Leaving my comrades concealed in the woods, I cautiously advanced through the edge of the woods until I got within three or four rods of the fire, when I could distinctly see a cavalryman with his sabre at his side, sitting by the fire smoking. His horse was tied to the fence. I had been

there but a short time when he got up, stirred up his fire, unfolded his blanket, and lay down beside it. I then very quietly returned to my comrades. We waited until the fire burned down, and we got near enough to hear him snoring. Being satisfied that he was safely locked in the arms of Morpheus, we advanced with noiseless tread and passed within eight feet of him.

Ransom, John, QM Sgt., 9th Michigan Cavalry, Marine Hospital, Savannah, Ga.:

None die through neglect here; all is done that could reasonably be expected.... For a week or ten days could take care of nothing. Winn took charge of the book that I am writing in now and Battese had the other two books, and now they are all together safe in my charge. Wonder if any one will ever have the patience or time to read it all? Not less than a thousand pages of finely written crow tracks, and some places blurred and unintelligible from being wet and damp. As I set up in my bunk my legs are just fitted for hanging down over the side, and have not been straightened for three or four months. Rub the cords with ointment furnished me by physician and can see a change for the better. Legs are blue, red and shiny and in some places the skin seems calloused to the bone.

## October 15 (Saturday)

Ransom, John, QM Sgt., 9th Michigan Cavalry, Marine Hospital, Savannah, Ga.:

A very little satisfies me as regards the upward tendency to health and liberty. Some would think to look at me almost helpless and a prisoner of war, that I hadn't much to feel glad about. Well, let them on through what I have and then see. Citizens look on me with pity when I should be congratulated. Am probably the happiest mortal anywhere hereabouts. Shall appreciate life, health and enough to eat hereafter. Am anxious for only one thing, and that is to get news home to Michigan of my safety.... Drizzling rain has set in. Birds chipper from among the trees. Hear bells ring about the city of Savannah. Very different from the city of Richmond; there it was all noise and bustle and clatter, every man for himself.... Everyone talks and treats you with courtesy and kindness. Don't seem as if they could both be cities of the Confederacy.

Conley, Capt., 101st Penna. Volunteers, escaped prisoner, S.C.:

We traveled until nearly morning without any further incident worthy of note, when we sought a hiding place, and having secured what we thought was a safe place, we proceeded to build our fire. In doing so, I took out my knife to split some kindling. Just after our fire was started, we heard a rooster crow quite near us. This satisfied us that we were too close to a building. So, gathering up our few effects, we moved some distance away.

The morning being foggy, it was difficult to secure a good location. When we stopped again and proceeded to build a fire, I discovered that I did not have my knife, having left it where we had first built a fire. After daylight I tried to find the place but could not, and consequently did not get my knife again. As we lay by our fire that forenoon, we saw a white man approaching us through the woods. He seemed to be coming directly towards us. What was to be done? If we attempted to run he would see us. He was walking quite rapidly, with his eyes to the ground. To our great relief, however, when he to got about twelve or fifteen rods from us he commenced to change his course a little to the right. Seeing this, we lay flat on the ground and he passed within four or five rods of us. Our fire at the time was burned down so that it made very little smoke. He had gone but a short distance from us when he met another man and they stopped to talk. The subject of conversation seemed to be about some horses that had broken into the field of one of the parties. We inferred that the horses belonged to the other party. After talking for some time, each turned back the way he came. Our man again passed by as he had gone without seeing us. We afterward discovered that he was following a path that led through the woods. We then took the precaution to move farther away from it.

### October 16 (Sunday)

Confederate Col. D.T. Chandler arrived at Cahaba in early October to inspect the prison as a part of the Inspector-General's routine visits. Chandler found the prison to be populated with over 2100 prisoners, 69 of whom were hospitalized and another 75, or more, requiring hospitalization. The hospital, however, was too small for the number of patients requiring treatment. The prisoners were short of almost every item imaginable. Food was issued to the prisoners as rations of raw meat and few utensils were available for use. No vegetables were issued to the prisoners, although the guards were issued peas or beans almost daily. Only three axes were available for use by the prisoners to cut wood for their cooking fires. The guards, totaling 179, worked a day-on-day-off schedule which was very tiring and their efficiency suffered because of this.

Chandler was also concerned about the prisoners overpowering the guards and escaping into the nearby countryside. There were no troops in the area to contain so many determined men. Chandler recommended that the prison be moved about 1 mile south of its present location to a more suitable site where accommodations could be made and the health of the prisoners would improve.

Conley, Capt., 101st Penna. Volunteers, escaped prisoner, S.C.:

That night we again made our usual march, passing within about two miles of Unionville, and halting the next morning a few miles above it. Although we had called on several slaves during the night, we had failed to get anything to eat. All were friendly, but had nothing to give us. So we decided, rather reluctantly, to observe this as a day of fasting. We were now suffering very greatly with sore feet. They had become so much inflamed that we could scarcely wear our shoes. That forenoon I took my position behind a log near the road to watch for a slave. I had not been there long before I heard children talking and laughing a short distance down the road. I judged that they were coming in my direction. While listening to them, a little dog came running around the log and commenced to bark at me. Seeing that the children were not yet in sight, and fearing that the dog might reveal my hiding place to the children, I threw a stick at him, at which he retreated, and I also beat a hasty retreat. After the children had passed, I again took my position behind the log and waiting for some time, a young colored man, apparently about 20 years of age, came along in a cart. I stepped out and spoke to him and asked him where he lived, and he answered on the Foster plantation, about two or three miles ahead. I then asked him whether he could get us something to eat, to which he replied that he could, and that he would have us a supply of corn bread ready when we came along that evening, but told me that he did not live on the main public road, but that, after passing the first plantation, we would find a road taking off to the right; to follow that road until we came to a field and there he would meet us. He also said he had a whistle, which he would blow, so as to attract our attention.

In order to save time, we started before it was entirely dark, and leaving the public road, passed around the first plantation, reaching the road just beyond it. By this time it was quite dark and though we searched for the road leading to the right, we failed to find it. After going some distance, we came to a small dwelling house beside the road. From the appearance of the house we supposed that it was occupied by a free colored family, or what is known to the South as "po' white trash," and we decided to make inquiry. Capt. Dawson went in and found it occupied by a white family. On inquiry he was told that we had passed the road. We then returned but still failed to find the road. Having reached the end of the lane leading through the plantation that we had just passed around that evening, I told my comrades to remain there and I would go and search for a slave and get more definite information. Passing along the lane, which was the public road, for some distance, I came to another lane leading to the left at right angles to the public road. Taking this lane, I had not gone far until I heard the voices of Colored men. As I got a little closer, I heard horses walking. They seemed to be just bringing the horses out to the road. Supposing that there was no white man about, I boldly approached them. Just as I reached them, I heard a white man's voice not more than ten feet from where I was. From the manner in which he spoke, I was convinced that he was either the planter himself or an overseer. He was just beside the road, and to go on I must pass within six or eight feet of him. Believing that I was too close to retreat without being discovered, I decided to walk boldly by him. As I did so, and just as I had passed him, he called out, "Who are you?" Then, with an oath, he said, "Halt, or I will shoot." Paying no attention to him, I kept right on, knowing that to halt or even hesitate would mean capture as he would command his slaves and they would be compelled to obey. I therefore went right on while he kept swearing fearful oaths that he would shoot. When I had gotten about four

or five rods from him he changed his tactics. Instead of shooting, as he had threatened, he commenced to call his dog, "Sumter." I was at that time just about opposite the house, which stood some distance back from the road. I heard "Sumter" give a bay. Dark as it was, I could see there were woods some distance ahead. From there until I reached the woods, I did some fine running. As I ran I passed some of the slaves on horseback. When I reached the woods I stopped and finding the dog did not follow me, I began to calculate how I was to get back to my comrades. It would not be safe to go by the road, and to leave the road for any distance I would be in danger of losing my bearings, the night being dark and cloudy. After studying the situation carefully, I decided to pass through the fields at the rear of the house. I crossed over into the field and had not gone far when I found a fence, I passed along of the opposite side of it. Just as I passed the house, I heard the darkies start up a song. I judged by the song that they were husking corn. I now cautiously approached the place where they were and finally located them. They were beside a stable husking and I took my position on the opposite side, and after satisfying myself that there were no white folks around, I passed around to where they were. They seemed to form a semicircle around a pile of corn. At the end of the line next to me sat a large colored woman with the usual handkerchief on her head. Stooping down, I laid my hand on her shoulder and whispered in her ear, "Tell one of the men to come around the stable, I want to talk to him." I then passed back and was quickly followed by one of the colored men but before I had time to speak to him, the colored woman came also and as she approached me, she said, "Now, you mind dat Ole Jack don't see you." I answered that we would be careful. She then said, "Who is you?" I replied, "I'm a Yankee." With a warning gesture of her hand, [she said] "Now you mind dat none of de white folks don't see you." Assuring her that I would be careful, she returned to her work and I then asked the colored man the road to Foster's plantation. He had just commenced to tell me when he stopped suddenly, and in a whisper said, "Dar's Old Jack," and leaving me he hastened around to his work. I then noticed that the singing had stopped and I recognized the same voice that had attempted to halt me at the road. The first thing I heard him saying was: "Did you see any more of that man that passed down there?" One of the slaves answered, "No, massa, we didn't see nuffin' more of him." He then asked, "Was he a white man or a nigger?" The reply was, "Sam dunno, mar'se, it was too dark; I couldn't see." He then asked, "Sam, which way was he going when you saw him last?" To which Sam replied, "De last I seen of him, he was going down towards de spring." I supposed that Sam was one of the boys I had ran past as they were riding down the road.

Seeming to be satisfied that his slaves knew nothing about me, he returned to the house, the slaves again started up their song and my man returned to me and as he did so, he said, "Ole Jack was 'quirin' about you." I replied that I had heard him. At which he said, "I 'spect you's the man dat walked past down dar." To which I replied in the affirmative. He then said, "We done tole him we didn't know nuffin' about you." I replied that I had heard him. I then secured the information I desired and he walked with me through the field to the public road. Just as we reached the lane fence we heard footsteps coming from the direction I had left my comrades. Concealing ourselves behinds the fence as they approached, I believed they were my comrades, at which I gave a signal which they answered and stopped. We had a system of signals arranged by which we might recognize each other in the dark. I then learned from them that they had heard the planter hail me, had heard him call his dog, and they supposed that I had been captured. Had I been five minutes later getting to the road, they would have been past and in all probability I would not have found them again. I had been absent from them more than an hour.

Bidding our colored friend good-bye with thanks for his information, we started out and found the road, which being covered with grass, was difficult to find in the night. We had not gone far on it when we heard the whistle of our colored boy. When we reached the field where he was to meet us, he was not there, but we heard the whistle some distance ahead. Following on the whistle finally stopped and we could hear nothing more of it. We went on until near the buildings, when we stopped and concealed ourselves. After waiting a while, we heard someone coming towards us and as he came near, he gave a whistle, by which we believed he was our boy. I stepped out and met him. He had with him some corn bread, which he gave us. But he had no idea how much three hungry men could eat. It was

scarcely enough for our supper. I asked him if he had any cornmeal. Replying that he had plenty, we gave him our haversack and asked him to fill it for us, which he did. From this darky we learned that the planter who had hailed me was "Mar's Jack Wright" who showed such a strong desire to form my acquaintance. He added, "Dey calls him Squire Wright." He also stated that he was a bitter rebel. After partaking of our supper of corn bread and learning all that we could about the roads we were to travel, we bade him good-bye and traveled until it was time to turn in for the day which we did about three or four miles southeast of Spartanburg. Here, as usual, we sought a secure hiding place, built our fire and lay down for a little rest.

Capt. Munger, inspector of the prison camp at Elmira, N.Y., was at it again. He reported on his inspection on this date:

I have made the weekly inspection of camp ... and find the police of grounds, quarters, &c., good. Drainage as perfect as the situation of camp will allow. During the past week over 1200 invalid prisoners, 300 of whom were from hospital, were paroled and sent South for exchange. There are now in hospital 588 patients, and receiving medical treatment, 1021 prisoners. During the four days since the removal of the sick there have been forty-four deaths. The cause of this amount of sickness and death is a matter of deep interest. That the existence of a large body of filthy, stagnant water within the camp has much to do with it can admit of no doubt. Low diet, indifferent clothing, and change of clothing doubtless have some effect. Most of the causes may be removed, and that it be done seems the plainest duty of humanity.

## October 17 (Monday)

Not having done much except annoy Sherman, John Bell Hood's Army of Tennessee moved towards Gadsden, Ala., relieving the pressure on Sherman. The torn track would be replaced shortly and the trains running again.

The continuing saga of the stagnant pond of water at Elmira, N.Y., gained some momentum today when Col. B.F. Tracy, commanding at Elmira, wrote Col. Wm. Hoffman, in Washington:

The continued prevalence of disease and death in this camp impels me to call the attention of the authorities to what is apparently the cause, to wit, the existence of a stagnant pond of water within the inclosure. Nothing else that I can see produces the large mortality among the prisoners. The camp is clean, water pure and abundant, and rations wholesome. The medical officers attribute the larger proportion of the sickness prevailing to the effects of this body of impure and material matter. The remedy for this evil, for such I conceive it to be, is attainable. A stream of water can be introduced from the river by digging a trench and laying pipe about 6000 feet. The cost of wooden pipe of six-inch diameter would be, as I learn upon inquiry, about 75 cents per foot. The digging and laying could be done principally with prison labor and at a small expense. I am informed that the estimated cost of laying pipe of this description is about $6000 per mile.

Your attention was first called to this almost intolerable nuisance in a letter from these headquarters, dated August 17, 1864, recommending that a ditch be dug from the river and allowing a stream of fresh water to play through it. A telegram from you of the date of August 20, 1864, requiring a report on the matter of introducing water into the camp from the city waterworks, was answered August 21, 1864, there then being made a full report in the matter, that it would be inexpedient to admit water from the city waterworks, as they failed to supply even the inhabitants of the city through the summer and fall months. A survey had been made, a copy of which was forwarded to you in letter of that date, of a ditch to be dug from the river. It seems to me that a due regard for the lives of the prisoners confined here requires that some method of introducing a running stream of water through this camp should be adopted, and in view of this I respectfully request authority to have the ditch constructed and the pipe laid after the plan proposed in this communication. The owners of the land do not object to the blind ditch, but did to the open ditch, as proposed by Lt. Col. Eastman in letter of August 17, 1864.

On August 19th, Col. Hoffman forwarded Tracy's letter, with enclosures, to Maj. Gen. Henry W. Halleck, Chief of Staff of the Army, for action:

The evacuation required can be done by the work of the prisoners at a trifling cost, and a pipe to be made of one-inch boards, with an opening six by six inch-es, would probably cost less than $500, and of two-inch plank not over $1000;... recommend that a pipe of two-inch plank be laid, the expense to be paid out of the prison fund.

On October 23rd, Gen. Halleck approved the plan and suggested it be carried out. *Somebody* finally made a decision.

Conley, Capt., 101st Penna. Volunteers, escaped prisoner, S.C.:

After daylight we got up and again built up our fire and soon we had a good bed of coals. We then commenced to mix our cornmeal with salt and water in a tin plate that we had with us. Making it into cakes about three or four inches in diameter and about three quarters of an inch thick. Wrapping these in green chestnut leaves, we buried them in the coals. Leaving them until thoroughly baked, we took them out. They came out nice and clean, the leaves having protected them from the ashes until they were thoroughly baked. To our surprise we found them better in flavor than any corn bread we had eaten before. We could not account for this unless it was that the leaves enclosing them prevented the escape of any of the flavor. During the forenoon we converted all of our cornmeal into corn bread.

During the afternoon I again took my position near the road behind a thick clump of chestnut bushes which grew up around a stump. I was about twenty or twenty-five feet from the road. After remaining there for some time, I heard a wheeled vehicle approaching. When it came into view it proved to be a carriage occupied by a very aristocratic-looking old gentleman and lady, with a very slight-looking colored driver who wore a black suit and a silk hat. Just as they got opposite me in the road, they met two ladies in an open buggy. To my great annoyance, both vehicles stopped and the occupants engaged in conversation. The ladies wanted some information about the roads, after which the health of the families and other subjects were discussed until it seemed to me that they would never get through. The carriage was on the side of the road next to me and I was afraid that pompous colored driver on his elevated seat might discover me but he did not look in my direction. I do not know what those high-toned Southern ladies would have done had they known that one of those hated "Yanks" lay concealed not more than twenty or twenty-five feet of them listening to their conversation. I could see the faces of each of them quite distinctly through the clump of bushes, and it appeared to me that they might have seen me, but, after talking for quite a while, they each started on their way, greatly to my relief.

I again returned to my comrades without accomplishing my purpose, which was to find a slave. That evening we did not find anything to eat but had still some corn bread left of what we had baked that day. During the night a slave at one of the plantations wanted to go with us, and pled very hard for us to take him along, but we thought it would be unwise. That night we passed through the suburbs of Spartanburg and halted the next morning about eight or ten miles northwest of it.

Abbott, A.O., 1st Lt., 1st N.Y. Dragoons, prisoner, Columbia, S.C.:

As the papers had informed us of the nomination of Abraham Lincoln for a second term to the Presidency,... it was determined to hold an election, and, if possible, send the returns through to our government. That they might get through in time, it was proposed, and agreed upon, to hold it on the 17th of October, which was accordingly done. Ballot-boxes were *improvised*, from a starch-box sent from home with "goodies" in it, to the whole hat of a "fresh fish," and a list posted up, appointing the senior officer belonging to the regiment of each state as the judge of election.... The following is the official report of the election, compiled by Capt. Piggott, 8th Pennsylvania Cavalry....

Number of votes for Lincoln, 1024; votes for McClellan, 143.

### October 18 (Tuesday)

Conley, Capt., 101st Penna. Volunteers, escaped prisoner, S.C.:

We noticed some fine buildings in Spartanburg. Here we spent the day by our fire with nothing to eat, having eaten the last of our corn bread during the night. That evening we started out and after more unsuccessful attempts at three or four plantations to get something to eat, I said to the last slave that I saw, "Is there any plantation where we will probably be able to get something to eat?" To my surprise, he answered, "Dis is de las' plantation on dis road." I asked if there were no other colored folks lived any farther up the road. He answered that there was a fine colored man named Henry Martin living some three or four miles ahead but a little distance off the main road. I asked for directions and he told me to go on that road for over three miles and after crossing the second stream, we should go on about a quarter of a mile where we would see a path leading off to the left which would lead to his house. Without difficulty we found the path and on reaching his house about 11 o'clock we rapped him up. The only thing he had to give us to eat was some cold sweet potatoes and then we inquired about the roads through the mountains, we being now in the foothills of the Blue Ridge.

Ransom, John, QM Sgt., 9th Michigan Cavalry, Marine Hospital, Savannah, Ga.:

Every day since last writing I have continued to improve, and no end to my appetite. Now walk a trifle with the aid of crutches. Coming cool, and agrees with me. Have fresh beef issued to us. Mike not yet gone. Battese went some days ago with others to our lines, at least it was supposed to our lines. Hope to see him sometime. Many have gangrene. Millen still talked of. See city papers every day, and they have a discouraged tone as if their cause were on its last legs.... Rebel guards I come in contact with are marines, who belong to rebel gunboats stationed in the mouth of Savannah River and are on duty here for a change from boat life.

### October 19 (Wednesday)

In Virginia's Shenandoah Valley the Confederates under Gen. Jubal Early surprised the Union forces at Cedar Creek early this morning and captured most of the Union camps before they could form to resist the attack. The Federals fled north down the Valley and were met by Maj. Gen. Philip Sheridan, who rallied them and returned to rout the Confederates. In the initial phases of the attack, many Union troops were captured and sent up the Valley towards Staunton after being searched and much of their clothing and equipment confiscated by the Confederate forces.

The prisoners were moved through Staunton to Richmond and then on to Salisbury, N.C., where they arrived late in the afternoon of November 5, looking ragged and filthy. None had a complete set of clothing. Most were without blankets, shoes, or hats. They joined nearly 7000 prisoners already at Salisbury in a facility originally intended for 2500.

Ransom, John, QM Sgt., 9th Michigan Cavalry, Marine Hospital, Savannah, Ga.:

Last night I talked with a guard while Mike Hoare went out of this tunnel and got away safely from the hospital.... It seems that Mike learned of some Union Irish citizens in the city and his idea is to reach them which he may do, as there are scarcely any troops about the city, all being to the front. Now I am alone, best friends all gone one way or the other.... It is said there are half a dozen hospitals similar to this in Savannah which are filled with Andersonville wrecks. They have need to do something to redeem themselves from past conduct.

Conley, Capt., 101st Penna. Volunteers, escaped prisoner, S.C.:

He told us that the roads through the passes in the mountains were all guarded. Finding that this would necessitate an entire change of plans, we asked him whether he could pilot us up into the mountains where we could reach the Union white men. He answered that he could not, as he was farming on the shares for a rebel and if he left home he would suspect something wrong. But he advised us to stop there for a few days and he would find us a guide. This idea struck us rather favorably as it would give us a chance to rest and to get our feet (which had become very sore and greatly inflamed) in better condition for traveling. He took us out about a half mile from the house into a thick wood and helped us to build a fire. Leaving us, he told us that he would bring our breakfast out in the morning and in the meantime see what he could do to secure us a guide. We had now been just two weeks on the way, having escaped Oct. 5th and reaching Henry Martin's Oct. 19th, and had made a distance of about 160 miles on our route but had traveled between 175 and 200 miles in accomplishing that. While these were two weeks of great hardship and exposure, yet we felt greatly encouraged with our success. We now lay down and enjoyed our first night's rest since our escape.

**October 20 (Thursday)**

In the Valley, fighting broke out with Early's stragglers as they fell back towards Fisher's Hill. Sheridan was getting his troops reorganized for an advance.

At Elmira, N.Y., it seemed that it would take a large bat applied to the heads of some of the major players in the tragedy of the stagnant pond of water in the prison compound to get them to work on a solution. Everyone talked about it, no one did anything about it. After the fiasco of the prisoner shipment, everyone in sight was looking for excuses and a scapegoat. Col. B.F. Tracy, commanding at Elmira, was looking for a way to clear his coattails when he wrote Col. Hoffman:

I desire to call the attention of the Commissary-General of Prisoners to the large number of sick in this camp. A little over a week since over 1200 sick prisoners were sent South from this camp. This I supposed would so relieve our hospitals that our accommodations would be ample, but I find they are still insufficient. The mortality in this camp is so great as to justify, as it seems to me, the most rigid investigation as to its cause. If the rate of mortality for the last two months should continue for a year you can easily calculate the number of prisoners there would be left to exchange. I have, therefore, the honor to request a thorough investigation be made into all the probable causes of disease in this camp, including the insufficiency of the present diet and clothing to maintain the standard of health in this climate, the effects of the pool of stagnant water in the center of the camp, and the compentency and efficiency of the medical officers on duty here. It seems to me that such an investigation, conducted by competent men, would do much to discover the cause and remedy the evil.

Conley, Capt., 101st Penna. Volunteers, escaped prisoner, S.C.:

The next morning our colored friend brought us out our breakfast and told us that he knew a deserter named Ray from a S.C. regiment living a few miles from there that he believed we could secure as a guide to pilot us up into N.C., and also stated that he was going to have a "Corn shucking" that night and that he was going into that neighborhood that day to ask some hands to his shucking and would see what he could learn about him. At noon, Martin's wife, who was a white woman, and another white woman, Mrs. Jones, brought us our dinner. Mrs. Jones, who was apparently about 70 years of age, we found to be an enthusiastic Union woman. She told us that her first husband was a man by the name of Hickcock from Connecticut whom she seemed to have almost idolized. To use her own language, "he was a heap smarter than our folks here." Seeing our destitute condition (we having neither overcoats nor blankets, and I had only a pair of canvas shoes without any hose) Mrs. Jones went home and returned with a good heavy bed comfort and a pair of home knit woolen half hose which she presented to me. We assured her that her kindness was very highly appreciated.

Towards evening Mr. Martin came through the woods on horseback on his return home and told us that he had been at Ray's house, had seen his wife, but that Ray was not at home, but was concealed in the woods. But that his wife expected him in two or three days as he would be compelled to come for supplies of provisions. He further told us that he had a brother-in-law named Hal who was a slave, living in the same neighborhood as Ray, that Hal's wife (who was a sister of Martin's) was a free woman and together with her mother owned a small farm on which they lived, that Hal lived on a plantation nearby, and that he would come over to his corn shucking that evening, and after shucking would take us over to his place and keep us there until they could find Ray.

About ten o'clock that night Martin came out and took us to the house where we found Hal, all other slaves having gone home. Mrs. Martin had killed a chicken and prepared a very good supper for us. After supper we started with Hal and after traveling about four miles we were taken into a piece of woods where Hal assisted us to build a fire just beside a little stream of pure spring water. Hal then left us saying, "de gals will bring out your breakfus' in de mo'nin'." It was now nearly one o'clock in the morning, so making a bed of leaves we lay down, spreading over us the comfort that kind Mrs. Jones had given us and slept soundly until morning.

### October 21 (Friday)

Conley, Capt., 101st Penna. Volunteers, escaped prisoner, S.C.:

It was nearly ten o'clock before "de gals" put in an appearance; when they did they proved to be Hal's wife and mother-in-law. They had two baskets which they handed to us and telling us that Hal would be out that evening, they at once started home. When we opened the baskets we found nicely cooked chicken and plenty of biscuits, corn bread and butter. So we had plenty for that day.

During the afternoon, Hal's wife and two white women came out to see us. These white women, we learned, were Ray's wife and sister. As soon as we learned who they were, we suspected the purpose of their visit. They feared we were rebels trying to entrap Mr. Ray, therefore without appearing to understand their purpose, we made it a point to convince them that we were indeed "Yankees." And they seemed to go away convinced that we were all right, and left us promising to find Ray as soon as possible. Taking advantage of the pure, fresh water, we bathed our feet frequently, thus soon allaying the inflammation. That night Hal came out with a supply of provisions for the next day and remained with us for several hours. Like all slaves, he showed an intense desire for freedom.

### October 22 (Saturday)

Ransom, John, QM Sgt., 9th Michigan Cavalry, Marine Hospital, Savannah, Ga.:

Lt. Davis commands the prison in Savannah. Is the same individual who officiated at Andersonville during Wirtz's sickness last summer. He is a rough but not a bad man. Probably does as well as he can.... I am hobbling about the hospital with the help of two crutches.... Sweet potatoes building me up with the luxuries they are traded for. Had some rice in my soup. Terrible appetite, but for all that don't eat a great deal. Have three sticks propped up at the mouth of our tent, with a little fire under it, cooking food. Men in tent swear because smoke goes inside. Make it all straight by giving them some soup. Rebel surgeons all smoke, at least do while among us. Have seen prisoners who craved tobacco more than food, and said of the two would prefer tobacco. I never have used tobacco in any form.

Abbott, A.O., 1st Lt., 1st N.Y. Dragoons, prisoner, Columbia, S.C.:

On the 22d of October they murdered Lt. Young, 4th Pennsylvania Cavalry. He was sitting in his chair, in the evening of that day, chatting gayly with his companions around his little fire. His term of service had expired the day before, and he was telling his messmates of his plans for the future, when "bang" went a sentinel's gun, and he fell over into the arms of a comrade. He was shot directly under the right shoulder, his back being towards the guard-line. Of course a rush was made to the spot, when the guard threatened *to shoot again* if the crowd did not disperse. The lieutenant spoke a few words concerning his wound, groaned a few times, and was gone.... The authorities furnished a plain coffin, and the next day permitted several of the officers to attend his burial.... The circumstances left a gloom upon the entire camp.

Conley, Capt., 101st Penna. Volunteers, escaped prisoner, S.C.:

The next morning after breakfast, feeling like taking a little exercise, I took a stroll down through the woods, keeping close to the stream. When I had gotten some distance from my comrades, in looking around, I discovered a man in a rebel gray suit with gun and full set of accoutrements sitting on a log not more than eight or ten rods to my right. I merely gave him a glance and turned my face in another direction and walked on as if I had not seen him. My first impulse was to pass on downstream until out of sight and then make a flank movement through the woods and go back to my comrades, but on reflection I found to attempt that I would run the risk of losing my bearings and not be able to find my comrades, and again if he was a rebel soldier and wanted me, he would not let me get out of his sight. Having noticed that he was of small size, I decided that my best plan was to face the situation at once and if he proved to be a rebel I would surrender to him and watch my chance to seize his gun and turn the tables on him. It also occurred to me that he might be our man Ray. While determining my course I had not walked more than four or five rods. I then looked again in that direction and saw him still sitting there watching me. I stood for a moment looking at him as if I had just discovered him, then started towards him. He sat still until I got within about two rods of him, when he got up, brought his gun to a ready, and called out, "Halt." Well, of course, I halted. He

then asked, "Who are you?" I replied, "Who are you?" He replied, "I want to know who you are first." I then asked, "What's your name?" To which he replied, "My name's Ray." I then said, "I guess you are just the man I am looking for." He then said, "Are you one of the Yankees?" Answering him that I was, I started towards him when he again brought his gun to the position of ready and called out, "Halt!" very sharply and then added "Just keep a little distance away." Well, there is something very persuasive about a loaded musket when the muzzle is pointed towards you. He then inquired where my comrades were and pointing upstream I asked him if he would go along with me. He replied, "Well, I reckon I will." As we walked along talking, I kept, thoughtlessly, getting a little closer to him when he again ordered me to keep a little distance saying, "There's plenty of room here." On reaching our comrades, I introduced Mr. Ray to them, at which they both got up and advanced to shake hands with him. Again bringing his gun up he said, "Just stay where you are. Don't come any closer."

A few minutes later Ray's wife and sister came to us. We then learned that Ray had been home the night before and they had arranged to meet him this morning at the point where I found him and pilot him to us. We then discussed the question of his piloting us up into the mountains of N.C. He stated that he was well acquainted with the country for about fifty miles in the direction we were going and would pilot us provided we would pay him for it. Our finances were at such a low ebb that we could not pay him any money, but I had a silver cased watch worth about twenty or twenty-five dollars which I offered to him if he would act as our guide for fifty miles and then leave us in communication with Union white men. To this proposition he readily assented. When that arrangement was made I asked him if he could start with us that evening. He answered, "No, I can't start before Monday evening." This being Saturday morning and being now well rested, we were anxious to be moving on. I therefore said to him, "You are not able to do anything here, having to keep concealed, why not go at once?" He answered, "I must get my family a supply of winter meat before I go, as I may not come back for some time." I suggested that he might make arrangements that day for his supply of meat. His reply was, "No, I can't get it in day time, I must get it at night." My curiosity prompted me to ask what kind of meat he was going to get, to which he replied, "I know where there is some nice fat sheep, but I can't get them in day time, but must get them at night." We then began to catch on to how he got his "Supply of winter meat." So it was arranged that we would start on Monday evening. During this meeting Ray's wife urged him very strongly to go on with us to Knoxville and remain there until the war was over as he was in daily danger of being killed here, but he would not consent, being anxious, I thought, to drive as good a bargain as he could with us.

That evening Hal came out again with a supply of provisions and spent about half the night with us.

## October 23 (Sunday)

The commander of the prison at Point Lookout, Md., had previously requested more, and replacement, tents for the prisoners at that facility. Today, Col. W. Hoffman, Federal Commissary-General of Prisoners, replied that: "the Secretary of War, by whom I am directed to say that no additional tents can be furnished while there are any on hand which can be used in any way to shelter the prisoners. The tents reported unservicable can be used by nailing them over frames having about the same dimensions of a wall tent. *The lumber and nails required for this purpose can be purchased from the prison fund*" [italics added]. Keep in mind that the "prison fund" was created from monies *saved* by cutting the rations of the prisoners.

Abbott, A.O., 1st Lt., 1st N.Y. Dragoons, prisoner, Columbia, S.C.:

Just at daylight that morning two strangers were discovered, closely locked, going through the camp, evidently with the intent of spying out the secret by which so many of the officers succeeded in making their escape. They had well-nigh succeeded, when the attention of some of the prisoners was called to their mysterious actions. It was decided they must not be allowed to leave camp with the knowledge they possessed, for it would prevent the escape of others. "They must be killed at once."

Bring an ax. It was brought, and the deed was done.

But now how to *hide* the deed was the question.

An old well answered the purpose, and into this the bodies were thrown, and hastily covered with earth. Roll-call followed soon after, when a search was made by the guard for our two *friends*. After an hour spent in vain, they formed a skirmish-line across the camp, drove us all between the deadline and the guard-line, and searched again for the missing members of the "chivalric society."

As the party came near the well, they discovered some fresh earth on the outside, and, upon closer examination, found that all was not right inside of the well. One of the party descended to a little excavation in the side of it, and, after a few minutes work, brought to light the missing—DOGS, dead *blood-hounds*—two of a pack that had been brought there on purpose to catch Yankees, and were put around the camp every morning to discover if any "Yankees" had made fresh tracks for liberty during the night.

As the dogs were dragged out by the guard, their resurrection was greeted with tremendous applause, groans, howls, barks, and some even pled that they might be left to make soup for dinner, as we had then been without an issue of meat since we left Charleston.

Conley, Capt., 101st Penna. Volunteers, escaped prisoner, S.C.:

During Sunday forenoon, Ray came out again and brought with him some cooked mutton for our dinner and said, "I got along pretty well last night, but it will take me another night to get enough." Hal spent most of Sunday with us again bringing us a supply in the evening.

Today, Col. Wm. Hoffman, Federal Commissary-General of Prisoners, wrote Col. B.F. Tracy, commanding at Elmira, N.Y., approving the installation of the drainage pipe requested by Tracy on the 17th.

The suggestion made by you that a pipe be laid to conduct the water from the river above into the pond within the inclosure, with a view to remove the material exhalations from the stagnant water, is approved, and will be carried into immediate effect if the soil through which the ditch is to be dug is of a character to be readily excavated and there are no other obstacles.

All the labor must be preformed by the prisoners,

and the cost must be paid out of the prison fund. The pipe will be constructed of two-inch plank, the opening to be six inches square, the joints to be well pitched to prevent leaking. To unite the several lengths of pipe let the end of one be beveled off five or six inches, while the other is made flaring, so that one may be forced into the other to make a close joint. Constructed in this way, the whole work should not cost over $120. Make inquiries in relation to the work in all its particulars and report to me before it is commenced.... The fall rains may be expected to come on very soon, which for this winter will do away with the necessity for the work.

On November 13th, Col. Tracy reported to Col. Hoffman that the work had been commenced. On November 20th, Tracy reported that 3000 feet of the ditch had been dug and 1000 feet of the pipe laid and covered. The ditch was completed by mid-December.

### October 24 (Monday)

On September 29th, Col. William Hoffman, Federal Commissary-General of Prisoners, sent instructions to the Commanding Officer, Elmira Prisoner Depot, Elmira, N.Y., concerning the shipment of sick and wounded rebel prisoners south for exchange. On October 13th, the train carrying the prisoners arrived at Baltimore, where the prisoners were to be loaded on a steamer for further transfer to City Point, Va. The senior officer on the train, Maj. Roberts, reported to the Office of the Medical Director, in Baltimore, that several of the prisoners had died en route and many were sick. The Medical Director, Surgeon J. Simpson, directed that the prisoners be examined by doctors from his staff before they departed. One Surgeon, C.F.H. Campbell, inspected the prisoners on the train before they were unloaded and sent sixty of them to the local general hospital and reported that another had died while being loaded into an ambulance. On October 14th, Surgeon Simpson forwarded the reports of Campbell and Surgeon Chapel to Col. Hoffman for disposition. Today, Hoffman forwarded the reports to the Secy. of War with his recommendations:

The accompanying copy of instructions given to Col. B.F. Tracy, One hundred and twenty-seventh Colored Troops, commanding at Elmira, shows that, so far as orders could effect it, every precaution was taken to guard against unnecessary suffering by the prisoners ordered South, but from the within reports it appears that both the commanding officer and the medical officers not only failed to be governed by these orders, but neglected the ordinary promptings of humanity in the performance of their duties towards sick men, thus showing themselves to be wholly unfit for the positions they occupy, and it is respectfully recommended that they be immediately ordered to some other service.

Ransom, John, QM Sgt., 9th Michigan Cavalry, Marine Hospital, Savannah, Ga.:

Did not write yesterday. Jumping right along towards health if not wealth. Discarded crutches and have now two canes. Get around considerable, a little at a time.... A smallpox case discovered in hospital and created great excitement. Was removed. Was loitering near the gate, when an Irish woman came through it with her arms full of wheat bread. All those able to rushed up to get some of it and forty hands were pleading for her favors. After picking her men and giving away half a dozen loaves her eyes lighted on me and I secured a large loaf. She was a jolly, good natured woman, and it is said that she keeps a bake shop. My bad looks stood me in well this time. As beautiful bread as I ever saw.

Conley, Capt., 101st Penna. Volunteers, escaped prisoner, S.C.:

On Monday, Ray reported to us that he had had good success again last night and would be ready to start with us at dark that evening. In the meantime we had become thoroughly rested; our feet had gotten well and having a good supply of provisions for several days, we were feeling strong and anxious to be moving on. That evening Hal brought us some more provisions and Ray a piece of roast mutton, his wife and sister coming out with him. After eating our supper, Ray said that he wanted to leave the watch with his wife. So I handed it over to him and he gave it to his wife, after which Mrs. Ray took me to one side and asked me to try to have Ray go on with us and stay inside the Union lines until the war was over as she feared if he stayed here that he would be killed. I promised her that I would use my influence with him. After bidding our colored friend Hal and the two ladies good-bye, with many thanks, especially to Hal for his kindness, we started. Our course for the first fifteen miles was among foothills of the Blue Ridge.

### October 25 (Tuesday)

Conley, Capt., 101st Penna. Volunteers, escaped prisoner, N.C.:

About daylight, we halted just over the crest of the Blue Ridge, which is quite a high mountain at that point, having travelled about twenty-five miles. Before our rest at Hal's, we had never been able to make more than 15 miles in a night and often before we had gone that far we were too much fatigued to go farther; but now we had travelled 25 miles over hills and up a mountain, and scarcely felt fatigued. We only now began to realize how much we had been benefitted by our rest. We stopped that morning in the woods near a small mountain farm owned and occupied by a man named Stanton, in Polk Co., N.C., just over the crest of the Blue Ridge.

Our guide left us there and went to the house. In about two hours he and Mr. Stanton brought us out our breakfast. During the day Mr. Stanton brought out to us his two sons, young men about 18 and 20 years of age, who as we learned were compelled to keep in hiding to escape the conscription which prevailed through the Confederacy and included every man able to do military duty. Mr. Stanton suggested that his sons join us and go with us to Knoxville, saying that he thought it would be best for them to get inside the Union lines and remain there until the close of the war. He also said that he thought it would be an advantage to us, as the boys' grandfather, Mr. Bishop, lived about thirty-five miles from them in Henderson Co. and another Mr. Bishop, an uncle of theirs, lived about 30 miles farther in Transylvania Co., and in about the direction we should travel. It was therefore decided that they should join us. By this time Ray had decided to go with us to our lines. So, about four o'clock that afternoon, having first been supplied with provisions, we started under the pilotage of the Stanton boys, our party now numbering six.

Leaving the roads, we traveled through the woods and byroads until after dark, when we again took to the roads and traveled steadily until after daylight, when we halted in the woods near Mr. Bishop's, the grandfather of the Stanton boys.

Ransom, John, QM Sgt., 9th Michigan Cavalry, Marine Hospital, Savannah, Ga.:

Am feeling splendid and legs doing nobly, and even taking on fat. Am to be a gallant nurse as soon as able, so Sergt. Winn says. Most of the men as soon as convalescent are sent to big prison, but Winn has spoken a good word for me. Papers say the prison at Millen, Ga., is about ready for occupancy and soon all will be sent there, sick and all. Nights cool and need more covering than we have. I am congratulated occasionally by prisoners who saw me at Andersonville. They wonder at my being alive. Rains.

### October 26 (Wednesday)

Ransom, John, QM Sgt., 9th Michigan Cavalry, Marine Hospital, Savannah, Ga.:

Time passes now fast; most a year since captured. When the Rebs once get hold of a fellow they hang on for dear life.... Walk better every day. Sometimes I overdo a little and feel bad in consequence.

Conley, Capt., 101st Penna. Volunteers, escaped prisoner, N.C.:

About daylight it commenced to rain quite heavily so that by the time we stopped we were quite wet. The Stanton boys went to the house and in a short time came out and took us in, where we were received very kindly and our wants provided for. Mr. Bishop, who was quite old, we soon learned had been a soldier in the war of 1812 and was a very zealous Union man. This being a small mountain farm through which no public highway passed, Mr. Bishop thought that it would be entirely safe for us to spend the day there, which we did by the open fire. It continued to rain very heavily all day. It was our intention to travel that night to the other Mr. Bishop's, the boys' uncle, but the rain continued so heavy that we decided not to travel that night. As we feared to sleep in the house, we went out and made our bed in a stable among some corn fodder.

### October 27 (Thursday)

Ransom, John, QM Sgt., 9th Michigan Cavalry, Marine Hospital, Savannah, Ga.:

A rebel physician (not a regular one), told me that it looked very dark for the Confederacy just now; that we need have no fears but we would get home very soon now, which is grand good news.... Everything points to a not far away ending of the war...

Conley, Capt., 101st Penna. Volunteers, escaped prisoner, N.C.:

Before daylight the family had our breakfast ready and after partaking of it, we bade our kind host and his family good-bye, and with many thanks for their kindness, we started, the rain having now ceased.

Avoiding all public roads, we traveled all day, much of the time through the woods, until a little after dark we reached the home of Mr. Bishop in Transylvania Co. There we were received very kindly and given our supper, but as he lived along a public highway, he said it would be unsafe for us to stay at his house, but said that about a mile from there two brothers (whose names I can not now recall) had built a shanty in the woods and were staying there to avoid the conscription, that he would take us there. Under his guidance, we reached the shanty and woke up the occupants. Mr. Bishop then told us that he had heard that there were a couple of recruiting officers in that county securing recruits for the Second N.C. Union Regiment, which was organizing at Knoxville, Tenn. and that the place of rendezvous, before starting, would probably be about 25 or 30 miles farther on in the direction we were going. But he advised us to remain where we were until he could secure for us the necessary information and that he would furnish us cornmeal, potatoes and apples, but said that he had no meat. He said, however, that deer were very plent[iful] in the mountains and that he would send us a noted hunter the next morning and also furnish us with an extra gun and that we should go out and kill a deer. The Stanton boys had brought their own guns with them. So, with the one Mr. Bishop found and those belonging to the Stantons, we were able to raise six guns.

### October 28 (Friday)

In northern Alabama, Hood kept moving across the state, going west towards a crossing of the Tennessee. Sherman, with Hood immediately out of his hair, turned his armies and headed back towards Atlanta, leaving Hood's fate to Thomas at Nashville.

Ransom, John, QM Sgt., 9th Michigan Cavalry, Marine Hospital, Savannah, Ga.:

Am feeling splendid, and legs most straight. Get fat fast. Am to be a nurse soon. Reported that they are moving prisoners to Millen. Over a thousand went yesterday. About ten thousand of the Andersonville prisoners came to Savannah.... Only the sick were left behind there, and it is said they died like sheep after the well ones went away. Great excitement among the Gray-coats. Some bad army news for them, I reckon. Negroes at work fortifying about the city.

Conley, Capt., 101st Penna. Volunteers, escaped prisoner, N.C.:

After breakfast the next morning, Mr. Bishop came out bringing his hunter with him. We at once set out, one hunter, the two Stanton boys, Capt. Dawson, Lt. Davidson and myself. The gun given to me was an old rusty Austrian rifle. I didn't have much confidence in it but was willing to try it. We deployed and travelled about three miles through the mountains without seeing a deer, but, then came upon two hogs feeding upon chestnuts. Deciding that pork would suit us just as well as venison, we undertook to kill them. I was not surprised that my gun would not go off. One of the Stanton boys killed a hog the first shot, but all the other guns proved to be of the same kind as mine. But one gun out of six being discharged. Stanton loaded his gun again and shot the other hog. We then dressed the two hogs (by skinning them) and, tying each one on a pole, two men took each hog, and the other two the guns, and travelled back to our camp. Here we gave our hunter part of one hog, and also some to our friend, Mr. Bishop. We now settled down to camp life. Mr. Bishop brought us a large Dutch oven which would at least hold a half bushel, and had a cast iron lid. This was our only cooking utensil. In this we baked our corn bread and cooked our pork and potatoes. Three times a day we would put on a large supply of pork and while it was cooking, we would pare enough potatoes to fill it and when cooked, we would set it down and our whole company now eight in number (including the two men who owned the shanty) would surround it. We seasoned with salt and cayenne pepper in pods. Having no plates, knives or forks or spoons, we made forks and spoons of wood and with them we all helped ourselves from the Spider, or Dutch Oven, as we call it in Pennsylvania. The Stanton boys, with Mr. Bishop's permission, would go to the orchard every day and bring us a good supply of apples. So with corn bread, pork and potatoes, and apples we were able to live very well.

## October 29 (Saturday)

Ransom, John, QM Sgt., 9th Michigan Cavalry, Marine Hospital, Savannah, Ga.:

I suppose we must be moved again, from all reports. Savannah is threatened by Union troops, and we are to be sent to Millen, Ga.... Can eat now anything I can get hold of, provided it can be cooked up and made into shape of soup. Mouth will not admit of hard food. This hospital is not far from the Savannah jail, and when the gate is open we can see it.... Last of my three pecks of sweet potatoes almost gone. For a dollar, Confed., bought two quarts of guber peas (peanuts), and now I have got them can't eat them. Sell them for a dollar a quart—two dollars for the lot. It is thus that the Yankee getteth wealth. Have loaned one cane to another convalescent and go around with the aid of one only. Every day a marked improvement.

Conley, Capt., 101st Penna. Volunteers, escaped prisoner, N.C.:

After dark on Saturday evening (we had been there 48 hours) Mr. Bishop came out to our camp and reported that a company of rebels was scouting the entire neighborhood and that for our safety we should retreat several miles back into the mountains. While here we had learned that every Union man who was liable to military duty and hence subject to conscription kept himself in hiding. Many of them, like the ones we were stopping with, had built little shanties in secluded spots in the woods and spent most of their time there. Mr. Bishop told us to be ready to move before daylight the next morning and he would have a guide there for us.

## October 30 (Sunday)

At Mobile, Ala., the South still held the city and the surrounding area, although the two forts at the entrance to Mobile Bay were in Northern hands. At that city were thousands of bales of cotton that had been there since the war had begun and the port effectively closed by blockade. Meanwhile, in the Northern prison camps there were thousands of Confederate prisoners who needed clothing and other necessities if they were to survive until exchanged—and the exchange was still deadlocked.

Someone in the South hit upon a plan to alleviate the suffering of their troops that was just short of ingenious. The South would make cotton available to be taken to New York and sold. The proceeds would be used to buy clothing, etc., for the Confederate prisons. Today, Robert Ould, Agent of Exchange for the Confederacy, started the process by writing Lt. Gen. U.S. Grant at City Point, Va.:

Sir: I beg leave respectfully to inquire whether the U.S. authorities will consent to a shipment of cotton from one of our ports to one of the Northern cities with the view of purchasing there, with the proceeds of sale, blankets, &c., for the immediate relief of our prisoners confined in Northern prisons. Of course we would give you due notice of the name of the vessel carrying the cargo, as well as the time of her sailing, together with such other particulars as you might request.

Conley, Capt., 101st Penna. Volunteers, escaped prisoner, N.C:

The next morning before daylight Mr. Bishop and the same man who had gone hunting with us came out and we prepared to start. Mr. Bishop said that as soon as it was safe for us to return he would send for us. Loading up our stock of cornmeal, potatoes, pork and apples, and our spider, we started and after travelling six or seven miles, we stopped at what our guide called a "Rock House," which was simply a large overhanging cliff, but which would furnish shelter for about 20 men. In this movement, we had crossed the crest of the Blue Ridge into S.C. The two brothers who owned the shanty accompanied us. On leaving us, our guide said that he would come back for us as soon as Mr. Bishop thought it would be safe.

The imagination could scarcely picture a more lonely spot. It was a place where there seemed to be a buck in the mountain. At the point where the "Rock House" was located, there was near it the base of a very precipitous mountain; indeed so steep was this mountain that it required the greatest care to keep one's feet. About four or five rods below, the Saluda River flowed over a rocky bed with a succession of falls which kept up a constant roar. On the opposite side of the stream the mountain rose almost perpendicularly for several hundred feet. There was no habitation for several miles. Here we spent that day with nothing to do but cook our food and eat it. But we could make ourselves comfortable by building our fire at the outer edge of the cliff.

Ransom, John, QM Sgt., 9th Michigan Cavalry, Marine Hospital, Savannah, Ga.:

It is said prisoners from main prison are being removed every day, and the sick will go last. Quite a batch of the nearest well ones were sent from here today to go with the others. Am to be a nurse pretty soon.... The surgeon who has had charge of us has been sent away to the front. It seems he had been wounded in battle and was doing home duty until able to again go to his command. Shall always remember him for his kind and skilful treatment. Came round and bid us all good-bye, and sick sorry to lose him....Considerable activity about the place. Trains run through at all hours of the night, evidently shifting their troops to other localities.LATER—Since the surgeon went away the rebels are drinking up our whiskey, and tonight are having a sort of carnival, with some of the favorite nurses joining in; singing songs, telling stories, and a good time generally.

## October 31 (Monday)

The fighting in the Petersburg area increased the prisoner count at Point Lookout, Md., dramatically during this month. Several hundred were also sent South on the sick list.

Ransom, John, QM Sgt., 9th Michigan Cavalry, Marine Hospital, Savannah, Ga.:

Reported that the well prisoners have all left this city for Millen and we go tonight or tomorrow. I am duly installed as a nurse, and walk with only one cane. Legs still slightly drawn up.... Am feeling very well. Will describe my appearance. Will interest me to read in after years, if no one else. Am writing this diary to please myself, now. I weigh one hundred and seventeen pounds, am dressed in rebel jacket, blue pants with one leg torn off and fringed about halfway between my knee and good sized foot, the same old pair of mismatched shoes I wore in Andersonville, very good pair of stockings, a "biled" white shirt, and a hat which is a compromise between a clown's and the rebel white partially stiff hat; am poor as a tadpole, in fact look just about like an East Tennessean, of the poor white trash order. You might say that I am an "honery looking cuss" and not be far out of the way. My cheeks are sunken, eyes sunken, sores and blotches both outside and inside my mouth, and my

right leg the whole length of it, red, black and blue and tender of touch. My eyes, too, are very weak, and in a bright sun I have to draw the slouch hat away down over them. Bad as this picture is, I am a beauty and picture of health in comparison to my appearance two months ago.... LATER—We are on the Georgia Central Railroad, en route for Millen, Ga., which is ninety miles from Savannah, and I believe north. Are in boxcars and very crowded with sick prisoners. Two nurses, myself being one of them, have charge of about a hundred sick. There are, however, over six hundred on the train.

Conley, Capt., 101st Penna. Volunteers, escaped prisoner, N.C.:

On Monday morning, the second day we were there, one of the Stanton boys shot another hog, which we dressed so we had a good supply of meat.

## November 1 (Tuesday)

Ransom, John, QM Sgt., 9th Michigan Cavalry, Camp Lawton, Millen, Ga.:

Arrived at our destination not far from midnight, and it was a tedious journey. Two died in the car I was in. Were taken from the cars to this prison in what they call ambulances, but what I call lumber wagons. Are now congregated in the southeast corner of the stockade under hastily put up tents. This morning we have drawn rations, both the sick and the well, which are good and enough. The stockade is similar to that at Andersonville, but in a more settled country, the ground high and grassy, with no swamp at all. It is apparently a pleasant and healthy location. A portion of the prison is timberland, and the timber has been cut down and lays where it fell, and the men who arrived before us have been busily at work making shanties and places to sleep in. There are about six thousand prisoners here, and I should judge there was room for twelve or fifteen thousand. Men say they are given food twice each day, which consists of meal and fresh beef in rather small quantities, but good and wholesome. The rebel officer in command is a sociable and kindly disposed man, and the guards are not strict, that is, not cruelly so. We are told that our stay here will be short. A number of our men have been detailed to cook the food for the sick, and their well-being is looked to by the rebel surgeon as well as our own men.... Barrels of molasses (nigger toe) have been rolled inside and it is being issued to the men, about one-fourth of a pint to each man, possibly a little more. Some of the men, luxuriantly, put their allowances together and make molasses candy of it.

Conley, Capt., 101st Penna. Volunteers, escaped prisoner, N.C.:

On Tuesday morning our guide came back to our camp. Mr. Bishop came out to see us and told us that the recruiting was going to start in a few days and he thought our best policy was to join them, as they would have guides who were familiar with the route and would also have some arms in case of attack. Believing the idea was a good one, we agreed to follow his advice. He then told us we should go at once to Ex-Sheriff Hamilton's in Transylvania Co. and there we would get all the information we desired, that the next morning he would furnish us a guide to show us the way, the distance being about 20 miles.

At Elmira, N.Y., Surgeon E.F. Sanger wrote a report to the Surgeon-General of the U.S. Army in Washington concerning the health conditions of the camp. The report is a good example of bureaucracy run amok:

Forward the monthly report of sick and wounded of prisoner's hospital, Elmira, N.Y., for the month of October. The ratio of disease and deaths has been fearfully and unprecedentedly large and requires an explanation from me to free the medical department from censure.

Since August, the date of my assignment to this station, there have been 2011 patients admitted to the hospital, 775 deaths out of a mean strength of 8347 prisoners of war, or 24 percent, admitted and 9 percent died. Have averaged daily 451 in hospital and 601 in quarters, an aggregate of 1052 per day, sick. At this rate the entire command will be admitted to hospital in less than a year and 36 per cent. die.

The prison pen is one-quarter of a mile square, containing forty acres, located in the valley of the Chemung River. The soil is gravel deposit sloping at two-thirds of its distance from the front towards the river to a stagnant pond of water 12 by 580 yards, between which and the river is a low sandy bottom subject to overflow when the river is high. This pond received the contents of the sinks and garbage of the camp until it became so offensive that vaults were dug on the banks of the pond for sinks and the whole left a festering mass of corruption, impregnating the entire atmosphere of the camp with its pestilential odors, night and day.

On my arrival the subject of drainage, sinks, enlargement of the hospitals, providing a kitchen, mess hall, laundry, dead-house, offices, and storerooms were all considered and their importance impressed upon the commanding officer.

On the 13th of August commenced making written reports of the following dates: August 13, August 23, August 26, September 3, 5, 16, October 5, 9 and October 17, calling attention to the pond, vaults, and their deadly poison, the existence of scurvy to an alarming extent (reporting 2000 scorbutic cases at one time); recommended fresh vegetables daily to scurvy patients and an increase in the capacity of the hospital; pointed out the necessity of a kitchen, laundry, mess-room, and dead-house, and presented plans for the same; called attention to improvements in cooking and method of serving the rations; great delay in filling my requisitions for the hospital; the sickness and suffering occasioned thereby; a more general observation of the sanitary laws governing human beings herded in crowded camps and the inevitable consequences following neglect. How does the matter stand today? The pond remains green with putrescence, filling the air with its messengers of disease and death, the vaults give out their sickly odors, and the hospitals are crowded with victims for the grave.

A single ration of vegetables was given for a while and discontinued. Three rations in five of onions and potatoes were allowed from the 1st of October for a fortnight and discontinued. The men are hurried in to their rations of bread, beans, meat, and soup, to half gulp it down on the spot or to carry it hastily away to their quarters in old rusty canteens and improvised dirty dippers and measures.

Hospital wards, with the addition of three barracks, buildings poorly adapted for hospital purposes, are insufficient to accommodate the sick. Kitchen half large enough. Washing and drying done in the open air at a time when we have not been able to dry our clothes for a month. Nurses, full-diet patients, &c., eat in the wards, kitchen, or wherever they can. Postmortems performed in a little tent exposed to the gaze of the camp and an office 12 by 20 feet, in which are crowded together drugs and druggists, stewards and clerks, doctors and dressings, commissary clerks and hospital supplies, in a state of confusion worst confounded.

While Lt. Col. Eastman, of the Regular Army, was in command I reported directly to him, and was able by direct communication to expedite business, personally explain the wants of the hospital department, and to a limited extent act as medical adviser of the medical interests of the prisoners. Since Col. Tracy, of the U.S. colored troops, has been in command, all direct communication has been cut off, and I am ordered by him to report to a junior military officer in camp, who has merely a forwarding power. So far as garrison duties are concerned, I do not object to reporting to a junior military officer, but in the administrative duties of a large hospital department the surgeon in charge must have direct communication with the commander, who is the only authorized executive officer. My provision returns, my bill of purchases, my requisitions for hospital fixtures and medical supplies, must all be forwarded to him, subject to his approval or disapproval, without any medical representations to advise or guide in the exercise of opinions and actions based upon common sense alone. Common sense is a very good thing, but does not work in physic. To illustrate: The requisition for medicine sent October 7 through the intermediate channel for approval was never heard from; the second was delayed two or three days; my provision returns are often forty-eight hours getting back to me, and applications for straw and fixtures for hospital are frequently made some three or four weeks before I receive the articles. My application for straw, put in October 21, for beds, is not filled yet, and the patients are compelled to lie on the floor. My application for caldron, stovepipe, and cover for washing purposes, put in on the 5th and 16th of September, was finally filled October 28. I was ordered to feed patients in quarters, and yet my requisition for cooking utensils came back disapproved. When the sick were sent from here for exchange I received no official information, nor was advised in reference to the matter. I was informed by a captain of the examining board, in the original examination, not to send those who were unable to travel. I was totally ignorant whether the journey would exceed two or three days, only as I judged from the number of days' rations

required, viz, two; although the day for forwarding prisoners' returns was the day before the prisoners started, October 11, and mine went in promptly. I did not receive my supplies, and the patients were sent off without coffee or sugar. The train started without reporting to the medical officer, and before the nurses were assigned, blankets distributed, and many had been fed after a fast of more than twelve hours. I was ordered to appoint a given number of nurses and doctors, and my application for an increased number received no attention. A camp inspector is appointed who takes the liberty of entering my wards at all times, instructs my ward-masters and nurses, finds fault to them of my management, and quizzes them in regard to the medical officers. Medical officers have complained that he changes beds of the patients, corrects and changes their diet, directs the washing of my wards without regard to my rules, orders pneumonia patients with blisters on their sides bathed, &c. I have entered a written protest without avail. I cannot be held responsible for a large medical department of over 1000 patients without power, authority, or influence. Our post is without a medical representative, and as senior medical officer of this post the whole administrative duties should be intrusted to my care, when it would be hoped that the interest of the sick would be consulted.

The report above, received at the Surgeon-General's office in Washington, caused immediate reaction. On the 10th, C.H. Crane, Surgeon-General of the U.S. Army, directed that an inspection be made of the Elmira facility and action taken to correct the deficiencies noted in Sanger's letter.

### November 2 (Wednesday)

Ransom, John, QM Sgt., 9th Michigan Cavalry, Camp Lawton, Millen, Ga.:

Have seen many of my old comrades of Andersonville, among whom is my tried friend Sergt. Wm. B. Rowe; were heartily glad to see one another; also little Bullock who has improved wonderfully in appearance. Everyone is pleased with this place and are cheerful, hoping and expecting to be released before many weeks; they all report as having been well treated in Savannah.... My duties as nurse are hard, often too much for my strength, yet the enforced exercise does me good and continue to improve all the time.

A cane will be necessary to my locomotion for a long time as am afraid myself permanently injured; my cane is not a gold-headed one; it is a round picket which has been pulled off some fence ... All who want to can take the oath of allegiance to the Confederacy and be released; am happy to say though that out of all here, but two or three has done so, and they are men who are a detriment to any army. The weather is now beautiful, air refreshing, water ditto; all happy and contented and await coming events with interest. Part of the brook, the lower part, is planked and sides boarded up for sanitary privileges; water has also been damned up and a fall made which carries off the filth with force. Plenty of wood to do cooking with.

Conley, Capt., 101st Penna. Volunteers, escaped prisoner, N.C.:

The next morning it was raining quite heavy, but soon after daylight Mr. Bishop and a middle-aged woman came to us. Mr. Bishop informed us that the lady was to be our guide. By this time, the two brothers with whom we had been stopping decided to join our party and go through to the Union lines. Bidding our very kind friend, Mr. Bishop, good-bye, with many acknowledgements of his kindness, we started through the woods, our clothing soon drenched with the rain. When we had travelled about 12 miles, all of which was through the woods, our guide told us to stop until she went to a farmhouse nearby. She was not gone long until she returned with a gentleman with her, whom she introduced as "Mr. Fisher." Mr. Fisher asked us to go the house, and our guide started back the way she had come. On reaching the house we found a family which showed more evidence of culture than any we had met with on our route. Mrs. Fisher prepared us a very good dinner, Fisher having informed us that he was to act as our guide after dinner.

When we were ready to start, Mrs. Fisher informed us that her daughter was upstairs just recovering from an attack of diphtheria, and that she was very anxious to see a Yankee, and asked whether one of us would take the risk of going to see her. Not feeling that I could refuse, after all their kindness, I told her that I would go up. On entering her room, I found her sitting before an open fire, dressed in a neat white wrapper; her face almost as white as the wrapper. I soon discovered that she was a young lady of culture and refinement. She informed me that she had a brother who had been forced into the rebel army, and at that time was a prisoner of war at Camp Douglas, Chicago, and asked me to write him and tell him how the family were, and ask him, for her, to take the oath of allegiance to the U.S. and remain north until the close of the war. I promised her that I would do just as she requested me. A promise which I fulfilled at the earliest possible date after reaching the lines. I never heard from him after. Bidding the young lady good-bye, I came down stairs and we at once started on our way with Mr. Fisher as our guide.

We travelled between four and five miles when we came to a ferry over the French Broad River. Here Mr. Fisher left us and returned soon after with an old Gentleman whom he introduced as Mr. Orr, telling us that Mr. Orr would ferry us across the river and then act as our guide, Mr. Fisher returning home. Mr. Orr had a large canoe or "dugout" in which he took us over the river and tying it up at the opposite side of the river, he went with us until we came in sight of Ex-Sheriff Hamilton's house, then bidding us good-bye, he returned to his home. The rain seemed to increase as evening approached. Sheriff Hamilton lived in a large log house standing back some distance from the road. Leaving the rest of my party concealed in the woods, I went to the house to see whether the coast was clear. Approaching the house, I rapped at the door. Instantly I heard some persons moving quietly about the room, which continued only for a moment, when all became quiet. I waited outside for about ten minutes, I thought, when I again heard footsteps in the house, and soon the door was opened by a young lady, addressing whom, I asked, "Is the Sheriff Hamilton at home?" To which interrogatory, she made no reply, but leaving me standing in the rain, she turned around, leaving the door open, and passed through another door. I stood for at least five minutes more, when the door through which she had passed was again opened and a middle-aged lady, who proved to be Mrs. Hamilton, entered, and, as she did so, asked me to walk in. As I did so, I saw a large fire burning in the big open fireplace. This was most agreeable to me, as my clothing was thoroughly drenched with the cold rain.

Stepping in front of the fire, I asked her the same question I had asked the young lady, who proved to be her daughter, but, like the daughter, she made no reply. Seeing she was in doubt about who I was, I said to her, "I am what you call in this country a Yankee. I have escaped from a rebel prison and am trying to make my way to the Union lines. The Sheriff has been recommended to me as a reliable Union man. That is why I am here." While thus addressing her, she seemed to be scrutinizing me from head to foot, then turned around and walked out, without making any reply. After standing by the fire probably five minutes longer, the door opened again and to my great surprise, in stepped Capt. C.S. Aldrich of the 85th N.Y. United States Infantry. We recognized each other at a glance. I exclaimed, "Capt. Aldrich, are you here?" Behind him came a gentleman, apparently about 55 years of age, whom Capt. Aldrich introduced to me as Sheriff Hamilton. Capt. Aldrich stepped back and opened the door and called out, "This is all right." To my further surprise, in came Capt. D.A. Longworth and First Lt. J.E. Twilliger of the 85th N.Y., Capt. G.H. Starr of the 104th N.Y., and First Lt. G.S. Hastings of the 2nd N.Y. Independent Battery, all of whom I was well acquainted with except Capt. Starr. The other four belonged to our garrison at Plymouth, N.C. and were captured when I was and we had all been together in prison.

After an exchange of greetings, Sheriff Hamilton asked me whether there was anybody else with me. I informed him that I had two comrades, four North Carolinians, and one South Carolinian with me. He asked, "Are the North Carolinians and South Carolinians all right?" Upon assuring him that they were, "Then," said he, "bring them in." Going to the door, I beckoned to them and they came in. I then learned that the five officers whom I met there had escaped from Columbia the same night we passed it, their camp being on the southwest side of the Broad River, whilst we passed Columbia on the northeast side of the river. Their route to the mountains lay considerably to the west of ours. While we were stopping at Bishop's, they coming by a different route, reached Hamilton's two or three days ahead of us and were waiting there to join the same recruiting party we were. I also learned that when I rapped at the door, the only persons in the room were these five officers, having just come in from the woods, were sitting around the fire drying their clothes, having their coats and shoes off. When they heard the rap, they hastily gathered up their effects, slipped quietly out, and going behind the kitchen (which as a separate building a few feet away) sent the young lady in to

see who was there. Here we learned that two other officers, Capt. Cady of the 24th N.Y. and Lt. Masters of the 2nd N.C. Union, who had escaped from the same train they had, were stopping a few miles from there in a deserted cabin in the mountains which they had named "The Pennsylvania House."

Mrs. Hamilton and her daughter prepared supper for us, and after supper, Sheriff Hamilton put on a rubber blanket and travelled about two miles to a neighbor's to ascertain whether there was any danger from rebels in the neighborhood. Returning, he told us that all was safe, and as it was still raining heavily, he said that we could sleep on his floor before the fire. We found the Sheriff to be a very earnest Union man who was willing to assist the Union cause in every way that he could. Though like many of his neighbors who were past the age for military duty, he was, however, compelled to serve in a company of home guards whenever called upon to do so. He told us that whenever they called on him to turn out, he always responded. As their principal duty was to hunt deserters, he said he always tried to manage to send word ahead that they were coming. On one occasion he said that they surrounded a house where it was supposed a deserter was concealed. He, with one or two others, were taken by the captain to search the house. While the others were in other parts of the house, he searched one room, and in doing so, discovered the man hiding under a bed. Without disturbing him he passed out, and at the door met the captain who asked him if he had searched that room. Answering that he did, they left the house with the deserter still under the bed. We found both the Sheriff and his family of more than the average intelligence and thoroughly Union. The evening was pleasantly passed, our five comrades relating to us their experience and we ours to them. From this interesting family we learned much of the hardships suffered by the Union men in this mountainous district, and of their being hunted as deserters and persecuted in every way by their rebel neighbors, being robbed of almost everything they had. Their houses had been confiscated, and many of them were compelled to work their milch cows in order to raise a little corn and a few potatoes to supply their families. Before retiring, it had been decided that our party of eight should go the next morning to the "Pennsylvania House" and remain there until Sunday morning, at which time it had been arranged that the party would start.

## November 3 (Thursday)

Ransom, John, QM Sgt., 9th Michigan Cavalry, Camp Lawton, Millen, Ga.:

About a hundred convalescents were taken outside today to be sent away to our lines the official told us. At a later hour the commander came inside and said he wanted twelve men to fall into line and they did so, myself being one of the twelve; he proceeded to glance us over and on looking at me said: "Step back out of the ranks, I want only able-bodied men." I stepped down and out considerably chagrinned, as the general impression was that they were to go to our lines with the convalescents who had been taken outside before. He marched off the twelve men and it then leaked out that they were to be sent to some prison to be held as hostages until the end of the war. Then I felt better. It is said all the sick will be taken outside as soon as they get quarters fixed up to accommodate them. Think that I shall resign my position as nurse. Would rather stay with the "boys."... But few die now; quite a number died from the removal, but now all seem to be on the mend.

Conley, Capt., 101st Penna. Volunteers, escaped prisoner, N.C.:

The next morning our breakfast was ready and eaten before daylight, and under a guide furnished by the Sheriff, we proceeded to this mountain cabin where we found Capt. Cady and Lt. Masters. This was Thursday morning, Nov. 3rd, and just three days before the time for starting for Tennessee. We were now informed that it would be necessary to secure five days rations before starting, as we would not be able to get any for that time. So we spent our time among the Union families in that neighborhood, with most of whom we became acquainted soon. We found them to be rugged stalwart mountaineers; most of them had little culture, but answering Union proclivities, most of them seemed to be determined to die rather than serve in the rebel army. All the men who were liable to military duty and consequently to conscription, spent most of their time in the woods, only coming home for supplies. All of them were heavily armed. I met a number of men here who carried, each, two guns and two revolvers. Posses of rebels had frequently been sent in there to hunt up these people, but had almost invariably met with defeat, as these mountaineers would band together and ambush them. We were told

that they also tried to capture them with bloodhounds, but that also proved a failure; as not one bloodhound brought in ever got out alive.

I went one afternoon to the home of a Mr. Case, living near, and was invited to stay for supper. There were three brothers of the Cases' and a brother-in-law named William Perry, but who was familiarly called "Bill Perry." While there, Mr. Case described to me a fight he and his two brothers and "Bill" Perry had had with the rebels. By previous arrangement, all four of them and their wives met there on a certain night. Next morning, just as day was breaking, having secured a supply of provisions, the men were about to start when they discovered that the house was surrounded by a company of rebels. Bolting the door, they opened fire through loopholes that had been purposely made between the logs. As the men fired, their wives loaded their guns, and in a very short time the rebels began to retreat, seeing which, the besieged opened the door, stepped out, and opened fire on them from the yard as they retreated. When the fight was over, seven or eight of the rebels lay dead about the house. The company of rebels was said to number about thirty. I have never anywhere else known such bitterness as existed between neighbors here. The persecution and hardship that the Union men had been subjected to, very naturally, brought a spirit of retaliation. It was not unusual, as we learned, for persons to be waylaid, and assassinated when passing along the public highways.

## November 4 (Friday)

At Richmond, Capt. John C. Rutherford, CSA, reported on his recent inspection trip to the prison at Columbia, S.C.:

The camp is a large one, in fact much too large for the number of prisoners confined (hence they have made themselves very comfortable), which requires a much larger guard than is necessary. Prisoners are constantly escaping during the dark nights. Five escaped the night before I arrived. I suggested that the lines be contracted, as a great deal more ground than necessary was inclosed, throwing the sentinels closer together; also, that light wood fires be kept up along the lines during the dark nights. Both of these changes I deemed necessary, and would have so ordered had Col. Means been regularly assigned to command under Gen. Gardner. In the first place, Col. M. being put in command by Gen. Hardee and reporting to him, I was not authorized to make any changes. In the second place, my orders could not have been recognized had I issued them.

Also at Richmond, Judge Robert Ould, Confederate Agent for Exchange, wrote Maj. Gen. McLaws in Savannah about the exchange of wounded:

I understand, from a press dispatch received here, that a large number of our prisoners were about to be delivered in the Savannah River. The Federals promised to notify me when they would do so, but have not done it. It was my purpose to send an agent to superintend the delivery on both sides. If I send one, will he arrive in time? Only the sick and wounded are to be delivered in return, if we have as many of that sort as the Yankees give us. If not, let the difference be made up from those whose term of service has expired. The prisoners south of Charleston are under Gen. Winder; those north of that place, under Gen. Gardner. There are many sick and wounded under both. The deficiency of sick and wounded under Gen. Winder can be made up from those under Gen. Gardner. There are numbers at Columbia and Salisbury. Let me know immediately what you contemplate doing, and whether an assistant can reach Savannah in time…

Conley, Capt., 101st Penna. Volunteers, escaped prisoner, N.C.:

During the three days of our stay there we succeeded in getting a supply of corn bread and a little meat for the next five days. In order to make ourselves as comfortable as possible while there, we gathered in some corn fodder that stood in a field nearby and made our beds of it.

Ransom, John, QM Sgt., 9th Michigan Cavalry, Camp Lawton, Millen, Ga.:

The fine weather still continues. Just warm enough, and favorable for prisoners. Food now we get but once a day—not all we want, but three times as much as issued at Andersonville and of good quality.

**November 5 (Saturday)**

Master John Y. Beall, Confederate States Navy, was into another plot against the U.S.S. *Michigan*,

Commander Carter, at Sandusky, Ohio. Beall had once before plotted to take over the *Michigan*, but the plot had failed when Carter smelled a rat and arrested the co-conspirators, but Beall escaped. Now, it seemed, that Beall and a Southern sympathizer, Dr. James Bates, had purchased the steamer *Georgian* in Toronto, Canada, and plotted to capture the *Michigan* and use both ships to attack the larger cities on Lake Erie. Strict surveillance by Union agents kept the plot from being fulfilled and eventually the *Georgian* was put into dock on the Canadian side and sold again.

Ransom, John, QM Sgt., 9th Michigan Cavalry, Camp Lawton, Millen, Ga.:

Hostages taken out. Everything is bright and pleasant and I see no cause to complain, therefore won't. Tomorrow is election day at the North; wish I was there to vote—which I ain't. Will here say that I am a War Democrat to the backbone. Not a very stiff one, as my backbone is weak.

Conley, Capt., 101st Penna. Volunteers, escaped prisoner, N.C.:

On Saturday evening, Sheriff Hamilton brought over the five officers that were stopping with him and we all slept in the cabin that night. Sheriff Hamilton remained with us all night.

**November 6 (Sunday)**

Confederate Agent for Exchange Robert Ould's letter of October 30 to Gen. Grant arrived at City Point this date. Grant, recognizing the possibilities of the arrangement, replied:

Sir: Your communication of the 30th of October, inquiring whether the U.S. authorities will consent to a shipment of cotton from a Southern port to a Northern city, with a view of purchasing blankets, &c., for the immediate relief of prisoners, &c., is just this moment received. I hasten to reply to send back by the same messenger who brought yours.

I will propose that the U.S. authorities send a vessel to receive the cotton at any place you may designate between the lines of the two parties and ship it to such Northern city as you may designate. A Confederate prisoner of war will be allowed to accompany the vessel going after the cotton, and to stay with it until it is sold. He will also be allowed to make the purchases with the proceeds and distribute them. A commissioned U.S. officer will accompany the officer selected by you during the whole of this transaction.

This much I can answer without referring to higher authority. If it is insisted that a Southern vessel run from a Southern to a Northern port direct, I will have to refer the matter to the Treasury Department for the views of the President.

The number of Union prisoners at Salisbury, N.C., on this date was recorded at 8740. This number was considerably over the capacity, which was to be 2500. This was 4500 more than were incarcerated at Andersonville, Ga., during the entire month of October 1864.

Ransom, John, QM Sgt., 9th Michigan Cavalry, Camp Lawton, Millen, Ga.:

One year ago today captured. Presidential election at the North between Lincoln and McClellan. Someone fastened up a box, and all requested to vote, for the fun of the thing. Old prisoners haven't life enough to go and vote; new prisoners vote for present administration. I voted for McClellan with a hurrah, and another hurrah, and still another. Had this election occurred while we were at Andersonville, four-fifths would have voted for McClellan. We think ourselves shamefully treated in being left so long as prisoners of war.... Yes, one year ago today captured. A year is a good while, even when pleasantly situated, but how much longer being imprisoned as we have been. It seems a lifetime, and I am twenty years older than a year ago. Little thought that I was to remain all this time in durance vile. Improving in health, disposition and everything else. If both breeches legs were of the same length should be supremely happy.

Abbott, A.O., 1st Lt., 1st N.Y. Dragoons, prisoner, Columbia, S.C.:

In the afternoon ... Capt. M ———— came to the guard-line with a list of officers in his hand, and began to call for them. Visions of prison walls and dungeons rose up before those called for, and it was with difficulty some of them could be persuaded to go out. Soon, however, it was found they were *"special"* exchanges, and then the aspect of the matter changed somewhat.

All of the sick, all of the nurses were included, besides some eighty others. Several names were called of officers who had escaped, and, when it could be done without detection, another took their place, signing the name of the absent to the parole rather than his own.... The party left the next day about three o'clock.

Conley, Capt., 101st Penna. Volunteers, escaped prisoner, N.C.:

The next morning when we woke there was about an inch of snow on the ground but it soon melted away when the sun came up. After breakfast we started to the place of meeting which was about a mile away. We of the "Pennsylvania House" now numbered fifteen and we were joined by fourteen others, making a company of twenty-nine men, including Sergt. Hamlin, who was one of the recruiting officers for the 2nd N.C., who now informed us that we would now proceed to the place of general rendezvous, which was about twelve or fifteen miles further on, and it was expected that a company of recruits numbering thirty or thirty-five would meet us there, most of them whom would be armed, and with whom would be a Lieutenant, who would be our guide. We started at once, taking byways.

When within a mile of the place of rendezvous, three of the recruits stopped at a farmhouse to get some more corn bread, the rest of us going on to the place appointed, which we found to be a secluded spot, in a very narrow valley, little more than a ravine, between two high and very steep hills. Here we unloaded our stuff and built a fire. We had been there probably an hour and a half when we were startled by a volley of musketry, apparently not more than three or four hundred yards down the ravine below us. At the same time we heard a scream which we believed to be that of a wounded man. Under direction of our guide, Sergt. Hamlin, we gathered up our supplies, and keeping together, reached the top of the hill east of us as quietly as possible. Here we formed a skirmish line with all the arms we had, consisting of four guns and three revolvers, while the rest of us formed in line in rear of the skirmishers and advanced to ascertain what the trouble was. We had only gone a few rods when the skirmishers came in sight of a company of rebels. Our guide hailed them and asked who they were. The answer was Capt. (whose name I do not recall) Company. This company was known to our guide as a company of home guards. Hamlin at once ordered the skirmishers to fire, at which the rebels retreated. At about the same time we could see a company of about thirty, all armed, marching down the road on the opposite hill, and scarcely a quarter of a mile from us. Sergt. Hamlin and the ten officers held a hasty consultation. The appearance of the company we saw coming down indicated that they were rebels, and if so, we were not prepared to meet them. On being assured by our guide that he was sufficiently acquainted with the route to act as guide, we decided not to wait for the other squad. Accordingly, we faced back into the mountains, it being now about sunset. After travelling about four or five miles, and until it was quite dark, we descended a very steep mountain, at the foot of which we came to a very rapid mountain stream. Pulling off our shoes and hose, and rolling up our trousers, we waded it. On the opposite side of this stream we found a level place several rods wide and covered with a thick growth of rhododendrons. This grew up and seemed to branch at a height of about five to six feet from the ground, forming a complete canopy overhead. Here we lay down for the night, believing that no human being could find us there.

At Ft. Monroe, Va., Lt. Col. John E. Mulford, U.S. Agent for Exchange, wrote Maj. Gen. Benjamin F. Butler, Federal Commissioner for Exchange, of his problems getting proper shipping for the transport of sick and wounded prisoners to Savannah, there to pick up Federal sick and wounded.

General: I ... inform you that I am still here awaiting transportation for the sick prisoners now on board steamers *Atlantic* and *Baltic*, and more particularly our own men whom I am to receive in return. It would be worse than barbarous, general, for me to undertake, in the ships now at my disposal, the transportation of those feeble and dying men now anxiously awaiting my arrival in Savannah, and whose sufferings are protracted and aggravated and whose mortality is fearfully increased by this needless delay. My fleet, as organized by yourself, was indeed a noble one, for a noble purpose; one that would reflect honor upon our Government and carry joy and gladness to many thousand anguished hearts. Of that portion still left me no fault can be found, but the most essential part for this expedition is withheld. I am, by an order from Washington

to Col. Webster, chief quartermaster of this department, deprived the use of the only hospital ships in the fleet, and knowing so well as I do for what a wretched freight I am to provide on my return trip, I feel assured you will approve my course in insisting upon some proper provision being made for the sick before I sail. I have now here loaded the steamers *Atlantic, Baltic, Northern Light II, Livingston,* and *New York,* in all some 3000 men; have lost over 50 since their arrival at this place. One other vessel, the *Crescent,* is loaded with stores, clothing, &c. I have turned over to the quartermaster five of the large vessels for the transportation of troops. The balance of the fleet is still here. Quartermaster-General informed Col. Webster he had ordered vessels from New York to relieve the *Atlantic* and *Baltic.* They have not yet arrived, nor have we further advice of them. Please direct me what to do...

In action around Cassville, Ga., a Union wagon train was captured. One of the teamsters was Pvt. Eliab Hickman, on detached service from Co. E, 92d Ohio Volunteer Infantry. The prisoners were hastily marched away from the battle area and forwarded to the prison at Andersonville, Ga., where they arrived on November 9th, were processed and incarcerated.

### November 7 (Monday)

Ransom, John, QM Sgt., 9th Michigan Cavalry, Camp Lawton, Millen, Ga.:

A rather cold rain wets all who have not shelter. Many ladies come to see us; don't come through the gate, but look at us through that loophole. Any one with money can buy extras in the way of food, but, alas, we have no money. Am now quite a trader— that is, I make up a very thin dish of soup and sell it for ten cents, or trade it for something. Am ravenously hungry now and can't get enough to eat. The disease has left my system, the body demands food, and I have to exert my speculative genius to get it.... A man belonging to the Masonic order need not stay here an hour. It seems as if every rebel officer was of that craft, and a prisoner has but to make himself known to the taken care of.... That is another thing I must do when I get home—join the Masons. No end of things for me to do: visit all the foreign countries that prisoners told me about, and not forgetting to take in Boston by the way, wear silk underclothing, join the Masons, and above all educate myself to keep out of rebel prisons.... Small alligator killed at lower part of the stream.

Conley, Capt., 101st Penna. Volunteers, escaped prisoner, N.C.:

During the night, it commenced to rain and by morning we were thoroughly wet. While the clouds were dark and lowering so that our guide had difficulty in taking any bearings, yet he appeared to be confident that he could find the way.

We travelled all day through the woods up and down mountains, it continuing to rain most of the day. As night approached, we halted in a ravine in the mountains, and built up a fire, and lay down to sleep while the cold November rain came down in torrents.

### November 8 (Tuesday)

Abraham Lincoln was reelected President and Andrew Johnson elected Vice-President by a 55 percent majority of the popular vote of the people of the United States. The Lincoln-Johnson ticket received 212 of the electoral votes to McClellan's 21. Although the people of the North were not happy with the bloodshed, they were more interested in keeping the Union. Interestingly, the soldiers' vote was almost entirely for Lincoln. The war would continue.

The prisoners at Andersonville were aware of the significance of the day and conducted their own election. Lincoln won there also.

Conley, Capt., 101st Penna. Volunteers, escaped prisoner, N.C.:

With the break of day, Tuesday morning, we again started out and travelled again up and down steep, rugged mountains, avoiding all settlements, until between two and three o'clock we halted and our guide told us that we now had a choice of routes. If we would cross the valley, which lay in front of us, about fifteen miles to the mountain on the opposite side, instead of following the mountain around, it would save us a distance of about twenty-five miles. We decided to risk the shorter route. Descending to the foot of the mountain, we halted and built a fire. It had been raining nearly all day and our clothing was wet. This was the day of Lincoln's second election.

Ransom, John, QM Sgt., 9th Michigan Cavalry, Camp Lawton, Millen, Ga.:

All eager for news.... Wonder who is elected? Feel stronger every day, and have a little flesh on my bones. As the weather gets cool, we are made painfully aware of the fact that we are sadly deficient in clothing.... One good sign—the rebels are making no more improvements about this prison; they say we are not to stay here long. We hear that our troops are marching all through the South.

### November 9 (Wednesday)

There was action at Shoal Creek near Florence, Ala., and skirmishing near Ft. Henry. The Union buildup at Nashville of Gen. George Thomas's army was progressing.

At Kingston, Ga., a major decision had been made concerning Sherman's armies. He would now start his drive for the sea, planning to live off the land.

Conley, Capt., 101st Penna. Volunteers, escaped prisoner, N.C.:

About nine o'clock we started. Moving carefully, we crossed the valley that night and about three o'clock next morning we reached the summit of the mountain very tired, it having rained nearly all night. There we rested until morning, and after a hasty breakfast of cold corn bread, started out again and travelled all day following the mountains and avoiding all settlements. We stopped for the night just at the base of Mt. Pisgah, one of the highest mountain peaks in that part of N.C. It had rained at intervals all day and as night approached the rain increased. We built fires and tried to make ourselves as comfortable as possible under the circumstances.

Ransom, John, QM Sgt., 9th Michigan Cavalry, Camp Lawton, Millen, Ga.:

A deadline has also been fixed up in Camp Lawton, but thus far no one has been shot. Rebel doctors inside examining men who may be troubled with disease prison life might aggravate. Those selected are taken outside and either put in hospitals or sent to our lines.... Have made a raise of another pair of pants with both legs of the same length, and I discard the old ones to a "poor" prisoner.

### November 10 (Thursday)

In the Valley, Jubal Early's weakened force was

now hardly effective. Early used what he had to make a demonstration north towards Sheridan from the New Market area.

In Tennessee, Forrest was moving to a junction with Hood which would provide Hood a more formidable force with which to face Thomas at Nashville.

Ransom, John, QM Sgt., 9th Michigan Cavalry, Camp Lawton, Millen, Ga.:

Pleasant and rather cool. My hair is playing me pranks. It grows straight up in the air and only on the topmost part of my head. Where a man is generally bald, it's right the other way with me.... We are not far from the railroad track, and can listen to the cars going by. Very often Confederate troops occupy them and they give the old familiar rebel yell. Once in a while the Yanks get up steam enough to give a good hurrah back to them. Seems to be a good deal of transferring troops now in the South.... Rumors that we are to be moved.

Conley, Capt., 101st Penna. Volunteers, escaped prisoner, Tennessee:

Towards morning the rain ceased and that (Thursday) morning the sun came out brightly, the first sunshine we had that week. From Sunday night until this time our clothing had never been dry. Our comfort that kind Mrs. Jones had given us had been thoroughly soaked every night and each morning we would wring it out. Thus by frequent wringings it had become so much torn that it was of little use to us so this morning we threw it away.

Near the eastern base of the Smoky Mountains, we came to where once had been a small farm but which apparently had been abandoned for years. The buildings were in a tumbledown condition, but near the house stood several large apple trees and under one of them there lay several bushels of good ripe apples. This was a treat. We stopped and ate all that we could and filled our pockets. That afternoon we crossed Smoky Mountains, the boundary between N.C. and Tennessee. While in N.C. we had passed through Polk, Henderson, Transylvania, Jackson, and Haywood Counties. We entered Tenn. in the southern part of Cook Co. About sunset that evening we approached the first farmhouse we had seen in Tenn., our guide having informed us that a Mr. Davis lived there and

that it would be a good place to stop for the night, our stock of provisions being now exhausted and it was necessary to look for something to eat.

As we approached the house we saw a man come out at the rear door and run for the woods. As we reached the fence in front of the house, a lady appeared at the front door evidently much excited and gesticulating wildly with her hands, called out: "Don't come in here. Just clear out with you; we don't want any rebels in here." Stopping outside the fence, we said to her: "Madam, we are not rebels, we are all Union men, and part of us are escaped Union prisoners." Her reply was, "I don't believe it. I believe you are rebels, and we don't want anything to do with you." After some delay, we succeeded in convincing her that we were all right, when she told us to come in. She afterwards told us that the first thing she did when she saw us coming was to hide her knives, forks and spoons. She had little to give us but corn bread, but she gave us enough of that to satisfy our hunger. After she had become satisfied that we were all right, she sent a couple of the children to hunt her husband and bring him home. They found him at a neighbor's two or three miles from home, but he would not risk to come home. That night we slept on her kitchen floor, the ten officers doing guard duty by turns. Before retiring, we told Mrs. Davis that she should not get us breakfast the next morning as it would be asking too much of her, but, that we would start out at daylight and take the risk of finding breakfast on the way. So at daylight we bade our kind hostess good-bye with many thanks.

## November 11 (Friday)

In Georgia, Sherman ordered the railroads destroyed. At Rome, Ga., the Union troops tore up the tracks, destroyed mills, foundries, etc., while the garrisons around Kingston were sent to pull up the rails and send them back to Chattanooga for later use.

In Richmond, Robert Ould, Confederate Agent for Exchange, today received U.S. Grant's reply concerning the movement of cotton from the South to alleviate the Confederate prisoners in the North. In his reply Ould outlined the basis for the agreement and the mechanics of how it would work:

General:... The Confederate Government will deliver on board one of your vessels near Mobile 1000 bales of cotton, to be forwarded to the city of New York and there be sold, the proceeds to be applied to the benefit of our prisoners.... The cotton will be ready to be delivered within a week. Whenever the Federal vessel is ready to receive it notification can be given to Maj. Gen. Maury, commanding at Mobile.

I venture to suggest some details, all of which I believe are in accordance with the tenor of your letter of the 30th ultimo.

First. Maj. Gen. Trimble, now at Ft. Warren, has been selected as the Confederate officer to whom the consignment shall be made at New York, who will there make the necessary and proper arrangements for the sale of the cotton.... In the event of the disability of Maj. Gen. Trimble, Brig. Gen. William N.R. Beall is designated as his alternate. The selected officer shall be put on such parole as will enable him to discharge the duties assigned....

Second. Such officer shall be allowed to make his purchases at those points where they can be made with the greatest advantage.

Third. As the Confederate Government proposes to forward without charge such supplies as you may send for the relief of your prisoners, we take it for granted that the cost of transportation from the place of purchase will be borne by the United States Government. The officer selected by us will make all necessary arrangements for such transportation.

Fourth. The reception of the supplies and their subsequent distribution amongst the prisoners on both sides shall be certified by a committee of officers confined in the prisons so supplied. Such a parole will be given to such officers as will enable them to carry out this agreement with due facility....

Fifth. Receipts will be given when the cotton is delivered on board your vessel and a bill of lading forwarded to Maj. Gen. Trimble or his alternate.

Sixth. I will thank your authorities to furnish Gen. Trimble or his alternate, as near as may be, the number of prisoners confined in your respective prisons in order that he may duly apportion the supplies. Similar information as to our prisons will be furnished whenever it is asked.

I trust that these details will be agreeable to you. If they are found to be inconvenient or defective, they can be amended by the consent of both parties.

I will thank you for a reply ... at your earliest convenience.

Ransom, John, QM Sgt., 9th Michigan Cavalry, Camp Lawton, Millen, Ga.:

Very well fed.... I have an appetite larger than an elephant.... Cannot possibly refrain from saying that I am feeling splendidly and worth a hundred dead men yet. Have two dollars in Confederate money and if I can sell this half canteen of dishwater soup shall have another dollar before dark.... Often hear the baying of hounds from a distance, through the night—and such strange sounds to the Northern ear.

Conley, Capt., 101st Penna. Volunteers, escaped prisoner, Tenn.:

It may be said that we were now between the lines but not out of danger. Stopping among the small mountain farmers, we all succeeded in getting breakfast. During the day, while crossing some fields, we came upon two men who were digging in the field while two others stood guard. When we approached them we learned that they were digging a grave for an old man who had been cruelly murdered the day before by some rebel cavalry. As told us, a company of cavalry came to his house and asked him to show them the road to some point a short distance, and as he walked before them to comply with their request, he was shot down. After passing over this farm, and while passing through the next one, near the house a woman came out and said to us: "You are going the wrong way. You should go this way." Pointing further to the right. But our guide answered, "This is the way we want to go." But she continued to insist on our going the other say, until we had gotten some distance past her. Her conduct was a mystery to us. We could not understand why she was so much interested in us as we had not asked for information. When we reached the woods, as our guide informed us, we found a path leading through the woods. We had not gone more than thirty rods along this path when we saw a man ahead of us, without hat or coat, running as if his life depended on the speed he made. When we reached the point where we first saw him, we found a small board shanty, about six by eight feet; in the end opposite the door was a mud chimney with a bright fire burning. On the ground was a shoemaker's bench and beside it lay the shoemaker's strap and a half-finished shoe; on two nails in the side of the shanty hung his coat and hat. To our minds this solved the mystery of the woman's great anxiety as to the route we should take. He was, in all probability, her husband, who, in order to escape conscription was pursuing his calling at this lonely spot, and she, supposing we were rebels, and fearing for his safety, undertook by that ruse to change our course. After examining his shanty, we proceeded without disturbing anything in it.

Towards evening we passed an old mill, and as we approached it we noticed a rather fine looking old gentleman sitting on a mule in front of the mill talking to the miller. He seemed to be scrutinizing us as we approached, and when we got within 15 or 20 feet of them the old gentleman called out, "I'm for Lincoln. I don't know who you are for." Something in our appearance, probably our uniforms, must have convinced him that we were not rebels. We assured him that we most heartily agreed with him in sentiment. He told us that he was a practicing physician and had been a Union man from the first. From inquiry as to where we could find a safe stopping place for the night, he advised us to go to Jones' Cove about three miles distant where there were only four or five families, and all Union families. He directed us on how to find it, and told us to call on Milt Spurgeon; that he was a good Union man and would take care of us. About sunset we entered the cove through a gap in the mountains and were making our way to the nearest house and while doing so we noticed a man in a field some distance from the house who seemed to be driving hogs towards the house. Presently he saw us, and giving a yell, he turned and ran for the mountains. Instantly the women commenced to sound the alarm. The cove was small and cleared from one end to the other. Inside of two minutes we could see men from every house running to the mountain and all seemed to be converging at a certain point. Seeing that we had created alarm, we halted and sent two men to the nearest house to try to convince the women that we were Union men. But they would not believe our story. They believed that we were rebels trying to entrap their men. Finding our efforts with the women futile, the only thing left was to find the men. For this purpose, we sent Capt. Aldrich and our guide to find them. The cleared land extended at the point for which they steered, to the base of a steep bluff. The top of the bluff was heavily wooded. When the two men got within 40 or 50 feet of

the base of the bluff, they were halted by a man who had taken his position behind a large tree. He asked who they were and what they wanted. On being told, he at first refused to believe. They called his attention to their blue uniforms. He answered, "Your clothes look all right and you talk all right, but if you are not all right, I've got enough men up here to blow you all to h———." After considerable parleying, he agreed that one of them might go up to him unarmed. At that Capt. Aldrich went up and soon convinced him that we were all right, and he gave permission for us to come up to him. When we reached him he proved to be Milt Spurgeon. But, up to this time, none of the others would venture out. Mr. Spurgeon called to them but they would not come. It was then suggested that the few guns we had be handed over to Mr. Spurgeon. He then called to them come on, that he had all the guns. At this they began to move towards us but with a great deal of caution. After they had all gotten there and began to feel satisfied that we were all right, the next thing was to make arrangements for the night.

After some discussion it was agreed that we should all go to the house of a man named Long as his house was in a secluded spot and the others would bring their cornmeal there and have it baked. Mr. Long said that he had one hog in the pen and that he would kill that in order to give us some meat. We protested against his doing so as it was his only hog, but he insisted on doing it. We started with him while the others returned home to send us cornmeal. In going to his place, we followed a path which led for some distance through a large thicket of rhododendrons, passing under the branches. When we reached there we found a small log cabin with the spaces between the logs all open, no chinking. Here he had his wife and two small children. We learned from him that he had built there so that the conscripting officers would not find him. As soon as we arrived at his place, he made preparations to butcher his hog, while his wife commenced to bake corn bread. It was nearly midnight before she had enough corn bread to satisfy twenty-six hungry men.

In the meantime, they had put on a large pot and boiled enough of the pork to satisfy the party. We built up large fires not far from the house and spent our time around them until midnight, when we lay down near them.

## November 12 (Saturday)

In Georgia, Sherman sent his last message to Grant while his army was tearing Atlanta down (except for the houses and churches), and Sherman's force of 55,000 men and 5000 cavalry and 2000 artillery was ready to march.

At Andersonville, Ga., Capt. Henry Wirz reported that he had received 399 blankets; 60 pairs of shoes; 240 pairs of pants; 396 pairs of drawers; 396 pairs of socks; and 324 shirts for distribution to the prisoners. A mere drop in the bucket for the prison population.

Conley, Capt., 101st Penna. Volunteers, escaped prisoner, Tenn.:

During the night a log rolled off one of our fires and fell on Lt. Master's ankle, injuring it so much that he was unable to walk the next day. One of the men in the cove who had a mule agreed to let him ride for about ten miles, he going along to take the mule back. With two forked sticks we made him two crutches and he travelled the balance of the distance on them. A little before noon we emerged from the mountains into the beautiful valley of the Little Pigeon River, a most fertile valley. Here we found a fine plantation. We scattered...and secured some dinner. About 2 o'clock we reached Sevierville, the county seat of Sevier Co. Here we found it necessary to cross the Pigeon River. At a mill near the village, we found a customer of the mill with two horses. He agreed to assist us in crossing. There was then also a large canoe used as a ferry. With the canoe and the horses, we were soon over.

Up to this time Knoxville had been our objective point, but learning that Strawberry Plains, sixteen miles further up the Holstone River, was nearer than Knoxville, and it was occupied by our troops, we changed our course towards that place. During the afternoon we met a rebel major in full uniform armed with sabre and revolvers. He bade us the time of day and passed. What he was doing along in that locality we did not know. About sunset, we reached the French Broad River, having travelled a little over thirty miles that day. A citizen ferried us across in a large dugout, taking eight or ten at a load. As soon as all were over, most of the party secured entertainment at several houses nearby but Capts. Dawson, Longworthy and Aldrich and Lt. Twilliger and myself pressed

on further. After going about a mile we met a man and inquired of him where we could find a good stopping place. He told us about a mile ahead there lived a Mrs. Jones, a widow, who was a good Union woman, where he thought we could stop. From him we learned the first news of the Presidential election held the Thursday before, this being Saturday evening, Nov. 12. We stopped at Mrs. Jones's and had a very good substantial supper. Mrs. Jones very kindly offered us the privilege of sleeping before her fire in her sitting room, which offer we decided at first to accept, but about 9 o'clock we asked Mrs. Jones whether the rebels ever made raids in there, and she answered that they did at times, and being now only about eight miles from where we had seen the rebel major that afternoon we feared that there [might] be some rebel cavalry in the neighborhood and decided to continue to our lines that night. Mrs. Jones gave us directions and told us that just outside of the picket lines we would come to an old mill, and the miller, whose name was Thompson, was a Union man and that we should stop there, and he could tell us whether we could get through the picket lines that night.

Bidding Mrs. Jones good-bye, we started. The night was cold and frosty, and we travelled briskly, reaching the old mill about half past eleven. We woke up the old miller and asked him whether we could get through the picket lines that night. He replied that he didn't think that we could but "You can stay here till morning and sleep on my floor." We accepted his offer; when he got up and dressed, and bringing some wood, built up a good fire in his capacious fire place. We had travelled about 40 miles that day. He proved to be an odd character. He entertained us for about two hours, with a recital of his adventures during the war and with several songs. There was not much music in his voice, but being his guests, we felt compelled to show some appreciation of his proficiency as a vocalist.

Ransom, John, QM Sgt., 9th Michigan Cavalry, Camp Lawton, Millen, Ga.:

Have just heard the election news—Mr. Lincoln again elected, and "Little Mac" nowhere. Just about what I expected. Returns were rather slow coming in, evidently waiting for the Camp Lawton vote. Well, did what I could for George; hurrahed until my throat was sore and stayed so for a week; know that I influenced twenty or thirty votes, and now can get no office because the political opponent was elected. 'Tis ever thus. Believe I would made a good postmaster for this place. There is none here and should have applied immediately, if my candidate had been elected. More sick taken away on the cars; rebels say to be exchanged.... Have lived rather high today on capital made yesterday and early this morning. Just my way—make a fortune and then spend it.

## November 13 (Sunday)

Conley, Capt., 101st Penna. Volunteers, back in Union lines, Holston River, Tenn.:

Between one and two o'clock he got us out some army blankets which he said some cavalrymen had left there and we lay down before his fire and slept until daylight, when we arose and thanking our kind host, we bade him good-bye. Passing through the timber for a short distance, we came out into the beautiful open valley of the Holston River. Just beyond the river on a gentle rise of ground we saw the white tents of the 10th Mich. Cavalry and over the camp floated the Stars and Stripes. It was the first sight we had of the old flag for nearly seven months. Reaching the pickets, and telling them who we were, they passed us through and directed us to the tent of Maj. Newell of the 10th Mich. Cavalry, commandant of the post there being part of the 10th Mich. Cavalry. On reaching his tent, we found him enjoying a morning nap. On learning who we were, he got up and very kindly set out the "applejack" and ordered breakfast for us. We found the major as well as all the other officers of the regiment very gentlemanly and courteous.

About 9 o'clock the balance of our party came in. After Sunday morning inspection, the officers of the post all called to see us, and invited the escaped prisoners among the different officers' messes for dinner. The writer and two or three others took dinner with the Quartermaster and the Chaplain. About the middle of the afternoon Maj. Newell furnished us each a horse and an escort to go to Knoxville that evening, which place we reached soon after dark. We were now within the Union lines, having reached our outpost on Sunday morning, Nov. 13, 1864, that being the fortieth day since our escape. While we were now within the Union lines, we were yet more than a thousand miles by rail from our commands. At Knoxville we reported to the Provost Marshal, who ordered us to our com-

mands. With the order we reported to the Quartermaster, who gave us transportation.

Ransom, John, QM Sgt., 9th Michigan Cavalry, Camp Lawton, Millen, Ga.:

Today had an incident happen to me; hardly an incident, but a sort of an adventure.... A rebel sergeant came inside at just about nine o'clock this morning and looked me up and said I was wanted outside, and so went. Was taken to a house not far from the stockade, which proved to be the officers' headquarters. There introduced to three or four officers, whose names do not occur to me, and informed that they were in need of someone to do writing and assist in making out their army papers, and if I would undertake the job, they would see that I had plenty to eat, and I should be sent North at the first opportunity. I respectfully, gently and firmly declined the honor, and after partaking of quite a substantial meal, which they gave me thinking I would reconsider my decision, was escorted back inside.... Always willing to do extra duty for our own men, such as issuing clothing on Belle Isle, also my nursing the sick or in any way doing for them, but when it comes to working in any way for any rebel, I shall beg to be excused.... Am still loyal to the Stars and Stripes and shall have no fears at looking my friends in the face when I do go home.

## November 14 (Monday)

In Georgia, the march to the sea was getting closer to its beginning. Federal cavalry under Gen. Judson Kilpatrick left Atlanta for Jonesborough and the southeast, moving towards Savannah. Sherman's left wing, Maj. Gen. Slocum, was in Decatur and Stone Mountain, where they demolished the railroad, bridges, and anything else of military value.

In Nashville, George H. Thomas assembled his troops, and Schofield's two corps at Pulaski were positioned as a blocking force. Hood, near Florence, Ala., waited for Forrest to come up from Corinth, Miss., before entering Tennessee.

Abbott, A.O., 1st Lt., 1st N.Y. Dragoons, prisoner, Columbia, S.C.:

After about four weeks, the hope of being supplied with tents, or any kind of shelter, died out of our hearts, and we set about building ourselves some kind of winter-quarters, for it was evident we were to stay there till spring. The rebels seemed to have come to the same conclusion, and, to enable us to build houses for ourselves, brought in for 1200 men *eight axes and ten shovels*. To facilitate matters also, *a kind-hearted sutler* sold us axes for the moderate price of forty-five dollars each, and a helve for five dollars.... That we might get at the timber, the commandant allowed a certain number to be paroled each day.... Two reliefs of the guard, usually about 80 men, were deployed around a piece of wood each day for a couple of hours, and we were allowed to get all the wood we could during that time. Some days we could get *much*, some days but little. This time was usually seized upon to "demoralize" the guard, *i.e.*, find one alone, and strike a bargain to let you run his beat at night for a consideration, or, better, let you stray past him *now* while in the woods. In many cases it succeeded. Generally fifty dollars, in Confederate money, would buy the best of them....

While we were trying to build our quarters, it was quite amusing to attempt to go through camp. The space was very much crowded, and no regularity in laying it out. Each one built his cabin just where he could find a place.

Ransom, John, QM Sgt., 9th Michigan Cavalry, Camp Lawton, Millen, Ga.:

Six hundred taken away this forenoon; don't know where to. As I was about the last to come to Millen, my turn will not come for some days if only six hundred are taken out each day. Rebels say they go straight to our lines, but their being heavily guarded and every possible precaution taken to prevent escape, it does not look like our lines to me. Probably go to Charleston; that seems to be the jumping off place. Charleston, for some reason or other, seems a bad place to go to. Any city familiar with the war I want to avoid. Shall hang back as long as I can, content to let well enough alone.

The inspection of Elmira Prison had been completed by Surgeon Wm. J. Sloan of the New York Medical Director's Office and today a report was forwarded to Surgeon C. McDougall, the Medical Director, Department of the East:

I made a special inspection of the prisoners' camp at Elmira, N.Y., on the 12th instant. No better

time could have been selected for this examination, with particular reference to its condition in unpleasant weather, as a severe storm of snow and rain was prevailing....

The statements made to the Surgeon-General by Surgeon Sanger in his report of November 1 were not exaggerated, although an undue warmth of language may have been exhibited, from the difficulties he had to encounter from the delays attending the filling of his requisitions and the little attention paid to his remonstrances.

In the latter part of September Surgeon Sanger, having represented the difficulties under which he labored, was instructed by you to make requisitions for everything necessary for the proper administration of his department, for your approval and the action of the general commanding the Department of the East. The reason why this was not done was explained to me. The instructions he received were submitted to the commanding officer of the prison camp, Col. Tracy, who stated that Col. Hoffman, Commissary-General of Prisoners, Washington, having sole charge of prisoners of war, gave all orders in relation to their management, and that all requisitions, &c. must be submitted to him for his action. To this view you made no objection, and, being informed of it, instructed Dr. Sanger accordingly, your sole object being to procure the necessary supplies and relieve the medical department of responsibility or censure.

The means suggested by Dr. Sanger for the better care of the prisoners were the drainage of an unhealthy pond, the erection of sinks, the enlargement of the hospital buildings, and the erection of the kitchen, mess hall, laundry, dead-house, offices, and storerooms, an increased issue of vegetable diet for the prevention of scurvy, increased means of cooking and distributing food, regularity in the issue of rations, and straw for the bed sacks. For all these objects he made frequent requisitions and applications at different dates between August 13 and October 17.

On the 5th of October the surgeon made application, accompanied by plans, for buildings needed in addition to those authorized by the Commissary-General of Prisoners, viz., dispensary and offices, additional wards, mess halls and sinks. These buildings have just been commenced, including a kitchen, but nothing has been done towards erecting the mess hall, dispensary, or laundry and drying room, all essentially needed. I was informed that work was about being commenced for draining and cleansing the fetid pond by introducing water from the Chemung River, through underground wooden tubing, thus creating a constant freshwater current, which, it is admitted, will remedy the existing difficulties. It is scarcely necessary to enumerate the causes of the great ratio of mortality and sickness at this camp, all important to suggest the means of reducing it to a healthier standard.

From a full examination of the whole subject with reference to the climate and the existing condition of things, I respectfully recommend: First, the lining and ceiling of all the buildings now erected; second, the erection of additional wards, to be lined and ceiled; third, the completion of the kitchen and erection of hospital mess hall, dispensary, offices, storerooms, laundry, and drying room, dead-house, and sinks; fourth, the erection of a mess hall for the camp; fifth, the use of larger stoves in the hospital; sixth, the erection of a quartermaster's and commissary storehouse at the camp for the prompt issue of quartermaster's and commissary supplies without reference to the town of Elmira, and that an officer be detailed at the camp as acting assistant quartermaster and acting assistant commissary of subsistence; seventh, an issue of vegetables three times a week to those in the hospital suffering from scurvy; eighth, an issue of clothing, including drawers and socks, to the prisoners.

The surgeon in charge complained with justice of the perplexities arising from the delay in furnishing the supplies, particularly the straw for bed sacks. The commanding officer, while maintaining the incorrectness of these complaints, admitted the tardiness of the quartermaster. The quartermaster justified himself by asserting the scarcity of lumber and straw, an excuse, it seems to me, which can hardly [be] sustained in that region of New York, in close proximity to the lumber and grain districts and on the lines of canals and the great Erie railway. The detail of an acting assistant quartermaster and commissary at the camp, as above suggested, would obviate all these difficulties by keeping on hand supplies in bulk equal to the demands of a force of 10,000 men.

I was informed that everything being referred to the Commissary-General of Prisoners, the requisition of lining the buildings to make them comfortable for the winter was disapproved and the stopping of cracks and open places ordered. A personal inspection convinced me that this measure would not remedy the evil. The winters are exceedingly cold and bleak at Elmira and the buildings were hastily erected of green lumber, which is cracking, splitting, and warping in every direction. An inside lining would prevent the access of cold winds, snow, and rain, and repay the expenditure in the end in the saving of fuel. I feel confident that if these suggestions are presented to the Commissary-General of Prisoners and the commanding general of the department, their force will be manifest and the proper steps be taken immediately on account of the approach of winter, and this prevent the progress of pneumonia and scurvy, now ravaging the camp. With protection from the weather and the climate and with an increase of vegetable food, the winter instead of adding to the mortality will exercise a beneficial influence.

## November 15 (Tuesday)

Ransom, John, QM Sgt., 9th Michigan Cavalry, Camp Lawton, Millen, Ga.:

At about six or seven o'clock last night six hundred men were taken away, making in all twelve hundred for the day; another six hundred are ready to go at a moment's notice. I don't know what to think. Can hardly believe they go to our lines. Seems almost like a funeral procession to me, as they go through the gate.... If it is an exchange there is no danger but all will go, and if not an exchange would rather be here than anyplace I know of now. LATER—Eight hundred have gone, with Rowe and Dakin in the crowd, and I am here alone as regards personal friends. Could not be induced to go with them. Have a sort of presentiment that all is not right. STILL LATER— Six hundred more have gone, making 2600 all together that have departed, all heavily guarded.

## November 16 (Wednesday)

Sherman, leaving Atlanta in ruins, the economy wrecked, and the people without means of livelihood, rode out with the Fourteenth Corps towards Lovejoy's Station.

In Tennessee, near the Alabama border, the Federals at Pulaski waited for Hood to enter the state. Forrest had finally arrived, increasing Hood's force with a good cavalry arm.

Ransom, John, QM Sgt., 9th Michigan Cavalry, Camp Lawton, Millen, Ga.:

A decided thinness in our ranks this morning. Still housekeeping goes right along as usual. Rebels not knowing how to figure give us just about the same for the whole prison as when all were here. Had a talk with a rebel sergeant for about an hour. Tried to find out our destination and could get no satisfaction.... He said he "reckoned we war goin' nawth." Well, I will write down the solution I have at last come to, and we will see how near right I am after a little. Our troops, Sherman or Kilpatrick or some of them, are raiding through the South, and we are not safe in Millen, as we were not safe in Andersonville, and as plainly evident we were not safe in Savannah.... Six hundred gone today.

**November 17 (Thursday)**

Sherman left the Atlanta area using four different routes and moved towards Augusta and Macon, cavalry out front and on the flanks.

Judge Robert Ould, Confederate Agent for Exchange, wrote to Col. William Hoffman, Federal Commissary-General of Prisoners, concerning Hoffman's communications with Confederate prisoners in the North:

Sir: I have lately received several communications from Confederate prisoners at the North, stating that they had received letters from you. Some of these letters state one thing and some another. Some of them contain extracts from your letters to them. Are not the sufferings of these people already sufficient without further torture? Why delude them with false hopes, why tell some of them we are opposed to exchanges, and others that if we would give equivalents for them they would be sent home?

In order that there should be no misunderstanding between us I now say that there is not one Confederate officer or soldier in captivity at the North for whom I will not give an equivalent just as soon as he is delivered to us.

These prisoners generally write that you have informed them that if I will request their delivery, promising to send an officer of the same rank, or soldier, as the case may be, they will be sent South to their own people. I request the delivery of any and every officer and soldier whom you have in confinement, and more particularly all to whom you have told this story. I will simultaneously deliver the

equivalent of each. If you refuse this, I beg in the name of common humanity that no more represenations of this kind be made to our captives.

Seems fair enough. Hoffman, stick to running the camps and let the exchange business be handled by others.

Abbott, A.O., 1st Lt., 1st N.Y. Dragoons, prisoner, Columbia, S.C.:

At this time about one third of the officers had succeeded, by hard work and indomitable energy, in building places that in part protected them from the inclemency of the season. It was now cold, and although we were in the "sunny South," yet the ground would freeze nights hard enough to bear a horse. Those who had still to live in their brush houses suffered very much from the cold.

A few boxes had been received from home in tolerably good condition, and some were indulging in the luxury of good clean new clothes, and also of sugar, coffee, and some other delicacies. The last we received was in November, and the day the officers left a mail was received, among which were letters addressed to several of the officers, stating that our government had revoked the order allowing boxes to be sent through the lines to prisoners.

Ransom, John, QM Sgt., 9th Michigan Cavalry, Camp Lawton, Millen, Ga.:

It is now said that the prisoners are being moved down on the coast near Florida. That coincides with my own view, and I think it very probable. Will try and go about tomorrow. Hardly think I can go today. LATER—The today's batch are going out of the gate. Makes me fairly crazy to wait, fearful I am missing it in not going. This lottery way of living is painful on the nerves.... I stick to my resolution that the rebels don't really know themselves where we are going. They move us because we are not safe here. They are bewildered.

The flap over the unhealthy situation at Elmira, N.Y., continued. On this date, Surgeon C. McDougall, Medical Director, Department of the East, wrote Col. William Hoffman, Federal Commissary-General of Prisoners, in Washington, enclosing copies of the original report, and the inspection report:

To transmit the report of Surgeon Sloan, U.S. Army, of his inspection of the prison camp at Elmira, N.Y., made by order of the Surgeon-General. The condition of affairs there requires the immediate attention to the report and ask that its recommendations may be carried out. Deeming your authority ample in the case, I have not asked the interposition of the commanding general of the department. As the responsibility connected with the management of the medical department at that places rests upon me, I beg that you will communicate your decision upon the matters and recommendations contained in this report at your earliest convenience.

The Surgeon at Elmira was not the only one having problems getting things done for a prison hospital. Surgeon Isaiah H. White, recently assigned as Medical Director for the Confederate prisons, was having a hard time with his own bureauacracy. He wrote from Lawton, Ga.:

Having been ordered to this post, I am lending my aid to the surgeon in charge in the construction of hospital accommodations. Temporary sheds are being constructed sufficient in number and capacity to accommodate 2000 sick.

Great difficulty is experienced in procuring from the Quartermaster's Department the necessary tools for the advancement of the work. Any number of laborers can be obtained among the prisoners, and with the necessary tools the work could soon be completed.

The law of Congress creating a hospital fund to provide for the comfort of sick and wounded is completely abrogated by the Commissary Department failing to fill requisitions for funds.

The authority granted in your telegram of September 22, to divide the excess of funds at Andersonville among the new prisons, has been thwarted by the commissary at that post in failing to supply funds. Thus we are crippled and embarrassed....

A large excess of funds at Andersonville will be turned over to the Treasury, because the commissary at that post has failed to supply himself with funds to met requistions, while thousands of sick both at this post and Andersonville are in a state of suffering that would touch the heart even of the most callous....

Humanity and the fame of the Government demand that the extreme suffering among the prisoners should be alleviated.

## November 18 (Friday)

Sherman, on the road to Augusta and Macon, was travelling in two large columns, cutting a swath about 60 miles wide. Nothing in his front except some scattered militia and weak cavalry units.

Hood, after a delay caused by the weather, was ready to move into Tennessee, crossing at Florence, Ala.

Malone, B.Y., Sgt., Co. H, 6th N.C. Infantry, CSA, prisoner, Point Lookout, Md.:

The 18th of Nov. was a cold raney day Our men are not dying here like they have bin they onley avridge about too a day now...

Ransom, John, QM Sgt., 9th Michigan Cavalry, Camp Lawton, Millen, Ga.:

None being taken away today, I believe on account of not getting transportation. Notice that rebel troops are passing through on the railroad and immense activity among them. Am now well satisfied of the correctness of my views as regards this movement. Have decided now to stay here until the last. Am getting ready for action however. Believe we are going to have a warm time of it in the next few months. Thank fortune I am as well as I am. Can stand considerable now. Food given us in smaller quantities, and hurriedly so too. All appears to be in a hurry.... My noble old coverlid is kept rolled up and ready to accompany me on my travels at any moment. Have my lame and stiff leg in training. Walk all over the prison until tired out so as to strengthen myself.... Even if we are not exchanged during the war, don't think we will remain prisoners long.

## November 19 (Saturday)

In Georgia, Gov. Brown called for every able-bodied man in the state to come forward to defend their homes from the deprivations of Sherman's marching columns. Very few came to that party, most of them content to let Sherman's 60,000 men go where they pleased. There was no way to stop them, anyway.

Ransom, John, QM Sgt., 9th Michigan Cavalry, Camp Lawton, Millen, Ga.:

A carload went at about noon, and are pretty well

thinned out. Over half gone—no one believes to our lines now; all hands afraid of going to Charleston. Believe I will try and escape on the journey, although in no condition to rough it.... The nights are cool, and a covering is of great benefit. My being the owner of a good blanket makes me a very desirable comrade to mess with.... Another load goes tonight or early in the morning. My turn will come pretty soon.

### November 20 (Sunday)

At Indianapolis, the officials at Camp Morton reported that:

During the past week the prisoners generally have been very insubordinate, and on the night of the 14th instant made a break on the guard and several prisoners escaped, a part of whom were recaptured. And on the night of the 18th instant preparations were made for another break, but owing to the extra vigilance used by the officers on duty at this camp, in connection with the guard, the plans concocted by the prisoners were ferreted out and broken up before being put into execution.

Ransom, John, QM Sgt., 9th Michigan Cavalry, Camp Lawton, Millen, Ga.:

None as yet gone today and it is already most night. Had a falling out with my companion Smith, and am again alone walking about the prison with my coverlid on my shoulders. Am determined that this covering protects none but thoroughly good and square fellows. LATER—Received for rations this day a very good allowance of hardtack and bacon. This is the first hardtack received since the trip to Andersonville, and is quite a luxury.

### November 21 (Monday)

John Bell Hood moved the remnants of the Army of Tennessee, about 30,000 infantry and a little over 8000 cavalry, including Forrest's, into Tennessee from Florence, Ala. First, his objective was to get between Schofield at Pulaski and Thomas at Nashville and try to defeat the Federals piecemeal.

Sherman hardly hiccuped when he took on Georgia state militia at Griswoldville, east of Macon, as his columns converged on Milledgeville and gave them a severe thumping. A little fighting along the route of march, but nothing to slow it down.

Ransom, John, QM Sgt., 9th Michigan Cavalry, Camp Lawton, Millen, Ga.:

Got up bright and early, went to the creek and had a good wash, came back, after a good walk over the prison, and ate my two large crackers and small piece of bacon left over from yesterday, and again ready for whatever may turn up.... NOON—Five hundred getting ready to go; my turn comes tomorrow, and then we will see what we will see. Decided rumors that Sherman has taken Atlanta and is marching towards Savannah, the heart of the Confederacy. All in good spirits for the first time in a week.

### November 22 (Tuesday)

Sherman's left wing entered Milledgeville, then the capital of Georgia, ransacked the state house, and generally made a real mess of things. Sherman's famous "bummers" now came into their own. They scoured the countryside for food, draft animals, wagons, carts, and anything that could be useful to an army on the march. State militia were absolutely ineffective against the Federal advance, being poorly equipped and worse led.

Today, Col. Wm. Hoffman's office forwarded the letters and inspection reports from the Surgeon-General's Office in Washington to Col. B.F. Tracy at Elmira. Tracy was in line for a good chewing-out for his lack of action on requests and his interference with the medical department:

Referred ... for immediate report as to what has been done, what is in the course of completion, and what is about being commenced to remedy the evils mentioned in within report. Full report required. Particular attention is called to the prevalence of scurvy and to the instructions from this office of August 1, 1864, in relation to the purchase of antiscorbutics. These papers to be returned with report.

It is very doubtful if Col. Tracy was ever recommended for brigadier general.

Ransom, John, QM Sgt., 9th Michigan Cavalry, Camp Lawton, Millen, Ga.:

And now my turn has come, and I get off with the next load going today. My trunk is packed and baggage duly checked; shall try and get a "lay over" ticket, and rusticate on the road. Will see the conductor about it.... Coverlid folded up and thrown across my shoulder, lower end tied as only a soldier knows how. My three large books of written matter on the inside of my thick rebel jacket, and fastened in. Have a small book which I keep at hand to write in now. My old hat has been exchanged for a red zouave cap, and I look like a red-headed woodpecker. Leg behaving beautifully.... LATER—On the cars, in vicinity of Savannah en route for Blackshear, which is pretty well south and not far from the Florida line. Are very crowded in a close boxcar and fearfully warm. Try to get away tonight.

## November 23 (Wednesday)

In Georgia, Sherman stayed overnight at Howell Cobb's plantation prior to entering Milledgeville. The Twentieth Corps was at Milledgeville. Lt. Gen. William Hardee had now taken command of the Confederate forces opposing Sherman.

Ransom, John, QM Sgt., 9th Michigan Cavalry, escaped, near Doctortown Station, Ga.:

A change has come over the spirit of my dreams. During the night the cars ran very slow, and sometimes stopped for hours on side tracks. A very long, tedious night, and all suffered a great deal with just about standing room only. Impossible to get any sleep. Two guards at each side door, which are open about a foot. Guards are passably decent, although strict. Managed to get near the door, and during the night talked considerable with the two guards on the south side of the car. At about three o'clock this A.M., and after going over a long bridge which spanned the Altamaha River and in sight of Doctortown, I went through the open door like a flash and rolled down a high embankment. Almost broke my neck, but not quite. Guard fired a shot at me, but as the cars were going, though not very fast, did not hit me. Expected the cars to stop but they did not, and I had the inexpressible joy of seeing them move off out of sight. Then crossed the railroad track going north, went through a large open field and gained the woods, and am now sitting on the ground leaning up against a big pine tree *and out from under rebel guard!* The sun is beginning to show itself in the east and it promises to be a fine day. Hardly know what to do with myself. If those on the train notified Doctortown people of my escape they will be after me. Think it

was so early an hour that they might have gone right through without telling anyone of the jump off. Am happy and hungry and considerably bruised and scratched up from the escape. The happiness of being here, however, overbalances everything else.... Am in a rather low country although apparently a pretty thickly settled one; most too thickly populated for me, judging from the signs of the times. It's now about dinner time, and I have traveled two or three miles from the railroad track, should judge and am in the edge of a swampy forest, although the piece of ground on which I have made my bed is dry and nice. Something to eat wouldn't be a bad thing. Not over sixty rods from where I lay is a path evidently travelled more or less by negroes going from one plantation to another. My hope of food lays by that road. Am watching for passersby. LATER—A negro boy too young to trust has gone by singing and whistling, and carrying a bundle and a tin pail evidently filled with somebody's dinner. Inasmuch as I want to enjoy this outdoor Gypsy life, I will not catch and take the dinner away from him. That would be the height of foolishness. Will lay for the next one traveling this way. The next one is a dog and he comes up and looks at me, gives a bark and scuds off. Can't eat a dog. Don't know how it will be tomorrow though. Might be well enough for him to come around later.... Have broken off spruce boughs and made a soft bed.... Not a crust to eat since yesterday forenoon.... Thus closes my first day of freedom and it is *grand*.

## November 24 (Thursday)

In Tennessee, the footrace north to Columbia was won by Schofield's two corps with Gen. Jacob D. Cox arriving with the Confederates on his heels. Forrest's cavalry, in the van of Hood's army, attacked and was repulsed by the strong Union infantry. Schofield secured a bridge crossing on the Duck River on the road to Nashville.

Ransom, John, QM Sgt., 9th Michigan Cavalry, escaped, near Doctortown Station, Ga.:

Another beautiful morning, a repetition of yesterday.... It is particularly necessary that I procure sustenance wherewith life is prolonged, and will change my headquarters to a little nearer civilization. Can hear someone chopping not a mile away.

Here goes. LATER—Found an old negro fixing up a dilapidated post and rail fence. Approached him and enquired the time of day. (My own watch having run down.) He didn't happen to have his gold watch with him, but reckoned it was nigh time for the horn. Seemed scared at the apparition that appeared to him, and no wonder. Forgave him on the spot. Thought it policy to tell him all about who and what I was, and did so. Was very timid and afraid, but finally said he would divide his dinner as soon as it should be sent to him, and for an hour I lay off a distance of twenty rods or so, waiting for that dinner. It finally came, brought by the same boy I saw go along yesterday. Boy set down the pail and the old darkey told him to scamper off home—which he did. Then we had a dinner of rice, cold yams and fried bacon. It was a glorious repast, and I succeeded in getting quite well acquainted with him. We are on the Bowden plantation and he belongs to a family of that name. Is very fearful of helping me as his master is a strong Secsh., and he says would whip him within an inch of his life if it was known. Promise him not to be seen by anyone and he has promised to get me something more to eat after it gets dark. LATER— After my noonday meal went back towards low ground and waited for my supper, which came half an hour ago and it is not yet dark. Had a good supper of boiled seasoned turnips, corn bread and sour milk, the first milk I have had in about a year. Begs me to go off in the morning, which I have promised to do. Says for me to go two or three miles on to another plantation owned by LeCleye, where there are good negroes who will feed me. Thanked the old fellow for his kindness. Says the war is about over and the Yanks expected to free them all soon.

### November 25 (Friday)

Ransom, John, QM Sgt., 9th Michigan Cavalry, escaped, near Doctortown Station, Ga.:

This morning got up cold and stiff; not enough covering. Pushed off in the direction pointed out by the darky of yesterday. Have come in the vicinity of negro shanties and laying in wait for some good benevolent colored brother. Most too many dogs yelping around to suit a runaway Yankee. Little nigs and the canines run together. If can only attract their attention without scaring them to death, shall be all

right. However, there is plenty of time, and won't rush things. Time is not valuable with me. Will go sure and careful. Don't appear to be any men folks around; more or less women of all shades of color. This evidently a large plantation; has thirty or forty negro huts in three or four rows. They are all neat and clean to outward appearance. In the far distance and towards what I take to be the main road is the master's residence. Can just see a part of it. Has a cupola on top and is an ancient structure. Evidently a nice plantation. Lots of cactus grows wild all over, and is bad to tramp through. There is also worlds of palm leaves, such as five-cent fans are made of. Hold on there, two or three negro men are coming from the direction of the big house to the huts. Don't look very inviting to trust your welfare with. Will still wait, McCawber like, for something to turn up. If they only knew the designs I have on them, they would turn pale. Shall be ravenous by night and go for them. I am near a spring of water, and lay down flat and drink. The Astor House Mess is moving around for a change; hope I won't make a mess of it. Lot of goats looking at me now, wondering, I suppose, what it is. Wonder if they butt? Shoo! Going to rain, and if so I must sleep in one of those shanties. Negroes all washing up and getting ready to eat, with doors open. No, thank you; dined yesterday. Am reminded of the song: "What shall we do, when the war breaks the country up, and scatters us poor darkys all around." This getting away business is about the best investment I ever made. Just the friendliest fellow ever was. More than like a colored man, and will stick closer than a brother if they will only let me. Laugh when I think of the old darky of yesterday's experience, who liked me first rate only wanted me to go away. Have an eye on an isolated hut that looks friendly. Shall approach it at dark. People at the hut are a woman and two or three children, and a jolly looking and acting negro man. Being obliged to lay low in the shade feel the cold, as it is rather damp and moist. LATER—Am in the hut and have eaten a good supper. Shall sleep here tonight. The negro man goes early in the morning, together with all the male darky population, to work on fortifications at Ft. McAllister. Says the whole country is wild at the news of approaching Yankee army. Negro man named "Sam" and woman named "Sady."

Two or three negroes living here in these huts are not trustworthy, and I must keep very quiet and not be seen. Children perfectly awestruck at the sight of a Yankee. Negroes very kind but afraid. Criminal to assist me. Am five miles from Doctortown. Plenty of "gubers" and yams. Tell them all about my imprisonment. Regard the Yankees as their friends. Half a dozen neighbors come in by invitation, shake hands with me, scrape the floor with their feet, and rejoice most to death at the good times coming. "Bress de Lord," has been repeated hundred of times in the two or three hours I have been here. Surely I have fallen among friends. All the visitors donate of their eatables, and although enough is before me to feed a dozen men, I give it a tussle. Thus ends the second day of my freedom, and it is glorious.

### November 26 (Saturday)

Ransom, John, QM Sgt., 9th Michigan Cavalry, escaped, near Doctortown Station, Ga.:

An hour before daylight "Sam" awoke me and said I must go with him off a ways to stay through the day. Got up and we started. Came about a mile to a safe hiding place, and here I am. Have plenty to eat and near good water. Sam will tell another trusty negro of my whereabouts, who will look after me, as he has to go away to work. The negroes are very kind, and I evidently am in good hands. Many of those who will not fight in the Confederate army are hid in these woods and swamps, and there are many small squads looking for them with dogs and guns to force them into the army in the South. It is possible I may be captured by some of these hunting parties. It is again most night and have eaten the last of my food. Can hear the baying of hounds and am skerry. Shall take in all the food that comes this way in the meantime. Sam gave me an old jackknife and I shall make a good bed to sleep on, and I also have an additional part of a blanket to keep me warm. In fine spirits and have hopes for the future. Expect an ambassador from my colored friends a little later. LATER—The ambassador has come and gone in the shape of a woman. Brought food, a man told her to tell me to go off a distance of two miles or so, to the locality pointed out, before daylight, and wait there until called upon tomorrow. Rebel guards occupy the main roads, and very unsafe.

### November 27 (Sunday)

Faulty intelligence from the cavalry caused Schofield to move all his men across the Duck River into the trenches dug on the north side at Columbia, Tenn. He thought Hood had crossed the river and was on his flank.

Ransom, John, QM Sgt., 9th Michigan Cavalry, escaped, near Doctortown Station, Ga.:

Before daylight, came where I am now. Saw alligators—small ones. This out in the woods life is doing me good. Main road three miles away, but there are paths running everywhere. Saw a white man an hour ago. Think he was a skulker hiding to keep out of the army, but afraid to hail him. Many of these stay in the woods day times, and at night go to their homes, getting food. Am now away quite a distance from any habitation, and am afraid those who will look for me cannot find me. Occasionally hear shots fired; this is a dangerous locality. Have now been out four days and fared splendidly. Have hurt one of my ankles getting through the brush; sort of sprain, and difficult to travel at all. No water nearby and must move as soon as possible. Wild hogs roam around through the woods, and can run like a deer. Palm leaves grow in great abundance, and are handsome to look at. Some of them very large. Occasionally see lizards and other reptiles, and am afraid of them. If I was a good traveler I could get along through the country and possibly to our lines. Must wander around and do the best I can however. Am armed with my good stout cane and the knife given me by the negro; have also some matches but dare not make a fire lest it attract attention. Nights have to get up occasionally and stamp around to get warm. Clear, cool nights and pleasant. Most too light, however, for me to travel. The remnants of yesterday's food, have just eaten. Will now go off in an easterly direction in hopes of seeing the messenger.

### November 28 (Monday)

Ransom, John, QM Sgt., 9th Michigan Cavalry, escaped, near Doctortown Station, Ga.:

No one has come to me since day before yesterday. Watched and moved until most light of yesterday but could see or hear no one. Afraid I have lost communication. In the distance can see a habitation and will mog along that way. Most noon. LATER—As I was poking along through some light timber, almost ran into four Confederates with guns. Lay down close to the ground and they passed by me not more than twenty rods away. Think they have heard of my being in the vicinity and looking me up. This probably accounts for not receiving any visitor from the negroes. Getting very hungry, and no water fit to drink. Must get out of this community as fast as I can. Wish to gracious I had two good legs. LATER— It is now nearly dark and I have worked my way as near direct north as I know how. Am at least four miles from where I lay last night. Have seen negroes, and white men, but did not approach them. Am completely tired out and hungry, but on the edge of a nice little stream of water. The closing of the fifth day of my escape. Must speak to somebody tomorrow, or starve to death. Good deal of yelling in the woods. Am now in the rear of a hovel which is evidently a negro hut, but off quite a ways from it. Cleared ground all around the house so I can't approach it without being too much in sight. Small negro boy playing around the house. Too dark to write more.

### November 29 (Tuesday)

Last evening Forrest's cavalry had crossed Duck River and was skirmishing in the area of Spring Hill by noon, while Schofield was still on the Duck River line disengaging his troops and sending them north along the Pike between Columbia and Spring Hill. The Pike was being held open by Gen. David S. Stanley's Union troops. By some weird circumstance, all of Schofield's men went up the Pike without being attacked by Hood's Confederates. The Federal force, wagon trains and all, escaped to take positions near Franklin, Tenn.

Sherman sent Kilpatrick towards Augusta, Ga., to divert Wheeler, while he, Sherman, kept up the line of march for Savannah. The objective was to get across the Ogeechee River near Savannah by November 30th without major opposition.

Ransom, John, QM Sgt., 9th Michigan Cavalry, escaped, near Doctortown Station, Ga.:

The sixth day of freedom, and a hungry one. Still where I wrote last night, and watching the house. A woman goes out and in but cannot tell much about her from this distance. No men folks around. Two or three negro boys playing about. Must approach the house, but hate to. NOON—Still right here. Hold my position. More than hungry. Three days since I have eaten anything, with the exception of a small potatoe and piece of bread eaten two days ago and left from the day before. That length of time would have been nothing in Andersonville, but now being in better health demand eatables, and it takes right hold of this wandering sinner. Shall go to the house towards night. A solitary woman lives there with some children. My ankle from the sprain and yesterday's walking is swollen and painful. Bathe it in water, which does it good. Chickens running around. Have serious meditations of getting hold of one or two of them after they go to roost, then go farther back into the wilderness, build a fire with my matches and cook them. That would be a royal feast. But if caught at it, it would go harder with me than if caught legitimately. Presume this is the habitation of some of the skulkers who return and stay home nights. Believe that chickens squawk when being taken from the roost. Will give that up and walk boldly up to the house.

### November 30 (Wednesday)

At Franklin, Tenn., Schofield was faced with Hood and the problem of repairing bridges to get the Union wagon trains up to Nashville, so while he waited, he took on Hood, who came swinging up the Pike from Columbia, swung his troops to the left and right, into line of battle and attacked the well-fortified Yankees about 4 P.M. The Confederate line behaved well, drove the Federals back to their second prepared line, and then withdrew. The Confederate casualties were very heavy—nearly 6300 out of a force of 27,000, more than 20 percent. Among them were six Confederate generals: States Rights Gist, H.B. Granbury, John Adams, O.F. Strahl, and the incomparable Patrick Cleburne. John C. Carter was mortally wounded. Four of the dead generals were laid on the porch of a local house. In addition, Hood also lost 54 regimental commanders killed, wounded, or captured. He now had fewer than 18,000 effective infantrymen. Federal losses were about 2300 from nearly 27,000 engaged. This evening, Schofield pulled his men out of Franklin and headed up the road to Nashville.

Sherman was across the Ogeechee River with no opposition.

Ransom, John, QM Sgt., 9th Michigan Cavalry, recaptured, Doctortown Station, Ga.:

Ha! Ha! My boy, you are a prisoner of war again. Once more with a blasted rebel standing guard over me, and it all happened in this wise: Just before dark I went up to that house I spoke of in my writings yesterday. Walked boldly up and rapped at the door; and what was my complete astonishment when a white woman answered my rapping. Asked me what I wanted, and I told her something to eat. Told me to come in and set down. She was a dark looking woman and could easily be mistaken from my hiding place of the day for a negro. Began asking me questions. Told her I was a rebel soldier, had been in the hospital sick and was trying to reach home in the adjoining county. Was very talkative; told how her husband had been killed at Atlanta, &c. She would go out and in from a shanty kitchen in her preparation of my supper. I looked out through a window and saw a little darky riding away from the house, a few minutes after I went inside. Thought I had walked into a trap, and was very uneasy. Still the woman talked and worked, and I talked, telling as smooth lies as I knew how. For a full hour and a half sat there, and she all the time getting supper. Made up my mind that I was the same as captured, and so put on a bold face and made the best of it. Was very well satisfied with my escapade anyway, if I could only get a whack at that supper before the circus commenced.

Well, after a while heard some hounds coming through the woods and towards the house. Looked at the woman and her face pleaded guilty, just as if she had done something very mean. The back door of the house was open and pretty soon half a dozen large bloodhounds bounded into the room and began snuffing me over; about this time the woman began to cry. Told her I understood the whole thing and she need not make a scene over it. Said she knew I was a Yankee and had sent for some men at Doctortown. Then five horsemen surrounded the house, dismounted and four of them came in with guns cocked prepared for a desperate encounter. I said: "Good evening, gentlemen." "Good evening," said the foremost, "We are looking for a runaway Yankee prowling around here." "Well," says I, "you needn't look any farther, you have found him." "Yes, I see," was the answer. They all sat down, and just then the woman said, "Supper is ready and to draw nigh." Drawed as nigh as I could to that supper and proceeded to take vengeance on the woman. The fellows proved to be home guards stationed here at Doctortown. The woman had mounted the negro boy on a horse just as soon as I made my appearance at the house and sent for them. They proved to be good fellows. Talked there at the house a full hour on the fortunes of war, &c. Told them of my long imprisonment and escape and all about myself. After a while we got ready to start for this place. One rebel rode in front, one on each side and two in the rear of me. Was informed that if I tried to run they would shoot me. Told them no danger of my running, as I could hardly walk. They soon saw that such was the case after going a little way, and sent back one of the men to borrow the woman's horse. Was put on the animal's back and we reached Doctortown not far from midnight. As we were leaving the house the woman gave me a bundle; said in it was a shirt and stockings. Told her she had injured me enough and I would take them. No false delicacy will prevent me taking a shirt. And so my adventure has ended and have enjoyed it hugely. Had plenty to eat with the exception of the two days, and at the last had a horseback ride. How well I was reminded of my last ride when first taken prisoner and at the time I got the coverlid. In the bundle was a good white shirt, pair of stockings, and a chunk of dried beef of two pounds or so. One of the captors gave me ten dollars in Confederate money. Now am in an old vacant building and guarded and it is the middle of the afternoon. Many citizens have visited me and I tell the guard he ought to charge admission; money in it. Some of the callers bring food and are allowed to give it to me, and am stocked with more than can conveniently carry. Have had a good wash up, put on my clean white shirt with standing collar, and new stockings and am happy. Doctortown is a small village with probably six or eight hundred population, and nigger young ones by the scores. Am treated kindly and well, and judge from conversations that I hear, that the battles are very disastrous to the rebels and that the war is pretty well over. All the negroes hard pressed, fortifying every available point to contest the advance of the Union Army. This is cheering news to me. My escape has given me confidence in myself, and I shall try it again at the first opportunity. A woman has just given me a bottle of milk and two dollars in money. Thanked her with my heart in my mouth. Having been captured and brought to this place, am here waiting for them to get instructions as to what they shall do with me. They say I will probably be sent to the prison at Blackshear, which is forty or fifty miles away. Think I should be content to stay here with plenty to eat. Am in a good clean room in a dwelling. Can talk with anyone who chooses to come and see me. The room was locked during the night, and this morning was thrown open, and I can wander through three rooms. Guard is off a few rods where he can see all around the house. Occasionally I go outdoors and am having a good time. LATER—Have seen a Savannah paper which says Sherman and his hosts are marching towards that city, and for the citizens to rally to repel the invader. My swollen ankle is being rubbed today with ointment furnished by an old darky. I tell you there are humane people the world over, who will not see even an enemy suffer if they can help it. While I have seen some of the worst people in the South, I have also seen some of the very best, and those, too, who were purely southern people and rebels. There are many pleasant associations connected with my prison life, as well as some directly to the opposite.

### December 1 (Thursday)

At Nashville, Maj. Gen. Schofield's troops entered the Union lines after eluding Hood's forces at Spring Hill, Columbia, and Franklin, Tenn. Hood brought his much-reduced and weary army to the front of Thomas's defenses and surveyed his options. The options were attack or retreat.

Ransom, John, QM Sgt., 9th Michigan Cavalry, recaptured, Doctortown Station, Ga.:

Still at Doctortown, and the town is doctoring me up "right smart." There is also a joke to this, but a weak one. The whole town are exercised over the coming of the Yankee army, and I laugh up my sleeve. Once in a while some poor ignorant and bigoted fellow amuses himself cursing me and the whole U.S. army. Don't talk back much, having too much regard for my bodily comfort. Orders have come to put me on a train for Blackshear. Have made quite a number of friends here, who slyly talk to me encouragingly. There are many Union people all through the South, although they have not dared to express

themselves as such, but now they are more decided in their expressions and actions. Had a canteen of milk, and many other luxuries. Darkys are profuse in their gifts of small things. Have now a comb, good jack-knife, and many little knicknacks. One old negress brought me a chicken nicely roasted. Think of that, prisoners of war, roast chicken! Shall jump off the cars every twenty-rods hereafter. Tried to get a paper of the guard, who was reading the latest, but he wouldn't let me see it. Looks rather blue himself, and I surmise there is something in it which he don't like. All right, old fellow, my turn will come some day. Young darky brought me a cane, which is an improvement on my old one. Walk now the length of my limit with an old-fashioned crook cane and feel quite proud. LATER—Got all ready to take a train at 3:30, and it didn't stop. Must wait until morning. Hope they won't stop for a month.

### December 2 (Friday)

Hood, outside of the fortifications of Nashville, began establishing his own lines, conforming to the Federal half-moon defenses.

Sherman turned his blue columns from an eastward course and, pivoting on Millen, Ga., headed in four columns almost directly south. Until now, Hardee had no idea of the direction of the march, except towards Augusta. The advance was now towards Savannah, down the peninsula formed by the Savannah and Ogeechee rivers.

Ransom, John, QM Sgt., 9th Michigan Cavalry, prison, Blackshear, Ga.:

In with the same men whom I deserted on the cars. We are near the Florida line. Was put in a passenger train at Doctortown and rode in style to this place. On the train were two more Yanks named David and Eli S. Buck, who are Michigan men. They were runaways who had been out in the woods nearly three months and were in sight of our gunboats when recaptured. Belong to the 6th Michigan Cavalry. David Buck was one of Kilpatrick's scouts; a very smart and brave fellow, understands living in the woods, and thoroughly posted. We have mutually agreed to get away the first chance, and shall get to our lines.... We three Yankees were quite a curiosity to the passengers on the train that brought us to this place. Some of them had evidently never seen a Yankee before, and we were stared at for all we were worth.... The ladies in particular sneered and stared at us. Occasionally we saw some faces which looked as if they were Union, and we often got a kind word from some of them. The railroads are in a broken-down condition, out of decent repair, and trains run very slow.

### December 3 (Saturday)

At Nashville, Hood had now settled his positions and sent Forrest's cavalry to probe the Union lines and to attempt a blockade of the river downstream from the city. Washington pressured Thomas to attack Hood, but Thomas again awaited developments.

Sherman was in Millen, Ga., looking upon the remains of the prisoner-of-war stockade. Sherman told Judson Kilpatrick to destroy the railroads around Millen.

Ransom, John, QM Sgt., 9th Michigan Cavalry, prison, Blackshear, Ga.:

Blackshear is an out-of-the-way place, and shouldn't think the Yankee army would ever find us here. The climate is delightful. Here it is December and at the North right in the middle of winter, and probably good sleighing, and cold; while here it is actually warm during the daytime, and at night not uncomfortably cold. The Buck boys are jolly good fellows, and full of fun.... We don't stay here but a few days, the guards say.... There is no wall or anything around us here, only guards. Encamped right in the open air. Have food once a day, just whatever they have to give us. Last night had sweet potatoes. I am getting considerably heavier in weight, and must weigh one hundred and forty pounds or more. Still lame, however, and I fear permanently so. Teeth are firm in my mouth now, and can eat as well as ever.... Found Rowe and Bullock, and Hub Dakin. They are well, and all live in jolly expectancy of the next move.... Some fresh beef given us today; not much, but suppose all they have got.

### December 4 (Sunday)

Malone, B.Y., Sgt., Co. H, 6th N.C. Infantry, CSA, prisoner, Point Lookout, Md.:

The 4th which was the Sabath I went to meating at the School house Mr. Morgan lectured on the Parable of the Sower & in the eavning I was at the

Same plaise and Mr. Carol preached a good Surmond.... We have a white gard now for patroles in camp of knights the Neagros got so mean that the General would not alow them in Side of the Prison they got so when they would catch any of the men out Side of thir tents after taps they would make them doubble quick or jump on thir backs and ride them and some times they would make them get down on thir knees and prey to God that they might have thir freadom and that his Soul might be sent to hell

Ransom, John, QM Sgt., 9th Michigan Cavalry, prison, Blackshear, Ga.:

Another delightfully cool morning. There are not a great many guards here to watch over us, and it would be possible for all to break away without much trouble. The men, however, are so sure of liberty that they prefer to wait until given legitimately. Would like to have seen this guard hold us last summer at Andersonville. Fresh meat again today. Rebels go out to neighboring plantations and take cattle, drive them here, and butcher for us to eat. Rice is also given us to eat. Have plenty of wood to cook with.... Blackshear is a funny name and it is a funny town, if there is any, for as yet I haven't been able to see it. Probably a barn and a hen-coop comprise this place. Cars go thundering by as if the Yanks were after them. About every train loaded with troops. Go first one way then the other. Think they are trying to keep out of the way themselves.

### December 5 (Monday)

Ransom, John, QM Sgt., 9th Michigan Cavalry, prison, Blackshear, Ga.:

Guard said that orders were not to talk with any of the prisoners, and above all not to let us get hold of any newspapers. No citizens are allowed to come near us. That shows which way the wind blows. Half a dozen got away from here last night, and guards more strict today, with an increased force. Going to be moved, it is said, in a few days. Why don't they run us right into the ocean?... Can see an old darky with an ox hitched to a cart with harness on, the cart loaded with sugar cane.... But few die now; no more than would naturally die in any camp with the same numbers. It is said that some men get away every night, and it is probably so.

### December 6 (Tuesday)

Grant sent a wire to Thomas at Nashville, directing him to attack Hood at once. Grant feared that Hood would slip past Thomas and head for the Ohio River. Thomas said he would attack at once without waiting for cavalry remounts.

On the 3rd of the month Col. Tracy at Elmira had asked Washington if an inspector from the Sanitary Commission could inspect the camp at Elmira and report on the condition at that location. Today, the answer came. Not just no, but h——— no. Civilians could not inspect the facility unless under the aegis of the War Department.

Ransom, John, QM Sgt., 9th Michigan Cavalry, prison, Blackshear, Ga.:

Thirteen months ago today captured—one year and one month. Must be something due me from Uncle Sam in wages, by this time.... Believe that we are also entitled to ration money while in prison. Pile it on, you can't pay us any too much for this business. This is the land of the bloodhound. Are as common as the ordinary cur at the North. Are a noble-looking dog except when they are after you, and then they are beastly. Should think that any one of them could whip a man; are very large, strong, and savage looking.... See no horses about here at all—all mules and oxen, and even cows hitched up to draw loads.

### December 7 (Wednesday)

Ransom, John, QM Sgt., 9th Michigan Cavalry, prison, Blackshear, Ga.:

Another day of smiling weather.... Have a good piece of soap, and have washed our clothing throughout, and are clean and neat for prisoners of war.... Guards denounce Jeff Davis as the author of their misfortunes. We also denounce him as the author of ours, so we are agreed on one point. Going to move. The "mess" will escape *en masse* at the first move, just for the sake of roaming the woods.

### December 8 (Thursday)

At Nashville, Thomas still had not attacked Hood. Grant, really perturbed with Thomas, told Halleck: "If Thomas has not struck yet, he ought to be ordered to hand over his command to Schofield." Grant again urged Thomas to attack, Thomas said his cavalry would not be ready before the 11th.

Ransom, John, QM Sgt., 9th Michigan Cavalry, prison, Blackshear, Ga.:

There are many men of many minds here.... A majority of the men here have about half enough to eat. Our mess has enough to eat, thanks to our own ingenuity. Now expect to go away from here every day. Have borrowed a needle, begged some thread, and have been sewing up my clothing; am well fixed up, as are also the Bucks.... If I always keep my ways mended as I do my clothes, I shall get along very well. Eli has come with four large yams bought of a guard and we will proceed to cook and eat a good supper, and then go to bed.... Drew cuts for the extra potato, and Dave won, and he cut that article of food into three pieces and we all had a share. Good boy.

### December 9 (Friday)

Brig. Gen. William N.R. Beall, CSA, had been selected as the Confederate officer to handle the purchase and distribution of supplies resulting from the sale of cotton brought from the South. Brig. Gen. H.E. Paine, USA, had been assigned as his counterpart and would coordinate the activities among the various Federal sites. To make things easier, Beall and Paine had devised a form letter to be sent to the various prison camps requesting information on the needs of that particular camp. The needs to be determined by committee, the number of officers, privates, and civilians at the site, and the names of the officers selected to distribute the information was requested.

Sherman's march to the sea was almost complete, at the outskirts of Savannah.

Grant issued an order relieving Gen. Thomas of command, replacing him with Schofield, then suspended the order when Thomas told him he planned to attack on the 10th but a heavy storm with freezing rain had made movement impossible. Grant waited.

Ransom, John, QM Sgt., 9th Michigan Cavalry, prison, Blackshear, Ga.:

Still in Blackshear, and quiet.... One of these days my

314        CIVIL WAR PRISONS & ESCAPES

Northern friends and relatives will hear from me. Am getting over my lameness, and have an appetite for more than my supply of food.... Of all my many messmates and friends in prison, have lost track of them all; some died, in fact nearly all, and the balance scattered, the Lord only knows where. What stories we can talk over when we meet at the North.

## December 10 (Saturday)

Federal Secy. of War Edwin M. Stanton today directed that all prisoners of war be removed from the Old Capitol Prison and sent to a permanent place of confinement. No further prisoners of war would be incarcerated there except for brief periods of time.

Ransom, John, QM Sgt., 9th Michigan Cavalry, prison, Blackshear, Ga.:

The grand change has come and a carload of prisoners go away from here today. Although the Bucks and myself were the last in prison, we are determined to flank out and go with the first to go. Our destination is probably Charleston, from what I can learn. We three will escape on the road, or make a desperate effort to do so, anyway. Can walk much better now than ten days ago, and feel equal to the emergency.... More guards have come to take charge of us on the road, and it looks very discouraging for getting away, although "Dave" says we will make it all right.... Now comes the tug-of-war.

Many Union prisoners in the South were offered a chance to take an *oath of neutrality* which permitted them to work in a parole status for the Confederacy. At Salisbury, N.C., the listing for this month showed prisoners working as music teachers, stage drivers, sawmill hands, railroad workers, gardeners, hospital attendants, nurses, clerks, and one as a barkeeper. Some had even helped put down the prison riot at Salisbury.

In Tennessee, the vicious storm that had coated everything with ice prevented any movement. Thomas and Grant both waited for an improvement.

Sherman was in front of Savannah, facing Hardee, with somewhat less than 18,000 men. Hardee had flooded the rice fields of the area, leaving only a few roads available for the approach. Sherman approached Ft. McAllister, which guarded the

Ogeechee River, south of the city, the obvious approach to the sea.

## December 11 (Sunday)

The Confederates had destroyed the bridge across the Ogeechee River to Ft. McAllister; the bridge would have to be rebuilt. Sherman's troops, using axes to fell trees and parts of dismantled houses, started rebuilding the 1000-foot bridge.

At Elmira, N.Y., clothing was issued to the needy prisoners during the past week which consisted of 2500 jackets; 2000 pairs of pants; 3011 shirts; 1216 pairs of drawers; 6065 pairs of socks; 3938 blankets; and 162 greatcoats.

From this date, Ransom's diary contains some error as to the actual days that events occurred.

Ransom, John, QM Sgt., 9th Michigan Cavalry, on the cars, north from Blackshear, Ga.:

We flanked out this morning, or rather paid three fellows two dollars apiece for their turn to go. Are now thirty miles from Blackshear; have been unloaded from the cars and are encamped by the side of the railroad track for the night. Most dark. Rebel soldiers going by on the trains, with hoots and yells. We are strongly guarded, and it augurs not for us to get away tonight. Our best hold is jumping from the cars. Ride on open platform cars with guards standing and sitting on the sides, six guards to each car. About sixty prisoners ride on each car, and there are thirty or forty cars. Were given rations yesterday, but none today. It is said we get nothing to eat tonight, which is bad; more so for the other prisoners than ourselves. Low country we come through, and swampy. Bucks think we may get away before morning, but I doubt it.

Abbott, A.O., 1st Lt., 1st N.Y. Dragoons, prisoner, Columbia, S.C.:

True to their promise "that, if we did not stop escaping, they would put us in a *pen*, as the enlisted men were," the 11th of December, a cold, cheerless, and windy day, an order came for us to be ready to move the following day to the city.

## December 12 (Monday)

Ransom, John, QM Sgt., 9th Michigan Cavalry, on the cars, north from Blackshear, Ga.:

Routed up at an early hour and loaded on to the cars, which stood upon a sidetrack, and after being loaded have been here for six mortal hours. Small rations given us just before loading up. All are cramped and mad. We will more than jump the first opportunity. We go to Charleston, via Savannah. Wish they would hurry up their old vehicles for transportation.... Worth four hundred dollars a day to see the rebel troops fly around. Would give anything to know the exact position now of both armies. Guards are sleepy and tired out from doing double duty, and I think we can get away if they move us by night, which I am afraid they won't do.

Abbott, A.O., 1st Lt., 1st N.Y. Dragoons, prisoner in the State Asylum, Columbia, S.C.:

The morning of the 12th found us all very busy packing up, preparing to move. With unprecedented liberality, they furnished some wagons to transport our baggage, and several expresses came up, which were hired at exorbitant rates, and used to transport baggage also. But little was left in the camp.... Before we left, however, we had one of the grandest sights we had seen for a long time, viz., a "camp on fire."...

After the wagons were loaded, they were formed in column, and the officers formed also near the "deadline," preparatory to their march through the capital of South Carolina. We reached the city in safety, the prisoners following the train....

We were marched through the principal street of the city, yet, compared with Northern cities, it had the appearance of a Sabbath. Men, women, and children looked out upon us as we passed, indulging in coarse, vulgar jest at our expense....

We reached the Insane Asylum yard about 3 P.M., and after some delay went inside. There we found for our accommodation two small buildings to be used as hospitals, and a *shell* of another, twenty-four feet square, with a part of a roof on.... The yard contained about two acres, surrounded by a brick wall on three sides ten feet high, and two feet thick. The fourth side was a board fence, which separated us from the asylum. In the other yard were planted two pieces of artillery, and portholes were cut through the board fence to allow the muzzles to come through in case of action.

Instead of a platform for sentries to walk on, as at Macon, they had sentry-boxes outside the wall. The water arrangements were very good, consisting of six large troughs placed in a line, supplied by a hydrant which kept them full all the time. Three of them we used for washing purposes, while in the other three the water was kept clean for cooking purposes. The water was always abundant, and of good quality.

### December 13 (Tuesday)

The attack on Ft. McAllister started about 5 P.M., Sherman and several officers having climbed atop a rice mill to watch the show. At his elevated platform, Sherman could see the sea.

Ransom, John, QM Sgt., 9th Michigan Cavalry, escaped again, somewhere near Savannah, Ga.:

Yesterday long towards night our train started from its abiding place and rolled slowly towards its destination, wherever that might be. When near Savannah, not more than a mile this side, David Buck jumped off the cars and rolled down the bank. I jumped next and Eli Buck came right after me. Hastily got up and joined one another, and hurried off in an easterly direction through the wet, swampy country. A number of shots were fired at us, although my cap was knocked off by a bullet hitting the fore-piece. Eli Buck was also singed by a bullet. It seemed as if a dozen shots were fired. Train did not stop, and we ran until tired out. Knew that we were within a line of forts which encircle Savannah, going all the way around it and only twenty rods or so apart. It was dark when we jumped off, and we soon came in the vicinity of a schoolhouse in which was being held a negro prayer meeting. We peeked in at the windows, but dared not stop so near our jumping-off place. Worked around until we were near the railroad again and guided by the track going south—the same way we had come. It was very dark. Dave Buck went ahead, Eli next and myself last, going Indian file and very slow. All at once Dave stopped and whispered to us to keep still, which you may be sure we did. Had come within ten feet of a person who was going directly in the opposite direction and also stopped, at the same time we did. Dave Buck says: "Who comes there?" A negro woman says "it's me," and he walked up close to her and asked where she was going. She says: "Oh! I knows you; you are Yankees and has jumped off de cars." By this time we had come up even with Dave and the woman. Owned up to her that such was the case. She said we were her friends, and would not tell of us. Also said that not twenty rods ahead there was a rebel picket, and we were going right into them. I think if I ever wanted to kiss a woman, it was that poor, black, negro wench. She told us to go about thirty rods away and near an old shed, and she would send us her brother, he would know what to do. We went to the place designated and waited there an hour, and then we saw two dusky forms coming through the darkness, and between them a wooden tray of food consisting of boiled turnips, corn bread and smoked bacon. We lay there behind that old shed and ate and talked, and talked and ate, for a full hour more. The negro, "Major," said he was working on the forts, putting them in order to oppose the coming of the Yankees, and he thought he could get us through the line before morning to a safe hiding place. If we all shook hands once we did fifty times, all around. The negroes were fairly jubilant at being able to help genuine Yankees. Were very smart colored people, knowing more than the ordinary run of their race. Major said that in all the forts was a reserve picket force, and between the ports the picket. He said pretty well south was a dilapidated fort which had not as yet been repaired any, and that was the one to go through or near, as he did not think there was any picket there. "Bress de Lord, for yo' safety," says the good woman. We ate all they brought us, and then started under the guidance of Major at somewhere near midnight. Walked slow and by a roundabout way to get to the fort and was a long time about it, going through a large turnip patch and over and through hedges. Major's own safety as much as ours depended upon the trip. Finally came near the fort and discovered there were rebels inside and a picket off but a few rods. Major left us and crawled slowly ahead to reconnoitre; returned in a few minutes and told us to follow. We all climbed over the side of the fort, which was very much out of repair. The reserve picket was asleep around a fire which had nearly gone out. Major piloted us through the fort, actually stepping over the sleeping rebels. After getting on the outside there was a wide ditch which we went through. Ditch was partially full of water. We then went way round near the railroad again, and started south, guided by the darky, who hurried us along at a rapid gait. By near daylight we were five or six miles from Savannah, and then stopped for consultation and rest. Finally went a mile further, where we are now laying low in a swamp, pretty well tired out and muddy beyond recognition. Major left us at daylight, saying he would find us a guide before night who would show us still further. He had to go back and work on the forts. And so I am again loose, a free man, with the same old feeling I had when in the woods before. We got out of a thick settled country safely, and again await developments. Heard drums and bugles playing reveille this morning in many directions, and "We are all surrounded." David Buck is very confident of getting away to our lines. Eli thinks it is so if Dave says so, and I don't know, or care very much. The main point with me is to stay out in the woods as long as I can. My old legs have had a hard time of it since last night and ache, and are very lame. It's another beautiful and cold day, this 13th of December. Biting frost nights, but warmer in the daytime. Our plan is to work our way to the Ogechee River, and wait for the Stars and Stripes to come to us.... The railroad is only a short distance off, and the river only three or four miles. As near as we know, are about twenty miles from the Atlantic coast.

Abbott, A.O., 1st Lt., 1st N.Y. Dragoons, prisoner in the State Asylum, Columbia, S.C.:

As before stated, we found a shell of a building twenty-four feet square, standing in the northwest corner of the yard. This was a model of the kind of houses we were all to have *at once*. They would furnish the lumber, timber, nails, tools, etc., if we would do the work for ourselves.... Each building was to contain thirty-six men, to be divided into two rooms, having a double fireplace and chimney in the centre. At the close of the third day, all of the frames were up for the thirty-two buildings necessary.... Many more would have been done, could we have had the materials as promised. The next morning Maj. Griswold informed us the government had impressed all the locomotives and cars, and they could get no more lumber till they could haul it from the country, sixteen miles....

To remedy this in part, they sent in some old tents and pieces of tents, which were used to the best advantage possible, and, by digging holes in the ground, crawling under the buildings, and making clay houses, nearly all had some place they called "quarters." Yet many, very many of them were no better than the open air, for they were poor protection against the storm and cold. The weather at this time was cold and freezing, our clothing was growing thinner and thinner, and it was not unusual to find officers walking at all times of the night to keep warm.

### December 14 (Wednesday)

Gen. George Thomas in Nashville decided that he would attack Hood on the 15th and so notified Grant.

Ransom, John, QM Sgt., 9th Michigan Cavalry, escaped again, somewhere near Savannah, Ga.:

We are now three miles from yesterday's resting place, and near the Miller plantation. Soon as dark last night we went to the negro huts and found them expecting us. Had a Jubilee. No whites near, but all away. The Buck boys passed near here before when out in the woods, and knew of many darkys who befriended them. Had a surfeit of food. Stayed at the huts until after midnight, and then a woman brought us to this place. Tonight we go to Jocko's hut, across the river. A darky will row us across the Little Ogechee to Jocko's hut, and then he will take us in tow. It is a rice country about here, with canals running every way. Negroes all tickled to death because Yankees coming. I am feeling better than yesterday, but difficult to travel. Tell the boys they had better leave me with the friendly blacks and go ahead to our lines, but they won't. Plenty to eat and milk to drink, which is just what I want. The whites now are all away from their homes and most of the negroes. Imagine we can hear the booming of cannon, but guess we are mistaken. Dave is very entertaining and good company. Don't get tired of him and his talk. Both of them are in rebel dress throughout, and can talk and act just like rebels. Know the commanders of different rebel regiments. They say that when out before they on different occasions mixed with the Southern army, without detection. Said they didn't wonder the widow woman knew I was a Yankee. Ain't up to that kind of thing.

Abbott, A.O., 1st Lt., 1st N.Y. Dragoons, prisoner in the State Asylum, Columbia, S.C.:

The wood ration was very small indeed, averaging a piece about as large and as long as your arm from the elbow for one man. It was totally insufficient for cooking purposes, to say nothing of an attempt to

keep warm by the fire. That was a luxury to be enjoyed hereafter. There was a wood screen before the sink: yet this was all torn down and burned up.... There was much suffering all this time for want of fuel both to cook and keep warm....

About rations... In the first place, they stopped the *meat*, and *we were one hundred and thirty-three days in the city of Columbia, S.C., without a particle of anything of the meat kind being issued to us.* In lieu thereof we received daily one gill of sorghum (made from the Chinese sugarcane, and what we got was usually black, sour, bitter, and very filthy. It gave the most of us diarrhoea), also one pint of coarse cornmeal, *often* ground cob and all; two tablespoonfuls of salt for five days, two tablespoonfuls of rice for five days, and this was ALL for *one hundred and thirty-three consecutive days.*

To atone in part for not giving us meat, they proposed, upon our arrival in Columbia, to give us flour. The first issue was tolerably fair, and consisted of about a pint to a man for five days. The second looked like plaster, and was as black as buckwheat flour or rye, and looked very much like the sweepings of some mill; even this failed, and then they gave us an issue of "shorts" from the tail end of the bolt, and then they gave us "bran," and that ended the flour issue....

To add to our troubles, they neglected to issue us any cooking utensils, although they often promised to do so. Had we not smuggled them through from other places, and bought others, we would have been compelled to have eaten our cornmeal raw.... Thus it went on day after day. The most of the cooking had to be done *at once* for the day, for want of wood. Those who had money, or could get it, of course fared better, being able to buy a little meat, sweet potatoes, flour, beans, pepper, etc.

As in most prisons, North and South, sutlers were available to provide the "extras" for a certain price. Gouging the customer was the normal thing. For example, some of the prices (Confederate money) listed in Abbott's diary were: sweet potatoes, $35/bushel; tea, $120/lb; writing paper, $225/ream; black sewing thread, $150/lb; pepper, $35/lb; and butter, $20/lb.

Sherman spent a busy day visiting the fleet and Maj. Gen. John G. Foster, commander of the Union Army troops in the area. The message was on its way north that Sherman was safe and on the coast.

## December 15 (Thursday)

In Tennessee, the first day of the Battle of Nashville began when George H. Thomas's blue lines slowly edged their way through heavy fog and struck Hood's left with about 35,000 men, the right being held by more Union forces. The Federal onslaught drove the gray-clad veterans more than a mile to the rear, where they held on the Franklin Pike, but barely. The weather was foul, being cold, wet, and sloppy with melting ice. The lines were adjusted somewhat during the night.

Ransom, John, QM Sgt., 9th Michigan Cavalry, escaped again, somewhere near Savannah, Ga.:

Jocko's hut was not across the river as I supposed and wrote yesterday, but on the same side we were on. At about ten o'clock last night we went to his abiding place as directed and knocked. After a long time an old black head was stuck out of the window with a nightcap on. The owner of the head didn't know Jocko or anything about him; was short and crusty; said "Go away from dar!" Kept talking to him and scolding at being disturbed. Said he had rheumatics and couldn't get out to let us in. After a long time opened the door and we set down on the doorstep. Told him we were Yankees and wanted help. Was the funniest darky we have met yet. Would give something for his picture as he was framed in his window in the moonlight talking to us, with the picturesque surroundings, and us Yankees trying to win him over to aid us. Finally owned up that he was Jocko, but said he couldn't row us across the river. He was lame and could not walk, had no boat, and if he had the river so swift he couldn't get us across, and if it wasn't swift, the rebels would catch him at it and hang him. Talked a long time and with much teasing. By degrees his scruples gave way, one at a time. Didn't know but he might row us across if he only had a boat, and finally didn't know but he could find a boat. To get thus far into his good graces took at least three hours. Went looking around and found an old scow, fixed up some old oars, and we got in; before doing so however, he had warmed up enough to give us some boiled sweet potatoes and cold baked fish. Rowed us way down the river and landed us on the noted Miller plantation and a mile in rear of the negro houses. Jocko, after we forced our acquaintance on him with all

kind of argument, proved to be a smart able-bodied old negro, but awful afraid of being caught helping runaways. Would give something for his picture as he appeared to us looking out of his cabin window. Just an old-fashioned, genuine negro, and so black that charcoal would make a white mark on him. Took us probably three miles from his hut, two miles of water and one of land, and then started back home after shaking us a dozen times by the hand, and "God blessing us." Said "Ole Massa Miller's niggers all Union niggers," and to go up to the huts in broad daylight and they would help us. No whites at home on the plantation. We arrived where Jocko left us an hour or so before daylight, and lay down to sleep until light. I woke up after a while feeling wet, and found the tide had risen and we were surrounded with water; woke up the boys and scrambled out of that in a hurry, going through two feet of water in some places. The spot where we had laid down was a higher piece of ground than that adjoining. Got on to dry land and proceeded to get dry. At about ten o'clock Dave went up to the negro huts and made himself known, which was hard work. The negroes are all afraid that we are rebels and trying to get them into a scrape, but after we once got them thoroughly satisfied that we are genuine Yanks they are all right, and will do anything for us. The negroes have shown us the big house, there being no whites around, they having left to escape the coming Yankee army. We went up into the cupola and looked way off on the ocean, and saw our own noble gunboats. What would we give to be aboard of them? Their close proximity makes us discuss the feasibility of going downriver and out to them, but the negroes say there are chain boats across the river farther down, and picketed. Still it makes us anxious, our being so near, and we have decided to go down the river tonight in a boat and see if we can't reach them. It is now the middle of the afternoon and we lay off from the huts eighty rods, and the negroes are about to bring us some dinner. During the night we traveled over oyster beds by the acre, artificial ones, and they cut our feet. Negroes say there are two other runaways hid a mile off and they are going to bring them to our abiding place. LATER—Negroes have just fed us with corn bread and a kind of fish about the size of sardines, boiled by the kettle full, and they are nice. Fully as good as sardines. Think I know now where nearly all of the imported sardines come from. Negroes catch them by the thousands, in nets, put them in kettles, and cook them a few minutes, [then] they are ready to eat. Scoop them out of the creeks. The two other runaways are here with us. They are out of the 3d Ohio Cavalry. Have been out in the woods for two weeks. Escaped from Blackshear and traveled this far. I used to know one of them in Savannah. We do not take to them at all, as they are not of our kind. Shall separate tonight, they going their way and we going ours. Have secured a dugout boat to go down the Ogechee River with tonight. The negroes tell us of a Mr. Kimball, a white man, living up the country fifteen miles, who is a Union man, and helps runaways, or anyone of Union proclivities. He lays up the river, and our gunboats lay down the river. Both have wonderful charms for us, and shall decide before night which route to take. Are on a rice plantation, and a valuable one. Before the "wah" there were over fifteen hundred negroes on this place. Cotton is also part of the production. Have decided to go down the river and try to reach our gunboats. It's a very hazardous undertaking, and I have my doubts as to its successful termination.

Money sent from the North to prisoners in the South was held by the prison officials, who set the exchange rate at which it would be used. This rate was always less than the market rate, the difference usually going to the official who had custody of the money. Brig. Gen. John H. Winder, commander of all prison camps in the South at this time, prohibited the issuing of *any* currency to the prisoners. This was mainly to prevent the bribing of guards by the prisoners, although it was not looked upon that way by those incarcerated. Abbott describes the method used in Columbia for handling money.

Abbott, A.O., 1st Lt., 1st N.Y. Dragoons, prisoner in the State Asylum, Columbia, S.C.:

The letter containing the money was first passed into the hands of the Rebel quartermaster, opened, the money and letter taken out, the amount it contained indorsed on the envelope, and that [the envelope and letter] would be sent in to you, and your name posted on the bulletin board, with the amount in the quartermaster's hands set opposite your name. But you did not draw the money, or any part of it, from the quartermaster, but would give him an order to convert your money in his hands into Confederate

money at government rates. You could not draw even *this* from him, but you would be obliged to give another order for the quartermaster to pay over to the sutler the Confederate money belonging to you, and he (the sutler), in turn, would give you a due-bill on himself, upon which you might trade....

It will be very plain to anyone that this plan was only one of swindling—a plan for the quartermaster and sutler to trade off their worthless currency for gold and greenbacks. [Gold exchange was 1 for 33, government rate; 1 for 47, market rate at this time.]

### December 16 (Friday)

Today was the second day of the Battle of Nashville. At 6 o'clock, with the air filled with rain and snow, Thomas's Union troops redeployed and prepared to assault the Confederates. The Confederate right was pressed back and then held at the line of their main entrenchments. The Union cavalry got in behind Hood's left flank and the Confederate rear was threatened. Late in the afternoon the Federals made their main assault and the firing became almost continuous for a period of time. The Confederate left caved in first, moving back, then the center folded and left the right to play rear guard. Thomas described the action as the Confederates being "hopelessly broken." The Confederate rear guard held off the pursuing Federals until late in the afternoon, when the entire line gave way and the Rebels fled the field. Hood lost most of his artillery and many of his wagons.

Thomas had engaged about 55,000 men and suffered 3600 casualties, mostly wounded (2562). Hood's force had little over 20,000 men, and he lost 4500 captured and another 1500 killed and wounded—over 25 percent lost. The Army of Tennessee was an army in name only, having suffered frightful casualties in the five months since Hood took command in front of Atlanta.

After the failure of the plot to capture the U.S.S. *Michigan* at Sandusky, Ohio, the previous September, John Yates Beall and a few of his trusty men went east and decided to wreck trains in upstate New York. They spent a couple of unproductive months trying to get a train off the track and finally were about to give the idea up. On this date, Beall boarded a train returning to Canada via the suspension bridge when he noticed that one of his men was not aboard. He returned to the station and found the man in the waiting room asleep. While trying to arouse him, he was questioned by the local police and then arrested. The Secret Service, of course, took the credit for the capture of this notorious "criminal," and he was whisked off to New York and placed in jail.

Ransom, John, QM Sgt., 9th Michigan Cavalry, escaped again, somewhere near Savannah, Ga.:

Another adventure, and a red-hot one. Started down the river in our dugout boat somewhere near midnight. Ran down all right for an hour, frequently seeing rebel pickets and camp fires. Saw we were going right into the lion's mouth, and the farther down the more rebels. All at once our boat gave a lurch and landed in a treetop which was sticking out of the water, and there we were, swaying around in the cold water in the middle or near the middle of the Ogechee. Dave went ashore and to a negro hut, woke up the inmates, and narrated our troubles. A negro got up, and with another boat came to our rescue. Were about froze with the cold and wet. Said not more than a mile farther down we would have run right into a chain boat, with pickets posted on it. It really seems as if a Divine providence were guiding us. After getting a breakfast of good things started off towards the Big Ogechee River, and have traveled three or four miles. Are now encamped, or rather laying down, on a little hillock waiting for evening, to get out of this vicinity, which is a dangerous one. In our river escapade lost many of our things, but still hang on to my coverlid and diary. There are three or four houses in view, and principally white residences, those of the poor white trash order, and they are the very ones we must avoid. Have caught cold and am fearfully out of travelling condition. But must go it now. A mistake in coming down the river.... No chance of getting out by the coast. Have enough food to last all day and night, and that is a good deal. Can't carry more than one day's supply.... If I could travel like my comrades, would get along. Bucks praise me up and encourage me to work away, and I do.... Storm brewing of some sort and quite chilly. Saw rebel infantry marching along the highway not more than eighty rods off.... Am writing with a pencil less than an inch long. Shall print this diary and make my everlasting

fortune, and when wealthy will visit this country and make every negro who has helped us millionaires.... The programme now is to go as straight to Mr. Kimball's as we can. He is probably twenty miles away; is a white Union man I spoke of a day or so ago in this same diary. Will stick to him like a brother. Can hear wagons go along the road towards Savannah, which is only thirteen or fourteen miles away. LATER—Most dark enough to travel and I have straightened up and am taking an inventory of myself. Find I can walk with the greatest difficulty. The boys argue that after I get warmed up I will go like a top, and we will see.

A scam was operated in Columbia by a man named Potter, a transplanted Rhode Islander who currently lived in Charleston, using bills of exchange. His method was to draw up a legal bill of exchange, get the prisoner to sign this, in duplicate, and then provide the prisoner with Confederate money at the rate of two Confederate dollars for one greenback, or six Confederate dollars for one in gold. This at a time when greenbacks were trading 1 for 20 and gold was trading at 1 for 50. This was all done with the Confederate prison officials being aware of the transactions, and with their help. The prisoners in Columbia took advantage of this because of the need to get funds to purchase food. Abbott continues:

Abbott, A.O., 1st Lt., 1st N.Y. Dragoons, prisoner in the State Asylum, Columbia, S.C.:

We were thus enabled to get a little money to buy something to eat to keep ourselves from starving. Watches, knives, jewelry, boots, hats, buttons, anything that would sell, was parted with to obtain money for this purpose.

It was no excuse for them to say they did not have it for us; they *did* have it, and every day they could bring it in to us and sell at rates one third higher than their market. Every five days we would buy *more* than the amount of our rations for that time, thus proving conclusively that the rations were not *one half* that we needed to keep us in health, saying nothing of comfort.

The following estimate was handed me by Capt. Cook, who was in the sutler's shop at the time. Read it, and then remember we ate all of this *in addition* to our rations, and then judge what those did who could not buy.

*Estimate of Provisions sold every five Days in Asylum Prison, Columbia, S.C.* Sweet Potatoes, 35 bushels; Bread, 4000 loaves; Beef, fresh, 3450 lbs.; Pork, 1200 lbs.

Is it any wonder our enlisted men starved to death on the Rebel government rations? This is the reason *why* the officers did not look as bad as the men when they came out of prison.

### December 17 (Saturday)

Ransom, John, QM Sgt., 9th Michigan Cavalry, escaped again, somewhere near Savannah, Ga.:

Another day of vicissitudes. We traveled last night about four miles, piloted by a young negro. It was a terrible walk to me; slow and painful. Were fed, and have food for today. Are now about three miles from a canal which we must cross before another morning. Negroes say "Sherman most here" and "Bress de Lord!" Mr. Kimball seems an impossibility for me to go so far. Are now in high and fine country, but too open for us. Have to lay down all day in the bushes. David is a thorough scout. Goes crawling around on his hands and knees taking in his bearings.... Every crossroad has its pickets, and it is slow business to escape running into them.

### December 18 (Sunday)

After the Battle of Nashville, Wilson's cavalry pursued Hood to Rutherford Creek near Columbia, Tenn., where the Federal chase was delayed, when the Federals found the stream flooded and impassable. Sherman waited quietly in Savannah, resupplying his troops with new uniforms, etc., while Hardee, who had refused Sherman's demand for surrender yesterday, pondered his next move.

At Elmira, N.Y., the weekly inspector found seventy men in the convalescent wards lying on the floor for lack of bunks. He also reported many cases of smallpox. One hundred and one prisoners arrived at the prison without blankets, theirs having been taken from them and being told they would receive blankets at Elmira. Some of the prisoners were poorly clad for the weather. Blankets were issued as required.

Ransom, John, QM Sgt., 9th Michigan Cavalry, escaped again, somewhere near Savannah, Ga.:

Six days of freedom and what a sight of hardship, sweetened by kind treatment and the satisfaction of being out from under guard. We traveled last night some four miles and now are in a very precarious position. When almost daylight we came to the canal, and found cavalry pickets all along the towpath; walked along until we came to a lock. A cavalryman was riding his horse up and down by the lock.... It was absolutely necessary that we get across before daylight. As the mounted picket turned his horse's head to go from us, Dave slid across the towpath and went across the timbers which formed the lock, and by the time the picket turned around to come back Dave was hid on the opposite shore. At the next trip of the rebel Eli went the same as Dave. The third one to go was myself, and I expected to get caught, sure. Could not go as quiet as the rest, and was slower. Thought the picket saw me when halfway across but kept right on going, and for a wonder made it all right. Was thoroughly scared for the first time since jumping off the train. Am very nervous. All shook hands when the picket turned about to go back the fourth time. Getting light in the east.... Dare not travel over half a mile, and here we are hid almost in a woman's dooryard, not over thirty rods from her very door.... It's now most noon, and have seen a rather elderly lady go out and in the house a number of times. The intrepid Dave is going up to the house to interview the lady soon. LATER— Dave crawled along from our hiding place until he came to the open ground, and then straightened boldly up and walked to the house. In fifteen minutes he came back with some bread and dried beef, and said the woman was a Union woman and would help us. Her daughter slept at her uncle's a mile off last night, and expected her back soon, and perhaps the uncle, who is a violent Secesh, with her. Said for us to lay low. LATER—The daughter came home on horseback and alone. Could see the old lady telling the daughter about us and pointing our way. About the middle of the afternoon the old lady started out towards us. Behind her came a young darky, and behind the darky came another darky; then a dog, then a white boy, then a darky, and then the daughter. Old lady peeked in, and so did the rest except the grown-up girl, who was too afraid. Finally came closer, and as she got a good view of us she says: "Why, mother, they look just like anybody else." She had never seen a Yankee before. Brought us some more food, and after dark will set a table for us to come to the house to eat. Her name is Mrs. Dickinson.... During the afternoon five rebel soldiers came to the house, one at a time. It is now most dark and we are about ready to go to the house and eat. Mr. Kimball lives only four miles away.

### December 19 (Monday)

Ransom, John, QM Sgt., 9th Michigan Cavalry, escaped again, somewhere near Savannah, Ga.:

We are now less than half a mile from Mr. Kimball's. After dark last night we went to Mrs. Dickinson's house and partook of a splendid supper. I wrote a paper directed to the officer commanding the first Yankee troops that should arrive here telling what she had done for us runaway Yankees. She talked a great deal, and I thought was careless leaving the front door open. Three or four times I got up and shut that door. We had taken off our blankets and other wraps and left them in a sort of a kitchen, and were talking in the best room. I heard the gate click, and on looking out saw two rebel officers coming to the house and not six rods off. We jumped into the other room and out of the back door and behind a corn house, bareheaded. The officers were asked into the front room by the daughter. They asked who the parties were who ran out of the backway. She said she reckoned no one. They kept at her and jokingly intimated that some of her skulking lovers had been to see her. She kept talking back and finally said: "Mother, did any one just go away?" And the old lady said: "Why, yes, brother Sam and his 'boy' just went off home." Them confounded rebels had come to see the girl and spent the evening, and we shivering out in the cold. Joked her for an hour and a half about her lovers and we hearing every word. Finally they got up and bid her good night, saying they would send back some men to guard the house and keep her lovers away. Just as soon as they were down the road a ways, the daughter came out very frightened and said for us to hurry off, as they would send back troops to look for us. Hurried into the house, got our things and some dried beef, and started off towards Mr. Kimball's house. Reached here just before daylight and lay down back of the house about eighty rods, in the corner of the fence, to sleep a little before morning. Just at break of day heard someone calling hogs. David got up and went

towards an old man whom we knew was our friend Kimball. Came to us, and was glad to shake hands with genuine Yankees. Said one of his neighbors was coming over early to go with him to hunt some hogs, and for us to go farther off and stay until night, and he would think up during the day what to do with us.... Mr. Kimball said that Sherman was not over fifty miles off, and coming right along twenty miles per day.... Mr. Kimball is an old man, probably sixty years old, white haired and stooped shouldered. He had five sons, all drafted into the rebel army. All refused to serve. Two have been shot by the rebels, one is in some prison for his Union proclivities, and two are refugees. The old man has been imprisoned time and again, his stock confiscated, property destroyed, and all together had a hard time of it. Still he is true blue, a Union man to the backbone.... LATER—Have been laying all day watching Kimball's house. Along in the morning the neighbor spoken of came to Kimball's, and they both went off on horseback to shoot hogs. The swine here roam over a large territory and become most wild, and when they want fresh pork they have to go after it with a gun.... A negro boy went with them with a light wagon and mule attached. At three or four o'clock the old man came down where we were, "to look after his boys," he said.... Said come to the house after dark and he would have a supper prepared for us, and has just left us. LATER—Have just eaten a splendid supper at Kimball's and getting ready to travel three miles to a safe hiding place.

### December 20 (Tuesday)

Ransom, John, QM Sgt., 9th Michigan Cavalry, escaped again, somewhere near Savannah, Ga.:

Well, we are just well fixed and happy. After partaking of a royal repast last night, served in an outbuilding near the main building of the Kimball home, we were directed to this place which is on the banks of the Big Ogechee river, in a most delightful spot. While we were at Kimball's he had negro sentinels stationed at different points on the plantation to announce the coming of any rebel soldiers or citizens that might see fit to come near. He gave us an axe, a quart of salt, a ham too big to carry conveniently, and all the sweet potatoes we could drag along; also a butcher knife. Went with us a mile as guide and then told us so we found the place pointed out. Also gave us some shelled corn to bait hogs and told Dave how to make a deadfall to catch them. We left the main road going directly west until we came to a fence, and when we had got to the end of it kept straight ahead going through a swampy low section. After a while came to higher and dry land and to the banks of the river. Is a sort of an island, and as I said before, a very pretty and pleasant spot. Out in the river grows tall canebrake which effectually hides us from any one going either up or down the river. Tall pines are here in abundance and nice grass plats, with as handsome palm clusters as ever I saw. Are going to build us a house to keep off the cold and rain.... Our government should give to Mr. Kimball a fortune for his patriotism and sacrifices to the Union cause. About eight miles above is a long bridge across the river and there it is thought a big fight will take place when Sherman attempts to cross, and so we will know when they approach.... NIGHT—We have built the cosyest and nicest little house to lay in.... Have eaten the ham half up; ditto potatoes.... I also wrote a letter for Mr. Kimball to the commanding Union officer who may first approach these parts.... We heard boats going by on the river today.... Rebels are too busy to look for us or anyone else. All they can do now is take care of themselves.... A beautiful night—clear and cold. And thus ends another day, and we are in safety.

### December 21 (Wednesday)

Ransom, John, QM Sgt., 9th Michigan Cavalry, escaped again, somewhere near Savannah, Ga.:

Got up bright and early.... Cooked and ate our breakfast, and would you believe it the ham is all gone. Incredible, the amount of food we eat.... Dave fixing up his deadfall for hogs.... Buzzards are very curious in regard to us. They light on the limbs in the trees, and if their support is a dead limb it breaks and makes a great noise in the still woods. Two or three hundred all together make a terrible racket, and scare us sometimes.... The main road is away about one and a half miles we think by the sound of the teams which occasionally rumble along. Often hear shouting on the road as if cattle were being driven along towards Savannah.... I am getting fat every day, yet lame, and have come to the conclusion that it will be a long time before I get over it. The cords have contracted so in my

right leg that they don't seem to stretch out again to their normal length. That scurvy business came very near killing me. LATER—I also went out of our hiding place, and saw away out in a field what I took to be a mound where sweet potatoes were buried. Came back and got a pair of drawers, tied the bottom of the legs together, and sallied forth. The mound of potatoes was a good way back from the house, although in plain sight. I crawled up and began digging into it with a piece of canteen.... Found some of the nicest potatoes that you can imagine, of the red variety.... Now if we can catch a porker will be fixed all right for some days to come. LATER—Dave has returned. He went to the main road and saw a negro. Was lucky enough to get a Savannah paper three days old in which there was nothing we did not know in regard to Sherman's coming. The negro said Yankee scouts had been seen just across the river near the bridge, and the main army is expected every day.... LATER—We went around a drove of hogs and gradually and carefully worked them up to the trap. Pretty soon they began to pick up the corn and one of them went under the figure four, sprung it and down came the logs and such a squealing and scrambling of those not caught.... Dave ran up and grabbed it and struck the animal on the head and cut his throat.... Exciting sport this trapping for fresh pork.... Have sliced up enough for about a dozen men and are now cooking it on sticks held up before the fire.... It's a clear moonlight night, and we can hear very plain a long distance. Can also see the light shining from camp fires in many direction...

### December 22 (Thursday)

Ransom, John, QM Sgt., 9th Michigan Cavalry, escaped again, somewhere near Savannah, Ga.:

Sleep so sound that all the battles in America could not wake me up. Are just going for that fresh pork today. Have three kinds of meat—fried pig, roast pork and broiled hog. Good any way you can fix it.... We begin to expect the Yankees along. It's about time. Don't know what I shall do when I again see the Stars and Stripes. Probably go crazy, or daft, or something. This is a cloudy, chilly day, and we putter around gathering up pine knots for the fire, wash our duds and otherwise busy ourselves.... Considerable travel on the highways, and going both ways as near as we can judge.... LATER—Considerable firing up in vicinity of the bridge. Can hear volleys of musketry, and an occasional boom of cannon. Hurrah! It is now four o'clock by the sun and the battle is certainly taking place. LATER—Go it Billy Sherman, we are listening and wishing you the best of success. Come right along we will be with you. Give 'em another— that was a good one. We couldn't be more excited if we were right in the midst of it. If we had guns would go out and fight in their rear; surround them, as it were. Troops going by to the front, and are cavalry, should think, also artillery. Can hear teamsters swearing away as they always do. LATER—It is now long after dark and we have a good fire. Fighting has partially subsided up the river, but of course we don't know whether Yankee troops have crossed the river or not. Great deal of travel on the road, but can hardly tell which way they are going. Occasional firing. No sleep for us tonight. In the morning shall go out to the road and see how things look. Every little while when the battle raged the loudest, all of us three would hurrah as if mad, but we ain't mad a bit; are tickled most to death.

From the problems indicated by Col. Ernest W. Holmstedt at Ship Island, Miss., someone picked a very poor place to put a prison camp. Today, the colonel wrote Capt. W.T. Hartz of the Office of the Federal Commissary-General of Prisoners in Washington:

Your communication dated Washington, D.C., November 21, 1864, inclosing an extract from inspection report of the condition of prisoners of war on Ship Island, made by Surg. T.M. Getty, medical inspector prisoners of war, was duly received, and in reply I have the honor to state that at the inspection of Surg. T.M. Getty there were no proper means at hand to provide for the prisoners. They arrived here destitute of tents and none could be furnished on the island. The cooking of the rations were, even until shortly, prepared in the open air, as not a board of lumber, even for coffins, could for a time be procured at this place. The prisoners must bring their firewood, stick for stick, on their shoulders about three miles and a half, and on pleasant days it is rather beneficial for them, but it is sometimes difficult to get 10 per cent. of them able to perform this necessary labor. Some provisions ought to be made

to supply the prison camp with fuel. For my own command, I have a detail of soldiers chopping firewood on Cat Island, fifteen miles from here, and by the occasional use of a light-draft steamer I am enabled to keep enough wood on hand for immediate use.... The sick of the prisoners of war are as well cared for as my own, and at present time they have no reason to complain.

Inclosed I have the honor to forward a report made to me by my post surgeon, Dr. John H. Gihon.

Dr. John H. Gihon, Surgeon for the Union prison camp at Ship Island, Miss., wrote a report outlining the situation and problems at that location:

Surg. T.M. Getty arrived at this post on his tour of inspection a very short time after the arrival here of a large number of prisoners of war, who came unannounced, and for whose reception and proper care no previous provision had been made. We were without houses, tents, blankets, bedding, or any of the necessary means for furnishing a hospital. The men themselves were in a most filthy condition—all regard to cleanliness, either of clothing or person, having been for a long time entirely neglected. Out of nearly 1500 there were not 300 who did not report themselves to the surgeon in charge here as being afflicted with disease. The prevailing complaints were measles, scurvy, smallpox, diarrhea, dysentery, typhoid and intermittent fevers, rheumatism, and almost every variety of contagious, cutaneous disease that results from the neglect of personal cleanliness.

Many of the these men were the refuse of rebel hospitals, taken from sickbeds to garrison forts. Others were lads from eleven to fifteen years of age, and old men of from fifty to seventy-five, who represented themselves, almost without exception, as having been forced into the rebel service. Many of them were so feeble and emaciated that it was necessary to carry them from the boats to the encampment, and it did not require the judgment of a medical officer to foresee a large amount of mortality.

As soon after their arrival as possible, active exertions were made in their behalf, and through the aid of the heads of the various departments at New Orleans they were quite as well provided for as are our own sick troops. The condition of these prisoners might now be vastly improved if they manifested a proper disposition to take care of each other or even of themselves. As a general thing they are filthy in their habits and about their persons. Unless forced to do so they will not use exercise enough to keep themselves in a healthy condition. Although their camp is located within a few feet of the beach (one of the finest bathing places in the world), to which they have free access, some of them have not washed their hands and faces since their arrival here, now nearly three months. They have not animation or decency enough to employ the means suggested to cleanse themselves of the vermin which infest their persons and clothing. Some of them die from absolute indolence and filthiness. Their cooks and nurses are selected from among their own body and furnished with everything that is afforded our own troops, and if there is any neglect of proper attention to diet, cooking, and care of the sick the fault rests with themselves.

At the time of Surgeon Getty's inspection the prisoners were without clothing to wash, and on that account no provision was made for washing. Since then the sick have been provided with beds, blankets, &c., and women have been employed to keep them clean.... Scurvy, with which very many of the prisoners were afflicted when they came here, has almost disappeared, from the use of acids and vegetable diet, and abundance of which has been procured. No new cases have occurred. Most of the deaths that have taken place were cases of chronic diarrhea and dysentery, pneumonia, consumption, typhoid and other fevers. All of these were sick, and most of them helpless, at the time of their arrival at this post. Vaccination was not attended to at the time of Surgeon Getty's inspection for want of the necessary means. As soon as reliable virus could be obtained it received the proper share of the surgeon's attention. The cases of smallpox were brought, not acquired, here.

In Louisville, Ky., Brig. Gen. Wm. Hoffman, Federal Commissary-General of Prisoners, wired Secy. of War Edwin Stanton that many of the Confederate prisoners passing through Louisville were without shoes. Hoffman suggested that shoes be provided and the cost reimbursed by the Confederacy through Gen. Beall, who was handling the cotton sales and purchase of clothing for the prisoners.

Stanton, a vindictive so-and-so, asked if these prisoners were "any part of that rebel army recently engaged in killing Union troops at Nashville, and whether they are more destitute or worse provided for now in food, shelter, and raiment than when engaged in that work." The noble Secy. of War said that if they were a part of that rebel force, then he "does not see any occasion for such sympathetic tenderness as to give them supplies provided for own troops, when their own leader at Richmond has stipulated to supply their wants."

Hoffman replied that the prisoners were indeed a part of those from Nashville, but it had been the practice to provide clothing to prisoners when required and he had seen no countermanding orders.

In Mobile, Ala., Maj. Gen. D.H. Maury indicated that he had another 1000 bales of cotton ready to be sent north for sale.

### December 23 (Friday)

In one of Benjamin F. Butler's less-than-brilliant escapades, he set off to capture Ft. Fisher, the controlling fort at Wilmington, N.C. The fleet that sailed from Hampton Roads the previous Sunday (18th) had run into a very heavy storm off Hatteras and had scattered. Today they reassembled off Wilmington— Maj. Gen. Benjamin F. Butler and 6500 troops. The assault on Ft. Fisher was set to begin.

Ransom, John, QM Sgt., 9th Michigan Cavalry, with Union troops, near Savannah, Ga.:

It is not yet daylight in the morning, and are anxiously awaiting the hour to arrive when we may go out to the road. Slept hardly any during the night. More or less fighting all night, and could hear an army go by towards Savannah, also some shouting directly opposite us. Between the hours of about twelve and three all was quiet, and then again more travel. We conjecture that the rebel army has retreated or been driven back, and that the Yankees are now passing along following them up. Shall go out about nine o'clock. LATER—Are eating breakfast before starting out to liberty and safety. Must be very careful now and make no mistake. If we run into a rebel squad now, might get shot. We are nervous, and so anxious can hardly eat. Will pick up what we really need and start. Perhaps good-bye, little house on the banks of the Ogechee, we shall always remember just how you look, and what a happy time we have had on this little island. Dave says: "Pick up your blanket and that skillet, and come along." NIGHT—Safe and sound among our own United States Army troops, after an imprisonment of nearly fourteen months. Will not attempt to describe my feeling now. Could not do it. Staying with the 80th Ohio Infantry, and are pretty well tired out from our exertions of the day. At nine o'clock we started out towards the main road. When near it Eli and I stopped, and Dave went ahead to see who was passing. We waited probably fifteen minutes, and then heard Dave yell out: "Come on boys, all right! Hurry up!" Eli and I had a stream to cross on a log. The stream was some fifteen feet wide, and the log about two feet through. I tried to walk that log and fell in my excitement. Verily believe if the water had been a foot deeper I would have drowned. Was up to my arms, and I was so excited that I liked never to have got out. Lost the axe, which Dave had handed to me, and the old standby coverlid which had saved my life time and again floated off down the stream, and I went off without securing it—the more shame to me for it. Dave ran out of the woods swinging his arms and yelling like mad, and pretty soon Eli and myself appeared, whooping and yelling. The 80th Ohio was just going by, or a portion of it, however, and when they saw first one and then another and then the third coming towards them in rebel dress, with clubs which they mistook for guns, they wheeled into line, thinking, perhaps, that a whole regiment would appear next. Dave finally explained by signs, and we approached and satisfied them of our genuineness. Said we were hard looking soldiers, but when we came to tell them where we had been and all the particulars, they did not wonder. Went right along with them, and at noon had plenty to eat. Are the guests of Co. I, 80th Ohio. At three the 80th had a skirmish, we staying back a mile with some wagons, and this afternoon rode in a wagon. Only came about three or four miles today, and are near Kimball's, whom we shall call and see the first opportunity. The soldiers all look well and feel well, and say the whole Confederacy is about cleaned out. Rebels fall back without much fighting. Said there was not enough to call it a fight at the bridge. Where we thought it a battle, they thought it nothing worth speaking of.... Hear that some Michigan cavalry is with Kilpatrick off on another road, but they do not know whether it is the 9th Mich. Cav., or not.... Soldiers forage on the plantations, and have the best of food; chickens, ducks, sweet potatoes, etc. The supply wagons carry nothing but hardtack, coffee, sugar and such things. Tell you, coffee is a luxury, and makes one feel almost drunk. Officers come to interview us every five minutes, and we have talked ourselves most to death today. They say we probably will not be called upon to do any fighting during this war, as the thing is about settled. They have heard of Andersonville, and from the accounts of the place did not suppose that any lived at all. New York papers had pictures in, of the scenes there, and if such was the case it seems funny that measures were not taken to get us away from there. Many rebels are captured now, and we look at them from a different standpoint than a short time since.

## December 24 (Saturday)

Some time previously, the Confederate government decided that they would recruit Federal prisoners into the Confederate Army and form a unit composed entirely of these men (except for the officers, of course). Today, Lt. Gen. W.J. Hardee, at Charleston, notified Richmond that the idea was not working out too well:

> Col. Brooks' battalion, composed of Federal prisoners of war enlisted from prison into Confederate service, was found at Savannah to be utterly untrustworthy. The men deserted in large numbers, and finally muntinied, and were narrowly prevented from going over in a body to the enemy. The ringleaders were shot and the remainder sent back to prison. These men were selected with great care, and were principally foreigners, and this is, therefore, a fair test of such troops. I recommend that all authority to organize similar commands be revoked.

Ransom, John, QM Sgt., 9th Michigan Cavalry, with Union troops, near Savannah, Ga.:

> This diary must soon come to an end. Will fill the few remaining pages and then stop. Co. "I" boys are very kind. They have reduced soldiering to a science. All divided up into messes of from three to five men each. Any mess is glad to have us in with them, and we pay them with accounts of our prison life. Know they think half we tell them is lies. I regret the most of anything, the loss of my blanket that stood by me

so well.... The infantry move only a few miles each day, and I believe we stay here all day. Went and saw Mr. Kimball. The officers commanding knew him for a Union man, and none of his belongings were troubled. In fact, he has anything he wants now.... Our good old friend Mrs. Dickinson did not fare so well. The soldiers took everything she had on the place fit to eat; all her cattle, pork, potatoes, chickens, and left them entirely destitute. We went and saw them, and will go to headquarters to see what can be done. LATER—We went to Gen. [John E.] Smith, commanding 3d Brigade, 2d Division [3rd Division, 15th Corps] and told him the particulars. He sent out foraging wagons, and now she has potatoes, corn, bacon, cattle, mules, and everything she wants. Also received pay for burned fences and other damages. Now they are smiling and happy and declare the Yankees to be as good as she thought them bad this morning.... Gen. Smith is a very kind man, and asked us a great many questions. Says the 9th Michigan Cavalry is near us and we may see them any hour. Gen. Raum also takes quite an interest in us, and was equally instrumental with Gen. Smith in seeing justice done to our friends the Kimballs and Dickinsons. They declare now that one of us must marry the daughter of Mrs. Dickinson, the chaplain performing the ceremony.... Many officers have read portions of my diary, and say such scenes as we have passed through seem incredible. Many inquire if we saw so and so of their friends who went to Andersonville, but of course there were so many there that we cannot remember them.... We marched about two or three miles and are again encamped for the night, with pickets out for miles around. Many refugees join the army prepared to go along with them, among whom are a great many negroes.

### December 25 (Sunday)

In a novel way to spend Christmas, at 10:30 this morning the gunboats of the Union fleet off Ft. Fisher opened again in a heavy bombardment. Gen. Ben Butler's troops landed north of the fort near Flag Pond Battery and advanced on the fort. The assault troops were near the works in the late afternoon but it was decided that the fort was too strong for so small a force, so an order to withdraw was given. The weather got worse, with heavy seas running, and some 700 of the 2000 were left on the beach,

covered by the fire of the U.S.S. *Santiago de Cuba*, which provided continuous support.

Malone, B.Y., Sgt., Co. H, 6th N.C. Infantry, CSA, prisoner, Point Lookout, Md.:

The 25th was Christmas day And a beautyfull one it was. But I had nothing Strong to drink and but little to eat I had Some loaf Bread fryed Meat & Corn Coffee for breakfast and for dinner I had a cup of Split Pea Soup.

In the eavning I went to the School house to meating Mr. Carrol preached his text was in Zachariah 15th capt 7 virse After preaching I went to the Comiseary and found that Mr. Walas had bet Mr. Barby five dollars that there was a man in Camp that could eat 5 lbs of Bacon and 3 Loafs of Bread each loaf weighing 2 lbs at one meal. When I left he had onley about ¼ of a pound of Bacon and a half of a loaf of bread they Said he eat it all befour he quit. This man belonged to the 11th Ala: Regiment.

Ransom, John, QM Sgt., 9th Michigan Cavalry, with the 9th Mich. Cav., near Savannah, Ga.:

Christmas day and didn't hang up my stocking. No matter, it wouldn't have held anything. Last Christmas we spent on Belle Island, little thinking long imprisonment awaiting us. Us escaped men are to ride in a forage wagon. The army is getting ready to move. Are now twenty-four miles from Savannah and rebels falling back as we press ahead. NIGHT—At about nine o'clock this morning as we sat in the forage wagon top of some corn riding in state, I saw some cavalry coming from the front. Soon recognized Col. Acker at the head of the 9th Michigan Cavalry. Jumped out of the wagon and began dancing and yelling in the middle of the road and in front of the troop. Col. Acker said "Get out of the road you ———— lunatic!" Soon made myself known and was like one risen from the dead. Maj. Brockway said: "Ransom, you want to start for home. We don't know you, you are dead. No such man as Ransom on the rolls for ten months." All remember me and are rejoiced to see me back again. Lt. Col. Way, Surgeon, Adjutant, Sergeant-Maj., all shake hands with me. My company "A" was in the rear of the column, and I stood by the road as they moved along, hailing those I recognized. In every case had to tell them who I was and then would go up and shake hands with them at the risk of being stepped on by the horses. Pretty soon Co. "A" appeared, and wasn't they surprised to see me. The whole company were raised in Jackson, Mich., my home, and I had been regarded as dead for nearly a year. Could hardly believe it was myself that appeared to them. Everyone trying to tell me the news at home all at the same time—how I was reported as having died in Richmond and funeral sermon preached. How so and so had been shot and killed, &c., &c. And then I had to tell them who of our regiment had died in Andersonville—Dr. Lewis, Tom McGill and others. Although Jimmy Devers did not belong to our regiment, many in our company knew him, and I told of his death. Should have said that as soon as I got to the company, was given Capt. Johnson's lead horse to ride, without saddle or bridle and nothing but a halter to hang on with. Not being used to riding, in rebel dress—two or three pails hanging to me—I made a spectacle for them all to laugh at. It was a time for rejoicing. The Buck boys did not get out of the wagon with me and so we became separated without even a good-bye. Before I had been with the company half an hour Gen. Kilpatrick and staff came riding by from the rear, and says to Capt. Johnson: "Captain, I hear one of your company has just joined you after escaping from the enemy." Capt. Johnson said, "Yes, sir," and pointed to me as a Sergeant in his company. Gen. Kilpatrick told me to follow him and started ahead at a breakneck pace. Inasmuch as the highway was filled with troops, Gen. Kilpatrick and staff rode at the side, through the fields, and any way they could get over the ground. The horse I was on is a pacer and a very hard riding animal and it was all I could do to hang on.... Having no saddle or anything to guide the brute, it was a terrible hard ride for me, and time and again I had thought I could fall off without breaking my neck should have done so.... After a while and after riding five or six miles, Kilpatrick drew up in a grove by the side of the road and motioning me to him, asked me when I escaped, etc. Soon saw I was too tired and out of breath. After resting a few minutes I proceeded to tell him what I knew of Savannah, the line of forts around the city, the location of the rivers, force of rebels, etc. Asked a great many questions and took down notes.... After an extended conversation a dispatch was made up and sent to Gen. Sherman, who was a few miles

away, with the endorsement that an escaped prisoner had given the information and it was reliable. Gen. Kilpatrick told me I would probably not be called upon to do any more duty as I had done good service as a prisoner of war. Said he would sign a furlough and recommended that I go home as soon as communication was opened. Thanked me for information and dismissed me with congratulations on my escape. Then I waited until our company, "A," came up and joined them, and here I am encamped with the boys, who are engaged in getting supper. We are only twelve or fourteen miles from Savannah and the report in camp is to the effect that the city has been evacuated with no fight at all. Ft. McAllister was taken today, which being the key to Savannah, leaves that city unprotected, hence the evacuation. Communication will now be opened with the gunboats on the coast and I will be sent home to Michigan.... Am invited to eat with every mess in the company, also at regimental headquarters, in fact, anywhere I am a mind to, can fill. And now this diary is finished and is full. Shall not write any more, though I hardly know how I shall get along, without a self-imposed task of some kind.

Unfortunately, John Ransom was not fated to return to Jackson, Mich., immediately. After the contact with the gunboats and supply ships was made at Savannah, Ransom got a furlough signed by his troop commander, Capt. Johnson. Further endorsed by the regimental surgeon and the regimental commander, Ransom took the furlough to Gen. Kilpatrick for approval. Kilpatrick gladly signed the furlough and wrote a personal note to Gen. Sherman requesting that he approve the furlough.

Ransom took the furlough papers to Savannah to see Gen. Sherman and was told that no men were being sent home now and no furloughs granted for any reason. Sherman said that if Ransom were disabled, he could be sent to a hospital in the North, or, if Ransom had been exchanged he could be sent to a parole camp in the North. However, there were no provisions for handling escaped prisoners of war. In short, Ransom could not go home. Sherman did, however, give Ransom a document releasing him from any and all duty during his stay with Sherman's army and promised that the first furlough given would go to him.

Ransom stayed with his old company during the

march through the Carolinas and was at Raleigh, N.C., when Lee surrendered in April 1865. He then returned home to Michigan. He went back to work in the composing room of the Jackson *Citizen* after regaining his health. He married and later moved to Clearwater, Mich., where he also worked in the printing trade. Several years later he moved to Chicago and worked for a Linotype company. Ransom first published his book, at his own expense, under the title *Andersonville* in Auburn, N.Y., in 1881. John Ransom died at the age of 76 in 1919, leaving a single daughter who died in California years later.

### December 26 (Monday)

John Bell Hood's bone-weary men finally crossed the Tennessee River at Bainbridge, and the Army of Tennessee, as an elite fighting unit, passed into history, to be remembered as a montage of long, cold marches, colder nights, and periods of hellish gunfire.

Sherman, now at the sea, began planning his next move.

### December 27 (Tuesday)

Brig. Gen. Hoffman, in Nashville, finally had a head-count on the prisoners taken during the Battle of Nashville about two weeks previously. He wrote Stanton of the situation:

The number of prisoners captured by the army of Gen. Thomas in the recent battles in front of this city, including the battle of Franklin, amounts to something over 8000. Of these, 439 officers have been sent to Johnson's Island and 3651 enlisted men to Camp Douglas. There are now ready for shipment to Camp Chase 19 officers and 2400 enlisted men, who will be forwarded on Friday and Saturday next, by which time the railroad bridge near Sonora, which was burned by guerrillas on the 24th instant will be repaired.

There are now in hospital in this city 67 wounded rebel officers and 1001 enlisted men. About 550 are expected to arrive from Franklin, and 200 will be kept there in hospital, being too badly wounded to admit of their transportation to this city. As those in hospital here recover sufficiently to bear removal they will be forwarded to Camp Chase. On the recommendation of Gov. Johnson, Maj. Gen. Thomas has ordered the discharge of such loyal persons who, without being mustered into service, were forced by the rebels to serve in their intrenchments, and were there captured and became prisoners of war.

Care will be taken that none but those whose loyalty is well established shall be discharged under this order.

The year had seen many changes. Lee was now boxed in at Petersburg. Sherman had reached the sea and was preparing for the tour through the Carolinas. The Confederacy had just about fallen apart. The prisoner exchange situation had improved somewhat

# 1865

The war now entered another year, but unlike the previous year, the end was in sight. Lee was tied down in Petersburg and before Richmond, and Sherman's powerful "army group" was flexing its muscle at Savannah, preparatory to its march through the Carolinas. The Mississippi River was open to the sea, and only one port, Wilmington, N.C., was still open for the South. The prison camps bulged, both North and South, because of the deadlock on the exchange of captives. The South used the cartel as a political weapon and the North violated its principles just as readily. Just how much more the prisoners would have to endure was the real question.

### January 1 (Sunday)

An inspection of the prison at Elmira, N.Y., indicated an improvement in the general condition of the camp. The report also showed that there were ninety-five cases of smallpox present and that nine prisoners had died during the past week. The problem of the stagnant pond in the camp was relieved by the "blind ditch," which brought a stream of water through the camp from the Chemung River and effectively flushed the pond. This would greatly improve the health of the camp.

An inspection report from Johnson's Island, Ohio, showed a prisoner strength of 3209, 44 in the hospital, and 3 deaths during the past week. The late decision to add more barracks for the prisoners created a problem in obtaining lumber to build them. Consequently, the additional influx of prisoners required the use of one of the mess halls for housing, which, in turn, caused a shortage of messing facilities for the additional men. A vicious cycle. Part of the problem was the ice on Lake Erie, which was frozen enough for normal traffic, but not thick enough for heavy loads to be drawn over it on sleds. The three miles from Sandusky could be very difficult to traverse during the winter months. Scurvy among the prisoners was on the increase. To counter this, the medical officer ordered that an issue of 60 pounds of onions would be given for every 100 rations per week until March 1. Only one case of smallpox was reported.

At Columbia, S.C., General Orders No. 1, issued by Headquarters, C.S. Military Prisons East of Mississippi River, designated the new location of the command to be at Columbia. Brig. Gen. John H. Winder had moved from Andersonville to Augusta, Ga., and now would base in South Carolina.

### January 2 (Monday)

Following the Battle of Nashville on December 15 and 16, 1864, the area was filled with prisoners and casualties. The Union had over 2500 wounded and the South had an estimated 1500 killed and wounded. Light overall casualties for such a battle. Hood had about 4500 of his men captured, which meant that they had to be accommodated within the Federal prison system somewhere. The wounded Confederates were of primary concern since they needed additional treatment—the nonwounded being shipped from Nashville to the prisons in the North by steamer. Brig. Gen. William Hoffman, Federal Commissary-General of Prisoners, wired Maj. Gen. George H. Thomas in Nashville that:

> General: I am informed that wounded rebel prisoners are being collected at Pulaski and Columbia, as well as at Franklin, and I have therefore the honor to request that the surgeons in charge of them may be instructed to forward them as rapidly as possible to this city. Those who are able to be moved should be sent forward at once, and others as soon as they are sufficiently recovered to bear the journey. It is not desirable to establish hospitals for prisoners south of this point [Nashville], but as for the present it is unavoidable to provide for extreme cases, it is desirable that all such cases should be collected in the hospital at Franklin, to be forwarded as soon as they recover. By this arrangement guards and attendants will be saved and the prisoners will be properly accounted for. I fear if special instructions are not given, wounded prisoners will not be forwarded as promptly as they might be.

Col. L.B. Northrop, Commissary-General of Subsistence for the South, had a major problem. Many of the supply lines previously used by the C.S. government to bring food and other supplies to the army in Virginia had now been severed or the source of the supply was now in Union hands. Many of the requirements had been shifted to North Carolina, especially the western portion of the state. That presented another problem. The prison containing 13,000 Union prisoners was located in Salisbury, N.C., and food for this group was also being obtained from the western part of the state. Northrop's solution to the problem was to remove the prisoners to some other place so that the food would be available for Lee's Army of Northern Virginia. Obviously, Northrop did not think this one through very well. If the prisoners were moved, they still had to be fed, and where was the food to come from?

Confederate Secy. of War James A. Seddon referred Northrop to Brig. Gen. John H. Winder, for coordination to reach a solution of where to put the prisoners. Winder and Northrop were old ene-

mies from the days when Winder was Provost-Marshal in Richmond. Winder replied on January 26 that he had already thought of the problem and was trying to find a solution. His first thought was to move the prisoners to southwest Georgia. However, since Sherman made that part of the country unsafe, he now had no refuge for them. Even South Carolina would not be feasible because that would appear to be on Sherman's line of march. He then informed the Secy. of War that there were *only 8000* prisoners at Salisbury, *not 13,000* as Northrop had stated.

The end result of the initial request was that it was returned to the Secy. of War, who by this time was John Cabell Breckinridge, on February 4—a month after it was initiated—and Breckinridge said no further action was to be taken on the request, this on February 7. Another exercise in futility.

Also on this date, Brig. Gen. John H. Winder in Columbia, S.C., notified the President of the Wilmington and Manchester Railroad, in Wilmington, that he would need trains to move about 10,000 prisoners from Florence, S.C., either towards Augusta, Ga., or Wilmington, N.C.

### January 3 (Tuesday)

Brig. Gen. John H. Winder, in Columbia, S.C., wrote Dr. S.P. Moore, Surgeon-General, CSA, concerning the chain of command among the surgeons attached to the various prison camps:

> All officers and men serving with the different prisons east of the Mississippi River are placed under my command. At the several prisons there are a large number of medical officers; some placed on duty in orders from the War Department, others by various medical directors. The location of these prisons is frequently changed, creating a necessity for the transfer of the officers beyond the limits of the department of [the] medical director, by whom they were assigned.... Great difficulty is sometimes experienced in obtaining the necessary supplies for the comfort of the sick in this command. Many of the administrative details of the medical department of this command necessarily pass through these headquarters. I have, therefore, placed Surg. Isaiah H. White on duty at these headquarters as chief medical officer of the prisons. I find this necessary and hope you will approve of this, and separate the prison hospitals

from all medical directors, and that he report directly to your office.

Not all prisoners taken were treated well by the capturing troops, as evidenced by the following report:

1st Lt. George W. Fitch, Twelfth U.S. Colored Infantry, Nashville, Tenn.:

I was captured on the 20th of December fourteen miles in a southeasterly direction from Murfreesborough, in company with two other officers, Lt. D.G. Cooke, Twelfth U.S. Colored Infantry, and Capt. Charles G. Penfield, Forty-fourth U.S. Colored Infantry, by a company of scouts belonging to Forrest's command, numbering thirty-six men, commanded by Capt. [Addison] Harvey. As soon as captured we were robbed of everything of any value, even to clothing. We were kept under guard for three days with some other prisoners (private soldiers of Gen. Steedman's division, who were captured near Murfreesborough) until we reached a small town called Lewisburg, some eighteen miles south of Duck River. There the officers were sent under a guard of four men to report, as I supposed, to Gen. Forrest's headquarters. The guard told [me] that was their destination. They took us along the pike road leading from Lewisburg to Mooresville, about four miles, and then left the road and turned to the right for the purpose, as they said, of stopping at a neighboring house for the night.

After leaving the road about half a mile, as we were walking along through a wooded ravine, the man in advance of us halted, partially turned his horse, and as I came up, drew his revolver and fired on me without a word. The ball entered my right ear just above the center, passed through and lodged in the bone back of the ear. It knocked me senseless for a few moments. I soon recovered, however, but lay perfectly quiet, knowing that my only hope lay in leading them to believe they had killed me. Presently I heard two carbine shots, and then all was still. After about fifteen minutes I staggered to my feet and attempted to get away, but found I could not walk. About that time a colored boy came along and helped me to a house nearby. He told me that the other two officers were dead, having been shot through the head. That evening their bodies were brought to the house where I lay. Next morning they were decently buried on the premises of Col. John C. Hill, nearby.

The shooting occurred on the 22d, and on the 23d, about midday, one of Forrest's men came to the house where I was lying and inquired for me; said he had come to kill me. The man of the house said that it was entirely unnecessary, as I was so severely wounded that I would die any way, and he expected I would not live over an hour. He then went away, saying that if I was not dead by morning I would be killed. After he left I was moved by the neighbors to another house, and was moved nearly every night from one house to another until the 27th, when I was relieved by a party of troops sent from Columbia and brought within the Federal lines.

The privates were sent off on a road leading to the right of the one we took; about in the direction of Columbia, I should judge. I cannot but think they were killed, as about that time our forces occupied Columbia, the rebel army having retreated. There were twelve privates, belonging, I think, to Cruft's brigade.

The above action resulted in a letter from Maj. Gen. George H. Thomas, USA, to Gen. John B. Hood, CSA, on January 13, in which the essence of the letter from Fitch was given. Thomas then read the riot act to Hood about the treatment of prisoners:

It is my desire as far as lies in my power to mitigate the horrors of this war as much as possible, but I will not consent that my soldiers shall be thus brutally murdered whenever the fortunes of war place them defenseless within your power. Such acts on the part of the soldiers of your army are by no means rare occurrences. A case which occurs to my mind now, and of which no mention has heretofore been made to either your predecessor in command or yourself, is that of the murder of ten prisoners of war by a portion of Ross' brigade, of Wheeler's command, at Wood's Gap, between Gordon's Mills and Dalton, early in April last. Should my troops, exasperated by the repetition of such acts, take no prisoners of war at all in future, I shall in no manner interfere in this exercise of their just vengeance, and you will fully understand their reasons as well as mine, and you will please remember that it is your army and not mine who is responsible for the inauguration of the dreadful policy of extermination.

The process of setting up shop to handle the cotton coming from the South to be sold in New York continued. Brig. Gen. William N.R. Beall, appointed as the Confederate officer to handle this business, and paroled for this purpose, had rented space and opened an office in New York City, put a sign up to announce his presence, and was almost ready. The New York newspapers, knowing what was afoot, wrote about the sign in such a way as to make it objectionable. These papers were seen by the Secy. of War in Washington. Maj. Gen. Halleck, Chief of Staff in Washington, wrote Lt. Gen. Grant at City Point, Va., on the developments:

> General:... [I] transmit to you all papers in regard to supply of prisoners of war.... The Secretary of War refused permission to purchase on credit before the arrival of the cotton, on the ground that such a proceeding would give the rebel Government and agents an acknowledged credit in our markets.... The transfer of commissioned officers to camps where there are none has been ordered. The release on parole of other officers to assist Gen. Beall is deemed objectionable on account of the facilities it would afford to communicate between the different camps and arrange plans of escape. But if the enemy should allow Gen. Hayes an assistant, probably the Secretary would permit one to Gen. Beall.
>
> Since commencing this letter I learn that Gen. Beall's course of conduct in New York has been so conspicuous and offensive that the Secretary of War has ordered his sign to be taken down. Gen. Paine has also been directed to suspend his parole and take him in custody till the cotton arrives. The selection of Gen. Beall was unfortunate, for he seems disposed to make all the trouble he can. His parole will be renewed the moment the cotton reaches New York.

At 2:07 P.M. today Maj. Gen. Halleck, in Washington, directed Brig. Gen. H.E. Paine, in New York, to "suspend Gen. Beall's parole and place him in Ft. Lafayette as a prisoner of war until the arrival of cotton from Mobile, when his parole will be renewed and he will enter upon the business as agreed."

### January 4 (Wednesday)

On December 29, 1864, Maj. Gen. Halleck, in Washington, had asked Maj. Gen. E.R.S. Canby, in New Orleans, about the delay in the arrangements for a Union steamer to pick up cotton at Mobile. Today, Gen. Canby wired Halleck that the steamer *Atlanta*, which had a capacity of 1500 bales of cotton, had been sent to Mobile on December 16, after a 3-day delay caused by weather, to find that the cotton was not ready to be loaded. The Confederate authorities were notified that unless the cotton was sent immediately, the *Atlanta* would not wait.

In New York, Brig. Gen. Halbert E. Paine, birddogging Confederate Brig. Gen. Wm. N.R. Beall, wrote Halleck that the sign that so incensed Secy. of War Stanton was only a small tin sign attached to the glass door on the inside and of not much consequence. Paine said that he did not think the sign that objectionable; however, he would take Beall to Ft. Lafayette tomorrow, weather permitting, tugs not being able to land at the island today.

Meanwhile, Beall requested that the removal to Ft. Lafayette be suspended, at least for two days, until he could return samples of cloth he had received from manufacturers. It had taken him about 2 to 3 weeks to gather the samples from which selection would be made for the uniforms and blankets to be purchased. This time was granted, but he would have to return to prison until the cotton arrived.

### January 5 (Thursday)

Today, John Yates Beall was removed from the city jail in New York City and taken to the military prison at Ft. Lafayette in New York Harbor. There he was confined with several other Confederate prisoners to await trial. He was to be tried before a military court as a spy rather than to be treated as a prisoner of war.

At Nashville, Tenn., Lt. O.O. Poppleton, 111th U.S. Colored Infantry, sent a letter to Maj. Gen. Benjamin F. Butler, Commanding Department of East Virginia, concerning the treatment of Union Negro troops when captured by the Confederacy:

> Sir:... I have in my possession a copy of the Mobile *Advertiser and Register* of October 1864, which contains a printed order from D.H. Maury, major-general, C.S. Army, giving the names of about 570 of our colored soldiers who belong to the One hundred and sixth, One hundred and tenth, and One hundred and eleventh U.S. Colored Infantry Regiments, and notifying the former owners of said soldiers that they were

at that time employed by the engineer department at Mobile, Ala., and for the owners to report and receive the pay due for the soldiers' services. If you desire me to send you the paper which contains the order, or a copy of the order, I will do so.

Col. B.F. Tracy, commanding at Elmira, N.Y., wrote today that he was in desperate need of 11,000 jackets, 2500 shirts, 3000 pair of trousers, 8000 drawers, 4000 bootees, 7000 socks, and 1500 caps for the prisoners at that depot. A requisition had been sent on December 1, 1864, which was partially filled and those items were issued. Since then he received word of the sale of the cotton to relieve the prisoners, but had heard nothing more on that subject. Meanwhile, his prisoners were suffering the cold in that northern clime. Tracy needed help now.

Two days later, Brig. Gen. H.W. Wessells, USA, agreed with Tracy and forwarded the request to the Quartermaster-General in Washington. Seven days later, Col. Alex J. Perry at the Quartermaster-General's office said that the requisition had not been received. However, if Tracy would submit one it would be filled. Typical. Perry could have taken action to fill the requisition and *then* had it submitted; at least that way the prisoners would have been warmer sooner.

Out in Nashville, Tenn., Brig. Gen. William Hoffman, Federal Commissary-General of Prisoners, made a decision without checking the status of the cotton sale in New York. His decision would adversely affect several hundred wounded and sick Confederate prisoners.

> The rebel wounded prisoners in the hospitals at this place and at Franklin are much in want of clothing suitable for sick men, and if it is thought advisable to consider their wants so far, I would suggest that Gen. Beall be notified accordingly. In the belief that arrangements for the supplying of clothing to rebel prisoners in our hands by the rebel authorities have been completed,... I have directed that no clothing, including blankets, shall be issued to prisoners forwarded from this city since my arrival.

Light was shed on the situation of getting the cotton out of Mobile, Ala., today by Capt. Frank G. Noyes, Federal Commissary of Subsistence, off Mobile on the U.S.S. *Chickasaw*.

The delay ... has been explained ... at two different times by flag of truce. The first time, under date of December 29 ultimo, he stated that the wind (a violent norther) had so lowered the water that the vessel on which the cotton was loaded could not go through the obstructions.... Yesterday another communication was received ... stating that the vessel ... had got aground, and that if she was not got off very soon the cotton would be transferred to another vessel and carried through the obstructions.... There is high tide this P.M., and the naval officers here state to me their belief that the rebel steamer will be got off, as we can see her plainly, and heavy clouds of smoke indicate a vigorous attempt to get her off.

So far as I can judge, I have no doubt that the delay has been unavoidable on the part of the rebel authorities…

Brig. Gen. Wm. N.R. Beall notified Confederate Agent for Exchange Robert Ould that his parole had been suspended, to be reinstated when the cotton arrived in New York.

### January 6 (Friday)

Malone, B.Y., Sgt., Co. H, 6th N.C. Infantry, CSA, prisoner, Point Lookout, Md.:

> The 6th my Self A.R. Moore James R. Aldridge Nathaniel Hooper & T.Y. Compton built us a hous out of cracker Boxes the house coust us $8.80 cts we bought a stove from the Sutlar the Stove coust us $8.00 the Stove and house totel $16.80.

Richmond *Examiner*, Richmond, Va.:

BLANKETS FOR UNION PRISONERS—THE DISTRIBUTION PROGRESSING—ONLY 2000 FEDERAL PRISONERS CONFINED AT RICHMOND—REASON WHY OUR CAPTURED MEN ARE SENT SOUTHWARD

Yesterday a commission from Grant's lines arrived at Varina, under flag of truce, bringing 1500 blankets for distribution among the Federal prisoners in Richmond, in addition to 1000 blankets received through the same source last week. Maj. Turner, the commandant of the Libby Prison post here, placed the distribution under the control of Lt. Col. Hutchins, a Federal officer and a prisoner, and the distribution of the blankets was progressing yesterday and will be concluded today.

This is an offset to the courtesy extended our prisoners in the North by the cargo of cotton sent from Mobile recently, which, converted into Federal currency, will go far towards supplying the wants of the suffering Confederate prisoners in the, to them, frigid zone of the North.

Of the fifty-odd thousand Yankee prisoners computed to be now held in the South, not over 2000 are confined in Richmond, and more than the half of these are in the hospital. A wise determination of the Government has constantly for a year past been shifting the great body of the prisoners southward, and the wisdom of the order is being demonstrated every day. Richmond, hard-pressed to feed its superabundant population and the large army defending its gates, is relieved from the incubus of an overstocked prison post in its midst.

## January 8 (Sunday)

An inspection report of this date showed that at Elmira, N.Y., the convalescent wards were unsafe for occupancy; ward six nearly blew down during the last storm; and, there were 126 cases of smallpox in camp, causing 10 deaths.

Wade, F.S., Sgt., McNeill's Texas Scouts, prisoner, Elmira, N.Y.:

If there ever was a hell on earth, Elmira prison was that hell, but it was not a hot one, for the thermometer was often 40 degrees below zero. There were about six thousand Confederate prisoners, mostly from Georgia and the Carolinas. We were housed in long prison buildings, say one hundred and twenty feet long and forty feet wide, three tiers of bunks against each wall. A big coal stove every thirty feet was always kept red hot; but for these stoves, the most of us would have frozen. Around each stove was a chalk mark, five feet from the stove, marking the distance we should keep, so that all could be warm. We were thinly clad and not half of us had even one blanket. Our rations were ten ounces of bread and two ounces of meat per day. My weight fell from 180 to 160 in a month. We invented all kinds of traps and deadfalls to catch rats. Every day Northern ladies came in the prison, some of them followed by dogs or cats, which the boys would slip aside and choke to death. The ribs of a stewed dog were delicious, and a broiled rat was superb.

One day I was at the guardhouse when about thirty-five of our boys had on barreled shirts, guards

marching them around. A barreled shirt was made by knocking out the head of a barrel then cutting a hole in the other head and putting it on the body. On these barreled shirts was written in big letters, "Stole a dog," "Stole a cat," "Stole a ration," "Stole a fur," etc. If a lady's fur was not fastened on, the boys would grab it off, and some of them had been caught.

All the Yankee soldiers were not cruel. The chalk marks were drawn around the stoves so that all could get some of the heat. One day a poor sick boy lay down near the chalk line and went to sleep. In his sleep he threw his leg over the chalk line. A big guard caught him by the shoulder and threw him against the wall, making his nose bleed. I popped my big fist against the guard's jaw, knocking him hells over head. He ran out cursing me. Of course I was scared. In a few minutes, a captain came in with a file of soldiers, having the guard I assaulted of the party, and asked: "Where is the man who knocked this soldier down?" I stepped out and said: "I am the man." Then I called up the sick boy and made him lie down, and I told the captain it made me so mad to see this poor boy so brutally treated that I could not help punishing the bully. He said to our men: "Has this man told the truth?" A dozen of our men stepped forward and said that they would swear that I had related the scene correctly. The captain slapped me on the shoulder and said to the brute: "I will put you in the guardhouse." I was called before a court-martial, and, being sworn, related the whole matter as it occurred. The Judge Advocate said to the bully: "You will wear a ball and chain for thirty days and forfeit your pay for a month for brutality to a prisoner."

Good luck came to me after I had been in this prison, say, a month. Some good Yankee ladies got up a lot of old schoolbooks and established a prison school, and I was appointed one of the teachers, the pay to be an extra ration. I soon got back my twenty pounds of flesh. This was the best pay I ever got for a job in my life....

My dear comrade, Jimmie Jones, took the smallpox and was sent to the smallpox hospital. I was immune and got permission to help nurse him. A young Chinese physician by the name of Sin Lu, had just been put in charge of the ward. The doctor had just become a Mason. Sin and I were very proficient in the work. All the doctor's spare time he spent in Jim's room learning the work. We became great friends. One day the doctor went over to Lake Erie, a few miles away. The next day he told me to go to Jim's room. To my great surprise, Jim was sitting in a coffin with a white sheet around him. He handed me a paper of flour and said: "Sprinkle my face and hands with flour, then slightly fasten the coffin lid down, and when the dead wagon comes around, be sure to put my coffin on top of the other dead." Soon the dead wagon, driven by a negro, came up. I got help and put Jim's coffin on top. It was forty years before I saw Jim again at a reunion of Greene's Brigade at Cuero, Tex.; but a day or two after, I got a letter from him telling me about his experiences. He said when the dead wagon got out of the prison walls, he raised the coffin lid, rapped on it, and said in a sepulchral voice: "Come to judgment." The darky looked around, jumped off the wagon, eyes like saucers, yelling: "Ghosties! Ghosties! Ghosties!" As soon as the darky was out of sight, he stripped off his sheet, wiped the flour off his face and hands, took one of the horses out of the wagon, mounted, and galloped to Lake Erie, where he found a boat awaiting him, and was soon in Canada.

Soon after, an order was issued for all prisoners from the subjugated States of Missouri, Kentucky, West Virginia, and Louisiana, to report for parole. All that night I rolled over in my bunk and wished I was from one of those States. Just before daylight, I had another inspiration. I slipped on my clothes, ran to the office where the prison rolls were kept, and asked the officer in charge to turn to the entry of a certain date. I ran my finger down the list till I came to the name, "F.S. Wade, sergeant of McNeill's Texas Scouts." I said to the officer: "I will give you $10 to erase Texas and substitute Louisiana." Said he: "Show me the money." I started to take it out of my vest pocket, but he put his hand over mine and saw the "X." Then he made the change, and I walked out with my parole.

Soon an officer came in my ward and called my name for parole. I stepped out and fell in line. The boys in the prison kept saying: "He always said he was from Texas." But I kept mum.

### January 9 (Monday)

In Montgomery, Ala., Gen. P.T.G. Beauregard, CSA, requested prisoners to be sent to him from Brig. Gen. John H. Winder, Confederate Commissary-General of Prisoners:

General: Gen. Beauregard desires that you will furnish Maj. J.M. Hottle, quartermaster, with thirty Federal prisoners to take out the torpedoes and shells in railroad cuts on the West Point and Atlanta Railroad. Maj. Hottle has been charged with the repair of the road.

Gen. Winder did not hesitate. On the 26th he forwarded the request to the Adjutant and Inspector General with the comment "I don't think this is legitimate work for prisoners of war. I have therefore declined to furnish the prisoners asked for. I request to be informed if I have decided properly."

The Adjutant and Inspector General's office kicked the letters upstairs to the Secy. of War, John Breckinridge, on February 4.

The Secy. of War agreed with Winder. This *was not* legitimate work for prisoners. The whole pile of paper was sent back to Beauregard, who then said that since McClellan supposedly did use prisoners to clear torpedoes during the Peninsular Campaign, he felt he could do the same. No other action.

### January 10 (Tuesday)

Lt. P.E. O'Connor, Adjutant of the Tenth Veteran Corps, Camp Fry, outside Washington, D.C., today wrote a letter to the Commissary-General of Prisoners concerning a Confederate prisoner, John Brusnan, being held at Elmira, N.Y. With his letter he enclosed an extract of a letter written by Brusnan to a sister (Brusnan's) living outside Baltimore, Md.:

Some time ago his friends represented to me that he (Brusnan) was loyal to the Union; that it was want of forethought placed him in the rebel ranks, and after being some time in the rebel service he repented his rashness, and on two occasions attempted to desert to the Union side. On this representation (which I have no doubt his friends believed to be true), and he being also a relative of mine, I wrote twice to the Commissary-General of Prisoners to effect his release, if possible, by the first of the new year, providing he would take the oath of allegiance. At present I am glad that he is not released; and further, I most respectfully request that no action be taken on the letters which I have written in his behalf. Whether he has or has not taken the oath of allegiance it does not make much difference, as it is evident from the inclosed extract he is an incorrigible and an ungrateful rebel. In my humble opinion he deserves (instead of the rations he now complains of) to be kept on bread and water during his remaining term of confinement.

One of the extracts from the letter:

My Dear Sister: I take this opportunity of writing you a letter (which the Yankees will not see). I wrote you a few days ago acknowledging the receipt of the money. I will give you some idea of my situation. I would never have written to you for money, but I am almost starved to death. I only get two meals a day, breakfast and supper. For breakfast I get one-third of a pound of bread and a small piece of meat; for supper the same quantity of bread and not any meat, but a small plate of warm water called soup. I would never take that oath if I was not starved to do it. You know that without my telling you. When I came here this prison contained 10,000 prisoners, and they have all died except about 5000. They are now dying at the rate of twenty-five a day. You know this is no place for me.

## January 12 (Thursday)

Grant, at City Point, Va., wrote Robert Ould, in Richmond that the cotton has not yet reached the Union ship. The waiting was costing money. Grant asked for any information available.

The availability of food within the Confederacy was a known fact. The transportation and distribution of that food was something else.

Jones, John B., Rebel War Clerk, Confederate War Dept., Richmond, Va.:

Maj. R.J. Echols, Quartermaster, Charlotte, N.C., says the fire there destroyed 70,000 bushels of grain, a large amount of sugar, molasses, clothing, blankets, etc. He knows not whether it was the result of design or accident. All his papers were consumed. A part of Conner's brigade, on the way to South Carolina, 500 men, under Lt. Col. Wallace, refused to aid in saving property, but plundered it! This proves that the soldiers were all poor men, the rich having bought exemptions or details!

## January 13 (Friday)

Off Wilmington, N.C., early this morning, the U.S.S. *New Ironsides*, Commodore William Radford, led the monitors *Saugus*, *Canonicus*, *Monadnock*, and *Mahopac* to within 1000 yards of Ft. Fisher and opened with their naval guns. The defenders, 1500 men under Col. Lamb, replied with

spirit. The U.S.S. *Brooklyn*, Capt. Alden, led the heavy wooden-hulled ships into line behind the ironclads and the bombardment lasted all day and into the night. Maj. Gen. Terry, in command of the Union Army forces, landed his 8000 men on a defensible beachhead out of range of the fort's guns. One Confederate soldier remembered the battle:

Davis, T.C., 40th Regt., N.C. troops, arrival at Ft. Fisher:

After the evacuation of Atlanta, five companies of the North Carolina Regiment of Hardee's command were ordered to reinforce the command at Ft. Fisher, N.C., which, at that time, was the "key to the Confederacy." We arrived on the 13th of January, 1865, at the beginning of the second attack on that fort, which was garrisoned with about twelve hundred soldiers. The Federals had a navy of eighty-four vessels, carrying six hundred heavy guns.

The quartermaster at Camp Douglas, Ill., today requisitioned clothing for the Confederate prisoners held at that facility. The clothing requisitions called for 8000 blankets, 2000 coats or jackets, 3000 pair trousers, 5000 shirts, 10,000 pair drawers, 12,000 pair stockings, and 3000 bootees.

At Mobile, Ala., the 1000 bales of cotton were finally out of the harbor and ready to load onto the seagoing vessel for shipment to New York. Capt. Frank G. Noyes was having a hard time getting stevedores to move the cotton from the rebel steamer *Waverly* to the *Atlanta*. Speed in movement was important because the *Waverly* was somewhat frail and a good "norther" could seriously damage her.

## January 14 (Saturday)

Federal naval fire was pouring 100 shells per minute into Ft. Fisher, N.C. The Confederates had suffered 300 casualties and could not bury their dead because of the lethal shrapnel flying around. Only one gun on the land face of the fort was left in a serviceable condition, all the others having been dismounted by the incessant naval gunfire.

Meanwhile, Gen. Terry had prepared defensive works facing the approaches from Wilmington to protect his rear from a possible assault by the 6000 Rebel troops at Wilmington under Gen. Braxton Bragg. During the day, the C.S.S. *Chickamauga*, based at Wilmington, came down and fired on Terry's Union troops from her position on the Cape Fear River.

Terry visited Porter aboard the flagship *Malvern* to coordinate the attack for the following day. The plan called for 4000 of Terry's troops to hold the defensive line and the other 4000 to attack the land face of the fort in midafternoon. At the moment of Terry's attack, 2000 sailors and Marines would assault the sea face of the fort at the northeast bastion.

Davis, T.C., 40th Regt., N.C. troops, defending Ft. Fisher:

After bombarding the fort for three days and nights, and disabling all of our guns except two or three, they landed eleven thousand infantry, under the guns of their navy, and assaulted the fort.

Abbott, A.O., 1st Lt., 1st N.Y. Dragoons, prisoner in the State Asylum, Columbia, S.C.:

About the middle of January, one morning, we were surprised by the officer of the day bringing in a guard, and, proceeding directly to one of the tents on the northeast side of the camp, drove out the inmates, and commenced searching for a "tunnel," and was rewarded by discovering a splendid one *nearly completed*. Two or three nights more, and it would have been ready for use. Hopes were again blasted, for we were ordered to remove the tent to another part of the camp, and thus the hard labor of many nights was unceremoniously destroyed.

Before night a paper was posted on the hospital, reading something like the following, viz.:

### NOTICE!

Gen. Winder directs that I inform the Federal prisoners under my command that, unless the tunneling is stopped, he will cause all the buildings, tents, lumber, boards, and shade-trees to be removed from the yard.

I would also say that I shall use force for force if any attempt is made to injure any prisoners suspected of reporting tunneling at these head-quarters.
(Signed), ——— Griswold,
Major Commanding Federal Prisoners.

The reason of inserting the last clause was the suspicion in camp that one of the prisoners had reported the tunnel to the Rebel authorities, and there was talk of lynching him on the spot. He was not seen

after we left Columbia, I believe.

That threat of Winder's was only the signal for tunneling to commence; for, at the time we were hurried away so unceremoniously, nearly a dozen were in progress, a part of them nearly completed, which would let out two persons per minute. They were not discovered till after we left, and, as Winder was gone, I suppose the buildings were left standing.

Lt. Col. Benjamin T. Hutchins, 1st New Hampshire Cavalry, a prisoner in Richmond, Va., had been selected as the agent to distribute blankets to the Federal prisoners in that city. He, in turn, selected Chaplain Emerson, 7th New Hampshire Infantry, and Asst. Surgeon Pierce, 1st New Hampshire Cavalry as assistants. Surgeon Strawbridge, medical director of the 18th Army Corps, also assisted part of the time.

On the evening of December 31, 1864, Hutchins had received ten bales of blankets, 100 to a bale, for distribution, being told by Mr. Robert Ould and Maj. Turner that he could commence the following morning. Col. Hutchins's account to Maj. Gen. Butler follows:

On Sunday, the 1st of January, 1865, we commenced to issue the blankets, and surely it was a welcome New Year's present to our suffering soldiers. After inspecting the different prisons we came to the conclusion that those prisoners who were confined in what is known as the Pemberton Building were the most destitute, although every soldier who was here confined was sadly in need of blankets and clothing. There were nearly 3000 prisoners in Richmond, and very few were in possession of blankets. In the Pemberton Building there are six large rooms in which our prisoners are confined. The three rooms in the northwest corner of this building were found to be the most open, and the prisoners here confined were the most exposed. We here issued one blanket to each enlisted man, there being 579 men confined in these rooms. We also found that up to this time there were but thirty-one blankets for all these men.

On Monday, the 2d of January, we completed distribution of the blankets to these prisoners confined in the south rooms. Not having a sufficient supply on hand, and wishing to make all as comfortable as possible, I took the responsibility to depart somewhat from the instructions I received from Brig. Gen. Turner and accordingly issued two blankets to every three men. Instead of murmuring or complaining, these men received them most gratefully, and frequent expressions of thankfulness were made for this token of remembrance by their Government. It was, indeed, a sad sight to see these brave soldiers, who have been suffering for months in this prison from cold and hunger, roll themselves up in their warm blankets and sink at once in a quiet slumber, forgetful of their food and mindful of nothing save sleep. In this connection allow me to say that not a single commissioned officer here confined would receive a blanket from this lot, all preferring that they should be distributed to the enlisted men.

On January 5, 1865, I received 1500 more blankets and on the following morning commenced to distribute them, assisted by Dr. Pierce and Maj. Owens, of the 1st Kentucky Cavalry. We issued the following number to prisoners confined in the rooms of Libby Prison: In room No. 1, 228; No. 2, 210; No. 3, 198. We issued to men who had just arrived from Western Virginia, captured in the late raid made by Gen. Stoneman, ninety-two blankets; and here I must say that among all of the prisoners whom I have yet seen these are the most destitute. None had blankets or overcoats. In most cases their hats and coats had been taken from them, and but very few had boots or shoes upon their feet. Many of them could hardly stand, and when the blankets were given to them they seemed too grateful to reply. We then went over to the Pemberton Building and distributed blankets to those men who did not receive them from the first consignment, numbering 588. The next lot was to a class of men whose situation I would most respectfully call your attention. They are a class of men who have been held as prisoners for a long time and are detailed as shoemakers, broom makers, cooks, carpenters, and tailors. These men say they do it because they were suffering so much for food, receiving double rations for their labor, but there is not one whom I conversed with who is not extremely anxious to be exchanged at once.... We distributed blankets to those officers who are held in close confinement as hostages (ten in number). I also issued blankets to the officers, and turned over fifty-six to Capt. Watson on the morning of my release from prison.

Thus I have completed the issue of blankets sent by you for our prisoners, and believe me, general, it has been a most pleasant duty, and our Government has received the thanks of nearly 3000 brave men who were suffering for the want of them.

Permit me to call your attention to the necessity of sending clothing to these men. A great many of them are almost destitute of clothes, so long have they been imprisoned. Several hundred are bootless and shoeless; as many are without socks, while a very large number are without coats and jackets. If you will permit me I would recommend that a supply of shoes, shirts, and blouses be sent with a less number of pants, for without them a large number will certainly die during the winter. In conclusion, I am happy to state that every facility was rendered me in the performance of my duty by Col. Ould and Maj. Turner.

### January 15 (Sunday)

When the naval guns ceased firing on Ft. Fisher at 3 P.M., the result must have been a deafening silence. The Confederate gunners, however, manned the guns that were left and began firing on the assaulting Federals. The naval landing force was the first target available, the Army troops having farther to come, and as the landing party crossed the beach the defenders' fire was point-blank, "ploughing lanes in the ranks." The naval landing force, under the command of Lt. Commander K. Randolph Breese, pressed the attack with one group headed by Lt. Commander Thomas O. Selfridge reaching the top of the parapet and temporarily breaching the defenses, but were driven back, the Confederates cheering the withdrawal.

The Confederates, too busy cheering the repulse of the naval force, suddenly realized that Terry's forces had taken the western end of the fort in strength. A counterattack was immediately launched and hand-to-hand fighting soon ensued. Reinforcements rushing to the western end from other points of the fort now were hit by naval gunfire firing with pinpoint accuracy and destroying the Confederate columns as they moved. Other ships fired on the riverbank behind the fort to prevent any reinforcements from that direction. Gen. Whiting was wounded during the assault and command was taken by Maj. James Reilly after Col. Lamb was hit in the hip by a bullet. Reilly fought doggedly and well but was overwhelmed by the onrushing Union troops and the naval gunfire. He was driven from the fort and surrendered his men later that night. Union casualties were heavy, nearly 1000 killed or wounded to about half that number for the Confederates.

Davis, T.C., 40th Regt., N.C. troops, defending Ft. Fisher:

They succeeded in making lodgment in the fort about three o'clock Sunday evening, January 15, and the contest kept up until ten o'clock at night. The fort, with its garrison, was captured. The Federal loss, as stated by Gen. Terry in his official report, was 1445. The Confederate loss is not known, though it is estimated at 500, including Gen. W.H.C. Whiting and Col. William Lamb.

An inspection report dated today showed the prisoner strength at Camp Douglas, Chicago, to be 11,540. During the past two weeks, twelve new cases of smallpox were reported along with four cases of varioloid. Twelve prisoners died of smallpox during the same period—a marked decrease in deaths from this dreaded disease.

From City Point, Va., Lt. Gen. Grant directed that Confederate Gen. Vance be paroled to work with Brig. Gen. Wm. N.R. Beall on the cotton transfer and sale.

From Mobile, Ala., Maj. Gen. Dabney H. Maury, CSA, added some light to the problem of getting the cotton to the Federal steamer:

General: Please inform the Secretary of War that the cotton for purchase of supplies for our prisoners was delivered to an officer appointed by Gen. Granger to receive it on the 13th instant. The lightest draft boat in this harbor capable of taking out the cotton was selected. Her draft when loaded was about four feet. There is only one point at which such a boat can pass in or out, and then only when the tide is high. After this boat was loaded no tide came up sufficient to take her out. The cotton was then transferred to flats, and the boat thereby enabled to pass out. Before she could be reloaded a violent storm came up and caused one of the flats with the cotton on it to break adrift. Two days' delay occurred from this cause. Every effort and means have been exerted to insure prompt execution of the instructions relative to this business, and no delay has occurred which it has been in my power to prevent.

### January 16 (Monday)

At Ft. Fisher, the cleanup began and the prisoners were taken aboard the ships offshore for transport to prisons in the North.

Davis, T.C., 40th Regt., N.C. troops, prisoner of war:

On January 16 we were put on board a ship and sent to Fortress Monroe, Va., from whence we were to be sent to Ft. Delaware; but we got stuck in the ice at the breakwater, and the ship backed out and took us to New York City.

Reports from Rock Island, Ill., prison indicate that 281 prisoners left this day for exchange at Cairo, Ill. Only 23 took the oath of allegiance, most of the other prisoners alleging that as soon as they were exchanged they would desert and return to their homes.

At Mobile, Ala., Capt. Frank G. Noyes reported on the status of the cotton being transferred for shipment to New York:

In checking off the cotton from the rebel steamer *Waverly* we found it to contain only 997 bales, and it was in very bad condition. I of course only signed bills of lading for the amount received and its condition. I inclose herewith a copy of my communication to Gen. Maury in forwarding the bills of lading. I forward by the schooner *Highlander* to Capt. Perkins, assistant quartermaster, New Orleans, for transportation to me at New York, 170 bales (under the statement I sent you yesterday), and shall sail on the *Atlanta* for New York today with 827 bales.

### January 17 (Tuesday)

Arriving at New York aboard ship, the prisoners from Ft. Fisher were transferred to the railroad for movement to the prison at Elmira, N.Y.

Davis, T.C., 40th Regt., N.C. troops, prisoner of war, Elmira, N.Y.:

We were sent by rail for that den of misery known as Elmira Prison, about one mile from Elmira, N.Y. Arrived about eight o'clock in the evening, in four feet of snow, and many prisoners had neither blankets or coats. We were kept standing in ranks in the street for half an hour before starting for the prison. We were halted in an old warehouse and robbed of all valuables by Lt. Groves and an unknown Sgt. Major; then we were sent to the barracks—board shanties about fifty yards long, containing one stove. Our beds were planks without blankets. There were about seven thousand prisoners confined there, and those who had preceded us were in much want. They were dirty, pale, emaciated, and scantily clothed. Our rations consisted of loaves of stale bread an inch thick, tough pieces of steak, and occasionally broth. When prisoners died, their bodies were put in a box and stacked in a "dead-house" as high as they could stack them before taking them out for burial. The Federal Sergeants who had charge of the prison "wards" (as they were called) were the meanest men I ever saw—demons in human flesh. There was a young soldier about eighteen years old, without blanket or coat, who had become deaf from exposure. When he was found near the stove, he was beaten and kicked about unmercifully.... After the war, we were turned out in squads of two hundred, by taking the oath. I was truly glad to get out of prison, but sorry to be deprived of my watch and ring, which were stolen by Lt. Groves and the Sgt. Major. I arrived at home on June 1, 1865, and while memory lasts I shall not forget the great war and the cruel prison.

Gen. Samuel Cooper, Adjutant-General of the CSA, wired Brig. Gen. John H. Winder in Columbia, S.C., yesterday concerning the status of the new prison to be built at Columbia. Today, Winder replied:

The original location for prison, five miles below Columbia, has been abandoned by order of the President. Another locality, fourteen miles above Columbia, on the Charlotte railroad, has been selected and a considerable quantity of timber has been gotten out, and we shall continue the construction unless you think it unsafe. We have been delayed, waiting for the opinion of the district attorney as to the title to the land and the want of the purchase money, and now we are delayed, as the time of the last year's labor has expired and that for this year we have not been enabled yet to procure. Ask the Quartermaster-General to send the purchase money at once. He has been telegraphed to.

### January 20 (Friday)

Having incarcerated John Yates Beall at Ft. Lafayette military prison in New York Harbor on January 5, the Federal authorities wasted no time in arraigning him on this date for violating the laws of war as a guerrilla and pirate and being a spy. James T. Brady, a prominent New York lawyer, came forward at this time and volunteered to act as the defense counsel for Beall. Beall's obvious defense was that he was acting in the capacity of a Confederate officer and under the recognized rules of warfare.

Brig. Gen. John H. Winder, at Columbia, S.C., had a dilemma on the movement of prisoners. He wired Gen. Samuel Cooper in Richmond:

I am at a loss to know where to send prisoners from Florence. In one direction the enemy are in the way. In the other the question of supplies presents an insuperable barrier. I again urge paroling the prisoners and sending them home. I have consulted the Governor and Gen. Chesnut, who both urge that they be paroled. The guard is very weak and insufficient to take care. At once give full instructions.

### January 21 (Saturday)

Lt. Gen. Ulysses S. Grant, commander of all Union armies, finally relented on this date and agreed to prisoner exchanges. It would be too late for many of the prisoners, both North and South.

Lt. O.O. Poppleton, 111th U.S. Colored Infantry, again reported to Maj. Gen. Benjamin F. Butler that the names of nearly 890 colored Union soldiers had appeared in the Mobile, Ala., paper as working on the defenses of Mobile. These soldiers had been captured by Gen. N.B. Forrest's men at Athens, Ala., on the 24th and 25th of September, 1864. The newspaper article called for the owners of these former slaves to come forth and claim the money due for their slaves' labor.

### January 22 (Sunday)

Malone, B.Y., Sgt., Co. H, 6th N.C. Infantry, CSA, prisoner, Point Lookout, Md.:

The 22d was cold and cloudy & it was my birthday which made me 26 years old. And about 600 prysnors come in today captured at Foat Fisher The men that came in Say that Gen. Whiten and Col. Lamb was captured and also wounded After knight a Neagrow Sentnal Shot one of our men and kild him.

### January 23 (Monday)

Brig. Gen. Wm. N.R. Beall, CSA, had his parole reinstated today so he could continue work on selling the cotton and buying clothing for the Confederate prisoners in the Northern prisons. Brig. Gen. Vance was also paroled on this date to assist Beall.

### January 24 (Tuesday)

Capt. Frank G. Noyes, USA, today notified Brig. Gen. Halbert E. Paine, USA, in New York that he [Noyes] had arrived with the cargo of cotton and was ready to consign it to the Confederate officers. That saga was over after trials and tribulations.

Wasting no time, Gen. Paine set a meeting with Capt. Noyes for the 25th, the next day, and then notified Gen. Beall that the cotton was now located at Pier 41, North River. Beall was invited to the meeting at noon.

### January 27 (Friday)

An inspection report of the Confederate prison at Florence, S.C., indicated that on this date there were a total of 7538 Union prisoners at Florence, of whom 537 were in the hospital. The mortality rate was about six per day, mostly from diarrhea. There were some few cases of smallpox and typhoid fever. The inspector did report that the subsistence department was entirely deficient, and the ration issued daily amounted almost to starvation. There had been but two issues of meat during the past two months. No quartermaster officer was posted at the prison and no transportation was available. Lumber for construction was carried by prisoners about a mile from the pickup point.

The report, sent to Brig. Gen. John H. Winder in Columbia, S.C., was forwarded to Gen. Samuel Cooper, Adjutant-General, CSA, on January 28. On February 2, it was passed from the Adjutant-General's office to the Commissary-General, L.B. Northrop, for comment. On February 4, Northrop endorsed the letter by saying that "Unless more money is furnished the bureau it will be impossible to continue to issue the present ration to prisoners of war, much less to increase it." Then the letter went through the Secy. of War's offices from Febru-

ary 9 through 14, when it was sent to the Secy. of the Treasury for comment. On February 18, G.A. Trenholm, Secy. of the Treasury, wrote that "Every effort is being made to supply the necessary funds for the pay of our returned prisoners. The means at the command of the Treasury is extremely limited, and no provision has yet been made by Congress for the replenishment of the Treasury." The papers were then returned to the Secy. of War.

It had now taken 21 days to find out that no money was available to buy rations for the prisoners at Florence, S.C., and in the meantime, those same prisoners were still on near-starvation rations.

### January 29 (Sunday)

An inspection report for Camp Douglas, Ill., submitted on this date indicated that a total of 11,312 prisoners were present. Since the last report, 83 had died and 41 were released. Additional remarks were a recommendation that "the sutler be directed to keep constantly on hand and for sale to the prisoners onions and cabbage whenever they can be procured." Fresh vegetables were not a part of the regular Army ration at this time.

### January 31 (Tuesday)

Undaunted, and still trying, Lt. Col. John F. Iverson, commanding the prison at Florence, S.C., tried again to improve the rations at his facility. Iverson's letter is illustrative of the declining position of the Confederacy:

The ration now being issued to the prisoners at this prison is totally insufficient for their sustenance, as large numbers are dying daily, and I am satisfied it is from not being properly fed. The post commissary informs me that he is not furnished with sufficient stores to warrant him in increasing the ration. The following are the instructions from the Commissary-General, dated Richmond, October 3, 1864: "Present scarcity of meat requires that prisoners be wholly subsisted on sorghum when practicable, and not on meat and sorghum, as provided in circular 1st October." I cannot construe this as entirely cutting the prisoners off from meat rations, especially when sorghum cannot be had, which has been the case at this post for some time past. I am informed that the prisoners at Andersonville, Ga., are receiving one-half pound of beef every day, besides their regular bread rations, which sustains me in my construction of the circular quoted above. Taking into consideration that these prisoners are not able to get anything but what is issued to them by the Government, for it is almost impossible for the sutler to procure supplies, coupled with the fact that they are very destitute of clothing, I feel it my duty to call the attention of the brigadier-general commanding to these facts, and I respectfully request that if it is out of his power to remedy the evil that this communication be forwarded to the War Department.... If the Government is really not able to give these prisoners more to eat then no blame can be attached to anyone; but if they are then I must think that the fault lies at the door of the Subsistence Department.

The present ration is as follows: One pound of meal, one-half pound of peas, three pounds of salt per 100 rations per day.

If a change in the ration can be made I will have the satisfaction of knowing that the prisoners under my charge are well housed, plenty of fuel, good hospital accommodations, and in as good a condition as could reasonably expect.

Brig. Gen. John H. Winder tried again to alleviate the problem. He forwarded the letter on to Gen. Samuel Cooper in Richmond on February 4. It was then sent to the Commissary-General's office on February 8. The Commissary-General, L.B. Northrop, sent it back with a comment to the effect that he had already answered a similar query on December 16, 1864. His reply at that time was:

The state of the commissariat will not allow the issue of a full ration to our own troops in the field, much less to prisoners of war. It is just that the men who caused the scarcity shall be the first to suffer from it.... Present appearances indicate the prospective necessity of a still greater reduction in the ration.

The letter was returned to Gen. Cooper, where it was filed with the notation that the prisoners had been ordered from Florence and that the prospects of a speedy exchange required no further action.

An abstract taken from a report of the sick and wounded at the prison at Andersonville, Ga., for the month of January 1865 indicated that on January 1 there were 813 sick and wounded and an additional 589 were hospitalized during the month—total: 1402. During the month, 267 were returned to the prison pen and 199 died, leaving 936 in the hospital. Quite a load of patients, considering the almost total lack of medical supplies.

### February 1 (Wednesday)

In New York the trial of John Yates Beall began. The military commission sitting on the case wasted little time in listening to witnesses or hearing clemency pleas.

At City Point, Va., U.S. Grant received a letter from Messrs. M. Lehman and I.T. Tichenor, Agents of the State of Alabama, requesting an audience to discuss the movement of cotton from Mobile to New York. They enclosed a letter written the month before, from Richmond, outlining the plan to bring cotton from Mobile on a U.S. government ship, to be sold in New York, the proceeds of the sale to be used to provide clothing, etc., to the prisoners of war from Alabama being held in Northern prisons. This effort was in addition to that already in process by the Confederate government.

In Richmond, Brig. Gen. Joseph Hayes, U.S. Volunteers, wrote the Adjutant-General in Washington that:

I have the honor to report my arrival in this city from Danville on Thursday, the 26th ultimo. Upon the following day I received official information from Mr. Ould, agent of exchange, of my appointment as agent to receive and distribute supplies for Union prisoners. Yesterday the supplies, consisting of 650 private packages and 50 bales of blankets, were transferred to me. I have been paroled to attend to this business, together with Lt. L. Markbreit, Twenty-eighth Ohio Volunteers, who will assist me. A suitable warehouse has been provided for storing the supplies, and I am assured by Mr. Ould that every facility for their transportation will be provided. I have this day issued 250 blankets to the Federal prisoners in this city, and shall in a day or two ... send the balance to the prisoners at Danville and Salisbury, who are in more pressing need. I have nominated three officers at each of those prisons to receive and distribute these supplies. A traveling agent will accompany them upon the road to insure safe delivery. In addition to the blankets I think there are needed at least 2000 complete suits of clothing (exclusive of overcoats, which are unnecessary) to clothe our men that are absolutely naked, or nearly so. I would recommend that they be sent. I find myself in need of funds to defray the public expenses incident to my present position, and therefore would request that $10,000 in Confederate funds be sent me by next flag of truce.

U.S. Grant, at City Point, Va., forwarded Gen. Hayes's report with the notation that the clothing requested would be provided from stocks in City Point.

At Raleigh, N.C., Gov. Zebulon B. Vance wrote the Confederate Secretary of War, J.A. Seddon, concerning the Federal prisoners at Salisbury, N.C.

Accounts reach me of the most distressing character in regard to their suffering and destitution. I earnestly request you to have the matter inquired into, and if in our power to relieve them that it be done. If they are willfully left to suffer when we can avoid it, it would be not only a blot upon our humanity, but would lay us open to a severe retaliation. I know how straitened our means are, however, and will cast no blame upon any one without further information.

On February 7, the new Secretary of War in Richmond, John C. Breckinridge, directed that an immediate investigation be conducted. This was begun.

Leaving no stone unturned, Gov. Vance also wrote Brig. Gen. Bradley T. Johnson, commanding at Salisbury, tendering what aid that could be provided the prisoners. Vance urged Johnson to greater efforts to alleviate the situation.

### February 2 (Thursday)

Part of Grant's problem in the prisoner exchange was that the Confederate prisoners who were able-bodied were immediately placed back in the ranks and become active enemies again. The fighting in the west had calmed somewhat since Sherman went through the South, and that, coupled with the distances involved in moving troops in the western theater, made the return of prisoners to that area less of a future problem. At 11:30 A.M., U.S. Grant wired Secy. of War Stanton in Washington that:

I am endeavoring to make arrangements to exchange about 3000 prisoners per week. This is as fast and probably faster than they can be delivered to us. Please have facilities given Lt. Col. Mulford to get rebel prisoners to comply with this arrangement. I would like disabled troops (troops from Missouri,

Kentucky, Arkansas, Tennessee, and Louisiana) sent first, as but few of these will be got in the ranks again, and as we can count upon but little re-enforcement from the prisoners we get.

In the North, the movement of supplies to the Confederate prisoners continued. In New York, Brig. Gen. H.E. Paine requested the head count of the number of prisoners being held at the various facilities so that the supplies could be shipped by Brig. Gen. W.N.R. Beall, CSA. The supplies were the product of selling the cotton sent by the South from Mobile, Ala., earlier.

### February 3 (Friday)

In prompt action, Brig. Gen. W.N.R. Beall, CSA, today received a listing of the prisoner strength at each of the prison facilities in the North. The largest population was at Camp Douglas, Ill. (11,676), followed by Point Lookout, Md. (11,097), Camp Chase, Ohio (9073), Ft. Delaware, Del. (7768), Elmira, N.Y. (7054). The remaining sites had fewer prisoners, only 26 imprisoned in Wheeling, W.Va.

In Chattanooga, Tenn., Col. L. Johnson, commanding the Forty-fourth U.S. Colored Infantry, wrote the Adjutant-General in Washington, D.C., about the treatment of colored soldiers captured by the Confederate forces.

General: I have the honor to forward inclosed the statement of an enlisted man of the Forty-fourth U.S. Colored Infantry, captured at Dalton, Ga., October 13, 1864, who subsequently escaped and is on duty at his company now.

I have already forwarded reports stating that although I surrendered my command at the place named above "as prisoners of war," their treatment was not that accorded to prisoners of war generally. They were, even under my own eyes a day after their capture, forced to tear up the railroad track between Dalton and Tunnel Hill. Since, I have heard from every man who escaped captivity and returned to the regiment, that they were not only deprived of their clothing, barbarously treated, and when sick sometimes shot down, but constantly worked in a most brutal manner that even surpassed the harshest treatment they had ever received in bondage.

The statement enclosed by Col. Johnson was one made by Sgt. John S. Leach, Co. A., Forty-fourth

U.S. Colored Infantry, excerpts from which are shown below:

> We ... were marched from Dalton to Selma, Ala. From thence we were forwarded to Corinth, Miss., at which place we were compelled to labor on railroads. The number of men of the Forty-fourth who labored on these roads I estimated at about 350. During the time I was in the hands of the rebels there were about 250 men of the Forty-fourth delivered to their former masters, or men who claimed to own them, thereby returning these men to slavery. The Forty-fourth arrived at Corinth, Miss., and commenced labor on or about the 1st of December, 1864, at which labor I remained until I effected my escape about the 25th of December, 1864, and arrived at Memphis, Tenn., and from thence I reported to my command at Chattanooga, Tenn.
>
> When I left the rebels there were about 125 men of the Forty-fourth still laboring on these railroads, the remainder having either been sent to the hospital to die, or turned over to civilians as slaves, or effected their escape. While with them our ration consisted of one pint of cornmeal per day and a small portion of fresh beef once or twice per week.

North Carolina Gov. Zebulon B. Vance had requested a report of the conditions at the prison at Salisbury, N.C., on February 1. A report by Capt. G.W. Booth, Gen. Johnson being absent, was sent to the Governor on this date:

> The C.S. prison when established at this place was contemplated for Confederate prisoners only, buildings and sufficient ground being purchased for that purpose. About the 5th of November, 1864, a large number of prisoners of war, some 8000, were suddenly sent here, the Government having no other place to send them. The grounds were enlarged and such preparations as could be made were arranged for their reception. A short time after their arrival tents were issued, and now they are all under shelter of some sort. The number of prisoners confined here has reached as high a figure as 10,000. When sent here they were in extremely bad condition. Wood in sufficient quantities is issued them. Only two days have they been without, and then unavoidable circumstances prevented its issue. The issue of wood is regulated in a measure by the weather.... As evidence that they have plenty, they offer to sell, and do sell,

to the sutler wood for his stove in exchange for tobacco....

> The matter of food receives the earnest attention of the commanding officers. They regularly receive one pound of good bread, one pint soup, besides small issues of meat or sorghum. Sometimes small quantities of both. As to clothing, their condition is truly deplorable, most of them having been prisoners some six or nine months. The Confederate Government cannot issue clothing to them, and none has been received at this post from the North. Gen. Johnson, in a communication to Commissioner Ould in early part of January, called attention to their condition in this respect.... Ten wells are in the prison, which afford them water. In addition, they are permitted every day to bring water in barrels from a neighboring creek. No stream of water runs through the prison.... A removal of prisoners to Columbia is contemplated and all improvements, buildings, &c., have been prohibited by Gen. Winder.... In consequence of the lack of transportation and the damages to the railroads of late the energy of the officers of the Commissary and Quartermaster Departments has been subjected to no mean test, but the prisoners have not suffered for wood or rations.

A postscript to the above indicated that the clothing and blankets shipped from Richmond on February 2nd were arriving for distribution.

The report was a good piece of creative writing on the part of Capt. Booth, who didn't have his facts straight, even on the reason for establishing the prison. It was at odds in many points with other reports from the same locality at that time. The situation was grim and getting worse at Salisbury.

### February 6 (Monday)

The winds were bitter cold at the railroad depot in Columbia, S.C., where on the open platform, among the gusts was an older man, Brig. Gen. John Henry Winder, Commissary-General of Confederate Prisons, waiting for a train to arrive going to Wilmington, N.C. The train would make an intermediate stop at Florence, S.C., some one hundred miles distant. The train arrived and the passengers and the General's party boarded. The train arrived at Florence late in the day, stopping at the depot on Front Street. The general departed for the local prison compound immediately, foregoing the comforts of the hotel across the street from the station. Upon arrival at the prison compound, Winder had entered in search of the prison commander when he suffered a massive heart attack and died almost immediately. Telegrams were sent to Richmond, and other points, notifying everyone of his death. His body was sent back to Columbia for burial.

In New York, Brig. Gen. William N.R. Beall, paroled prisoner handling the distribution of supplies to the Confederate prisoners, had, almost, been assigned an assistant. Brig. Gen. Robert B. Vance, currently at Ft. Delaware, Del., was to be released on parole and work with Beall getting the supplies out as rapidly as possible. Today, Beall wrote Brig. Gen. H.E. Paine, in Washington, on the progress being made:

> I ask that you make, if there is no objection, an arrangement with the Quartermaster's Department to furnish transportation on requisitions made direct from me for supplies to go to the several prisons. This, if done, will save much time and will save you the work of forwarding my requisitions.... I ... ask that Brig. Gen. R.B. Vance, who is to be my assistant, be permitted to visit such prisons as I may desire, to look to the distribution of supplies. This privilege is, I see from the papers, granted the U.S. officers in the South.... On Saturday I shipped to Point Lookout 2000 blankets, 1000 socks; to Elmira, 1000 blankets, 1000 socks, have also supplies to ship today to Ft. Delaware. I purchased 15,000 pair socks and 7000 pair shoes on Saturday. The delay in the cotton transshipped by Capt. Noyes will cause me great inconvenience, I fear. Can he not hurry it up?

### February 8 (Wednesday)

Abbott, like so many prisoners of war in the South, held Gen. Winder directly responsible for the short rations, lack of housing, poor medical treatment, etc., that befell them during their incarceration. Winder tried all within his power to do his duty and care for the prisoners in his custody. Circumstances overtook his control of the situation and he failed.

Abbott, A.O., 1st Lt., 1st N.Y. Dragoons, prisoner in the State Asylum, Columbia, S.C.:

The 8th of February we first heard of Winder's death, which caused great joy through all the prison camps—joy that he could no longer torture Union prisoners.

He was directly and the immediate cause of all the unnecessary suffering among us. He was the commissary general of prisoners, and he had it in his power to say what they should have to eat, where and what kind of quarters they should occupy, and what they should have to minister to their comfort....

The following story concerning the cause of Winder's death obtained much circulation among the prisoners. I do not vouch for the truth of the statement, only the story.

When Gen. Winder was first placed in command of the Federal prisoners, he made an arrangement with his Satanic Majesty that he (*Winder*) should have unlimited power to torment Union prisoners while the war lasted; and, farther, that there should be no "general exchange" while he lived; that when an exchange *did* take place, his work was done, and his master might come and claim him.

Certain it is exchange *has* taken place, and Winder is—gone.

In New York, the trial of John Yates Beall ended with a verdict of guilty on all charges of being a guerrilla and spy. He was sentenced to die by hanging on February 18. Beall was not notified of his impending death until February 13th. Meanwhile he was removed to Ft. Columbus on Governor's Island and placed in a dungeon lighted by one gas jet. He was given a small table and writing materials for his use.

Gen. Samuel Cooper, Adjutant-General, CSA, was notified today that Brig. Gen. John Henry Winder, CSA, died at Florence, S.C., the previous day. A successor to the command was immediately necessary. Col. H. Forno was inbound for duty. Would he be appointed?

### February 9 (Thursday)

Gen. James Chesnut, husband of the famed diarist Mary Chesnut, had made the funeral arrangements for Brig. Gen. Winder. Services were held late in the afternoon after Winder had lain in state at city hall, and the body was taken, under escort, to the cemetery at Trinity Church. The pallbearers included Gens. Joseph E. Johnston,

Mansfield Lovell, and Wade Hampton. The body was placed in an unmarked grave because of the proximity of Sherman's armies coming up from Savannah, by way of Orangeburg. After the war the body was taken to Maryland and reinterred.

In New York, Brig. Gen. Beall asked that 170 bales of cotton on hand in that city be furnished him in lieu of the same amount that had been left aboard the *Highlander* by Capt. Noyes when he had sailed for New York the previous month. On the 13th, Noyes disputed, to some degree, giving the cotton to Beall because that which he had left in the South he described as "in very bad condition, many of the bales being torn open, the roping broken, and there being consequently a large quantity of loose cotton. The marks on many of the bales were illegible...." This situation would take time to resolve.

Jones, John B., Rebel War Clerk, Confederate War Dept., Richmond, Va.:

Gen. Lee writes that desertions are caused by the bad management of the Commissary Department, and that there are supplies enough in the country, if the proper means were used to procure them.

### February 10 (Friday)

In an interesting development, Col. A.A. Stevens, commanding Camp Morton at Indianapolis, Ind., reported to the Federal Commissary-General of Prisoners, in Washington, today:

In pursuance of instructions received by telegram from the Commissary-General of Prisoners, dated Washington, D.C., February 4, 1865, I have carefully examined all prisoners of war confined in this camp from the five States mentioned in said telegram, viz, Missouri, Kentucky, Tennessee, Arkansas, and Louisiana, 1822 in number, and can find out of that number but 366 who want to go on exchange. The remaining 1516 express freely their desire to remain in prison until such time as they can be released by taking the oath as prescribed in the President's proclamation, December 8, 1863.

In essence, the prisoners did not want to return to active service in the Confederate armies.

The cotton trade in Mobile, Ala., was brisk. John C. Breckinridge, Confederate Secy. of War, directed Gen. D.H. Maury, at Mobile, to send 1500 bales of cotton through N. Harleston Brown, a local agent, to a shipping point for further movement to New York. The sale of the cotton was to subsidize the purchase of clothing, etc., for the Confederate prisoners in the North.

Gen. Samuel Cooper, Adjutant-General of the CSA, today notified Brig. Gen. Gideon J. Pillow, CSA, currently at Montgomery, Ala., that Pillow had been assigned as Confederate Commissary-General of Prisoners to replace the late Brig. Gen. John H. Winder.

### February 11 (Saturday)

More prisoner exchange was in the offing. Judge Robert Ould, Confederate Agent of Exchange, wrote Grant today:

Sir: I propose to deliver to you by James River, Wilmington, or any other practicable points, all the Federal prisoners now in our custody without delay, upon receiving an assurance from you that you will deliver an equal number of Confederate prisoners within a reasonable time. Of course I would prefer that such reasonable time should be as early a day as will be practicable or convenient to you.

I can deliver to you at Wilmington 1000 prisoners per day, commencing at any early date you may designate. I can have even a larger number in readiness at any named day. Deliveries of a like number per day can be made at Cox's Wharf, on James River, at the same time. I will be obliged for an early answer.

An inspection report from the prison at Camp Chase, Ohio, indicated that many of the prisoners taken during the battles of Franklin and Nashville, Tenn., were now hospitalized at Camp Chase and in bad condition. The battles, fought on the last day of November and in mid-December 1864, took place in severe weather and the exposure of the troops, on both sides, caused many non-battle-related casualties. All precautions were being taken at Camp Chase to aid the prisoners.

### February 12 (Sunday)

At Elmira, N.Y., the prison hospital was overflowing, and from 12 to 20 patients remained in their barracks, as no room was available in the hospital.

An increase in sickness was caused by the arrival of prisoners from the battle for Ft. Fisher, fought the previous month. More than half of these prisoners were sick when they arrived. The prison doctors were trying to cope.

Federal prisoners began shuffling around the South in increasing numbers because of the advance of Sherman into South Carolina. Today, telegrams were sent to direct the movement of 10,000 prisoners at Florence, S.C., towards Wilmington, N.C., with a view to exchange them at that point. In addition, it was directed that Charlotte, N.C., be prepared to receive 1800 officer prisoners from Columbia, S.C.

Brig. Gen. Bradley T. Johnson, commanding the prison at Salisbury, N.C., reported that "It is impossible to subsist any larger number of prisoners than are at this post." He also notified Brig. Gen. Martin, CSA, in Raleigh, N.C., that a large number of Confederate deserters were gathering to the west of Salisbury, in the area of Yadkin, for an attack on Salisbury. The western part of North Carolina, always a collecting ground for Union supporters, was becoming more bold as the power of the South ebbed.

Col. H. Forno, commanding the prisoners at Columbia, S.C., had 1200 officer prisoners camped in the State Asylum and was interested in removing them because of Sherman's rapid approach on the city. Gen. Beauregard wanted the prisoners at Florence, S.C., removed to Andersonville, Ga., but Forno had no men to guard them. A new prison being built at Killian Mills, 11 miles north of Columbia, was being rushed to completion to contain the prisoners at Florence and Columbia. It would never be finished.

In South Carolina, captured U.S. Colored troops were being used to construct a new prison camp, called Camp Maxcy Gregg. Today, Col. Forno ordered work to cease on the stockade. Maj. Gen. Wade Hampton would receive the impressed Negroes from the local plantations for use elsewhere. The "Yankee" Negroes were to be put to work getting wood to the railroad for use at that point. All tools and equipment not needed would be turned over to Wade Hampton's officers.

### February 13 (Monday)

A major problem for some time had been the handling of Confederate prisoners who did not desire to be paroled and returned South. Many had publicly stated the desire to take the oath of allegiance and be discharged from prison. This would present problems of where to send them. Obviously, they could not just be turned loose in the North. How would they live? For the time being, they would remain incarcerated.

At Hilton Head, S.C., the commander of the Union forces requested permission to return to the North 495 prisoners previously sent to that location to be placed under fire of Confederate guns.

Lt. Col. John F. Iverson, commanding the prison at Florence, S.C., reported he had 7000 prisoners, 3000 of whom were sick, but not sufficient guards to move them. Rations were short, no meat at all.

Abbott, A.O., 1st Lt., 1st N.Y. Dragoons, prisoner in the State Asylum, Columbia, S.C.:

> The month of February was full of rumors to us. Upon every breeze was borne tidings of an "exchange" soon to take place....
>
> Our hopes were still farther heightened on the 13th of February, when an order came for 600 to be ready to move to Charlotte, North Carolina, with the assurance that we would remain there but a few days, and then be sent to Richmond. We also learned from the faithful negro that Sherman was approaching Columbia, and it was unsafe to keep us longer there. "The old story," said we, as we packed up, meanwhile making our arrangements to escape from the train on its way to Charlotte.

### February 14 (Tuesday)

Brig. Gen. William Hoffman, Federal Commissary-General of Prisoners, recommended to Grant, at City Point, Va., that the 600 prisoners held at Hilton Head, S.C., be exchanged rather than being sent north. Grant, in reply, indicated that he had already given directions to Maj. Gen. J.G. Foster at Hilton Head on the 5th of February to accomplish this very thing.

At Charleston, S.C., Gen. Beauregard suggested that the prisoners at Florence, S.C., be sent to Wilmington, N.C., on parole, "thus relieving us and embarrassing the enemy." The CSA Adjutant-General's office directed that prisoners be sent to the vicinity of Wilmington in anticipation of exchange.

Col. Forno, at Columbia, directed that the prisoners at Florence be sent to Abbeville, S.C. Forno was to send the officer prisoners at Columbia to Charlotte, N.C., today. The entire movement of prisoners to safety was muddled and chaos reigned.

Abbott, A.O., 1st Lt., 1st N.Y. Dragoons, prisoner, to Charlotte, N.C.:

We left Asylum Prison-yard the 14th of February, bag and baggage, making about the appearance we usually did when we moved. Soon after we reached the cars it began to rain, turned cold, the rain became sleet, making the trip decidedly uncomfortable. We were stowed in boxcars, as usual, forty together. Many of the guards, who attempted to ride outside by order of Maj. Griswold, nearly perished, and were finally obliged to come inside. The cars were old and rickety, and during the night two of them broke down and had to be abandoned. Once the train broke, leaving six of the cars on the track, while the locomotive ran off to the station, five miles distant, before the accident was discovered by the engineer. It was nearly time for an up express. We had no tail-lights, or anything to show we were in the way, and it was only by threatening to leave the train *en masse* that we could persuade them to build a fire on the track to warn trains of danger. Fortunately, the "runaway" came back in time....

As the night was so bad, many who had determined to escape were deterred. Such a storm I have seldom seen. It was almost impossible to live out in the woods, as one escaping would be obliged to. Yet some braved it, the majority only to be recaptured after several days and nights of starvation and travel.

Lt. Col. H.A.M. Henderson, former commander of the Cahaba prison in Alabama, began negotiations at Vicksburg for the exchange of the prisoners immediately. Working with his Federal counterpart, Col. A.C. Fisk, the two devised a means of paroling the prisoners at Vicksburg, both North and South, and placing them into separate camps where they could be fed and controlled until finally released. Their plan, once submitted, was approved quickly and put into effect. The camps for the parolees were established at Four-Mile Bridge, east of Vicksburg.

## February 15 (Wednesday)

Surgeon Henry Palmer, Medical Inspector, Baltimore, Md., notified Surgeon J. Simpson, Medical Director, Baltimore, of his inspection of the Confederate prisoners who had just arrived from the Elmira, N.Y., prison camp. He found that 19 were unable to continue on their exchange journey. Eighteen were sent to the West Hospital and one to the smallpox ward. Three bodies of prisoners who had died en route, due to chronic diarrhea, were sent to the National Hospital for burial. Palmer suggested that proper screening of the prisoners had not been done prior to their departure from Elmira.

This incident led to several days of correspondence between Brig. Gen. Hoffman, Federal Commissary-General of Prisoners, the Medical Director at Baltimore, and the commander of the prison at Elmira. The result was a report by Col. B.F. Tracy, at Elmira, on the condition of the travel:

The train left Elmira at 5 P.M. February 13 and reached Baltimore, via Northern Central Railroad, at 10 A.M. February 15, after many delays. During the night of February 14 neither water nor lights were provided for any car upon the train, as required by the terms of the contract, and three of the prisoners died from the continued exposure. The train consisted of seventeen cars, with only one brakeman for the entire number, to which ten or more cattle cars were added when the train left Williamsport.... I would beg leave to call attention to the indifference of the officials of the Northern Central Railroad, who paid not the least attention to repeated applications for lights for the cars, which I was finally compelled to purchase myself. Neither did they supply any water or fuel after the train left Elmira.

Col. Tracy further pointed out that it took a pretty strong man to survive a railroad journey of forty-one hours in winter weather without heat, light, or water.

Abbott, A.O., 1st Lt., 1st N.Y. Dragoons, prisoner, Charlotte, N.C.:

We arrived at Charlotte, N.C., at four o'clock on the afternoon of the 15th, and, disembarking in the mud and water, marched three-quarters of a mile to a little pine grove, which was called by some "Camp Necessity," by others "Camp Bacon," for here we received the first meat we had had in over one hundred thirty days....

Here we had a few old "A" tents for shelter, otherwise there was not the least convenience or preparation for our comfort.... The ground was soft and wet, and the water we drank was obtained from an old goose-pond. We had been there but a little while when Capt. Stewart (in whose charge we now were, and he was a gentleman) informed us that we would not stay there long, for he had just received a communication from Col. Hoke, commandant of the post, stating that he had received a dispatch from Richmond saying that the terms of a "general exchange" had been agreed upon, and it would commence in a few days...

### February 16 (Thursday)

The problem of Confederate prisoners not wanting to be exchanged and to stay in the Federal prisons until the end of the war took on a new twist today. Lt. Gen. Grant, at City Point, Va., notified Maj. Gen. E.A. Hitchcock:

I see it stated in the papers that there were some prisoners in the West were paraded to be sent forward for exchange; those who preferred Northern prisons to a return to rebel service were invited to step to the front. I think this is wrong. Those who do not wish to go back are the ones whom it is most desirable to exchange. If they do not wish to serve in the rebel army they can return to us after exchange and avoid it.

A general exchange of prisoners had finally been agreed to by all parties and Gen. Cooper, Adjutant-General, CSA, notified the commanders of the prisons at Florence, S.C., and Charlotte and Salisbury, N.C., that the prisoners in their care could be so informed.

Abbott, A.O., 1st Lt., 1st N.Y. Dragoons, prisoner, Charlotte, N.C.:

The day following Col. Hoke himself rode down to our camp, and had an interview with our senior officer, Col. Shedd, 30th Illinois, in which he reiterated all he had written to Capt. Stewart.... Another thing that added weight to all this was the fact that the Rebel guard that surrounded us was totally inefficient and terribly demoralized, yet no effort was made to increase its efficiency.... Officers could and did escape both day and night while we were there.... We were

joined here by those left at Columbia, so that we were all together again.

### February 17 (Friday)

The prisoners at Florence, S.C., had been jerked around like yo-yos for some time. At last, they were to be sent to Wilmington, N.C., for exchange.

In a rather belated report, Inspector T.A. Hall from Richmond sent information on his inspection of the prison at Salisbury, N.C., to Adjutant-General Samuel Cooper. Although the report covered a lot of background material, a significant item covered was the lack of hospital facilities at the site and the number of deaths among the prisoners.

The excessive rate of mortality among the prisoners, as shown by the prison returns herewith forwarded, merits attention. Out of 10,321 prisoners of war received since October 5, 1864, according to the surgeon's report, 2918 have died. According to the burial report, since the 21st of October, 1864, a less period by sixteen days, 3479 have been buried. The discrepancy is explained by the fact that in addition to the deaths in hospital, six or eight die daily in their quarters without the knowledge of the surgeons, and of course without receiving attention from them. This discrepancy, which in December amounted to 223, and in January to 192, in the first two weeks of February had diminished to 21. The actual number of deaths, however, outside of hospital during that period would show probably little falling off, if any, from the number in previous months. Pneumonia and diseases of the bowels are the prevalent diseases. The prisoners appear to die, however, more from exposure and exhaustion than from actual disease.

In Washington, Maj. Gen. Halleck wrote Lt. Gen. Grant at City Point, Va., of Secy. of War Stanton's concerns about the equipping of the Confederate prisoners with blankets, clothing, etc. Stanton, ever the worrywart, was prone to see bad behind everything that transpired.

It will be seen ... that all the proceeds of the rebel cotton are devoted to supplying the rebel prisoners with new clothing, shoes, and blankets. Not a cent is expended for provisions. The result is that we feed their prisoners and permit the rebel Government to send cotton within our lines, free of all charge, to purchase and carry back the means of fitting out their own men in the field. Under these circumstances the Secretary of War is not disposed to sanction the admission of any more cotton on the same terms.

The provisions for a general exchange of prisoners moved apace. Brig. Gen. Wm. Hoffman, Federal Commissary-General of Prisoners, today notified the commander of the prison at Ft. Delaware to begin planning for the movement of prisoners to Point Lookout, Md., on short notice. No prisoner who did not wish to be exchanged would be included, nor any held as guerrillas.

## February 18 (Saturday)

This was to be the day for the execution of John Yates Beall at Ft. Columbus, Governor's Island. Due to a technical snag in the wording of the order, the hanging was postponed until the 24th. Meanwhile, Beall's friends were attempting to get a stay of execution from President Lincoln.

In reply to Gen. Halleck's message of the day before, February 18, about the equipping of Confederate prisoners with blankets and clothing, Grant today replied:

The arrangement for the relief of prisoners of war was made at a time when exchange could not be made, and under it I see no way to prevent rebel prisoners from being clothed. Having, however, a very large excess of prisoners over the enemy, we can in making exchanges select those who have not been furnished with new clothing or blankets. By this means but a very limited number of rebel soldiers will be returned with new uniforms.

Should it become necessary prisoners for exchange can be required to turn their blankets over to their comrades who remain.

## February 19 (Sunday)

Abbott, A.O., 1st Lt., 1st N.Y. Dragoons, prisoner, Charlotte to Goldsboro', N.C.:

On Sunday the 19th, an order for 200 to leave at 5 P.M., which they did in good spirits, arriving the next morning at Greensboro'.

## February 20 (Monday)

Abbott, A.O., 1st Lt., 1st N.Y. Dragoons, prisoner, Charlotte to Goldsboro', N.C.:

200 others left the next morning, passed the first detachment at Greensboro' and went on towards Raleigh, the capital of the state. Passed it in the night and arrived at Goldsboro' the next morning at four o'clock.

## February 21 (Tuesday)

Within the Confederacy, the movement of prisoners for exchange was building rapidly. Unfortunately, the information was not reaching the Union forces who were to receive the prisoners rapidly enough. On this day, Maj. Gen. John M. Schofield, commanding the Union forces near Wilmington, N.C., wrote Maj. Gen. R.F. Hoke, in Wilmington, that:

General: I have the honor to acknowledge the receipt of your communication of the 19th instant, proposing to deliver to me 2500 prisoners which have been set apart for exchange at Wilmington. I presume this proposition is based upon some new arrangement for the exchange of prisoners of which I have not been officially informed. Please inform me on what terms you propose to deliver the prisoners.

This action on the part of Schofield created much consternation among the Confederate command in Richmond and North Carolina. Orders, and counterorders, were issued to send, not to send, go-ahead-and-send, stop all movement, etc. from nearly everyone. The Southern commanders, especially Gen. Hoke at Wilmington, believed that Schofield was using this proximity to the prisoners as a means to recapture them and was pushing his operations into the interior.

The whole problem was that Schofield had not yet received the orders from Grant to accept the prisoners. All his orders had been to move by steamer from Ft. Monroe to Ft. Fisher. No telegraph wires were available. The problem would be solved the next day.

Abbott, A.O., 1st Lt., 1st N.Y. Dragoons, prisoner, Goldsboro', N.C.:

We at once disembarked, and built some little fires as best we could, and waited for morning, to see what would "turn up." Soon it came, and with it a train of 700 of our starved prisoners from Florence and Salisbury. They had been sent forward to Wilmington for exchange, but Gen. Foster, who was conducting the campaign there, had had no orders from Gen. Grant to receive prisoners at that point, and hence he refused to entertain the flag of truce the Rebels sent out to him.... Hence they were obliged to come back to Goldsboro' again, and await further orders.

I wish it were in my power to portray on this page the scene of suffering that met us as those men attempted to get off the train. They had ridden all night in open flatcars, without a particle of shelter or fire. It was in February, and a bitter cold, damp night, and, scantily clothed as they were, they had suffered beyond account. Three had died during the night, and were still on the train. Not one of them had a whole garment on, while nearly all were destitute of shirts or coats. A ragged or patched pair of pants, and a piece of an old blanket, constituted the wardrobe of the majority. Their faces were blackened by the pitch-pine smoke from the fires over which they had cooked their rations, while traces of soap and water were lost altogether. Hair and beard in their natural state. Yet all of this was nothing compared to their diseased, starving condition. In short, no words can describe their appearance. The sunken eye, the gaping mouth, the filthy skin, the clothes and head alive with vermin, the repelling bony contour, all conspired to lead to the conclusion that they were the victims of starvation, cruelty, and exposure to a degree unparalleled in the history of humanity. Many of them were unable to walk, or stand even, and would fall upon their knees as soon as they touched the ground. They informed us they had had nothing to eat for twenty-four hours, and were suffering from both hunger and thirst. We gathered everything we had with us that was eatable or wearable, and attempted to take it to them, when the guards presented their bayonets to us, with orders to have no communication with them whatever. Doubling clothes and rations into one bundle, we pitched them over the guards' heads, and oh! such a sight. Never were dogs more ravenous for a bone than were those poor boys for something to eat and wear.... As a specimen, I pulled off an old hospital gown, and threw it to one poor fellow who had neither coat, vest or shirt. As it struck his bare back, he turned around and picked it up. "Put it on," said I. He looked at me with a demented stare, when I repeated the command. He hugged it to his naked breast, and was moving off, when I called to him again to "put it on." He

seemed to realize for the moment that it was something to wear, when he made one or two feeble efforts to get his arms through one of the sleeves; but his mind seemed to wander again, and, hugging it as before, he marched off....

They soon marched them off out of our sight, and the commandant of the post issued an order that none of the citizens should visit them, or minister in any way to their comfort. *Three others died* in attempting to go two hundred rods, while more than twenty were obliged to fall out from exhaustion; and these they told us were the *well* ones....

As they were marching off, Lt. Powell, of South Carolina, who had them in charge, turned to several of us officers and remarked, "They have generally been well treated and well fed, but for a few days past they have had rather a hard time of it."... He *lied*, and he knew it....

Orders were finally received, and at eight o'clock we left for Greensboro' and Richmond, to go through the lines on the James River; but, on arriving at Raleigh again, we were sent by a down train, containing Capt. Hatch, who was on his way to Wilmington with a special order from Gen. Grant to Gen. Foster to receive us at that point, or one near there that might be agreed upon.

### February 22 (Wednesday)

Today, Lt. Gen. U.S. Grant got through to Maj. Gen. John M. Schofield at Ft. Fisher, N.C., with the instructions to receive the prisoners:

Gen. Lee reports to me today that you refused to receive our prisoners sent by him to Wilmington for exchange. I informed him in reply that you had not probably received my directions at that date. You will please receive all prisoners that the rebels may have to deliver to you and forward them to Annapolis. They were sent to Wilmington by special agreement, and should they fall into our hands by the fortunes of war, we should still be honor bound to regard them as delivered to us by the enemy.

Grant, at 7:30 P.M., also notified Brig. Gen. W. Hoffman, Federal Commissary-General of Prisoners, that approximately 15,000 prisoners would be returning in the next six days. The prisoners had been held in Virginia, North Carolina, and South Carolina.

Abbott, A.O., 1st Lt., 1st N.Y. Dragoons, prisoner, en route to Wilmington, N.C.:

We remained on the train till daylight, when we discovered a large proportion of those we had left at Charlotte bivouacked on the bank near us, and during the day the rest of them arrived. We found that about half of those left at Charlotte had been paroled preparatory to exchange, and this day and part of the following was spent in making out our papers.

### February 24 (Friday)

At Ft. Columbus, Governor's Island, N.Y., John Yates Beall was hanged on this date for treason, guerrilla warfare, and being a spy. His last letter was to his brother in Virginia:

Dear Will: Ere this reaches you you will have most probably heard of my death through the newspapers, that I was tried by a military commission and hung by the enemy, and hung, I assert, unjustly. It is both useless and wrong to repine over the past. Hanging, it was asserted, was ignominious, but crime only can make dishonor. "Vengeance is mine, saith the Lord, and I will repay," therefore, do not show unkindness to the prisoners, they are helpless. Remember me kindly to my friends. Say to them I am not aware of committing any crime against society. I die for my country. No thirst for blood or lucre animated me in my course, for I had refused, when solicited, to engage in enterprises which I deemed not only destructive, but illegitimate. And but a few months ago I had but to have spoken and I would have been red with the blood and rich with the plunder of the foe. But my hands are clear of blood, unless it be spilt in conflict, and not a cent enriches my pocket. Should you be spared through the strife, stay with mother and be a comfort to her old age. In my trunk you can get plenty of old clothes. Give my love to mother and the girls, too. May God bless you all now and evermore is my prayer and wish for you.

John Yates Beall's body was removed to his family home in Jefferson County, W.Va., after the war and reinterred. His tombstone reads: "Died in the Service and Defense of his Country."

### February 26 (Sunday)

Confederate prisoners arrived at Varina, Va., and were exchanged for Federal prisoners. The problem of moving these prisoners from Varina to Richmond in an expeditious manner had yet to be solved. The Adjutant-General of the CSA, Samuel Cooper, directed Lt. Gen. Richard S. Ewell, CSA, commanding the Richmond area:

General: It has been represented to the Secretary of War that the prisoners received on yesterday from the U.S. authorities are greatly scattered between the city and Varina, and undergoing much suffering from sickness and other causes, if not neglect. He therefore directs that you will immediately detail a competent energetic officer to inquire into the matter and ascertain the causes of this state of things. He will also ascertain their wants, have them relieved, and superintend their transportation to Richmond. When this is done he will make a full report of this inspection through you to this office without delay.

At Andersonville, Ga., Capt. Henry Wirz, commanding the prison, wrote a letter to his headquarters outlining a problem concerning shoes:

Sir:... There are a large number of paroled prisoners of war who are doing work for the Government which if not done by them would have to be done by impressment or other hire and thus be a heavy expense to the Government. These men are, almost without exception, barefooted, having been so long at work that what shoes they had are entirely worn out. I wish to know if I cannot be authorized to make a requisition on the Quartermaster's Department to supply their wants in this line, or else buy the leather through the quartermaster and have the shoes made, as there are plenty of shoemakers among the prisoners.

### February 27 (Monday)

At Mobile, Ala., Maj. Gen. Dabney H. Maury, CSA, commanding the district, wrote Maj. Gen. G. Granger, USA, at Ft. Gaines, Ala., that he would be happy to transport the proffered clothing to the prison at Cahaba, Ala., for use by the Federal prisoners. However, these prisoners were in the process of being exchanged and the clothing might not arrive before they left. From all records, the clothing was held at Ft. Gaines and the prisoners were sent to Vicksburg for exchange in their old clothes.

Abbott, A.O., 1st Lt., 1st N.Y. Dragoons, prisoner, en route to Wilmington, N.C.:

We remained here till Monday afternoon, when a train came up and took 300, and at 9 P.M. 570 more of us got on and into eight boxcars, while the balance came on the next day. At this time, I believe, there were no complaints about being crowded or of poor accommodations.

At 11:30 we found ourselves again at Goldsboro', and we camped one and a half miles from the city, on the Weldon Road, with the promise that we should go on at eight o'clock.

Acting Volunteer Lt. Frederick Crocker, USN, had been trying to get a number of captured naval personnel currently held at Camp Ford, Tex., exchanged, with little result. A part of the problem was that some of these naval personnel were free Negroes and the South did not recognize this status, treating all captured Negroes as recaptured slaves. Crocker explains:

In a conversation with Col. Szymanski I called his attention to a letter written by Gen. Lee to Gen. Grant in answer to one addressed him by Gen. Butler, which said that free negroes in our service were, when captured, to be treated as prisoners of war. Col. Szymanski denied ever having seen any such letter, and assured me that if he was furnished with an official copy of it he would at once treat all free negroes now prisoners in the Trans-Mississippi Department as prisoners of war. I therefore respectfully request that the necessary steps may be taken to furnish him the official copy he requests in order that the free negroes captured on the *Clifton, Sachem, Morning Light*, and ram *Queen of the West*, and now held to labor, may be treated as prisoners of war. I furnish herewith a partial list of free negroes captured on the above vessels, and have reason to believe that there are still more, besides contrabands whose names I have been unable to learn.

The three men captured on the *Queen of the West* are now at work on the steamboat *Doubloon*, at Shreveport, La.

### February 28 (Tuesday)

February was a momentous month for Sgt. Malone of the 6th N.C. Infantry. The prisoner exchange was activated after a long hiatus and the population of Point Lookout, Md., was being depleted. On the 4th, the Federal government decided that all prisoners from Kentucky, Missouri, Louisiana, Tennessee, and Arkansas would be paroled and returned to the Confederacy. The release extended through the 6th of the month. On the 17th, those who were captured at Gettysburg were paroled and left for the South on the 18th.

Sgt. Malone was paroled on the 21st and placed in a parole camp awaiting shipment. On the 24th, Malone boarded the steamer *George Leary* and departed for Ft. Monroe, Va., arriving there about dark. On the 25th they were further transported to the exchange point at Aiken's Landing and marched from there to Richmond, where they were housed at Camp Lee. On the 27th they were transferred to Camp Winder near Richmond for processing.

Abbott, A.O., 1st Lt., 1st N.Y. Dragoons, prisoner, en route to Wilmington, N.C.:

However, as we expected, we staid till the next day at 5 P.M. There was also a camp of enlisted men about a mile from us, and they were suffering all it was possible for them to suffer and live. Many of them *did not live*. Some of the "ladies," God bless them, loyal women of North Carolina, heard of the sufferings of these poor men, and, regardless of the "order" of the commandant of the post, *visited* them, ministering to their wants as best they could. Some of them came eight miles on foot, through the mud and wet. And one old lady and her two daughters (a Mrs. Scott, of Wilson County, Black Creek District, N.C.) came in an ox cart, twenty miles, to do what they could. I was able to obtain only the names of the following. There were others; let them be remembered by every patriot, for they were liable to arrest at the time they were there. Mary Ann Peacock, Goldsboro', N.C.; Mary Starling, Mary A. Worrel, Rachel Worrel, Hepsey Jackson, Martha Sicer, Pikeville, N.C. It may be truly said of them, as of one of old, "They have done what they could."

While here we received a magnificent donation of a wagon load of provisions from Snow Hill, North Carolina. Before it was unloaded, all said, "Send it to the enlisted men," and there it went, with a contribution of $470 from the officers with it. I would also mention that several gentlemen at Raleigh remembered us kindly in the shape of provisions, and prominent among them was Gov. Holden. We left Goldsboro' at 6 P.M., crowded, piled, jammed on the train, inside and out, and, amid songs and cheers, started for Wilmington, which was now in our possession.

## March 1 (Wednesday)

The Confederate prison at Cahaba, Ala., located at the conflux of the Cahaba and Alabama rivers, began flooding during the afternoon on this date. The water came up slowly at first, but by midnight it was several feet deep over the prison area. The Federal prisoners, now about 3000 in number, climbed upon the bunks to escape the water, several of those wooden structures collapsing under the weight.

Abbott, A.O., 1st Lt., 1st N.Y. Dragoons, paroled, Wilmington, N.C.:

Rode all night, and daylight found us standing on the track, three miles from Northeast Bridge, fourteen miles from Wilmington. This place, we found, was the outpost picket line of the Rebels. At eight o'clock down came Col. Hatch (late captain) on a special train, with a white flag flying from the engine. As he ran on to a switch, we backed up and passed him, giving him one of our good loyal Union songs. He then took the lead, and we followed. All this certainly looked like exchange. As we neared the bridge our expectations began to rise, and each one was looking ahead to catch a sight, as soon as possible, of something that was not "Rebel." "Three cheers for Col. Mulford and the boys in blue," said one, and we gave them with a will. As the train came to a stand, all seemed impressed with the idea that we must be silent, or the spell would be broken. We now disembarked, and, forming in line, were counted through the ranks of our soldiers (the escort being about twenty), they presenting arms to us.

No doubt it would have been an interesting sight to our friends (it was to us) to see us march through, ragged, destitute, hungry, lean, and gaunt, yet feeling well, I assure you.

As soon as one passed the line of the soldiers he would start on a "double-quick" down the road, swinging his piece of a hat (if he had one), and cheer most lustily. About a quarter of a mile out they stopped us, to form for marching. Here the scene that took place beggars description. We laughed, cried, hurrahed, hugged, kissed, rolled in the sand, and—rejoiced generally. Many declared it was the happiest day of their lives. Up to this point we had transported all our baggage, and now you could see it "high in air," or lying around promiscuously; ration-bags of cornmeal, pots, pails, pans, kettles, pieces of old blankets—all went, and glad were we to leave them, too. This was the first time we had seen plenty of cornmeal since captured. We also cheered for Gen. Grant, Sherman, Lincoln, Johnson, and General Exchange, all voting that the latter personage was the "biggest general" of the whole.

After a little delay, which was necessary to count all through, we started for Cape Fear River, where our forces were encamped. A mile and a half brought us, for the first time, in sight of our flag. As soon as the head of the column came in sight of it, it began to cheer, which ran down its whole length.

The 6th Connecticut was encamped on the bank of the river, and at the end of the pontoon bridge they had erected a bower of evergreens. In the centre of the arch was a card, surrounded by a beautiful wreath of evergreens, on which was printed

### WELCOME, BROTHERS

From the centre of this arch were flung out the national colors, while their band played

"Hail to the chief who in triumph advances."

Cheer followed cheer, and shout followed shout, till we reached the river. This we crossed in silence, and passed the flags with uncovered heads—many in tears, while not a few stepped out of the ranks and kissed the sacred emblem of freedom—a blessed privilege they had not enjoyed for many long months.

As we reached the top of the hill, we found the whole division turned out with sidearms to meet us, and they gave us a hearty welcome. We were marched to a pine grove, where we were served with hard bread, cold boiled fresh beef, and coffee. Our friends can judge what we did with it, for it was a full meal, the *first* for a long time. Dinner, or rather breakfast over, we ... started to march to Wilmington—nine miles; and such marching! We made it in less than three hours, for each walked as though he feared to be behind, lest he should be "gobbled" by some stray Rebel. As we arrived at Wilmington we were taken to a "retreat," supplied with supper, and allowed the freedom of the city.

In Washington, Brig. Gen. William Hoffman, Federal Commissary-General of Prisoners, sent the following message to the commanders of the prisons at Ft. Delaware, Elmira, Camp Chase, Camp Morton, Rock Island, and Camp Douglas:

> The transfer of prisoners to City Point will be resumed, as directed in my telegram of the 23d. Send an ordinary roll to this office on the departure of each party. Guerrillas will not be forwarded until further notice, nor any who are bad characters. Reply.

At Ship Island, Miss., Col. Ernest W. Holmstedt, commanding the prison, reported that the tents now occupied by the prisoners were so rotten that a high wind tears them down by the dozen. He requested that prison funds be used for building wooden barracks. On March 28, Holmstedt was mildly reprimanded for not following directions for requesting lumber to build the barracks—the rebuke intimated that much time had been lost through his negligence. On April 18, he replied that he had done what was necessary as far back as November 24, 1864, in submitting his plans, but was told to wait. One bureaucracy is as bad as another. In any event, the prisoners were out in the weather when the tents came down.

### March 2 (Thursday)

The water flooding the Confederate prison at Cahaba, Ala., had not relented. By morning several of the prisoners requested an audience with the prison commander, Lt. Col. Jones, to see if they could move to higher ground. The Colonel refused, believing that the prisoners might try to escape if released from the stockade. The prisoners would remain inside for two more days existing on hardtack that the guards supplied. No fires were possible and many of the men were without shoes or jackets, which resulted in many of the prisoners becoming ill from exposure. In addition, the water flooded the latrine facility and overflowed, spilling the contents into the prison compound.

Abbott, A.O., 1st Lt., 1st N.Y. Dragoons, paroled, Wilmington, N.C.:

> The next day we embarked on board a steamer for Annapolis, which place we reached after five days and a *comfortable* amount of seasickness. Here we were

promptly met by officers who did all they could for us, prominent among whom was our old friend Uncle Sam. If we had ever supposed he had forgotten us in our imprisonment, these fears were dispelled upon our arrival here. We quickly obtained new outfits, and, after a few days, received a "leave of absence" for thirty days…

A.O. Abbott had kept a journal during his confinement by the Confederate government and in 1866 published his account of prison life. No information is available on his life after the war.

### March 3 (Friday)

To alleviate the hardship of the flooding at Cahaba, Ala., Lt. Col. Jones, the camp commander, sent about 700 prisoners to Selma, Ala., for further transportation eastward. There remained about 2300 at Cahaba.

### March 4 (Saturday)

In Richmond, Va., Special Orders, No. 53, dated this date, dashed the hopes of the returning Confederate prisoners of war of getting a furlough home before reporting to their regiments. The South was in desperate straits on manpower and every gun was needed.

> XXIX. All furloughs granted under Special Orders, No. 46, Adjutant and Inspector General's Office, current series, to enlisted men who are … declared exchanged are hereby revoked, and all enlisted men who are exchanged will at once report for duty, those whose commands are beyond the North Carolina line selecting companies temporarily, in accordance with special orders referred to. Commissioned officers exchanged will report to their respective commands without delay.

A real blow to a prisoner who had not been home for months, or even years. This move did not do much for the morale of the troops.

### March 5 (Sunday)

Three days previously Sgt. Bartlett Y. Malone received his furlough. The following day, the 3rd, he was paid off—$237.00 in Confederate money. He went to the railroad depot and left Richmond about 6 P.M., arriving at Barksdale, N.C., about 10 A.M.

the following day. Today, after breakfast with a Mr. Maxtons, he arrived home about 1 P.M. Sgt. Bartlett Yancey Malone's wandering was done.

Sgt. Malone married Mary Frances Compton on November 15, 1866. Together they raised a family of ten children on the farm at Hyco Creek, Corbett, N.C. He died on May 4, 1890, of tuberculosis.

## March 10 (Friday)

Col. H. Forno, former commander of prisoners in South Carolina (his charges having been exchanged), wrote from Goldsborough, N.C., to Confederate Brig. Gen. Gardner:

I have the honor to transmit herewith a report of the removal of the prisoners of war from Columbia and Charlotte, N.C., to Magnolia, N.C., for exchange.

I should, I feel, be derelict to duty were I in doing this to pass unnoticed the condition of the "Fair Grounds Hospital" at Goldsborough, in which about 360 of the sick prisoners were temporarily placed, and which from neglect, filth, and squalor presented a sight which for misery I have rarely seen equaled. This establishment was nominally in charge of Surgeon Holt, but I was unable to learn that he ever visited it in person. Having no control over the officers in charge, and only learning that such a hospital existed the day prior to that on which the patients were removed from it for exchange, I was unable to apply any corrective to the state of affairs that I felt disgraced our character for humanity.

## March 14 (Tuesday)

The agreement reached at Vicksburg for the prisoner exchange finally bore fruit at the Confederate prison at Cahaba, Ala. Lt. Col. Jones informed the prisoners that they were being freed on parole. The first Federals to be moved were the sick who were able to travel. From that time, the boats plied the Alabama River daily, removing the prisoners as fast as possible. Many of the prisoners were taken upstream to Selma, Ala., where they were transferred to railcars for transport to Vicksburg. Others went down on the Alabama River to the junction of the Tombigbee River and then headed north to McDowell's Bluff and via railroad to Meridian, Miss., and then to Vicksburg.

## March 15 (Wednesday)

Adjutant-Gen. Samuel Cooper, CSA, wanted the prison facility at Salisbury, N.C., for use as an ordnance workshop, but some Federal prisoners were still there. Cooper inquired of Gen. Gardner if the prisoners could be removed to Danville, Va., to vacate the prison buildings.

## March 16 (Thursday)

Maj. Gen. Howell Cobb, at his headquarters in Macon, Ga., notified Maj. Gen. Grover, USA, in Savannah, that he would deliver 5000 prisoners of war now held in Georgia to Doctortown on the Altamaha River, or some other convenient point, for exchange.

The commander of the prison at Elmira, N.Y., Col. B.F. Tracy, reported on the recent ordeal at that facility:

Relative to our embarrassment occasioned by the recent inundation of the Chemung River, and ... now submit more explicit detail of the case. The rapid rise of the stream on the night of the 16th instant made it clear that the low flat upon which the smallpox ward was located would be whelmed and the fence swept away. Although I felt that the ward would not be carried away, still, as it was obvious that the freshet was to be an extraordinary one, it would not do to imperil between 200 and 300 lives. Rafts were accordingly built to convey this number from the part of the camp isolated by water from the camp proper, and the removal was accomplished without any casualty. They were placed in six old barracks on the highest ground of the camp. These barracks are very old and nearly useless, having been kept standing through the winter only by means of props and braces outside. Their destruction will now be necessary, as it would not be safe again to occupy them as barracks. In consequence of the great reduction of the camp it will not be necessary to erect new ones in their places. The river continued to rise until the entire camp, except about an acre, was flooded. It even crossed the road and flooded the camp of the Nineteenth Veteran Reserve Corps on the opposite side. We were compelled to remove the sick of the camp to the Nineteenth Veteran Reserve Corps barracks. This was accomplished with great promptness; with no escape of prisoners, and, what is still more remarkable, with but slightly increased loss of life. I immediately took measures to rebuild the fence. It will be completed in a few days. About 2700 feet were carried away. I shall sink the posts six feet and anchor them and build floodgates across the lowest part. There was no loss of buildings and none of stores, except a very small quantity stolen by prisoners during their removal. No prisoners can pass over the Northern Central Railroad, as we are at present advised, within less than two weeks.

## March 17 (Friday)

Jones, John B., Rebel War Clerk, Confederate War Dept., Richmond, Va.:

We shall have a negro army. Letters are pouring into the department from men of military skill and character, asking authority to raise companies, battalions, and regiments of negro troops. It is the desperate remedy for the very desperate case—and may be successful. If 300,000 efficient soldiers can be made of this material, there is no conjecturing where the next campaign may end. Possibly "over the border," for a little success will elate our spirits extravagantly; and the blackened ruins of our towns, and the moans of women and children bereft of shelter, will appeal strongly to the army for vengeance.

## March 18 (Saturday)

Brig. Gen. W.M. Gardner, commanding the prison at Salisbury, N.C., wired Adjutant-Gen. Samuel Cooper in Richmond that the remaining Federal prisoners would be removed within a few days and the facility could be used for ordnance shops.

## March 21 (Tuesday)

At City Point, Va., Grant asked Col. John Mulford for information on the delivery of Federal prisoners in the western theater. The only news Grant had came from the newspapers.

Mulford, at Varina, Va., replied that he had no information on the western theater but that he had sent agents to the various exchange points with full power to make the exchanges. He further stated:

I have been expecting our deliveries of Confederate prisoners at this point would fall off, but as yet there is no abatement. I would suggest that Gen. Hoffman be requested to limit the shipments for the pre-

sent to some 2000 or 3000 per week, at least until we learn what is being done at other points. Have you any information concerning the officers who were at Ft. Pulaski?

The last question from Mulford was in reference to the prisoners who had been held "under fire" as retaliation for the Federal prisoners held in Charleston. Their status had since been converted to that of normal prisoners. Grant replied to Mulford:

I do not know what has been done with the officers at Ft. Pulaski. I sent orders to have them delivered at Charleston. Before the order was received Charleston had fallen into our possession. I then sent orders to have them sent to the James River. Before that order was received Gen. Gillmore wrote to me that, having received my first order, which had been directed to Gen. Foster, he had sent a flag to find an enemy to deliver the prisoners to. I have heard nothing since.

At this point in the exchange process there were literally thousands of prisoners in transit, all of whom had to be accounted for when they left their prison and when they were physically exchanged. The amount of paperwork was staggering.

## March 22 (Wednesday)

In what certainly was a first for the Confederacy, the Negro units formed just weeks previously were to be paraded in front of the capitol. The Confederates who had died to this time were probably turning in their graves.

Jones, John B., Rebel War Clerk, Confederate War Dept., Richmond, Va.:

Today some of our negro troops will parade in the Capitol Square.

## March 23 (Thursday)

In a head count of prisoners exchanged up to March 22 (yesterday), Col. John E. Mulford reported:

Federals prisoners received at Savannah, Charleston, and the James River: 19,264

Confederate prisoners delivered to the same locations: 26,053

The movement of the Federal prisoners from Andersonville, Ga., and Cahaba, Ala., was slow due to transportation problems and the weather. Brig. Gen. M.L. Smith, USA, at Vicksburg, was concerned about the welfare of the prisoners in transit:

Col. Watts ... started them upon the receipt of a dispatch from Gen. Grant, furnished him by Gen. G.H. Thomas.... He says there are 9000 en route, including those already arrived. He don't claim anything under my contract, but claims under Gen. Grant's arrangement that the residue is to be held by the captors in their favor. He says he expects to hear every day of the delivery of prisoners to balance the lot, when he is willing to let these go. He says the camps at Andersonville and Cahaba are broken up and no rations there, and the suffering that will attend the turning of them back will be without a parallel. There being a gap between the Cahaba and Andersonville lots of about a week, we can hear from you in time to stop all that are now the other side of Jackson. It is my opinion, general, that at least one-fourth of them will die and be killed if they are turned back. They won't let them know they are to be turned back till they get force enough to shoot all who try to escape. The public service cannot suffer by keeping them here a few days.... I await your decision.

A joint resolution of the Legislature of the Commonwealth of Pennsylvania was approved on this date concerning the release of *civilian* prisoners taken by the Confederacy at Gettysburg, Pa., in July 1863. No mention was made of the reason for the capture and imprisonment. The resolution stated:

JOINT RESOLUTION of request to the Secretary of War to secure the release of certain unarmed citizens of this Commonwealth from rebel imprisonment.

Whereas, during the battle of Gettysburg certain unarmed citizens of this Commonwealth were captured by the rebel forces, taken to Richmond, and afterward sent to Salisbury, where they yet remain in close confinement in rebel prisons: Therefore,

*Resolved by the Senate and House of Representatives of the Commonwealth of Pennsylvania in General Assembly met,* That the Secretary of War be respectfully requested to use his utmost official exertions to secure the release of J. Crawford Gwinn, Alexander Harper, George Codori, William Harper, Samuel Sitzer, George Patterson, George Arendt, and Emanuel Trostle, and such other civil-

ians, citizens of Pennsylvania, as may now be in the hands of the rebel authorities, from rebel imprisonment and have them returned to their respective homes in Pennsylvania.

### March 24 (Friday)

Jones, John B., Rebel War Clerk, Confederate War Dept., Richmond, Va.:

There is a rumor of a great victory by Gen. Johnston in North Carolina, the taking of 4500 prisoners, 70 guns, etc.—merely a rumor, I am sure. On the contrary, I apprehend that we shall soon have news of the capture of Raleigh by Sherman. Should this be our fate, we shall soon have three or four different armies encompassing us.

### March 25 (Saturday)

At Marietta, Ohio, Mathias Fox, born at Muriella, Monroe Co., Ohio, aged 26, a farmer, being 6 feet tall, with black eyes, dark hair, and dark complexion, was enlisted in Co. D, 197th Ohio Volunteer Infantry, one-third of a bounty of $100.00 being paid at this time. He was mustered in on this date and sent to Camp Chase, near Columbus, Ohio, on March 28th.

### March 27 (Monday)

Many of the prisoners in Andersonville and Macon, Ga., were transferred by rail to the parolee camps at Vicksburg. Many were too weak to stand the journey, dying along the road. Confederate Col. N.G. Watts, commander of the area through which the prisoners were passing, notified his commander, Lt. Gen. Taylor, that he had agreed to have the Union send ambulances and surgeons into Confederate territory to collect the sick Federal prisoners and return them to Vicksburg. Watts notified Taylor in an "after the fact" message and asked for approval. Taylor immediately approved.

In Washington, Maj. Gen. E.A. Hitchcock was concerned about the number of prisoners arriving at Annapolis without muster rolls, since the accounting of the prisoners is important to maintain the "balance" of those exchanged on a man-for-man basis. Brig. Gen. William Hoffman, Federal Commissary-General of Prisoners, notified Lt. Gen.

Grant that since February 1, the Union had returned 24,200 prisoners, and 16,700 Union prisoners had arrived at Annapolis, a 7500 surplus for the Union, in their accounting.

### March 28 (Tuesday)

Pvt. Mathias Fox, with the rest of the recruits, arrived at Camp Chase, Ohio, on this date to begin his basic instruction to the life of a soldier. Gen. Robert E. Lee would surrender in Virginia in just a little over two weeks. Pvt. Fox's tour would be a short one. Fox would remain in Ohio until July 31, 1865, at which time he was mustered out at Camp Bradford. At this time he owed the Government $3.76 for equipment lost or destroyed. The government, however, still owed him $66.66, the remainder of his enlistment bounty.

Fox returned to Monroe Co., Ohio, to his farm. In the 1870s he would move to Wirt Co., W.Va.

### March 30 (Thursday)

With his world crashing around him, rations for Richmond and the troops around Petersburg were on Jones's mind. Again, distribution was the problem.

Jones, John B., Rebel War Clerk, Confederate War Dept., Richmond, Va.:

We have 2,000,000 bread rations in the depots in North Carolina.

### March 31 (Friday)

Capt. J. Louis Smith, of Gen. Samuel Cooper's staff, submitted a report this date concerning the accounting of prisoners during the recent movement and exchange. Capt. Smith reported that prior to the exchange being made, a total of 13,521 prisoners were present. Of these, 5149 were located at Salisbury, N.C., 7187 at Florence, S.C., and 1185 (all officers) at Columbia, S.C.

Subsequently, 2279 of the prisoners at Salisbury were sent to Richmond and 700 were left at Florence, S.C., as being too ill to transport. Between that and the 8684 exchanged at Northeast River, N.C., a deficiency exists of 1858 prisoners. He then deducted 125 who died in transit and added 30 who were recaptured, the net loss was 1703 on the movement.

Of the 1185 officers who were shipped from Columbia, only 1003 arrived at Goldsborough, N.C., 182 having escaped en route. An additional 11 escaped at Goldsborough. Twenty prisoners from Salisbury died en route.

Mass confusion seemed to be the order of the day on the route to exchange. Different gauges in the railroads required changes of stations at Goldsborough and Danville for those going to Richmond.

Capt. Smith continued his comments:

Complaint has been made of Lt. Snead, in charge of one of these detachments [sick prisoners], and of the assistant surgeons in charge of the sick....

Loud complaint has been made in Greensborough, N.C., by the officers of the post and prominent citizens to the inefficiency of the officers and the looseness of discipline exercised over the prisoners marched from Salisbury, N.C. Prisoners were allowed to straggle over the country and town, to purchase liquor, and to annoy the citizens. Col. John F. Hoke, commanding Fourth Regiment North Carolina State Reserves, was in command of the guard forces, and, in view of his responsibility, I have preferred charges against him, which I inclose with this report....

The inclosed reports of Col. H. Forno, commanding military prisons in South Carolina, and specially charged with the removal of prisoners from South Carolina, and of Maj. E. Griswold, assistant adjutant-general, commanding military prison, Columbia, are herewith filed. These reports show what difficulties were encountered in the removal of prisoners by the inefficiency of guards, imperfect transportation, and the confusion attending the proximity of the enemy.

From all the evidence I can gather,... it is apparent that Maj. Griswold is chargeable with inefficiency as an officer. The loss of some prisoners during the delay and darkness of the night at the depot at Columbia on the 14th of February was unavoidable, but no such excuse is admissible for the loss of thirty-eight officers by concealment in the prison roof. The fact that a detachment of 500 officers had already been sent off made the care and accountability for the reduced number so much less onerous. Again, at Charlotte a number made their escape—thirty going off in one body with two of the guard. I am officially informed by Col. Forno that at this point he was compelled to order Maj. Griswold three times out of his camp, the third time under threat of arrest. At Goldsborough, almost at the point of delivery, eleven more made their escape.

Lt. Col. John F. Iverson, Fourth Georgia, commanded the prison at Florence, and superintended the removal of prisoners from that point. An order from Lt. Gen. Hardee, received a few days before the removal of prisoners, to this officer to rejoin his command, has, I presume, prevented this officer from sending in a report.... I was officially informed by Col. Forno that a large loss of these prisoners occurred in the evacuation of Wilmington. It was found impossible to drive out the troops, numbers of these men, enfeebled by long imprisonment and crippled by scurvy and other diseases. This loss of prisoners is greatly to be deplored in view of the present exchange of man for man. My observation leads me to state that confusion and want of management have characterized the removal of prisoners on this occasion, but also the management of prisons during the war. The fact that 14,000 prisoners of war died at Andersonville alone, startling and shocking as it is, leads one to hope that, as a mere matter of policy, the Government will hereafter insist upon and enforce more system in the management of prisons…

Maj. E. Griswold, former commander of the prison at Columbia, S.C., and currently charged with inefficiency in handling of the prisoner transfer, explains the difficulties of moving the prisoners from Columbia to Charlotte, N.C. Having ordered a train to move the officer prisoners, Griswold formed them up and marched them to the depot through streets crowded with refugees fleeing Columbia in the darkness, only to find that a train was *not* available until 6 o'clock the following morning. In the confusion and darkness he had already lost nearly sixty prisoners. He continued his report:

It could not be prevented. My officers with myself went up and down the line constantly, but no guard, especially such as I had, could have prevented escapes on such an occasion and in such darkness. I regard the fact of being assured of transportation under the circumstances and failing to get it as most unwarrantable misinformation and recklessness.

I moved my prisoners back to their quarters and refused to bring them out again upon information of a train until the train I was to use was actual-

ly pointed out to me and put in my charge. At 11 o'clock on the 15th I got the balance of the prisoners upon the train and moved off. When within a mile of Winnsborough, at about 12 o'clock, we came into a drove of Government cattle, which had been left by the agent or persons in charge to roam and sleep on the railroad, the drivers having gone off to rest. The engine ran over and killed three cows and was thrown off the track and rendered utterly useless. We had to remain here until a new track was made around the wreck, and at about 2 o'clock the 16th we reached Winnsborough, there being then some five or six trains behind us. At Winnsborough the president of the road showed me a telegram from the road transportation agent, saying that it was understood a raid was then on its way to Winnsborough. He also suggested that it would be well for my train to go off on a sidetrack to allow lighter trains to pass. To this I utterly objected, stating politely and firmly that having a guard I must take possession of the road to get off these prisoners. Upon a representation of danger to the country if these prisoners were not got off, the president gave me the road. We arrived at Charlotte that night, the 16th, and went into camp, a most inadequate and unsafe place to keep them, being an old field, and with a small guard utterly worthless, so much so that notwithstanding every diligence and personal orders and urgency upon each relief as it went on guard, a sergeant and three men of the guard were bribed and went off in one night with thirty prisoners, and nightly they were escaping. I could not keep my own guard in quarters, not having enough men for a camp guard, and I could not punish one-half who deserved, because they were so few that they were doing double duty.

In the west, the Governor of Louisiana, now at Shreveport, wrote Col. Ig. Szymanski, the Confederate Agent for Exchange:

Sir: Learning that the C.S. prisoners have left Johnson's Island, I have the honor to request that you sell the fifty bales of cotton, placed in your custody for the benefit of Louisiana prisoners of war, in New Orleans for Federal currency, and retain in your hands the proceeds of the sales until you can ascertain where the Louisiana prisoners are now stationed and how the donation can be transmitted to them.

South of Petersburg, Va., the defenses of Richmond were unraveling rapidly. Union forces were expanding westward and actions were reported at Dinwiddie Court House and White Oak road.

### April 1 (Saturday)

The number of prisoners at Andersonville, Ga., had taken a steep drop with the shipments to Vicksburg. Capt. Henry Wirz, commanding at Andersonville, reported a beginning strength on March 1 of 5851, of whom 1378 were hospitalized. During the month, 118 prisoners died, 2 escaped, 1 was sent to another post, and 2553 were exchanged. On this date, Wirz had a total of 3319 prisoners, of whom 263 were hospitalized. The place must have seemed almost empty.

At Five Forks, Va., the Confederates had dug in around the road junction. In late afternoon, Sheridan's cavalry and infantry arrived and almost immediately went into battle. The fighting was intense, but brief. The Confederates were beaten and Petersburg was almost surrounded.

### April 2 (Sunday)

With Five Forks gone, Petersburg would fall rapidly. Lee sent word to President Davis to evacuate Richmond as soon as possible. Lee began to pull his troops out of the lines at Petersburg, and those lines were filled with Union troops. Lee moved to Amelia C.H., to the west. As Richmond was evacuated, military stores and other materials were set afire by the military officials. The fires soon got out of control and the Richmond riverfront was burning.

An eyewitness inside Richmond described the chaos:

Jones, John B., Rebel War Clerk, Confederate War Dept., Richmond, Va.:

No doubt our army sustained a serious blow yesterday; and Gen. Lee may not have troops sufficient to defend both the city and the Danville Road at the same time.

It is true! The enemy have broken through our lines and attained the South Side Road. Gen. Lee has dispatched the Secretary to have everything in readiness to *evacuate the city tonight*.... The Secretary of

War intends to leave at 8 P.M. this evening. The President and the rest of the functionaries, I suppose, will at the same time....

The negroes stand about mostly silent, as if wondering what will be their fate. They make no demonstrations of joy.

Several hundred prisoners were brought into the city this afternoon—captured yesterday. Why they were brought here I am a loss to conjecture.

### April 3 (Monday)

Early today the Federal cavalry moved into the streets of Richmond. The first Union flag was raised above the State House by Maj. Atherton H. Stevens, Jr., of Massachusetts. The infantry arrived shortly thereafter and the Mayor of Richmond surrendered the city at 8:15 A.M. to Maj. Gen. Godfrey Weitzel, USA. The troops immediately stacked arms and began to fight the fires raging along the riverfront.

Jones, John B., Rebel War Clerk, Confederate War Dept., Richmond, Va.:

Another clear and bright morning. It was a quiet night, with its million of stars. And yet how few could sleep, in anticipation of the entrance of the enemy!...

At dawn there were two tremendous explosions, seeming to startle the very earth, and crashing the glass throughout the western end of the city. One of these was the blowing up of the magazine, near the new almshouse—the other probably the destruction of an ironclad ram. But subsequently there were others. I was sleeping soundly when awakened by them....

At 7 A.M. Committees appointed by the city government visited the liquor shops and had the spirits (such as they could find) destroyed. The streets ran with liquor; and women and boys, black and white, were seen filling pitchers and buckets from the gutters....

A dark volume of smoke rises from the southeastern section of the city, and spreads like a pall over the zenith. It proceeds from the tobacco warehouse, ignited, I suppose, hours ago, and now just bursting forth.

At 8½ A.M. the armory, arsenal, and laboratory (Seventh and Canal Streets), which had been previously fired, gave forth terrific sounds from thousands of bursting shells. This continued for more than an hour. Some fragments of shell fell within a few hundred yards of my house.

The pavements are filled with pulverised glass.

Some of the great flour mills have taken fire from the burning government warehouses, and the flames are spreading through the lower part of the city. A great conflagration is apprehended....

Eleven A.M. I walked down Broad Street to the Capitol Square. The street was filled with *negro troops*, cavalry and infantry, and were cheered by hundreds of negroes at the corners.... The leaping and lapping flames were roaring in Main Street up to Ninth; and Goddin's Building (late General Post Office) was on fire, as well as all the houses in Governor street up to Franklin....

Shells are still bursting in the ashes of the armory, etc.

All the stores are closed; most of the largest (in Main Street) have been burned.

An officer told me, at 3 P.M., that a white brigade will picket the city tonight; and he assured the ladies standing near that there would not be a particle of danger of molestation.... He said we had done ourselves great injury by the fire, the lower part of the city being in ashes, and declared that the United States troops had no hand in it. I acquitted them of the deed, and told him that the fire had spread from the tobacco warehouses and military depots, fired by our troops as a military necessity.

## April 4 (Tuesday)

Jones, John B., Rebel War Clerk, Confederate War Dept., Richmond, Va.:

I walked around the burnt district this morning. Some seven hundred houses, from Main Street to the canal, comprising, the most valuable stores, and the best business establishments, were consumed. All the bridges across the James were destroyed, the work being done effectually. Shells were placed in all the warehouses where the tobacco was stored, to prevent the saving of any.

The War Department was burned after I returned yesterday; and soon after the flames were arrested, mainly by the efforts of the Federal troops....

The troops do not interfere with the citizens here any more than they do in New York—yet....

Confederate money is not taken today.

While Richmond was burning and Lincoln visited the Confederate Capitol, the business of prisoner exchange moved apace. As fast as the Confederate prisoners could be exchanged they were sent on to their commands for immediate integration into the ranks.

In the North, the large number of Confederate prisoners to be sent out for exchange had created much confusion. Washington, giving directions for the movement of the prisoners, was not quite sure how many prisoners were where. It seems that some who were already reported as exchanged were still in the prisons scattered around the country. A general "sorting out" was required.

In Nashville, Maj. Gen. George H. Thomas, USA, directed a letter to Lt. Gen. R. Taylor, commanding the Dept. of Alabama, Mississippi, and East Louisiana, concerning one of the Federal officers who was to be tried as a spy:

General: I learn from a letter of Maj. Carlin, Seventy-first Ohio Volunteer Infantry, that Capt. Hanchett, Sixteenth Illinois Volunteers (Cavalry), and acting assistant adjutant-general on the staff of Col. Capron, is being tried by court-martial at Cahaba, Ala., on the charge of being a spy. Capt. Hanchett is an officer of the U.S. Army; has never been within Confederate lines, except in the performance of his duties as an officer with troops. Should he be convicted and punished as a spy I assure you I shall make most ample retaliation.

## April 5 (Wednesday)

Jones, John B., Rebel War Clerk, Confederate War Dept., Richmond, Va.:

Stayed with my next-door neighbors at their request last night—all females. It was quiet; and so far the United States pickets and guards have preserved perfect order....

This morning thousands of negroes and many white females are besieging the public officers for provisions. I do not observe any getting them, and their faces begin to express disappointment....

Three P.M. I feel that this Diary is near its end.

The burnt district includes all the banks, money changers, and principal speculators and extortioners. This seems like a decree from above!

Four P.M. The Square is nearly vacated by the negroes. An officer told me they intended to put them in the army in a few days, and that the Northern people did not really like negro equality any better than we did.

At Danville, Va., communications to the northeast, towards Richmond, were cut at Burke's Station, when Sheridan's blue-clad troops reached the railroad to Danville. President Davis, in Danville, prepared to move south with his greatly reduced staff. At this time, most of the prisoners located at Danville had been forwarded for exchange or moved to other locations.

### April 6 (Thursday)

Lee's Army of Northern Virginia, retreating westward, today clashed with its old rival, the Army of the Potomac, at Sayler's Creek. The Confederate column was inadvertently split, leaving Lt. Gen. Richard Ewell and Maj. Gen. R.H. Anderson east of and behind the main column. The Federals didn't miss their chance. Although the Confederate troops made a good showing, they were nearly surrounded and overwhelmed within a short period of time. Ewell surrendered his troops. For all practical purposes, the war in Virginia was over.

### April 7 (Friday)

Lee's weary columns were still moving west towards Lynchburg, losing stragglers along the way, who were picked up as prisoners of war and held in the Union rear. Sheridan's cavalry and infantry moved west and then north to attain a position between Lee and Appomattox Station.

In Danville, Va., there was much discussion about the status of the prison at Salisbury, N.C. The Ordnance Department had designs on the buildings used for the prison, and at the same time the departments responsible for the prisoners needed a place to house them. Today, Brig. Gen. Daniel Ruggles, Commissary-General of Prisoners, wired Confederate Adjutant-Gen. Samuel Cooper for a decision, not realizing that the government in Richmond no longer existed, but that it had become mobile and was on its way south.

### April 8 (Saturday)

This day, Grant received Lee's message of yesterday asking what terms would be granted for surrender. Grant complied with the request, outlining the terms. Lee, upon receipt of Grant's message, replied that he was not, as yet, ready to surrender.

At Vicksburg, Miss., Maj. Gen. N.J.T. Dana, USA, informed the Adjutant-General's office in Washington that:

> The rebel commissioners, Col. Watts and Lt. Col. Henderson, have now near this place about 5000 of our prisoners under flag of truce awaiting exchange, and refuse to allow them to be sent on parole to Benton Barracks till they receive an equivalent. I request that a sufficient number of rebel prisoners be sent me from Rock Island and Alton for the exchange. There are no rebel prisoners at present in this department or that of the Gulf.

Col. R.C. Wood, Assistant Surgeon General, USA, at Louisville, Ky., was notified from the U.S. Hospital Steamer *R.C. Wood* that the condition of the returning Federal prisoners was "most deplorable." After receiving the prisoners, they were clothed and fed and made as comfortable as possible. However, twenty died on the trip to St. Louis. It was estimated that about 2500 sick in the same condition were awaiting transportation.

In Danville, Va., Lt. Col. R.C. Smith, commanding the prison, was directed to prepare the prison at that location to receive 1200 Federal prisoners.

### April 9 (Sunday)

Lee had finally reached the end of his rope. Outnumbered, nearly surrounded, and out of ideas, he accepted the terms of surrender and hostilities all but ceased in Virginia. All of the Army of Northern Virginia, except for the cavalry, became prisoners of war, even if briefly.

### April 10 (Monday)

The surrendered Army of Northern Virginia lay quiet in its camps, being fed by Federal rations, while Lee and Grant conversed.

### April 11 (Tuesday)

In Mobile, Ala., Confederate Gen. D.H. Maury ordered the evacuation of the city and the destruction of the stores and public works. All cotton was fired as well as other valuable stores. No Confederate prisoners were taken.

## April 12 (Wednesday)

Surrender ceremonies took place at Appomattox Court House today. The Confederates marched in between rows of Union troops and laid down their arms and battle standards. There was many a tear shed, both North and South. For these men, the war was over. For the armies in the west, days of action were to come.

The city of Mobile, Ala., surrendered on this date, following the Confederate evacuation of the city the day before, the troops under Gen. D.H. Maury heading north, out of the city.

## April 13 (Thursday)

Sherman's armies entered Raleigh, N.C., destined to follow Confederate Gen. Joseph E. Johnston towards Hillsboro, N.C.

In the North, the draft was discontinued and plans were made to release the prisoners of war being held at the various prisons.

## April 14 (Friday)

In Washington, President Lincoln was shot while attending Ford's Theater. Secy. of War Edwin M. Stanton took charge of the government.

On this day, Union Maj. Gen. N.J.T. Dana, commander of Union forces around Vicksburg, informed the War Department in Washington that the Confederacy had released 4700 men and sent them to Vicksburg. Of these, 1100 from Andersonville were sick. The remainder of the prisoners were in better shape, especially those from the Cahaba prison.

In Washington, Maj. Gen. E.A. Hitchcock, Commissioner of Exchange, directed that Gen. William Hoffman, Federal Commissary-General of Prisoners, have lists prepared at each prison site of the applicants for discharge among the prisoners of war. The lists would be forwarded daily until the number of prisoners was exhausted. When approved by the Secy. of War, the lists would serve as the roster for prisoners to be released.

## April 15 (Saturday)

At 7:22 A.M., without ever speaking, President Lincoln died in a house across the street from Ford's Theater. Vice President Andrew Johnson, of Tennessee, was sworn in as the seventeenth President.

In Andersonville, Ga., former Union prisoners were being shipped from the prison as rapidly as they could be moved and sent to points where they would be turned over to Union authorities. Pvt. Eliab Hickman, Co. E, 92nd Ohio Volunteer Infantry, was released from Andersonville and sent to Jacksonville, Fla., for processing.

## April 28 (Friday)

At Jacksonville, Fla., a group of former prisoners at Andersonville, Ga., were paroled and sent to a parole camp at Camp Chase, Columbus, Ohio. Among these was Pvt. Eliab Hickman, an Ohio native, who had been incarcerated at Andersonville on November 9, 1864, and was released from there on April 15, 1865.

## May 2 (Tuesday)

The Confederate armies were either surrendered or in disarray, and the soldiers were moving towards home by any means at hand. Those who had surrendered were placed on parole, in most cases given transportation, and released to follow their normal pursuits. There were, however, restrictions on what activities they could engage in, according to the terms of surrender:

Prisoners of war on parole within the Department of the Gulf, and all officers and soldiers who have been connected with the rebel Army and are not registered, are required to report to the provost-marshal-general forthwith. The neglect of this duty will be followed by forfeiture of rights conferred by the parole, or arrest and imprisonment.

Prisoners of war on parole granted by competent authority are allowed to return "to their homes not to be disturbed by the U.S. authorities so long as they observe their parole, and the laws in force where they may reside." But they are to be regarded as prisoners of war. They will not be allowed to bear arms, to wear in public the uniform of the rebel Army, the uniform of the United States, or any distinctive badge of military service.

They are not entitled to participate in the management of public affairs or to enter upon business pursuits.

All persons will be required strictly to conform to regulations of the department in their intercourse with paroled prisoners of war.

No person who has been engaged in civil employments, within or by the rebel Government, will be allowed to return to or to remain in the department, except upon reporting to the provost-marshal, and a compliance with the conditions established by law.

### May 3 (Wednesday)

Maj. Gen. Halleck, in Richmond, reported to Secy. of War Edwin Stanton today that "at least part of the money sent from the North for the use of our prisoners of war was diverted to other purposes, and the evidence seems to implicate Robert Ould and his assistant, Hatch. I have arrested both, and shall keep them in prison till a full investigation can be made." Stanton approved the action.

Later the same day, Halleck told Stanton that the arrest of Ould and Hatch would be kept secret; even they would not know why they were arrested. Halleck believed that he was on the trail of the money.

### May 6 (Saturday)

Grant had given Lee's army the benefit of amnesty, and the Confederate veterans had been paroled and sent home. The western armies were still in the surrendering stage. Grant provided Maj. Gen. George Thomas some guidance:

Paroled prisoners surrendered by Lee and Johnston and others entering into the same arrangement will be allowed to return to their homes if within any of the States which seceded. If belonging to other States they must take the oath of allegiance first, under the decision of the Attorney-General. Prisoners captured in battle are not to be allowed paroles nor the privilege of discharge in any way except on authority of the War Department.

### May 7 (Sunday)

Capt. H.E. Noyes, Fourth U.S. Regular Cavalry, and a squad of troopers, today visited Andersonville, Ga., to arrest Maj. Henry Wirz, commandant of the prison. Noyes, upon arrival, demanded the records of the prison, which were given him by Wirz. He then informed Wirz that he was arrested and would be taken to Macon, Ga., to the headquarters of Maj. Gen. J.H. Wilson, USA. Wirz invited Noyes to eat with them before they left, to which Noyes agreed.

After eating a simple meal of corn bread and bacon, they departed for Macon. This would be the last that Cora Wirz would see of her father. While at Macon, Wirz wrote Maj. Gen. J.H. Wilson, USA, concerning his status:

General: It is with great reluctance that I address you these lines, being fully aware how little time is left you to attend to such matters as I now have the honor to lay before you; and if I could see any other way to accomplish my object I would not intrude upon you. I am a native of Switzerland, and was before the war a citizen of Louisiana, by profession a physician. Like hundreds and thousands of others I was carried away by the maelstrom of excitement and joined the Southern Army. I was very severely wounded at the battle of Seven Pines, near Richmond, Va., and have nearly lost the use of my right arm. Unfit for field duty, I was ordered to report to Bvt. Brig. Gen. J.H. Winder, in charge of Federal prisoners of war, who ordered me to take charge of a prison in Tuscaloosa, Ala. My health failing me, I applied for a furlough and went to Europe, from whence I returned in February 1864. I was then ordered to report to the commandant of military prisons at Andersonville, Ga., who assigned me to the command of the interior of the prison. The duties I had to perform were arduous and unpleasant, and I am satisfied that no man can or will justly blame me for things that happened there which were beyond my power to control. I do not think that I ought to be held responsible for the shortness of rations, for the overcrowded state of the prison (which was in itself a prolific source of the fearful mortality), for the inadequate supplies of clothing, want of shelters, &c. Still I now bear the odium, and men who were prisoners here seem disposed to wreak their vengeance upon me for what they have suffered, who was only the medium, or, I may better say, the tool in the hands of my superiors. This is my condition. I am a man with a family; I lost all my property when the Federal army besieged Vicksburg; I have no means at present to go any place, and even if I had I know of no place where I could go. My life is in danger, and I most respectfully ask of you help and relief. If you will be so generous as to give me some sort of a safe-conduct, or, what I should greatly prefer, a guard to protect myself and family against violence, I shall be thankful to you, and you may rest assured that your protection will not be given to one who is unworthy of it. My intention is to return with my family to Europe so soon as I can make the arrangements.

## May 10 (Wednesday)

Today, Maj. Henry Wirz, arrested at Andersonville, Ga., arrived at Washington, D.C., and was placed in the Old Capitol Prison, awaiting disposition.

## May 15 (Monday)

The work of releasing prisoners of war from the various sites continued. The officers confined at Ft. Delaware wrote Lt. Gen. Grant requesting that they be released on parole so they might return home. Lt. H. Coffey, Co. I, First Texas Legion, and Capt. John Humphrys, Fiftieth Virginia Infantry, and forty-seven others, earnestly solicited Gen. Grant:

The persons whose names are appended to this respectfully solicit that they may be released from the military prison at Ft. Delaware on taking the oath of allegiance to the Government of the United States. Many of them have been in confinement since the battle of Gettysburg. Many are crippled for life. All have either wives or children or mothers or sisters dependent upon them, and all will take the oath from a sense of duty and an earnest determination to fulfill its obligations in the strictest sense.

On this date, former Union prisoners from Andersonville, Ga., arrived at Camp Chase, Ohio, for processing and discharge. Among them was Pvt. Eliab Hickman, Co. E, 92nd Ohio Volunteer Infantry. Hickman's discharge would be issued from Washington, D.C., and would be effective on June 10, 1865, at which time he would be paid three months extra pay and the remaining $75.00 of his enlistment bounty.

## May 16 (Tuesday)

At Point Lookout, Md., Brig. Gen. James Barnes called attention to the number of prisoners remaining at that location and requested, and recommended, disposition:

General: I beg leave to invite your attention to the patients in the prison camp hospital. There are in this hospital 1859 men, including the attendants, belonging to the following States, viz: Maryland, 6; Virginia, 391; North Carolina, 521; South Carolina, 184;

Georgia, 233; Florida, 25; Alabama, 154; Louisiana, 20, Mississippi, 216; Arkansas, 19, Tennessee, 60; Kentucky, 4; Missouri, 7; Texas, 22; numbering in all as above, 1859. Some 1600 of them could be sent home with proper means of conveyance, say, by steamer, to the most advisable ports. The oath of allegiance could be administered to them all, for they all are ready to take it and would be glad to be sent home. Many are disabled by loss of limbs and otherwise by wounds and the expense of taking care of them here is considerable. You will be able to judge of the places which they might be sent by the statement above of the States to which they belong. These steamers would take them, say to Wilmington, Savannah, and Mobile. There would remain between 200 and 300 not in condition to be furloughed for the present.

Gen. Hoffman recommended to the Secretary of War that this action be approved. Action was taken to implement the decision immediately. At last, many of the Confederates who had struggled so hard and lost so much would be permitted to return home.

At Macon, Ga., Maj. Gen. John H. Wilson, USA, wired the Adjutant-General in Washington:

General: I have the honor to report that I have arrested Capt. H. Wirz, C.S. Army, notorious as commandant of the Andersonville prison, and have sent him under guard to Gen. Thomas. I forward herewith all the records, &c., of the prison that could be found, and also other papers relating to his cruel treatment of our men. I respectfully request that this miscreant be brought before a general court-martial in Washington, D.C., where the evidence in his case can be more readily obtained.

## May 18 (Thursday)

Gen. U.S. Grant, now in Washington, responded to the request sent three days previously from Ft. Delaware by recommending to Secy. of War Stanton:

I hope early means may be devised for clearing our prisons as far as possible. I would recommend that all who come within the amnesty proclamation be allowed the benefit of it. By going now they may still raise something for their subsistence for the coming year and prevent suffering next winter. Prisoners living west of the Mississippi, those from States which never passed the ordinance of secession, and those from the District of Columbia, might be made an exception for the present.

The arrest of Henry Wirz was reported on this date. Since the 1st of May, 1870 prisoners had left Camp Chase, Ohio, for the South. About 3400 remained in the camp.

## May 19 (Friday)

Today, the former President of the Confederate States of America, under escort of Lt. Col. B.D. Pritchard, 4th Michigan Cavalry, arrived at Ft. Monroe to be incarcerated.

I have just arrived at this point on board the steamer *Clyde*, in charge of a party of prisoners from Macon, Ga., consisting of Jeff. Davis and family, Alexander H. Stephens, C.C. Clay and wife, Maj. Gen. Wheeler and staff, Postmaster General Reagan, Col. Johnston and Col. Lubbock, aides-de-camp to Davis, and Harrison, his private secretary, besides several other unimportant names. The *Clyde* is under the convoy of the steam sloop-of-war *Tuscarora*. We will depart for Washington at once.

## May 26 (Friday)

Capt. Henry Wirz, late commandant of the prison at Andersonville, Ga., was ordered taken to Washington, D.C., under guard for disposition.

## May 31 (Wednesday)

Today, Secy. of War Edwin Stanton directed that an officer be sent immediately to take charge of Capt. Henry Wirz, currently in the Washington Central Guardhouse, and incarcerate him in the Old Capitol Prison.

## June 12 (Monday)

Rosanna Hickman had remained on the farm in Centre Township, Noble County, Ohio, with her three children while Eliab Hickman went off to war with the 92nd Ohio Volunteer Infantry. She had heard very little from him since his capture at Cassville, Ga., and incarceration at Andersonville, in 1864. With the end of the war, she expected Eliab to come home, but heard that he, along with five other prisoners, had been hung at Andersonville. On this day, while working in a field near the house, she noticed a tall figure coming down the

road who look familiar. It was Eliab. Emaciated and sick, he was at last home. He and Rosanna would later move to Wirt County, W.Va., and raise 13 children.

## June 20 (Tuesday)

At Camp Chase, Ohio, less than 50 prisoners remained in the camp. All the others had left for the South. These were gone within a few days.

## July 5 (Wednesday)

By midsummer, the prisoners were nearly all gone and the camps were being closed as rapidly as possible. Brig. Gen. William Hoffman, Commissary-General of Prisons, wrote Lt. Gen. Grant, in Washington:

General: I have the honor to report that, except a few sick who have been transferred to the post hospitals, all prisoners of war have been released from the following named military prisons, viz: Point Lookout, Newport News, Hart's Island, Elmira, N.Y., Camp Chase, near Columbus, Ohio, Camp Morton, near Indianapolis, Ind., Camp Douglas, near Chicago, Ill., Rock Island, Ill., and the military prison at Alton, Ill., and the forces stationed at these several places as guards to the prisons may now be relieved.

There are now but 150 rebel officers confined at Johnson's Island, and if it is thought advisable they may be transferred to Ft. Warren or Ft. Delaware, by which arrangement the guard can be relieved and the island may be returned to its owner.

## July 8 (Saturday)

In contrast to previous reports on the condition of the prison at Elmira, N.Y., the inspector on this date gave the operation high marks and noted that the buildings were now being used as a general hospital. He also recommended that flowers be planted along the paths and roads to enhance the beauty of the post and provide pleasure to the invalids. This stands in stark contrast to the conditions previously reported, which showed this prison to be one of the worst in the nation, North or South.

## July 13 (Thursday)

Special Orders No. 168, this date, discontinued Point Lookout, Md., as a garrisoned post. All general and general staff officers serving there were to report to their respective homes and report to the Adjutant-General of the Army, by letter, upon arrival.

The pubic property at Point Lookout was to be protected by a strong company of the Twenty-fourth Regiment of U.S. Colored Troops. The remaining troops of the Regiment were to be sent to Richmond, Va., for disposition.

On this date, Lt. Col. O.E. Babcock wrote Col. T.S. Bowers, in Washington, of the results of his inspection trip at several prisons:

I made an inspection of the prison at Alton, Ill., on the 3d of July. Found no inmates, all having been discharged or transferred to Jefferson City and St. Louis, Mo.... I examined such of the records as remained at Alton and found them in apparent good order, but could not verify them, as the prisoners had all been removed. The prison fund on hand amounts to near $35,000. I would recommend the breaking up of this post at once, the prison to be turned over to its owners, the public property to be sold or transferred to other depots.

I inspected the military prison at Rock Island on the 6th of July. This prison is also empty.... The prison fund here amounts to $174,068.15. As this island is to be the place of deposit of a large amount of ammunition I would recommend the preservation of the buildings. The locality has the appearance of being very healthy, and would, in my opinion, be a fine location for a general hospital....

I inspected the prison at Indianapolis on the 10th of July and found eight prisoners—one citizen and seven prisoners of war. Citizen William E. Munford, supposed to be a lieutenant in the C.S. Army, held as a spy, was arrested with one Maj. J.B. Castleman on same charge. Castleman has been released on condition that he would leave the country not to return. I would recommend Munford to be released on taking the oath of allegiance or required to leave the country. The seven turned over as prisoners of war are held as deserters from our own Army.... I would recommend their discharge on taking the oath of allegiance, as their trial would be attended with many difficulties and great expense, and they can do no harm if released.... The prison fund amounts to about $100,000.... I also found some forty of the Veteran

Reserve Corps prisoners in the guardhouse guilty of mutiny. The major-general commanding says their guilt is clear and recommends their dishonorable discharge without pay as an economical and judicious disposition.

**July 15 (Saturday)**

By Executive Order of President Andrew Johnson, dated July 5, 1865, the place of confinement for the convicted Lincoln assassination conspirators who were not to be executed was changed from the penitentiary at Albany, N.Y., to the military prison at Dry Tortugas, Fla. The transportation of Samuel Arnold, Samuel A. Mudd, Edman Spangler, and Michael O'Laughlin to Dry Tortugas was immediately effected.

The military commission which conducted the trial was dissolved.

Today, after months of investigation, former Agent for Exchange Robert Ould and his assistant, Hatch, were exonerated of any charges of taking monies belonging to Federal prisoners and were released from prison.

**August 2 (Wednesday)**

Brig. Gen. William Hoffman, Federal Commissary-General of Prisoners, today informed the Adjutant-General of the Army that the prisons at Elmira, N.Y., Hart's Island, N.Y., Point Lookout, Md., Camp Chase, Ohio, Camp Morton, Ind., Camp Douglas, Ill., and Rock Island, Ill., had all been vacated and the buildings and facilities could be disposed of by the Quartermaster Department.

**August 23 (Wednesday)**

The military commission convened to try Maj. Henry Wirz on this day in Washington by order of the President of the United States, Andrew Johnson.

**August 25 (Friday)**

The trial of Maj. Henry Wirz began this date in Washington. One hundred and sixty witnesses were called by the government for the prosecution. Most were former prisoners of war at Andersonville and could hardly be called nonbiased. The charges, and their validity, are as follows:

### CHARGE 1:

That he shot a prisoner on July 8, 1864 with his own hand, the prisoner dying the following day.

The *name* of the prisoner who was shot was never determined by the court.

### CHARGE 2:

That Wirz maliciously stomped, kicked, and bruised a prisoner on September 20, 1864.

The *name* of the prisoner was not determined by the court.

### CHARGE 3:

That Wirz shot a prisoner, with his own hand, on June 13, 1864.

The *name* of the prisoner was not determined by the court.

### CHARGE 4:

That Wirz shot a prisoner, with his own hand, on May 30, 1864.

The *name* of the prisoner was not determined by the court.

### CHARGE 5:

That Wirz placed a prisoner in the stocks for punishment on August 20, 1864.

Wirz was *not even present at Andersonville* during the month of August 1864, and, again, the *name* of the prisoner was never determined.

### CHARGE 6:

That Wirz caused a man to be placed in the stocks, which resulted in his death, on February 1, 1864.

Wirz had *not yet arrived at Andersonville* on this date. He arrived about April 12, nearly eight weeks after the alleged event occurred.

### CHARGE 7:

That Wirz, on July 20, 1864, chained several prisoners together and made them carry around large iron balls fastened to their feet. The result was that one of the prisoners died.

Again, *no names* were determined by the court.

### CHARGE 8:

That Wirz, on May 15, 1864, ordered a sentry to shoot a prisoner, which resulted in the prisoner's death.

This shooting supposedly took place during the daylight hours, in view of thousands of witnesses, but *no one knew the name of the prisoner*.

### CHARGE 9:

That Wirz, on July 1, 1864, ordered a sentry to shoot a prisoner, which resulted in the prisoner's death.

Again, this shooting supposedly took place during the daylight hours, in view of thousands of witnesses, but *no one knew the name of the prisoner*.

### CHARGE 10:

That Wirz, on August 20, 1864, ordered a sentry to shoot a prisoner, which resulted in the prisoner's death.

Wirz was not present at Andersonville during August 1864. Yet again, the *name* of the prisoner was never determined.

### CHARGE 11:

That Wirz, on July 1, 1864, allowed bloodhounds to attack and wound a prisoner which resulted in the death of the prisoner six days later.

The *name* of the prisoner was not determined by the court, although the man lived for six days after the attack.

### CHARGE 12:

That Wirz, on July 27, 1864, ordered a sentry to shoot a prisoner, which resulted in the prisoner's death.

Again, this shooting supposedly took place during the daylight hours, in view of thousands of witnesses, but *no one knew the name of the prisoner*.

### CHARGE 13:

That Wirz, on August 3, 1864, beat a prisoner with his pistol to the extent that the prisoner died the following day.

This beating supposedly took place during the daylight hours, in view of thousands of witnesses, but *no one knew the name of the prisoner.*

The main witness at the Wirz trial was a former prisoner called Felix de la Baume, who had a very glib tongue and was believed without question. This witness was appointed to a position in the Department of the Interior even before the trial began. On November 21, eleven days after Wirz was hanged, de la Baume was unmasked as a Federal deserter named Felix Oeser, a former member of the Seventh New York Volunteers. Nothing was done to question the validity of his testimony at the trial and he was quietly dismissed from his position at Interior and then disappeared from view.

In some cases during the trial, documents were tampered with to show different dates in an effort to further incriminate Wirz. But perhaps the most glaring omission was the full report of Dr. Joseph Jones, a noted medical researcher in the South, who had visited Andersonville in late summer of 1864 and wrote a lengthy report to the Confederate Surgeon-General on the conditions at the prison. The Federal government, learning of the report, *directed* that Jones come to Washington with the report so it could be used as evidence in the trial. The report was brought and delivered to the government, *who then selectively used only what they wanted* to help incriminate Wirz. Jones protested loud and strong but was not allowed to testify or to explain about the report.

In general, the trial was a witch-hunt and Wirz was the witch. A gross miscarriage of justice was perpetrated by the government and no apology was ever given.

### November 3 (Friday)

The Judge Advocate General of the United States Army, Joseph Holt, today forwarded information to Secy. of War Edwin M. Stanton concerning former Confederate officials who should be apprehended for trial for their treatment of prisoners during the late war. In some cases, the trials would be unjust and unnecessary; in others, a just retribution.

Sir: In the cases of sundry rebel officials ... I have the honor to return the papers referred to me and to submit thereon as follows:

The testimony evolved in the course of the recent trial of Wirz, and by means of recent investigations in the Southern military departments, fully confirms and strengthens this conclusion and I have not formally recommended as follows in all these cases:

First. That Lt. Col. Iverson, Forty-seventh Georgia Volunteers, and his subordinate, Lt. (or Capt.) Barrett, be arrested and brought to trial for their treatment of our soldiers when prisoners of war at Florence, S.C. The testimony fixes upon them not only a series of the most cruel and inhuman acts of neglect, abuse, assault, robbery, &c., but a considerable number of well established homicides. In these Barrett was the principal agent, but Iverson, as his commanding officer, was clearly no less criminal.

Second. That Maj. John H. Gee should be tried for homicides and acts of similar atrocity committed by him while in charge of the rebel prison at Salisbury, N.C....

Third. That J.W. Duncan be also tried for at least one case of murder and numerous cases of robbery and cruelty, committed by him while commissary-sergeant at Andersonville....

Fourth. That Dr. Nesbit, of Salisbury, N.C., be forthwith brought to trial ... for the wanton murder of a Union prisoner on the occasion of a slight outbreak at the prison, which occurred last winter.

Fifth.... In the case of R.B. Winder, while the evidence at the trial of Wirz was deemed by the court to implicate him in the conspiracy against the lives of all Federal prisoners in rebel hands, no such specific overt acts of violation of the laws of war are as yet fixed upon him as to make it expedient to prefer formal charges and bring him to trial.

Nowhere in the record does it show that the Union personnel who caused such suffering to the Confederate prisoners at Camp Douglas, Ill., by making them ride the "Morgan horse" in freezing weather were even investigated, let alone recommended for trial. Nor does the record show that the many Union jailers who robbed the Confederate prisoners of their valuables, their blankets, etc., were ever brought to justice. No record of investigation into the lack of firewood at Point Lookout, Md., or Elmira, N.Y., that caused such misery and death from pneumonia is available.

The victor writes the history.

### November 6 (Monday)

President Andrew Johnson today approved the sentence of death by hanging for Maj. Henry Wirz. Said sentence to be carried out in Washington on Friday, November 10, 1865, between the hours of 6 o'clock A.M. and 12 o'clock noon.

### November 10 (Friday)

Maj. Henry Wirz, former commander of the interior prison at Andersonville, Ga., was today hanged at the Old Capitol Prison in Washington. The government refused to turn over his body to his widow so he could get a decent burial. His final words were, "I know what orders are, Major—I am being hung for obeying them."

It was over. In many cases the innocent were punished, the guilty rewarded, just as it had been for centuries in war, and would continue to be forever. The soldiers went home and tried to reconstruct their lives with some meaning, not always being successful. Many would go west, plagued by cruel memories and driven by a need to forget. Many former prisoners would suffer years of agony from the sicknesses contracted in the prison pens and would die early because of it. The veterans would not forget, and some never forgive, their jailors. One case was the exception. One commander of the prison at Camp Morton, outside Indianapolis, Ind., would be remembered with such fondness that a statue would be erected to his memory by the former prisoners.

It is unfortunate that more relationships were not like that.

# APPENDIXES

## APPENDIX I

# THE PRISONER EXCHANGE CARTEL OF JULY 22, 1862

### BETWEEN THE UNITED STATES AND THE CONFEDERATE STATES GOVERNMENTS

Executed at Haxall's Landing, on the James River, Va., the cartel provided for:

**Article 1.** It is hereby agreed and stipulated that all prisoners of war held by either party, including those taken on private armed vessels known as privateers, shall be discharged upon the conditions and terms following:

Prisoners to be exchanged man for man and officer for officer; privateers to be placed upon the footing of officers and men of the navy.

Men and officers of lower grades may be exchanged for officers of a higher grade, and men and officers of different services may be exchanged according to the following scale of equivalents:

A general commanding-in-chief or an admiral shall be exchanged for officers of equal rank, or for sixty privates or common seamen.

A flag-officer or major-general shall be exchanged for officers of equal rank, or for forty privates or common seamen.

A commodore carrying a broad pennant or a brigadier-general shall be exchanged for officers of equal rank, or for twenty privates or common seamen.

A captain in the navy or a colonel shall be exchanged for officers of equal rank, or for fifteen privates or common seamen.

A lieutenant-colonel or a commander in the navy shall be exchanged for officers of equal rank, or for ten privates or common seamen.

A lieutenant-commander or a major shall be exchanged for officers of equal rank, or for eight privates or common seamen.

A lieutenant or a master in the navy or a captain in army or marines shall be exchanged for officers of equal rank, or for four privates or common seamen.

Masters' mates in the navy or lieutenants and ensigns in the army shall be exchanged for officers of equal rank, or for four privates or common seamen.

Midshipmen, warrant-officers in the navy, masters of merchant vessels, and commander of privateers shall be exchanged for officers of equal rank, or for three privates or common seamen.

Second captains, lieutenants, or mates of merchant

vessels or privateers, and all petty officers in the navy, and all noncommissioned officers in the army or marines shall be severally exchanged for persons of equal rank, or for two privates or common seamen, and private soldiers or common seamen shall be exchanged for each other, man for man.

**Article 2.** Local, State, civil, and militia rank held by persons not in actual military service will not be recognized, the basis of exchange being the grade actually held in the naval and military service of the respective parties.

**Article 3.** If citizens held by either party on charges of disloyalty or any alleged civil offenses are exchanged, it shall only be for citizens. Captured sutlers, teamsters, and all civilians in the actual service of either party to be exchanged for persons in similar position.

**Article 4.** All prisoners of war to be discharged on parole in ten days after their capture, and the prisoners now held and those thereafter taken to be transported to the points mutually agreed upon at the expense of the capturing party. The surplus prisoners not exchanged shall not be permitted to take up arms again, nor to serve as military police or constabulary force in any fort, garrison, or fieldwork held by either of the respective parties, nor as guards of prisons, depots, or stores, nor to discharge any duty usually performed by soldiers, until exchanged under the provisions of this cartel. The exchange is not to be considered complete until the officer or soldier exchanged for has been actually restored to the lines to which he belongs.

**Article 5.** Each party, upon the discharge of prisoners of the other party, is authorized to discharge an equal number of their own officers or men from parole, furnishing at the same time to the other party a list of their prisoners discharged and of their own officers and men relieved from parole, thus enabling each party to relieve from parole such of their own officers and men as the party may choose. The lists thus mutually furnished will keep both parties advised of the true condition of the exchange of prisoners.

**Article 6.** The stipulations and provisions above mentioned to be of binding obligation during the continuance of the war, it matters not which party may have the surplus of prisoners, the great principles involved being, first, an equitable exchange of prisoners, man for man, officer for officer, or officers of higher grade exchanged for officers of lower grade or for privates, according to the scale of equivalents; second, that privateers and officers and men of different services may be exchanged according to the same scale of equivalents; third, that all prisoners, of whatever arm of service, are to be exchanged or paroled in ten days from the time of their capture, if it be practicable to transfer them to their own lines in that time; if not, as soon thereafter as practicable; fourth, that no officer, soldier, or employee, in the service of either party, is to be considered as exchanged and absolved from his parole until his equivalent has actually reached the lines of his friends; fifth, that the parole forbids performance of field, garrison, police, or guard, or constabulary duty.

Signed:        John A. Dix, Major-General, USA
               D. H. Hill, Major-General, CSA

## APPENDIX II

# LETTER OF MARQUE

## ISSUED BY THE CONFEDERATE GOVERNMENT

TO ALL WHO SHALL SEE THESE PRESENTS, GREETING:

Know ye, that by virtue of the power vested in me by law I have commissioned and do hereby commission, have authorized and do hereby authorize the schooner or vessel called the *Savannah*, whereof T. Harrison Baker is commander, to act as a private armed vessel in the service of the Confederate States on the high seas against the United States of America, their ships, vessels, goods and effects and those of their citizens during the pendency of the war now existing between said Confederate States and the said United States.

This commission to continue in force until revoked by the President of the Confederate States for the time being.

Given under my hand seal of the Confederate States at Montgomery this 18th day of May, A.D. 1861.

JEFFERSON DAVIS

# APPENDIX III

# ARTICLE XXXVI OF U.S. ARMY REGULATIONS

745. Prisoners of war will be disarmed and sent to the rear and reported as soon as practicable to the headquarters. The return of prisoners [report of prisoners taken] from the Headquarters of the Army to the War Department will specify the number, rank and corps.

746. The private property of prisoners will be duly respected, and each shall be treated with the regard due his rank. They are to obey the necessary orders given them. They receive for subsistence one ration each without regard to rank, and the wounded are to be treated with the same care as the wounded of the Army. Other allowances to them will depend on conventions with the enemy. Prisoners' horses will be taken for the Army.

747. Exchanges of prisoners and release of officers on parole depend on the orders of the general commanding-in-chief under the instructions of Government.

## APPENDIX IV

# AN ACT RELATIVE TO PRISONERS OF WAR APPROVED MAY 21, 1861

*The Congress of the Confederate States of America do enact*, That all prisoners of war taken whether on land or at sea during the pending hostilities with the United States shall be transferred by the captors from time to time and as often as convenient to the Department of War; and it shall be the duty of the Secretary of War with the approval of the President to issue such instructions to the Quartermaster-General and his subordinates as shall provide for the safe custody and sustenance of prisoners of war; and the rations furnished prisoners of war shall be the same in quantity and quality as those furnished to enlisted men in the Army of the Confederacy.

Sec. 2. That the eighth section of the act entitled "An act recognizing the existence of war between the United States and the Confederate States, and concerning letters of marque, prizes and prize goods," shall not be so construed as to authorize the holding of prisoners of war the officers or crew of any unarmed vessel, nor any passengers on such vessel, unless such passengers be persons employed in the public service of the enemy.

Sec. 3. That the tenth section of the above-recited act shall not be so construed as to allow a bounty for prisoners captured on vessels of the enemy and brought into port unless such prisoners were captured on board of an armed ship or vessel of the enemy equal or superior force to that of the private armed vessel making the capture.

# APPENDIX V

# PAROLE TO BE USED FOR CAPTURED OFFICERS

## AS DIRECTED BY GENERAL WINFIELD SCOTT IN JULY 1861

We and each of us for himself severally pledge our words of honor as officers and gentlemen that we will not again take up arms against the United States nor serve in any military capacity whatsoever against them until regularly discharged according to the usages of war from this obligation.

But we must remember the times in which our cast of characters lived and the ideals they adhered to during the struggle. These were more romantic, gallant times in which men quoted Shakespeare and poetry and believed in the virtues expounded for the knights of old by Sir Walter Scott. Ivanhoe did indeed live! Honor was to be protected and death was preferable to dishonor.

Today we know little of the concept of paroling a prisoner of war. The concept died out in the 19th century and probably will never be resurrected. Its entire philosphy is based on the concept of personal honor—that once an oath is taken, it cannot be broken. A soldier of the Civil War would pledge upon his honor not to bear arms against the government giving the parole unless exchanged or otherwise released from the parole.

## APPENDIX VI

# DEATHS IN NORTHERN PRISONS

| Location | No. of Prisoners | Deaths | Percent |
|---|---|---|---|
| Point Lookout, Md. | 38,073 | 3,446 | 9.0 |
| Ft. Delaware, Del. | 22,773 | 2,502 | 10.9 |
| Camp Douglas, Ill. | 22,301 | 3,759 | 16.8 |
| Camp Chase, Ohio | 14,227 | 2,108 | 15.0 |
| Camp Morton, Ind. | 10,319 | 1,763 | 17.0 |
| Elmira, N.Y. | 9,167 | 2,980 | 32.5 |
| Louisville, Ky. | 8,438 | 139 | 1.7 |
| Alton, Ill. | 7,717 | 1,613 | 20.9 |
| Johnson's Island, Ohio | 7,357 | 275 | 3.7 |
| Old Capitol, Washington, D.C. | 5,761 | 457 | 7.9 |
| Newport News, Va. | 5,459 | 89 | 1.6 |
| Ft. McHenry, Md. | 5,325 | 33 | .6 |
| Ship Island, Miss. | 4,789 | 162 | 3.3 |
| St. Louis, Mo. | 4,585 | 589 | 1.3 |
| Camp Butler, Ill. | 4,154 | 816 | 19.6 |
| Harts Island, N.Y. | 3,117 | 230 | 7.4 |
| Rock Island, Ill. | 2,184 | 1,922 | 77.4 |
| Totals | 170,136 | 22,878 | 12.9 |

There were 43,764 prisoners at Ft. Warren, Ft. Lafayette, and other prisons not reported as to deaths.

Deaths of Union prisoners in Confederate prisons, under 9 percent.

Number of Union prisoners, 270,000; deaths, 22,570.

Number of Confederate prisoners, 220,000; deaths, 26,436.

Excess of Confederate deaths, 3,866.

[Sent to *Confederate Veteran* by Henry T. Williams, of Charleston, S.C., as taken from the Confederate Handbook compiled by the late Col. Robert C. Wood, of New Orleans, La.]

# BIBLIOGRAPHY

Abbott, A.O. *Prison Life in the South*. New York: Harper & Bros., 1866.

Bateman, Francis M. Letter to his parents, Feb. 23, 1862. Library of Congress.

Baylor, H.B. *Confederate Veteran*, IX (1901), 83.

Beall, John Yates. *Confederate Veteran*, VII (1899), 66-69.

Benson, P.H. *Confederate Veteran*, IX (1901), 271, 391.

Berry, Thomas F. *Confederate Veteran*, XX (1912), 65-67.

Blakey, Arch Fredric. *General John H. Winder, C.S.A.* Gainesville, FL: Univ. Florida Press, 1990.

Branch, J.T. *Confederate Veteran*, VIII (1900), 71-72.

Breeden, James O. *Joseph Jones, M.D.: Scientist of the Old South*. Lexington, KY: The Univ. of Ky. Press, 1975.

Brown, Daniel Patrick. *The Tragedy of Libby and Andersonville Prison Camps*. Ventura, CA: Golden West Hist. Pub., 1980.

Brown, Louis A. *The Salisbury Prison*. Wilmington, NC: Broadfoot Pub. Co., 1992.

Bryant, William O. *Cahaba Prison and the Sultana Disaster*. Tuscaloosa, AL: Univ. of Alabama, 1990.

Buford, Charles. Letter to his wife, August 3, 1864. Library of Congress.

Davis, T.C. *Confederate Veteran*, VII (1899), 65, 486.

"Deaths in Northern Prisons," *Confederate Veteran*, XXXVII (1929), 157.

Denney, Robert E. *The Civil War Years: A Day-by-Day Chronicle of the Life of a Nation*. New York: Sterling Publishing Co., Inc., 1992.

Dodson, W.C. *Confederate Veteran*, VIII (1900), 121-122.

Glazier, Willard. *Sword and Pen: or Ventures and Adventures*. Phila: P.W. Ziegler & Co., 1883

Hawes, Jesse. *Cahaba: A Story of Captive Boys in Blue* New York: Burr Printing House, 1888.

Hesseltine, William B. *Civil War Prisons*. Kent, OH: Kent State University Press, 1962.

_____. *Civil War Prisons: A Study in War Psychology*. Columbus: Ohio State University Press, 1920.

Jervey, Edward D. *Prison Life among the Rebels*. Kent, OH: Kent State Univ. Press, 1990.

Jones, John Beauchamp. *A Rebel War Clerk's Diary, Vol I & II*. Onancock, VA: 1866.

Knauss, William H. *Story of Camp Chase*. Dallas: Methodist Episcopal Church, 1906.

Livermore, Thomas L. *Numbers and Losses in the Civil War in America: 1861-1865*. Boston: Houghton, Mifflin, 1901.

Long, E.B. *The Civil War Day by Day: An Almanac 1861-1865.* New York: Da Capo Press, 1971.

Malone, Bartlett Y. *Whipt 'em Everytime.* Jackson, TN: McCowat-Mercer Press, Inc., 1960.

Parker, Sandra. *Richmond's Civil War Prisons.* Lynchburg, VA: H.E. Howard Inc., 1990.

Ransom, John. *Andersonville.* Auburn, NY: John Ransom, 1881.

Richmond Lady, A. *Richmond During the War: Four Years of Personal Observation.* London: G.W. Carleton & Co., 1867.

Riley, J.S. *Confederate Veteran,* IX (1901), 3-4.

Stanfield, N.B. *Confederate Veteran,* VII (1899), 60-61.

Tench, John W., Major, CSA *Confederate Veteran,* IX (1901), 125.

The Reports of Committees of the House of Representatives made during the Third Session of the Fortieth Congress, 1869. Washington: GPO, 1869.

*The War of the Rebellion: A Compilation of the Official Records of the Union and Confederate Armies.* Washington: GPO, 1889.

Urban, John W. *Battle Field and Prison Pen.* Philadelphia: Hubbard Brothers Publishers, 1882.

Wade, F. S. "Mc Neill's Texas Scouts." *Confederate Veteran,* XXXIV (1926), 379-80.

Ward, Col. W.W. *For the Sake of My Country: The Diary of Col. W. W. Ward* [Volume VIII of the *Journal of Confederate History,* edited by R. B. Rosenberg]. Murfreesboro, TN: Southern Heritage Press, 1992.

Williams, George. Letter to Charles Buford, March 9, 1863. Library of Congress.

# INDEX

341, 344, 345, 349, 351, 359
Cold Harbor, 195, 197, 198, 199, 203, 205
Corrick's Ford, 25
Crampton's Gap, 77
Crew's Farm, 69
Culpeper Court House, 172
Danville, 148, 358, 361, 365
Deep Run, 100
Dinwiddie Court House, 363
Evan's Mill, 180
Fair Grounds, prison, Lynchburg, 66
Fair Oaks, 60
Fairfax Court House, 75, 101, 102
Falls Church, 75
Falmouth, 82, 101
Fisher's Hill, 253, 265, 269, 278
Five Forks, 363
Fleetwood Hill, 100
Flint Hill, 75
Franklin's Crossing, 100
Fredericksburg, 82, 83, 85, 98, 100, 187
Front Royal, 59, 253
Gaines Mill, 67, 68
Goochland Court House, 159, 160
Good Hope Church, 195
Gordonsville, 73, 178
Grafton, 21
Guiney's Station, 193
Halltown, 239, 242
Hampton Roads, 42, 55, 325
Hanging Rock Pass, 41
Hanover Junction, 193, 193
Hanovertown, 194, 195
Harpers Ferry, 16, 60, 76, 77, 101, 216, 218, 219, 220, 232
Harrison's Landing, 68
Henrico County, 54
James River, 68
Kelly's Ford, 100
Kernstown, 227
King and Queen Court House, 160
King William Court House, 160
Laurel Hill, 24, 25
Leesburg, 35, 75, 223
Libby Prison, 26, 37, 38, 77, 79, 80, 98, 102, 108, 111, 114, 151, 159
Lynchburg, 66, 71, 133, 203, 265
Malvern Hill, 68, 114
Manassas, 25, 26, 57, 115, 74, 75, 169
Manassas, First Battle of, 34, 38, 40
Manassas Junction, 20
Mantapike Hill, 160
Marye's Heights, 83
Mechanicsville, 67
Mechum River, 58
Middletown, 253
Mine Run, 123
Moorefield, 43
New Market, 296
Norfolk, 34, 43, 45, 50, 54
Norfolk Navy Yard, 58
North Anna River, 194

Opequon Creek, 237
Orange Court House, 178
Page County, 69
Pamunkey River, 194, 195
Petersburg, 83, 86, 196, 203, 205, 209, 216, 217, 231, 237, 245, 249, 286, 319, 331, 361, 363
Philippi, "Philippi Races," 21, 24
Po River, 191
Port Republic, 255
Portsmouth, 54
Potomac River, 235
Rapidan River, 119, 178, 179, 196, 159
Rappahannock River, 74, 82, 86, 115
Rich Mountain, 24, 25
Richmond, **1861**, 16, 22, 26, 28, 30, 32, 37; **1862**, 43, 45, 50, 54, 56, 57, 58, 62, 63, 64, 66, 71, 72, 74, 77, 79, 80, 82; **1863**, 86, 87, 89, 90, 93, 97, 98, 100, 108, 113, 114; **1864**, 144, 147, 148, 150, 158, 159, 160, 161, 163, 169, 179, 180, 184, 193, 194, 195, 197, 198, 199, 203, 204, 205, 208, 209, 210, 211, 213, 217, 220, 223, 228, 249, 254, 256, 277, 291, 292, 296, 325, 326; **1865**, 338, 344, 347, 351, 352, 354, 355, 361; mayor surrenders city, 363, 364, 365, 370; Richmond General Hospital No. 10, 167; Richmond General Hospital No. 21, 167
Romney, 21, 41, 43, 169
Sayler's Creek, 365
Seven Pines, 60, 61
Shenandoah Valley, **1862**, 41, 56, 58, 59, 60, 65; **1864**, 200, 217, 219, 226, 227, 235, 236, 239, 242, 244, 245, 247, 250, 251, 253, 254, 255, 256, 269, 277, 278
Spotsylvania, 181, 182, 184, 185, 186, 187, 191
Staunton, 25, 200, 254, 277
Stephenson's Depot, 101
Stevenburg, 100
Strasburg, 253
Sudley Springs, 75
Suffolk, 90
Thoroughfare Gap, 75
Tom's Brook, 265
Totopotomoy River, 195
Unger's Store 41, 42
Varina, 354, 359
Vienna, 75
Warrenton Turnpike, 75
Warwick River, 57
Waynesborough, 254, 256
West Point, 58
Weyer's Cave, 255
White Oak Road, 363
White Oak Swamp, 68
White's Ford, 223
Wilderness/Old Wilderness Tavern/Wilderness Crossroads, 178, 179, 180, 193, 196
Williamsburg, 58
Winchester, 43, 59, 75, 100, 216, 236, 251
Yellow Tavern, 185, 186
York Peninsula, 66, 69
Yorktown (peninsula), 56, 57, 58
*Virginia* (was *Merrimack*), 56, 58
Virginia Infantry (50th), 368

## ABOUT THE AUTHOR

ROBERT E. DENNEY served with the U.S. Marines in China and on Guam. In 1950 he entered the Army, serving in the Korean and Vietnam Wars. He was wounded in action in Korea and was awarded the Silver Star, Bronze Star with "V" device, and Purple Heart. Graduating from the Warrant Officer's Flight Program in 1956 as a helicopter pilot, he went on to become an Assistant Project Officer for the testing of low-level navigation systems for helicopters. For his performance during these tests, he was awarded the Army Commendation Medal. For various actions in Vietnam, he was awarded the Distinguished Flying Cross, Bronze Star (OLC), several Air Medals, and another Purple Heart. On retirement in 1967 as a major in the Signal Corps, Denney pursued his lifelong interest in the Civil War, an avocation which he attributed to the influence of a high-school history teacher who in the early 1940s "peppered his American History classes with tales he remembered [from his youth] as told by the veterans, and stories of rural Indiana in the late 1800s." A computer systems consultant, Denney is married, has four children and three grandsons, and is a past president of the Civil War Round Table of Washington, D.C. He is also the author of *The Civil War Years: A Day-by-Day Chronicle of the Life of a Nation.*